T0211038

Lecture Notes in Computer Science 13227

Founding Editors

Gerhard Goos
Karlsruhe Institute of Technology, Karlsruhe, Germany

Juris Hartmanis
Cornell University, Ithaca, NY, USA

Editorial Board Members

Elisa Bertino
Purdue University, West Lafayette, IN, USA

Wen Gao
Peking University, Beijing, China

Bernhard Steffen
TU Dortmund University, Dortmund, Germany

Gerhard Woeginger
RWTH Aachen, Aachen, Germany

Moti Yung
Columbia University, New York, NY, USA

More information about this series at https://link.springer.com/bookseries/558

Alex Orailoglu · Matthias Jung ·
Marc Reichenbach (Eds.)

Embedded Computer Systems: Architectures, Modeling, and Simulation

21st International Conference, SAMOS 2021
Virtual Event, July 4–8, 2021
Proceedings

Editors
Alex Orailoglu
University of California, San Diego
La Jolla, CA, USA

Matthias Jung
Fraunhofer IESE
Kaiserslautern, Germany

Marc Reichenbach
Brandenburg University of Technology
Cottbus, Germany

ISSN 0302-9743 ISSN 1611-3349 (electronic)
Lecture Notes in Computer Science
ISBN 978-3-031-04579-0 ISBN 978-3-031-04580-6 (eBook)
https://doi.org/10.1007/978-3-031-04580-6

© Springer Nature Switzerland AG 2022
This work is subject to copyright. All rights are reserved by the Publisher, whether the whole or part of the material is concerned, specifically the rights of translation, reprinting, reuse of illustrations, recitation, broadcasting, reproduction on microfilms or in any other physical way, and transmission or information storage and retrieval, electronic adaptation, computer software, or by similar or dissimilar methodology now known or hereafter developed.
The use of general descriptive names, registered names, trademarks, service marks, etc. in this publication does not imply, even in the absence of a specific statement, that such names are exempt from the relevant protective laws and regulations and therefore free for general use.
The publisher, the authors and the editors are safe to assume that the advice and information in this book are believed to be true and accurate at the date of publication. Neither the publisher nor the authors or the editors give a warranty, expressed or implied, with respect to the material contained herein or for any errors or omissions that may have been made. The publisher remains neutral with regard to jurisdictional claims in published maps and institutional affiliations.

This Springer imprint is published by the registered company Springer Nature Switzerland AG
The registered company address is: Gewerbestrasse 11, 6330 Cham, Switzerland

Preface

SAMOS is a conference with a unique format. It brings together every year researchers from both academia and industry on the topic of embedded systems in the perfect setting of Samos island. Due to the COVID-19 crisis, the SAMOS 2021 conference was held as a virtual live event on a virtual island, where people could walk around with their virtual avatars and chat with their peers, and listen to interesting talks.

The SAMOS 2021 keynote with the title "Spectres, Meltdowns, Zombies, Orcs: Can formal methods banish the ghosts that haunt your hardware?" was given by Wolfgang Kunz from University of Kaiserslautern. He presented a new formal method in order to detect hardware vulnerabilities systematically without demanding the clever thinking of a human attacker. A specific focus was also placed on virtual prototyping and simulation through a tutorial by Jakob Engblom from Intel.

The SAMOS 2021 proceedings comprise a selection of publications targeting either systems themselves - through their applications, architectures, and underlying processors - or methods created to automate their design. A total of 45 papers were submitted to the conference and 17 papers were selected by the Program Committee for presentation at the conference (38% acceptance rate). Four special sessions were organized in the program to report recent results of European projects, coalesce novel work on next generation computing (NGC) and security and put a special focus on the lessons learnt from meaningful negative results.

The SAMOS 2021 committee would like to acknowledge the generous support of the many reviewers who contributed to the quality of these proceedings. We hope that you enjoy reading them!

July 2021

Alex Orailoglu
Matthias Jung
Marc Reichenbach

Organization

General Chair

Alex Orailoglu — University of California, San Diego, USA

Program Chairs

Matthias Jung — Fraunhofer IESE, Germany
Marc Reichenbach — Brandenburg University of Technology, Germany

Special Session Chairs

Innovative Architectures and Tools for Security

Francesco Regazzoni — Università della Svizzera italiana, Switzerland, and University of Amsterdam, The Netherlands

Next Generation Computing

Matthias Jung — Fraunhofer IESE, Germany
Jens Krüger — Fraunhofer ITWM, Germany
Marc Reichenbach — Brandenburg University of Technology, Germany

Insights from Negative Results

Karol Desnos — IETR, France
Shuvra Bhattacharyya — University of Maryland, College Park, USA, and IETR, France

Reports from Research Projects – Digital Services and Platforms: Application Areas Automotive Industry, Energy, Agriculture, Healthcare, and Industry 4.0 Workshop

Giovanni Agosta — Politecnico di Milano, Italy
Jasmin Jahic — University of Cambridge, UK
Dimitrios Soudris — National Technical University of Athens, Greece

Tutorial Chair

Jakob Engblom — Intel, Sweden

Submission Chair

Anuj Pathania — University of Amsterdam, The Netherlands

Web Chair

Jasmin Jahic — University of Cambridge, UK

Proceedings and Finance Chair

Carlo Galuzzi — Swinburne University of Technology, Australia

Publicity Chair

Andy D. Pimentel — University of Amsterdam, The Netherlands

Steering Committee

Shuvra Bhattacharyya	University of Maryland, College Park, USA, and IETR, France
Holger Blume	Leibniz Universität Hannover, Germany
Ed F. Deprettere	Leiden University, The Netherlands
Nikitas Dimopoulos	University of Victoria, Canada
Carlo Galuzzi	Swinburne University of Technology, Australia
Georgi N. Gaydadjiev	Maxeler Technologies, UK
John Glossner	Optimum Semiconductor Technologies Inc., USA
Walid Najjar	University of California, Riverside, USA
Andy D. Pimentel	University of Amsterdam, The Netherlands
Olli Silvén	University of Oulu, Finland
Dimitrios Soudris	National Technical University of Athens, Greece
Jarmo Takala	Tampere University of Technology, Finland
Stephan Wong	TU Delft, The Netherlands

Program Committee

Giovanni Agosta	Politecnico di Milano, Italy
Ammar Ben Khadra	Fraunhofer IESE, Germany
Shuvra Bhattacharyya	University of Maryland, USA
Holger Blume	Leibniz Universität Hannover, Germany
Luigi Carro	UFRGS, Brazil
Jeronimo Castrillon	TU Dresden, Germany
Ricardo Chaves	INESC-ID, Portugal
Francesco Conti	UniBo, Italy
Karol Desnos	IETR, France

Vassilios V. Dimakopoulos	University of Ioannina, Greece
Giorgos Dimitrakopoulos	Democritus University of Thrace, Greece
Nikitas Dimopoulos	University of Victoria, Canada
Lide Duan	University of Texas at San Antonio, USA
Xin Fang	Qualcomm and Northeastern University, USA
Holger Flatt	Fraunhofer IOSB-INA, Germany
Carlo Galuzzi	Swinburne University of Technology, Australia
Georgi N. Gaydadjiev	Maxeler Technologies, UK
Andreas Gerstlauer	University of Texas at Austin, USA
Michael Glaß	University of Erlangen-Nuremberg, Germany
John Glossner	Optimum Semiconductor Technologies Inc., USA
Diana Goehringer	Ruhr University Bochum, Germany
Xinfei Guo	University of Virginia, USA
Rajiv Gupta	University of California, Riverside, USA
Soonhoi Ha	Seoul National University, South Korea
Frank Hannig	University of Erlangen-Nuremberg, Germany
Christian Haubelt	University of Rostock, Germany
Pekka Jääskeläinen	Tampere University of Technology, Finland
Matthias Jung	Fraunhofer IESE, Germany
Christoforos Kachris	Athens Information Technology, Greece
Georgios Keramidas	Technical Educational Institute of Western Greece, Greece
Leonidas Kosmidis	BSC, Spain
Angeliki Kritikakou	Inria and IRISA, France
Kevin Martin	Université Bretagne Sud, France
John McAllister	Queen's University Belfast, UK
Paolo Meloni	UniCa, Italy
Alexandre Mercat	Tampere University of Technology, Finland
Daniel Mueller-Gritschneder	Technical University of Munich, Germany
Chrysostomos Nicopoulos	University of Cyprus, Cyprus
Alex Orailoglu	University of California, San Diego, USA
Andrés Otero	Universidad Politécnica de Madrid, Spain
Gianluca Palermo	Politecnico di Milano, Italy
Francesca Palumbo	UniCa, Italy
Anuj Pathania	National University of Singapore, Singapore
Guillermo Payá Vayá	Leibniz Universität Hannover, Germany
Maxime Pelcat	Université Européenne de Bretagne, France
Andy Pimentel	University of Amsterdam, The Netherlands
Oscar Plata	University of Malaga, Spain
Dionisios Pnevmatikatos	FORTH-ICS and NTUA, Greece
Ann Ramirez (Gordon-Ross)	University of Florida, USA

Francesco Regazzoni	Università della Svizzera italiana, Switzerland, and University of Amsterdam, The Netherlands
Marc Reichenbach	Brandenburg University of Technology, Germany
Ruben Salvador	CentraleSupelec and IETR, France
Carlo Sau	UniCa, Italy
Muhammad Shafique	NYU Abu Dhabi, UAE
Magnus Själander	Uppsala University, Sweden and NTNU, Norway
Dimitrios Soudris	NTUA, Greece
Ioannis Sourdis	Chalmers University of Technology, Sweden
Leonel Sousa	INESC-ID and Instituto Superior Técnico, Portugal
Todor Stefanov	Leiden University, The Netherlands
Christos Strydis	Erasmus MC, The Netherlands
Sander Stuijk	Eindhoven University of Technology, The Netherlands
Wonyong Sung	Seoul National University, South Korea
Jarmo Takala	Tampere University of Technology, Finland
Jean-Pierre Talpin	Inria and IRISA, France
George Theodoridis	University of Patras, Greece
Stavros Tripakis	Northeastern University, USA
Theo Ungerer	University of Augsburg, Germany
Carlos Valderrama	University of Mons, Belgium
Norbert Wehn	University of Kaiserslautern, Germany
Stefan Weithoffer	IMT Atlantique, France
Stephan Wong	TU Delft, The Netherlands
Roger Woods	Queen's University Belfast, UK
Jun Xiao	University of Amsterdam, The Netherlands
Hoeseok Yang	Ajou University, South Korea

Secondary Reviewers

Ali, Muhammad
Arvanitis, Petros
Beichler, Benjamin
Bruschi, Nazareno
Dias, Tiago
Drewes, Anna
Eldstal-Ahrens, Albin
Fiolhais, Luís
Friesen, Andrej
Gautam, Pushpak
Gruetzmacher, Florian
Heller, Marc
Kalms, Lester
Kyl, Troya
Leppnen, Topi
Loroch, Dominik
Mallya, Neethubal
Marques, Diogo
Medina, Alfonso Rodriguez
Mueller, Luise
Ozen, Elbruz
Rachuj, Sebastian
Sharoodi, Taha
Siddiqi, Muhammad Ali

Weis, Christian
Willig, Michael
Zadnik, Jakub
Zahedi, Mahdi

Contents

Simulation and Design Space Exploration

The 3Cs - Cache, Cluster and Cloud

Heterogeneous SoC

Novel CPU Architectures and Applications

Dataflow

Special Session on Innovative Architectures and Tools for Security

Special Session on Reports from Research Projects

Special Session on Next Generation Computing

Special Session on Insights from Negative Results

Simulation and Design Space Exploration

Accurate LLVM IR to Binary CFGs Mapping for Simulation of Optimized Embedded Software

Alessandro Cornaglia[1(✉)], Alexander Viehl[1], and Oliver Bringmann[2]

[1] FZI Research Center for Information Technology, Karlsruhe, Germany
{cornaglia,viehl}@fzi.de
[2] University of Tübingen, Tübingen, Germany
oliver.bringmann@uni-tuebingen.de

Abstract. In this paper, we present a new approach for mapping LLVM IR to binary machine code for overcoming the current limitations of host-based simulations of performance-critical embedded software imposed by compiler optimizations. Our novel, fully automated mapping approach even copes with aggressive compiler optimizations without requiring any modification to the compiler or the need of expert supervision. Experimental results show that accurate mappings are produced even when compiling with the highest level of optimization (average error below 2%). The proposed simulation methodology provides a speedup of at least 26 compared to the widely used gem5 simulator.

Keywords: Performance estimation · Host-based simulation · IR to binary CFGs mapping · Design space exploration

1 Introduction

The design of embedded systems requires dealing with the complexity of the actual processor architectures, the constant need for reducing the waste of precious resources and the strictness of the non-functional requirements. The performance of a program is generally optimized by applying compiler optimizations that focus on increasing the instruction-level parallelism (ILP) by making the best run-time use of the physical resources available on the processor. In this context, the designers need early feedback about the performance of the software program regarding its execution on a given target platform. The evaluation is usually conducted by simulating the target system on a development host machine.

Traditional simulators like instruction-set simulators (ISS) or gate level RTL simulators often cover too many unnecessary details in too much depth that make them too slow and unsuitable for supporting the design activities. Fast host-based simulation techniques are an alternative for tackling this limitation. Host-based simulators execute a software binary version that differs from the

© Springer Nature Switzerland AG 2022
A. Orailoglu et al. (Eds.): SAMOS 2021, LNCS 13227, pp. 3–15, 2022.
https://doi.org/10.1007/978-3-031-04580-6_1

one produced for the target. The target performance can be simulated by compiling the program for the host machine and executing it. The simulation can be executed on different software representations such as the source code, its compiler intermediate representation (IR) or the host binary simulation code.

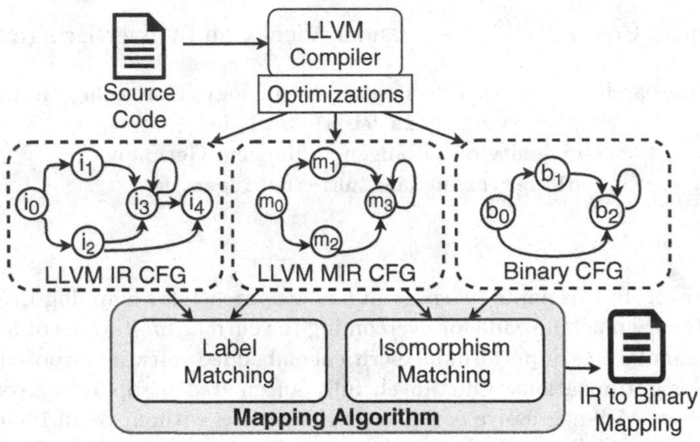

Fig. 1. Proposed two-steps approach for accurately mapping LLVM IR to binary code dealing with the effects of the compiler optimizations.

The simulation speedup provided by the host-based simulation techniques comes at the price of mapping the simulation code representation to the target binary machine code. Unfortunately, this task can be extremely hard and complex because, especially in typical industrial settings, it is desirable to highly optimize the program at compile-time. Aggressive compiler optimizations can substantially change the structure of a program in comparison to the structure of the original source code. In most cases, when the program is highly optimized, these transformations make a direct match between the different representations of the control flow graphs (CFGs) impossible. It is easier to map IR to binary code rather than trying to map the source code directly. The IR is a lower level representation of the source code that is internal to the compiler and it is designed to support architecture-independent compilation passes. Its structure is closer to the binary representation because it already includes the effects of some of the compiler optimizations. Mapping IR to binary machine code only requires considering the effects of the missing back-end transformations.

The main contribution of this paper is the definition of a new and fully automatic approach for generating a precise mapping between LLVM IR and binary machine code that can deal with aggressive compiler optimizations. The methodology relies on the LLVM MIR representation, a machine dependent low-level code representation designed for applying architecture-dependent optimizations. The mapping problem is decomposed by initially mapping LLVM IR to MIR code and consequently mapping the MIR to binary machine code. As a result, the precise mapping allows defining a fast host-based simulation methodology for accurately evaluating non-functional properties of an embedded system, such as timing, performance and power estimations.

The rest of the paper is organized as follows: Sect. 2 introduces other existing mapping approaches. An introduction to fundamental LLVM concepts is provided in Sect. 3. The proposed mapping approach is presented in Sect. 4 and the host-based simulation methodology is described in Sect. 5. Section 6 shows the experimental results and Sect. 7 concludes the paper.

2 Related Work

Mapping the structure of the simulation's code representation to the cross-compiled binary code is a common requirement for executing host-based simulations. Unfortunately, this is a hard task, especially in the presence of aggressive compiler optimizations. Some approaches try to directly map the source code to the binary instructions. Others instead rely on the IR code because its structure already includes the effects of the architecture-independent compiler optimizations. The IR structure is consequently closer to the binary in comparison to the structure of the source code. Our mapping relies on a lower level code representation but the methodology is mainly inspired by three different approaches [5,12,13] that belong to both of the two categories.

The concept described in [13] proposes an automatic approach for mapping source code statements to the respective binary instructions generated after the program's cross-compilation. This approach relies exclusively on the DWARF debug information generated by the compiler. Unfortunately, even if this information is available, the mapping may turn out to be imprecise or ambiguous due to the effects of aggressive compiler optimizations that break the full traceability between source code and binary instructions [2]. Possible improvements are proposed in [17] and [16], imprecision and ambiguities are reduced by substituting the source code parts subjected to aggressive compiler optimizations with functionally-equivalent optimized IR code. The optimized IR code has a structure closer to the binary representation, helping in generating the mapping but without fully solving the problem even considering hierarchical subgraphs of a CFG as proposed in [11].

An automated flow for mapping IR to binary code is described in [5]. This algorithm implements a heuristic for mapping the basic blocks of the two different program representations relying on their similarities. The similarities are defined considering two numerical metrics: flow value and nesting level. In some cases, the heuristic fails in producing a complete mapping because of ambiguities in the CFGs. If this happens, the mapping process requires the supervision of an expert. The authors in [6] proposed a tracing-based enrichment for making the algorithm fully automatic. The improvement consists in filling the mapping gaps by comparing IR and binary execution traces. On the one hand, the solution can fix the ambiguities problem, but on the other hand, it can be hard to identify the exact input data that leads the execution to visit the desired control flow path.

A different approach for mapping IR to binary code with the purpose of performance estimation in native simulation is presented in [12]. By analyzing optimized IR code, this approach can focus on managing only the hardware-dependent optimizations applied during the back-end compilation. In particular, this approach is focused on identifying, characterizing and finally mapping the loops in the two different program representations. The experimental results show that an increase in accuracy can be reached only if all the loop optimizations are correctly identified and managed. However, every single imperfection may introduce a substantial percentage of error.

3 LLVM Background

The LLVM Compiler Infrastructure [9] provides tools for analysis and for both static and dynamic compilation of programs. The compiler's front-end, `clang`, translates the source code to bitcode. The bitcode is the LLVM IR, it is architecture independent and it is structured in modules. The architecture-independent optimization passes performed by `opt`, the middle-end, are applied to this intermediate representation. It is possible to link multiple IR modules together via `llvm-link`. The compilation, or cross-compilation, process is concluded by `llc`, the back-end, that finally translates the bitcode to binary machine code.

Two further architecture-dependent code representations are considered in LLVM: The LLVM Machine Code (MC) [15] and the LLVM Machine IR (MIR) [14]. The former is a representation for an object file that is similar to the binary representation and does not contain any high-level information stored in the bitcode. The latter is an architecture specific translation of the bitcode that is utilized by the back-end for applying architecture-dependent optimizations. The structure of an MIR module resembles the structure of its original IR module. At the same time, the MIR structure is closer to the binary representation because it includes most of the effects caused by the architecture-dependent optimizations, including the ones that change the program structure. For instance, an MIR module already includes the effects of aggressive loop optimizations such as loop unrolling, loop-invariant code motion, loop inversion and others. During the final compilation phases, for every function in the MIR module, the MIR basic blocks are sequentially translated in order into LLVM MC instructions.

The key idea of our novel mapping mechanism consists in also considering the program's structure at the MIR level. Instead of directly map the IR structure to its corresponding binary, we propose to perform an additional step that requires matching the MIR representation to both the IR and binary representations. As shown by the consequent IR, MIR and binary CFG representations of a given function in Fig. 2, this double mapping mechanism allows to reduce the problem complexity even when aggressive architecture-dependent optimizations are applied. The problem's simplification derives from the fact that: 1) There exists an implicit direct connection between the IR and MIR basic blocks' labels and, 2) The MIR structure is very close to the structure of the resulting executable.

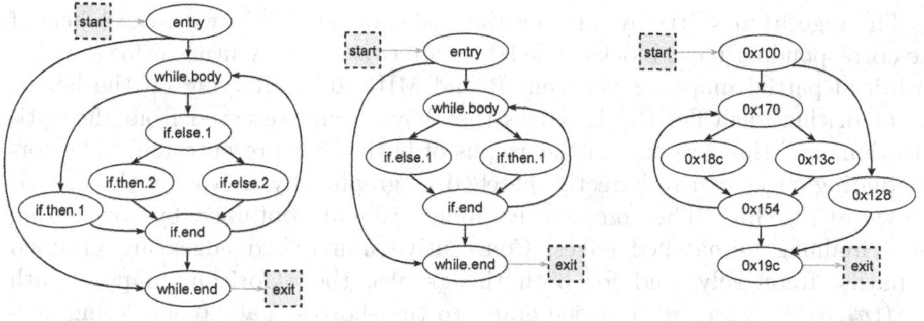

(a) Optimized IR CFG. (b) Optimized MIR CFG. (c) Optimized binary CFG.

Fig. 2. Control flow graphs at different code representations for the same function.

4 Mapping Algorithm

The proposed novel mapping approach consists of two separate phases, as shown in Fig. 1. The first one allows the generation of a mapping between IR and MIR CFGs relying on the definition of the label matching algorithm. The second one allows mapping MIR to binary CFGs relying on the isomorphism matching algorithm that automatically generates an isomorphism between them. The combination of these two mappings together allows producing a precise mapping from LLVM IR to binary machine code. The two phases are presented in the next sections with the help of the support of the CFGs provided in Fig. 2. The terms basic block and node will be utilized in an interchangeable way by following this definition: a CFG is a directed graph $CFG = (N, E)$ where every node $n \in N$ corresponds to a basic block and each edge $e = (n_i, n_j) \in E$ identifies a connection between two blocks. The mapping is intended to define a match between paths (sequence of edges) in the CFGs. This granularity allows considering, for every single function in the program, only the effects of the optimizations that change the structure of a graph. The mapping is not intended to model any of the optimizations that can change the internal structure of the basic blocks. This assumption does not limit the possibility of future finer granularity extensions.

4.1 Label Matching

The basic block labels are used to support the automatic mapping of IR to MIR CFGs. The labels are internal to the compilor, specific per function, completely independent from the debug symbol information (that can be unavailable or imprecise) and each of them identifies a specific node in the graph. An example is given in Fig. 2(a) and Fig. 2(b). The two graphs are similar but a direct mapping between the labels of the two representations is not possible because of the effects of potential optimizations. MIR nodes can be removed or inserted [1]. An insertion implies the appearance of a new MIR node identified by a new synthetic label. These labels are not present in the IR CFG. On the opposite, a removal causes the IR CFG to contain a label not present in the MIR CFG.

The algorithm starts by labeling the nodes of the CFGs with the labels of the corresponding basic blocks. The labels are consequently utilized for defining an initial partial mapping between IR and MIR edges. Relying on the labels, the algorithm identifies the IR edges that have been preserved from the optimizations and that are part of the graphs of both the representations. The corresponding edges can be directly matched as graphically shown by the dashed arrows in Fig. 3(a). The complete mapping is finally obtained by considering the remaining unmatched edges. Consecutive unmatched edges are grouped in paths. Iteratively, and for both the graphs, the algorithm maps a path $p = ((n_i, n_j), \ldots, (n_x, n_y))$ of one graph to the shortest path (considering possible back-edges) in the other graph between the nodes identified by the labels of nodes n_i and n_y. These matches, represented as dotted arrows in Fig. 3(a), complete the IR to MIR mapping.

4.2 Isomorphism Matching

The process for defining an MIR to binary mapping requires the generation of an isomorphism between their CFGs. The isomorphism can be obtained by modifying the structure of the graphs of both the representations while preserving their original control flow paths. In fact, similarly to certain compiler optimizations, specific nodes can be removed in order to obtain two graphs with an isomorphic structure. The isomorphism ensures the definition of a unique mapping between the edges and paths of the original graphs as described in Algorithm 1.

The algorithm starts by labeling the nodes of the two graphs with unique IDs. These IDs are essential for the isomorphism-based direct mapping. As discussed in Sect. 3, the basic blocks translation from MIR to binary machine code reflects the order of their appearance in the MIR module. Therefore, every node in the MIR CFG is labeled with an integer ID relying on the order of appearance in the MIR function. In a similar way, it is possible to label the binary nodes relying on their start address (or offset) reported in the binary file.

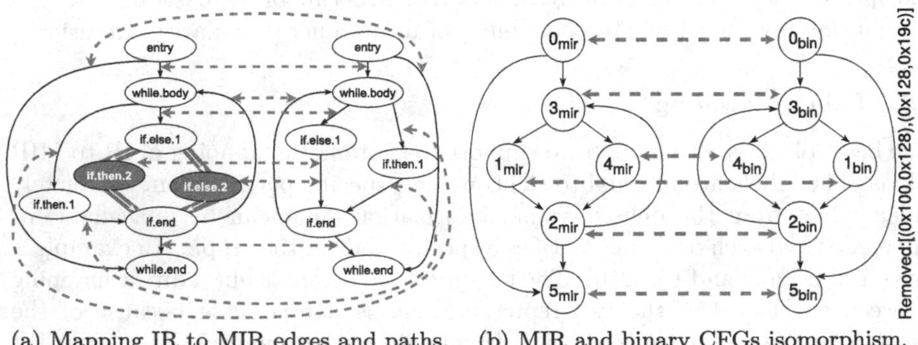

(a) Mapping IR to MIR edges and paths. (b) MIR and binary CFGs isomorphism.

Fig. 3. Steps of the procedure for mapping IR to MIR to binary paths relying first on labels and later on the CFGs isomorphism.

Algorithm 1. Isomorphism Mapping(CFG_{mir}, CFG_{bin})

mapping := ∅
sortByAppearance(N_{mir}); *sortByAddress*(N_{bin})
assignIntegerIds(N_{mir}, N_{bin})
colorNodes(N_{mir}, N_{bin})
CFG^{iso}_{mir},CFG^{iso}_{bin} := *remove&Annotate*(CFG_{mir}, CFG_{bin})
sortAndupdateIntegerIds($N^{iso}_{mir}, N^{iso}_{bin}$)
// *Isomorphism completed between* CFG^{iso}_{mir} *and* CFG^{iso}_{bin}
for all $(n_i, n_j)^{iso}_{mir} \in E^{iso}_{mir}$ **do**
    $\text{annotatedEdges}_{mir}$:= *getAnnotation*$\big((n_i, n_j)^{iso}_{mir}\big)$
    p_{mir} := *extractPath*$\big((n_i, n_j)_{mir}, \text{annotatedEdges}_{mir}\big)$
    $\text{annotatedEdges}_{bin}$:= *getAnnotation*$\big((n_i, n_j)^{iso}_{bin}\big)$
    p_{bin} := *extractPath*$\big((n_i, n_j)_{bin}, \text{annotatedEdges}_{bin}\big)$
    mapping := mapping $\bigcup$ map(p_{mir}, p_{bin})
return mapping

The algorithm continues by coloring the graphs for identifying the necessary nodes that have to be removed for obtaining the isomorphism. Initially, all the nodes are colored in white. Consequently, all the nodes that are eligible to be removed are colored in black. A node has to be colored in black if, ignoring potential back-edges, its in-degree is equal to one and its out-degree is at maximum one. In order to preserve the original structure of the paths in the final isomorphic graphs, it is necessary to refine the set of nodes that have to be removed by further coloring. Any node n_j is colored in dark gray if: 1) It is the direct successor of at least two distinct black nodes or, 2) It is the direct successor of the last node n^b_n of an uninterrupted path of black nodes $(n^b_0, \ldots, n^b_n)$ and it shares a common direct predecessor n_p with the first node of the path n^b_0. All the blocks having a dark gray successor instead are colored in light gray. The nodes that are still colored in black at the end of the coloring have to be removed. The node removal requires to: 1) Preserve the control flow and nesting levels of the graphs by updating any affected original edge (or back-edge) and, 2) Update the node IDs for preserving the initial incremental labeling scheme, 3) Annotate the removed edges information in the updated edges. For example, the graph on the right side of Fig. 3(b) is the result of the removal of the only remaining black node from its colored CFG.

Finally, as shown in Fig. 3(b), a direct match can be identified by relying on the isomorphic versions of the two CFGs. Mixing the information from the node IDs and the annotated edges in the direct match, it is possible to define the mapping between the two original graphs. Two possibilities have to be considered while generating the mapping: 1) An edge is part of the original graph only if it has not been annotated. In this case, the original edge can be mapped with the corresponding edge or path in the other graph. 2) An annotated edge is not part of the original graph because it is the result of some node removal operations. Therefore, if an annotated edge represents a supposed edge (n_i, n_j) in one of the original graphs and its annotation is composed of a list of removed edges $\big((n^r_0, n^r_1), \ldots, (n^r_{n-1}, n^r_n)\big)$, the path $p = \big((n_i, n^r_0), \ldots, (n^r_n, n_j)\big)$ has to be mapped with the corresponding edge or path in the other graph. As a result, the two steps matching approach allows to accurately map the LLVM IR paths to their corresponding binary paths by first translating them into MIR paths.

5 Host-Based Simulation

The detailed workflow designed for executing LLVM IR host-based simulations is described in Fig. 4. The `lli` tool, which is used as the simulator's core, allows executing bitcode on a host machine via Just-In-Time compilation (JIT). The host-execution cannot directly execute bitcode generated for a different target architecture but retargeting the IR module requires only minimal effort. This can be done by implementing an appropriate modification pass for `opt`.

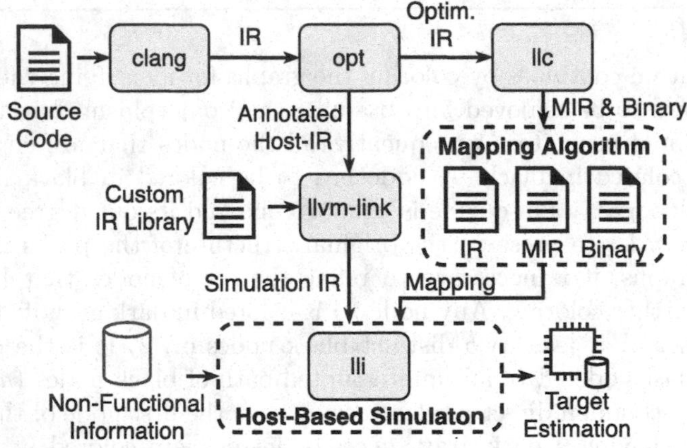

Fig. 4. Combined and detailed workflows proposed for producing the accurate mapping and enabling fast host-based simulations.

The simulation requires three different inputs: the bitcode to simulate, the CFGs mapping and a source of non-functional information, which is used for updating the simulation results. The simulation bitcode is the result of the linkage of the annotated retargeted IR module with a custom IR library. The annotation consists in the insertion of a function call at the beginning of every basic block. At run-time, the function call forces the simulator to execute the code in the custom library for computing and updating the simulation estimations.

The LLVM IR to binary code mapping is produced as described in Sect. 4 by analyzing and comparing the different CFGs of the IR, MIR and binary representations. The IR module that is considered during the mapping process is the final IR version optimized by `llc`. This version of the bitcode includes some of the effects of the architecture-dependent optimizations. The MIR module is generated at the end of the last `llc` optimization pass and it includes most of the possible structural changes produced by the back-end.

Finally, the source of non-functional information can be any kind of information that is desired to be considered while simulating. The preference has to be defined in the custom IR library and it can be a model, a database, an external simulator or others.

6 Experimental Evaluation

During compilation, the compiler optimizations are commonly applied in groups of optimization levels rather than individually. Most of them are not independent and applying them in different orders may lead to different results. In our evaluation, we considered all the possible combinations of standard middle-end and back-end optimization levels. Compared with lower optimization levels, the highest level of optimization `-O3` allows observing substantial changes in the structure of the different program representations and is therefore harder to map. For this reason, here we show only the results for the highest level of optimization and omit more accurate results caused by a lower mapping complexity. The evaluation has been conducted on an Intel Core i7-2600K workstation running at 3.4 GHz. An ARM Cortex-A15 with out-of-order superscalar execution and multiple cache levels was chosen as target processor. The analyzed benchmarks are part of the widely-used Mälardalen benchmark suite [7]. The complexity of the benchmarks, expressed by the quantitative metrics Line Of Codes (LOC) and Cyclomatic Complexity Number (CCN), is reported in Table 1. We excluded the benchmarks that introduce non-available library sources because this may introduce inaccuracies that are not caused by the mapping algorithm's accuracy.

6.1 Mapping Accuracy

A direct validation of the mapping accuracy is not feasible. Therefore, we took an indirect approach that consists of measuring the number of executed instructions and the program execution time and comparing them to the respective results of a simulation based on our mapping approach. The two measured metrics strongly depend on the executed control flow. Consequently, a high level of accuracy in the simulated values indicates a precise mapping of the CFGs.

A fixed number of instructions has been assigned to every binary basic block by statically analyzing the binary file. It is assumed that the execution of a basic block implies the execution of all its instructions starting from its start address. However, the execution time of a basic block can vary depending on the program's execution history due to the possible different timing behavior of the stateful resources included in the processor (e.g. cache memories, pipelines, etc.). Multiple execution times have been consequently measured for every binary basic block, extracted from the target via non-intrusive tracing measurements, allowing to account for the variation caused by the different execution contexts.

The simulator updates both the metrics at run-time relying on the IR execution paths and the mapping information. The evaluation results are summarized in Table 1 showing that the difference between the measured and simulated values is minimal. In most of the cases, the accuracy is close to 100%. This implies a high level of accuracy of the simulation results and consequently of our mapping approach. One reason for the deviation in the results is that the ARM instruction set includes conditional execution instructions that partially invalidates our assumption on the complete execution of a basic block. Nevertheless, the effectiveness of the mapping is proven by the accuracy of the simulation results.

Compared to other mapping approaches the one we propose is fully automatic and achieves a high level of precision. However, since it relies on the information contained in the LLVM MIR, it requires the analyzed programs to be compiled with LLVM and cannot simply be ported to other compilers. Furthermore, for us it has proven to be sufficient to match sequence of edges of the IR CFG to the binary CFG's paths. For other approaches requiring the mapping to be performed on basic blocks or instructions, this may not be suitable.

6.2 Host-Based Simulation Speed

A second evaluation objective has been to determine the potential simulation speed. We have measured the time required for simulating the benchmarks. The simulation speed is measured in Million of simulated Instructions Per Second (MIPS). In Fig. 5 the results of our measurements are shown. For consistency reasons, the chart shows only the results for benchmarks compiled with `-O3`

Table 1. Measured mapping's accuracy with `-O3` optimization level.

Benchmark	Metrics		Instructions count			Execution time (us)		
	LOC	CCN	Measured	Simulated	Accuracy	Measured	Simulated	Accuracy
bs	144	9	51	51	**100%**	7	7	**100%**
bsort100	128	8	45949	44286	**96.38%**	2380	2301	**96.68%**
cnt	267	3	1525	1525	**100%**	165	165	**100%**
crc	128	9	11661	11661	**100%**	635	635	**100%**
duff	86	10	537	537	**100%**	37	37	**100%**
edn	285	4	84992	84301	**99.19%**	5989	5945	**99.27%**
fdct	239	3	1834	1834	**100%**	159	159	**100%**
fir	276	5	133588	133588	**100%**	9270	9340	**99.24%**
insertsort	92	8	1108	1083	**97.74%**	92	90	**97.83%**
ludcmp	147	14	1512	1506	**99.61%**	235	231	**98.30%**
matmult	163	4	35229	35229	**100%**	3015	3040	**99.17%**
ndes	231	11	28625	28566	**99.79%**	1502	1489	**99.13%**
prime	47	4	4233	4223	**99.76%**	449	448	**99.78%**
qsort_exam	121	15	851	867	**98.12%**	79	76	**96.23%**
qurt	166	5	514	514	**100%**	135	135	**100%**
select	144	16	368	368	**100%**	34	34	**100%**
sqrt	77	5	447	447	**100%**	124	124	**100%**
st	177	4	70067	70067	**100%**	4548	4518	**99.34%**
ud	163	11	1205	1161	**96.35%**	109	106	**97.24%**

optimization level. We considered only the results for the benchmarks that ensure simulating more than ten thousand ARM instructions. The maximum observed simulation speed value has been of 69 MIPS while simulating the benchmark `crc`. The same benchmark compiled with `-O2` showed the highest value of our entire evaluation reaching the value of 90 MIPS. We observed that the simulation speed is directly related to the number of simulated instructions. The simulation of a substantial number of instructions reduces the minimal overhead due to the basic blocks instrumentation and the JIT compilation. We are confident that this will be advantageous for real applications considering that they typically execute more instructions than the used benchmarks. We also observed that the type of instructions in a program influences the simulation speed. Arithmetic intensive benchmarks showed higher speed than others.

An additional evaluation has been conducted for comparing the performance [4] of our host-based simulation approach with the well-known and public available gem5 simulator [3]. We compared the amount of time required for simulating the benchmarks with our simulation approach against the time required by gem5. We compiled gem5 configuring the fast mode of the full system simulation mode [10]. The histogram's columns in Fig. 5 show the speedup resulting from simulating the benchmarks with our approach and requiring a logarithmic scale. The light gray columns represent the comparison results when gem5 only simulates ARM instructions without timing or physical resource consideration. The darker columns show the comparison with a full timing gem5 simulation. We observed a maximum speedup of 20 comparing the simulation of the `edn` benchmark without timing considerations. The maximum observed speedup increased to 527 simulating the `crc` benchmark with gem5 and by enabling the consideration of the timing behavior of caches, pipeline and branch predictor. The average observed speedup in case of timing simulation is 144. The results demonstrate

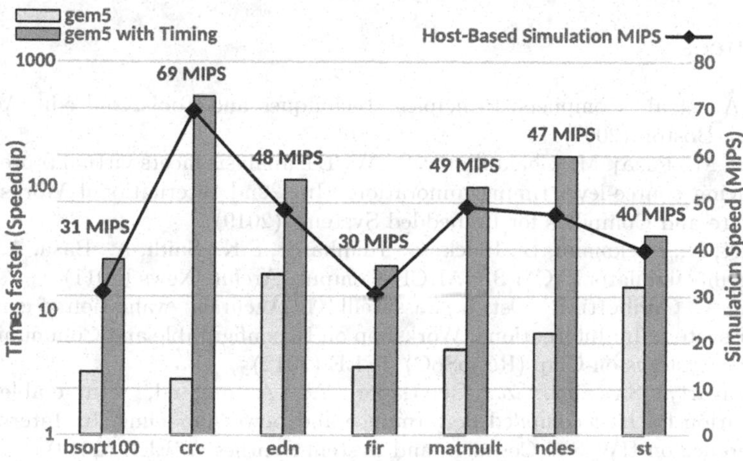

Fig. 5. Simulation speedup compared with the performance of the gem5 simulator executed with and without timing considerations.

that our approach allows executing accurate simulations requiring an amount of simulation time that is orders of magnitude shorter than simulating with gem5.

7 Summary and Conclusions

In this paper, we presented a new approach for automatic mapping of LLVM IR to binary embedded code for the purpose of host-based simulations in support of system design decisions. The mapping approach relies on the information extracted from the intermediate LLVM MIR representation that is internal to the compiler without requiring any modification. Overall experiments results show a high level of accuracy even in presence of aggressive compiler optimizations (average error smaller than 2%). The conducted evaluation activities prove that our mapping can be utilized for evaluating the execution cost of embedded programs in addition to the quantification of code coverage metrics [8] at different program representations. Furthermore, the proposed LLVM IR host-based simulation approach shows a substantial speedup of several orders of magnitudes compared with the gem5 simulator (144 average observed speedup).

Future work will focus on the further evaluation of different target architectures and benchmarks. Prospectively, we intend to refine the granularity of the mapping algorithm for identifying a direct mapping between the LLVM IR and binary instructions. Furthermore, a straightforward extension has been planned for additionally mapping the source code to LLVM IR. The extension will enable the possibility of source-level simulations and consequently improving the simulation speed while keeping the showed level of accuracy.

Acknowledgements. This work has been partially supported by the German Federal Ministry of Education and Research (BMBF) within the projects COMAPCT under grant 01|S17028C and progressivKI under grant 19A21006M.

References

1. Aho, A., et al.: Compilers: Principles, Techniques and Tools, 2nd edn. Addison-Wesley, Boston (2007)
2. Becker, M., Pazaj, M., Chakraborty, S.: WCET analysis meets virtual prototyping: improving source-level timing annotations. In: 22nd International Workshop on Software and Compilers for Embedded Systems (2019)
3. Binkert, N., Beckmann, B., Black, G., Reinhardt, S.K., Saidi, A., Basu, A., et al.: The gem5 simulator. ACM SIGARCH Comput. Archit. News (2011)
4. Butko, A., Garibotti, R., Ost, L., Sassatelli, G.: Accuracy evaluation of gem5 simulator system. In: International Workshop on Reconfigurable and Communication-Centric Systems-on-Chip (ReCoSoC). IEEE (2012)
5. Chakravarty, S., Zhao, Z., Gerstlauer, A.: Automated, retargetable back-annotation for host compiled performance and power modeling. In: International Conference on HW/SW Codesign and System Synthesis. IEEE (2013)
6. Cornaglia, A., Hasan, M.S., Viehl, A., Bringmann, O., Rosenstiel, W.: JIT-based context-sensitive timing simulation for efficient platform exploration. In: 25th Asia and South Pacific Design Automation Conference (ASP-DAC). IEEE (2020)

7. Gustafsson, J., Betts, A., Ermedahl, A., Lisper, B.: The Mälardalen WCET benchmarks: past, present and future. In: 10th International Workshop on Worst-Case Execution Time Analysis (WCET 2010) (2010)
8. Jahić, J., Kuhn, T., Jung, M., Wehn, N.: BOSMI: a framework for non-intrusive monitoring and testing of embedded multithreaded software on the logical level. In: 18th International Conference on Embedded Computer Systems: Architectures, Modeling, and Simulation (2018)
9. Lattner, C., Adve, V.: LLVM: A compilation framework for lifelong program analysis and transformation. In: International Symposium on Code Generation and Optimization. IEEE (2004)
10. Lowe-Power, J., Ahmad, A.M., Akram, A., Alian, M., et al.: The gem5 simulator: Version 20.0+. arXiv preprint arXiv:2007.03152 (2020)
11. Lu, K., Müller-Gritschneder, D., Schlichtmann, U.: Hierarchical control flow matching for source-level simulation of embedded software. In: 2012 International Symposium on System on Chip (SoC). IEEE (2012)
12. Matoussi, O., Pétrot, F.: A mapping approach between IR and binary CFGs dealing with aggressive compiler optimizations for performance estimation. In: 23rd Asia and South Pacific Design Automation Conference (ASP-DAC). IEEE (2018)
13. Stattelmann, S., Bringmann, O., Rosenstiel, W.: Dominator homomorphism based code matching for source-level simulation of embedded software. In: International Conference on HW/SW Codesign and System Synthesis (2011)
14. The LLVM Compiler Infrastructure: Machine IR (MIR) Format Reference Manual. https://llvm.org/docs/MIRLangRef.html
15. The LLVM Compiler Infrastructure: The LLVM Target-Independent Code Generator. https://llvm.org/docs/CodeGenerator.html
16. Wang, Z., Henkel, J.: Accurate source-level simulation of embedded software with respect to compiler optimizations. In: Design, Automation and Test in Europe Conference and Exhibition (DATE). IEEE (2012)
17. Wang, Z., Herkersdorf, A.: An efficient approach for system-level timing simulation of compiler-optimized embedded software. In: 46th Design Automation Conference (DAC). IEEE (2009)

RVfplib: A Fast and Compact Open-Source Floating-Point Emulation Library for Tiny RISC-V Processors

Matteo Perotti[1(✉)], Giuseppe Tagliavini[2], Stefan Mach[1], Luca Bertaccini[1], and Luca Benini[1,2]

[1] ETH Zürich, Gloriastrasse 35, 8092 Zürich, Switzerland
{mperotti,smach,lbertaccini,lbenini}@iis.ee.ethz.ch
[2] University of Bologna, Viale del Risorgimento 2, 40136 Bologna, Italy
giuseppe.tagliavini@unibo.it

Abstract. Small, low-cost IoT devices rely on floating-point (FP) software emulation on 32-bit integer cores when the cost of a full-fledged FPU is not affordable. Thus, the performance and code size of the FP emulation library are decisive for meeting energy and memory-size constraints. We propose RVfplib, the first ISA-optimized open-source library for single and double-precision IEEE 754 FP emulation on RV32IM[C] cores. RVfplib is 59% smaller and 2× faster than the GCC emulation library, on average. On benchmark programs, code size reduction is 39%, and performance boost 1.5×. RVfplib is 5.3% smaller than the leading closed-source RISC-V commercial library.

Keywords: RISC-V · Embedded · IoT · Floating-point · Library · Size · Performance

1 Introduction

Low-cost Internet of Things (IoT) devices are often subject to tight constraints on their silicon area and memory, which are precious resources in the embedded systems domain and impact cost and energy consumption [8]. At the same time, processing FP workloads is a common requirement for many applications. FP support enables programmers to satisfy the requirements on dynamic range and precision. In addition, deriving the fixed-point variant of an algorithm proven to be safe with floating-point numbers is often time-consuming and, in some cases, very challenging. However, small cores cannot always afford hardware Floating Point Units (FPUs) and rely on software emulation of FP instructions. Consequently, the code to be stored in memory is inflated, inducing performance overhead and increased total energy consumption due to higher execution times and added memory accesses. The code size cost is particularly relevant since FP emulation support can dominate the total code size of small programs, reaching

© Springer Nature Switzerland AG 2022
A. Orailoglu et al. (Eds.): SAMOS 2021, LNCS 13227, pp. 16–32, 2022.
https://doi.org/10.1007/978-3-031-04580-6_2

up to 8 kB just for the single and double-precision basic operations. In this scenario, using small and fast FP emulation libraries is necessary to be competitive in the market.

The RISC-V Instruction Set Architecture (ISA) is gaining industrial traction in IoT applications where cost is a major concern. The main challenge for RISC-V low-cost microcontroller units (MCUs) is to reduce code size [3], as currently experimental evidence shows that the Arm ISA (ARMv7-M), its mature compilers, and highly size-optimized libraries generate smaller code on average [12,15]. The code size issue mainly affects applications that require FP arithmetic. In this case, long FP software emulation functions add a remarkable code size overhead, even if only a few FP computations are needed.

In this work, we present the following contributions:

1. *RVfplib*, the first open-source IEEE 754[1] FP library for RISC-V, manually optimized for low code size and high performance for both single and double-precision FP. RVfplib is compatible with the RV32IM[C] ISA, and implements addition, subtraction, multiplication, division, as well as comparisons and conversions. Double-precision division is optional in RVfplib; it targets low code size and is compatible with cores without an integer divider.
2. *RVfplib_nd*, the reduced version of RVfplib that considers subnormal inputs/outputs as correctly signed zeroes. RVfplib_nd is compatible with the RV32EM[C] ISA and has smaller code size than RVfplib, making it the perfect candidate for tightly memory-constrained devices.
3. A comparison of the code size and performance of all RVfplib functions with their counterparts provided by *libgcc*. Moreover, we perform a code size comparison between the functions in RVfplib_nd and the ones available within SEGGER *emFloat*, the current state-of-the-art closed-source competitor. We also compare code size of RVfplib with the Arm-optimized libgcc code.
4. An analysis of the real code size and performance impact that RVfplib has on full programs.

The rest of the paper is organized as follows: in Sect. 3, we describe the structure of RVfplib and the main ideas that led to its development, as well as the techniques used to optimize it and a code comparison with libgcc. In Sect. 4, we present the experiments used to evaluate RVfplib figures of merit, and we show the corresponding results in Sect. 5. We close our work with insights about further improvements to RVfplib and the conclusion of the analysis in Sects. 6 and 7.

2 Related Work

Researchers have proposed different solutions to provide FP capabilities to a core when the system area is strictly constrained. When a full-fledged FPU leads

[1] The library presents some deviations from the standard. It does not support exception flags, it produces only fixed quiet NaNs, and it provides nearest-even or toward-zero rounding only.

to an excessive area increase, designers can integrate a slower but tiny FPU, crafted for tightly constrained IoT cores [2]. Another possibility is to implement hardware/software approaches, in which hardware optimizations in the integer datapath speed up critical operations used in the FP emulation libraries [13]. Nonetheless, both the solutions can be adopted only if the system tolerates the related area overhead, and do not apply to systems that already exist.

Integer-only cores that cannot afford an area increase can execute FP programs only through FP emulation libraries, usually provided by compiler vendors along with their compilation toolchain. For example, the Arm Keil compiler comes with the IEEE 754-1985 compliant fplib [1], and GCC with FP support within libgcc, its low-level runtime library [10]. Since the optimization of these libraries is essential for producing fast code with a low memory footprint, FP emulation libraries can also be manually crafted at the assembly-level to ensure the best code size and performance possible. libgcc provides optimized code for well established ISAs like Arm but lacks customized support for relatively new ISAs like RISC-V, which should rely on compiling the generic high-level FP emulation C functions. The novelty of the RISC-V solution results in sub-optimal code size and performance that makes it less attractive with respect to the Arm-based alternatives.

In addition to what is available in compiler ecosystems, designers have implemented optimized FP libraries for specific processors [5,14] and for the maximum flexibility and compliance with the IEEE 754 standard, like SoftFloat [19]. However, these solutions are non-RISC-V specific.

To the best of our knowledge, the only available assembly-optimized RISC-V FP library is emFloat, designed by SEGGER [17]. However, this library is closed-source and does not support subnormal values, flushing them to correctly signed zeroes instead.

3 RVfplib Design

RVfplib is the first open-source optimized FP emulation library for RISC-V processors, for both single and double-precision FP. Its main goals are low code size and increased performance. Implicitly, this implies lower energy consumption thanks to the reduced memory bandwidth and execution time.

RVfplib is wholly written in RV32IM assembly. Thanks to the modularity of the RISC-V C extension, it is also compatible with RV32IMC ISA since the compiler can compress all the compressible instructions on request.

Functions in RVfplib adhere to the interface of the corresponding libgcc functions [10] and have their same names to ensure compatibility with GCC and a fast porting to real programs. The aliasing induces GCC to automatically link using RVfplib functions, if implemented, instead of the ones from libgcc, without additional modifications to the program. Therefore, there is no need to explicitly call the RVfplib functions, as the compiler does it automatically.

RVfplib functions have been obtained with ISA-specific assembly level optimizations starting from the libgcc FP functions, with an approach similar to the one used for Arm [9]. Compliance with the IEEE 754 standard rules for FP encoding and computation presents the same deviations that hold for the libgcc FP support compiled with the default options, namely:

- Exception flags are not supported, and exceptional events only provide their pre-defined output (i.e., divisions by zero result in a NaN).
- All the produced NaNs are quiet, in the form of `0x7FC00000` for single-precision and `0x7FF8000000000000` for double-precision.
- Only the default *round to nearest, ties to even* rounding mode is supported for the majority of the operations (as in the default libgcc implementation, some of the conversion functions round toward zero).

3.1 Structure

RVfplib is a static library that comes in two different variants:

- `RVfplib.a`: the standard version, which targets low code size and increased performance.
- `RVfplib_nd.a`, which treats subnormal values as signed zeroes and shows an even smaller code size.

Each variant includes the functions listed in Table 1, in which both the SoftFloat and the libgcc names are reported. The two *not-equal* functions are aliased with the *equal* ones, as they have the same behavior. Both libraries can be compiled with particular code that can increase performance in the presence of specific input operands, with an additional code size overhead. For example, the multiplication can include code to deal with power-of-two operands, speeding up the processing of specific patterns while increasing the code size. Choosing between one implementation or the other depends on the system constraints and input workloads.

To further push toward reducing the memory footprint of the library, we also implemented part of the same FP support environment provided by SEGGER emFloat, treating subnormal values as correctly signed zeroes. Thanks to the reduced requirement for registers in its design, RVfplib_nd is compliant with the RV32EM ISA (i.e., with only 16 registers in the register file). The library currently comes with a double-precision division that does not use any integer hardware divider, which cannot be included in such small cores[2]. For this reason, this function is optional and is only included when targeting the smallest code size possible. If performance is a more critical constraint, the standard double-precision division from libgcc is used instead.

[2] Such a processor would not be fully compliant with the RV32IM/RV32EM ISA since the M extension also requires an integer divider. Nevertheless, the compiler allows for avoiding hardware divisions even when compiling RV32IM code.

3.2 Design Choices

RVfplib benefits from some essential ideas that, together with the functional algorithmic choices, contribute to crafting optimized RISC-V functions that reduce code size and execution times.

1. *Make the common case fast*: FP algorithms take different decisions depending on the received inputs and create different control paths within the code. The latency of each function strongly depends on the inputs since different data patterns are processed differently. Optimizing the paths taken by the common input patterns (normal values) is a methodology for reducing the average latency.
2. *Avoid memory references*: RVfplib minimizes data memory bandwidth reducing register spilling in function prologues/epilogues. This is accomplished by using only caller-saved registers. libgcc functions, on the contrary, do not limit register usage and have bloated prologues/epilogues.
3. *No function calls*: Whenever the code makes a call, it must also save the return address and, in general, any other already-used caller-saved registers. This process leads to additional memory operations, stack pointer adjustments, and additional jumps to/from the called function, with a consequent code size increase and degraded performance. RVfplib contains only leaf-functions (i.e., functions that do not make other function-calls). This property enables RVfplib to be independent of other external libraries, minimizing the extra code linked in the final binary. This is not the case for libgcc, as some of its functions depend upon *__clzsi2()* calls and the related table *__clz_tab*.
4. *Maximize potential compression*: The RISC-V C extension allows for compressing the most common RISC-V instructions when precise register patterns are used. For example, the majority of the instructions can be compressed when using registers from the *RVC* (i.e., registers in the set a0, a1, a2, a3, a4, a5, s0, s1). Since s0 and s1 are callee-saved registers, RVfplib does not use them.
5. *Register re-use*: Register allocation is optimized at function level to overcome heuristics of the compiler, whose analysis is mainly limited to the boundaries of basic blocks. As a basic rule, an operand is placed in the first free register; when it is no longer used, the register becomes free again.
6. *Performance vs. code size tradeoff*: Some RVfplib functions use loops to perform iterative processes. For example, the leading zeroes count after a numerical cancellation of an effective subtraction can be reduced to a shift-and-check loop, in which the result is left-shifted until the implicit one returns to its original position. This iterative process is convenient in terms of code size, but it is slow and inefficient. For this reason, it is also possible to use a bisection algorithm to count the leading zeroes, with better performance and increased code size. The choice can be taken at compile time. In general, when the taken-branch penalty is critical, unrolling the loop helps in maximizing the number of non-taken branches.

3.3 Comparison with Libgcc

FP functions from libgcc use a complex set of hierarchical C macros to be as flexible and generic as possible. When compiling the library, it is possible to set specific high-level parameters to control how the library will treat exceptions, subnormals, roundings, etc. With the default settings, no exception is raised or handled, subnormal values are not flushed to zero, and the rounding mode is rounding to nearest, ties to even (RNE). Even with these minimalistic options, the generated code is sub-optimal in terms of size and performance.

In Listing 1.1, we report the assembly code of `__eqsf2()` compiled with GCC 10.2.0 and optimized for size (`-Os`), together with comments and labels that we added to help the reader understand the code. This function, one of the smallest of the library, returns `1` if the inputs are not equal, and `0` if they are equal. The algorithm is straightforward:

1. If at least one input is `NaN`, return `1`.
2. In the case of `+0` and `-0`, return `0`.
3. If the numbers are equal, returns `0`; otherwise, return `1`.

The libgcc function unpacks both the operands in their sign, exponent, and mantissa before starting the comparison. In `__eqsf2()`, this operation is unnecessary and is probably performed to adopt a common coding standard for the library design. Moreover, separately comparing sign, exponent, and mantissa improves the code readability but discards possible optimizations.

```
__eqsf2:
# Unpack operands, prepare checks
  srli  a3,a0,0x17
  lui   a5,0x800
  addi  a5,a5,-1
  srli  a2,a1,0x17
  andi  a3,a3,255
  li    a7,255
  and   a6,a5,a0
  srli  a4,a0,0x1f
  and   a5,a5,a1
  andi  a2,a2,255
  srli  a1,a1,0x1f
# Check and compare
checks_0:
  li    a0,1
  bne   a3,a7,checks_1
  bnez  a6,return
  bne   a2,a3,return
  beqz  a5,checks_2
return:
  ret
checks_1:
  beq   a2,a7,return
```

```
    bne   a3,a2,return
    bne   a6,a5,return
checks_2:
    li    a0,0
    beq   a4,a1,return
    li    a0,1
    bnez  a3,return
    snez  a0,a6
    ret
```

Listing 1.1. __eqsf2() disassembled libgcc code

In Listing 1.2, we show the __eqsf2() function extracted from RVfplib. Writing in assembly allows to have a better control over the used instructions and registers when the functions are sufficiently small. All the checks are performed without unpacking the operands, and we opportunistically reuse the register a5 to reach the desired outcome during the final snez comparison.

```
__eqsf2:
    lui   a5,0xff000
# Check for NaNs
    slli  a2,a0,0x1
    bltu  a5,a2,end
    slli  a3,a1,0x1
    bltu  a5,a3,end
# Check for +0, -0
    or    a5,a2,a3
    beqz  a5,end
# Effective comparison
    xor   a5,a0,a1
end:
    snez  a0,a5
    ret
```

Listing 1.2. __eqsf2() RVfplib code

We aimed to reach the same optimization level implementing the algorithm of Listing 1.2 using C, and we managed to halve the code size of the libgcc function from 84 B to 42 B, showing the importance of choosing an optimized algorithm. However, the generated code is still 16% larger than the one generated from our assembly.

Forcing the compiler to reuse precise registers and take branches in a deterministic way is more natural in assembly than in C; during the compilation of our C function, the compiler creates unexpected intermediate operations and register moves, with negative effects on both code size and performance.

The same is true for the more complex functions of the library. Functions from libgcc are safe, generic, flexible, and parametric, but this comes at the expense of possible critical optimizations in key functions, where more precise control over the registers and the branch choices would be preferred. Assembly language helps consider a register as a container for a value, without a precise label and meaning as in C; therefore, a more opportunistic usage of the registers comes more natural, without the need of forcing the compiler to behave in a precise way.

3.4 Testing

To test RVfplib, we relied on TestFloat [20], which provides an extensive IEEE 754 testing suite for generating test-cases and checking the correctness of custom FP implementations. Internally, TestFloat uses the fully IEEE 754 compliant SoftFloat library [19] as a golden reference. We generated the inputs for each function with the TestFloat engine and compared the function outputs with both SoftFloat and libgcc golden models. Since not all functions in RVfplib have a SoftFloat implementation, we used libgcc as a golden model when it was needed (e.g., for the "greater [or equal] to" functions).

4 Experimental Setup

To analyze the impact of RVfplib, we evaluated its code size and performance metrics in both a synthetic environment and using real programs. In the first set of experiments, we extracted the code size of each function; in the second one, we evaluated the behavior of RVfplib on real benchmarks.

4.1 Benchmarks

Since we evaluate an FP library useful for area-constrained embedded devices, we selected all the Embench benchmark suite applications [4] that use FP numbers (`cubic`, `minver`, `nbody`, `st`, `ud`, `wikisort`). On the other hand, we selected three popular algorithms that can be run on small systems at the edge, on both single and double-precisions: a convolution (`conv`), a fast Fourier transform (`fft`), and a discrete wavelet transform (`dwt`).

4.2 Code Size

RVfplib implements most of the FP functions provided by libgcc and all the implicit arithmetic functions available in emFloat. Therefore, we evaluated the code size of the functions of our library and compared them against the two competitors. The code size of the emFloat functions is publicly available for RV32IMC ISA [17]; thus, we compiled both RVfplib and libgcc functions with the same target using GCC 10.3 and libgcc originally compiled with the *-Os* flag enabled, its default setting. The functions were linked to a fixed C program, and the code size of the functions extracted from its disassembly-dump. To create realistic conditions for embedded devices and avoid intricate dependencies and code size bloating, we always linked our programs against `libc_nano` and `libm_nano`. For a fair analysis, we compared RVfplib and libgcc since both are compiled for minimum code size and support subnormal values, and RVfplib_nd with emFloat since both flush subnormal values to zero and target minimum code size as well.

Since libgcc is freely available, we extended our comparison linking our real benchmarks against RVfplib and RVfplib_nd first, and then libgcc. To measure the code size impact that the libraries have on the read-only memory footprint, we added the size of the .text and the .rodata sections. Since some programs use the FP division, we also measured their code size when linked against RVfplib with fast divisions (the double-precision one belongs to libgcc).

To complete the code size analysis, we measured the code size of the Arm-optimized libgcc FP library and compared it with the code size of both the generic RISC-V libgcc support and RVfplib.

4.3 Performance

On the performance side, a full profiling of RVfplib and libgcc was performed for both the single average latencies of the functions and the execution time of the benchmarks. In the following, when referring to a function, the term *latency* indicates the number of cycles required to execute it.

To evaluate the function latencies, we simulated a synthetic C program on the CV32E40P processor [6] with single-cycle latency memories using Mentor QuestaSim, repeating the experiment for each function of the compared libraries. The C program is composed of a loop that makes an explicit call to the function under test during each iteration and measures the latency of each function execution, including the jump/return to/from function cycles, and then averages the total cycle count on the number of iterations. Each function is fed with 10000 randomly generated values within (0,1), and the overhead of the load/store operations before and after the call is not considered. Using 1-cycle fixed-latency memories is a best-case scenario for libgcc performance, as libgcc accesses the stack inside its FP functions while RVfplib does not, as we avoided in-function memory requests. Additional memory latency/miss penalties negatively affect only the functions from libgcc.

We also compare our results to the average latencies reported by SEGGER emFloat [17]. It is unclear, however, whether this reported performance includes latency overheads from function calls and function returns. These overheads, as well as processor-specific branch- and jump penalties, can strongly affect performance, especially for small functions. SEGGER extracted performance metrics using a GigaDevice GD32VF103 [18], which is based on a variable 2-stage pipeline RISC-V core [7]. It is likely that the jump/branch penalties of CV32E40P (from 2 to 4 cycles) [11] are higher. Moreover, SEGGER only reports latency results of their "performance-optimized" emFloat library, which is different from the one used for the code size results. For this reason, we used our fast single-precision division and the double-precision division from libgcc to perform this comparison.

To provide insight into how RVfplib affects the execution time, we simulated our benchmarks with SPIKE, a RISC-V simulator for a simple processor that executes one instruction per cycle, and reported the different instruction counts linking with libgcc, RVfplib, and RVfplib_nd. Since some benchmarks use the double-precision division, we also reported the execution times of the programs linked with RVfplib with fast divisions (the 64-bit division is taken from libgcc).

5 Results

5.1 Code Size

We show the code size of the single functions of RVfplib, libgcc, and emFloat in Table 1. Comparing the total code size of the libraries, we achieve a net gain of ≈60% by replacing libgcc FP functions with the ones in RVfplib. In absolute terms, the memory savings reach 7.5 kB, which is a significant code size reduction, especially for small programs. The small embedded systems we target are area/memory size constrained and do not have hardware FPUs. Most commonly, they require performing computations on single-precision data. As such, our high code size reduction for the most frequent single-precision FP operations (i.e., addition, subtraction, multiplication), which is around 67% on average, is very significant. libgcc subtraction is automatically re-linked as a function different from the addition, even if their code is shared except for one initial sign change of the second operand. RVfplib subtraction flips the sign and then executes an addition, without any other jump that would cause extra latency.

Passing from RVfplib to RVfplib_nd, which flushes subnormal values to correctly signed zeroes, allows saving another 21.6% of the library code size. This significant gain comes for free when supporting subnormal numbers is not a requirement. RVfplib_nd is almost 5.3% smaller than emFloat, even if the double-precision division from emFloat is 30% smaller than the one from RVfplib_nd. The functions that gain the most from removing the subnormal support are multiplication and division, as the addition needs only small adjustments to process the denormalized inputs.

In Fig. 1, we summarize the code size results of our benchmarks. The code size savings on libgcc span from 16% of `cubic` (with libgcc double-precision division) to 60% (`st` with RVfplib_nd) and are relatively high also for large code size programs like `fft64`, which passes from almost 13.8 kB to 8.4 kB with more than 39% of saving. The average code size reductions with respect to libgcc are 39.3%, 36%, and 46.5% for RVfplib, RVfplib with libgcc fast divisions, and RVfplib_nd, respectively.

5.2 Performance

Average latencies of each function of RVfplib and libgcc FP support are summarized in Table 2. RVfplib functions are always faster than the ones from libgcc, except for the two small divisions, which are 1.45× and 2× slower for single and double-precision, respectively. This fact underlines the importance of trying to re-implement these operations, changing the core algorithm; nevertheless, RVfplib divisions do not use the hardware integer divider, allowing for more flexibility, and the division operation is not common in simple algorithms used on small

Table 1. Code size comparison between RVfplib, libgcc FP support, RVfplib_nd, and emFloat. Only the functions implemented in RVfplib are reported. Target ISA: RV32IMC

Function	libgcc name	Code size [B]			
		RVfplib	libgcc	RVfplib_nd	emFloat
f32_add	__addsf3	320	804	274	410
f32_sub	__subsf3	6	818	6	10
f32_mul	__mulsf3	310	542	172	178
f32_div	__divsf3	294 (416)*	590	188 (280)*	184
f32_lt	__ltsf2	56	120	56	58
f32_le	__lesf2	60	120	60	54
f32_gt	__gtsf2	52	120	52	50
f32_ge	__gesf2	60	120	60	62
f32_eq	__eqsf2	36	84	36	44
f32_ne	__nesf2	-	-	-	-
f32_i32	__fixsfsi	58	96	58	74
f32_ui32	__fixunssfsi	50	88	50	50
f32_i64	__fixsfdi	120	136	120	146
f32_ui64	__fixunssfdi	80	100	80	98
i32_f32	__floatsisf	60	186	60	66
ui32_f32	__floatunsisf	48	154	48	52
i64_f32	__floatdisf	106	258	106	96
ui64_f32	__floatundisf	82	214	82	70
f32_f64	__extendsfdf2	88	150	56	64
f64_add	__adddf3	736	1542	572	724
f64_sub	__subdf3	6	1560	6	10
f64_mul	__muldf3	506	1080	288	286
f64_div	__divdf3	742 (1334)*	1334	396 (1334)*	278
f64_lt	__ltdf2	94	166	94	70
f64_le	__ledf2	96	166	96	70
f64_gt	__gtdf2	90	166	90	70
f64_ge	__gedf2	104	166	104	70
f64_eq	__eqdf2	60	106	60	52
f64_ne	__nedf2	-	-	-	-
f64_i32	__fixdfsi	62	100	62	84
f64_ui32	__fixunsdfsi	54	96	54	54
f64_i64	__fixdfdi	130	164	130	146
f64_ui64	__fixunsdfdi	94	126	94	96
i32_f64	__floatsidf	44	102	44	46
ui32_f64	__floatunsidf	32	78	32	34
i64_f64	__floatdidf	114	372	114	128
ui64_f64	__floatundidf	90	328	90	106
f64_f32	__truncdfsf2	158	284	104	130
Total		5100	12636	3994	4220

*RVfplib small divisions can be replaced with faster versions, yielding better performance and extra code size.

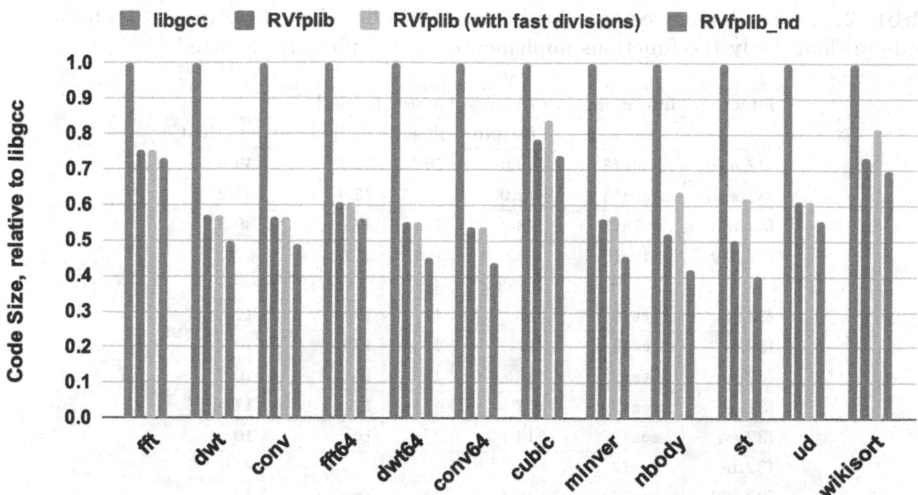

Fig. 1. Relative code size (.text+.rodata) of benchmarks linked against libgcc, RVfplib, RVfplib with fast divisions, RVfplib_nd. The reference is libgcc.

embedded systems. The fast 32-bit division in RVfplib is slightly faster than one from libgcc, and the 64-bit one is the same. The single-precision comparisons and both the multiplications show important speedups (up to 2.57× for the multiplication), and the single-precision addition in RVfplib is faster than the one from libgcc by more than 1.5×. These data are promising, as these operations are ubiquitous in almost every FP algorithm. The conversions from integers to FP numbers are the functions that obtain the highest speed gain, which peaks for converting a 64-bit unsigned integer to a double-precision FP value with more than 4× lower latency. Replacing the whole set of libgcc functions with RVfplib gives an average speedup of 2×.

As already pointed out, making a comparison between RVfplib_nd and emFloat performance using the average latencies reported by SEGGER is not straightforward. We could not reproduce the experiment in the same conditions since they used a device that is likely to show a lower cycle count if compared to the CV32E40P core. Moreover, it is not specified whether the latency of the jumps to/from functions was taken into account. This is especially valid for the smaller functions, that can be strongly biased by the jump to/from function latency overhead. However, if we focus on the bigger functions, the double-precision addition in emFloat (the subtraction shares the code with the addition) and both divisions are faster than the ones from RVfplib by factors around 2.7× and 1.9×, for single and double-precision, respectively.

When we measure the instruction count of the real benchmarks linked against RVfplib and libgcc, we obtain the data shown in Fig. 2. We chose these benchmarks to have a good mix of realistic examples, and we found for RVfplib and RVfplib_nd an average speedup of 1.5× even if the benchmarks that use the

Table 2. Average latency comparison between RVfplib, libgcc FP support, RVfplib_nd, and emFloat. Only the functions implemented in RVfplib are reported.

Function	libgcc name	Average latency [cycles]			
		RVfplib	libgcc	RVfplib_nd	emFloat*
f32_add	__addsf3	50.6	79.5	52.1	49.5
f32_sub	__subsf3	72.9	114.7	72.4	62.2
f32_mul	__mulsf3	48	120	47	39.3
f32_div	__divsf3	252 (182.2)†	190	252 (182.2)†	67
f32_lt	__ltsf2	18	41	18	11
f32_le	__lesf2	17	41	17	10
f32_gt	__gtsf2	16	41	16	10
f32_ge	__gesf2	17	41	17	11
f32_eq	__eqsf2	14	26.5	14	10
f32_ne	__nesf2	-	-	-	-
f32_i32	__fixsfsi	18.5	21	18.5	14
f32_ui32	__fixunssfsi	16	23	16	13
f32_i64	__fixsfdi	22	48	22	23.2
f32_ui64	__fixunssfdi	18	44	18	18.9
i32_f32	__floatsisf	29.5	88.5	29.5	32.6
ui32_f32	__floatunsisf	22	78.7	22	33
i64_f32	__floatdisf	41.5	131.4	41.5	49.1
ui64_f32	__floatundisf	32.5	122	32.5	44.1
f32_f64	__extendsfdf2	19	33	18	14.1
f64_add	__adddf3	87.2	101.1	83.9	62.8
f64_sub	__subdf3	116.5	138.5	114.9	82.8
f64_mul	__muldf3	85	219	85	75
f64_div	__divdf3	769.5 (382.2)†	382.2	769.5 (382.2)†	197.2
f64_lt	__ltdf2	27	46.2	27	16
f64_le	__ledf2	26	46.2	26	16
f64_gt	__gtdf2	25	46.2	25	16.1
f64_ge	__gedf2	27	46.2	27	16.1
f64_eq	__eqdf2	24	30.5	24	14
f64_ne	__nedf2	-	-	-	-
f64_i32	__fixdfsi	19	19	19	16.8
f64_ui32	__fixunsdfsi	17	21	17	13.8
f64_i64	__fixdfdi	33	38.4	33	26.9
f64_ui64	__fixunsdfdi	30.5	43	30.5	21.5
i32_f64	__floatsidf	24.9	61	24.9	31.6
ui32_f64	__floatunsidf	18.5	53	18.5	23.9
i64_f64	__floatdidf	41	142	41	45.1
ui64_f64	__floatundidf	31	134	31	39.3
f64_f32	__truncdfsf2	25	61	28	25.1

*emFloat data were obtained from [17]. It is unclear whether reported numbers include function call/function return latency overheads.

†RVfplib small divisions can be replaced with faster versions, yielding better performance and extra code size.

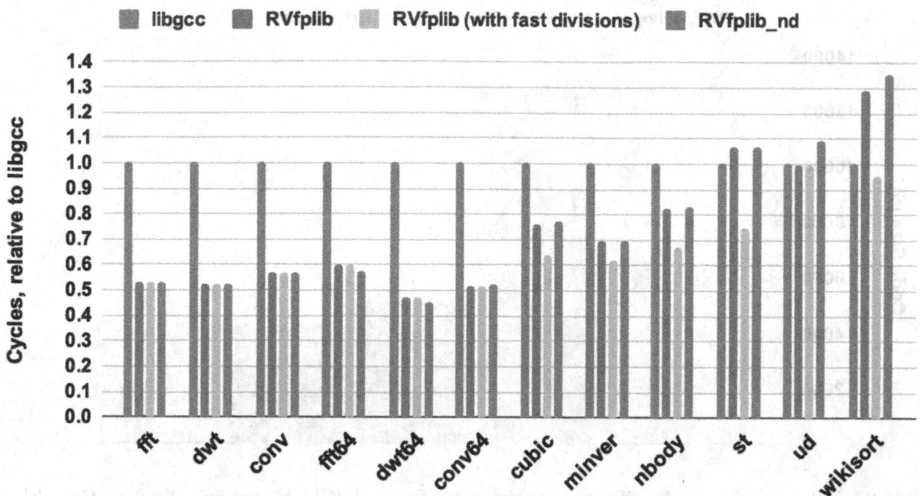

Fig. 2. Relative SPIKE instruction count of benchmarks linked against libgcc, RVfplib, RVfplib with fast divisions, RVfplib_nd. The reference is libgcc.

double-precision division in RVfplib are actually slower than the ones linked against libgcc. In particular, `wikisort` uses the square root operation that uses the double-precision division, which is also used by `st`. In some benchmarks (e.g., `ud`), RVfplib_nd performance decreases because of its 64-bit addition, which does not have a fast-path for equal operands. All the other programs show high-speed gains thanks to the massive use of multiplications and additions. For RVfplib with fast divisions, the average speedup grows to 1.6×, and the programs linked with RVfplib are always faster than the ones linked with libgcc.

5.3 Comparison with Arm

In Fig. 3, we show the code size comparison between the generic RISC-V libgcc FP support, RVfplib, and the Arm-optimized libgcc FP support. RVfplib brings the existing FP library code size gap between RISC-V and Arm from 8376 B to 840 B (10× less), reducing the Arm to RISC-V code size inflation from 196.6% to 19.7%. Arm addresses many comparison-function calls to a generic *compare*, reducing the total number of implemented functions and the library code size. This choice can be implemented in future versions of RVfplib as well.

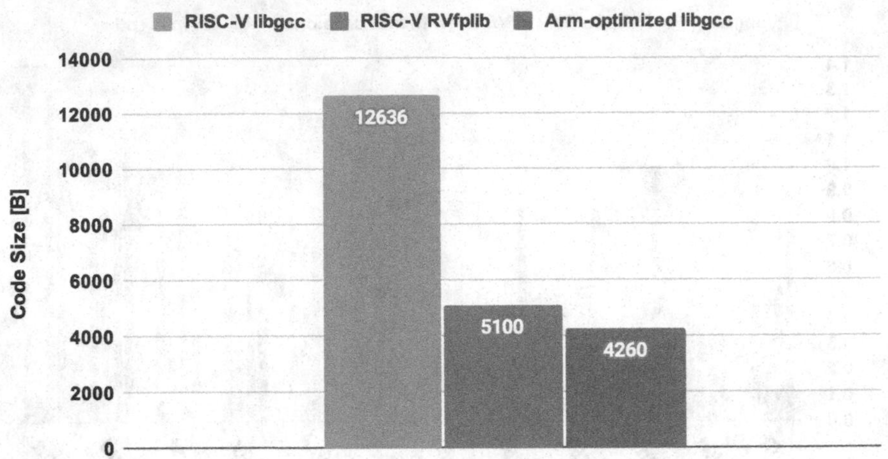

Fig. 3. FP libraries code size comparison between RISC-V generic libgcc, RVfplib, Arm-optimized libgcc.

6 Further Improvements

RVfplib will be released as an open-source project under GPL license, and everyone will be allowed to contribute to its enhancement, improving and extending it. SEGGER results unequivocally show that the 64-bit addition in RVfplib can be further improved to decrease its average latency. Both the divisions can reach increased code size and performance, maybe with different algorithmic choices and exploiting the hardware divider. The optimal solution would be to offer both a version that exploits the divider and one independent from it. On the other hand, the library misses important functions, such as the square root and the trigonometric ones, to be more versatile and further save precious memory space and cycle counts. As already evaluated in [13], hardware support for Count Leading Zeroes (CLZ) helps in speeding up the FP functions (e.g., addition, truncation) and can also decrease their code size, replacing a block of instructions with only one. Such support is already present in the PULP extension and in the draft of the RISC-V B extension [16]. Another improvement to further save code size would be merging in common functions the repeated code for dealing with subnormals/special cases, especially when such input patterns are uncommon, and various comparison into one.

7 Conclusion

In this paper, we presented RVfplib, the first open-source assembly-optimized FP emulation library for RISC-V small integer-only processors. The library implements the primary and most common single and double-precision FP operations like addition, subtraction, multiplication, division, comparisons, conversions, and adopts the same interface as libgcc to be easily linked by GCC against real programs without any source-code modification. The library follows IEEE 754 standard guidelines for encodings and computations, with only minor and easily modifiable differences. RVfplib is smaller than the libgcc FP support by almost 60% and, on average, 2× faster. We showed that, on real benchmarks, RVfplib reduces the code size by 39% and speeds up the execution by 1.5× on average, even when considering benchmarks that heavily use the less optimized functions in RVfplib. If compared to the Arm-optimized libgcc library, RVfplib reduces the Arm to RISC-V code size inflation from 196.6% (vs. RISC-V general libgcc FP support) to 19.7%. We also presented RVfplib_nd, which treats subnormal values as correctly signed zeroes, and shown that its code size is 5.3% smaller than the SEGGER emFloat FP library, the only available RISC-V optimized FP emulation library, which is closed-source and treats subnormal values in the same way.

References

1. Arm Keil - fplib. https://www.keil.com/support/man/docs/armlib/armlib_chr1358938941317.html
2. Bertaccini, L., Perotti, M., Mach, S., Schiavone, P.D., Zaruba, F., Benini, L.: Tiny-FPU: low-cost floating-point support for small RISC-V MCU cores. In: 2021 IEEE International Symposium on Circuits and Systems (ISCAS), pp. 1–5 (2021). https://doi.org/10.1109/ISCAS51556.2021.9401149
3. Code size reduction official sub-committee. https://lists.riscv.org/g/tech-code-size
4. Embench benchmark suite. https://github.com/embench/embench-iot
5. FLIP library. http://flip.gforge.inria.fr/
6. Gautschi, M., et al.: Near-threshold RISC-V core with DSP extensions for scalable IoT endpoint devices. IEEE Trans. Very Large Scale Integr. (VLSI) Syst. **25**(10), 2700–2713 (2017). https://doi.org/10.1109/TVLSI.2017.2654506
7. GigaDevice Semiconductor Inc.: GD32VF103 RISC-V 32-bit MCU User Manual, Revision 1.2, October 2019
8. Gottscho, M., Alam, I., Schoeny, C., Dolecek, L., Gupta, P.: Low-cost memory fault tolerance for IoT devices. ACM Trans. Embed. Comput. Syst. **16**(5s), 1–25 (2017). https://doi.org/10.1145/3126534
9. libgcc - Arm floating-point support. https://github.com/gcc-mirror/gcc/blob/master/libgcc/config/arm/ieee754-sf.S
10. libgcc library. https://gcc.gnu.org/onlinedocs/gccint/Soft-float-library-routines.html
11. OpenHW Group CV32E40P user manual. https://core-v-docs-verif-strat.readthedocs.io/projects/cv32e40p_um/en/latest/index.html
12. Perotti, M., et al.: HW/SW approaches for RISC-V code size reduction (2020). https://doi.org/10.3929/ethz-b-000461404
13. Pimentel, J.J., Bohnenstiehl, B., Baas, B.M.: Hybrid hardware/software floating-point implementations for optimized area and throughput tradeoffs. IEEE Trans. Very Large Scale Integr. (VLSI) Syst. **25**(1), 100–113 (2016)
14. Qfplib library. https://www.quinapalus.com/qfplib.html
15. RISC-V - Arm comparison, Embench. https://riscv.org/wp-content/uploads/2019/12/12.10-12.50a-Code-Size-of-RISC-V-versus-ARM-using-the-Embench%E2%84%A2-0.5-Benchmark-Suite-What-is-the-Cost-of-ISA-Simplicity.pdf

16. RISC-V Bit-Manipulation extension draft. https://github.com/riscv/riscv-bitmanip/blob/master/bitmanip-0.92.pdf
17. SEGGER emFloat. https://www.segger.com/products/development-tools/runtime-library/technology/floating-point-library/
18. SEGGER wiki. https://wiki.segger.com/SEGGER_Floating-Point_Library
19. SoftFloat. http://www.jhauser.us/arithmetic/SoftFloat.html
20. TestFloat. http://www.jhauser.us/arithmetic/TestFloat.html

Exploiting Similarity in Evolutionary Product Design for Improved Design Space Exploration

Luise Müller(✉), Kai Neubauer, and Christian Haubelt

Applied Microelectronics and Computer Engineering, University of Rostock, Rostock, Germany
{luise.mueller,kai.neubauer,christian.haubelt}@uni-rostock.de

Abstract. The design of new products is often an evolutionary process, where product versions are built on one another. This form of *(PGE)* reuses some parts of previously developed systems, while others have to be designed from scratch. In consideration of subsequent design steps, i.e., verification, testing, and production, PGE may significantly reduce the time-to-market as these steps can be skipped for reused parts. Thus, deciding which components have to be replaced or added to meet the updated requirements while preserving as many legacy components as possible is one of the key problems in PGE. A further aspect of PGE is the potentially more efficient search for valid design candidates. An already optimized base system can be systematically extended by new functionality without the necessity to search the entire design space. To this end, in this work, we propose a systematic approach, based on Answer Set Programming, to exploit the ideas of PGE in electronic system-level design space exploration. The idea is to gather information on a previous design, analyze the changes to a new version, and utilize the information to steer the search towards potentially good regions in the design space. Extensive experiments show that the presented approach is capable of finding near-optimal design points up to 1,000 times faster than a conventional approach.

Keywords: Design space exploration · Heuristic · Answer Set Programming · Evolutionary design

1 Introduction

Embedded computer systems continuously advance into more areas of everyday life such as medical devices, automotive industry, and telecommunications. In addition to the growing number of application areas, the complexity of individual systems, influenced by the number of internal components, processes,

This work was funded by the German Science Foundation (DFG) under grant HA 4463/4-2.

© Springer Nature Switzerland AG 2022
A. Orailoglu et al. (Eds.): SAMOS 2021, LNCS 13227, pp. 33–49, 2022.
https://doi.org/10.1007/978-3-031-04580-6_3

and heterogeneity, grow simultaneously. Due to the growing complexity, for each system, a vast amount of design decisions has to be made that influence the characteristics of the system. This includes the allocation of hardware resources, the partitioning of functionalities into hardware and software, and the synthesis of the communication infrastructure. The aim is not only to design a valid system, but also to optimize the resulting characteristics of a product. Furthermore, stringent time-to-market requirements, imposed by the pace of technological progress, aggravate the problem of designing optimal products. Hence, an efficient design space exploration is imperative to deliver high-quality products in a reasonable timeframe. To this end, the design process is started at high abstractions with lower degrees of detail mitigating complexity and allowing for a quick exploration of promising design points. Although the DSE is started at a high abstraction level to accelerate decision-making, the high complexity of today's computer systems prevents a complete exploration of the search space. Hence, finding optimal design points remains complicated.

In reality, many electronic systems do not have to be developed entirely from scratch. Instead, it is often aspired to have an entire product line with multiple variants of the system as well as potential successor devices where only marginal changes to the specification are made. Thus, the development of systems can be recognized as an evolutionary process where product versions are built on one another. This form of product design, called *product generation engineering* (PGE) [1], reuses components of previous versions, while others have to be designed from scratch. Deriving a version of an existing product can mitigate the design time and limits verification and testing to the new parts of the system.

Assume, for example, the product line of current smartphone manufacturers. Regularly, typically in a one-year interval, a new generation is released. Here, a generation consists of a base device and derivatives that either have specialized camera sub-systems, less processing capabilities, or varying display and battery sizes. While the transition from one generation to the next may be larger than the changes within one generation, core parts, such as the wireless interface (e.g., WiFi, Bluetooth, GSM) or parts of the operating system remain subject to reuse.

To exploit the general trend towards PGE, in this paper, we propose a methodology that detects similarities of systems in an evolutionary design process. The obtained information is subsequently used in the design process aiming to keep implementation decisions. Our contribution is threefold:

1. We provide an extension to a state-of-the-art system-level design space exploration framework. The information of design decisions of previous product versions is extracted and used to steer the search towards promising regions in the design space exploration of the new product version.
2. We propose a declarative encoding of the problem through the utilization of Answer Set Programming (ASP). This results in a succinct and elaboration tolerant formulation that is easily extensible for future problems.
3. An extensive study is executed that evaluates the proposed approaches with a varying number of changes. The results indicate a large improvement on the quality of found solutions when compared to traditional approaches where no

information of previous generations can be used. While the overall exploration time is not reduced with the presented approach, the exploration yields good solutions three orders of magnitude faster on average.

2 Related Work

In previous works, an effective design reuse model has been developed in [3] and the question of reusability addressed in [6]. Therefore, the necessity of knowledge reuse in connection with product design tasks has been discovered already decades ago. Nevertheless, the advantages of design reuse, like time savings, the prevention of faults as well as an increased extensibility and predictability [3,6] are still valid nowadays and are targeted by the approach of this paper. To make a design applicable for reuse, steps, such as documentation, standardization, parameterization and modularization are carried out [3] enabling that the concept of design reuse is used in processes like design exchange, design evolution or component-based design [3,6].

As an example, the composition of existing subsystems can be implemented by the use of hierarchical mapping encodings, which represent the assignment of functionality to architectural resources [10]. While in that concept subsystems are modeled and combined during the system synthesis steps, the proposed approach aims at identifying similarities between two product versions to reuse parts from one another on design decision level. The synthesizing problem can successfully be encoded using SAT [10] or answer set programming (ASP) [2,11,12]. Contrary to SAT, ASP is based on a closed-world assumption which allows an efficient implementation in particular for densely connected networks and multi-hop communication [2,12].

As another application, the concept of PGE combines reuse mechanisms with significant new developments during the generation of a new technical product. That allows to build up generations of products based on a reference product. Such product management expands the view by an economic perspective. Concrete technical use cases are illustrated by the product generations of the Porsche 911 or of the iPhone [1]. A platform-based design, moreover, enables the creation of either module-based or scale-based product families. For those, metrics and optimization algorithms have been classified [15].

To be able to make use of prior design decisions, similarities and differences between two product versions have to be identified. In this approach, the components of a specification graph are considered whereas in [4] a similarity analysis and scoring is performed on call graphs from different control software projects. In another approach, equivalent mappings for symmetrical transformations of the architecture are determined, thus reducing the number of feasible solutions [7].

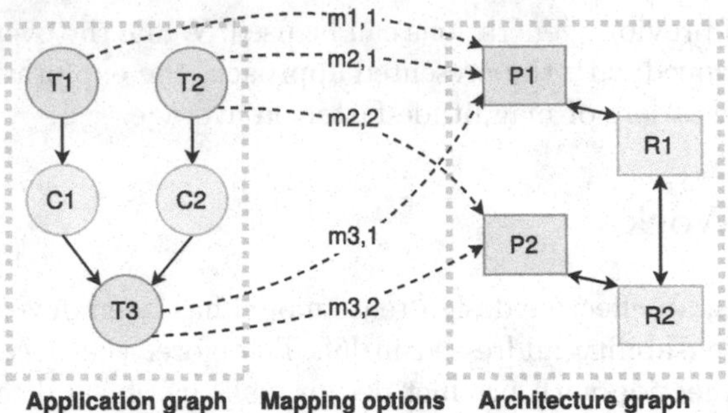

Fig. 1. An example of a specification graph

3 Fundamentals

In this section, we will give an overview of the key prerequisites for the remainder of the paper. To this end, we first present the underlying system model used throughout the paper. Subsequently, the exploration approach is defined, that includes the concept of Pareto optimality and the synthesis model used. Finally, we introduce Answer Set Programming as the symbolic solving technology that is employed to realize the concept.

3.1 System Model

In this paper, we specify the system at the electronic system level (ESL). The specification $S = (A, H, M)$ is split into an application, modeling the behavior of the system, and a hardware template constraining the structure of the system. Both the application $A = (V_A, E_A)$ and the hardware template $H = (V_H, E_H)$ are modeled through directed graphs and are connected through a set of mapping options M, as depicted in Fig. 1. The application is modeled at a task-level granularity with the set of vertices $V_A = T \cup C$ consisting of computational tasks T and communication messages C. The edges $E_A \subseteq T \times C \cup C \times T$ represent the data flow of the application and therefore, the interdependencies of individual tasks. Tasks can send and receive messages to exchange data packets according to their behavior. Each message $c \in C$ is required to be sent and received exactly once, i.e., $\nexists c : \{(c, t_i), (c, t_j)\} \subset E_A$ and $\nexists c : \{(t_i, c), (t_j, c)\} \subset E_A$. In other words, only point-to-point communication among tasks can be modeled directly. Hence, multicast communication is modeled through multiple messages that are all sent by the same task but have different receivers.

The vertices of the hardware template $V_H = P \cup R$ represent hardware devices and are separated into processing elements P and routing units R. While the processing elements are used to execute the tasks of the application graph, the routing units cannot execute code but rather form the communication infrastructure. The latter is completed by the edges $E_H \subseteq V_H \times V_H$ representing links that establish communication channels between devices. In contrast to the application graph, the links are not constrained, i.e., potentially each device may be connected to another device through a link. In this work, we focus on networks on chip (NoC) with regular mesh topologies. However, in principle, the same approach can be used to model bus-based or mixed hardware architectures. Note that the bidirectional edges in Fig. 1 represent two individual links. For example, the edge between routers R1 and R2 is modeled through the two links $l_1 = (R_1, R_2)$ and $l_2 = (R_2, R_1)$.

The set of mapping options $M \subseteq T \times P$ connects the application and hardware graphs. At least one mapping option $m \in M = (t_i, p_j)$ is defined for each task that signifies that the task t_i may be executed on p_j. For the messages, no mapping options have to be specified explicitly as they are constrained implicitly by their sending and receiving tasks, respectively, and can be routed over the entire communication infrastructure. The function $w : M \to \mathbb{N}$ assigns an integer number to each mapping option $m = (t, p)$, signifying the worst case execution time of the task t on the processing element p. Analogously, further properties are assigned to the remaining elements of the specification graph to model heterogeneous architectures. In the present paper, we define the functions $P_{stat} : V_H \to \mathbb{N}$, $area : V_H \to \mathbb{N}$, and $E_{dyn} : M \to \mathbb{N}$ that assign the static power consumption and area costs to each hardware device as well as the dynamic energy requirements to each mapping option, respectively. Finally, a periodicity $\mathcal{P}$ and a routing energy E_r are assigned to the specification that specifies the time, after which the execution is restarted and the energy a single message hop consumes when routed over the network, respectively[1].

In order to transform the specification into an implementation, a valid allocation, binding, routing, and schedule have to be determined. The allocation α is composed of devices and links from the heterogeneous architecture template H, i.e., $\alpha \subseteq V_H \cup E_H$ that shall be used in the specific system implementation and is separated into the device and link allocation α_D and α_L. The static binding $\beta \subseteq M$ and routing $\gamma \subset C \times 2^{E_H}$ select exactly one mapping option for each task and a cycle-free route for each message, depending on the binding of the sending and receiving tasks, respectively. Finally, the schedule τ assigns start times to each task and message, i.e., $\tau : T \cup C \mapsto \mathbb{N}$.

3.2 Exploration Model

The aim of the design space exploration (DSE) is the determination of a set of Pareto-optimal implementations of a specification $S = (A, H, M)$. To this end, each implementation x has to be evaluated according to a set of desired objective functions. In this paper, we focus on the overall latency $lat(x)$ of the system, its area costs $area(x)$, and the energy requirements $E(x)$. Without loss of generality, the DSE is formulated as a multi-objective minimization problem:

$$\begin{aligned} &\textbf{minimize } f(x) = (lat(x), area(x), E(x)),\\ &\text{subject to:}\\ &\quad x \text{ is a feasible system implementation.}\end{aligned}$$

[1] For simplicity, we restrict the properties to integer values. The proposed ASPmT-based [5] approach, however, also allows for real-valued properties in principle.

The area costs of an implementation are calculated as the accumulated area costs of each allocated hardware device, i.e., $area(x) = \sum_{d \in \alpha_D} area(d)$. The energy requirement is the sum of the systems dynamic and static energy requirements:

$$E(x) = \mathcal{P} \cdot \sum_{d \in \alpha_D} P_{stat}(d) + \sum_{m \in \beta} E_{dyn}(m) + \sum_{r \in \gamma} E_r \cdot hops(r).$$

Note that we refer the static energy to one iteration of the system, i.e., the consecutive execution of all tasks within the given period $\mathcal{P}$. The latency of the system is defined as the difference between the maximum end time ($\tau(t) + w((t,p))$, i.e., depending on β) and the minimum start time ($\tau(t)$):

$$lat(x) = \max_{(t,p) \in \beta} (\tau(t) + w((t,p))) - \min_{t \in T}(\tau(t)).$$

For the sake of brevity, we will forgo the exact details of the evaluation steps as they are not particularly relevant for the proposed approach at hand. Instead, we refer to [11] for further information.

As is common in multi-objective optimization problems with conflicting objectives f_i, a single optimal solution generally does not exist as solutions are not totally, but only partially ordered through the dominance relation $\succ$. The dominance relation $\succ$ is defined for n-dimensional quality vectors of two distinct solutions. A candidate solution x dominates another solution y ($x \succ y$) if x evaluates at least as good in every objective and better in at least one objective compared to y. Without loss of generality, for a minimization problem with n objectives, it is formally defined as follows:

$$x \succ y \leftrightarrow \forall i \in \{1, \ldots, n\} : f_i(x) \leq f_i(y) \ \wedge \exists j \in \{1, \ldots, n\} : f_j(x) < f_j(y). \quad (1)$$

A solution x is said to be Pareto-optimal if no dominating solution y exists. Hence, by definition, Pareto-optimal solutions in the Pareto set X_P for a given problem are mutually non-dominated to each other: $\nexists x, y \in X_P : x \succ y \vee y \succ x$.

3.3 Answer Set Programming

In the paper at hand, we implement the DSE with ASP, a programming paradigm that stems from the area of knowledge representation and reasoning. In the following, we will introduce the basics of ASP that are imperative to understand the core concepts of the present work. Based on the stable model semantics, ASP is tailored towards NP-hard search problems. The input is a logic program formulated in a first-order language that is typically separated into a general problem description and a specific problem instance. While the former consists of rules that define how new knowledge is inferred, the latter contains facts representing the initial knowledge. A stable model, or *answer set*, of a logic program conforms to a feasible variable assignment that can be inferred by the rules applied to the facts. The knowledge is encoded by n-ary predicates, i.e., *atoms*, consisting of a predicate name and n parameters. For example, the unary atom `task(ti)` may encode the existence of a task $t_i \in T$, while the binary atom `map(t,p)` indicates that task t may be executed on the processing element p.

An ASP rule consists of a head and a body, and indicates that its head can be inferred if the body holds. In its simplest form, a rule has an empty body and therefore holds unconditionally, i.e., represent the facts to model initial knowledge. In contrast, a rule with an empty head, called an integrity constraint, forces the body not to hold. This way, specific assignments can be excluded from a stable model. To allow for the general problem description to be applicable to each problem instance, the rules are encoded with variables, generally indicated by uppercase letters in the encoding. For instance, the rule `1{bind(T,P) : map(T,P)}1 :- task(T).` encodes the binding constraint. The rule states that exactly one mapping option $(t, p) \in M$ has to be selected for each task $t \in T$. Internally, the rule is grounded into a variable-free representation resulting in a set of $|T|$ individual rules. Afterwards, the variable-free atoms are inferred according to the rules given by the problem definition. Therefore, the ASP solver employs a conflict-driven clause learning (CDCL) strategy where atoms are inferred subsequently until a conflicting assignment causes the generation of a conflict clause and the back-jump to a previous decision level.

The order, in which (variable-free) atoms are assigned, is decided by a heuristic that is generally influenced by a generic set of rules, the characteristics of the problem. These rules can be disparate and usually influence the performance of the search differently for varying problem classes. The utilized ASP solver clingo, for example, employs the heuristic Variable State Independent Decaying Sum (VSIDS) [8] in its default configuration. Here, variables are assigned initial activities that decay over time and increase if they appear in a learned conflict clause. Whenever the search branches, the solver selects the atom with the highest activity. Although VSIDS is considered to be one of the most efficient branching heuristics [8], it does not embody domain knowledge. In the paper at hand, we will propose the use of domain specific heuristics to accelerate the evolutionary product design. This is discussed in more detail in Sect. 4.3.

Note that an elaborate discussion of ASP solving and the detailed presentation of the encoding are out of the scope of this paper. The interested reader is referred to [5,9] and [12], respectively.

4 Similarity of Design Points

The aim of this project is to enhance the development step of the DSE by applying the idea of evolutionary product design. The therefore required prior knowledge is provided by a previously developed system representing a product present on the market. It is given by the parent configuration in Fig. 2 and is consisting of a specification and an implementation. It has to be noted that this solution is not guaranteed to be optimal, but very good concerning its application. Besides, Fig. 2 illustrates the steps of the proposed approach.

As a comprehensive example, a cellphone shall be improved. By modifying the specification of the parent configuration, a new derived version is created, namely

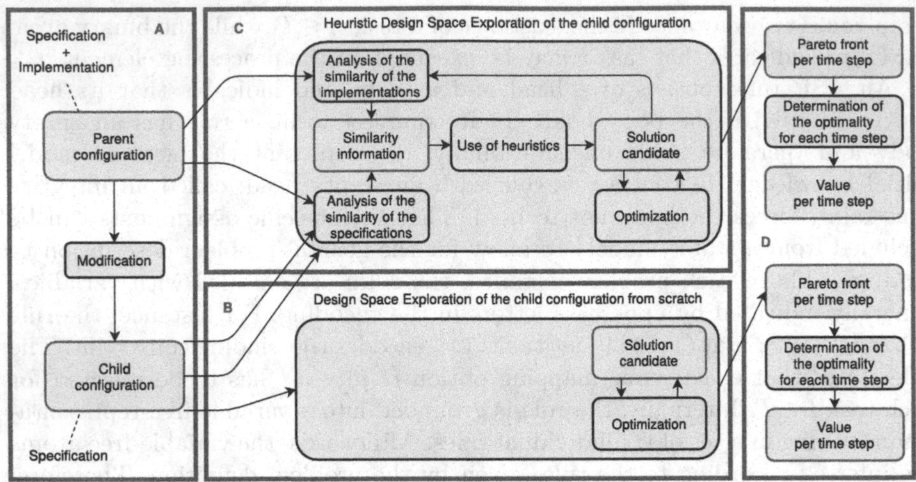

Fig. 2. Overview of the proposed approach (A+C) and its comparison (D) to a state-of-art approach (B)

the child configuration. Since all elements of the specification offer modification potential, it might be planned to extend the device functionality by changing its application as well as to equip the cell phone with additional hardware components, like a new processor or a second camera to improve its performance. Depending on the extent of the modification and the affected sections, a change in the specification can have a considerably large as well as nearly no impact on the final implementation. To refer to the example given above, an additional processor is only allocated, when a task is bound on it. If done so, additional interconnections are required to ensure the communication ability of the new processor. The modification stage is shown in block A in Fig. 2. The specific modifications applied in the experiments are given in Sect. 5.

To determine the implementation of the child configuration, two approaches are distinguished. Block B in Fig. 2 represents the DSE from scratch where solution candidates are generated. Only valid intermediate solutions are kept and further optimized concerning the factors latency, energy consumption and area costs. This procedure is enhanced by the use of heuristics during the DSE shown in block C in Fig. 2. The heuristic DSE aims at retaining as many design decisions from the parent implementation as possible. To gain knowledge about reusable concepts and design decisions from the parent configuration, the specifications of both systems are analyzed to identify the similarities and differences and thus, the reuse potential. The corresponding steps are explained in detail in the following subsections.

Finally in block D, the results of both approaches are compared. Therefore, for each the optimality of the Pareto front of the final and of all intermediate solutions is evaluated and set in context to the time when the individual solution has been found.

4.1 Analysis of the Specifications

Firstly, as shown in Fig. 2, all elements of the specification graph as well as all characteristics of both configurations are examined and compared to identify each similarity and difference. From the perspective of the child configuration, for each instance of each component type, it is recorded whether it is a common (*equal*), an own, i.e., newly *added*, or an unknown and therefore already deleted (*missing*) component. These three cases are demonstrated by means of the component type *task* in Code snippet 1. The comparison is carried out on the basis of the parameters of the component instances. A *task* is defined by three constants: an ID, an application number, and a configuration assignment. If for two instances all parameters except for the configuration constant are identical, these present a single instance which is common to both systems. Similarly, instances can be found which only exist in one configuration.

For all other component types in the specification, the procedure is the same.

```
% Equal tasks in both configurations
equal_task(task(NUM,A,child)) :- task(NUM,A,child), task(NUM,A,parent).
% Missing tasks in child configuration with regard to parent configuration
missing_task(task(NUM,A,child)) :- not task(NUM,A,child),
    task(NUM,A,parent).
% Added tasks in child configuration with regard to parent configuration
added_task(task(NUM,A,child)) :- task(NUM,A,child),
    not task(NUM,A,parent).
```

Code snippet 1. The analysis of all instances of the component type *task*

4.2 Analysis of the Implementations

Besides the specification, the implementation of the parent configuration is clearly determined and available. To be able to take on a design decision from the previous system, the prospective decisions made to generate a solution candidate for the child configuration have to be evaluated. Like Fig. 2 illustrates, the results from the evaluation alongside with the optimization objectives influence the selection of favorable solutions.

To compare two implementations, each decision, including the allocation, binding, routing and scheduling, is considered. In the following Code snippet 2, the decision on the task binding is taken as a representative case.

```
% Equally decided bindings in both configurations
equal_bind(bind(M,task(T,A,child),processor(R,child))) :-
    bind(M,task(T,A,child),processor(R,child)),
    bind(_,task(T,A,parent),processor(R,parent)).
% Not equally decided binding for equal tasks in both configurations
not_equally_bind(bind(M1,task(T,A,child),processor(R1,child)),
    bind(M2,task(T,A,child),processor(R2,child))) :-
    bind(M1,task(T,A,child),processor(R1,child)),
    bind(M2,task(T,A,parent),processor(R2,parent)), R1!=R2.
```

```
% Missing binding in child configuration with regard to parent configuration
missing_bind(bind(M,task(T,A,child),processor(R,child))) :–
    bind(M,task(T,A,parent),processor(R,parent)), missing_task(task(T,A,child)).
% Added binding in child configuration with regard to parent configuration
added_bind(bind(M,task(T,A,child),processor(R,child))) :–
    bind(M,task(T,A,child),processor(R,child)), added_task(task(T,A,child)).
```

Code snippet 2. The analysis of all instances of the decision on the binding

It is identified by a mapping id and a corresponding task mapped to a certain processor, each belonging to a configuration. Analogical to the scheme presented in Sect. 4.1, three result types are expected: *equal*, *missing*, *added* and evaluated from the perspective of the child configuration. The similarity information generated by use of the terms in Code snippet 1 is used to decide on similarities in the implementations. For example, a task which was added or deleted cannot be bound equally and therefore causes an *added* or a *missing* bind. Furthermore, the type *not_equally* is introduced to ensure an unambiguous evaluation. Otherwise, for two configurations, which might have tasks and processors in common, but do not share the same binding decision, bindings might be simultaneously classified as *missing* and *added* and, this way, be counted twice. For all other decision types in the implementation, the analysis is done likewise.

4.3 Use of Heuristics During Design Space Exploration

Through analyzing the specifications and the implementations, an extensive knowledge is built up which is particularly useful for the development of the new derived product. It is assumed that, in the search space, a good solution for the child configuration is to be found near to the design point of the implementation of the parent configuration. Hoping that the optimal solution of the DSE for the child configuration is similar to the implementation of the parent configuration, the gained similarity information is used in heuristics to select appropriate design decisions from the previous system and set them as an initial design point. Thus, the exploration starts in a defined area of the search space and is controlled. At the same time, the search space is not restricted and no solution is excluded. If there are similarities in the specifications, all related decisions made in the development of the previous version are adopted and every variable assignment is preferably decided as previously done for the parent configuration.

Considering the example from Sect. 4.2, the similarity information about the decision on the task binding is taken up in a heuristic in Code snippet 3.

```
% Highest priority for deciding the binding equally to the parent configuration
#heuristic equal_bind(bind(M,T,R)). [23,true]
```

Code snippet 3. The heuristic influencing the decision on the binding

In the implementation of the heuristic in ASP, a so-called *modifier* is used. It prioritizes the individual term in a way that it, if possible, is assigned a specified value (*true* or *false*) and evaluated earlier during the DSE. In the code sample, the decision to set a binding equally compared to the parent configuration is assigned a static priority of *23*. At the same time, the decision on the allocation is indirectly made when a hardware resource is used in a binding. In case of a task that is only specified in one system, it is impossible to decide the binding identically. Hence, another heuristic is set whose aim is to, at least, bind the task to a common processor. Thus, the allocation of a new and additional resource might become superfluous, if no task is bound to it in the final solution.

The design decision on the binding is considered in the following step of the routing. If there is a common binding of a task on a processor, the communication path to and from that processor is adopted from the parent configuration. This approach is given in Code snippet 4. The heuristics deciding on the scheduling is considering the execution order of the tasks and similarly implemented.

Further, the synthesis steps are executed in order. According to their priority, the binding decisions are determined first, followed by the routing and the scheduling step. It is conceivable as well to decide on all equal elements first and then to consider the differences. This offers the advantage of a clear separation between the similarities and the differences.

```
% If binding was equally decided in both configurations, decide for the same
    routing like in the parent-configuration
#heuristic equal_reached(reached(comm(T1,_,_,child), processor(P,child),
    router(R,child))) : equal_bind(bind(_,T1,P)). [13,true]
#heuristic equal_reached(reached(comm(_,T2,_,child), router(R,child),
    processor(P,child))) : equal_bind(bind(_,T2,P)). [13,true]
#heuristic equal_reached(reached(C,router(R1,child),router(R2,child))). [13,true]
```

Code snippet 4. The heuristic influencing the decision on the routing

Starting with a good implementation for the child configuration consisting of adopted design decisions from the parent configuration, a faster converge to optimal solutions is expected.

5 Experiments

The implementation of this project consists of ASP and C++ code as well as bash scripts for the project execution. The tool clingo is used in version 5.2.2 [13]. To set time stamps and to interrupt a DSE at a certain time (timeout) the tool runsolver in version 3.4 is used [14]. The experiments introduced subsequently are tested on Intel Core i7-4770 CPUs with ×86-64 architecture and 32 GiB RAM. The surrounding environment is Ubuntu version 16.04.7 LTS.

5.1 Experimental Setup

As a setup, 24 parent instances of different characteristics are taken from a set of test cases generated by an ASP-based benchmark generator [12]. A 3×3 grid structure, consisting of nine routers bidirectionally connected to each other and additionally to one processor each, is common to all configurations while their

Table 1. Overview of the modification classes specifying the test cases

Change hardware elements			Change software elements			Combined changes		
	p_t	p_p		p_t	p_p		p_t	p_p
I	0	20	V	20	0	IX	20	20
II	0	40	VI	40	0	X	40	40
III	0	60	VII	60	0	XI	60	60
IV	0	80	VIII	80	0	XII	80	80

application graphs are structured differently. These are generated as "series-parallel graphs" (SPG) having twelve different sizes in the range of 17 to 115 tasks.

To assume good solutions for the parent instances as a basis for the experiments, a DSE for each has been executed for 48 h. Randomly, one of the best but not necessarily optimal solutions is taken as implementation of the parent configuration. From each parent specification, ten modified child specifications are generated. The modification is composed of a randomly decided combination of different changes including the deletion, addition or exchange of components. In the experiments, either tasks as representatives of the software side (p_t), processors as elements of the architecture graph (p_p), or combinations of both are considered. Table 1 gives an overview about the chosen test cases.

In total, we have conducted $2 * 24 * 12 * 10 = 5,760$ DSE runs for up to 30 min to explore the child configurations. This relatively short time was chosen to be able to consider different modification classes and a sufficient number of randomly generated modifications to obtain a generally valid statement. The resulting fronts are evaluated concerning their ϵ-dominance [16]. Therefore, a reference front, each consisting of the best solution front found up to a timeout of the DSE with and without the use of heuristics, is generated. It is considered as the optimal solution front. Additionally, all intermediate solutions found during the DSE are assigned with a time stamp and evaluated as well. The results together with their corresponding time stamps are plotted to identify the quality improvements over time. Per test case and per parent configuration each, an average curve is presented along with the individual results for the ten children.

5.2 Experimental Results

The test execution results in 24 diagrams per test case, each illustrating the progression of the ϵ-dominance during the DSE with and without heuristics over time for one parent instance. Until a timeout, which is set as a vertical line at 1,800 s, is reached, each curve approximates an ϵ-dominance equals one. Matching this value indicates that the respective solution front is covering the reference front in every design point. Obtaining this result at an early time is the desirable outcome. All in all, four types of curve progressions are identified and pictured in Fig. 3.

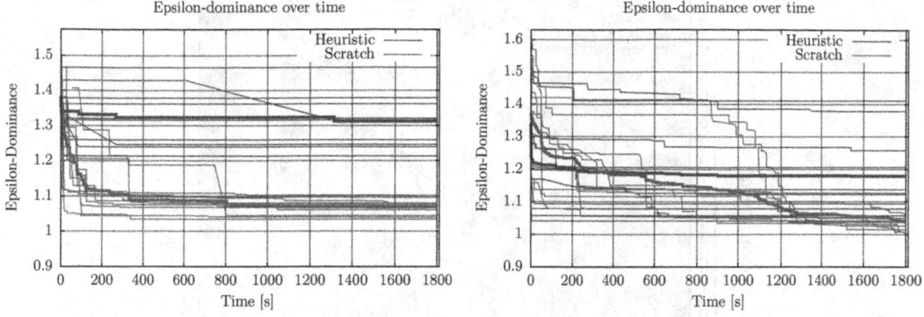

(a) Type 1 - Scratch better than Heuristic (b) Type 2 - Both with similar performance

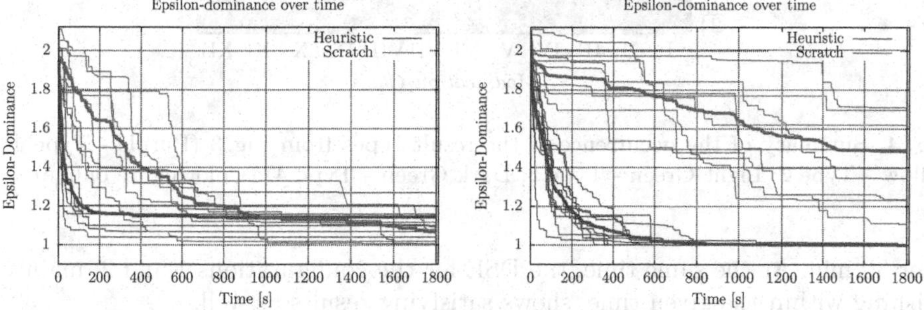

(c) Type 3 - Heuristic with good start is overtaken by Scratch (d) Type 4 - Heuristic better than Scratch

Fig. 3. The four resulting average curve types

The first and fourth type mark a course where either the scratch or the heuristic curve is obviously faster approximating the value one. Whereas for the third type, the heuristic curve is developing to low values fast, but is overtaken by the scratch curve during the exploration. The second type represents a case which does not allow a clear determination. Figure 4 aggregates the occurrences of the four types given in Fig. 3 for all modification classes and considering the 24 configurations. The types 1 (= purple), 2 (= yellow), 3 (= light green), 4 (= dark green) are colored and rated in ascending order with type 4 indicating the superiority of our proposed approach. Having this overview, a considerable trend can be detected. The usefulness of the usage of heuristics depends on the considered configuration. Noting that an increasing configuration number signifies a larger amount of applications and tasks, the use of heuristics tend to work better for large configurations. With an increasing size of a configuration, the time to exhaustively explore the respective design space grows exponentially. Thus, controlling the DSE by the use of any heuristics is essential to find good solutions in a reasonable time. For large configurations, the proposed heuristics provide excellent results, but it can not be evaluated how close these are towards the real Pareto-optimal solution front because the design space is hardly explored

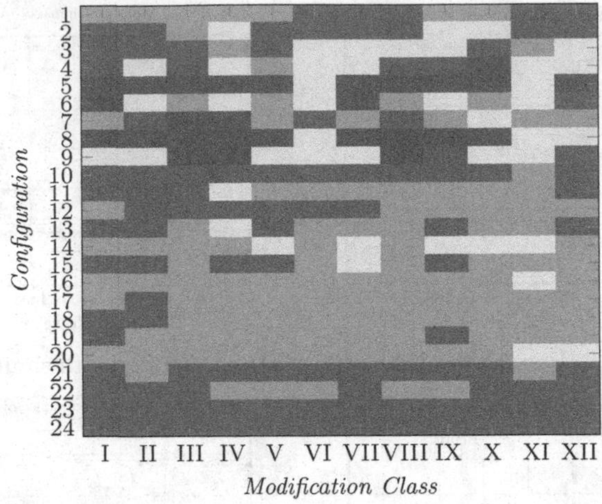

Fig. 4. Summary of the occurrence of the result types from Fig. 3 (Purple - Type 1; Yellow - Type 2; Light Green - Type 3; Dark Green - Type 4) (Color figure online)

after 30 min. At the same time, the DSE for the configurations 1 and 2, mainly finishing within the given time, shows satisfying results as well.

Considering the kind of modification, a few differences for cases with a lot of changes like III, IV, VII or XI are visible, but in overall no clear classification is identifiable.

In a second evaluation, the results for the configuration 11, which contains 55 tasks distributed over two applications, are analyzed in more detail. Table 2 lists for every change type the time it takes to reach a specified ϵ-dominance value. A table entry consists of a number of the explorations reaching the respective level, an average time value and a corresponding standard deviation. The behavior of the DSE with and without heuristics is compared.

Thereby, two aspects become visible. At first, not all explorations even reach an ϵ-dominance equal to two because large changes on the architecture graph (p_p and $p_p + p_t$), mainly in case of deletion of processors, cause the creation of unsatisfiable child instances. Furthermore, the heuristic DSE for satisfiable child instances, which are derived by purely changing the hardware side (p_p), provides significantly better results. This becomes more clear, the closer an ϵ-dominance equal to one is approximated. More heuristic instances are reaching lower stages and the results are found up to 1,000 times faster with lower deviations. These cases are perfect examples for the type 4 from Fig. 3.

Secondly, the results when considering only the modifications on the application graph (p_t) are ideal representatives for type 3 from Fig. 3. By using the own heuristics, the first three levels are reached within a few seconds. But as time goes on, the DSE from scratch is more successful. At the same time, most cases of both exploration types are finally not reaching an ϵ-dominance of one, which means that different design points exclusively were found and several valid implementations with good properties exist.

Table 2. Comparison of the influence of different change types

		2		1.5		1.3		1.1		1.0	
		$\mathcal{S}$	$\mathcal{H}$	$\mathcal{S}$	$\mathcal{H}$	$\mathcal{S}$	$\mathcal{H}$	$\mathcal{S}$	$\mathcal{H}$	$\mathcal{S}$	$\mathcal{H}$
p_p	20	10 0.70 s 6.26%	10 0.73 s 7.59%	10 0.70 s 6.00%	10 0.73 s 6.59%	10 101.62 s 182.06%	10 0.81 s 8.1%	5 566.03 s 120.87 %	9 0.91 s 7.71%	0 – –	4 315.77 s 87.74%
	40	9 0.66 s 7.75%	9 0.69 s 7.53%	9 3.84 s 248.05%	9 0.70 s 8.15%	9 70.11 s 91.26%	9 0.76 s 6.78%	6 822.49 s 63.46%	8 0.87 s 14.90%	0 – –	1 558.36 s –
	60	10 0.66 s 11.56%	10 0.67 s 14.14%	10 0.66 s 11.56%	10 0.67 s 14.14%	100 101.28 s 138.32%	10 0.75 s 23.35%	6 653.43 s 94,56%	10 0.96 s 22.85%	0 – –	5 803.26 s 81.10%
	80	5 0.64 s 12.66%	5 0.63 s 13.28%	5 0.80 s 46.39%	5 0.63 s 13.28%	5 134.22 s 84.79%	4 0.66 s 11.46%	1 849.31 s –	3 0.76 s 15.63%	0 – –	0 – –
p_t	20	10 0.74 s 12.97%	10 0.76 s 7.89%	10 6.85 s 132.70%	10 0.80 s 5.77%	10 175.78 s 105.01%	10 0.93 s 10.76%	9 694.56 s 78.29%	6 14.43 s 227.26%	1 1573.48 s –	0 – –
	40	10 120.73 s 146.54%	10 0.93 s 23.44%	10 129.55 s 132.63%	10 0.94 s 22.50%	10 185.42 s 124.74%	9 1.05 s 19.56%	8 752.76 s 71.24%	7 1.64 s 47.87%	5 1627.63 s 14.51%	1 49.54 s –
	60	10 0.77 s 20.52%	10 0.81 s 18.08%	10 52.94 s 172.62%	10 0.90 s 16.33%	10 175.09 s 111.62%	10 1.74 s 112.44%	9 453.64 s 53.79%	8 305.82 s 174.50%	4 1377.95 s 25.85%	0 – –
	80	10 0.81 s 31.61%	10 0.81 s 22.40%	10 36.85 s 10.14%	10 1.37 s 65.70%	10 215.07 s 132.61%	10 4.25 s 177.05%	8 591.55 s 85.23%	6 6.68 s 154.22%	1 1380.83 s –	2 6.50 s 54.11%
$p_p + p_t$	20	10 0.80 s 36.66%	10 0.73 s 11.02%	10 20.09 s 154.13%	10 0.74 s 10.09%	10 123.77 s 144.38%	10 0.89 s 19.69%	9 328.02 s 72.60%	9 1.13 s 33.53%	1 1739.00 s –	1 407.36 s –
	40	10 0.80 s 32.34%	10 0.74 s 13.67%	10 9.68 s 108.62%	9 0.76 s 17.35%	10 116.54 s 78.60%	9 0.89 s 21.32%	5 372.73 s 120.13%	5 1.13 s 23.52%	2 1730.17 s 0.84%	1 1042.53 s –
	60	5 120.51 s 112.08%	5 184,54 s 217.65%	5 120.52 s 112.07%	5 184.57 s 217.60%	5 162.42 s 82.09%	5 186.84 s 214.29%	3 590.29 s 42.76%	1 1.21 s –	1 1099.08 s –	0 – –
	80	6 152.49 s 243.92%	6 0.80 s 16.71%	6 188.32 s 211.23%	6 0.94 s 24.13%	6 412.54 s 144.05%	5 1.13 s 19.42%	3 435.72 s 63.92%	3 5.03 s 87.86%	1 1415.28 s –	0 – –

In general, Table 2 shows that the average times and the standard deviations for the first solutions from the DSE with and without heuristics are similar. If the heuristic DSE reaches a low ϵ-dominance, it takes a significantly shorter time. Likewise, the deviation is lower. This is an important result, showing that good results can be found at an early exploration stage without the necessity to search the entire design space.

6 Conclusion

Within this paper, a systematic approach based on ASP to enhance the DSE of embedded systems is proposed. It aims at supporting an evolutionary product design process in the context of *Product Generation Engineering*. Exploiting the similarities between a base system and its derivatives allows to identify parts that can be reused unchanged. The gained domain knowledge is utilized in heuristics to steer the search towards regions in the design space potentially containing solutions with optimal properties.

To ensure a meaningful evaluation of the impact of the used heuristics, an extensive amount of test cases, consisting of a variety of different configurations and several systematically derived child instances, was used in the experiments. As expected, the usage of heuristics in the DSE helps to find good solutions earlier. While small systems are less likely to profit from the introduction of the proposed heuristics, particularly in large system configurations, the application of heuristics shows a significantly high exploration quality. For the product development, it is not required to find the optimal implementation because that goes along with an inestimable long exploration time and high costs. Much more preferably is a good solution found at an early time. Likewise, in the majority of the test cases, excellent results were achieved just in a few seconds.

Finally, the implementation at hand can be extended by new heuristics and further use cases. The experiments have shown that there is more potential for identifying reusable parts, especially when analyzing how the structure of a configuration is influencing its reusability.

References

1. Albers, A., et al.: Product generation development-importance and challenges from a design research perspective. In: Proceedings of ME, pp. 16–21, May 2015
2. Andres, B., Gebser, M., Schaub, T., Haubelt, C., Reimann, F., Glaß, M.: Symbolic system synthesis using answer set programming. In: Cabalar, P., Son, T.C. (eds.) LPNMR 2013. LNCS (LNAI), vol. 8148, pp. 79–91. Springer, Heidelberg (2013). https://doi.org/10.1007/978-3-642-40564-8_9
3. Duffy, S., et al.: A design reuse model. In: Proceedings of ICED, pp. 490–495, August 1995
4. Fahimipirehgalin, M., Fischer, J., Bougouffa, S., Vogel-Heuser, B.: Similarity analysis of control software using graph mining. In: INDIN, vol. 1, pp. 508–515 (2019). https://doi.org/10.1109/INDIN41052.2019.8972335
5. Gebser, M., et al.: Theory solving made easy with Clingo 5. In: Proceedings of ICLP, pp. 2:1–2:15 (2016). https://doi.org/10.4230/OASIcs.ICLP.2016.2
6. Girczyc, E., Carlson, S.: Increasing design quality and engineering productivity through design reuse. In: Proceedings of DATE, pp. 48–53 (1993). https://doi.org/10.1145/157485.164565
7. Goens, A., Siccha, S., Castrillon, J.: Symmetry in software synthesis. ACM TACO **14**(2), 1–26 (2017). https://doi.org/10.1145/3095747
8. Liang, J.H., Ganesh, V., Zulkoski, E., Zaman, A., Czarnecki, K.: Understanding VSIDS branching heuristics in conflict-driven clause-learning SAT solvers. In: Piterman, N. (ed.) HVC 2015. LNCS, vol. 9434, pp. 225–241. Springer, Cham (2015). https://doi.org/10.1007/978-3-319-26287-1_14
9. Lifschitz, V.: What is answer set programming? In: Proceedings of AAAI, pp. 1594–1597, July 2008

10. Neubauer, K., et al.: Supporting composition in symbolic system synthesis. In: Proceedings of SAMOS, pp. 132–139, July 2016. https://doi.org/10.1109/SAMOS.2016.7818340
11. Neubauer, K., et al.: Exact multi-objective design space exploration using ASPmT. In: Proceedings of DATE, pp. 257–260, March 2018. https://doi.org/10.23919/DATE.2018.8342014
12. Neubauer, K., et al.: Exact design space exploration based on consistent approximations. Electronics **9**(7), 1057 (2020). https://doi.org/10.3390/electronics9071057
13. Potassco: Clingo homepage. https://potassco.org/clingo/. Accessed 13 Mar 2021
14. Roussel, O.: Controlling a solver execution: the runsolver tool. JSAT **7**, 139–144 (2011). https://doi.org/10.3233/SAT190083
15. Simpson, T.W.: Product platform design and customization: status and promise. AI EDAM **18**(1), 3–20 (2004). https://doi.org/10.1017/S0890060404040028
16. Zitzler, E., et al.: Performance assessment of multiobjective optimizers: an analysis and review. IEEE TEVC **7**(2), 117–132 (2003). https://doi.org/10.1109/TEVC.2003.810758

Automatic Search-Space Compression in System-Level Design Space Exploration Using Deep Generative Models

Valentina Richthammer(✉) and Michael Glaß

Institute of Embedded Systems/Real-Time Systems, Ulm University, Ulm, Germany
{valentina.richthammer,michael.glass}@uni-ulm.de

Abstract. Major challenges for system-level Design Space Exploration (DSE) include (a) tremendous search-space sizes for modern many-core architectures and networked systems and (b) the preponderance of infeasible solutions in the search space from which no actual implementations can be derived. Since current DSE approaches are not equipped to handle these developments, we propose the integration of deep generative models into DSE to automatically compress large-scale search spaces, thus (I) reducing problem complexity faced by the optimizer while (II) learning a model of feasible solutions to focus the optimization on. The proposed approach is seamlessly integrated into state-of-the-art DSE flows, is complementary to existing search-space pruning techniques, and its potential to improve optimization quality by up to ≈ 66% is demonstrated for a variety of DSE problems.

Keywords: Design automation · Deep learning · Compression

1 Introduction

Design automation at the Electronic System Level (ESL) is a combinatorial Multi-Objective Optimization Problem (MOOP) where application-to-architecture mappings are optimized for a variety of conflicting design objectives simultaneously. To this end, system-level Design Space Exploration (DSE) techniques need to derive a multitude of implementation options from an input specification that defines the application, architecture, as well as functional and non-functional requirements on feasible solutions in the form of data dependencies, energy budgets, latency, etc. Deriving a single feasible implementation is an NP-complete problem [19], also known as system synthesis, which makes DSE a *hard-constrained* MOOP. With increasingly complex system specifications, as, e.g., introduced by large-scale many-core architectures or networked automotive applications with extensive communication requirements, exact techniques are no longer able to exhaustively analyse the complete search space of all implementation possibilities [17]. Thus, metaheuristic optimization techniques are employed to efficiently traverse these large-scale search spaces [12].

© Springer Nature Switzerland AG 2022
A. Orailoglu et al. (Eds.): SAMOS 2021, LNCS 13227, pp. 50–61, 2022.
https://doi.org/10.1007/978-3-031-04580-6_4

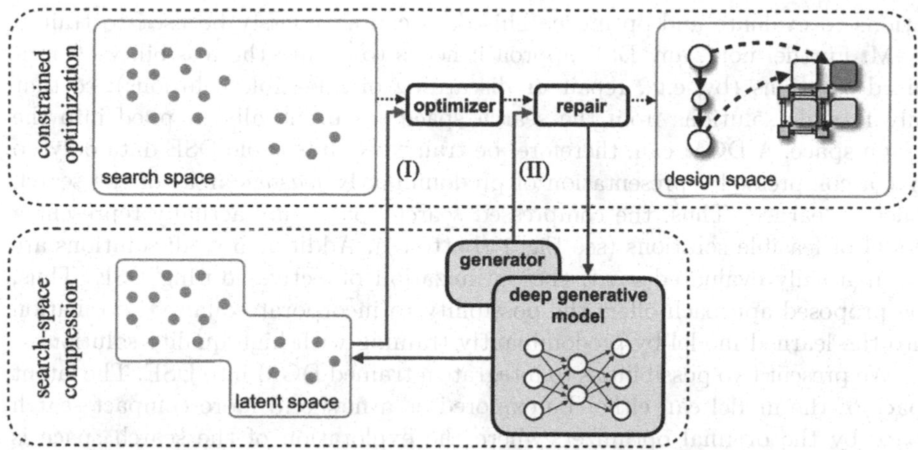

Fig. 1. Optimization flow for hard-constrained combinatorial MOOPs (top) and proposed *search-space compression* using Deep Generative Models (bottom).

These metaheuristics require an encoding of solutions from the design space into a suitable *search space* that can be efficiently explored by an optimizer. For hard-constrained combinatorial problems as DSE, an encoding that is feasible by construction is impossible. Thus, DSE search spaces are mainly populated by *infeasible solutions* with few and scattered feasible solutions inbetween (see Fig. 1 (top), where green dots in the search space represent feasible solutions, while the rest of the search space is infeasible). During the optimization, a dedicated *repair mechanism* needs to be integrated when deriving solutions in the design space from the search space to guarantee that only feasible solutions are evaluated and optimized. Nevertheless, the *predominance of infeasible search-space areas* combined with *tremendous search-space sizes* hinder its efficient exploration.

Contributions: As a remedy, this work presents an *automatic search-space compression* scheme using Deep Generative Models (DGMs), as also illustrated in Fig. 1. DGMs learn a compressed representation, i.e., an encoding of data together with the corresponding encoding and decoding functions. Thus, we propose to train a DGM to learn a compression of the original search space, so that a new *compact search space* can be used for further exploration. The DGM's decoder is used to reconstruct the compressed solutions in the original search space that can then be mapped into the design space as in standard DSE.

Since the compressed search space is much smaller than the original search space due to the dimensionality reduction performed by the DGM, problem complexity for the optimizer is reduced, facilitating the optimization. Finally, a DGM architectural pattern to be integrated into DSE is proposed that suits a variety of DSE problems across a range of application domains.

The proposed integration of Deep Learning (DL) techniques into DSE is well-suited, since DSE already generates hundreds of thousands of implementations to evaluate and optimize. This data can seamlessly be used to train a DGM. Furthermore, any DSE approach needs to ensure the feasibility of optimized solutions (by, e.g., repair or discarding of infeasible solutions), so that only feasible solutions from the search space are eventually mapped into the design space. A DGM can, therefore, be trained with feasible DSE data only, so that a compressed representation of predominantly *feasible* areas of the search space is learned. Thus, the compressed search space may actually represent a model of feasible solutions (see Fig. 1 (bottom)). Additionally, all solutions are automatically evaluated w.r.t. the optimization objectives during DSE. Thus, the proposed approach offers the possibility to incorporate quality information into the learned model by predominantly training with high-quality solutions.

We present two possibilities to integrate a trained DGM into DSE: The latent space of the model can either be explored as a new and more compact search space by the original optimizer, where the exploration of the search space is facilitated for conventional techniques by reducing search-space size (Fig. 1(I)). Alternatively, DGMs offer the possibility to generate novel instances of the model directly via a *generator* (Fig. 1(II)).

However, since the DGM is not able to learn an *exact* model of feasibility in practice, the newly generated solutions in both cases (I) and (II) still need to undergo the same feasibility check and repair as in the original optimization flow when being mapped into the design space. Furthermore, DGMs are designed for lossy compression to avoid overfitting the model. Thus, high-quality solutions may potentially be lost during the compression. Despite this, we demonstrate using experimental results that compact search spaces generated by encoding via a DGM can be explored more efficiently and solutions of superior optimization quality are found for different problem domains, compared to full-size DSE search spaces. This is in line with related works on search-space pruning (e.g. [17]), where an improved exploration of compact search spaces is already shown.

2 Related Work

Deep Generative Models (DGMs) are unsupervised-learning techniques that are able to produce new data points from a trained model. Two prevailing types are Generational Adversarial Networks (GANs) and Variational Autoencoders (VAEs) that have been applied to a wide array of problem domains, ranging from image, video, or music generation [14] to the synthesis of arithmetic expressions and molecules [7]. In this work, we focus on VAEs, since they are explicitly designed for dimensionality reduction by concurrently training an encoder coupled with the respective decoder, so that its latent space is a compressed representation of the input training data.

In DSE, Machine Learning (ML) has been applied for two main purposes up until now: First, overall DSE time is reduced by approximating the design objectives during the evaluation of solutions using ML techniques where a simulative or analytical evaluation may be expensive or infeasible. For example, [4] proposes Recurrent Neural Networks for latency estimation, [18] investigates predictive modelling techniques in DSE for high-level synthesis, while [9] evaluates different ML approaches to approximate cost, area, power, and performance for DSE of reconfigurable accelerator systems—among many others. Secondly, ML methods are used to improve the *traversal* of the search space, i.e. the exploration phase of the optimization. This is done by, e.g., improving local search based on ML predictions in many-core DSE [5] or by applying reinforcement learning to generate high-quality system configurations in Network-on-Chip (NoC) design [15]. In contrast, this work presents an ML-based *search-space compression* that allows continued optimization using standard optimization techniques on a *simplified search space* for a variety of constrained MOOPs.

For an overview of recent DSE techniques, see [12]. However, these algorithms are mostly geared towards specific DSE problem instances with no particular focus on the general problem of large-scale and sparse combinatorial search spaces, as present for any DSE problem. While other search-space pruning techniques for constrained optimization and DSE do exist [13,17], the compression approaches presented in the work at hand are orthogonal to any other technique and can be applied in conjunction before or after other such measures.

3 Fundamentals

This section introduces a DSE system model commonly used in literature together with a description of DSE as hard-constrained Multi-Objective Optimization Problem (MOOP).

3.1 System Model

Many current DSE techniques use a graph-based system model to represent application, architecture, and mapping possibilities [19]. All feasible implementation possibilities are represented in a *system specification* that defines a set of *mapping edges* E_M between an *application graph* G_T and an *architecture graph* G_R (see Fig. 2(a)).

Definition 1 (Application Graph). *The application graph is a bipartite directed acyclic graph* $G_T(V_T, E_T)$*, with vertices* $V_T = T \cup C$ *representing processing tasks* T *and messages* C *for data dependencies. Sender-receiver relations of messages are modelled by edges* $E_T \subseteq (T \times C) \cup (C \times T)$ *connecting tasks and messages (or vice versa).*

Definition 2 (Architecture Graph). *The architecture graph is a directed graph* $G_R(R, L)$ *with resources* R *as vertices and edges* L *modeling available communication links.*

Definition 3 (Mapping Edges). *The set of mapping options between tasks* T *and resources* R *is given by mapping edges* $E_M \subseteq T \times R$*, where mapping edge* $m_{t,r} \in E_M$ *represents a feasible binding of task* $t \in T$ *to resource* $r \in R$*.*

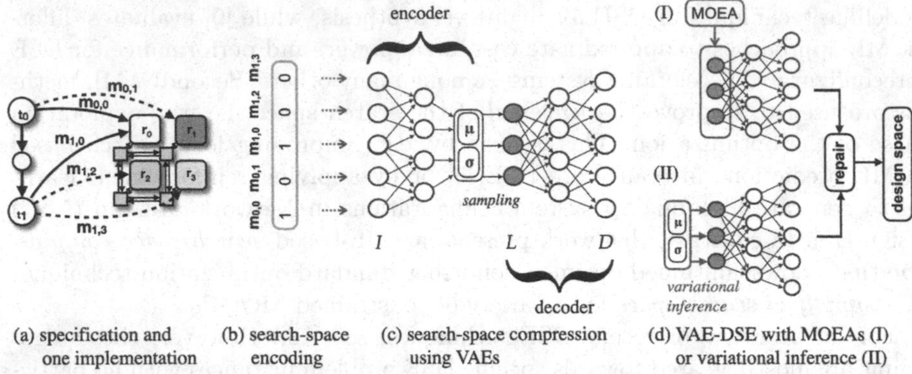

Fig. 2. System specification of DSE with one feasible implementation (a), search-space representation of an implementation (b), automatic search-space compression using VAEs (c), and DSE using VAE-compressed search spaces (d).

The specification in Fig. 2(a) shows an application with two tasks t_0, t_1 with a total of 5 mapping edges $m_{0,0} - m_{1,3}$ to the 2×2 architecture. A concrete implementation, that may be derived during DSE by selecting one feasible binding for each task, is shown using solid mapping arrows $m_{0,0}, m_{1,0}$.

3.2 DSE as Hard-Constrained MOOP

During DSE, *feasible implementations* need to be derived from the specification by determining an *allocation* of resources, a *binding* for each task, a *routing* of messages, and a *schedule* for the execution of tasks. This in itself is an NP-complete problem that is further subject to functional and non-functional design constraints, e.g., on physical system properties such as limited link bandwidth, maximal energy budgets, etc. DSE is, therefore, a hard-constrained MOOP:

Definition 4 (DSE as MOOP)

$$minimize \{\mathbf{f}(\mathbf{x}) \mid A\mathbf{x} \leq \mathbf{b}\} \tag{1}$$

$$with\ A \in \mathbb{Z}^{m,n}, \mathbf{b} \in \mathbb{Z}^m,\ and\ \mathbf{x} \in \{0,1\}^n.$$

$\mathbf{f}(\mathbf{x}) = (f_1(\mathbf{x}), \ldots, f_z(\mathbf{x}))$ is a vector of z objective functions to evaluate implementations represented by an n-dimensional binary *decision vector* $\mathbf{x} \in \{0,1\}^n$. A straight-forward encoding of implementation options is a representation by a *mapping vector* (cf. Fig. 2(b)), where each mapping edge $m_{t,r} \in E_M$ is encoded as one binary variable whose value indicates whether this mapping is activated in an implementation ($m_{t,r} = 1$) or not ($m_{t,r} = 0$). However, when decoding a mapping vector from the search space to the design space, it needs to be ensured that all design constraints $A\mathbf{x} \leq \mathbf{b}$ are satisfied by each solution. If any constraint is violated, a repair scheme must be applied or the solution is discarded from the optimization.

Since efficient symbolic repair techniques have been integrated into state-of-the-art DSE flows [10,11], feasible solutions can automatically be derived from the search space. Further non-linear constraints (e.g. on schedulability, reliability, etc.) must be considered separately using background theories or other specialised analyses. By repairing or discarding any solutions violating these additional constraints, DSE is guaranteed to optimize feasible solutions only.

However, an efficient exploration of largely infeasible search spaces is still a problem for many optimizers, so that techniques to prune DSE search spaces—without eliminating feasible and high-quality solutions—are much-needed.

4 VAEs for Search-Space Compression

To address these issues, we propose to integrate automatic *search-space compression* using Variational Autoencoders (VAEs) into DSE, see Fig. 2(c). A VAE is an unsupervised-learning technique that learns a compressed representation of an input data space with the corresponding encoding and decoding, i.e., reconstruction scheme. Furthermore, it is able to *generate* new data from the learned model [6,16]. This is achieved by learning the probability distribution of the latent space L for an input data set I. VAEs combine a symmetric Deep Neural Network (DNN) architecture representing the encoder and decoder. The encoder compresses the input space I to the mean μ and standard deviation σ of the probability distribution over the latent space L, while the corresponding decoder maps from L to the output space D. During training, an encoder-decoder combination is learned by adjusting the weights and biases of the network, so that the error between the original training samples in I and their reconstructions in D after encoding and decoding are minimized.

Formally, this is defined as follows [6]: Let $\mathbf{x} \in I$ be an input sample and $\mathbf{z} \in L$ its representation in the latent space. A probabilistic encoder $q_\theta(\mathbf{z}|\mathbf{x})$ infers a conditional distribution of the latent space based on hidden variables $\mathbf{z}$ that generate an observation $\mathbf{x}$. This distribution is typically modelled as a Gaussian distribution, so that the encoder network outputs the mean and variance parameters of this distribution.

A probabilistic decoder $p_\phi(\mathbf{x}|\mathbf{z})$ reverses this process: Given a latent representation $\mathbf{z}$, its output is a distribution over the observation $\mathbf{x}$ it is caused by. The output can then be mapped to a reconstruction of the original input.

In VAEs, DNNs are used to model encoder and decoder. Consequently, encoder and decoder are parametrized with weights and biases θ, ϕ, respectively, that are parameters of the corresponding networks. During training of the VAE, they are adjusted by minimizing a *loss function* $\mathcal{L}$: Let the VAE be trained with N data points l_i whose separate losses $l_i(\theta, \phi)$ can be calculated independently as follows:

$$l_i(\theta,\phi) = -\mathbb{E}_{z\sim q_\theta(z|x_i)}[\log p_\phi(x_i|z)] + \mathbb{KL}(q_\theta(z|x_i)||p(z)) \quad (2)$$

The first term in Eq. (2) measures the *reconstruction loss* between encoded and decoded solutions as expected log-likelihood of the ith data point l_i, so that the network is trained to closely reconstruct the input data points. The second term is added to enforce the regularity of the latent representation. This allows to generate new instances by sampling from the latent space. Regularity is enforced by minimizing the loss of the compression. This is done by minimizing the Kullback-Leibler divergence between the encoder distribution $q_\theta(\mathbf{z}|\mathbf{x})$ and the prior $p(z)$ on the latent space[1]. The total loss $\mathcal{L}$ is aggregated over all N training samples:

$$\mathcal{L} = \sum_{i=1}^{N} l_i(\theta, \phi) \tag{3}$$

4.1 Training VAEs in DSE

VAEs learn an efficient encoding that performs a lossy dimensionality reduction of the input space, so that a reduced number of features describing the original space are extracted. For automatic search-space compression in constrained optimization, we propose to train a VAE using *feasible* decision vectors $\mathbf{x} \in \{0,1\}^n$ as input I to the encoder. These training samples are automatically generated during any DSE, since feasibility of design points needs to be guaranteed by either repair or a filtering of infeasible solutions. Parameters θ, ϕ of the VAE's encoder and decoder are trained using gradient descent for a set number of iterations, or until they converge.

4.2 Proposed VAE Pattern

We propose the following VAE pattern that is well-suited to a variety of DSE problems, as demonstrated in the experimental evaluation in Sect. 5: The first layer of the VAE consists of n input neurons with relu activation functions, where n is the dimension of the original DSE search space. The input layer is followed by three hidden layers; the first increases in dimension by 10% to buffer the input, while the remaining layers evenly decrease in dimension to a set latent-space size d. All layers are fully connected to their predecessor and successor layer. A fourth hidden layer represents the latent space by two d-dimensional vectors μ, σ that correspond to mean and standard deviation of the Gaussian distribution describing the latent space. For the decoder, this architecture is simply reversed. Depending on the selected dimension d of the latent space, the VAE learns a more or less compact compression of the feasible search space, i.e. a simplified search space of the problem that can be exploited for the remaining DSE in the following ways:

4.3 Optimization Using VAEs

Variational Inference. As discussed, the latent spaces of VAEs are designed to be regularized, so that random sampling from the latent space allows to generate

[1] which is set to a standard Normal distribution $\mathcal{N}(0,1)$ to enforce maximal diversity between encoded values $\mathbf{z}$.

new data points by feeding the samples through the learned decoder. Consequently, we propose to replace the optimizer of DSE by the sampling process (Fig. 2(d)(II)). Since a model of the *feasible* search space is learned, sampling (or a systematic traversal) of this search space has the potential to improve optimization, since vast infeasible areas are no longer considered. However, since feasibility of generated samples cannot be guaranteed by the learned VAE-model, the synthesized solutions still need to undergo the same feasibility check (and potential repair) as before; since this is a necessary step of any DSE flow in any case, variational inference can seamlessly be integrated. Newly generated solutions are, subsequently, mapped to the design space to be evaluated w.r.t. the optimization objectives, and a systematic or random exploration can be continued until sufficient optimization quality is reached.

Exploration of Compressed Search Spaces. Since the previously discussed variational inference lacks the ability to explicitly improve solutions based on optimization-quality numbers, we propose to explore the compressed search space using conventional optimization techniques, as already applied in DSE. W.l.o.g., we illustrate this using Multi-Objective Evolutionary Algorithms (MOEAs) as an example (Fig. 2(d)(I)): MOEAs explore a search space using standardized operators that perform mutation or a crossover between high-quality solutions. Thus, the optimization quality is implicitly utilized during optimization, since new solutions are created by predominantly varying selected high-quality solutions. In standard search spaces, such variations frequently result in infeasible solutions that need to be discarded or repaired—where the repair may destroy high-quality properties or even reverse any operations performed, thus not advancing the optimization. By repurposing the MOEA to traverse the compressed search space after training of the VAE is complete, the simplified search space, i.e. the feasible model of the full-size search space, can be explored, *while* solution quality is taken into account. Solutions chosen by the optimization algorithm are, again, decompressed using the decoder of the VAE and subjected to the feasibility check and/or repair before evaluation.

5 Experimental Evaluation

This section presents an experimental evaluation of the proposed search-space compression using VAEs in DSE and compares them to a reference DSE *EA-ref* using an MOEA [2,10] on the original, uncompressed search space. All presented approaches use the same SAT-based repair mechanism [10] and DSE parametrization, implemented in the open-source DSE framework OpenDSE, so that the impact of the proposed search-space compression can be examined in isolation. Since VAE-based compression is orthogonal to other pruning approaches and can arbitrarily be combined with other techniques, an exhaustive comparison of such combinations is out of scope for this work.

The VAE is implemented in tensorflow [1] and its parameters θ, ϕ of the encoder and decoder are trained using gradient descent, as for standard DNNs.

The VAEs investigated in this work are trained with 10,000 feasible samples over 125 training epochs. The approach *VAE-EA* explores the VAE-compressed search space using a ranking-based MOEA NSGA-II [2] as frequently employed in multi-objective optimization. Approach *VAE-VarInf* utilizes the VAE's in-built generator capabilities that allow to directly generate new solutions by sampling from the latent space, thus removing the need for a dedicated optimizer in the subsequent DSE. Samples are selected from a normal distribution. To compare this to an iteration-based MOEA, we have implemented a sampling scheme that iteratively generates a fixed number of new solutions for a set number of iterations, so that the same number of solutions can be compared for all approaches. Furthermore, we present the results of a *random sampling* of the uncompressed search space to verify the effectiveness of the compression.

5.1 Experimental Setup

We evaluate the proposed approaches for large-scale embedded many-core systems. The benchmarks *telecom* and *automotive* are taken from the Embedded Systems Synthesis Benchmarks Suite (E3S) [3] and evaluated for 8×8 and 12×12 heterogeneous tiled many-core architectures. The benchmark specifications—including original search-space sizes—are summarized in Table 1.

Optimization Quality. We evaluate DSE quality using the ϵ-dominance measure [8] for multi-objective optimization quality. ϵ-dominance determines the distance between the solutions obtained by one optimization approach to a reference set of non-dominated solutions in the objective space. Thus, values $\rightarrow 0$ indicate *higher* optimization quality. For complex optimization problems as DSE, where the true Pareto set of solutions is unknown, the reference set is approximated by aggregating the non-dominated solutions across *all* optimizations performed for an experiment.

Table 1. System specifications, VAE training times, and compressed search-space sizes for all benchmarks.

Benchmark	E3S [3]		
	Telecom	Automotive 8×8	Automotive 12×12
Application size	18	24	24
Architecture size	64	64	144
Search-space size	$2^{1,144}$	$2^{1,536}$	$2^{3,456}$
Compressed search-space ($d \approx 0.06\,n$)	2^{75}	2^{100}	2^{225}
Training time (avg.) [s]	97.5	98.8	3144.2

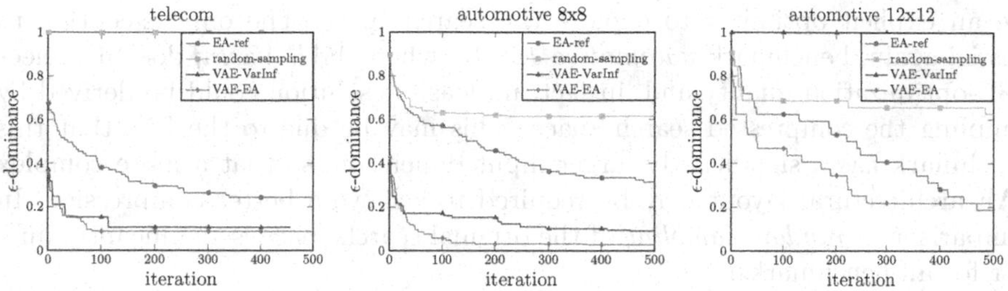

Fig. 3. Optimization quality in ϵ-dominance over DSE time for 500 DSE/sampling iterations.

5.2 Experimental Results

Preliminary Exploration of Latent-Space Size d. To determine suitable VAE patterns for search-space compression in DSE, we vary the size of the latent space d, i.e. the degree of search-space compression, for both *VAE*-DSE approaches. While a strong compression may result in a smaller and more tractable search space, more information is potentially lost during encoding. On the other hand, too large latent spaces may be good models of the original data; however, since search-space size is a major challenge in system-level DSE, too small a compression may have no effect on the optimizer's performance. Choosing a suitable latent-space size is, therefore, a crucial trade-off.

We systematically analyse latent-space sizes d, depending on input-space size n by performing preliminary experiments for various d, ranging from $d = 0.05\,n$ to $d = 0.75\,n$ and the corresponding VAEs. When the compressed search space is explored using an actual optimizer *VAE-EA*, strong compressions to $d \approx 0.06\,n$ result in optimization quality increases for most benchmarks. It is therefore used in the following experimental evaluation. Larger latent-space sizes, however, result in quality decreases, indicating that the search.space compression in these cases is not strong enough for more efficient exploration.

Optimization Quality. All experimental results are averaged over 5 runs for each approach to compensate for the randomly generated starting solutions of the MOEA. Figure 3 presents the optimization quality, measured in ϵ-dominance, after 500 iterations of the MOEA with 24 newly generated solutions per iteration. For the sampling approaches (*random sampling* (as reference) and the proposed *VAE-VarInf*), 500 × 24 solutions are sampled for a fair comparison.

The actual exploration of the simplified search space using *VAE-EA* improves optimization quality in both 8×8 benchmarks by up to 66% in ϵ-dominance. For *automotive 12*×12, both EA-based approaches achieve comparable optimization quality, while the proposed *VAE-EA* offers an advantage in quicker convergence.

Variational inference also significantly improves optimization quality compared to a standard DSE *EA-ref* in two out of three benchmarks; however, the effect is not as strong as when employing an actual optimization algorithm. This validates the effect of the search-space compression, since *VAE-VarInf* does not use an explicit optimizer to explore the search space. The only exception to this is, again, benchmark *automotive 12×12*, where *VAE-VarInf* does not meet DSE-optimization quality and, in fact, no feasible solution could be derived by sampling the compressed search space. This may be due to the fact that this benchmark has a significantly larger input dimension, so that a more complex VAE-architectural layout may be required to achieve a better compression. In comparison, a *random sampling* of the original search space is significantly inferior for all benchmarks.

Optimization Time. Optimization times for all new approaches, compared to the original DSE, vary between benchmarks. While VAE-optimization time for *automotive 8 × 8* is halved compared to *EA-ref*, approximately the same amount of DSE time is required for *automotive 12 × 12*. For *telecom 8 × 8*, DSE time is increased by a factor of ≈1.5. Thus, the additional required decoding step from the compressed search space to original search-space does add varying overhead that cannot always be compensated by reduced repair times. Furthermore, the time to train each VAE needs to be taken into account, which is in the range of ≈1.5–51 min (cf. Table 1), compared to an average DSE time of 1.25 h.

On the other hand, optimization quality in DSE typically stagnates after some time [17], so that more DSE time is not guaranteed to—and in practice typically will not—yield new high-quality solutions after a certain point.

6 Conclusion

This work investigates the need for search-space compression in hard-constrained multi-objective optimization, since vast and sparse search spaces are detrimental to effective exploration using standard optimizers. As a remedy, we propose automatic search-space compression using VAEs for facilitated optimization on a learned and compressed model of the *feasible* search space. Alternatively, novel solutions can directly be extracted from the model using VAE's built-in generator capabilities. Experimental results for a variety of application domains demonstrate the compression's potential to significantly improve DSE in terms of optimization quality with limited runtime overheads.

References

1. Abadi, M., et al.: TensorFlow: large-scale machine learning on heterogeneous systems (2015). https://www.tensorflow.org/
2. Deb, K., Pratap, A., Agarwal, S., Meyarivan, T.: A fast and elitist multiobjective genetic algorithm: NSGA-II. IEEE Trans. Evol. Comput. **6**(2), 182–197 (2002)
3. Dick, R.: Embedded System Synthesis Benchmarks Suite (E3S) (2018). http://ziyang.eecs.umich.edu/~dickrp/e3s/
4. Hu, Y., Mettler, M., Mueller-Gritschneder, D., Wild, T., Herkersdorf, A., Schlichtmann, U.: Machine learning approaches for efficient design space exploration of application-specific NoCs. ACM Trans. Des. Autom. Electron. Syst. **25**(5), 1–27 (2020)

5. Kim, R.G., Doppa, J.R., Pande, P.P.: Machine learning for design space exploration and optimization of manycore systems. In: Proceedings of the International Conference on Computer-Aided Design, ICCAD 2018. Association for Computing Machinery, New York (2018)
6. Kingma, D.P., Welling, M.: Auto-encoding variational bayes. In: 2nd International Conference on Learning Representations (ICLR2014) (2014)
7. Kusner, M.J., Paige, B., Hernández-Lobato, J.M.: Grammar variational autoencoder. In: ICML (2017)
8. Laumanns, M., Thiele, L., Deb, K., Zitzler, E.: Combining convergence and diversity in evolutionary multiobjective optimization. Evol. Comput. **10**(3), 263–282 (2002)
9. Lopes, A.S.B., Pereira, M.M.: A machine learning approach to accelerating DSE of reconfigurable accelerator systems. In: 2020 33rd Symposium on Integrated Circuits and Systems Design (SBCCI) (2020)
10. Lukasiewycz, M., Glaß, M., Haubelt, C., Teich, J.: SAT-decoding in evolutionary algorithms for discrete constrained optimization problems. In: IEEE Congress on Evolutionary Computing (2007)
11. Neubauer, K., Wanko, P., Schaub, T., Haubelt, C.: Exact multi-objective design space exploration using ASPmT. In: Design, Automation Test in Europe Conference Exhibition, pp. 257–260 (2018)
12. Panerati, J., Sciuto, D., Beltrame, G.: Optimization strategies in design space exploration. In: Ha, S., Teich, J. (eds.) Handbook of Hardware/Software Codesign, pp. 189–216. Springer, Dordrecht (2017). https://doi.org/10.1007/978-94-017-7267-9_7
13. Piscitelli, R., Pimentel, A.: Design space pruning through hybrid analysis in system-level design space exploration. In: Design, Automation and Test in Europe (DATE), pp. 781–786 (2012)
14. Radford, A., Metz, L., Chintala, S.: Unsupervised representation learning with deep convolutional generative adversarial networks. In: Bengio, Y., LeCun, Y. (eds.) 4th International Conference on Learning Representations, ICLR (2016)
15. Reza, M.F.: Reinforcement learning based dynamic link configuration for energy-efficient NoC. In: 2020 IEEE 63rd International Midwest Symposium on Circuits and Systems (MWSCAS), pp. 468–473 (2020)
16. Rezende, D.J., Mohamed, S., Wierstra, D.: Stochastic backpropagation and approximate inference in deep generative models. In: ICML (2014)
17. Richthammer, V., Fassnacht, F., Glaß, M.: Search-space decomposition for system-level design space exploration of embedded systems. ACM Trans. Des. Autom. Electron. Syst. **25**(2), 1–32 (2020)
18. Schafer, B.C., Wakabayashi, K.: Machine learning predictive modelling high-level synthesis design space exploration. IET Comput. Digit. Tech. **6**(3), 153–159 (2012)
19. Blickle, T., Teich, J., Thiele, L.: System-level synthesis using evolutionary algorithms. Design Autom. Embed. Syst. **3**(1), 23–58 (1998)

The 3Cs - Cache, Cluster and Cloud

A Case for Partial Co-allocation Constraints in Compressed Caches

Daniel Rodrigues Carvalho(✉) and André Seznec

Univ Rennes, Inria, CNRS, IRISA, Rennes, France
odanrc@yahoo.com.br, andre.seznec@inria.fr

Abstract. Compressed cache layouts require adding the block's size information to the metadata array. This field can be either constrained—in which case compressed blocks must fit in predetermined sizes; thus, it reduces co-allocation opportunities but has easier management—or unconstrained—in which case compressed blocks can compress to any size; thus, it increases co-allocation opportunities, at the cost of more metadata and latency overheads. This paper introduces the concept of partial constraint, which explores multiple layers of constraint to reduce the overheads of unconstrained sizes, while still allowing a high co-allocation flexibility. Finally, Pairwise Space Sharing (PSS) is proposed, which leverages a special case of a partially constrained system. PSS can be applied orthogonally to compaction methods at no extra latency penalty to increase the cost-effectiveness of their metadata overhead. This concept is compression-algorithm independent, and results in an increase of the effective compression ratios achieved while making the most of the metadata bits. When normalized against compressed systems not using PSS, a compressed system extended with PSS further enhances the average cache capacity of nearly every workload.

Keywords: Cache · Hardware compression · Cache organization

1 Introduction

Cache compressors process data in uncompressed format to generate compressed output. Typically, compressors focus on reaching good compression factors or fast decompression latencies to improve system performance or cache capacity [17]. However, compression by itself is not enough to achieve these goals; a *compaction scheme* (or *cache organization*, or *compactor*) must be used to determine what to do with the compressed data. That is, compaction schemes expand the capabilities of conventional tag-data mapping methods to account for compressed blocks and their ability to share data entries.

Some compaction techniques limit compression to fixed sizes (*e.g.*, 25% and 50% of the line size), adding padding to lines smaller than these sizes [18,19]. These *constrained* methods have low metadata overhead, but limit co-allocation by removing opportunities. Moreover, while cache compressors may be successful

© Springer Nature Switzerland AG 2022
A. Orailoglu et al. (Eds.): SAMOS 2021, LNCS 13227, pp. 65–77, 2022.
https://doi.org/10.1007/978-3-031-04580-6_5

in some workload regions, there is still plenty of data that fails to attain favorable compressed sizes for compaction; the average compressed size in SPEC 2017 for multiple state-of-the-art compressors [1,3,4,6,11,12,15], is still far above 50% of the uncompressed size (Fig. 1), making it hard to effectively co-allocate blocks with such limitations.

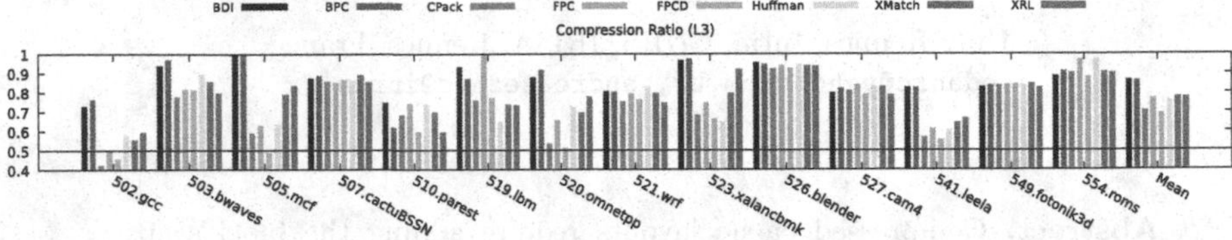

Fig. 1. Average compression ratio of SPEC 2017 workloads for multiple state-of-the-art cache compression methods applied to the Last-Level Cache (L3). Lower is better.

Other proposals remove these limits, allowing blocks to be compressed to any size [2,6]—a concept we will refer to as *unconstrained* methods. Although these methods allow compression to reach its full potential, they significantly increase metadata overhead due to the number of bits needed to represent the compressed size. Besides, locating lines becomes non-trivial: they can be found anywhere in the data entry. This results in a few more cycles being added to the access path.

We have come up with **Pairwise Space Sharing (PSS)**, a technique that achieves the best trade-off between limiting the number of possible sizes and having an unconstrained representation. PSS introduces the notion of a partially-constrained representation: blocks are stored in groups of two—*block pairs*—and although each pair must fit in a fixed-size entry, the blocks within a pair have less restrictions. As a result, **PSS keeps line location trivial, and requires far less metadata bits than conventional unconstrained methods, while still making the most out of co-allocation opportunities**. Moreover, Pairwise Space Sharing can be applied in conjunction with most state-of-the-art cache compaction proposals.

This paper makes the following contributions:

- We show a particular case of size constraints that significantly reduce metadata and latency overheads of existing methods.
- We demonstrate that having a fully unconstrained representation is sub-optimal when the compression design is focused on neighbor-block co-allocation.
- We group these benefits to propose Pairwise Space Sharing, an expansion to compaction layouts which allows the benefits of unconstrained compaction with minimal tag overhead and no extra latency.

The following terms will be used throughout this paper: **compression ratio** is the ratio between the compressed size and the cache line size [16]; and **compaction ratio**—also referred to in the literature as *effective cache capacity*—is the number of valid blocks in a data entry. The former measures how *efficient* a compressor is, while the latter exposes the *efficacy* of the compressed system (compression + compaction).

2 Size Constraints of Compressed Blocks

After a block is compressed, a compaction method is used to determine if it can be co-allocated with other block(s). These techniques may use different approaches to decide how to co-allocate, but they must always rely on one piece of information: the block size. Co-allocated blocks must fit in their designated space, which means that each block's size must always be retrievable; thus, a compressed block's size is an inherent metadata overhead. Sizes are typically represented at a byte granularity to slightly reduce this overhead [2,6].

The size field can be either **unconstrained**—*i.e.*, all sizes are possible—or **constrained**—*i.e.*, compressed blocks are padded to fit in predetermined sizes. While unconstrained sizes are theoretically ideal to make the most out of compression, they come at a high cost: large metadata overhead. Furthermore, its placement process is fairly complex due to varying available sizes and higher number of location possibilities, which may require a few extra cycles to process.

Constrained sizes use larger granularities to ease these drawbacks—*e.g.*, at half-line granularities a compressed block can either be compressed to half or be left uncompressed, which would require a single-bit size field, and generate only two possible block locations—but add a penalty to the compression efficiency: data entries routinely end up wasting many bits with padding [18,19].

2.1 Partial Constraint

We hereby define a third possibility: **partially constrained** sizes. *A partially constrained entry is split into multiple constrained segments, and each of those segments uses an unconstrained layer.* For example, a 512-bit data entry can be divided into four 128-bit segments. Each segment can co-allocate blocks without constraints, as long as they fit in its 16-byte space, as depicted in Fig. 2.

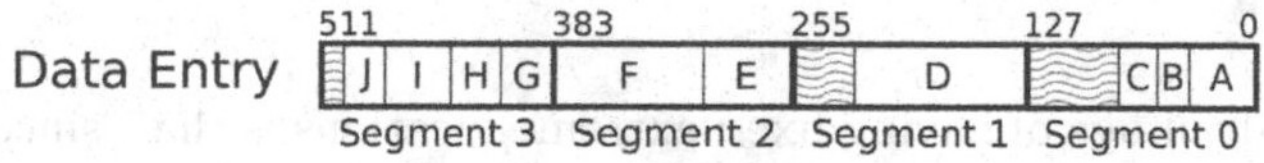

Fig. 2. Example of a data entry split into four constrained segments. Each segment co-allocates blocks in an unconstrained fashion: blocks can be compressed to any size, as long as their sum fits in their segment's 128 bits.

One possible goal of smaller constrained entries is to allow restricting placement. If a rule is applied so that, for example, a given block B can only be assigned to S specific segments, then $\frac{P-S}{P}$ of the P placement locations are removed from the possibilities. This reduces the number of size bits by $\lfloor \log_2(P - S) \rfloor$. Nonetheless, this restriction is not enough to satisfy latency requirements, because B can still be stored anywhere within its allowed segments, which may still be a large gamma of placement possibilities.

2.2 A Case for Latency-Efficient Partial Constraint

There are, however, two special cases of partial constraint that deserve distinct attention: when the number of blocks allowed per segment are, respectively, 1 and 2. When only one block can be allocated per segment, there are two possibilities: either it is an uncompressed cache (the segment size matches the cache line's size); or it is a general constrained method—the segment size is smaller than the cache line's, and compressed blocks must fit in fixed-sized entries.

The other case, when there are up to two blocks per segment, has a peculiarity that can be exploited to greatly simplify locating blocks. Within a constrained segment, no matter its size, there are two invariable locations: its leftmost bit, and its rightmost bit (*i.e.*, the extremities). These can be used as markers that define the beginning of a sub-block, with one of the sub-blocks being stored in reverse order (the MSB becomes the LSB and vice-versa) (Fig. 3a). *Since these locations are statically defined, there is no latency overhead to locate blocks within a segment.* We will refer to segments that contain up to two blocks as a **block pair (BP)**.

(a) Block placement in an entry containing a single BP. E is stored conventionally, and F is stored with its bits reversed.

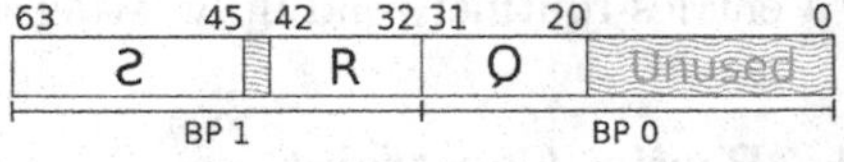

(b) A data entry with two segments supports up to four sub-blocks — there are two BPs. R and S are paired up in a BP 1, and Q is in BP 0. Q's companion is not present. Q and S are stored reversed.

Fig. 3. Overview of the sub-block placement in BPs. Each sub-block is stored relative to an extremity of its BP.

Another advantage of having fixed extreme locations is that, since the bits in between the sub-blocks are unused, *data contractions and expansions that still fit in the pair do not need recompaction.*

3 Pairwise Space Sharing

We herewith introduce **Pairwise Space Sharing (PSS)**: *a partially constrained co-allocation technique that uses block pairs (BPs).* Contrary to previous approaches, *Pairwise Space Sharing stores metadata implicitly, and reduces the* *likelihood of data expansions*—*i.e.*, it reduces the metadata overhead, yet yields better results. PSS is independent of the space available; thus, it can be applied to compressed cache layouts that allow more than two blocks per data entry.

For instance, in YACC [19] a superblock's compression factor (CF) defines the minimum size a sub-block must attain to be compressed: a quarter ($CF = 4$), and half of the data entry ($CF = 2$). If, for example, PSS is applied on top of YACC, this limitation is lessened, and the ***pair's size*** must fit in a half or a whole data entry instead, respectively. No further modifications are needed, and sub-blocks are paired like in YACC: when $CF = 2$ there is only one BP, and any of its four sub-blocks can be paired in it (Fig. 3a); when $CF = 4$, there are at most two pairs, and each sub-block's position in the data entry is fixed—sub-block 0 can only be paired with 1, and sub-block 2 with 3. Figure 3b shows an example of data entry containing more than one BP.

It is important to notice, however, that PSS is not limited to a YACC-like design, so it could handle placement differently (*e.g.*, by adding a position field to the metadata when the CF is 4 too to allow sub-blocks to be placed in any of the available extremities—see Sect. 3.4 for more information on that). In short, PSS decides *where* and *how*, not *which* blocks are allocated in a data entry; thus, it can be applied to non-superblock-based layouts too.

3.1 Decreasing the Number of Unsuccessful Co-allocations

A BP's size is fixed, but dependent on the CF (see Eq. 1). For example, given 64B cache lines, a superblock with $CF = 2$, has one BP; so, the size fields of its two blocks would naively require $2 \cdot 6$ bits; when $CF = 4$, two BPs can reside in the superblock, so $4 \cdot 5$ bits would be needed for the size fields, per tag entry. This naive approach assumes that any size is valid; however, the probability distribution of compressed sizes follows a non-uniform cumulative distribution function: barely compressing a block is significantly more frequent than compressing it to a tiny size (as seen in Fig. 1).

$$BPSize_{CF} = 2 \cdot \frac{cacheLineSize}{CF} \tag{1}$$

Consequently, *a large block will likely not co-allocate, and impose an unnecessary decompression latency fee on hits.* This observation is especially true for superblock-based compaction methods, since neighbor blocks tend to have similar compressibility [14], so a large sub-block will probably have a comparably sized counterpart. *Hence, one can limit the range of possible sizes within a segment to increase the likelihood of co-allocating blocks.*

Sizes are stored as a number relative to $minSize_{CF}$. By limiting the range of valid compressed sizes ($[minSize_{CF}{:}maxSize_{CF}]$, with values respecting Eq. 2), *not only does the likelihood of having non-co-allocated blocks reduce, but also the size field's width is also decreased* (Eq. 3 if $2 \cdot maxSize_{CF} \neq BPSize_{CF}$; 0 otherwise). This means that sizes are stored as numbers relative to $minSize_{CF}$. As a consequence, blocks whose size is smaller than $minSize_{CF}$ are rounded up to $minSize_{CF}$.

$$minSize_{CF} = BPSize_{CF} - maxSize_{CF} \quad (2)$$

$$sizeBits_{CF} = \log_2 (2 \cdot maxSize_{CF} - BPSize_{CF}) \quad (3)$$

In the previous example, if the **size-field range** is set so that $maxSize_{CF} = 62.5\% \cdot BPSize_{CF}$ of the uncompressed line ($minSize_2 = 24B$, $maxSize_2 = 40B$, $minSize_4 = 12B$, $maxSize_4 = 20B$), the width of a size entry is reduced to $sizeBits_2 = 4$, and $sizeBits_4 = 3$. Therefore, an absolute size of 30B would be stored as a relative size of 6B ($30B - minSize_2 = 6B = 0110_2$), and an absolute size of 10B would be stored as 0B.

3.2 Halving the Number of Size Fields

Since the segment's size and location, and the blocks' location are always known, one can further reduce the size-related metadata overhead: *only one of the sub-blocks' sizes needs to be stored in the tags, in the pair's respective size field entry*, and the other (e.g., the non-reversed sub-block's) can be implicitly estimated as its complement. If only the non-reversed block is present in the pair, the stored size represents the available space for the reversed sub-block.

This optimization has the drawback that the reversed block must be decompressed and re-compressed to retrieve the real available size in the BP whenever its companion suffers a data expansion (*i.e.*, a write larger than its current size occurs). Figure 4 presents how the size field is interpreted under different CFs, for both non-optimized and optimized configurations. Nonetheless, this event is rare, not on the critical path, and the re-compression step can be removed by adding a delimiter code to the end of the companion's compressed data.

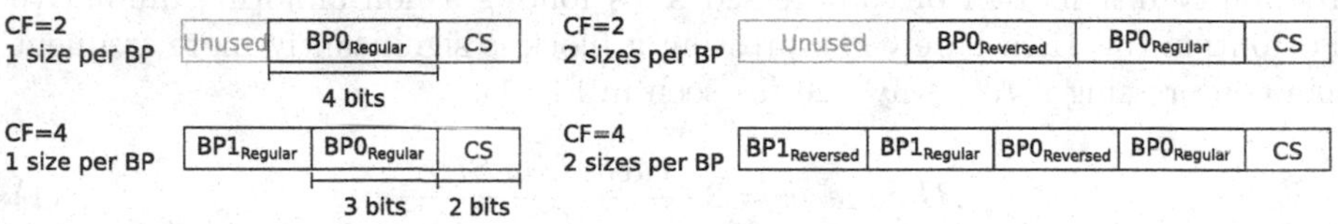

Fig. 4. A comparison of size-related metadata used at different compression factors for different configurations. CS is the compressibility state (whether CF is 1, 2, or 4). When CF=1, only the CS field is used (*i.e.*, the block is not compressed).

3.3 Total Size-Related Overhead

A data entry in a cache layout using Pairwise Space Sharing needs enough size-field bits to cover the worst-case scenario, in which the maximum amount of blocks compressed to the best compression factor ($maxCF$) are co-allocated (Fig. 4). This means that besides the usual tag, replacement state and coherence fields, each data entry must dispose of $\log_2 (maxCF)$ bits to inform the number of BPs in the data entry (equivalent to a conventional field informing the compressibility state—CS); and $\log_2(\frac{maxCF}{2})$ size field entries to bear the size of the smallest possible BP entry ($sizeBits_{maxCF}$), taking into account whether the single-size-per-BP optimization is being used—see Eq. 4.

$$total_{entry} = \log_2(maxCF) + \log_2(\frac{maxCF}{2}) \cdot sizeBits_{maxCF} \cdot numSizesPerBP \tag{4}$$

For instance, the case of PSS where the maximum compressed size allowed is 50% is similar to constrained methods allowing three possible sizes—25%, 50% and 100%—such as YACC [19] and SCC [18]: $maxCF = 4$, $BPSize_2 = 64B$, $BPSize_4 = 32B$, $maxSize_2 = 32B$, $maxSize_4 = 16B$, $sizeBits_2 = sizeBits_4 = 0$, thus $total_{entry} = 2$ bits.

3.4 Position Bits

It is important to notice that a block's size may not be the only piece of metadata needed to locate blocks: starting-position bits may also be necessary. When no positional information is explicitly provided the sizes are used to deduce the blocks' starting position. This means that a size can only be updated along with a recompaction step (see Fig. 5). If the design chooses not to update a block's size right away on a data contraction or eviction, these bits must be added to the size of the previous block in the sequence so that the starting positions of the following blocks are kept correct - *i.e.*, those bits are wasted.

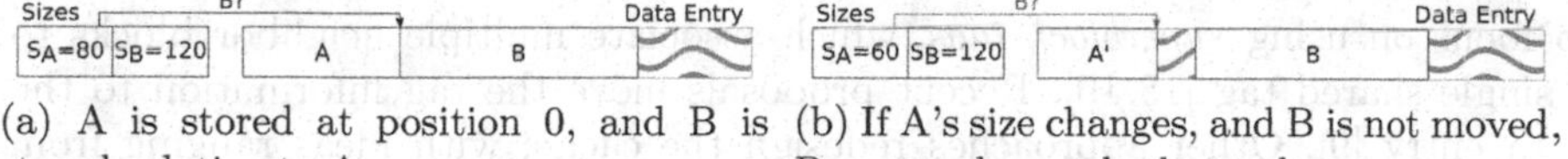

(a) A is stored at position 0, and B is stored relative to A.

(b) If A's size changes, and B is not moved, B can no longer be located.

Fig. 5. Locating blocks without a position field.

Under these circumstances, some layouts may opt to add a position field to the blocks' metadata. Assume that C is the number of coherence bits, up to four blocks can co-allocate in a data entry, and that the number of tag bits is the same for all methods: an unconstrained layout's metadata bits would include 1 compression-state (CS) bit per data entry, and 6 size bits and 6 position bits per block (Eq. 5); a constrained layout needs 1/2 CS bits per data entry, and 1/2 index bits per valid sub-block (depends on the CS) (Eq. 5); finally, PSS reduces the size restrictions of the constrained approach, so it adds one or two 3/4 size bits per valid block pair on top of T_{cons} (Eq. 7).

$$T(otal)_{uncons} = 1 + 4 \cdot 6 \cdot 6 + 4 \cdot C \tag{5}$$

$$T_{cons} = \max(T_{consCF4}, T_{consCF2}) = \max(1 + 4 \cdot (2 + C), 2 + 2 \cdot (2 + C)) \quad (6)$$

$$T_{PSS} = \max(T_{consCF4} + 2 \cdot (1|2) \cdot 3, T_{consCF2} + 1 \cdot (1|2) \cdot 4) \quad (7)$$

For example, if C is 3, $T_{uncons} = 157$, $T_{cons} = 21$, and $T_{PSS} = 27|33$. As seen, **PSS has a huge metadata advantage over the unconstrained approach, while not adding much when compared to the constrained technique.**

4 Related Work

Dictionary-based compressors use the values in a cache line to fill a dictionary of previously seen values. While parsing a line, the dictionary entries are compared against patterns for full or partial matches, which are referred to by the compressed data, along with the discrepant bits in case of a partial match.

C-Pack [6] applies the basic ideas of dictionary-based compressors; X-Match and X-RL reorder the dictionary to apply Huffman code on the most-recently seen value [12]; BDI [15] limits the dictionary to two entries, which are matched through delta comparisons to achieve 1-cycle decompression; DISH [14] improves BDI's low compression efficiency by sharing dictionaries between multiple lines.

COCO [21] applies BDI's idea to objects, instead of cache lines; FPC-D [1] uses a 2-entry FIFO as its dictionary to reduce decompression latency. FPC [3] has no dictionary (*i.e.*, a pattern-only scheme); BPC [11] further compresses base-delta-like compressed data with bit-plane transformations; and SC^2 [4] uses probabilistic models to build a global dictionary.

Compressors must be associated with a compaction scheme to increase the effective cache capacity. Some compacted layouts allow any pair of lines to co-allocate by doubling the number of tags and informing the compressed sizes in the metadata [2,6,13]. This overhead is cumbersome, so modern proposals tend to focus on using *superblock tags*, which associate multiple neighbor blocks to a single shared tag [18,19]. Recent proposals move the tag information to the data entry [9]. Other approaches redesign the cache, with ideas ranging from adding extra caches holding the compressed data [8] to a full overhaul of the cache organization [21]. PSS is orthogonal to these design decisions.

Chen *et al.* introduced *pair-matching* [6], which co-allocates blocks in pairs as long as the sum of their compressed sizes' fits in a data entry, requiring one size field per sub-block. Pairwise Space Sharing has up to 73% less size-related metadata overhead due to its insights on the probabilities of co-allocation, and removal of the partially redundant companion's size information. Besides, since sub-block location is fixed, and unused bits are located in-between blocks, PSS greatly simplifies data insertion, removes the need for recompaction, and minimizes the likelihood of data expansions.

5 Methodology

Our simulations have been performed using gem5 [5]. Compression-related statistics are averaged across all (de)compressions. Compaction-related statistics are averages of snapshots (taken every 100K ticks) of the cache's contents. We took multiple checkpoints per benchmark of the SPEC 2017 benchmark suite [7] using SimPoints [20]. Workloads were warmed up for 100M instructions, and then executed for 200M instructions. The average of each benchmark's statistics has been calculated with the arithmetic mean of its checkpoints, and the total geometric mean of the benchmarks was normalized to a baseline system without compression. Benchmarks whose number of Misses Per Kilo-Instruction (MPKI) was lower than 1 were discarded from the analysis—as they barely benefit from having larger caches, compression is not useful.

The baseline model executes out-of-order (OOO), and is detailed in Table 1. All compression and compaction algorithms are applied to the L3 on top of this common configuration.

Table 1. Baseline system configuration.

Cache line size	64B	*DRAM*	DDR4 2400MHz 17-17-17, tRFC=350ns, 4GB
L1 I/D	32KB, 4-ways, 4 cycles, LRU	*Processor*	1 core, OOO, 8-issue
L2	256KB, 8-ways, 12 cycles, RRIP [10]	*Architecture*	ARM 64 bits
Shared L3	1MB, 8-ways, 34 cycles, RRIP	*Clock*	4GHz
MSHRs and write buffers	64	*Image*	Ubuntu Trusty, Little Endian

6 Results

In this section we analyse which size range provides the most cost-effective results. We also compare the efficiency and effectiveness of PSS when applied on top of multiple state-of-the-art compressors. Finally, we provide an area estimate comparison.

6.1 Selecting the Size-Field Range

As stated previously, neighbor blocks tend to have similar data contents, and thus similar compressibility. If a line compresses to a size greater than 50% of the BP's size, its companion has a high likelihood of compressing to a size greater than 50% too; consequently, there is lower co-allocation chance. This means that reducing size constraints may actually degrade performance.

To find out the best number of bits to be used in the size field, we have analysed the different compaction ratios achieved, as well as the proportion of blocks that co-allocated with another block at the moment it was compressed. *The highest ratio of successful co-allocations is achieved when block sizes are within the absolute range* [37.5%: 62.5%] *of the BP's size* (Fig. 6, left). This is reflected in compaction ratio improvements (Fig. 6, right). **Unless stated otherwise, future references to PSS use the** [37.5%: 62.5%] **range.**

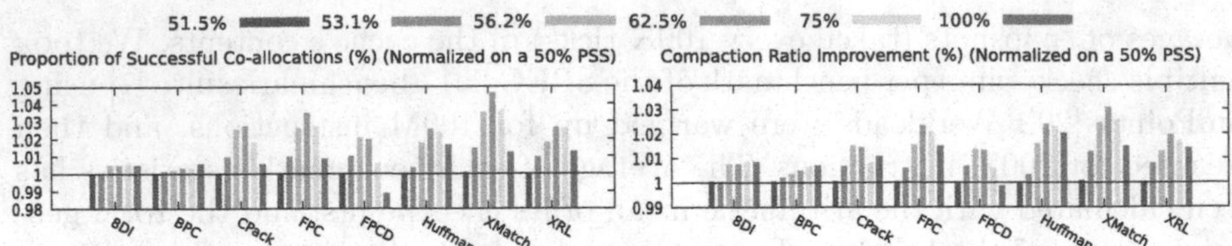

Fig. 6. Comparison of the best range choice for multiple state of the art compression methods under a YACC layout with PSS. Values for each compressor are normalized to the respective compressor using a PSS of 50%. Left plot is the ratio of successful co-allocations ($\frac{numCoAllocations}{numCompressions}$). Right plot is the compaction ratio.

6.2 Compaction Ratio

Figure 7 shows the difference in compaction ratio for various state-of-the-art compressors while coupling YACC [19] to PSS. *All PSS configurations outdo their non-PSS counterpart* because of the better ratio of successful co-allocations.

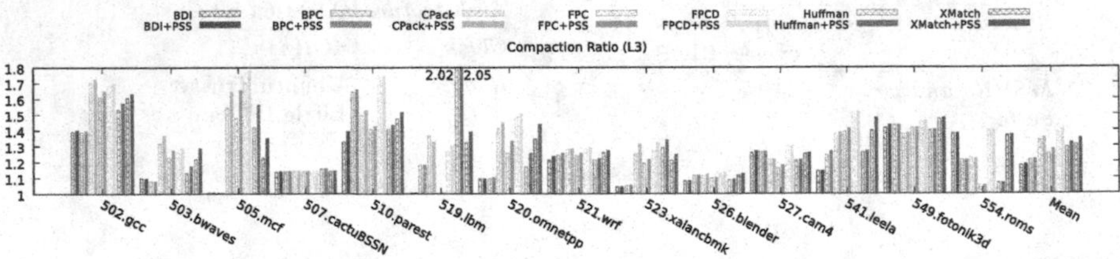

Fig. 7. Compaction ratio of multiple state of the art compression methods under a YACC layout without and with PSS applied to them. X-RL's results are similar to X-Match's, and are not shown due to space constraints.

6.3 Number of Size Fields per BP

Having a single size per BP has a drawback in case the block whose size is stored expands: the exact size of its companion is unknown, so the companion's data must be read, decompressed and re-compressed to check if evictions are needed. We simulated a worst case scenario where the latency of a read was added to every block overwrite, and the differences in IPC and compaction ratio were far below 1% because these steps could often be done off the critical path; hence, **halving the number of size fields has marginal negative impact**.

6.4 Effects on Data Expansions

Although rare, data expansions can be inconvenient. We compare the number of data expansions of YACC using PSS with 1) a conventional 50% constrained design (Con_{50}), and 2) a PSS design that co-allocates at non-extremities locations (*i.e.*, blocks are allocated sequentially, at the first available bit), at a byte granularity (PSS_{NE}). PSS generates a much smaller data-expansion footprint, as seen in Fig. 8.

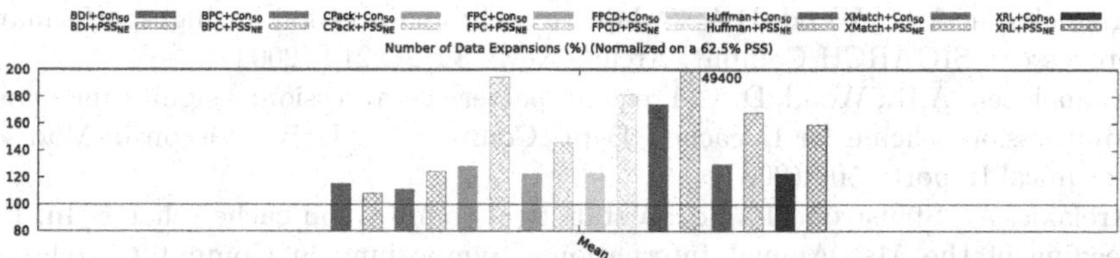

Fig. 8. Number of data expansions with Con_{50} and PSS_{NE} (normalized on PSS—*e.g.*, there are 15% more data expansions in BDI+Con_{50} than in PSS). Only the means of the benchmarks are shown due to space constraints. The number of data expansions is normalized on top of the selected PSS configuration, so any value above the horizontal line signifies that its respective configuration has more data expansions than PSS. All other configurations are above the horizontal line; thus, PSS has significantly less data expansions than any other compared configuration.

6.5 Area Overhead

We have implemented the placement decisioning logic under a generic unconstrained, a generic constrained, and the PSS approaches using Quartus II Web Edition v21.1 and assuming that the metadata contains a position field. Constrained and PSS require, respectively, 4% and 14% of the area of the unconstrained method. *These two techniques also manage to always calculate new positions in a single cycle, while the unconstrained approach needs multiple cycles at a much slower clock rate.*

7 Conclusion

This paper explores Pairwise Space Sharing (PSS), a special case of pairwise block compression which uses implicit information to reduce compression-size metadata, increase co-allocation opportunities, and remove re-compaction needs. This concept is layout-independent, but highly advantageous for spatially close block co-allocation techniques (*e.g.*, superblocks). PSS reaches an effective metadata-bits usage, and improves the compaction ratio of nearly every compressed-system configuration, while still being simple enough to handle compressed-line placement decision in a single cycle.

References

1. Alameldeen, A.R., Agarwal, R.: Opportunistic compression for direct-mapped dram caches. In: Proceedings of the International Symposium on Memory Systems, MEMSYS 2018, pp. 129–136. Association for Computing Machinery, Alexandria (2018). https://doi.org/10.1145/3240302.3240429
2. Alameldeen, A.R., Wood, D.A.: Adaptive cache compression for high-performance processors. SIGARCH Comput. Archit. News **32**(2), 212 (2004)
3. Alameldeen, A.R., Wood, D.A.: Frequent pattern compression: a significance-based compression scheme for l2 caches. Dept. Comp. Scie., Univ. Wisconsin-Madison, Technical Report 1500 (2004)
4. Arelakis, A., Stenstrom, P.: Sc2: a statistical compression cache scheme. In: Proceeding of the 41st Annual International Symposium on Computer Architecuture, ISCA 2014, pp. 145–156. IEEE Press, Minneapolis (2014). https://doi.org/10.1109/ISCA.2014.6853231
5. Binkert, N., et al.: The gem5 simulator. SIGARCH Comput. Archit. News **39**(2), 1–7 (2011)
6. Chen, X., Yang, L., Dick, R.P., Shang, L., Lekatsas, H.: C-pack: a high-performance microprocessor cache compression algorithm. IEEE Trans. Very Large Scale Integr. (VLSI) Syst. **18**(8), 1196–1208 (2010). https://doi.org/10.1109/TVLSI.2009.2020989
7. Corporation, S.P.E.: Spec cpu (2017). https://www.spec.org/cpu2017/, Accessed 10 Oct 2019
8. Dusser, J., Piquet, T., Seznec, A.: Zero-content augmented caches. In: Proceedings of the 23rd International Conference on Supercomputing, ICS 2009, pp. 46–55. Association for Computing Machinery, Yorktown Heights (2009). https://doi.org/10.1145/1542275.1542288
9. Hong, S., Abali, B., Buyuktosunoglu, A., Healy, M.B., Nair, P.J.: Touché: towards ideal and efficient cache compression by mitigating tag area overheads. In: Proceedings of the 52nd Annual IEEE/ACM International Symposium on Microarchitecture,MICRO '52, pp. 453–465. Association for Computing Machinery, Columbus (2019). https://doi.org/10.1145/3352460.3358281
10. Jaleel, A., Theobald, K.B., Steely, S.C., Emer, J.: High performance cache replacement using re-reference interval prediction (rrip). In: Proceedings of the 37th Annual International Symposium on Computer Architecture, ISCA 2010, pp. 60–71. Association for Computing Machinery, Saint-Malo (2010). https://doi.org/10.1145/1815961.1815971
11. Kim, J., Sullivan, M., Choukse, E., Erez, M.: Bit-plane compression: transforming data for better compression in many-core architectures. SIGARCH Comput. Archit. News **44**(3), 329–340 (2016)
12. Kjelso, M., Gooch, M., Jones, S.: Design and performance of a main memory hardware data compressor. In: EUROMICRO 96. Beyond 2000: Hardware and Software Design Strategies., Proceedings of the 22nd EUROMICRO Conference, pp. 423–430. IEEE, IEEE Computer Society, Prague (1996). https://doi.org/10.1109/EURMIC.1996.546466
13. Lee, J.S., Hong, W.K., Kim, S.D.: Design and evaluation of a selective compressed memory system. In: IEEE International Conference on Computer Design, 1999, (ICCD 1999), pp. 184–191. IEEE Computer Society, Austin (1999). https://doi.org/10.1109/ICCD.1999.808424

14. Panda, B., Seznec, A.: Dictionary sharing: an efficient cache compression scheme for compressed caches. In: The 49th Annual IEEE/ACM International Symposium on Microarchitecture. MICRO-49. IEEE Press, Taipei (2016). https://doi.org/10.1109/MICRO.2016.7783704
15. Pekhimenko, G., Seshadri, V., Mutlu, O., Gibbons, P.B., Kozuch, M.A., Mowry, T.C.: Base-delta-immediate compression: practical data compression for on-chip caches. In: Proceedings of the 21st International Conference on Parallel Architectures and Compilation Techniques, PACT 2012, pp. 377–388. Association for Computing Machinery, Minneapolis (2012). https://doi.org/10.1145/2370816.2370870
16. Salomon, D.: Data Compression: The Complete Reference, 3rd Edn. Springer (2004). http://www.davidsalomon.name/DC3advertis/DComp3Ad.html
17. Sardashti, S., Arelakis, A., Stenström, P., Wood, D.A.: A primer on compression in the memory hierarchy. Synth. Lect. Comput. Arch. **10**(5), 1–86 (2015)
18. Sardashti, S., Seznec, A., Wood, D.A.: Skewed compressed caches. In: Proceedings of the 47th Annual IEEE/ACM International Symposium on Microarchitecture, MICRO-47, pp. 331–342. IEEE Computer Society, Cambridge (2014). https://doi.org/10.1109/MICRO.2014.41
19. Sardashti, S., Seznec, A., Wood, D.A.: Yet another compressed cache: a low-cost yet effective compressed cache. ACM Trans. Archit. Code Optim. **13**(3) (2016). https://doi.org/10.1145/2976740
20. Sherwood, T., Perelman, E., Hamerly, G., Calder, B.: Automatically characterizing large scale program behavior. In: Proceedings of the 10th International Conference on Architectural Support for Programming Languages and Operating Systems, ASPLOS X, pp. 45–57. Association for Computing Machinery, San Jose (2002). https://doi.org/10.1145/605397.605403
21. Tsai, P.A., Sanchez, D.: Compress objects, not cache lines: an object-based compressed memory hierarchy. In: Proceedings of the Twenty-Fourth International Conference on Architectural Support for Programming Languages and Operating Systems, ASPLOS 2019, pp. 229–242. ACM, Providence (2019). https://doi.org/10.1145/3297858.3304006

PoCL-R: A Scalable Low Latency Distributed OpenCL Runtime

Jan Solanti[1](✉), Michal Babej[1], Julius Ikkala[1], Vinod Kumar Malamal Vadakital[2], and Pekka Jääskeläinen[1]

[1] Faculty of Information Technology and Communication Sciences (ITC), Tampere University, Tampere, Finland
{jan.solanti,michal.babej,julius.ikkala,pekka.jaaskelainen}@tuni.fi

[2] Nokia Technologies, Tampere, Finland
vinod.malamalvadakital@nokia.com

Abstract. Offloading the most demanding parts of applications to an edge GPU server cluster to save power or improve the result quality is a solution that becomes increasingly realistic with new networking technologies. In order to make such a computing scheme feasible, an application programming layer that can provide both low latency and scalable utilization of remote heterogeneous computing resources is needed. To this end, we propose a latency-optimized scalable distributed heterogeneous computing runtime implementing the standard OpenCL API.

In the proposed runtime, network-induced latency is reduced by means of peer-to-peer data transfers and event synchronization as well as a streamlined control protocol implementation. Further improvements can be obtained streaming of source data directly from the producer device to the compute cluster. Compute cluster scalability is improved by distributing the command and event processing responsibilities to remote compute servers. We also show how a simple optional dynamic content size buffer OpenCL extension can significantly speed up applications that utilize variable length data.

For evaluation we present a smartphone-based augmented reality rendering case study which, using the runtime, receives 19× improvement in frames per second and 17× improvement in energy per frame when offloading parts of the rendering workload to a nearby GPU server. The remote kernel execution latency overhead of the runtime is only 60 ms on top of the network roundtrip time. The scalability on multi-server multi-GPU clusters is shown with a distributed large matrix multiplication application.

1 Introduction

End-user applications are increasingly moving to battery-powered devices, and at the same time, the computational complexity of their functionalities increase. Offloading parts of applications to an edge node that resides within a short network round-trip from the user device is a solution that is becoming more feasible

© Springer Nature Switzerland AG 2022
A. Orailoglu et al. (Eds.): SAMOS 2021, LNCS 13227, pp. 78–94, 2022.
https://doi.org/10.1007/978-3-031-04580-6_6

with low-latency next-gen networking technologies such as 5G and WiFi6. The overall concept of utilizing edge cluster resources across low latency network links, called *Multi-access Edge Computing (MEC)* [29] is now an active field of research and development.

In the application layer, the MEC paradigm calls for a solution that both minimizes end-to-end latency overheads and allows utilizing all the heterogeneous compute resources in the remote edge cluster in a scalable and portable manner. To this end, we propose a scalable low-latency distributed heterogeneous computing runtime that implements the standard OpenCL API [15] and is targeted for usage by the application layer either directly or transparently as a backend for higher level interfaces with OpenCL backends such as SYCL [16] and oneAPI [10].

Unlike the previous distributed OpenCL projects, the proposed runtime called *PoCL-R* focuses on latency and the edge cluster side scalability at the same time. Furthermore, *PoCL-R* also provides support for low latency distributed streaming applications where data is read from a remote input device to the end user (client) device, which then needs to be further processed to produce the output. With *PoCL-R*, the input data can be streamed directly to the remote compute node, reducing the client's bandwidth use and overall latency. Overall, a key benefit of *PoCL-R* is that the whole edge cluster workload distribution can be orchestrated from the client application logic side without application-specific server-side software, thanks to the generality and power of the heterogeneous OpenCL API.

We identify the following novel aspects in the runtime presented in this paper:

- Utilization of edge cluster compute resources with *peer-to-peer (P2P)* communication and synchronization for improved compute scalability.
- Capability of supporting applications with both high performance and low latency demands to support distributed compute offloading scenarios of MEC with a wide complexity range.
- Enable transfers of input data straight from a producer server to the edge cluster before passing it to the client device while still only utilizing the standard OpenCL API's features.
- A minimal (optional) OpenCL API extension that can improve transfer times of dynamic-size buffers dramatically. This is especially useful for taking advantage of buffers with compressed data.
- The first distributed OpenCL runtime that is integrated to a long-maintained widely used open source OpenCL implementation framework *PoCL* [13] and is thus usable and extensible for anyone freely in the future.[1]

In order to test the latency of the runtime in a real-time context, we present a real-time augmented reality mobile case study, which receives significant improvements in both *frames per second (FPS)* and *energy per frame (EPF)* by offloading parts of the object rendering workload to a remote GPU server. The edge compute cluster side performance is reported separately with a remote

[1] The source code is available at http://code.portablecl.org/.

kernel execution latency overhead measurement and a multi-server multi-GPU cluster scaling experiment.

The paper is organized as follows. Section 2 gives an overview of the *PoCL-R* top level design and its usage aspects. Section 3 describes the most relevant techniques in the proposed runtime to achieve the low latency while retaining scalability. Section 4 lays out the results in terms of latency and throughput measurements, and Sect. 5 presents the MEC offloading case study. Section 7 describes some plans for future work and concludes the paper.

2 Architecture

The focus of *PoCL-R* is on minimizing the end-to-end latency to enable high quality user experience in responsive real-time edge cluster use scenarios as well as enable scalable use of diverse compute resources in the cluster.

The whole application logic is defined in a single host application, as specified by the OpenCL standard. The application includes both the main program running in the local device as well as the kernel programs that are executed on local, or in the case of *PoCL-R*, remote OpenCL devices. The OpenCL standard allows the kernel programs to be defined in a portable source code or an intermediate language, and alternatively using target-specific binary formats. This can be used to bypass long synthesis steps at application runtime when using FPGA-based accelerators.

PoCL-R runtime is implemented as a standard client-server architecture. The *client* is implemented as a special *remote driver* in *Portable Computing Language (PoCL)* [13], an open source implementation of the OpenCL API with flexible support for custom device backends. The remote driver acts as a "smart proxy" that exposes compute devices on a remote server through the OpenCL platform API the same way as local devices, making the use of remote devices in OpenCL applications identical to using local devices at the program logic level. Features of the remote devices depend on what their native drivers support.

A *host application* using the OpenCL API can use *PoCL-R* as a drop-in implementation without recompilation. When the *host application* is linked against *PoCL-R*, OpenCL calls are made to the *PoCL-R client* driver, which in turn connects to one or multiple *remote* servers, each providing one or more *remote compute devices*. The remote servers can form interconnected *clusters* visible and controlled by *PoCL-R* as *peers* to avoid round-trips back to the client whenever synchronization or data transfers are needed between the remote devices. The application can identify remote devices by the device name string that contains an additional "pocl-remote". This allows optimising choices of command queues and kernel implementations.

The server side is a daemon that runs on the remote servers and receives commands from the client driver, and dispatches them to the OpenCL driver of the server's devices accompanied with proper event dependencies.

The daemon is structured around network sockets for the client and peer connections. Each socket has a reader thread and a writer thread. The readers

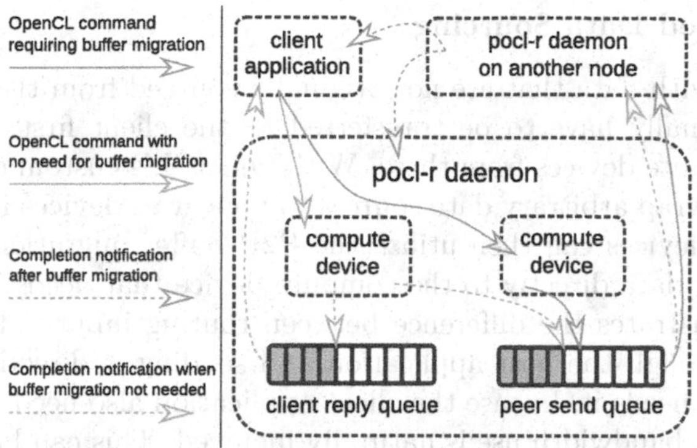

Fig. 1. The information flow from an application to the *PoCL-R* daemon and between remote servers. Two different commands are illustrated, one that transfers buffer contents from one remote node to another and one that doesn't.

do blocking reads on the socket until they manage to read a new command, which they then dispatch to the underlying OpenCL runtime, store its associated OpenCL event in a queue and signal the corresponding writer thread. The server writer thread iterates through commands in the queue and when it finds one that the underlying OpenCL runtime reports as complete, writes its result to the socket representing the host connection. Peer writers have separate queues, but work otherwise similar to the server writer. Figure 1 illustrates this architecture and the flow of commands and data through it.

3 Latency and Scalability Optimizations

The following subsections describe the essential latency and scalability optimization techniques of *PoCL-R*.

3.1 Peer-to-Peer Communication

PoCL-R supports transferring buffers directly between devices on the same remote server (provided that the server's OpenCL implementation supports it), P2P transfers of buffers between servers, as well as distributed event signaling.

Figure 2a illustrates the various possible links between the host application running in the client device that communicates with remote servers and devices. In a typical edge cluster use case, the client connection to the remote servers is much slower than the interconnect between servers in the cluster, thus the bandwidth savings versus transferring data always to the client application and back to another remote device can affect the overall performance dramatically. In addition, the number of network requests from the client are reduced drastically, since the host application only needs to send the migration command to the source server.

3.2 Distributed Data Sourcing

When working with data that are not originally sourced from the client device, they would normally have to be transferred to the client first, and then distributed to compute devices from there. With OpenCL's custom devices feature it is possible to wrap arbitrary data sources to appear as devices in the OpenCL platform. Such devices can then utilize the P2P buffer migration functionality to transfer input data directly to the compute device that needs it.

Figure 2b illustrates the difference between routing input data from a producer device through the host application and sending it directly to the compute device that needs it. In case the client application also needs the raw input data, some extra bandwidth use is naturally incurred. This can be mitigated by compressing the data in flight, at the cost of a slight latency and throughput overhead.

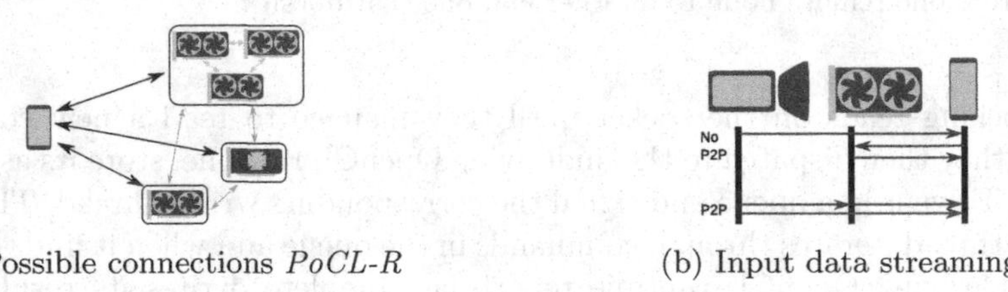

(a) Possible connections *PoCL-R* (b) Input data streaming

Fig. 2. Various connections between devices in a *PoCL-R* context. Roundtrips to the client device are avoided when possible.

3.3 Low-Overhead Communication

The base of the client-server communication is a pair of raw TCP sockets. One socket is dedicated to commands and the other to buffer data transfers, their send and receive buffer sizes tuned for their respective purposes. To minimize latency on the network level, TCP fast retransmission is enabled for both sockets.

While optimization of serialization protocols has been researched a lot and some extremely low-overhead protocols such as *FlatBuffers* [9] and *MessagePack* [7] have emerged, using a separate wire format for communication still adds overhead both on the sending and receiving side. *PoCL-R* uses the in-memory representation of commands as its wire format, avoiding this. The only added data is a fixed-size integer indicating the length of the next command structure.

The trade-off of this approach is that all remote servers as well as the client device running the host application need to have the same integer byte order. In practice we consider this not a noticeable limitation after successfully testing *PoCL-R* across a range of devices, from commodity mobile SoCs to PC and server room hardware. A bigger hurdle is the OpenCL C application code itself, as OpenCL has no knowledge about buffer contents' endianness and makes mixed endianness related swapping the application writer's responsibility [15]: Applications meant to work on platforms with mixed endianness need their kernels to be adapted to account for the difference and swap the byte order of multi-byte values stored in OpenCL buffers when crossing devices with different byte orders.

3.4 Decentralized Command Scheduling

OpenCL provides command completion events as a synchronization mechanism between commands. *PoCL-R* relies heavily on these for keeping execution in sync across nodes with minimal overhead. Commands are pushed to the remote servers immediately when OpenCL enqueue API calls are made by the client. Event dependencies are mapped to platform-local events on each server and events for commands running on other servers are substituted with user events. This way the heterogeneous task graph based on event dependencies defined by the application stays intact on the remote servers and the runtime can apply optimisations utilizing the dependency rules outlined in [12].

In addition to the control and data connections to the client, each remote server keeps a direct connection to each of its peers. This is used for peer-to-peer buffer migrations and to signal event completions to other servers for use in command scheduling as illustrated in Fig. 1. Thanks to this setup, enqueuing a command that depends on a buffer produced by a command on a different device only requires two network requests from the host application to the source server, which then signals other servers as needed.

3.5 Dynamic Buffer Content Size Extension

OpenCL allows applications to allocate memory in the form of buffers whose size is fixed once they are created. However, for many applications the amount of data actually produced or consumed varies greatly over time. As a means to improve performance when dealing with kernels dealing with varying size data, we propose a simple yet powerful OpenCL extension named *cl_pocl_content_size*. The extension provides an optional way to signal the actual used portion of an OpenCL buffer to the runtime as well as the consuming kernels. It works by designating a separate buffer, just large enough to hold a single unsigned integer, that holds the number of bytes actually being used by the buffer for valid data. *PoCL-R* runtime reads the content size buffer as an hint to only transfer the meaningful portion of buffers when migrating them between remote servers.

An example of using the extension is shown in the code snippet of Fig. 3. The only addition to the standard OpenCL API calls is the call which associates a content size buffer with a data buffer (`clSetContentSizeBufferPOCL`), and the addition of this "size buffer" to the kernels' arguments.

```
cl_mem data_buffer;
cl_mem data_size;
cl_event ev;
...
/* Attach data_size to data_buffer to hold
 * the content size. */
clSetContentSizeBufferPOCL(data_buffer, data_size);

/* Kernel writes an unknown amount of data to
 * data_buffer, and its size to the data_size
 * argument. */
clSetKernelArg(kernel1, 0, sizeof(cl_mem), &data_buffer);
clSetKernelArg(kernel1, 1, sizeof(cl_mem), &data_size);
clEnqueueNDRangeKernel(command_queue, kernel1, 1,
                       NULL, NULL, NULL,
                       0, NULL, &ev);

/* The second kernel uses information from data_size
 * to restrict its processing to the meaningful part
 * of data_buffer. */
clSetKernelArg(kernel2, 0, sizeof(cl_mem), &data_buffer);
clSetKernelArg(kernel2, 1, sizeof(cl_mem), &data_size);
clEnqueueNDRangeKernel(command_queue, kernel2, 1,
                       NULL, NULL, NULL,
                       1, &ev, NULL);
...
clFinish();
```

Fig. 3. Example of using the proposed dynamic buffer extension in a sequence of two kernels. The user defines a designated buffer where the kernel stores the size, which can be then used by the runtime to optimize the buffer transfers and migrations, as well as by the consumer kernels of the buffer to read the input size.

4 Latency and Scalability Results

The following subsections describe the experiments performed to measure the latency and scalability of the *PoCL-R* runtime and the results obtained. In order to more accurately measure the performance overhead of *PoCL-R*, wired network connections were preferred. In real-world use, client connections would generally be wireless and introduce network-dependent latency and jitter.

4.1 Command Overhead

Since low latency is a key priority of *PoCL-R*, we constructed a synthetic benchmark to measure the overheads imposed by the runtime itself using a kernel that simply exists. Some runtimes don't handle this well but it is a good indicator for command handling overhead. We compare the numbers against the roundtrip time reported by the *ping* utility which is generally accepted as a good baseline for network latency.

This benchmark creates a no-op kernel, enqueues it and waits for it to complete using `clFinish`. This is repeated 1000 times and the results are averaged. The client is a desktop PC with a 100-Mbps wired connection to the server. Time stamps are taken in the application code before the `clEnqueueNDRangeKernel` and after a `clFinish` call to ensure the completion of the command has been registered by the client application. The duration between the two is used for the host-measured timings.

Two machines with a Ryzen Threadripper 2990wx CPU and two Geforce 2080 Ti GPUs each were used for testing. The machines were connected to a 100Mbit LAN.

The results of this test are shown in Fig. 4a. For reference, the ICMP round-trip latency as reported by the `ping` utility fluctuates around 0.122 ms. On localhost the ICMP round-trip latency was measured to average at 0.020 ms. The average command duration was observed to be consistently around 60 ms more than ping. We consider this to be a good result given that connections between consumer devices and application servers usually measure in tens to hundreds of milliseconds even in realtime applications and even on our 100-Mbps LAN with a ping delay two to three orders of magnitude less than the aforementioned case, the overhead on top of ping is only a fraction of the full command duration. Running the application and server on the same machine confirms that the overhead is constant.

The closest related work that we could successfully make run and benchmark against was the latest version (1.3.3) of SnuCL [18] (released in 2015). SnuCL has a similar idea to *PoCL-R* but seems to focus more on datacenter-side throughput scalability.

In order to compare *PoCL-R* imposed minimum runtime latencies to SnuCL, a simple passthrough kernel that simply copies its single integer input to an output buffer was implemented. Kernel runtimes as reported by the OpenCL event profiling API were measured for three setups of interest: The proprietary NVIDIA driver used without any distribution layer, the SnuCL Cluster implementation and *PoCL-R*. The runtime differences here are indicative of internal command management overhead of the respective frameworks on top of the native driver and the additional overhead imposed by the MPI runtime in case of SnuCL. The results of this benchmark as shown in Fig. 4b put *PoCL-R* noticeably ahead of SnuCL with the average command duration in *PoCL-R* being only around $\frac{1}{6}$ of SnuCL's. In comparison to running without a distribution layer, *PoCL-R* takes almost twice as long, indicating some room for improvement.

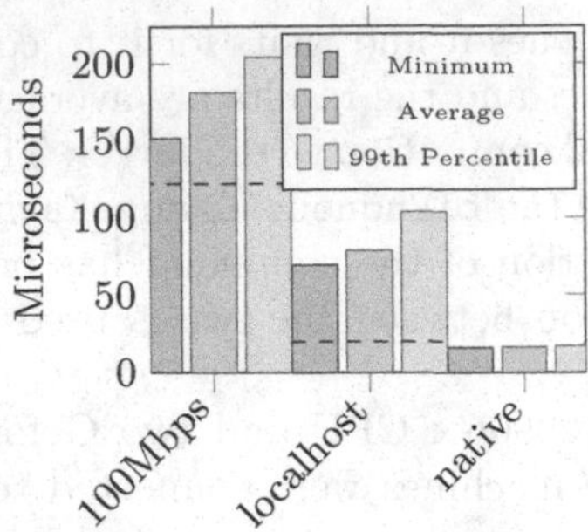

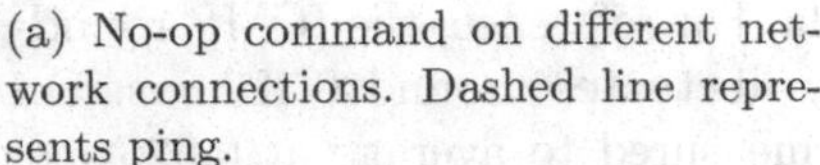

(a) No-op command on different network connections. Dashed line represents ping.

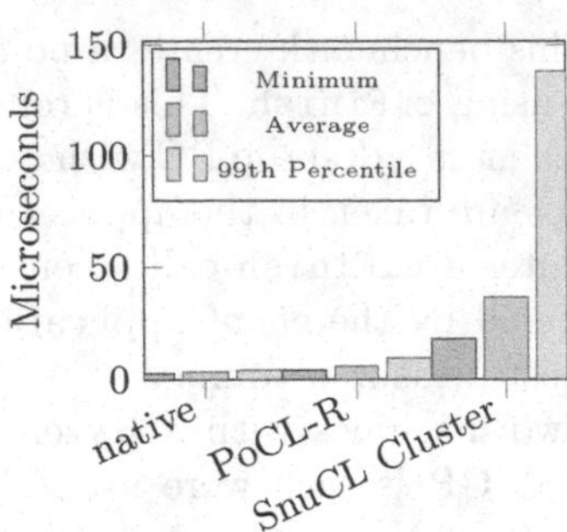

(b) Passthrough kernel on different OpenCL runtimes.

Fig. 4. Comparison of runtime duration of a no-op command in various network conditions.

4.2 Data Migration Overhead

The authors of SnuCL report data movement being the bottleneck in some of their benchmarks [18]. In order to get a general idea of how much the runtime affects the communication overhead due to data movement, it is interesting to measure the minimum time a buffer migration between devices takes due to runtime overhead. This is done separately from the no-op command overhead measurements because *PoCL-R* remote servers communicate directly with each other in a P2P fashion: the host application only has to send a migration command to the source server which in turn forwards the command to the destination server.

The test triggers 1000 migrations between remotes and averages the durations at the end. A buffer of 4 bytes is used to minimize the effect of transfering the actual contents and better measure runtime overhead. All kernel invocations were enqueued in sequence and after waiting for completion of all commands the buffer migrations inserted by the *PoCL-R* runtime were extracted and their timing information was analyzed. The results are shown in Fig. 5. When using a 100-Mbps ethernet connection between the remote servers the average timings add up to around 3× the overhead of a no-op command on top of network ping, which seems reasonable for a 3-step roundtrip (from the host to the first server, to the second server and back to the host) with extra buffer management on the intermediate hops.

Using an 40-Gbps direct infiniband link shortens the total duration in comparison to the ping noticeably, mostly because this is a dedicated direct connection between the two machines with no switches or other network equipment on the way and no interference from other traffic from the operating system. The benchmark was also run with two *PoCL-R* daemons running on the same machine as well as one daemon migrating data between two GPUs installed on one machine. However, the native OpenCL implementation used by the dae-

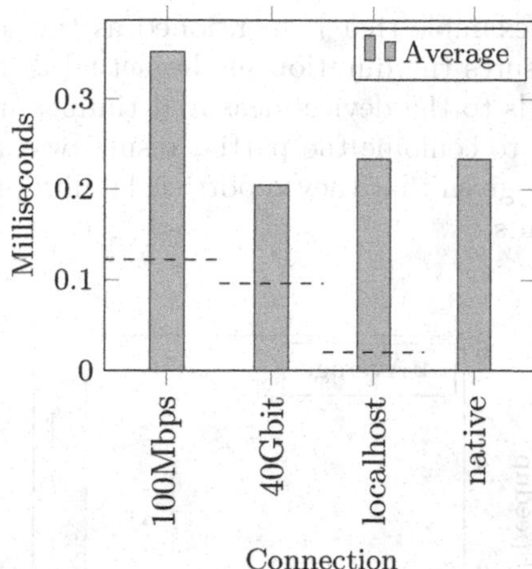

Fig. 5. Duration of a migration of a 4-byte buffer between two devices using different connectivity between servers, as well as using the native NVIDIA driver for reference. Numbers are averaged across 1000 migrations. The dashed line represents the average ICMP ping for the given connection.

mon turned out to exhibit a notable performance regression when using two GPUs simultaneously instead of just one, making this configuration impossible to compare.

A comparison with SnuCL was attempted, but calling *clEnqueueMigrateMemObjects* consistently resulted in a segmentation fault.

Two machines with an AMD Ryzen Threadripper 2990wx CPU and two NVIDIA Geforce 2080 Ti GPUs each were used for testing. The machines were connected to a 100 Mbit LAN and had an additional direct 40 Gbit infiniband link between them.

4.3 Distributed Large Matrix Multiplication

For a non-trivial throughput scalability benchmark, we constructed a distributed matrix multiplication application. This benchmark multiplies two NxN matrices using as many devices as the OpenCL context has available. Every device gets the full data of both input matrices and calculates a roughly equal number of rows of the output matrix. Five independent multiplications are run in parallel in order to keep all GPUs saturated and demonstrate total throughput. While the actual calculations are an embarrassingly parallel task, the partial results from each device have to be collected into a single buffer for the final result, which makes the workload as a whole non-trivial to scale.

This is largely similar to the matrix multiplication used in the benchmarks of SnuCL [18] with the exception that here the parts of the output matrix are combined to a single buffer on one of the GPUs and this is included in the host timings. The NVIDIA example that is mentioned as the source for the benchmark in [18] only measures the duration of the actual compute kernel invocations, which corresponds to the device-measured timings in our benchmark. It is unknown if the time to combine the partial results was accounted for in the SnuCL benchmark, but given that they report scalability problems it likely was part of the measurements.

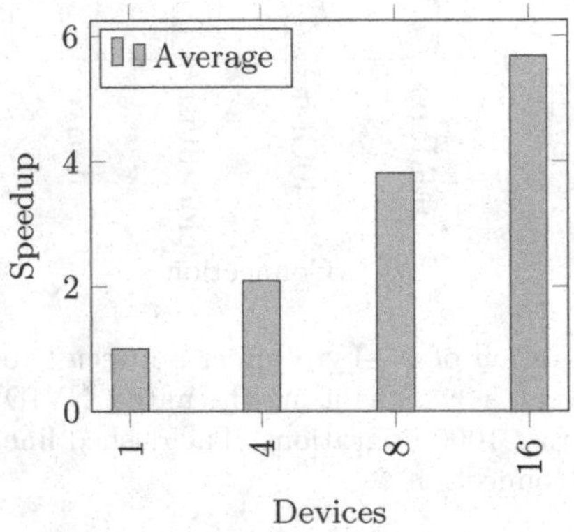

Fig. 6. Relative speedup when multiplying two 8192×8192 matrices using 1 to 16 remote devices spread across 4 servers.

Benchmarking was done on a cluster with three servers with an *Intel^{TM} Xeon^{TM} E5-2640 v4* CPU and four *NVIDIA Tesla P100* GPUs. An additional server with an *Intel^{TM} Xeon^{TM} Silver 4214* CPU and four *NVIDIA Tesla V100* GPUs was used to fill the number of usable compute devices to a total of 16 GPUs. All cluster servers were connected to each other and to the machine running the host application with a 56-Gbps infiniband link.

The relative speedup when multiplying two 8192 by 8192 matrices with an increasing number of GPUs is shown in Fig. 6. We observe logarithmic speedups compared to using a single GPU up to slightly below 6× with 16 GPUs. This is roughly in line with the results reported in [18] with the version of SnuCL that uses their proposed MPI collective communication extensions. Our implementation also doesn't exhibit the performance regression suffered by the unextended P2P version of SnuCL when using more than 8 devices.

5 Real-time Point Cloud Augmented Reality Rendering Case Study

In this section, we describe a full application task offloading case study, a smartphone application [21] that renders a streamed animated point cloud in augmented reality (AR). Figure 7 shows the application in action. The point cloud is received as an HEVC-encoded [22,28] VPCC (Video-based Point Cloud Compression) stream [8] which is decompressed using the mobile device's hardware decoder and reconstructed using OpenGL [30] shaders [26]. A more in-depth explanation of this process is given in [24].

Fig. 7. Screenshot of the AR application used to measure the effect of offloading heavy computation. A streamed animated point cloud of a person holding a small tablet device is displayed in augmented reality on top of a real-world chair.

Visual quality can be greatly improved by using alpha blending to hide point boundaries, but this requires sorting the points by distance to the viewer, which is a costly operation and a prime candidate for remote offloading. When offloading is enabled, the VPCC stream is sent to both the device and directly to the remote compute server and decoding and point reconstruction are performed on both. However the point sorting is only done on the remote and the sorted point indices are sent back to the mobile device for rendering.

The remote daemon makes use of the OpenCL 1.2 custom device type feature to provide a virtual device that exposes the server's video decoding capabilities using VDPAU and OpenGL; the decoder appears to the application as a fully conformant OpenCL device of type `CL_DEVICE_TYPE_CUSTOM` and thus does not require the use of any API extensions. The decoded result is made available as an OpenCL buffer with the OpenGL-OpenCL interoperation feature. The proposed dynamic buffer size extension can optionally be used to speed up transfers of the buffers between the OpenCL devices as their sizes vary wildly between frames – especially the compressed VPCC stream which on average has a much smaller chunk size than its worst case.

Framerates measured from the application are shown in Fig. 8a. The first two measurements are obtained using the local (mobile) GPU only for reconstruction sorting and AR positioning. The next two measurements offload point sorting to a GPU on a *PoCL-R* remote server with P2P buffer transfers disabled and enabled, for a roughly 2.3× speedup over the full reconstruction, sorting and AR workload done on the mobile GPU. Finally, the figure shows an almost 19× speedup when using the dynamic buffer size extension.

Figure 8b shows energy consumption per frame (EPF) measured on the mobile device in the same offloading configurations. The power usage of the smartphone was retrieved using Android's Power Stats HAL interface. Offloading the sorting of the point cloud compensates for most of the added energy consumption from AR positioning even without further optimizations. Enabling P2P buffer transfers and the content size extension further cuts energy consumption per frame to a mere fifth of the non-AR case. Overall the results point to *PoCL-R* being a powerful enabler for rendering advanced content on handheld devices.

Testing was done on a PC with an Intel Core i7-6700 CPU and a NVIDIA GeForce 1060 3 GB GPU that was connected to an ASUS ROG Rapture GT-AX11000 WiFi6 router via gigabit ethernet. The mobile device used was a Samsung Galaxy S10 SM-G973U1 with a Qualcomm® Snapdragon™ 855 chipset. The streaming data source emulated a camera feed by looping a prerecorded stream from a file.

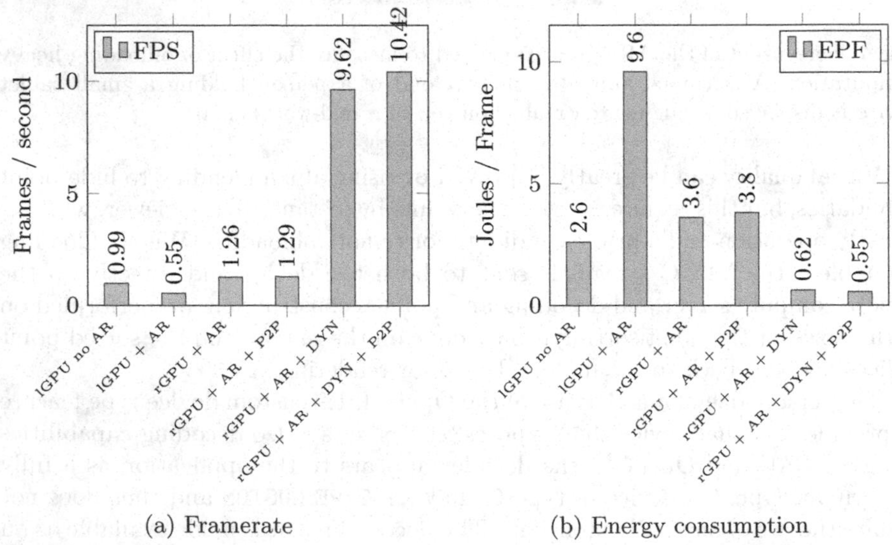

(a) Framerate (b) Energy consumption

Fig. 8. Performance of the AR demo application in various offloading configurations. lGPU and rGPU refer to the mobile device's local GPU and the remote GPU exposed via *PoCL-R*. AR indicates live position tracking. P2P refers to transferring buffer data from the (remote) data source directly to the remote GPU and DYN indicates that the buffer content size extension is used.

6 Related Work

Multiple projects [14,20,23,31] have expanded the scope of originally single server targeting heterogeneous APIs for distributed use in the past, but most of them have long since faded into obscurity and their implementations are no longer available for use and comparison, let alone for further development.

Various projects [1–4,14] also solely target HPC clusters with their existing library ecosystem and optimize purely for throughput. By contrast, our proposed runtime targets to support both compute clusters and realtime applications, and most interestingly, their combination.

Among the previous projects we found, the closest to *PoCL-R* is SnuCL [18]. It provides an implementation of the standard OpenCL API that enables execution of OpenCL commands on remote servers. However, it focuses solely on throughput in HPC cluster use cases with no consideration of latency. For communication it relies on the MPI framework. SnuCL supports peer-to-peer data transfers, but they report scaling problems in some tasks such as the matrix multiplication we used in our benchmarking. SnuCL solves these scaling issues with a proposed OpenCL extension that maps MPI collective operations to a set of new OpenCL commands. In contrast, *PoCL-R* uses plain TCP sockets with a custom protocol and socket settings tuned for low latency. SnuCL also handles command scheduling on the host machine, whereas *PoCL-R* lets remotes do their scheduling autonomously.

Further work on SnuCL also exists in the form of SNUCL-D [17], which further decentralizes computation by duplicating the control flow of the entire host program on each remote server. This results in great scalability improvements in theory, but requires the host application to be fully replicable on all servers which is naturally not possible by default.

Another very close project in terms of the overall idea is rCUDA[5]. At the time of this writing, rCUDA is one of the most actively developed related projects, but being based on the proprietary CUDA API it is limited in hardware support and portability.

There is also a recent open source project by the name RemoteCL [6] that takes the same approach with plain network sockets as *PoCL-R*. However, it only aims to fit the needs of the author and makes no attempt at providing a full conformant implementation of the OpenCL API. It also does not appear to support more than one remote server.

In a wider point of view, when used for accelerating graphics rendering of interactive content, *PoCL-R* could be thought of as an alternative to already commercialized *game streaming* services such as *Google Stadia*. The key difference is that when using *PoCL-R* for rendering acceleration, the use cases can be more flexible and adaptable to the available resources: A lightweight client device can render content using slower local resources and opportunistically exploit edge servers to improve quality instead of rendering exclusively on the server.

7 Conclusions and Future Work

In this paper we proposed a scalable low-latency distributed heterogeneous computing runtime *PoCL-R* which is based on the standard OpenCL API's features. We also proposed an API extension that significantly improves buffer transfer times for cases with varying data sizes. The unique latency and scalability enhancing features were tested with a distributed real-time augmented reality case study which reached 19× improvement in FPS and 17× in EPF by remote offloading a rendering quality enhancement kernel using the runtime. The remote kernel execution latency overhead was measured to be at 60 ms while the scalability at multi-server multi-GPU cluster level was shown with a logarithmic scaling of a distributed large matrix multiplication. These results indicate the significance of the proposed runtime as an enabler for high-performance low power distribution of computation and application deployment without needing additional distribution API layers.

In the future, we will research various low hanging fruits for improving the performance of the runtime further, e.g., by transparent and intelligent use of RDMA [25], GPUDirect [19] and similar technologies for improving cross-server and cross-GPU data transfer latencies. We will also investigate improvements to dynamic multi-user scheduling and load balancing such as the approaches described in [27] and [11]. Wireless networks can be unreliable for various reasons, so we will add handling for network instability.

Acknowledgements. This project has received funding from the ECSEL Joint Undertaking (JU) under grant agreement No 783162. The JU receives support from the European Union's Horizon 2020 research and innovation programme and Netherlands, Czech Republic, Finland, Spain, Italy. It was also supported by European Union's Horizon 2020 research and innovation programme under Grant Agreement No 871738 (CPSoSaware) and a grant from the HSA Foundation

References

1. Alves, A., Rufino, J., Pina, A., Santos, L.P.: clOpenCL-supporting distributed heterogeneous computing in HPC clusters. In: European Conference on Parallel Processing (2012)
2. Alves, R., Rufino, J.: Extending heterogeneous applications to remote co-processors with rOpenCL, pp. 305–312 (2020). https://doi.org/10.1109/SBAC-PAD49847.2020.00049
3. Barak, A., Shiloh, A.: The VirtualCL (VCL) cluster platform (2013)
4. Diop, T., Gurfinkel, S., Anderson, J., Jerger, N.E.: DistCL: a framework for the distributed execution of OpenCL kernels. In: 2013 IEEE 21st International Symposium on Modelling, Analysis and Simulation of Computer and Telecommunication Systems (2013)
5. Duato, J., Peña, A.J., Silla, F., Mayo, R., Quintana-Ortí, E.S.: rCUDA: reducing the number of GPU-based accelerators in high performance clusters. In: 2010 International Conference on High Performance Computing Simulation (2010)

6. Ferreira, P.O.: RemoteCL. https://github.com/silverclaw/RemoteCL, Accessed 16 Oct 2020
7. Furuhashi, S.: Messagepack: It's like json. but fast and small. https://msgpack.org/, Accessed 19 Oct 2020
8. Group, D., et al.: Text of ISO/IEC CD 23090–5: Video-based point cloud compression. ISO/IEC JTC1/SC29/WG11 Doc. N18030
9. Inc., G.: Flatbuffers. https://google.github.io/flatbuffers/, Accessed 19 Oct 2020
10. Intel: oneAPI Specification. https://spec.oneapi.com/versions/1.0-rev-1/oneAPI-spec.pdf, Accessed 16 Oct 2020
11. Iserte, S., Prades, J., Reaño, C., Silla, F.: Improving the management efficiency of GPU workloads in data centers through GPU virtualization. Concurr. Comput. Pract. Exp. **33**(2), e5275 (2021)
12. Jääskeläinen, P., et al.: Exploiting task parallelism with OpenCL: a case study. J. Signal Process. Syst. **91**, 33–46 (2019)
13. Jääskeläinen, P., de La Lama, C.S., Schnetter, E., Raiskila, K., Takala, J., Berg, H.: pocl: a performance-portable OpenCL implementation. Int. J. Parallel Program. **43**(5), 752–785 (2015)
14. Kegel, P., Steuwer, M., Gorlatch, S.: dOpenCL: towards a uniform programming approach for distributed heterogeneous multi-/many-core systems. In: 2012 IEEE 26th International Parallel and Distributed Processing Symposium Workshops & PhD Forum (2012)
15. Khronos® OpenCL Working Group: The OpenCL™ Specification. https://www.khronos.org/registry/OpenCL/specs/3.0-unified/pdf/OpenCL_API.pdf, Accessed 16 Oct 2020
16. Khronos® SYCL™ Working Group: SYCL™ Specification. https://www.khronos.org/registry/SYCL/specs/sycl-1.2.1.pdf, Accessed 16 Oct 2020
17. Kim, J., Jo, G., Jung, J., Kim, J., Lee, J.: A distributed OpenCL framework using redundant computation and data replication. SIGPLAN Not. **51**(6) (2016)
18. Kim, J., Seo, S., Lee, J., Nah, J., Jo, G., Lee, J.: SnuCL: an OpenCL framework for heterogeneous CPU/GPU clusters. In: Proceedings of the 26th ACM International Conference on Supercomputing, pp. 341–352 (2012)
19. Li, A., Song, S.L., Chen, J., Li, J., Liu, X., Tallent, N.R., Barker, K.J.: Evaluating modern GPU interconnect: PCIe, NVLink, NV-SLI, NVSwitch and GPUDirect. IEEE Trans. Parallel Distrib. Syst. **31**(1), 91–110 (2020)
20. Liang, T.-Y., Lin, Y.-J.: JCL: an OpenCL programming toolkit for heterogeneous computing. In: Park, J.J.J.H., Arabnia, H.R., Kim, C., Shi, W., Gil, J.-M. (eds.) GPC 2013. LNCS, vol. 7861, pp. 59–72. Springer, Heidelberg (2013). https://doi.org/10.1007/978-3-642-38027-3_7
21. Nokia Technologies Ltd.: Video point cloud coding (V-PCC) AR demo. https://github.com/nokiatech/vpcc/, Accessed 16 Oct 2020
22. Rec, I.: H. 265 and ISO/IEC 23008–2: High efficiency video coding (HEVC) (2013)
23. Reynolds, C.J., Lichtenberger, Z., Winter, S.: Provisioning OpenCL capable infrastructure with infiniband verbs. In: 2011 10th International Symposium on Parallel and Distributed Computing. IEEE (2011)
24. Schwarz, S., Pesonen, M.: Real-time decoding and AR playback of the emerging MPEG video-based point cloud compression standard. IBC 2019, Helsinki, Finland (2019)
25. Shpiner, A., et al.: RoCE rocks without PFC: detailed evaluation. In: Proceedings of the Workshop on Kernel-Bypass Networks, KBNets 2017 (2017). https://doi.org/10.1145/3098583.3098588

26. Simpson, R.J., Baldwin, D., Rost, R.: OpenGL ES® shading language version 3.20.6. https://www.khronos.org/registry/OpenGL/specs/es/3.2/GLSL_ES_Specification_3.20.pdf, Accessed 19 Oct 2020
27. Soldado, F., Alexandre, F., Paulino, H.: Execution of compound multi-kernel opencl computations in multi-cpu/multi-gpu environments. Concurr. Comput. Pract. Exp. **28**(3), 768–787 (2016)
28. Sullivan, G.J., Ohm, J.R., Han, W.J., Wiegand, T.: Overview of the high efficiency video coding (HEVC) standard. IEEE Trans. Circ. Syst. Video Technol. **22**(12), 1649–1668 (2012)
29. Taleb, T., Samdanis, K., Mada, B., Flinck, H., Dutta, S., Sabella, D.: On multi-access edge computing: a survey of the emerging 5G network edge cloud architecture and orchestration. IEEE Commun. Surv. Tutor. **19**(3), 1657–1681 (2017)
30. The Khronos Group Inc.: OpenGL® ES version 3.2 (2019). https://www.khronos.org/registry/OpenGL/specs/es/3.2/es_spec_3.2.pdf, Accessed 19 Oct 2020
31. Xiao, S., Bet al.: VOCL: an optimized environment for transparent virtualization of graphics processing units. In: 2012 Innovative Parallel Computing (InPar) (2012)

An Analytical Model for Loop Tiling Transformation

Vasilios Kelefouras[1,4(✉)], Karim Djemame[2], Georgios Keramidas[3,4], and Nikolaos Voros[4]

[1] University of Plymouth, Plymouth, UK
v.kelefouras@plymouth.ac.uk
[2] University of Leeds, Leeds, UK
[3] Aristotle University, Thessaloniki, Greece
[4] University of Peloponnese, Tripoli, Greece

Abstract. Loop tiling is a well-known loop transformation that enhances data locality in memory hierarchy. In this paper, we initially reveal two important inefficiencies of current analytical loop tiling models and we provide the theoretical background on how current analytical models can address these inefficiencies. To this end, we propose a new analytical model which is more accurate that the existing ones. We showcase, both theoretically and experimentally, that the proposed model can accurately estimate the number of cache misses for every generated tile size and as a result more efficient tile sizes are opted. Our evaluation results provide high cache misses gains and significant performance gains over gcc compiler and Pluto tool on an x86 platform.

Keywords: Loop tiling · Data cache · Data reuse · Analytical model · Cache misses

1 Introduction

Loop tiling is a loop transformation that exploits locality of data accesses in loop nests; the reused data stay in the cache and thus the number of cache misses is reduced. Although loop tiling does not always align with performance, it is one of the key optimizations for memory-bound loop kernels. The selection of an efficient tile size is of paramount importance as tiles of different sizes can lead to significant variations in performance. In this paper, we define a tile size as efficient if it achieves a reduced number of cache misses.

The two main strategies to address the tile size selection problem are analytical [16] and empirical [24]. The former refers to static approaches in which the tile size is selected based on static code analysis of the loop kernel and the memory configuration (number of caches, cache sizes, associativity, line size). Typically, the analytical model outputs the cache misses as a function of tile sizes, input size (of the executed kernel), and cache characteristics. The second strategy refers to empirical (experimental-based) approaches that rely on auto-tuning. In auto-tuning, the input program is executed multiple times assuming

© Springer Nature Switzerland AG 2022
A. Orailoglu et al. (Eds.): SAMOS 2021, LNCS 13227, pp. 95–107, 2022.
https://doi.org/10.1007/978-3-031-04580-6_7

different tile sizes, until the best solution is found. The input program is considered as a black-box and no information of the source code is extracted.

In this paper, we first demonstrate two important inefficiencies of current analytical models and provide the theoretical background on how current models can address these inefficiencies. Second, we propose a new more accurate analytical model for loop tiling, for single-threaded programs.

The first drawback of current analytical models is that they do not accurately calculate the tiles sizes and as a consequence additional unforeseen cache misses occur (not captured by the model). The second drawback is that the tiles cannot remain in the cache in most cases due to the cache modulo effect. This is because the cache line size, cache associativity and data reuse of tiles, are not efficiently taken into account. Therefore, current models cannot accurately calculate the number of cache misses for each tile size, leading to sub-optimal tile sizes. On the contrary, the proposed method provides efficient tile sizes by accurately estimating the number of cache misses for each tile size.

Our experimental results show that by using our method it is possible to estimate the number of cache misses with an accuracy of about 1% using simulation and about 3% and 5.5% by using the processor's hardware counters on L1 data cache and L3 cache, respectively, leading to more efficient tile sizes for static loop kernels.

The remainder of this paper is organized as follows. In Sect. 2, the related work is reviewed. The proposed methodology is presented in Sect. 3 while experimental results are discussed in Sect. 4. Finally, Sect. 5 is dedicated to conclusions.

2 Related Work

In [20], an analytical model for loop tile selection is proposed for estimating the memory cost of a loop kernel and for identifying the optimal tile size. However, cache associativity is not taken into account. In [8], the authors combine loop tiling with array padding in order to improve the tile size selection process for specific array sizes. In [4], authors use Presburger formulas to express cache misses, but they fail to accommodate the high set associativity values of modern caches. In [16], an improved analytical model is proposed where associativity value is taken into account, but the cache hardware parameters (cache line size and associativity) and data reuse, are not efficiently taken into account.

As we showcase in this work there is ample room for improvement in existing analytical approaches, as cache line size and associativity and the arrays' memory access patterns, are not fully exploited.

Due to the problem of finding the optimum tile size is very complex and includes a vast exploration space [9], in addition to general methods, a large number of algorithm-specific analytical models also exist for Matrix-Matrix Multiplication (MMM) [12,14], Matrix-Vector Multiplication [13], tensor contractions [15], Fast Fourier Transform [10], stencil [23] and other algorithms, but the proposed approaches cannot be generalized. In particular, regarding stencil applications, there has been a long thread of research and development tackling data locality and parallelism, where many loop tiling strategies have been proposed such as overlapped tiling [5,26], diamond tiling [2] and others.

The second line of techniques for addressing the tile size selection problem relies on empirical approaches. A successful example is the ATLAS library [25] which performs empirical tuning at installation time, to find the best tile sizes for different problem sizes on a target machine. The main drawback in empirical approaches is the enormous search space that must be explored.

Moreover, there are several frameworks able to generate tiled code with parameterized tiles such as PrimeTile [7] and PTile [1]. Parameterized tiling refers to the application of the tiling transformation without employing predefined tiles sizes, but inserting symbolic parameters that can be fixed at runtime [19]. In [1], a compile-time framework is proposed for tiling affine nested loops whose tile sizes are handled at runtime. In [19], authors present a formulation of the parameterized tiled loop generation problem using a polyhedral set. Pluto [3] is a popular polyhedral code generator including many additional optimizations such as vectorization and parallelization.

In [6], a thorough study on the major known tiling techniques is shown. In [21], authors use an autotuning method to find the tile sizes, when the outermost loop is parallelised. In [11], loop tiling is combined with cache partitioning to improve performance in shared caches. Finally, in [22], a hybrid model is proposed by combining an analytical with an empirical model. However, this model ignores the impact of set associativity in caches.

3 Proposed Methodology

3.1 Inefficiencies of Current Analytical Models

A. Current analytical models do not accurately calculate the tiles sizes Current methods, such as [16,20], calculate the number of cache lines occupied by a tile, by using the following formula:

$$number.lines = \lceil \frac{tile.size.in.bytes}{line.size.in.bytes} \rceil \quad (1)$$

However, Eq. 1 is not accurate as different tiles (of the same size) occupy a varied number of cache lines. Let us give an example (Fig. 1). Consider an one-dimensional (1-d) array of 200 elements and non-overapping tiles consisting of 25 elements each. Also consider that each array element is of 4 bytes and the cache line size is 64 bytes. The array elements are stored into consecutive main memory locations and thus into consecutive cache locations. Current methods assume that each tile occupies two cache lines ($\lceil \frac{25 \times 4}{64} \rceil = 2$) (Eq. 1), therefore just two cache misses are assumed when loading the tile into the cache. However, as it can be shown in Fig. 1, half of the tiles occupy two cache lines and the other half occupy three cache lines.

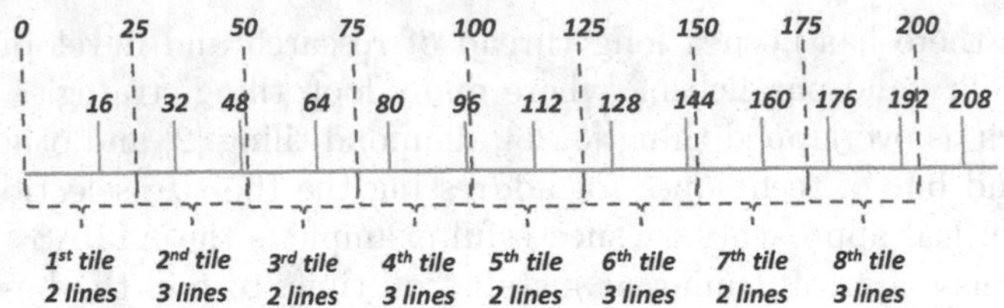

Fig. 1. An 1-d array is partitioned into tiles. 25 element tiles occupy a varied number of cache lines

The number of cache lines occupied by a tile is given by Eq. 2, where $a = 0$ or $a = 1$, depending on the tile size and cache line size values.

$$number.cache.lines = \lceil \frac{tile.size.in.bytes}{line.size.in.bytes} \rceil + a \tag{2}$$

There are cases where the tiles occupy a varied number of cache lines (e.g., in Fig. 1, $a = 0$ holds for some tile sizes and $a = 1$ holds for others) and cases where the tiles occupy a constant number of cache lines.

To ascertain that the tiles remain in the cache, in Subsect. 3.2, we show that the cache size allocated must equal to the largest tile size value.

B. The tiles proposed by current analytical models cannot remain in the cache. Related works such as [20] assume that if the aggregated size of the tiles is smaller than the cache size, then the reused tiles will remain in the cache; however, this holds true only in specific cases because even the elements of a single tile might conflict with each other due to the cache module effect. An improved model is proposed in [16], where the cache associativity value is taken into account, but still the tiles cannot remain in the cache in many cases, leading to a significant number of unforeseen cache misses.

Let us showcase the above problem with another example, the well-known Matrix-Matrix Multiplication (MMM) algorithm (Fig. 2). Although different tiles of A and B are multiplied by each other, the tile of C is reused $N/Tile$ times (data reuse), where $Tile$ is the tile size and N is the arrays size in each dimension. The current analytical models, such as [16], will consider data reuse in this case and therefore they will include this information to their cache misses calculation model; therefore, current models do assume that the tile of C is loaded just once in the cache, not $N/Tile$ times, which is accurate. However, **the tile of C cannot remain in the cache unless all the following three bullets hold** (in current analytical models only the first condition is satisfied):

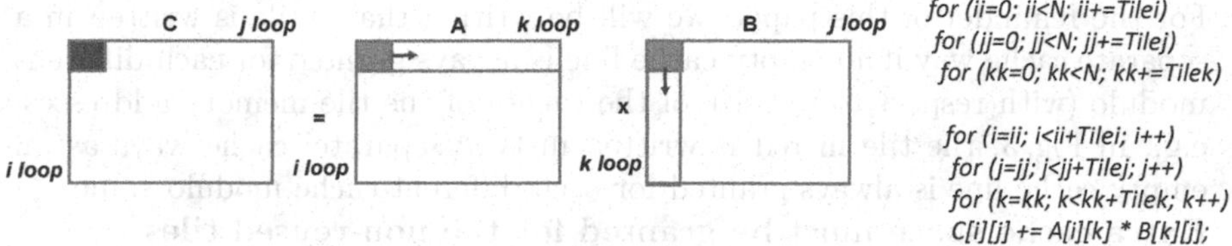

Fig. 2. An example. Loop tiling for MMM algorithm

- **Each tile must contain consecutive memory locations**
  The sub-rows of tile of C are not stored into consecutive main memory locations and therefore cache conflicts occur due to the cache module effect.
  A solution to this problem is array copying transformation; an extra loop kernel is added prior to the studied loop kernel where it copies the input array to a new one, in a tile-wise format; therefore, the tile elements are stored in consecutive main memory locations.
- **A cache way must not contain more than one tiles, unless they are stored into consecutive memory locations.**
  Assume an L1 data cache of 32 KB 8-way associative and $(Tilei, Tilej, Tilek) = (112, 32, 32)$; the size of tile of C, A and B is 14336 ($Tilei \times Tilej \times 4$ bytes), 14336 and 4096 bytes, respectively (32768 bytes in total) and they occupy $(3.5, 3.5, 1)$ cache ways, respectively (each way is 4096 bytes), assuming that each element is 4 bytes. Therefore, one cache way will be used to store part of the tiles of C and A (Way-0 in Fig. 3). In this case, Way-0 will store part of Tile of C and part of A; when the next tiles of A are loaded into the cache, they will be stored into different cache lines and therefore part of the C tile will be removed from the cache due to the cache module effect. This problem does not occur when $(Tilei, Tilej, Tilek) = (64, 64, 32)$, as the tiles occupy $(4, 2, 2)$ cache ways, respectively (Fig. 3).

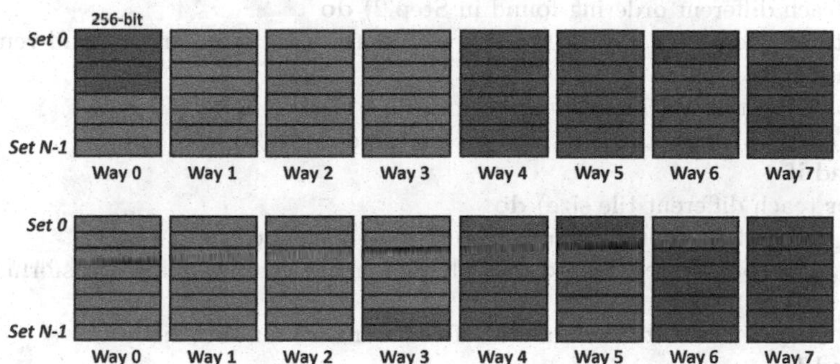

Fig. 3. An illustration of how tiles might be allocated to the cache, for the example shown in Fig. 2. On the top, $(Tilei, Tilej, Tilek) = (112, 32, 32)$ is shown, while in the bottom $(Tilei, Tilej, Tilek) = (64, 64, 32)$. Each tile is shown in a different colour. (Color figure online)

For the reminder of this paper, we will be writing that a tile is written in a separate cache way if an empty cache line is always granted for each different modulo (with respect to the size of the cache) of the tile memory addresses, e.g., in Fig. 3, the tile in red is written in two 'separate' cache ways as an empty cache line is always granted for each different cache modulo value.

- **Extra cache space must be granted for the non-reused tiles**
  Even if the two aforementioned bullets hold, it is false to assume that the C tile will remain in the cache just because the aggregated size of the three tiles is smaller than the cache size. This is because there is no cache space allocated for the next tiles of A and B; therefore, when the next tiles of A and B are loaded into the cache they will evict cache lines from the tile of C (LRU cache replacement policy is assumed). However, if $(Tilei, Tilej, Tilek) = (64, 64, 16)$ is selected instead of $(Tilei, Tilej, Tilek) = (64, 64, 32)$, then cache space for 2 tiles of A and B is allocated and therefore the Tile of C will remain in the cache.

We evaluated the above assumptions on a PC (see Sect. 4) using Cachegrind tool [17] (simulation) and the following tile sets $(Tilei, Tilej, Tilek)$ $= (112, 32, 32)$, $(64, 64, 32)$, $(64, 64, 16)$ give $(10.2, 9.8, 5.2)$ million dL1 misses and $(3.1, 3, 3, 7.4)$ Gflops, respectively (square matrices of size $N = 1344$).

3.2 The Proposed Analytical Model

Our approach is given in Algorithm 1. The proposed method generates the iterators to be tiled, their order as well as their tile sizes, for a given cache memory.

Algorithm 1. Proposed Loop Tiling Algorithm

Step.1 Specify the iterators that loop tiling is eligible to (n iterators)
for (i=1,n) **do**
  Step.2 Generate all different iterator orderings using i out of n iterators
  for (each different ordering found in Step.2) **do**
    Step.3 Construct Eq. 3. Eq. 3 holds all the tiles sizes that fit and remain in the cache
    if (If the tiles' memory locations overlap) **then**
      Step.4 Merge the tiles into one and update Eq. 3
    end if
    for (each different tile size) **do**
      if (the tiles contain non-consecutive memory locations) **then**
        Step.5 Either discard this tile size or use array copying transformation
      end if
      Step.6 Estimate the number of cache misses for each tile set
    end for
  end for
end for
Step.7 Choose the tile set achieving the minimum number of cache misses

STEP.1: The iterators that loop tiling is applicable to are manually provided; not all the loops are eligible to loop tiling mainly because of dependencies.

Step.2: The next step is to specify the iterators that loop tiling will be applied to as well as their nesting level values. For example, in a loop kernel with three iterators (i, j, k) eligible to loop tiling, such as the original (non-tiled) version of MMM in Fig. 2, the following 15 loop tiling implementations will be generated: $(i), (j), (k), (i,j), (i,k), (j,i), (j,k), (k,i), (k,j), (i,j,k), (i,k,j), (j,i,k), (j,k,i), (k,i,j), (k,j,i)$. All different orderings are processed so as not to exclude any efficient implementations.

Step.3: In Steps.3–6, the main part of the proposed loop tiling algorithm takes place. First, a mathematical inequality is constructed holding the tile sizes for which the tiles fit and remain in the cache:

$$m \leq \lceil \frac{Tile_1}{L_i/assoc} \rceil + \lceil \frac{Tile_{1\_next}}{L_i/assoc} \rceil + ... + \lceil \frac{Tile_n}{L_i/assoc} \rceil + \lceil \frac{Tile_{n\_next}}{L_i/assoc} \rceil \leq assoc \quad (3)$$

where $Tile_i$ is the tile size in bytes, L_i is the cache size in bytes, n is the number of tiles, $assoc$ is the L_i associativity and m defines the lower bound of the tile sizes and it equals to the number of arrays in the loop kernel. The tile sizes not included in Eq. 3 are discarded as they cannot remain in the cache.

In Eq. 3, a separate tile exists for each array reference (in the loop kernel) and thus an array might have multiple tiles. Furthermore, for each tile, we grant cache space for its next tile too (to address the third bullet in Sect. 3.1.2). Note that the overlapping tiles are merged into Step.4. All the tiles contain consecutive memory locations (1st bullet in Subsect. 3.1.2). The value of $(\lceil \frac{Tile_1}{L_i/assoc} \rceil)$ is an integer representing the number of L_i cache ways used by Tile1, or equivalently, is an integer representing the number of L_i cache lines with identical cache addresses used for Tile1. Equation 3 satisfies that the array tiles directed to the same cache subregions do not conflict with each other as the number of cache lines with identical addresses needed for the tiles is not larger than the $assoc$ value (second bullet in Sect. 3.1.2).

$Tile_i$ which contains consecutive memory locations is given by Eq. 4:

$$Tile_i = max.number.cache.lines \times cache.line.size \times element.size \quad (4)$$

where $cache.line.size$ is the size of the cache line in elements, $element.size$ is the size of the array's elements in bytes and the $max.number.cache.lines$ gives the maximum number of cache lines occupied by the tile (Eq. 2).

Step.4: In this step, the overlapping tiles in Eq. 3 are merged to one, normally bigger tile, which consists of their union; if the tiles match, then the new tile's size remain unchanged. Step.4 is needed so as there are no tile duplicates in the cache. For the rest of this paper we will write that two tiles overlap, if their memory locations overlap.

Consider the example where the following two array references exist in the loop body $A[i][j-2]$, $A[i][j+2]$ and j loop spans from 2 to N-2. By applying loop tiling to j loop with tile size T, the 1st tile of the 1st array reference spans within (0,T) and the 1st tile of the 2nd array reference spans within (4, T+4). These tiles are merged and a single bigger tile is created of size $(T+4)$.

Step.5 in Algorithm 1: In Step.5, all the remaining tile sizes with no consecutive memory locations are either discarded as they cannot remain in the cache or array copying transformation is applied.

It is common practice to apply array copying transformation before loop tiling in order all the tiles to contain consecutive memory locations. An extra loop kernel is added prior to the studied loop kernel where it copies the input array to a new one, in a tile-wise format. This adds an extra overhead and this is why it is performance efficient only in limited number of loop kernels.

Step.6 in Algorithm 1: In Step.6, the number of cache misses is approximated theoretically, considering the cache hardware parameters, the array memory access patterns of each loop kernel and the problem's input size. To do so, we calculate how many times the selected tiles (whose dimensions and sizes are known) are loaded/stored from/to the cache.

We are capable of approximating the number of cache misses because the number of unforeseen misses has been minimised (the reused tiles remain in the cache). This is because only the proposed tiles reside in the cache, the tiles are written in consecutive memory locations, an empty cache line is always granted for each different modulo and we use cache space for two consecutive tiles and not one (when needed). Additionally, we refer to CPUs with an instruction cache; in this case, the program code typically fits in L1 instruction cache; thus, it is assumed that the shared cache or unified cache (if any) is dominated by data.

The number of cache misses is estimated by Eq. 5.

$$Num\_Cache\_Misses = \sum_{i=1}^{i=sizeof(Tiles.List)} (repetition\_i \times cache.lines\_i) \tag{5}$$

where *repetition_i* gives how many times the array of this tile is loaded/stored from/to this cache memory (given by Eq. 7), *cache.lines_i* is the number of cache lines accessed when this tile traverses the array (given by Eq. 6) and *Tiles.List* contains all the tiles that contribute to Eq. 5.

The *Tiles.List* is initialised with all the tiles specified in Eq. 3, after the merging process (Step.3b) in Algorithm 1 (the 'next' tiles are not included; the only reason they exist in Eq. 3 is to grant extra cache space). There are cases where not all the tiles contribute to Eq. 5 and this is why some tiles might be deleted from the *Tiles.List*. This happens when an array has multiple array references (in the loop body) and therefore multiple tiles. Thus, different tiles of the same array might access memory locations that have already been accessed just before and thus the tile resides in the cache; in this case, accessing the tile will lead to a cache hit, not a miss.

The *cache.lines* value in Eq. 5 is given by

$$cache.lines = \begin{cases} \frac{N}{Ty} \times \sum_{j=1}^{j=M/Tx} (\lceil \frac{j \times Tx}{line} \rceil - \lfloor \frac{(j-1) \times Tx}{line} \rfloor), \text{row-wise data array layout} \\ \sum_{j=1}^{j=tiles} (\lceil \frac{j \times (Tx \times Ty)}{line} \rceil - \lfloor \frac{(j-1) \times (Tx \times Ty)}{line} \rfloor), \text{tile-wise} \end{cases} \tag{6}$$

where (Tx, Ty) are the tile sizes of the iterators in the (x,y) dimension of the array's subscript, respectively, (N, M) are the corresponding iterators' upper bounds (for 1D arrays $Ty = 1$), *line* is the cache line size in elements, *tiles* is the total number of the array's tiles and $(tiles = N/Ty \times M/Tx)$ or $(tiles = M/Tx)$ whether for 2D/1D arrays, respectively.

Let us give an example for the first branch of Eq. 6, consider a 2D floating point array and a tile of size (10×10) traversing the array in the x-axis. Also consider that $(line = 16)$ array elements. The first tile occupies $10 \times (\lceil \frac{10}{16} \rceil - \lfloor \frac{0}{16} \rfloor) = 10$ cache lines while the second tile occupies $10 \times (\lceil \frac{20}{16} \rceil - \lfloor \frac{10}{16} \rfloor) = 20$ cache lines. Although the array's tiles are of equal size, they occupy a different number of cache lines. Equation 6, gives the number of cache lines occupied in the case where array copying has been applied and therefore the array is written tile-wise in memory; in this case, the first tile lies between $(0, 100)$, the second between $(100, 200)$ etc.

The *repetition* value in Eq. 5 is given by

$$repetition = \prod_{j=1}^{j=U} \frac{(up_j - low_j)}{T_j} \times \prod_{k=1}^{k=Q} \frac{(up_k - low_k)}{T_k} \tag{7}$$

where U is the number of new/extra iterators (generated by loop tiling) that a) do not exist in the corresponding array's subscript and b) exist above of the iterators of the corresponding array, e.g., regarding the B tile in Fig. 2, this is the ii iterator. Q is the number of new/extra iterators that a) do not exist in the array and b) exist between of the iterators of the array, e.g., regarding the A tile in Fig. 2, this is the jj iterator; the ii iterator forces the whole array of B to be loaded $N/Tile$ times, while the jj iterator forces the whole array of A to be loaded $N/Tile$ times.

4 Experimental Results

The experimental results are extracted in a host PC (Intel i7-4790 CPU at 3.60 GHz, Ubuntu 18.04) and the codes are compiled using gcc 7.5.0 compiler.

The benchmarks used in this study consists of six well-known memory-bound loop kernels taken from 4.1 PolyBench/C suite [18]. These are: gemm, mvm, gemver, Doitgen, Bicg and gesumv. The input size of the loop kernels is specified with letter 'N' (square matrices are taken of size $N \times N$).

Table 1. The error in cache misses is measured for five different tile sizes using Eq. 8 and the maximum value is shown.

kernel		dL1 cache				L3 cache			
		Cachegrind	Perf (HW counters)	Cachegrind	Perf (HW counters)	Cachegrind	Perf (HW counters)	Cachegrind	Perf (HW counters)
gemm	Input size	**N=1000**		**N=2000**		**N=3000**		**N=6000**	
	Tile sizes	(25,25,25), (40,40,25) (-,2,-),(-,4,-),(25,25,40)		(20,20,50),(25,25,25) (25,25,40),(-,2,-),(40,40,25)		(500,500,600), (-,250,-) (500,500,500) (-,200,-),(600,600,300)		(500,500,600), (-,100,-) (500,500,500) (600,600,300), (-,75,-)	
	Error	**0.8%**	**2.8%**	**0.8%**	**2.9%**	**0.8%**	**5.4%**	**0.8%**	**5.8%**
mvm	Input size	**N=6000**		**N=9000**		**N=10000**		**N=12000**	
	Tile sizes	(-,2000), (-,1000), (6,1000) (3,2000), (4,1000)		(-,2000), (-,1000), (6,1000) (3,2000), (4,1000)		(100,2000), (50,2000), (100,2500) (50,2500), (125,2500)		(20,2000), (40,2000), (80,2000) (80,3000), (60,3000)	
		0.7%	**2.8%**	**0.7%**	**2.7%**	**0.7%**	**1.9%**	**0.7%**	**2.0%**
doitgen	Input size	**N=128**		**N=256**		**N=512**		**N=600**	
	Tile sizes	(-,32,32,32), (-,16,16,64) (-,16,64,16) (-,64,16,16),(-,16,16,32)		(-,32,32,32), (-,16,16,64) (-,16,64,16) (-,64,16,16),(-,16,16,32)		(-,512,256,512), (-,512,512,256) (-,256,256,256) (-,256,512,256),(-,512,512,512)		(-,600,300,600), (-,600,600,300) (-,300,600,600) (-,300,300,600),(-,600,300,300)	
	Error	**0.9%**	**2.5%**	**0.9%**	**3.1%**	**0.9%**	**2.5%**	**0.9%**	**2.6%**
gemver	Input size	**N=6000**		**N=9000**		**N=10000**		**N=12000**	
	Tile sizes	(-,1500), (-,1000), (2,1000) (3,1000), (1,1000)		(-,1500), (-,1000), (2,1000) (3,1000), (1,1000)		(100,2000), (50,2000), (125,2000) (50,1250), (80,1250)		(20,2000), (40,2000), (80,2000) (80,1500), (60,1500)	
	Error	**0.9%**	**2.9%**	**0.8%**	**2.9%**	**0.8%**	**2.0%**	**0.8%**	**2.0%**
bicg	Input size	**N=6000**		**N=9000**		**N=10000**		**N=12000**	
	Tile sizes	(3,1000), (1,1000), (2,1000) (-,1500), (-,1000)		(-,1500), (-,1000), (2,1000) (3,1000), (1,1000)		(100,2000), (50,2000), (125,2000) (50,1250), (80,1250)		(20,2000), (40,2000), (80,2000) (80,1500), (60,1500)	
	Error	**0.9%**	**2.9%**	**0.8%**	**2.9%**	**0.8%**	**2.0%**	**0.8%**	**2.0%**
gesumv	Input size	**N=4000**		**N=8000**		**N=8000**		**N=12000**	
	Tile sizes	(2,800), (1,1000), (2,1000) (-,800), (-,1000)		(2,800), (1,1000), (2,1000) (-,800), (-,1000)		(40,2000), (40,1000), (20,2000) (20,1000), (25,2000)		(20,2000), (20,1500), (10,2000) (30,2000), (30,1500)	
	Error	**0.9%**	**2.7%**	**0.9%**	**2.7%**	**0.9%**	**2.1%**	**0.9%**	**2.1%**

4.1 Validation of the Proposed Methodology

In this sub-section we showcase that i) the tiles generated by the proposed methodology fit and remain in the cache and ii) the proposed equations (Step.6) can accurately estimate the number of cache misses. To validate the proposed method, we have applied the proposed methodology to L1 data cache (dL1) (32 KB, 8-way) and L3 cache (8 MB, 16-way). The tile sizes and the iterators to be tiled are given by Algorithm 1.

The number of cache misses is measured for five tile sizes and the maximum error value is calculated (Eq. 8) using i) Cachegrind tool [17] (simulation) and ii) Perf tool using the 'l1d.replacement', 'LLC-load-misses' and 'LLC-store-misses' hardware counters.

$$error\% = \frac{|cache.misses.measured - Eq.\,5.misses|}{Eq.\,5.misses} \times 100 \qquad (8)$$

Cachegrind and Perf give different cache misses values, because the perf measures the number of cache misses of all the running processes, not just the process we are interested in.

In Table 1, we compare the dL1 and L3 misses as extracted from Eq. 5 against the measurements from Cachegrind and Perf. As Table 1 indicates the proposed equations provide roughly the same number of cache misses as Cachegrind. This means that first, the proposed tiles fit and remain in the cache and second, the proposed equations give a very good approximation of the number of misses.

Regarding dL1, the error values are higher (about 3%) when using the dL1 hardware counter (Table 1), as other processes are loading/storing data from/to this memory too. Note that Table 1 shows only the tile sizes that need roughly the size of seven out of eight cache ways, or less; the tiles that use more cache space give a much higher error value, which is up to 20%. Given that this inconsistency holds only for the Perf measurements and not for Cachegrind, it is valid to assume that this is due to the fact that other processes using the dL1. In this case, each dL1 access of another process leads to an unforeseen miss.

For the same reason, on the right of Table 1, we show the tile sizes that need roughly the size of 9 out of 16 L3 cache ways, or less. mvm, doitgen, bicg, gesumv and gemver give a small L3 error value as their arrays fit and remain in L3 even without using loop tiling. This is not the case for gemm and this is why the error value in gemm is higher.

Table 2. Comparison over gcc on Intel i7-4790.

	Tiling for dL1 only							Tiling for dL1 and L3						
kernel	**dL1 misses gain**	**perf. gain**	**tile size**	**dL1 misses gain**	**perf. gain**	**tile size**	**Pluto perf. gain**	**L3 misses gain**	**perf. gain**	**tile size**	**L3 misses gain**	**perf. gain**	**tile size**	**Pluto perf. gain**
gemm	**N=600**			**N=900**				**N=1800**			**N=3400**			
	x40.9	x3.7	(60,60,10)	x61.0	x4.1	(60,60,10)	1.01	x57.2	x4.09	(900*,60,900*) (60,60,10)	x59.3	x4.2	(850*,50,850*) (50,50,20)	1.01
mvm	**N=9000**			**N=12000**				**N=9000**			**N=12000**			
	x1.5	x0.98	(-,3000)	x1.5	x0.98	(-,3000)	x0.91	x1.00	x1.01	(120,3000)	x1.00	x1.01	(100,3000)	x0.91
doitgen	**N=256**			**N=512**										
	x34.2	x1.79	(64,64,16)	x41.4	x1.93	(64,64,16)	x0.99	-	-	-	-	-	-	-
gemver	**N=8000**			**N=12000**				**N=8000**			**N=12000**			
	x2.0	x1.08	(-,2000)	x2.0	x1.09	(-,2000)	x0.89	x1.00	x1.09	(80,2000)	x1.00	x1.18	(60,2000)	x0.89
bicg	**N=8000**			**N=12000**				**N=8000**			**N=12000**			
	x2.0	x0.92	(-,2000)	x2.0	x0.92	(-,2000)	x0.42	x1.00	x1.03	(80,2000)	x1.00	x1.04	(60,2000)	x0.42
gesumv	**N=8000**			**N=12000**				**N=8000**			**N=12000**			
	x1.25	x0.91	(-,2000)	x1.25	x0.91	(-,2000)	x0.87	x1.00	x1.01	(40,2000)	x1.00	x1.01	(30,2000)	x0.87

4.2 Evaluation over Gcc Compiler and Pluto

In all cases, the six studied loop kernels are compiled using 'gcc -O2 -floop-block -floop-strip-mine' command and the generated binaries are those that the proposed methodology is compared to. The '-floop-block -floop-strip-mine' option enables gcc to apply loop tiling transformation. The C codes of the proposed method are compiled using 'gcc -O2' command.

On the left of Table 2, the proposed methodology has been applied to dL1 only. The proposed method provides significant dL1 miss gains at all cases but performance gains just for gemm, doitgen and gemver. Reducing the number of dL1 misses does not always align with performance; in this case, the selected tile sizes for mvm, bicg and gesumv (which minimize dL1 misses) slighly increase the number of L3 misses and this is why performance is degraded. Note that the dL1 miss gain is higher in gemm and doitgen comparing to the other loop kernels, as all their tiles achieve data reuse; the tiles remain in L1 and also being loaded many times from L1, highly reducing the number of L1 misses.

It is important to note that the baseline binary code that we compare our method to for mvm, bicg and gesumv in Table 2, does not include loop tiling (although the loop tiling option has been enabled, gcc disables its application in gesumv, bicg and mvm, by considering it not performance efficient).

On the right of Table 2, the proposed methodology has been applied first to dL1 and then to L3. Applying loop tiling for mvm, gemver, bicg and gesumv just for L3 cache is pointless as their arrays fit and remain in the cache even for very large input sizes and as a consequence the number of L3 misses cannot be reduced. However, applying loop tiling for L3 to the implementations shown on the left of Table 2 is beneficial, as these implementations give a higher number of L3 misses than the no tiled implementations. Regarding doitgen, applying loop tiling to L3 cannot give any gain as the arrays fit in the cache. The '*' in Table 2 indicates that these iterators are interchanged.

The proposed methodology has been also evaluated using Pluto [3] (version 0.11.4). For a fair comparison, only the loop tiling phase of Pluto is activated. Pluto applies square tile sizes of size 32 at all cases and this is why gcc perfomrs better. Pluto is a powerful tool which is not limited to loop tiling and if we enable all its phases, then it provides higher speedup values than gcc.

5 Conclusions and Future Work

In this article, we first demostrate two important inefficiencies of current analytical loop tiling models and provide insight on how current models can overcome these inefficiencies. Second, we propose a new model where the number of cache misses is accurately estimated for each generated tile size. This is achieved by leveraging the target memory hardware architecture and data access patterns.

As far as our future work is concerned, the first step includes the validation and evaluation of the proposed method to other CPUs. Second, we plan to work towards correlating the number of cache misses with execution time.

Acknowledgements. This work has received funding from the European Union's Horizon 2020 research and innovation programme under Grant Agreement No 957210 - XANDAR: X-by-Construction Design framework for Engineering Autonomous & Distributed Real-time Embedded Software Systems.

References

1. Baskaran, M.M., Hartono, A., Tavarageri, S., Henretty, T., Ramanujam, J., Sadayappan, P.: Parameterized tiling revisited. CGO 2010 (2010)
2. Bondhugula, U., Bandishti, V., Pananilath, I.: Diamond tiling: tiling techniques to maximize parallelism for stencil computations. In: IEEE TPDS, pp. 1285–1298 (2017)
3. Bondhugula, U., Hartono, A., Ramanujam, J., Sadayappan, P.: A practical automatic polyhedral parallelizer and locality optimizer. In: SIGPLAN, vol. 43, no. 6 (2008)
4. Chatterjee, S., Parker, E., Hanlon, P.J., Lebeck, A.R.: Exact analysis of the cache behavior of nested loops. SIGPLAN Not. **36**(5), 286–297 (2001)
5. Cohen, A., Zhao, J.: Flextended tiles: a flexible extension of overlapped tiles for polyhedral compilation. ACM TACO (2020)

6. Hammami, E., Slama, Y.: An overview on loop tiling techniques for code generation. In: 2017 IEEE/ACS AICCSA, pp. 280–287 (2017)
7. Hartono, A., et al.: Parametric multi-level tiling of imperfectly nested loops. In: ICS 2009, NY, USA, p. 147–157. New York (2009)
8. Hsu, C.H., Kremer, U.: A quantitative analysis of tile size selection algorithms. J. Supercomput. **27**(3), 279–294 (2004)
9. Kelefouras, V., Djemame, K.: A methodology correlating code optimizations with data memory accesses, execution time and energy consumption. J. Supercomput. **75**(10), 6710–6745 (2019). https://doi.org/10.1007/s11227-019-02880-z
10. Kelefouras, V.I., Athanasiou, G.S., Alachiotis, N., Michail, H.E., Kritikakou, A.S., Goutis, C.E.: A methodology for speeding up fast Fourier transform focusing on memory architecture utilization. IEEE Trans. Sig. Process. **59**, 6217–6226 (2011)
11. Kelefouras, V., Georgios, K., Nikolaos, V.: Combining software cache partitioning and loop tiling for effective shared cache management. ACM Trans. Embed. Comput. Syst. **17**(3), 72:1-72:25 (2018)
12. Kelefouras, V., Kritikakou, A., Mporas, I., Kolonias, V.: A high-performance matrix–matrix multiplication methodology for CPU and GPU architectures. J. Supercomput. **72**(3), 804–844 (2016)
13. Kelefouras, V., Kritikakou, A., Papadima, E., Goutis, C.: A methodology for speeding up matrix vector multiplication for single/multi-core architectures. J. Supercomput. **71**(7), 2644–2667 (2015). https://doi.org/10.1007/s11227-015-1409-9
14. Kelefouras, V., Kritikakou, A., Goutis, C.: A matrix–matrix multiplication methodology for single/multi-core architectures using SIMD. J. Supercomput. **68**(3), 1418–1440 (2014). https://doi.org/10.1007/s11227-014-1098-9
15. Li, R., et al.: Analytical cache modeling and tilesize optimization for tensor contractions. In: SC 2019 (2019)
16. Mehta, S., Beeraka, G., Yew, P.C.: Tile size selection revisited. ACM Trans. Archit. Code Optim. **10**(4), 1–27 (2013)
17. Nethercote, N., Walsh, R., Fitzhardinge, J.: Building workload characterization tools with valgrind. In: IISWC, p. 2. IEEE Computer Society (2006)
18. POUCHET, L.: Polybench/c. http://web.cse.ohio-state.edu/~pouchet.2/software/polybench/. Accessed 10 Oct 2020
19. Renganarayanan, L., Kim, D., Strout, M.M., Rajopadhye, S.: Parameterized loop tiling. ACM Trans. Program. Lang. Syst. **34**(1), 1–41 (2012)
20. Sarkar, V., Megiddo, N.: An analytical model for loop tiling and its solution. In: IEEE ISPASS, pp. 146–153 (2000)
21. Sato, Y., Yuki, T., Endo, T.: An autotuning framework for scalable execution of tiled code via iterative polyhedral compilation. In: ACM TACO (2019)
22. Shirako, J., et al.: Analytical bounds for optimal tile size selection. In: CC 2012 (2012)
23. Stoltzfus, L., Hagedorn, B., Steuwer, M., Gorlatch, S., Dubach, C.: Tiling optimizations for stencil computations using rewrite rules in lift. ACM Trans. Archit. Code Optim. **16**(4), 1–25 (2019)
24. Tavarageri, S., Pouchet, L.N., Ramanujam, J., Rountev, A., Sadayappan, P.: Dynamic selection of tile sizes. In: HIPC 2011 (2011)
25. Whaley, R.C., Petitet, A., Dongarra, J.J.: Automated empirical optimization of software and the ATLAS project. Parallel Comput. **27**(1–2), 3–35 (2001)
26. Zhou, X., Giacalone, J.P., Garzarán, M.J., Kuhn, R.H., Ni, Y., Padua, D.: Hierarchical overlapped tiling. In: CGO 2012 (2012)

Interference-Aware Workload Placement for Improving Latency Distribution of Converged HPC/Big Data Cloud Infrastructures

Achilleas Tzenetopoulos[1(✉)], Dimosthenis Masouros[1], Sotirios Xydis[1,2], and Dimitrios Soudris[1]

[1] National Technical University of Athens, Athens, Greece
{atzenetopoulos,dmasouros,sxydis,dsoudris}@microlab.ntua.gr
[2] Harokopio University of Athens, Athens, Greece

Abstract. Recently, High Performance, Big Data, and Cloud Computing worlds tend to converge in terms of workload deployment with containerization technology acting as an enabler towards this direction. In such cases of application diversity and multi-tenancy, a universal scheduler able to satisfy the end-user needs for seamless, yet, efficient application deployment is required. While Kubernetes container orchestrator seems to be the answer that enables application-agnostic deployment, it still depends highly on coarse system metrics for its scheduling policies, thus, neglecting the performance degradation due to resource contention in the underlying system.

In this paper, we design and implement an interference-aware modular framework, able to balance incoming workload based on low-level metrics monitoring. We evaluate our proposed solution over different workload mixes and co-location scenarios showing that against the state-of-art, but interference unaware Kubernetes scheduler the proposed framework significantly improves the latency distribution of the converged cloud infrastructure, improving median latency up to 27% and reducing standard deviation up to 25%.

Keywords: Resource management · Kubernetes · Interference-aware · High-Performance Computing · Cloud computing

1 Introduction

Recently, High-Performance Computing (HPC) and Cloud worlds are getting more and more close. The latest advancements and performance improvements of containerization technology [14] have driven many HPC applications to be containerized, enabling increased productivity through prompt and seamless updates and rollbacks to previous versions. Respectively, cloud computing over the past twelve years has relieved users of physical infrastructure management as various technologies such as virtual machines, containers, and serverless have

© Springer Nature Switzerland AG 2022
A. Orailoglu et al. (Eds.): SAMOS 2021, LNCS 13227, pp. 108–123, 2022.
https://doi.org/10.1007/978-3-031-04580-6_8

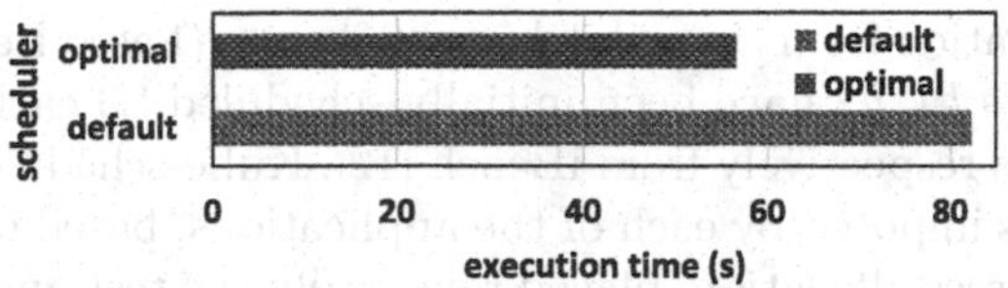

Fig. 1. Kube-scheduler sub-optimal node selection, neglecting the L3 cache stress

emerged. Thus, containers seem to be the common ground between cloud and HPC. However, containerization has led to a proliferation of virtual resources to be managed. The small resource footprint resulting in decreased startup latency, as well as a previously unseen flexibility regarding dependency packaging, have contributed to the adaptation of this technology by more and more users. Hence, since fleets of containers were deployed on data-center machines, the need for container orchestration frameworks in order to manage and automate the essential infrastructure operational tasks has arisen. Kubernetes [9] is currently the de facto solution for cloud infrastructure management. More specifically, in modern data-centers, in which HPC, Cloud and Big Data workloads co-exist, the infrastructure offerings by Kubernetes are indispensable to manage heterogeneous kinds of applications such as batch style (MapReduce), HPC stateful services, and others. In addition, heavy computation and unprecedented dataset sizes need to be combined with efficient resource sharing and ease of use. Thus, multi-tenancy is a critical, emerging factor, since different users run their heterogeneous workloads on top of a pool of finite shared resources.

While the cloud is becoming more and more popular, the amount of applications deployed and executed on cloud providers' shared hardware, competing for shared resources usage, has also radically increased. The increment in the number of workloads uploaded and executed on the cloud, has forced data-center (DC) operators and cloud providers, such as Google Cloud Platform [1] and Amazon Web Services [5], to embrace workload co-location and multi-tenancy as first-class system design concerns. On top of that, they need to provide QoS guarantees to foster the needs of the users. Academia [35] has identified that contention on the low-level shared resources of a system, i.e. low-level caches and bus bandwidth, can lead to unpredictable performance variability and degradation, which highly reduces the QoS of applications and may lead to Service Level Agreements violations.

Cloud users have their clusters mostly managed by container orchestrators, e.g., Kubernetes. Even though container orchestrators provide major benefits, such as ease of use and deployment, the abstraction of resources, scaling, and others, they are focusing mostly on availability rather than performance optimization, relying on coarse metrics, e.g., CPU or memory utilization, thus neglecting interference effects, overlooking the specifications of the underlying infrastructure and the nature of the imposed stress on the shared resources. In fact, Kubernetes scheduler (kube-scheduler) fails to select the most appropriate node when it comes to undetected low-level resources contention. To quantitatively motivate further the above discussion, we consider a kube-scheduler assigned the task of placing an incoming application from the scikit-learn [26] suite (Lasso Regression). In the two candidate hosts $h1, h2$ have been initially scheduled L3 cache and compute-intensive workloads respectively from iBench [12]. Kube-scheduler neglecting the nature of the stress imposed by each of the applications, based on coarse policies such as CPU resources allocation, placed repeatedly the test application into the host $h1$ which was suffering from L3 cache contention. However, by placing the scikit-learn application in $h2$, where it experiences less interference on the delay prone Last Level cache resource, we achieve an average speedup of 1.46x as it is also illustrated in Fig. 1 with optimal and default placement bars.

In this work, we propose an interference-aware custom scheduler as a Kubernetes in-tree extension, able to efficiently place applications on a cluster of available machines. Specifically, a) we try to identify interference and depict the contention volume of a system by utilizing low-level system metrics. b) By analyzing various benchmarking libraries' performance under resource pressure, we propose a custom metric achieving high correlation with performance degradation. c) We design and implement a modular Kubernetes scheduler extension, which distributes incoming workload leveraging the aforementioned custom metric. Using a universal approach for every kind of workload behaviour and duration our framework aims to minimize application execution delays provoked by interference phenomena by achieving a fairer resource utilization. d) Finally, we evaluate the median execution latency in the deployed applications' distribution. Compared to prior works [21,32], which employ offline application execution to identify implications of interference per application, our approach characterizes the contention in socket-level. Our scheduler outperforms the default one of Kubernetes, improving the performance of the scheduled workloads up to 27%, by efficiently equilibrating the usage of the resources between the available cluster machines. As tail-latency of the distribution, we signify the applications that suffer the most and experience higher volumes of performance degradation. Thus, we aim to result in a more equal resource exploitation in order to lift up the average tail-latency rather than to decrease the tail-latency for each application.

2 Related Work

Co-scheduling: Multi-tenancy and workload co-scheduling [16] to improve resource utilization has been issues that attracted the research community's attention over the years. Interference-aware methods are known to improve the distribution of the performance of applications in environments where large-scale resources are shared among multiple parties. As regards the existing interference-aware co-scheduling methods, a scheduling policy is set up that lowers the interference rate. Zhuravlev et al. [35] propose a contention-aware scheduling approach to mitigate contention for shared resources. Their approach classifies the application into four classes and identifies applications that should and should not be scheduled together. Mars et al. [22] used models so as to predict performance interference and QoS degradation by identifying co-locations of pre-characterized workloads aiming to improve data-center utilization. Different approaches have determined the sensitivity of applications to memory pressure, either statically [21] or dynamically [32], in order to co-schedule high-priority services with best-effort workloads. Finally, other works follow a separated, workload-specific scheduler approach for different classes of workloads [18]. In orchestration platforms such as Kubernetes, there are several *priority functions* provided, enabling system operators to customize the scheduling policies according to their application needs. Those functions include workload placement policies based on user- explicitly-defined resource allocation i.e. CPU cores and memory. Thus, orchestration platforms cherish application availability rather than performance optimization. In the proposed solution, incoming workloads are treated as black boxes, without any offline nor online application classification or profiling [29]. We identify interference at the socket level utilizing a custom scoring function composed of micro-architectural events monitoring and apply a best-fit heuristic for initial workload placement.

Performance Monitoring: Performance monitoring in data-center multi-core server architectures is essential to provide insights regarding the load that the cluster nodes experience. Today, state-of-the-art orchestrators [4], such as Kubernetes and Mesos, rely on naive metrics to manage workloads. However, much research has been conducted regarding monitoring approaches [7] and several frameworks have been developed to enable lightweight logging and fusion of micro-architectural events [27,28]. Moreover, services like Prometheus [6] allow for custom monitoring and optimization of running workloads, forming a promising area for low-level monitoring tools. In contrast to the aforementioned works, we monitor the system on a socket-level granularity and store the extracted metrics on a time series database with short retention policies.

Low-Level Metrics: The exploitation of performance characteristics of a system through hardware performance counters has been identified as a prominent step for improving the efficiency of data centers [20]. In addition, prior works has shown that hardware performance counters can also improve the scheduling policies inside modern NUMA multi-cores [8]. While the importance of low-level performance counters has been pinpointed, there has been minimal work regarding their exploitation, or even how these values are affected by interference effects. Even though various works [30,33], present state-of-the-art benchmark suites along with information about the low-level metrics of the included workloads, they provide no analysis regarding the fluctuation of these metrics when the workloads are executed in multi-tenant environments. Masouros D. et al. [23], utilize low-level counters "on-the-fly" to provide application-specific, runtime performance predictions under interference leveraging Long Short-term Memory (LSTM) networks. In this work, we utilize hardware performance counters (e.i. IPC, memory reads/writes etc.) to identify socket-level contention and place incoming applications accordingly.

3 Contention Analysis

Containerization technology contributed to application resource isolation by utilizing *cgroups*. Cgroups organize processes into namespaces and allocate and/or limit the resource usage for each of them. The aforementioned resources include the CPU time and memory. However, lower-level system resources such as cache misses, memory, disk, and network I/O bandwidth are not isolated as well. Thus, interference on those resources can still lead to unpredictable performance variability. On top of that, container orchestrators such as Kubernetes, taking into account the previously defined coarse resources on a compute node abstraction level, place incoming applications in a manner that the anticipated node availability is maximized. However, Kubernetes scheduler fails to select the most appropriate node, neglecting contention at low-level resources.

3.1 Benchmarks

Modern data-center server machines accommodate a wide range of workloads, which are basically either batch/best-effort (BE), or user-interactive /latency-critical (LC) applications. The former type of workloads require the highest possible throughput, whereas the latter demand to meet their QoS constraints. In order to cover both BE and LC workloads, we consider workloads from four popular scientific benchmarking libraries, i.e., scikit-learn [26], SPEC CPU 2006 [19] and HPCG [13] (as BE) and cloudsuite [15] (as LC) suite.

Regarding the scikit-learn suite, we examine workload skeletons, which are representative of modern machine learning applications. The datasets used in the training phase of these workloads are comprised of 40,000 instances, with 784 features per instance. The SPEC CPU 2006 benchmarks are computational heavy workloads as well as everyday operations deployed in cloud environments (e.g. sphinx3 performs speech recognition). For SPEC CPU 2006, we use the default settings.

Next, the cloudsuite benchmarks are based on real-world online services hosted in modern data-centers. In-Memory analytics utilizes Apache Spark [34] and runs a collaborating filtering algorithm on a movie ratings dataset. Data-Serving relies on the Yahoo! Cloud Serving Benchmark [11] and the Cassandra data store [10]. For the data-serving benchmark we increased the amount of operations to 300,000. Data-caching, uses the Memcached data caching server, simulating the behavior of a Twitter caching server using a Twitter dataset.

The High-Performance Conjugate Gradients (HPCG) [13] project is a benchmark suite for ranking HPC systems. It is designed to exercise computational and data access patterns that match a broad set of applications. HPCG is a complete, written in C++, standalone code that implements sparse matrix-vector multiplication, vector updates, and many other operations. It also supports MPI and OpenMP frameworks.

Deployment in Kubernetes: For the purposes of this evaluation, we containerized all the benchmarks utilizing the Docker runtime. More specifically, regarding the cloudsuite benchmarking suite, for the data-serving benchmark, we deploy two docker containers implementing a client-server architecture. The client is deployed only after the server and the implemented database service are up and running. The same applies for the web-serving benchmark. In order to deploy those benchmarks in our Kubernetes cluster, we needed to create the appropriate *deployment, pod* and *services* utilizing YAML configuration files. For the in-memory-analytics benchmark, we use a single node deployment.

3.2 Socket-Level Contention

Resources such as Last Level Cache (LLC) and memory bandwidth are shared between sub-system components, the sockets. In this work, we seek to identify contention aiming to improve node selection and to specify the deployment environment at socket level.

Proper scheduling requires a score that reflects the interference on the system, in our case the socket. For this purpose, in order to detect some correlation pattern between the imposed stress and the performance of applications, we tentatively co-schedule cloudsuite, scikit-learn and SPEC CPU 2006 workloads as described in Table 1 with iBench [12].

iBench provides contentious micro-benchmarks that can simulate stress in different intensities and for different shared resources, ranging from core up to memory levels (e.g. compute/L1i/L1d etc.). At the same time, we monitor the socket low-level metrics utilizing Intel Performance Counter Monitoring (PCM) [28]. We extract L3 cache misses, C0-state percentage, reads and writes from and to the memory and instructions per cycle(IPC). C0-state describes the percentage of physical cores in executing state (not being idle). Memory reads and writes are the requests for data on behalf of LLC misses, as well as DRAM traffic due to prefetching, providing a low-level performance counter able to depict the number of memory accesses. Thus, the count of those memory I/O operations seems to be a great indicator for the contention status of a system. On the other hand, IPC value is not a reliable metric since it depends both on system utilization and contention levels. In other words, IPC is low both in an empty and on a contended cluster. However, during a high volume of interference, different processes are competing for memory access, and as the available bandwidth is not able to support all requests at the same time, neither memory reads and writes number nor L3 cache misses are any longer valuable indicators of the contention beyond this point. Therefore, we compose the custom metric $S = \frac{Reads+Writes}{IPC}$ (1) in order to detect contention levels beyond the memory bandwidth limits. Higher values of this metric indicate a more contended system.

Table 1. Summary of workloads used as cloud applications.

Suite	Benchmarks	Type
Scikit-Learn	Lasso, Linear Regression, Linear Discriminant Analysis, Ada Boost Classifier, Random Forest Regressor, Random Forest Classifier	Best-Effort
SPEC CPU 2006	astar, leslie, cactus, sphinx, mcf, lbm	batch
Cloudsuite	web-serving, in-memory analytics, data-serving	Latency-critical
HPCG	Sparse matrix-vector multiplication, Vector updates, Global dot products. Local symmetric Gauss-Seidel smoother etc.	HPC

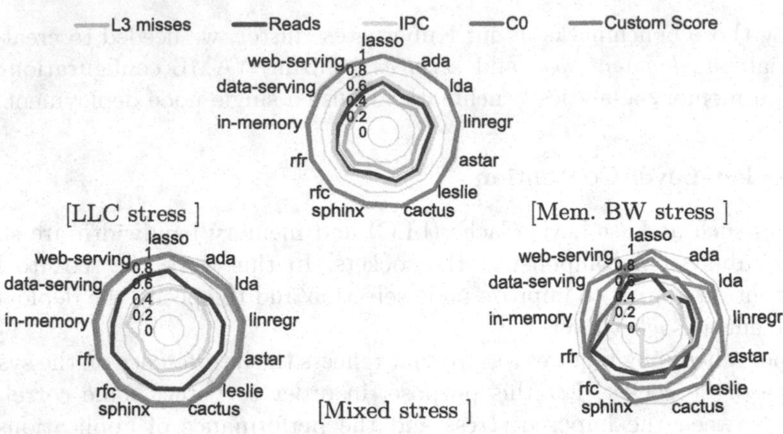

Fig. 2. Correlation between applications performance degradation and system metrics.

To show the effectiveness of the proposed metric, we compare different metrics' accuracy on reflecting the system's condition utilizing the Pearson's correlation between the performance of each application and the metric's average value prior to the application's scheduling. Figure 2 shows the correlation between the applications' normalized performance under different levels of stress and the corresponding metrics' values. We use the execution time when the application runs isolated as reference for the normalization. Our custom metric seems to be highly correlated with the application's performance in most scenarios. In L3-iBench, the custom score and the C0-state of the sockets are competing for the first place. Furthermore, in the memory bandwidth-iBench stress, L3 misses seem to be correlated with applications performance too. In those two previous scenarios, the high value of C0-state in performance correlation is disorienting. C0-state percentage will keep increasing as the number of pre-scheduled contentious benchmark increases. However, in Fig. 2c, when various resource stressing benchmarks are deployed and the contention is heterogeneous, C0 is not a reliable system state indicator anymore. The same applies for our custom metric to a lesser extent, due to the impact of core availability which is not captured. Therefore, we take into consideration this parameter in our proposed solution (Sect. 5.2).

4 Target Cluster Infrastructure

Architecture: Virtualization technology has led to the democratization of High-Performance Computing. Therefore, in many cases, clusters of high-end multi-processor systems are designed in order to serve multiple tenants. The target infrastructure setup in this paper is such a multi-node system. More specifically, the cluster is composed of 4 dual-socket worker nodes. Each one of them consists of two Intel® Xeon® E5-2690 processors, and 132 GB RAM. Additional specifications are described in Table 2.

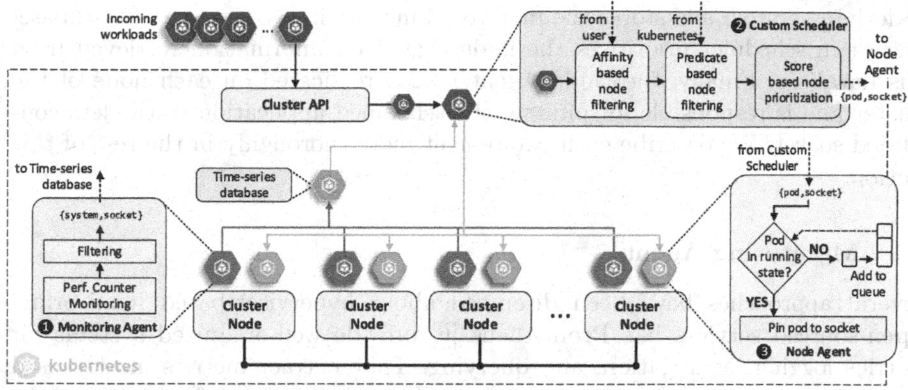

Fig. 3. Overview of our custom framework

Use-Case Scenario: The cluster we refer to in the rest of this paper is used by multiple parties, which execute a big variety of workload types. On top of those nodes, we deployed the Kubernetes container orchestrator. Kubernetes is an application-agnostic framework, designed to remove the burden of management and scheduling tasks from the end-users, providing seamless scalability and high availability for them at the same time. More specifically, workloads varying from web services that are mostly executed on the cloud to resource-hungry HPC tasks, will need to be co-scheduled under the same system. In this manner, in the following sections, we describe our proposed framework that aims to unburden both the scientists as well as the application developers from exercising resource management, and workload placement tasks depending on the current state of the different nodes of the system.

5 Interference-Aware Orchestration Framework

In this section, we describe the implementation of our custom interference-aware placement mechanism. The proposed framework is highly modular; therefore an easily scalable framework closely integrated with Kubernetes. Thus, except for its additional functionality, it also exploits any utilities provided by the open-sourced Kubernetes scheduler. The schema of our framework is illustrated in Fig. 3. Our framework is based on four different components, (i) the Monitoring Agent (❶), (ii) a time-series storage database, (iii) the interference-aware scheduler (❷) and (iv) the Node Agent (❸). The Monitoring Agent is replicated on each node of the cluster. Each Monitoring Agent continuously monitors the

Table 2. Hosts specifications

Processor Model	Intel® Xeon® E5-2690 v3	L2 Cache	256 KB
Cores per socket	12 (24 logical)	L3 Cache	30 MB
Base/Turbo Frequency	2.60 GHz/3.5 GHz	Memory	132 GB @2133 MHz

underlying system and stores the monitored metrics in the time series database. The main scheduler prioritizes the nodes based on information retrieved from this database. Finally, the Node Agent is also replicated on each node of the cluster and is responsible for pinning the scheduled application in the less contended socket. We describe each component more thoroughly in the rest of this section.

5.1 Monitoring Agent

Several approaches have been discussed about hypervisor-based monitoring. Open-sourced services like Prometheus [6] provide well-organized systems for metrics logging, aggregation, and querying. They extract metrics mostly used for alert generation and security insight, only providing a brief overview of the system's condition. As a result, the resource under contention cannot be identified and the root cause of application degradation remains unmanageable. Contrarily, low-level metrics, which describe micro-architectural events, can provide useful information regarding the resource under contention, namely the origin of a system's inability to serve workloads' needs efficiently.

As a first step, we need to get an insight into the low-level system metrics. Those metrics describe micro-architectural events of the host machine. For this purpose, we use the Performance Counter Monitor (PCM) [28], a tool developed by Intel. It is used as an agent ❶, extracting metrics from the system it is running on. We deploy one PCM agent per node. The Intel Performance Counter Monitor provides sample C++ routines and utilities to estimate the internal resource utilization of the latest Intel Xeon and Core processors.

Using PCM we were able to extract system and socket metrics. Most of the metrics provide useful information about the state of the system (Instructions per Cycle, L3 cache misses, Memory reads/writes etc.). Since, PCM extractor is written in C++, we added an influxDB [25] client [31] and store the desired metrics in a 500 ms interval, in batch mode for increased throughput on a time-series database. Intervals larger than 1 s can result to undetected system metrics' spikes [17], while much smaller ones provide non-essential granularity. We store information retrieved from the socket up to the system-level. The end-to-end latency from storing the metric in the database to getting it consumed by the scheduler is ~15 ms. InfluxDB provides real-time monitoring with the precision of nanosecond, allowing the user to define short retention periods for data that are no longer needed. It was proved to be very efficient for the purposes of our framework compared to MySQL [24].

5.2 Interference-Aware Custom Scheduler

Kubernetes Vanilla Scheduler: The popular, state-of-the-art, widely used container orchestrator Kubernetes, offers a scheduler that is responsible for node selection for any incoming pod's placement. Upon the pod creation by the user/controller, the scheduler monitoring the object store for unassigned pods, will assign the pod to a node. Kubernetes also exploits container tags, called labels. Users can explicitly define node/pod affinity/anti-affinity for their application (pod) or set of applications (deployment). User's preferences can be either preferred or required during scheduling, which indicate soft and hard requirements respectively. Any preference defined as a hard requirement bypasses the procedure described below.

The scheduling process uses node scoring, accounting for constraints, and load balancing, and consists of two stages. The first one is the node filtering, when the scheduler determines the set of feasible placements, which is the set of nodes that meet a set of given constraints. All filter functions must yield true for the node to host the pod. Those constraints called predicates are related to resources such as disk, volumes, memory, cores, network and ports availability as well as inter-pod affinity and node tolerations and taints. The node prioritization phase comes second. After the filtering, with only the feasible nodes remaining, Kubernetes scheduler (kube-scheduler) using a set of predefined rating functions, determines the viability of each node. Those functions are mostly related to resources availability, as well as node affinity provided by the user. The pod will be scheduled in the host with the highest viability. Kubernetes also supports resources declaration at the time of pod creation. The user is able to request any fraction of virtual cores and memory (RAM) which will be a guarantee for the deployed applications' minimum resource usage. This resource reservation prevents usage from other applications by offering runtime isolation. However, this constitutes only the lower bound of resources usage. The upper bound is set by defining the resource limits.

On the other side, the proposed framework supports application-agnostic deployment, removing the burden of workload profiling and resource allocation from the end-users. While the absence of such resource allocation policies may decrease the quality of service of the target application, macroscopically, it will increase resource utilization by exploiting any available system resource and fairly placing the incoming workload into the isolated parts of the cluster.

Custom Implementation: The main component ❷ of our implementation is an extended version of the vanilla Kubernetes scheduler. Since the Kubernetes scheduler consists of different predicate and priority functions, we added a custom priority function in the code of the Kubernetes open-source project. First, it filters the available nodes, applying user and system-defined strict requirements if any. Then, our custom function prioritizes the remaining nodes based on their most viable socket leveraging the proposed metric in Eq. 1. Thus, instead of selecting the predominant node, we select the node with the predominant socket. The main scheduler gets acquainted with system specifications down to the socket level through a configuration file.

- **Retrieve latest low-level socket metrics:** In order to acquire the most recent system condition information, by the time of a scheduling request, we query the time-series database, retrieving the moving average of the last 5 s metrics. This information allows our custom scheduler to greedily schedule applications in a manner that minimizes interference.

Algorithm 1. Calculate Score for server i

```
for ∀i do
    for ∀s_j^i do
        if s_j^i⟨c6⟩ * o_j > 1 then
            space ← space + 1
        end if
        if space ≥ 1 then
            c ← o_j
        else
            c ← o_j * s_j^i⟨c6⟩
        end if
        min, j ← min(min, s_j^i⟨reads⟩ + s_j^i⟨writes⟩) / s_j^i⟨ipc⟩ * c)
    end for
    return j
end for
```

- **Node prioritization:** In our implementation, we prioritize the candidate nodes based on their most viable socket. By convention, each server is uniquely identified by an identifier $i \in \mathbb{N}^{\leq n}$, where n is the total number of servers available on the cluster. We also denote the $j^{th}, j \in \mathbb{N}^{\leq m_i}$ socket of server i as s_j^i, where m_i is the total number of sockets of server i. Every socket $s_j^i \forall i, j$ is characterized by its attributes $\langle C6, IPC, Reads, Writes \rangle$ and is consisted of o_i number of cores.
  During the node scoring (Algorithm 1), we calculate our custom score according to the following two factors: a) *cache interference* and b) *core availability*. We use the custom metric described in Eq. 1, in order to take into consideration the contention in the last level cache (LLC) and the memory bus. Respectively, in cases of limited core availability in the examined socket, we multiply our previous result by the core-C6 state, which describes the percentage of further parts of the core that are shut down or power-gated.

Except for adding the additional code of our custom function, we needed to tweak the native code in various additional points as well. One of those points is the function that selects the most viable node. In our case, we wanted to schedule the incoming pod in a specific socket of the node. Thus, we implemented a gRPC [2] client, which sends a request to the winning node with the name of the pod and the desired socket to be placed, using a protocol buffer [3] file. More details about the gRPC server will be described in Sect. 5.4.

5.3 Node Agent

This framework applies distributed node management using node agents ❸. The exploitation of this component is currently limited to placing the incoming application (pod) into the desired socket. A gRPC [2] server running in the agent manages the aforementioned task. After the node selection, the main scheduler sends a gRPC request containing the name of the pod and the desired socket to be consumed by the node agent. On receipt of the request, the node agent adds the pod to a list of the awaiting pods to be executed. A background process checks iteratively whether a pod has been successfully started running, removes it from the queue, and pins it in the appropriate socket. We have also set a timeout for a pod's existence in the list in order to get rid of failed or delayed pods. In that case, the pod gets scheduled without core affinity. However, such cases only occur on large, unseen images that need to be downloaded.

5.4 Components Intercommunication

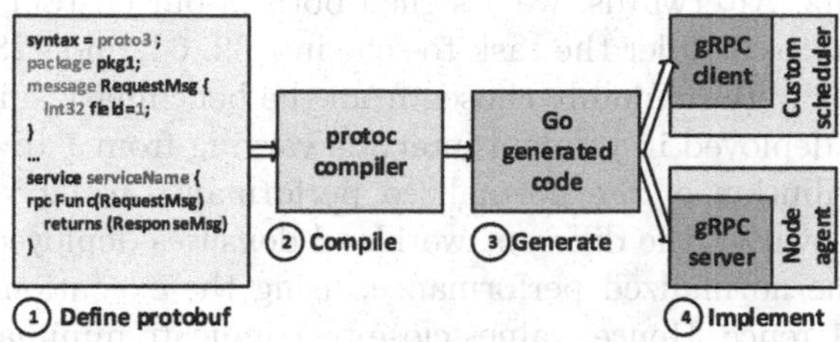

Fig. 4. gRPC code generation

PCM monitoring agents communicate with the centralized influxDB through a C++ client that implements the HTTP protocol. Respectively, a Go client is implemented in Kubernetes scheduler that queries the database on scheduling events. Regarding scheduler-node agent communication, we utilize gRPC. gRPC is a modern open-source high-performance remote procedure call (RPC) framework that can run in any environment. The end-to-end flow, from definition to implementation is illustrated in Fig. 4. It uses HTTP/2 for transport and Protocol Buffers as the interface description language. We defined the request and response messages in protocol buffer format, compiled them, and used Golang both for the client and the server implementations. While the server resides in the node agent, the client is embedded inside the main scheduler. The gRPC communication service we used is unary. Once the client calls a stub method, the server is notified that the RPC has been invoked with the client's metadata for this call, the method name, and the specified deadline if applicable.

6 Evaluation

In this section we evaluate our custom approach in terms of a) workload awareness, b) co-location with HPC workloads, and c) fair placement. In order to avoid warm-up cache effects, we flush the cache between any consecutive experiments.

Workload awareness: As the first stage of our evaluation, we examined the awareness of the Kubernetes scheduler regarding the running workload and the contention in the nodes of the system. Thus, leveraging deployments' feature replica sets, we scheduled 20 pods running a *sleep* command in an infinite loop

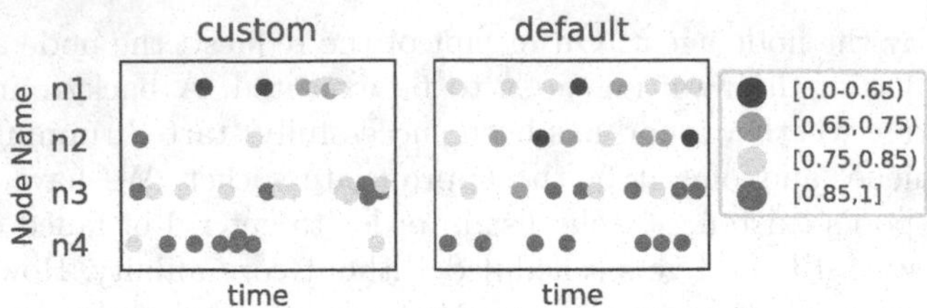

Fig. 5. Incoming workload placement and performance of 32 application scenario

in nodes n1 and n2. Afterwards, we assigned both in our custom scheduler and Kubernetes' default scheduler the task to schedule 32, 64, and 128 applications. Those applications were randomly chosen from the benchmark suites referred in Table 1 and were deployed in random intervals varying from 1 to 5 s. In Fig. 6a, we plot the distribution of the normalized performance using violin plots. In the X axis, are shown all the different workload densities deployed, while in the Y axis we plot the normalized performance, using the execution time without interference as reference. Hence, values close to 1 indicate minimal performance degradation. As we can see the distribution of our framework in all cases is more robust, achieving both higher median and lower standard deviation, providing a more predictable performance across the deployed workloads. A conclusion derived from those results and logical reasoning is that Kubernetes is unaware of workload's resource usage behaviour.

Co-scheduling with HPC Workloads: Next, by utilizing the HPCG benchmark, we scheduled MPI workloads on half of the available nodes of our evaluation. More specifically, the benchmark was configured to run with 4 MPI workers in nodes n{1, 2, 5, 6}. Each worker included one process per socket (two processes per worker in total). On top of this workload, we repeated the previous procedure and scheduled randomly picked benchmarks from Table 1 in different densities. While this time, there was no excessive number of idle pods to mislead the decision of the scheduler, it kept on scheduling any incoming workload in a round-robin approach. Figure 5, illustrates the workload distribution among the available nodes, as well as the normalized performance of each application for each node over time. We observe a contention unaware application placement in the default scheduler's case. On the other hand, our custom approach does not neglect the contention and acts towards a more balanced resource usage. The performance degradation of an application is also related to other conditions (e.g. network bandwidth contention, the sensitivity of each application to different kinds of interference), but such an analysis is not part of the current work.

Regarding the distribution of the normalized performance of the deployed applications, according to Fig. 6b, there is a more predictable performance achieved. In lower densities, the mean of the distribution is higher in the custom approach, because unused resources are exploited. However, as long as the system becomes more and more saturated, the performance gain is eliminated,

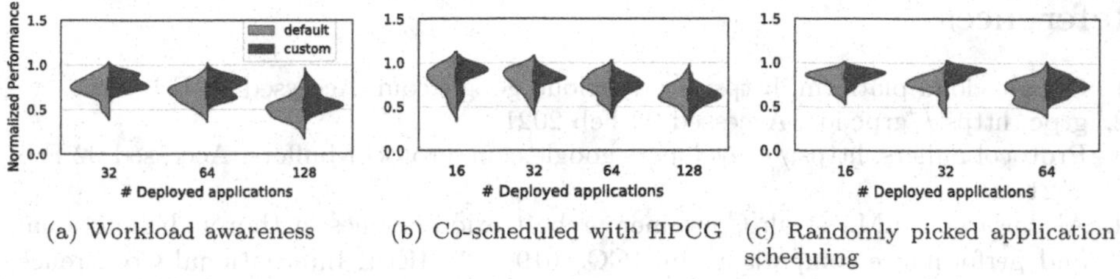

(a) Workload awareness (b) Co-scheduled with HPCG (c) Randomly picked application scheduling

Fig. 6. Applications relative performance distribution

since even a bad distribution will benefit from applications running on a less contended system. In such a scenario, further performance degradation in a highly contended system reaches a plateau. Still, the distributions in higher densities are more robust, providing results with a smaller by 25% on average standard deviation. The median is up to 19% higher, while the 95th tail latency of the distribution is improved up to 13.5% in the 32 application scenario.

Workload Placement Without Prior Application Scheduling: Finally, we evaluated the scenario of placing different densities of applications in nodes with no prior application scheduling. The distribution occurred by our custom scheduler placements, presented a 25–27% smaller expected value, and up to 19% greater median. The tail latency is constantly higher by 12–30% (Fig. 6c).

7 Conclusion

In this paper, we address the problem of interference in multi-tenant, converged HPC/Big Data cloud infrastructures. More specifically, we discuss the emergence of such environments due to HPC and Big Data democratization, as well as the need for a global, application-agnostic scheduler. In addition, we try to identify interference and depict the contention volume of a system by utilizing PCM. We analyzed workloads from different scientific benchmarking libraries' performance under pressure on various resources in different intensities. Thus, we identified resource contention and we proposed a highly correlated with application slowdown indicator able to depict the system's condition. We designed an integrated with Kubernetes and highly modular interference-aware custom scheduler implementing a fair resource usage policy by identifying contentious nodes using a custom scoring function composed of low-level metrics. Finally, we experimentally evaluated the workload placement of our proposed scheduler using different scenarios and compared it with the default Kubernetes scheduler. Our results showed that our custom approach can improve the overall performance of the deployed workloads, while, at the same time, it achieves a more balanced resource utilization.

References

1. Google cloud platform. https://www.cloud.google.com. Accessed 02 Feb 2021
2. grpc. https://grpc.io/. Accessed 02 Feb 2021
3. Protocol buffers. https://developers.google.com/protocol-buffers. Accessed 02 Feb 2021
4. Al Jawarneh, I.M., et al: Container orchestration engines: a thorough functional and performance comparison. In: ICC 2019–2019 IEEE International Conference on Communications (ICC), pp. 1–6. IEEE (2019)
5. Amazon, E.: Amazon web services (November 2012) (2015). http://aws.amazon.com/es/ec2/
6. Authors, P.: Prometheus-monitoring system & time series database (2017)
7. Bauman, E., Ayoade, G., Lin, Z.: A survey on hypervisor-based monitoring: approaches, applications, and evolutions. ACM Comput. Surv. (CSUR) **48**(1), 10 (2015)
8. Blagodurov, S., Fedorova, A.: User-level scheduling on NUMA multicore systems under Linux. In: Linux Symposium, vol. 2011 (2011)
9. Burns, B., Grant, B., Oppenheimer, D., Brewer, E., Wilkes, J.: Borg, omega, and Kubernetes: lessons learned from three container-management systems over a decade. Queue **14**(1), 70–93 (2016)
10. Cassandra, A.: Apache Cassandra. Website 13 (2014). http://planetcassandra.org/what-is-apache-cassandra
11. Cooper, B.F., Silberstein, A., Tam, E., Ramakrishnan, R., Sears, R.: Benchmarking cloud serving systems with YCSB. In: Proceedings of the 1st ACM Symposium on Cloud Computing, pp. 143–154 (2010)
12. Delimitrou, C., Kozyrakis, C.: ibench: quantifying interference for datacenter applications. In: 2013 IEEE International Symposium on Workload Characterization (IISWC), pp. 23–33. IEEE (2013)
13. Dongarra, J., Heroux, M.A., Luszczek, P.: HPCG benchmark: a new metric for ranking high performance computing systems. Knoxville, Tennessee, pp. 1–11 (2015)
14. Felter, W., Ferreira, A., Rajamony, R., Rubio, J.: An updated performance comparison of virtual machines and Linux containers. In: 2015 IEEE International Symposium on Performance Analysis of Systems and Software (ISPASS), pp. 171–172. IEEE (2015)
15. Ferdman, M., et al.: Clearing the clouds: a study of emerging scale-out workloads on modern hardware. In: Proceedings of the Seventeenth International Conference on Architectural Support for Programming Languages and Operating Systems (2012)
16. Ferikoglou, A., Masouros, D., Tzenetopoulos, A., Xydis, S., Soudris, D.: Resource aware GPU scheduling in Kubernetes infrastructure. In: 12th Workshop on Parallel Programming and Run-Time Management Techniques for Many-core Architectures and 10th Workshop on Design Tools and Architectures for Multicore Embedded Computing Platforms (PARMA-DITAM 2021), pp. 4:1–4:12 (2021)
17. Gan, Y., Zhang, Y., Hu, K., Cheng, D., He, Y., Pancholi, M., Delimitrou, C.: Seer: Leveraging big data to navigate the complexity of performance debugging in cloud microservices. In: Proceedings of the Twenty-Fourth International Conference on Architectural Support for Programming Languages and Operating Systems, pp. 19–33 (2019)
18. Garefalakis, P., Karanasos, K., Pietzuch, P., Suresh, A., Rao, S.: Medea: scheduling of long running applications in shared production clusters. In: Proceedings of the Thirteenth EuroSys Conference, p. 4. ACM (2018)

19. Henning, J.L.: Spec cpu2006 benchmark descriptions. ACM SIGARCH Comput. Archit. News **34**(4), 1–17 (2006)
20. Kanev, S., et al.: Profiling a warehouse-scale computer. In: Proceedings of the 42nd Annual International Symposium on Computer Architecture, pp. 158–169 (2015)
21. Mars, J., Tang, L., Hundt, R., Skadron, K., Soffa, M.L.: Bubble-up: increasing utilization in modern warehouse scale computers via sensible co-locations. In: Proceedings of the 44th Annual IEEE/ACM International Symposium on Microarchitecture, pp. 248–259. ACM (2011)
22. Mars, J., Vachharajani, N., Hundt, R., Soffa, M.L.: Contention aware execution: online contention detection and response. In: Proceedings of the 8th Annual IEEE/ACM International Symposium on Code Generation and Optimization, pp. 257–265. ACM (2010)
23. Masouros, D., Xydis, S., Soudris, D.: Rusty: runtime interference-aware predictive monitoring for modern multi-tenant systems. IEEE Trans. Parallel Distrib. Syst. **32**(1), 184–198 (2020)
24. MySQL, A.: Mysql (2001)
25. Naqvi, S.N.Z., Yfantidou, S., Zimányi, E.: Time series databases and influxdb. Studienarbeit, Université Libre de Bruxelles p. 12 (2017)
26. Pedregosa, F., et al.: Scikit-learn: machine learning in python. J. Mach. Learn. Res. **12**, 2825–2830 (2011)
27. Terpstra, D., Jagode, H., You, H., Dongarra, J.: Collecting performance data with PAPI-C. In: Müller, M., Resch, M., Schulz, A., Nagel, W. (eds.) Tools for High Performance Computing 2009, pp. 157–173. Springer, Heidelberg (2010). https://doi.org/10.1007/978-3-642-11261-4_11
28. Thomas Willham, R.D.: Intel® performance counter monitor - a better way to measure CPU utilization. https://software.intel.com/content/www/us/en/develop/articles/intel-performance-counter-monitor.html
29. Tzenetopoulos, A., Masouros, D., Xydis, S., Soudris, D.: Interference-aware orchestration in Kubernetes. In: Jagode, H., Anzt, H., Juckeland, G., Ltaief, H. (eds.) ISC High Performance 2020. LNCS, vol. 12321, pp. 321–330. Springer, Cham (2020). https://doi.org/10.1007/978-3-030-59851-8_21
30. Wang, L., et al.: Bigdatabench: a big data benchmark suite from internet services. In: 2014 IEEE 20th international symposium on high performance computer architecture (HPCA), pp. 488–499. IEEE (2014)
31. Wegrzynek, A.: Influxdb C++ client. https://github.com/awegrzyn/influxdb-cxx (2019)
32. Yang, H., Breslow, A., Mars, J., Tang, L.: Bubble-flux: Precise online qos management for increased utilization in warehouse scale computers. ACM SIGARCH Comput. Archit. News **41**(3), 607–618 (2013)
33. Yasin, A., Ben-Asher, Y., Mendelson, A.: Deep-dive analysis of the data analytics workload in cloudsuite. In: 2014 IEEE International Symposium on Workload Characterization (IISWC), pp. 202–211. IEEE (2014)
34. Zaharia, M., Chowdhury, M., Franklin, M.J., Shenker, S., Stoica, I., et al.: Spark: cluster computing with working sets. HotCloud **10**(10–10), 95 (2010)
35. Zhuravlev, S., Blagodurov, S., Fedorova, A.: Addressing shared resource contention in multicore processors via scheduling. ACM SIGPLAN Notices **45**(3), 129–142 (2010)

Heterogeneous SoC

Energy-Efficient and High-Throughput CNN Inference on Embedded CPUs-GPUs MPSoCs

Erqian Tang(✉), Svetlana Minakova, and Todor Stefanov

LIACS, Leiden University, Leiden, The Netherlands
{e.tang,s.minakova,t.p.stefanov}@liacs.leidenuniv.nl

Abstract. Nowadays, many application scenarios, such as mobile phones, drones, mobile robots, require Convolutional Neural Networks (CNNs) inference on embedded CPUs-GPUs MPSoCs. CNN model inference is usually computation intensive while the embedded CPUs-GPUs MPSoCs are usually energy consumption constrained. Therefore, how to achieve computationally-intensive CNN inference in an energy-efficient and high-throughput way is an important issue. However, existing Deep Learning (DL) frameworks only pay attention to achieving high-throughput inference when deploying CNN models on CPU or GPU processors without specifically considering the energy consumption.

In this paper, we propose a novel methodology which features design-time optimization techniques in order to achieve energy efficiency and high throughput when deploying CNN models on embedded CPUs-GPUs MPSoCs. Our methodology finds Pareto-optimal mappings of a CNN model onto a CPUs-GPUs MPSoC with voltage and frequency scaling (VFS) configurations with the help of a two-objective Genetic Algorithm (GA) which optimizes the system throughput and energy consumption simultaneously. Moreover, we propose two analytical models, that are used as fitness functions in the two-objective GA to evaluate very fast the system throughput and energy consumption of CNNs mapped onto embedded CPUs-GPUs MPSoCs. Also, we confirm the high accuracy of these two analytical models by experimental evidence. Finally, our experimental results show that our novel methodology is able to achieve both energy efficiency and high throughput when deploying CNN models on embedded CPUs-GPUs MPSoCs, in comparison with TensorRT which is the best-known CNN deployment optimizer designed for NVIDIA embedded MPSoCs.

Keywords: Convolutional Neural Networks · SDF · Pareto-optimal mapping · High-throughput · Energy-efficient · MPSoCs · TensorRT

1 Introduction

Convolutional Neural Networks (CNNs) are biologically inspired graph computational models, characterized by high degree of available parallelism. Due to their

© Springer Nature Switzerland AG 2022
A. Orailoglu et al. (Eds.): SAMOS 2021, LNCS 13227, pp. 127–143, 2022.
https://doi.org/10.1007/978-3-031-04580-6_9

ability to handle large, unstructured data, CNNs are widely used to perform various tasks in areas such as computer vision and natural language processing [1]. The CNNs execution typically includes two phases: training and inference [1]. At the training phase the optimal CNN parameters are established. At the inference phase, a trained CNN is applied to the actual data and performs the task for which the CNN is designed. Due to the high complexity of state-of-the-art CNNs, their training and inference phases are usually performed by high-performance platforms, and provided as cloud services. However, some applications, e.g. [2–4], require high-throughput execution of the CNNs inference, which cannot be provided as a cloud service. These applications are typically deployed on embedded devices.

Many modern embedded devices are based on multi-processor systems-on-chip (MPSoCs) [5]: complex integrated circuits, that consist of processing elements with specific functionalities. Due to their specific design, MPSoCs offer energy-efficient and high-throughput solutions for applications running on embedded devices. In addition to hosting various processing elements, capable of running the CNN inference, such as central processing units (CPUs), embedded graphics processing units (embedded GPUs), and field-programmable gate arrays (FPGAs), MPSoCs integrate many other components, such as communication network components and video accelerators, that allow to deploy the entire embedded application on a single chip. Therefore, MPSoCs seem to be a promising solution for the deployment of the CNN inference phase on embedded devices.

Embedded CPUs-GPUs MPSoCs are usually energy consumption constrained while the CNN model inference is computation intensive. For example, in many application scenarios requiring CNN inference on embedded MPSoCs, such as mobile phones, drones, mobile robots, the battery capacity is usually very limited. So, how to achieve computationally-intensive CNN inference in an energy-efficient way on embedded CPUs-GPUs MPSoCs is an important issue.

However, existing Deep Learning (DL) frameworks [6–16], that enable execution of the CNN inference on embedded CPUs-GPUs MPSoCs, only pay attention to achieving high-throughput inference when deploying CNN models on CPU or GPU processors without specifically considering the energy consumption, which can be influenced by the utilized number of processors and by the possibility for CPUs-GPUs voltage and frequency scaling (VFS). These frameworks rely on the operating system to determine the utilized number of processors and the CPUs-GPUs operating frequency at run-time and do not support design-time optimizations for energy-efficient deployment of the CNN inference.

Therefore, in this paper, we extend the methodology in [16], with design-time optimization techniques in order to achieve energy efficiency and high throughput when deploying CNN models on embedded CPUs-GPUs MPSoCs. We propose to extend [16] because it exploits explicitly both task- and data-level parallelism, available in a CNN, thereby achieving higher throughput compared to the other existing DL frameworks [6–15]. We exploit this higher throughput in combination with different CPUs and GPUs utilization and VFS configuration possibilities to reduce the energy consumption and to optimize the CNN inference on an MPSoC at design-time. The goal of our optimization is to find an MPSoC configuration which achieves the same or higher throughput with less energy consumption compared to existing DL frameworks.

Paper Contributions

In this paper, we extend the methodology in [16], which consists of three main steps, introduced in Sect. 3.1. In Step 1, a CNN model is automatically converted to a functionally equivalent Syndchronous Dataflow (SDF) model. In Step 2, an efficient mapping of the SDF model onto a CPUs-GPUs MPSoC is obtained using a single-objective genetic algorithm (GA) to achieve high throughput by utilizing the hardware resources as much as possible. Our main novel contributions are related to Step 2 and include: 1) We propose to use a two-objective GA in order to optimize for system throughput and energy consumption simultaneously. To enable such two-objective GA-based optimization, we propose novel and very accurate analytical models and use them as fitness functions in the GA to evaluate very fast the system throughput and energy consumption of CNNs mapped onto embedded CPUs-GPUs MPSoCs; 2) We confirm the high accuracy of our aforementioned analytical models by comparing the system throughput and energy consumption numbers provided by our models with measured numbers obtained by deploying real-world CNNs on the Nvidia Jetson-TX2 embedded platform; 3) We use the extended methodology and models, mentioned above, to find pareto-optimal mappings of real-world CNNs onto the Nvidia Jetson-TX2 MPSoCs platform. The obtained results, in terms of system throughput and energy consumption, are compared with results obtained by the best-known DL framework for Jetson MPSoCs called TensorRT [15]. This comparison shows that our extended methodology can achieve CNN inference on embedded CPUs-GPUs MPSoCs with the same or higher throughput but with less energy consumption.

The remainder of the paper is organized as follows: Sect. 2 gives an overview of the related work. Section 3 introduces the background material needed for understanding the contributions of this paper. Section 4 presents our proposed extension of the methodology in [16], briefly introduced in Sect. 3.1, including our two novel analytical models. Section 5 shows the experimental results and Sect. 6 ends the paper with conclusions.

2 Related Work

Among the existing DL frameworks [6–15], NVidia TensorRT [15] is the best-known CNN deployment optimizer designed for embedded MPSoCs such as Nvidia Jetson TX2. This optimizer is built on top of CUDA and includes several optimizations techniques to deliver high throughputs and low latencies for deep neural network applications. TensorRT tries to minimize the memory footprint of a CNN by reusing memory and applying fusion operations. Also, it exploits data-level parallelism, available in a CNN, for efficient utilization of embedded GPUs. However, TensorRT relies on layer-by-layer (sequential) execution of CNN layers and only one CPU processor is utilized for launching GPU engines and sending data. In this way, the available CPUs-GPUs MPSoC hardware resources are not utilized in the most efficient way in terms of high-throughput. Moreover, the focus of TensorRT is only to improve the system throughput, so optimizing the energy consumption is not considered. The CPUs and GPUs processors do not operate at proper frequency configurations, which is not a good solution for some energy constrained DL applications, such as drones or other light battery mobile robots. In contrast, our extended methodology exploits both data-level parallelism within the same layer and task-level parallelism among different layers of a CNN. At the same time, our methodology also considers different number of processors to be utilized and different CPUs-GPUs VFS to be applied. Therefore, compared to TensorRT, our methodology can achieve same or better inference system throughput, and lower energy consumption at the same time. Moreover, our extended methodology is implemented on top of TensorRT, thereby inheriting some benefits of TensorRT as well, such as minimizing the memory footprint and applying fusion operations.

In [16], a novel methodology for execution of the CNN inference on embedded CPUs-GPUs MPSoCs is proposed. It takes full advantage of all CPU and GPU resources, available in an MPSoC, and ensures high-throughput CNN inference execution on CPUs-GPUs MPSoCs by efficiently exploiting task-level (pipeline) parallelism, available among CNN layers, together with data-level parallelism, available within CNN layers. [16] achieves higher CNN inference throughput on embedded CPUs-GPUs MPSoCs compared to the aforementioned NVidia TensorRT [15] deployment optimizer. However, utilizing all possible CPU and GPU resources increases the energy consumption, which may fail to meet the energy consumption budget of some battery constrained applications. In contrast, in this paper, we extend [16] in order to enable fast and accurate multi-objective design space exploration to find more efficient utilization of CPU and GPU resources at proper VFS configurations. Therefore, we reduce the energy consumption while still achieving high CNN inference throughput.

3 Background

In this section, we briefly introduce the methodology in [16] for execution of the CNN inference on embedded CPUs-GPUs MPSoCs as well as we describe the specific features of the embedded CPUs-GPUs MPSoCs, we consider in this paper, and the Synchronous Dataflow (SDF) model [17]. All these are essential for understanding our paper contributions.

3.1 CNN Inference on Embedded CPUs-GPUs MPSoCs

[16] proposes a novel methodology to deploy a CNN model on embedded CPUs-GPUs MPSoCs. This methodology consists of three main steps. An overview of this methodology is shown in Fig. 1. In Step 1, a CNN model is converted into a functionally equivalent Synchronous Dataflow (SDF) model. Unlike the

CNN model, the SDF model explicitly specifies task- and data-level parallelism, available in a CNN, as well as it explicitly specifies the tasks communication and synchronization mechanisms, suitable for efficient mapping and execution of a CNN on an embedded MPSoC. Thus, a conversion of a CNN model into a SDF model is necessary for efficient mapping and execution of a CNN on an embedded CPUs-GPUs MPSoC. In Step 2, a Genetic Algorithm (GA) is utilized to find an efficient mapping of the SDF model, obtained on Step 1, on an embedded CPUs-GPUs MPSoC. The mapping, obtained by the GA, describes the distribution of the CNN inference computational workload on an embedded MPSoC, that exploits efficiently both task-level and data-level parallelism, available in the CNN. In Step 3, the mapping obtained in Step 2 is utilized to convert a CNN model into a final platform-aware executable Cyclo-Static Dataflow (CSDF) application model [18]. The CSDF model, obtained in Step 3, describes the CNN inference as an executable application, efficiently distributed over embedded MPSoC processors and exploiting the right amount of task- and data-level parallelism, which matches the computational capacity of an embedded MPSoC. Thus, this methodology takes full advantage of all CPU and GPU resources, available in an MPSoC, and enables high-throughput execution of the CNN inference on embedded CPUs-GPUs MPSoCs.

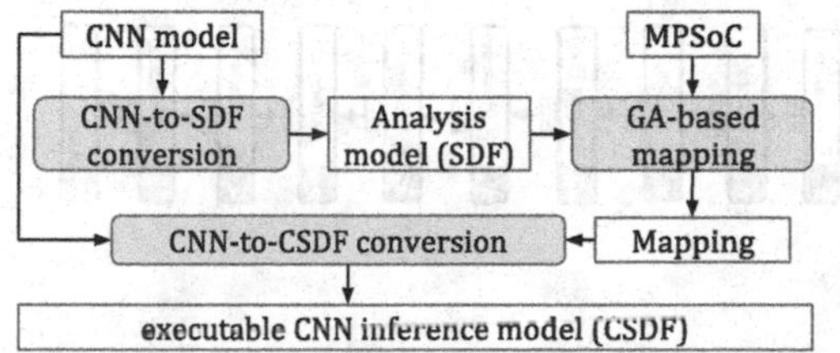

Fig. 1. An overview of the methodology in [16]

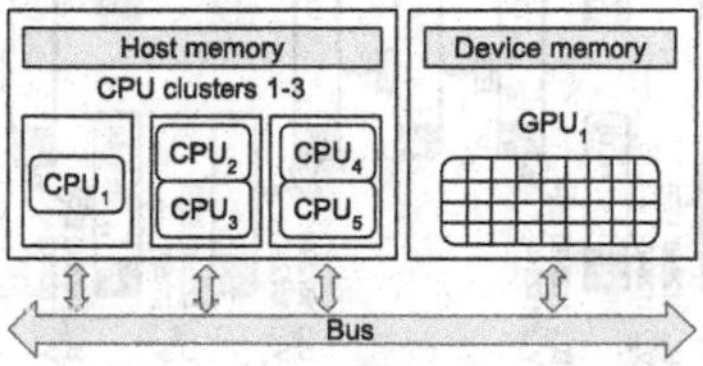

Fig. 2. Embedded MPSoC

3.2 Embedded CPUs-GPUs MPSoCs

We define an embedded MPSoC as a tuple $MPSoC(cpu, gpu)$, where $cpu = \{cpu_1, cpu_2, ..., cpu_n\}$ is a set of all CPU cores, available in the MPSoC; $gpu = \{gpu_1, gpu_2, ..., gpu_m\}$ is a set of all GPU devices, available in the MPSoC, and typically $m \leq n$. An example of an embedded CPUs-GPUs MPSoC with $n = 5$ CPU cores and $m = 1$ GPU device is shown in Fig. 2. CPU cores are usually divided into several clusters. The CPU cores in a cluster can operate at one of the frequencies from the set $f_{cpu} = \{f_{c1}, f_{c2}, ..., f_{cp}\}$. Each GPU can also operate at one of the frequencies from the set $f_{gpu} = \{f_{g1}, f_{g2}, ..., f_{gq}\}$.

3.3 Synchronous Dataflow (SDF) Model

The SDF model [17] is a well-known dataflow model of computation, widely used in the embedded systems community for efficient mapping of applications on embedded devices, including embedded CPUs-GPUs MPSoCs. An application, modeled as a SDF, is a directed graph $G(A, C)$, which consists of a set of nodes A, also called actors, communicating through a set of FIFO channels C. An example of a SDF model with $|A|$=23 actors and $|C|$=24 FIFO channels is given in Fig. 3. Every actor $a_i \in A$ is a task, which performs certain application functionality, represented as a function F_i. An example of SDF actor a_3 is shown in Fig. 3. Actor a_3 performs function $F_3 = \{ReLU\}$. Every FIFO channel $c_{ij} \in C$ represents data dependency and transfers data in tokens between actors a_i and a_j. c_{ij} has data production rate U_{ij} and data consumption rate V_{ij}. U_{ij} specifies the production of data tokens into channel c_{ij} by actor a_i. V_{ij} specifies the consumption of data tokens from channel c_{ij} by actor a_j. An example of a communication FIFO channel c_{36} is shown in Fig. 3. Channel c_{36} transfers data between actors a_3 and a_6. It has production rate U_{36}=[112640], specifying, that, at each firing, actor a_3 produces 112640 data tokens into channel c_{36} and consumption rate V_{36}=[112640], specifying, that, at each firing, actor a_6 consumes 112640 data tokens from channel c_{36}.

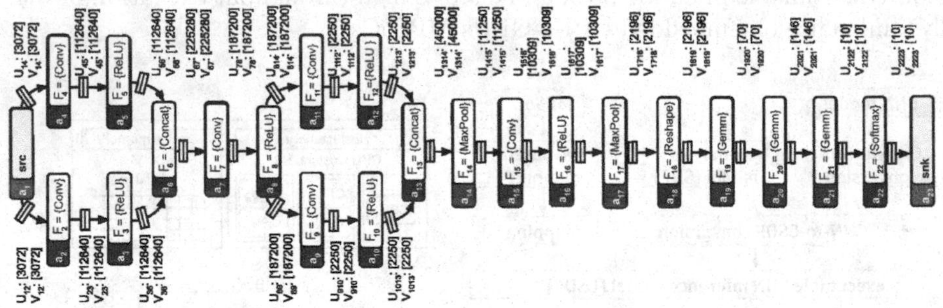

Fig. 3. An example of a SDF model

4 Methodology Extension

In this section, we present our proposed extension of the methodology, introduced in Sect. 3.1, to find an energy-efficient mapping of a SDF model, obtained automatically from a CNN model, onto an embedded CPUs-GPUs $MPSoC(cpu, gpu)$, defined in Sect. 3.2, with a proper configuration (proper utilization of the processors and VFS). In order to achieve this, first, we give our definition of a mapping of a SDF model onto an MPSoC with certain VFS configuration - see Sect. 4.1. Then, we use a two-objective GA in order to optimize the MPSoC system throughput and energy consumption simultaneously - see Sect. 4.2. To enable such two-objective GA-based optimization, we propose novel and very accurate analytical models, see Sect. 4.3, and use them as fitness functions in the GA to evaluate very fast the system throughput and energy consumption of CNNs mapped onto embedded CPUs-GPUs MPSoCs.

4.1 Mapping with VFS Configuration

In our extended methodology, the CNN inference tasks, explicitly specified as SDF actors, are executed on embedded CPU cores, that are able to efficiently handle the task-level parallelism among the different tasks. To efficiently utilize the data-level parallelism, available within the tasks, some of the CPU cores offload computations on the embedded GPUs. Since the number of embedded GPU devices is limited, it may occur, that the efficient exploitation of task-level parallelism, by embedded CPUs, is disrupted due to CPUs competition for the limited embedded GPU devices. To avoid such disruption, for every embedded GPU $gpu_j \in gpu$, we allocate a single CPU core $cpu_i \in cpu$, which offloads computations on gpu_j.

Based on the discussion above, we define a mapping of SDF model $G(A, C)$ onto $MPSoC(cpu, gpu)$ with a VFS configuration, as a partition of actors set A into n subsets, where $n = |cpu|$ is the number of CPU cores, available in the MPSoC. We denote such mapping as ${}^nA = \{{}^nA_1, {}^nA_2, ..., {}^nA_n\}$, where each ${}^nA_i \in {}^nA$ is a subset of actors, mapped on cpu_i, such that $\cap_{i=1}^{n} {}^nA_i = \emptyset$, and $\cup_{i=1}^{n} {}^nA_i = A$. The first $m = |gpu|$ number of CPU cores in mapping ${}^nA$ offload computations on the corresponding embedded GPUs, i.e., the computations within every actor $a_k \in {}^nA_j, j \in [1, m]$ are performed on gpu_j, and the computations within every actor $a_k \in {}^nA_i, i \in [m+1, n]$ are performed on cpu_i. Each cpu_i operates at a frequency $f_{cp} \in f_{cpu}$, and CPUs of the same cluster operate at the same frequency. Each gpu_j operates at a frequency $f_{gq} \in f_{gpu}$.

An example of a mapping with a VFS configuration, ${}^5A = \{{}^5A_1, {}^5A_2, {}^5A_3, {}^5A_4, {}^5A_5\}$ of the SDF model $G(A, C)$, shown in Fig. 3 and explained in Sect. 3.3, on the embedded MPSoC, shown in Fig. 2 and explained in Sect. 3.2, is given in Table 1. In this example, we consider that $f_{cpu} = \{f_{c1}, f_{c2}, f_{c3}, f_{c4}\}$ and $f_{gpu} = \{f_{g1}, f_{g2}, f_{g3}, f_{g4}, f_{g5}\}$. Every Column in Table 1 corresponds to a subset ${}^5A_i, i \in [1, 5]$. For example, Column 1 in Table 1 corresponds to subset ${}^5A_1 = \{a_1, a_2, a_3, a_4, a_5, a_6, a_7\}$. The actors within subset ${}^5A_1$ are mapped on cpu_1, which offloads computations on gpu_1. cpu_1 and gpu_1 operate at frequencies f_{c1} and f_{g2}, respectively. Column 2 in Table 1 describes subset ${}^5A_2 = \{a_8, a_9, a_{10}, a_{13}\}$. Every actor $a_i \in {}^5A_2$ is mapped on cpu_2, and cpu_2 operates at frequency f_{c3}. Since the MPSoC does not have gpu_2, all computations within actors in ${}^5A_2$ are performed only on cpu_2. Since cpu_2 and cpu_3 belong to the same cluster, as shown in Fig. 2, cpu_3 also operates at frequency f_{c3}. Similarly, cpu_4 and cpu_5 operate at frequency f_{c4}.

Table 1. Example of a Mapping with a VFS configuration

$cpu_1@f_{c1}/gpu_1@f_{g2}$	$cpu_2@f_{c3}$	$cpu_3@f_{c3}$	$cpu_4@f_{c4}$	$cpu_5@f_{c4}$
$a_1, a_2, a_3, a_4, a_5, a_6, a_7$	a_8, a_9, a_{10}, a_{13}	a_{11}, a_{12}	$a_{14}, a_{15}, a_{16}, a_{17}, a_{18}, a_{21}, a_{22}, a_{23}$	a_{19}, a_{20}

a_1	a_2	a_3	a_4	a_5	a_6	a_7	a_8	a_9	a_{10}	a_{11}	a_{12}	a_{13}	a_{14}	a_{15}	a_{16}	a_{17}	a_{18}	a_{19}	a_{20}	a_{21}	a_{22}	a_{23}
$cpu_1@f_{c1}$ $gpu_1@f_{g2}$	$cpu_1@f_{c1}$ $gpu_1@f_{g2}$	$cpu_1@f_{c1}$ $gpu_1@f_{g2}$	$cpu_1@f_{c1}$ $gpu_1@f_{g2}$	$cpu_1@f_{c1}$ $gpu_1@f_{g2}$	$cpu_1@f_{c1}$ $gpu_1@f_{g2}$	$cpu_1@f_{c1}$ $gpu_1@f_{g2}$	$cpu_2@f_{c3}$	$cpu_2@f_{c3}$	$cpu_2@f_{c3}$	$cpu_3@f_{c3}$	$cpu_3@f_{c3}$	$cpu_2@f_{c3}$	$cpu_4@f_{c4}$	$cpu_4@f_{c4}$	$cpu_4@f_{c4}$	$cpu_4@f_{c4}$	$cpu_4@f_{c4}$	$cpu_5@f_{c4}$	$cpu_5@f_{c4}$	$cpu_4@f_{c4}$	$cpu_4@f_{c4}$	$cpu_4@f_{c4}$

Fig. 4. Mapping chromosome example

4.2 Two-objective GA Optimization

With the aforementioned mapping in Sect. 4.1, we associate two system characteristics, (1) the system throughput: the amount of data processed per unit of time, for example measured in images per second (img/s); (2) the system energy consumption: the total energy needed to process a unit of data, for example measured in joules per image (J/img). We assume a mapping to be efficient if the system throughput is maximized and the system energy consumption is minimized. As these two objectives are conflicting, i.e., the increase of the throughput will cause increase of the energy consumption, we note, that obtaining such an efficient mapping of an SDF graph onto a CPUs-GPUs MPSoC with a VFS configuration is not possible. Thus, we have to perform a complex Design Space Exploration (DSE) in order to find a set of Pareto-optimal mappings [19] that we will consider efficient in our case. In our extended methodology, to solve this problem, we propose to use a two-objective Genetic Algorithm (GA) [20]: a well-known heuristic approach, widely used for finding Pareto-optimal solutions for complex DSE problems. We use a GA with standard two-parent crossover, a single-gene mutation, and standard user-defined GA parameters, such as initial offspring size, number of epochs, mutation and crossover probabilities [20]. To utilize such a GA for searching of Pareto-optimal mappings with a VFS configuration, we have to specify problem-specific GA attributes, namely a chromosome and fitness functions [20]. The chromosome is a representation of a GA solution (in our extended methodology a solution is a mapping with a VFS configuration) as a set of parameters (genes), joined into a string [20]. We represent mapping ^nA, as a string of length $|A|$, where every gene is a CPU core $cpu_i \in cpu$ running at a frequency $f_{cp} \in f_{cpu}$. For a CPU core which offloads computations on a GPU, the gene also includes the GPU frequency $f_{gq} \in f_{gpu}$. An example of the chromosome, corresponding to the mapping with the VFS configuration, shown in Table 1, is given in Fig. 4.

4.3 Analytical Models as Fitness Functions

The aforementioned fitness functions are special functions that estimate the quality of the GA solutions and guide the GA-based search. We propose two analytical models and use them as fitness functions ϕ_1 and ϕ_2 during the GA-based search.

On the one hand, ϕ_1 estimates the system throughput during the GA search and is given as the following equation:

$$\phi_1 = 1/\tau \tag{1}$$

Note that our SDF model, for CNN inference, features pipeline execution of actors on CPUs to exploit both task-level and data-level parallelism (see Sect. 3.3). The bottleneck CPU in such pipeline execution will determine the system throughput $\phi_1 = 1/\tau$, where τ is the execution time needed for all SDF actors, mapped on the bottleneck CPU, to process one unit of data given as an input to the pipeline. So, we can compute τ as follows:

$$\tau = \max\{\max_{\forall cpu_i, i\in[m+1,n]}\{\tau_{cpu_i}\}, \max_{\forall cpu_i, i\in[1,m]}\{\tau_{cpu_i}{}'\}\} \tag{2}$$

where $\tau_{cpu_i}{}'$ and τ_{cpu_i} are the execution times needed for all SDF actors mapped on cpu_i to process one unit of data given as an input to the pipeline, when cpu_i offloads and does not offload tasks on a GPU, respectively. For every $cpu_i \in cpu$, τ_{cpu_i} or $\tau_{cpu_i}{}'$ is computed as:

$$\tau_{cpu_i} = \tau^t_{cpu_i} + \tau^{com}_{cpu_i} \tag{3}$$

$$\tau_{cpu_i}{}' = \tau^t_{cpu_i}{}' + \tau^{com}_{cpu_i} \tag{4}$$

where $\tau^t_{cpu_i}{}'$ and $\tau^t_{cpu_i}$ are the times cpu_i spends only on computations for all actors mapped on cpu_i, when cpu_i offloads and does not offload tasks on a GPU, respectively. $\tau^{com}_{cpu_i}$ is the time, spent by cpu_i, on communication with other embedded processors. $\tau^t_{cpu_i}$ and $\tau^t_{cpu_i}{}'$ are computed as:

$$\tau^t_{cpu_i} = \sum_{a_k \in {}^n A_i} \tau_{(F_k, cpu_i, f_{cp})} \tag{5}$$

$$\tau^t_{cpu_i}{}' = \sum_{a_k \in {}^n A_i} \tau_{(F_k, cpu_i, f_{cp}, f_{gq})} \tag{6}$$

where ${}^n A_i$ is the set of actors, mapped on cpu_i; F_k is the function of actor $a_k \in {}^n A_i$; $f_{cp} \in f_{cpu}$ is the frequency of cpu_i. $\tau_{(F_k, cpu_i, f_{cp})}$ is the time, taken by cpu_i to execute F_k at frequency f_{cp}; $\tau_{(F_k, cpu_i, f_{cp}, f_{gq})}$ is the time, taken by cpu_i at frequency f_{cp} to execute F_k, when the computation of F_k is offloaded on a GPU running at frequency $f_{gq} \in f_{gpu}$. The time $\tau^{com}_{cpu_i}$ is computed as:

$$\tau^{com}_{cpu_i} = \sum_{a_k \in {}^n A_i} (\tau_w(f_{cp}) * \sum_{c_{kj} \in C} U_{kj} + \tau_r(f_{cp}) * \sum_{c_{jk} \in C} V_{jk}) \tag{7}$$

where ${}^n A_i$ is the set of all actors, mapped on cpu_i; $c_{kj} \in C$ is an output channel of actor $a_k \in {}^n A_i$, to which, at each firing, actor a_k produces U_{kj} data tokens; $c_{jk} \in C$ is an input channel of actor a_k, from which, at each firing, actor a_k consumes V_{jk} data tokens; $\tau_r(f_{cp})$ and $\tau_w(f_{cp})$ specify the times, needed by a CPU core, to read and write one data token, at specific CPU frequency f_{cp}, respectively.

The accuracy of the analytical model ϕ_1 to estimate the system throughput depends on the accuracy of the parameter values $\tau_{(F_k, cpu_i, f_{cp})}$, $\tau_{(F_k, cpu_i, f_{cp}, f_{gq})}$,

$\tau_r(f_{cp})$ and $\tau_w(f_{cp})$. These values can be obtained accurately by real measurements on the target CPUs-GPUs MPSoC. An experimental confirmation of the accuracy of ϕ_1 is given in Sect. 5.2.

On the other hand, ϕ_2 estimates the system energy, consumed to process one unit of data given as an input to the system pipeline, during the GA search and is given as the following equation:

$$\phi_2 = \sum_{\forall cpu_i, i\in[m+1,n]} E_{cpu_i} + \sum_{\forall cpu_i, i\in[1,m]} E_{cpu_i}{}' + \sum_{\forall gpu_j \in gpu} E_{gpu_j} \tag{8}$$

where $E_{cpu_i}{}'$ and E_{cpu_i} are the energy consumption needed for all SDF actors, mapped on cpu_i, to process one unit of data given as an input to the pipeline, when cpu_i offloads and does not offload tasks on a GPU, respectively; E_{gpu_j} is the energy consumption needed for all offloaded SDF actors on gpu_j to process one unit of data given as an input to the pipeline. For every cpu_i and gpu_j, E_{cpu_i}, $E_{cpu_i}{}'$ and E_{gpu_j} are computed as:

$$\begin{aligned} E_{cpu_i} &= P_{idle}(cpu_i, f_{cp}) * T \\ &+ (P(cpu_i, f_{cp}, A) - P_{idle}(cpu_i, f_{cp})) * \tau_{cpu_i} \end{aligned} \tag{9}$$

$$\begin{aligned} E_{cpu_i}{}' &= P_{idle}(cpu_i, f_{cp}) * T \\ &+ (P(cpu_i, f_{cp}, A) - P_{idle}(cpu_i, f_{cp})) * \tau_{cpu_i}{}' \end{aligned} \tag{10}$$

$$\begin{aligned} E_{gpu_j} &= P_{idle}(gpu_j, f_{gq}) * T \\ &+ (P(gpu_j, f_{gq}, A) - P_{idle}(gpu_j, f_{gq})) * \tau_{gpu_j} \end{aligned} \tag{11}$$

where $P_{idle}(cpu_i, f_{cp})$ and $P_{idle}(gpu_j, f_{gq})$ are the power consumption of cpu_i and gpu_j, when there are no actors mapped on them, and they operate at frequencies f_{cp} and f_{gq}, respectively; $P(cpu_i, f_{cp}, A)$ and $P(gpu_j, f_{gq}, A)$ are the average power consumption of cpu_i and gpu_j when all actors of the SDF model (i.e., actor set A) are mapped on them, and they operate at frequencies f_{cp} and f_{gq}, respectively. T is the total time, taken by the system pipeline, to process one unit of data given as an input to the pipeline and is computed as follows:

$$T = \sum_{\forall cpu_i, i\in[m+1,n]} \tau_{cpu_i} + \sum_{\forall cpu_i, i\in[1,m]} \tau_{cpu_i}{}' \tag{12}$$

τ_{cpu_i} and $\tau_{cpu_i}{}'$ are calculated as shown in Eq. (3) and (4), respectively. τ_{gpu_j} is the time needed for gpu_j to execute all tasks offloaded by its corresponding cpu_i and is computed as follows:

$$\tau_{gpu_j} = \sum_{a_k \in^n A_j} \tau(F_k, gpu_j, f_{gq}) \tag{13}$$

where ${}^{n}A_j$ is the set of actors mapped on cpu_i and offloaded by cpu_i for execution on gpu_j; F_k is the function of actor $a_k \in {}^{n}A_j$; f_{gq} is the frequency of gpu_j. $\tau_{(F_k, gpu_j, f_{gq})}$ is the time, taken by gpu_j to execute F_k at frequency f_{gq}.

If no actors are mapped on cpu_i or gpu_j, then τ_{cpu_i}, $\tau_{cpu_i}{}'$ or τ_{gpu_j} will be 0. In this case, E_{cpu_i}, $E_{cpu_i}{}'$ or E_{gpu_j} equals to the idle energy consumption, i.e., $P_{idle}(cpu_i, f_{cp}) * T$ or $P_{idle}(gpu_j, f_{gq}) * T$, as shown in Eq. (9), (10), (11).

The accuracy of the analytical model ϕ_2 to estimate the system energy consumption depends on the accuracy of the parameter values $P_{idle}(cpu_i, f_{cp})$, $P_{idle}(gpu_j, f_{gq})$, $P(cpu_i, f_{cp}, A)$ and $P(gpu_j, f_{gq}, A)$. These values can be obtained accurately by real measurements on the target CPUs-GPUs MPSoC. An experimental confirmation of the accuracy of ϕ_2 is given in Sect. 5.2.

5 Experimental Results

In this section, we present our results from experiments, in which real-world CNNs from the ONNX models zoo [21] are mapped and executed on the NVIDIA Jetson TX2 embedded CPUs-GPUs MPSoC [22]. The goal of the experiments is to demonstrate that, thanks to our contributions presented in this paper, our extended methodology can deliver CNN inference on embedded CPUs-GPUs MPSoCs with the same or higher throughtput but with lower energy consumption compared to existing DL frameworks that support CNN inference on such MPSoCs. First, we explain the setup for our experiments in Sect. 5.1. Then, in Sect. 5.2, we confirm the accuracy of our analytical models, introduced in Sect. 4.3. Finally, in Sect. 5.3, we use our extended methodology and models, introduced in Sect. 4, to find Pareto-optimal mappings and analyze our experimental results.

5.1 Experimental Setup

We use three real-world CNNs, namely Vgg19, Alexnet and Emotion_fer, from the ONNX models zoo [21] that take images as input for CNN inference. These CNNs are utilized in different applications and have diverse number and type of layers. Such diversity leads to a diverse scale of system throughtput and energy consumption when these CNNs are mapped and executed on the same hardware platform. Vgg19 and Alexnet are used for image classification and they have 19 layers and 8 layers, respectively. Emotion_fer is used for body, face, and gesture analysis and it has 10 layers. So, these three CNN models are sufficiently representative and good examples to apply our extended methodology on and to demonstrate its merits.

The three CNN models, mentioned above, are mapped and executed on the NVIDIA Jetson TX2 embedded CPUs-GPUs MPSoC [22] which features 6 CPUs (Quad-Core ARM and Dual-Core NVIDIA Denver 2) plus 1 Pa GPU device. The 6 CPUs are divided into two different clusters, where the CPUs from the same cluster can operate at 12 different frequencies and the GPU can operate at 13 different frequencies. We select NVIDIA Jetson TX2 as our experimental hardware platform because it is a well-known and easy-to-use embedded platform. Moreover, we can easily and accurately acquire the needed system throghput data and energy consumption data of each processor by setting timers within the executed code and by sampling the integrated power sensors onboard, respectively. In addition, NVIDIA Jetson TX2 is supported by the TensorRT framework [15], which is the best-known CNN deployment optimizer designed for NVIDIA embedded MPSoCs, as mentioned in Sect. 2. The results obtained by using our extended methodology are compared with TensorRT implementation results as reference in order to show the benefits of our extended methodology.

For every optimized reference system implementation, obtained by using TensorRT, the system throughput and energy consumption is directly measured on the NVIDIA Jetson TX2 platform, as the average value over 50 CNN inference executions. For the Pareto-optimal systems, obtained by using our extended methodology, the system throughput and energy consumption data is provided by our analytical models, introduced in Sect. 4.3. The two-objective GA of our methodology is executed with initial population size 5000, number of generations = 100, mutation probability = 5%. For all experiments, the original data precision (i.e., float32) is utilized in order to preserve the original CNN accuracy.

5.2 The Accuracy of Our Analytical Models

In this section, we confirm the accuracy of our system throughput and energy consumption analytical models, introduced in Sect. 4.3. We compare the estimated system throughput ϕ_1 and system energy consumption ϕ_2, obtained by our analytical models, with the corresponding numbers, obtained by direct measurements, on the reference system implementations, as described in Sect. 5.1. The results are shown in Table 2. In Column 1, we list the three experimental CNN models, mentioned in Sect. 5.1. For each CNN model, the experiments are performed with 9 different CPU and GPU frequency configurations. For the CPU and GPU frequencies, we use the maximum frequency, the minimum frequency, and a frequency in the middle, as shown in Column 2 and 3. For example, Row 2 shows that, when we perform the experiment on Vgg19 with CPU frequency 2.0 GHz and GPU frequency 1.3 GHz, we obtain system throughput of 14.30 img/s by a direct measurement, as shown in Column 4. Then, we obtain the estimated system throughput of 14.11 img/s by our analytical model, as shown in Column 5. Based on the data in Column 4 and 5, we calculate the error for the system throughput as $(14.11 - 14.30)/14.30 = -1.3\%$, shown in Column 6. In Column 6, a negative error value means that the system throughput is under-estimated and a positive value means that the system throughput is over-estimated. Similarly, Column 7 shows the system energy consumption of 0.58 J/img, obtained by a direct measurement and Column 8 shows the estimated system energy consumption of 0.56 J/img, obtained by our analytical model. Column 9 shows the error rate for the system energy consumption. We can see in Table 2 that the error rate for the system throughput is below 6% and the error rate for the energy consumption is below 9%. This fact confirms that our analytical models are accurate enough for finding pareto optimal points during a complex design space exploration because such accuracy is sufficient to relatively compare different design points [23].

Table 2. Accuracy evaluation for our analytical models

CNN model	CPU frequency (GHz)	GPU frequency (GHz)	System throughput by measurement (img/s)	ϕ_1 (img/s)	Throughput error (%)	System energy consumption by measurement (J/img)	ϕ_2 (J/img)	Energy error (%)
Vgg19	2.00	1.30	14.30	14.11	−1.3	0.58	0.56	−3.4
	2.00	0.73	10.45	10.94	4.7	0.44	0.47	6.8
	2.00	0.11	1.89	1.96	3.7	1.32	1.27	−3.8
	1.27	1.30	13.04	12.67	−2.8	0.54	0.52	−3.7
	1.27	0.73	10.28	10.55	2.6	0.30	0.32	6.7
	1.27	0.11	1.88	1.91	1.6	0.59	0.62	5.1
	0.35	1.30	6.52	6.53	0.2	1.04	1.08	3.8
	0.35	0.73	6.23	6.55	5.1	0.44	0.42	−4.5
	0.35	0.11	1.85	1.79	−3.2	0.54	0.57	5.6
Alexnet	2.00	1.30	81.17	82.02	1.0	0.055	0.051	−7.3
	2.00	0.73	70.82	70.44	−0.5	0.049	0.048	−2.0
	2.00	0.11	13.47	13.56	0.7	0.148	0.159	7.4
	1.27	1.30	70.92	69.89	−1.5	0.054	0.055	1.9
	1.27	0.73	61.69	62.22	0.9	0.045	0.044	−2.2
	1.27	0.11	11.74	11.85	0.9	0.110	0.115	4.5
	0.35	1.30	38.88	38.69	−0.5	0.090	0.088	−2.2
	0.35	0.73	30.90	31.21	1.0	0.068	0.072	5.9
	0.35	0.11	6.46	6.50	0.6	0.155	0.161	3.9
Emotion_fer	2.00	1.30	224.7	220.5	−1.9	0.017	0.016	−5.9
	2.00	0.73	178.6	181.1	1.4	0.017	0.018	5.9
	2.00	0.11	35.2	35.9	2.0	0.062	0.059	−4.8
	1.27	1.30	192.3	189.3	−1.6	0.015	0.015	0
	1.27	0.73	164.7	166.8	1.3	0.012	0.013	8.3
	1.27	0.11	32.55	33.01	1.4	0.034	0.032	−6.3
	0.35	1.30	57.77	58.21	0.8	0.033	0.032	−3.0
	0.35	0.73	46.73	45.99	−1.6	0.023	0.024	4.3
	0.35	0.11	27.26	27.61	1.3	0.033	0.034	3.0

5.3 Pareto-optimal Mappings

In this section, we show the benefits of using our extended methodology, introduced in Sect. 4, through a comparison between the Pareto-optimal mappings, found by our methodology and the Pareto-optimal mappings, found by exhaustive search when using TensorRT for CNN inference implementation because TensorRT [15] is the best-known CNN deployment optimizer designed for NVIDIA embedded MPSoCs such as the NVIDIA Jetson TX2.

First, in order to find the Pareto-optimal mappings by using our methodology, we perform a design space exploration (DSE), by using the two-objective GA of our methodology, introduced in Sect. 4.2, among possible mappings with a CPU and GPU VFS configuration, when Vgg19, Alexnet, and Emotion_fer are executed on the NVIDIA Jetson TX2 platform. The reason for using the two-objective GA for DSE is that the design space, which has to be explored and is supported by our methodology, consists of $|A|^{|cpu|*|gpu|*|f_{cpu}|*|f_{gpu}|}$ possible mappings. This is a huge number of mappings considering our experimental setup, thus exhaustive search is not feasible.

Second, in order to find the Pareto-optimal mappings when using TensorRT only, we perform a DSE by exhaustive search, among all possible mappings with a CPU and GPU VFS configuration, when Vgg19, Alexnet, and Emotion_fer are executed on the NVIDIA Jetson TX2 platform. Since TensorRT utilizes only one fixed CPU to offload all CNN inference tasks to one fixed GPU on NVIDIA Jetson TX2, the size of the design space when using only TensorRT depends on the possible CPU frequency levels $|f_{cpu}|$ and the possible GPU frequency levels $|f_{gpu}|$. Therefore, in this case, the design space consists of $|f_{cpu}| * |f_{gpu}| = 12 * 13 = 156$ design points to explore. Such small design space can be explored by exhaustive search in order to find all Pareto-optimal mappings with 100% guarantee.

Finally, we present and compare the Pareto-optimal mappings found by using the aforementioned two methods. The experimental results are shown in Fig. 5, 6 and 7. The horizontal axis shows the system throughput in images per second (img/s). The vertical axis shows the system energy consumption to process one image in joules per image (J/img). Each point in Fig. 5, 6 and 7 represents a Pareto-optimal mapping with certain system throughput and energy consumption. The red (+) points in the figures represent the Pareto-optimal mappings found by using our extended methodology. The green (×) points represent the Pareto-optimal mappings found by exhaustive search and using TensorRT only.

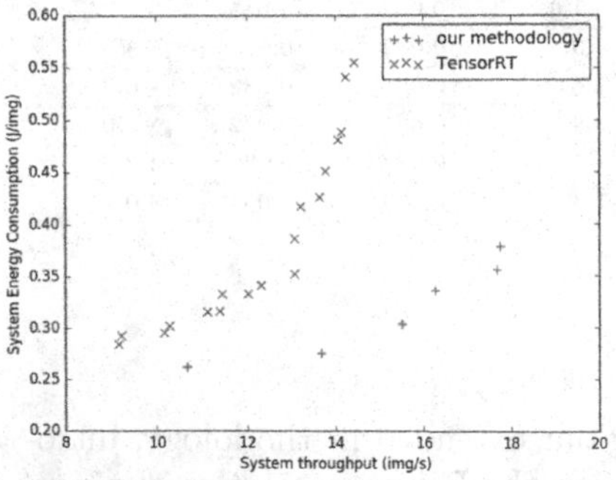

Fig. 5. Pareto-optimal mappings for Vgg19

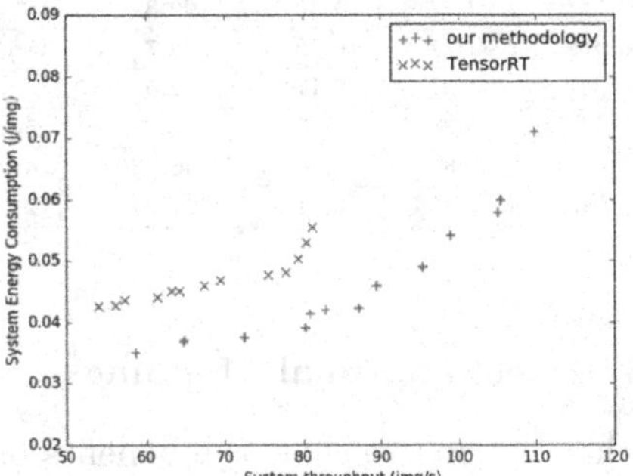

Fig. 6. Pareto-optimal mappings for Alexnet

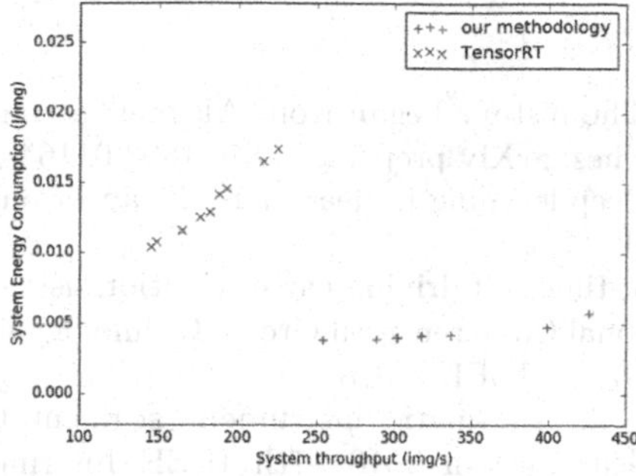

Fig. 7. Pareto-optimal mappings for Emotion_fer

From the experimental results, we can see that: (1) For Vgg19, as shown in Fig. 5, our methodology can deliver the same or better system throughput with a lower system energy consumption compared with TensorRT; (2) For Alexnet, as shown in Fig. 6, when the system throughput is lower than 100 img/s, our methodology can deliver the same or better system throughput with a lower system energy consumption compared with TensorRT. When the system throughput is higher than 100 img/s, only our methodology can deliver such system throughput but with a higher system energy consumption; (3) For Emotion_fer, as shown in Fig. 7, our methodology can always deliver a better system throughput with a lower system energy consumption compared with TensorRT. So, in conclusion, our extended methodology is able to achieve both energy efficiency and high throughput when deploying CNN models on embedded CPUs-GPUs MPSoCs.

6 Conclusions

In this paper, we propose an extended methodology to achieve energy efficiency and high throughput when deploying CNN models on embedded CPUs-GPUs MPSoCs. Our methodology finds Pareto-optimal mappings of a CNN model onto a CPUs-GPUs MPSoCs with VFS configurations with the help of a two-objective GA which optimizes the system throughput and energy consumption simultaneously. Moreover, we propose two analytical models, that are used as fitness functions in the two-objective GA to evaluate very fast the system throughput and energy consumption of CNNs mapped onto embedded CPUs-GPUs MPSoCs and we confirm the high accuracy of these two analytical models by experimental evidence. Finally, the experimental results of real-world CNNs execution on the NVIDIA Jetson TX2 platform show that, compared with the best-known CNN deployment optimizer TensorRT, our extended methodology is able to achieve both energy efficiency and high throughput when deploying CNN models on embedded CPUs-GPUs MPSoCs.

References

1. Alom, Md.Z., et al. The history began from Alexnet: a comprehensive survey on deep learning approaches. arXiv preprint arXiv:1803.01164 (2018)
2. Diamant, A., et al.: Deep learning in head & neck cancer outcome prediction. Sci. Rep. **9**(1), 1–10 (2019)
3. Do, T.-D., et al.: Real-time self-driving car navigation using deep neural network. In: 2018 4th International Conference on Green Technology and Sustainable Development (GTSD), pp. 7–12. IEEE (2018)
4. Alexey A Shvets et al. Automatic instrument segmentation in robot-assisted surgery using deep learning. In 2018 17th IEEE International Conference on Machine Learning and Applications (ICMLA), pp. 624–628. IEEE (2018)
5. Martin, G.: Overview of the MPSOC design challenge. In 2006 43rd ACM/IEEE Design Automation Conference, pp. 274–279. IEEE (2006)
6. Wang, S., et al.: High-throughput CNN inference on embedded arm big little multi-core processors. IEEE Trans. Comput.-Aided Des. Integr. Circ. Syst. **39**, 2254–2267 (2019)
7. Linpeng Tang et al. Scheduling computation graphs of deep learning models on manycore cpus. arXiv preprint arXiv:1807.09667 (2018)
8. Abadi, M., et al.: Tensorflow: large-scale machine learning on heterogeneous systems (2015)
9. Jia, Y., et al.: Caffe: convolutional architecture for fast feature embedding. In: Proceedings of the 22nd ACM International Conference on Multimedia, pp. 675–678 (2014)
10. Parvat, A., et al.: A survey of deep-learning frameworks. In 2017 International Conference on Inventive Systems and Control (ICISC), pp. 1–7. IEEE (2017)
11. Song, L., et al.: Hypar: towards hybrid parallelism for deep learning accelerator array. In: 2019 IEEE International Symposium on High Performance Computer Architecture (HPCA), pp. 56–68. IEEE (2019)
12. Kang, D., et al.: C-good: C-code generation framework for optimized on-device deep learning. In: Proceedings of the International Conference on Computer-Aided Design, pp. 1–8 (2018)
13. Huynh, L.N., et al.: Deepsense: a GPU-based deep convolutional neural network framework on commodity mobile devices. In: Proceedings of the 2016 Workshop on Wearable Systems and Applications, pp. 25–30 (2016)
14. Huynh, L.N., et al.: Deepmon: mobile GPU-based deep learning framework for continuous vision applications. In: Proceedings of the 15th Annual International Conference on Mobile Systems, Applications, and Services, pp. 82–95 (2017)
15. Nvidia tensorrt framework. https://developer.nvidia.com/tensorrt
16. Minakova, S., Tang, E., Stefanov, T.: Combining task- and data-level parallelism for high-throughput CNN inference on embedded CPUs-GPUs mpsocs. In: 20th International Conference on Embedded Computer Systems: Architectures, Modeling and Simulation (SAMOS 2020), July 05–09 (2020)
17. Lee, E.A., Messerschmitt, D.G.: Static scheduling of synchronous data flow programs for digital signal processing. IEEE Trans. Comput. **100**(1), 24–35 (1987)
18. Bilsen, G., et al.: Cycle-static dataflow. IEEE Trans. Signal Process. **44**(2), 397–408 (1996)
19. Deb, K., Gupta, H.: Searching for robust pareto-optimal solutions in multi-objective optimization. In: Coello Coello, C.A., Hernández Aguirre, A., Zitzler, E. (eds.) EMO 2005. LNCS, vol. 3410, pp. 150–164. Springer, Heidelberg (2005). https://doi.org/10.1007/978-3-540-31880-4_11

20. Sastry, K., et al.: Genetic algorithms. In: Search Methodologies, pp. 97–125. Springer, Heidelberg (2005). https://doi.org/10.1007/3-540-29623-9_7150
21. Onnx models zoo. https://github.com/onnx/models
22. Nvidia Jetson TX2. https://developer.nvidia.com/embedded/jetson-tx2
23. Palesi, M., Givargis, T.: Multi-objective design space exploration using genetic algorithms. In: The Tenth International Symposium on Hardware/Software codesign, pp. 67–72 (2002)

Evaluating System Identification Methods for Predicting Thermal Dissipation of Heterogeneous SoCs

Joel Öhrling, Sébastien Lafond(✉), and Dragos Truscan

Åbo Akademi University, Turku, Finland
{sebastien.lafond,dragos.truscan}@abo.fi

Abstract. In this paper we evaluate the use of system identification methods to build a thermal prediction model of heterogeneous SoC platforms that can be used to quickly predict the temperature of different configurations without the need of hardware. Specifically, we focus on modeling approaches that can predict the temperature based on the clock frequency and the utilization percentage of each core. We investigate three methods with respect to their prediction accuracy: a linear state-space identification approach using polynomial regressors, a NARX neural network approach and a recurrent neural network approach configured in an FIR model structure. We evaluate the methods on an Odroid-XU4 board featuring an Exynos 5422 SoC. The results show that the model based on polynomial regressors significantly outperformed the other two models when trained with 1 h and 6 h of data.

1 Introduction

In recent years, heterogeneous System-on-Chip (SoC) platforms have permeated many types of IT systems [11,16] due to the efficient balance they provide between their computing power and power consumption. However, the challenge they provide is in choosing the correct configuration for a specific application workload. This is particularly difficult due to the very large configuration space.

Performing exhaustive testing on these types of systems becomes unfeasible, as the number of possible configurations is vast and requires the presence of hardware setups to experiment with. In order to speed up the exploration process, we investigate system identification methods to build a model of the platform that can be used to predict the temperature of different configurations quickly without the need of hardware.

Modeling a processor based on theoretical relationship between the power and thermal dissipation requires extensive knowledge about the characteristics of the processor and its environment. For some processors, numerical values

Part of this work was carried out with financial support from the Nordic Master programme (contract NMP-2016/10169) and ECSEL-JU AIDOaRt project (grant agreement No. 101007350).

© Springer Nature Switzerland AG 2022
A. Orailoglu et al. (Eds.): SAMOS 2021, LNCS 13227, pp. 144–160, 2022.
https://doi.org/10.1007/978-3-031-04580-6_10

for the thermal characteristics of the materials and placement of the processor parts are readily available. However, for many processors, these values are not provided and have to be estimated or measured. Therefore, in this work, we focus on modeling approaches that can predict the temperature based on the clock frequency and the utilization percentage of each core. In this paper, we only consider an asymmetric single-ISA CPU, however including other computational units (like GPUs and DSPs) would only impact the number of configuration parameters of the platform and require different types of workload.

To that extent, we evaluate three system identification methods with respect to their prediction accuracy: a linear state-space identification approach using polynomial regressors, a NARX neural network approach and a recurrent neural network approach configured in an FIR model structure. We evaluate the three methods on an Odroid-XU4 board featuring an Exynos 5422 SoC and perform a set of experiments to evaluate their prediction accuracy using a 1-h and a 6-h dataset. The Exynos 5422 SoC is composed of a big.LITTLE octa-core mobile processor combining a Cortex-A15 and Cortex-A7 quad-core. We acknowledge the Odroid XU4 is a few years old platform at the time of writing this paper, however we consider that the proposed approach, with its benefits and drawbacks, can be applied to other modern SoC platforms.

2 System Identification and Selection of Methods

System identification [10] is a field which deals with creating mathematical models of dynamical systems through statistical and machine learning approaches.

Several works have utilized neural networks for thermal modeling and have been proposed in the past. Some of them [5,12] propose white-box approaches that are based on the theoretical equation that governs the power and heat dissipation of a processor. These implement a bottom-up technique, where the thermal model is based on the layout of the SoC, the conditions of the external environment and the conductive properties of materials. These approaches simulate the thermal dissipation directly at chip-level with some level of abstraction. This type of modeling relies heavily on the accuracy of the technical parameters and how much detail is lost through abstractions and simplifications.

Another approaches [7,8] use the thermal-electrical analogy, in which the chip is broken down into small parts; each part is represented as a combination of current sources, resistors and capacitors. A common tool for these is HotSpot [19]. These approaches also rely heavily on knowledge about the characteristics as well as the location of components within the chip.

Several researchers applied gray-box identification approaches to model the thermal characteristics of a processor. Beneventi et al. [2] propose an approach where a multi-core processor is modeled as a thermal-electrical circuit. In their approach, the processor is divided into blocks that correspond to each core and the section of the copper heat spreader directly above each core. The parameters of the model are then optimized using an Output-Error approach. A similar approach was proposed by Aguia et al. [3]. They suggested an implementation where the cores of a multi-core processor and the cache memory are represented as blocks in a thermal-electrical-equivalent circuit. The subspace identification method, N4SID, is then applied to find the optimal parameters for the model. Another approach that utilizes a state-space identification method has been proposed in [9]. Here, the researchers deploy a piece-wise linear subspace identification method that estimates a linear model for each temperature range. Shetu et al. [14], however, suggest a different approach with a polynomial model for approximating the temperature of a CPU. In their study, a thermal model is constructed by creating polynomials based on the size and intensity of the workload.

Several black-box approaches based on neural networks have been proposed. Vincenzi et al. [17] and Sridhar et al. [15] predict thermal dynamics of an integrated circuit using ARX linear neural networks. These approaches were shown to be effective at simulating heat flow in three-dimensional and highly granular, integrated circuits. Zhang et al. [20] use a feed-forward neural network to simulate the heat dissipation in processors By comparing the performance of a Gaussian process model, a neural network model and a linear regression model the researchers showed that the neural network model outperformed the linear model in terms of prediction accuracy by 30%, but was approximately three times more computationally expensive. The Gaussian process model also showed good prediction accuracy, at the expense of twice the computational overhead of the neural network model.

Pérez et al. [13] compared recurrent and feed-forward neural network structures for thermal prediction of immersive cooling computer systems. The core frequency and processor utilization measurements from the past minute were used for temperature predictions.

Differently from the previous approaches which rely on power measurements to predict the temperature of a processor, work has been done on predicting the power dissipation of a processor. Walker et al. [18] predict the power consumption of a multi-core processor by utilizing core frequencies, core voltages and event counters (e.g., cycle counter, bus and cache accesses) to train a linear regression model. Zhang et al. [21] built a linear regression model based on data collected from a CPU, where they utilized the idle states and idle time of each core. In addition, Balsini et al. [1] deploy a genetic algorithm to find the optimal parameters for a function that represents the theoretical relationship between power dissipation and quantities such as the core voltage and clock frequency.

In reality, as most models are constructed based on some knowledge and observations of a system, their corresponding modeling approaches can be viewed as being gray-box approaches to some degree [6]. Most of the white-box and gray-box approaches utilize power as an input variable or *regressor*. When the thermal properties and the blueprint are not directly available for the ARM CPUs, a white-box approach is not suitable. Many gray-box approaches also relied on the close-to-linear relationship between temperature and power. This also makes these approaches less appealing when the objective of this work is to perform modeling based only on measurable processor state variables, like frequency and processor utilization. However, some previous works exploit the theoretical relationship between frequency, voltage and utilization to estimate the power dissipation of a processor [1,18]. Therefore, combining such an approach with a linear model identification technique, such as the N4SID method suggested in [3], was selected as an approach to be evaluated in this work.

Other approaches that have produced promising results are neural network-based approaches [15,20]. A neural network in an ARX structure, could through the addition of a nonlinear hidden layer, learn to replicate the nonlinear dynamics of the heterogeneous processor. This would create a Hammerstein type of NARX model. As the dynamics of a heterogeneous processor is rather deterministic and the noise component in measurements can be expected to be rather low, an ARX-based model was also selected as an approach to be evaluated in this work.

Recurrent neural network approaches have not seen much attention in applications related to thermal modeling of computing systems. However, the approach in [13], where an RNN model is trained in an FIR structure, showed promising results. We therefore selected such RNN-based model as an approach to be evaluated.

The above approaches were not applied to create prediction models for thermal dissipation of heterogeneous SoCs. Thus in this paper we provide two contributions: a) we evaluate some of the proposed methods in the context of thermal dissipation and b) we propose a new approach, polynomial N4SID, as a combination of two existing methods.

3 Evaluated Methods

Based on the surveyed literature three methods have been selected for comparison. They will be described in the following: the first is a polynomial extension to N4SID, which we denote hereafter as Polynomial N4SID, a nonlinear state-space model structure using nonlinear regressors. The second is a NARX approach, where a neural network is recursively trained to predict the temperature. The third approach is an FIR model structure that utilizes an RNN layer to predict the thermal dissipation. The performance of these three modeling approaches has been assessed for two different lengths of training data: 1 h and 6 h. The error of each model has been measured using Mean Squared Error (MSE) as the metric. All three methods start with 10 regressors, i.e., the two cluster frequencies and the utilization of each of the eight cores.

3.1 Polynomial N4SID

The first model structure is a parametric approach based on the state-space identification method N4SID to estimate a linear state-space model. There is a direct relationship between the power dissipation of a processor and its thermal dissipation. This relationship could, therefore, be exploited to construct a linear model of the system. This type of approach has been suggested in both [2] and [3]. In this work, however, the objective is to compare modeling approaches that can predict the temperature based on the clock frequency and the utilization percentage of each core. The power consumption has a nonlinear relationship with the core frequency, the core voltage and the core utilization. While the dynamic power dissipation is linearly dependent on the core utilization, the core utilization cannot, on its own, be used to describe it, as it is also dependent on the core frequency and voltage. Therefore, a non-linearity relation had to be introduced to approximate the power dissipation, in the form of new nonlinear regressors as polynomial combinations of the core frequency and core utilization.

In our work, we approximate the relation between the voltage and the core frequency as $V \underset{\sim}{\propto} \sqrt{f}$. The dynamic part of the power consumption is expressed as $P_{dyn} \underset{\sim}{\propto} f^2$, while the static part of the power consumption was estimated to be approximately proportional to $f^{1.5}$. In this scenario, the core utilization is expected to be directly proportional to the dynamic power consumption.

Using these approximate relationships as a basis, the polynomials were created as the product of the core utilization to a power of 0 or 1 and the core frequency to a power of between 1 and 3 in increments of 0.5. This was performed for each core and resulted in 58 new nonlinear regressors with a total of 68 regressors, including the original 10.

The N4SID algorithm does not have many parameters that can be tuned. However, the model order can be viewed as a hyperparameter. In this implementation, the selection of nonlinear regressors can also be considered as hyperparameters. Optimization of the utilized regressors was performed using correlation analysis and grid search.

A randomized search was performed over 500 iterations on values measured over a one hour workload execution time, as describe in Sect. 4. In each iteration, three random combinations of core frequency to a power between 1 and 3 and core utilization to a power of 0 or 1 were selected. The combinations were then applied to the regressors belonging to each core to create the new regressors. At the end of each iteration, the average mean square error (MSE) was measured. Using the results, a pair-wise correlation analysis was performed to detect overall contribution of each regressor to the error. Figure 1 shows that most of the regressors with only a single frequency component showed a positive correlation. That is, they increased the error when they were utilized. Those that showed a negative correlation produced a decrease in the error when they were utilized. The regressors with a positive correlation were therefore removed from the regressor set.

Grid search and cross-validation were performed as an additional reduction step. During the grid search, the model order was set to 5 for all iterations. This was implemented to reduce computational time. The model order that produces the best performance was, however, expected to be higher than 5. An assumption was made, though, that a fifth-order model would be representative enough for this hyperparameter validation step. All permutations of the remaining regressors were tested and the best regressor configuration was saved. The

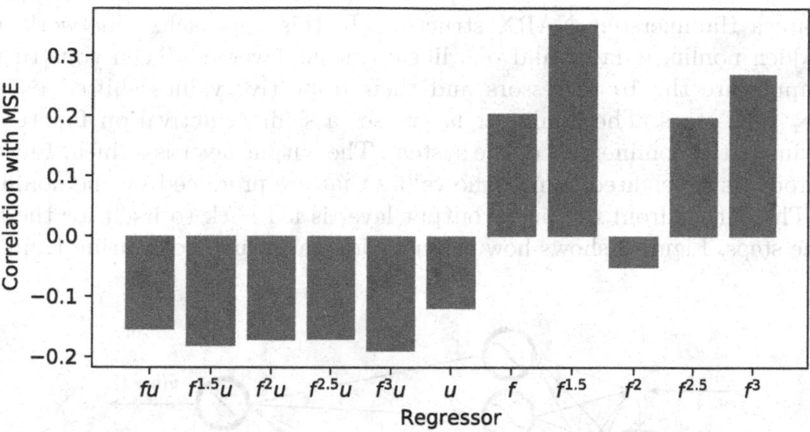

Fig. 1. Correlation between regressor and MSE.

best regressor set is shown in (1), where f is core frequency, u is core utilization and i indicates the number of cores.

$$U_{nl} = [f^{1.5}u_i, f^2u_i, f^3u_i, u_i, f^2], i = 1..8 \tag{1}$$

The final number of regressors utilized in this approach is 34. Furthermore, these regressors were selected for implementation for both 1-h and 6-h block lengths. The average validation error was measured for orders between 2 and 60. Figure 2 shows the model performance for each order. We presented this approach in detail in [4].

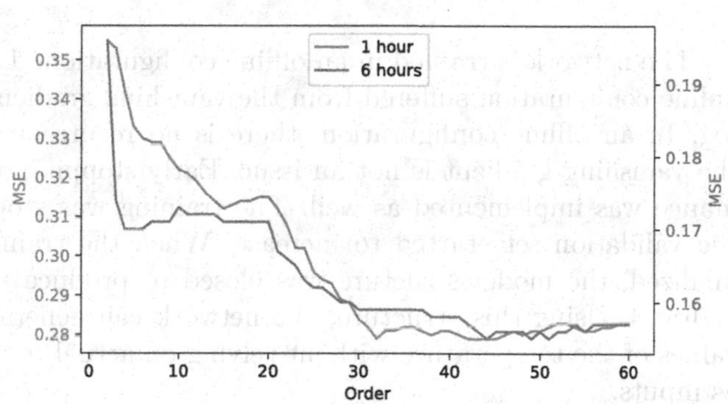

Fig. 2. Validation error and model order.

3.2 Hammerstein-NARX

The second model structure chosen was an NARX approach implemented as an artificial neural network. As shown by Zhang et al. [20] and Sridhar et al. [15], a neural network can be trained to predict the temperature at the next time step based on previous temperature values and some exogenous inputs that affect the temperature. The two approaches were in this implementation combined to create a Hammerstein-NARX structure. In this approach, a network with one hidden nonlinear layer and one linear output layer has been constructed. The inputs are the 10 regressors and their respective values shifted back in time n_x time steps. The nonlinear layer uses a sigmoid activation function to approximate the nonlinearity of the system. The output layer is a linear function that produces a weighted sum of the values that are produced by the nonlinear layer. The output from the linear output layer is fed back to itself for the past n_y time steps. Figure 3 shows how the network was structured during training.

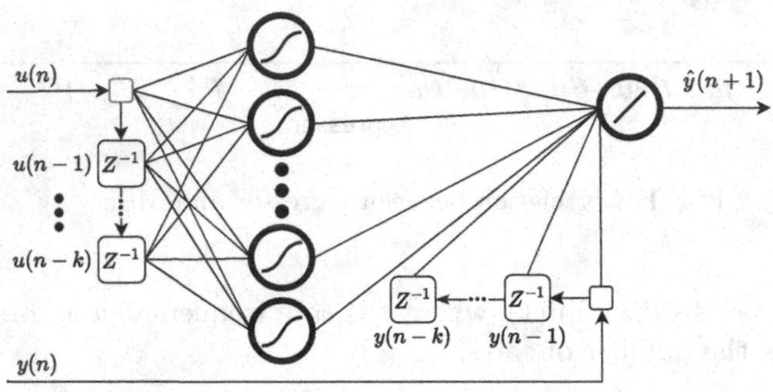

Fig. 3. Offline Hammerstein-NARX structure used for training.

The network is trained in an offline configuration. This was chosen since the online configuration suffered from the vanishing gradient problem during training. In an offline configuration, there is no recurrence in the network. Thus, the vanishing gradient is not an issue. Early stopping on the validation performance was implemented as well. The training was stopped when the error on the validation set started to increase. When the training of the network was finalized, the model structure was closed to produce the online layout shown in Fig. 4. Using this structure, the network can generate predictions of future values of the temperature without relying on actual temperature measurements as inputs.

A few hyperparameters for this approach were selected based on the network structures suggested in [20] and [15], as well as some empirical experience. The activation function was selected to be a sigmoid function. Additionally, only a shallow structure with one hidden layer was tested. The selected optimization algorithm, Levenberg-Marquardt, was also not changed and its associated parameters were kept as the default for the *trainlm* function in Matlab's Deep Learning Toolbox. The Levenberg-Marquardt optimization algorithm was chosen since it was the only algorithm that could successfully converge to a solution during training on the offline configuration.

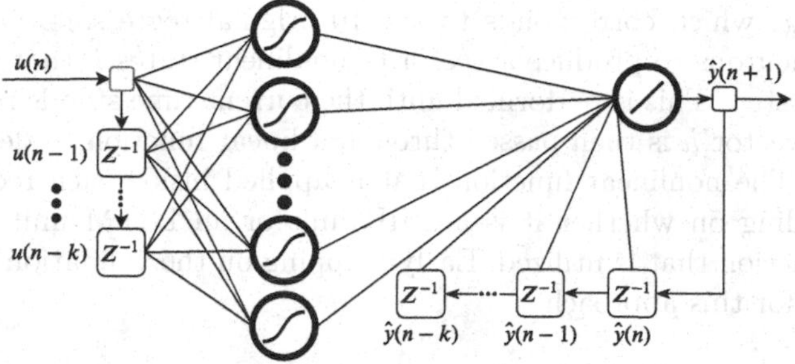

Fig. 4. Online Hammerstein-NARX structure used to produce predictions.

In Fig. 5, the validation performance for different layer sizes is shown. For the 1-h block length, 3 neurons in the hidden layer produced the best validation performance on average. When training the model structure using 6 h of data, 5 neurons yielded the lowest average prediction error.

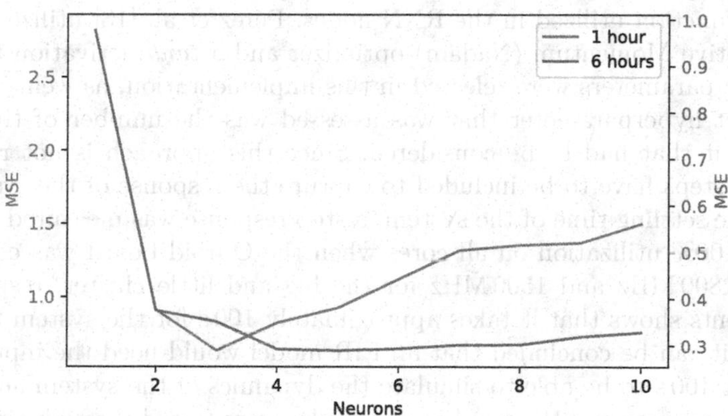

Fig. 5. Validation error per size of the hidden nonlinear layer.

3.3 FIR-RNN

The final model structure that was assessed is based on a recurrent neural network. This structure has one recurrent layer followed by a single linear layer. This is based on an FIR structure, where the output is predicted solely based on n_x previous inputs.

This modeling approach is based on the structure utilized by Pérez et al. [13]. They found that a shallow structure with either GRU or LSTM layers produced the best performance in their immersive cooling experiment. A similar approach is therefore implemented, as shown in Fig. 6. A single layer of RNN neurons is followed by a single linear layer. Each time step, the RNN layer takes the input vector x, which corresponds to the 10 original regressors, and passes it through the neurons to produce a vector of nonlinear states h that is passed to the next time step. This is performed until the current time step is reached. The hidden state vector h is then passed through a linear function to determine the prediction $\hat{y}$. The nonlinear function that is applied inside each recurrent unit differs depending on whether it is a GRU unit or an LSTM unit and on the activation function that is utilized. Early stopping on the validation set has also been utilized for this approach.

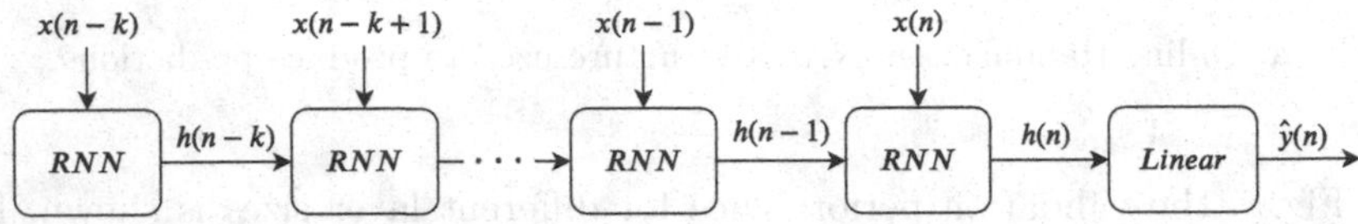

Fig. 6. FIR-RNN model structure.

The hyperparameters that were selected empirically were the optimizer and activation function utilized in the RNN nodes. Pérez et al. [13] utilize the Nesterov Adaptive Momentum (Nadam) optimizer and a *tanh* activation function. Thus, these parameters were selected in this implementation, as well.

The first hyperparameter that was assessed was the number of time steps for the input that had to be considered. Since this approach is not recursive, many time steps have to be included to capture the response of the system. To estimate the settling time of the system, a step response was measured by going from 0 to 100% utilization on all cores when the Odroid board was configured to run at 1800 MHz and 1500 MHz for the big and little cluster, respectively. Measurements shows that it takes approximately 100 s for the system to settle. Therefore, it can be concluded that an FIR model would need the input values for the past 100 s to be able to simulate the dynamics of the system accurately.

The sample rate and the number of samples were tested through grid search and cross-validation. Three other hyperparameters were also tested in conjunction: the unit type (LSTM or GRU), the number of units and the batch size. For both the 1-h and 6-h block lengths, a sample length of 50 samples spread out logarithmically between 0 and 100 s, performed the best. The GRU unit also outperformed the LSTM unit using both block lengths. A batch size of 1 and a unit size of 10 was found to be the optimal values for the 1-h block length. Using the longer block length, a batch size of 4 and a unit size of 18 generated the lowest average validation error.

4 Experimental Setup

For this study, a desktop experiment setup to benchmark and measure the temperature of a heterogeneous processor was created. The experimental setup in Fig. 7 was used to generate and gather data in this study.

System Under Test. In this case the system under test was an Odroid XU4 Exynos 5422 board - a single-board computer allows the control of the frequency on a per cluster basis between 200 MHz and 2000 MHz for the big cluster and 200 MHz and 1500 MHz for this little cluster. The operating frequency cannot be controlled independently for each core inside the clusters. The voltage levels can also be set for each cluster. However, in the Linux operating system for this platform, these are set to static values for each operating frequency by the kernel. The operating voltage levels are, therefore, not considered as a variable in the implementations in this work.

The Odroid board has been configured to trigger a thermal throttle when the core temperature for the big cores reaches 90° C. This means that the processor's frequency governors will reduce the maximum available frequency when the temperature is reached to prevent the processor from overheating.

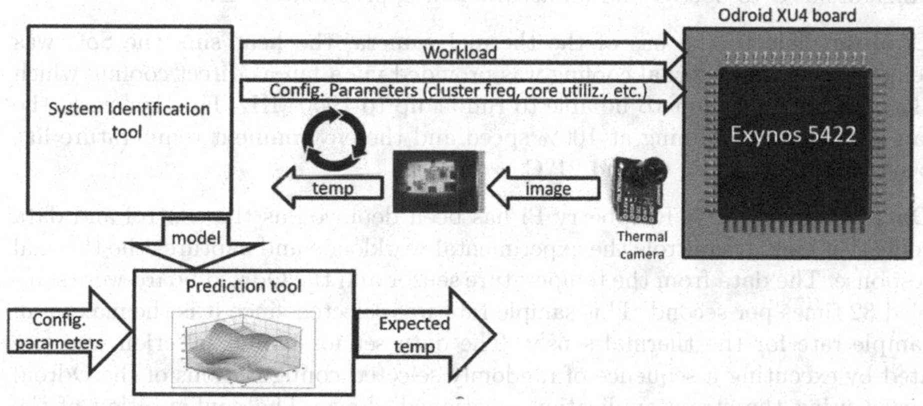

Fig. 7. Overview of the experimental setup

Experimental workload utilized in this experiment was an RGB-YUV image conversion. This image conversion was chosen as the workload because it is a highly parallel workload that can be distributed to many cores.

A custom-built stress configures the platform by setting the utilization of each core, the frequency of each cluster, and the amount of time for the execution of the workload. Inside the application, a thread for each core in the system is created. Each core thread runs its assigned workload independently from the other cores.

The cluster frequencies are controlled using the *Performance* frequency governor. The used application does not adjust the frequencies directly, it sets the maximum allowed frequency and the frequency governor then adjusts the frequency accordingly.

The workload is in this work constant. Thus, the total number of possible configurations can be calculated using Eq. (2), where U is the number of utilization levels, C is the number of cores, f_b is the clock frequency of the big cluster and f_l is the frequency of the little cluster.

$$N_c = U^C f_b f_l \tag{2}$$

Each core has five different utilization levels, and the big and little clusters have ten and six discrete clock frequency levels, respectively. For the implementation in this work, this yields a total of approximately 23 million possible configurations of the heterogeneous SoC.

Thermal Measurements. Due to the absence of a core temperature sensor for each core on the Odroid-XU4, a Melexis MLX90640 thermal camera was used. The camera, with a resolution of 32×24 pixels, has been mounted close to the SoC of the Odroid-XU4 in order to obtain a more accurate reading of the temperature across the surface of the SoC. The camera sensor has a temperature range of 40 °C to 300 °C and an accuracy of approximately ±1 °C.

Cooling. Due to the use of the thermal camera, the heat sink the SoC was removed and the external cooling was provided via a fan as direct cooling which allowed the big cluster to be able to run at up to 1900 MHz. For this work, the fan is constantly running at 100% speed and the environment temperature has been kept constant at around 21°C.

Data Collection. A Raspberry Pi has been deployed as the control and data collection unit. It controls the experimental workloads and captures the thermal response. The data from the temperature sensor and the Odroid board were sampled 32 times per second. This sample rate was selected since it is the maximum sample rate for the thermal sensor. The data set for model selection was created by executing a sequence of randomly selected configurations of the Odroid board using the stress application mentioned above. The configuration of the board was changed after a random amount of time in the range of 10 to 60 s. Both the selection of configuration parameters (cluster frequencies and core utilization) and execution period followed a uniform distribution. Throughout the experiment, the ambient temperature was kept steady at 21°C.

5 Model Selection and Evaluation

The performance of the three selected modeling approaches has been assessed for two different lengths of training data: 1 h and 6 h. The error of each model has been measured using MSE as the metric. A flowchart of the entire model identification methodology is shown in Fig. 8.

The previously collected data set was divided into two sets, a development set and a test set. The first 79% of the data became the development set. This is the portion of the data that the models were trained on and the models' hyperparameters were evaluated with. The last 20% of the data were chosen as the test set. This is the data set that the final prediction error was assessed upon and was not utilized for model training and selection. A small set of data

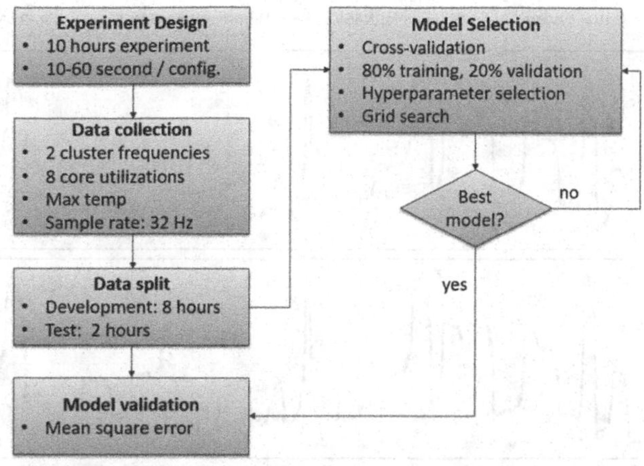

Fig. 8. Flowchart of system identification procedure.

corresponding to 1% of the total data, lodged between the development and test sets, is omitted to ensure that there is no interference between the development set and the test set. Furthermore, the same data split was utilized for all three modeling approaches.

1-h Performance. Using the hyperparameters and model structures described in the previous section, the models were validated through 10-fold cross-validation. Table 1 shows the result for the model on the 1-h block length.

Table 1. MSE for the implemented approaches trained with 1 h of data.

	Folds										
Method	1	2	3	4	5	6	7	8	9	10	**Avg**
Polynomial N4SID	0.16	0.15	0.15	0.16	0.16	0.14	0.16	0.16	0.17	0.14	**0.16**
Hammerstein-NARX	0.53	1.28	0.61	0.74	0.74	0.55	0.65	0.85	0.79	0.54	**0.73**
FIR-RNN	2.28	2.14	1.42	1.44	1.05	2.12	1.60	1.30	2.77	0.80	**1.69**

Table 1 shows that the Polynomial N4SID approach showed the lowest average MSE. It can also be noted that the N4SID based approach has, by far, the lowest variance, with a standard deviation of just 0.01. The other two approaches had significantly worse performance on the test data.

Figure 9 shows the models' performance on the test set when trained on the seventh fold. This fold is selected since it is the fold that is the closest to the average for all three approaches. The configuration parameters of the board were randomly changed every 10 to 60 s. This means that approximately 57 different board configurations were utilized in the 2000 s window.

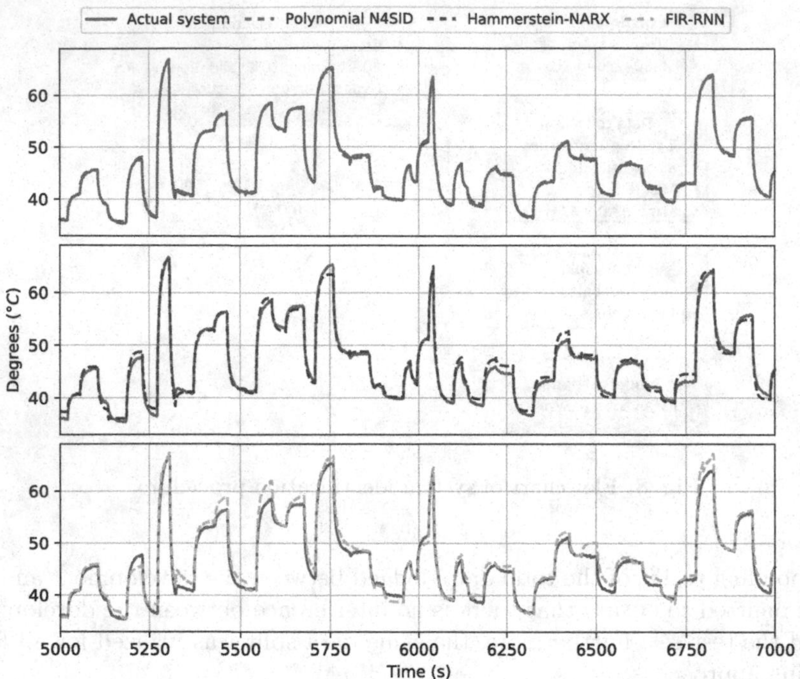

Fig. 9. 1-h model predictions on the last 2000 s of the test data.

Looking at the above figure, it can be seen that the Polynomial N4SID model produced a good approximation of the true measured temperature. The other two models produced less desirable results, but they still yielded a decent approximation of the true temperature. Furthermore, the Polynomial N4SID model does not appear to have any particular problem areas or specific configurations that it struggles with. The other two models and especially the FIR-RNN show varying performance in regards to the different board configurations.

The average training time, average prediction time and the number of parameters were also measured for the three model structures. Table 2 shows that the N4SID-based model structure has the lowest training and prediction time. However, it is closely followed by the Hammerstein-NARX model structure. The FIR-RNN model takes the longest both to train and to make predictions. The training time is especially significant as it is about 100 times that of the other two approaches.

6-h Performance. The same procedure was utilized for the 6-h block length. The models were validated through 4-fold cross-validation. Table 3 shows the result for the model when trained with 6 h of data.

The prediction error of the Polynomial N4SID model was reduced even further when trained with 6 h of data. It improved by approximately 50% compared to its 1-h performance. The FIR-RNN model, however, has improved substantially.

Table 2. Average training time, average prediction time and number of parameter for the 1-h models.

Method	Training time (s)	Prediction time (s)	Number of parameters
Polynomial N4SID	6	0.25	2144
Hammerstein-NARX	7	0.558	347
FIR-RNN	987	4.9	671

Table 3. MSE for the implemented approaches trained with 6 h of data.

	Folds				
Method	1	2	3	4	Avg
Polynomial N4SID	0.11	0.11	0.11	0.11	**0.11**
Hammerstein-NARX	0.26	0.25	0.28	0.28	**0.27**
FIR-RNN	0.24	0.21	0.18	0.19	**0.21**

It yields a prediction MSE of 0.21 when trained with more data. The Hammerstein-NARX model did also improve compared to the 1-h block length, but it did not see the same level of improvement as the recurrent FIR model. Figure 10 shows the three modeling approaches' performance on the final 2000 s of the test set when trained on the second fold.

The average training time, average prediction time and the number of parameters for the three model structures on 6 h of training data is shown in Table 4. Just as for 1 h of training data, the N4SID and NARX-based models have significantly lower training and prediction times. Interestingly, the Hammerstein-NARX model's prediction time only increased slightly and is more than twice as fast as the Polynomial N4SID model.

Table 4. Average training time, average prediction time and number of parameter for the 1-h models.

Method	Training time (s)	Prediction time (s)	Number of parameters
Polynomial N4SID	60	1.34	3354
Hammerstein-NARX	67	0.65	571
FIR-RNN	2580	10.5	1639

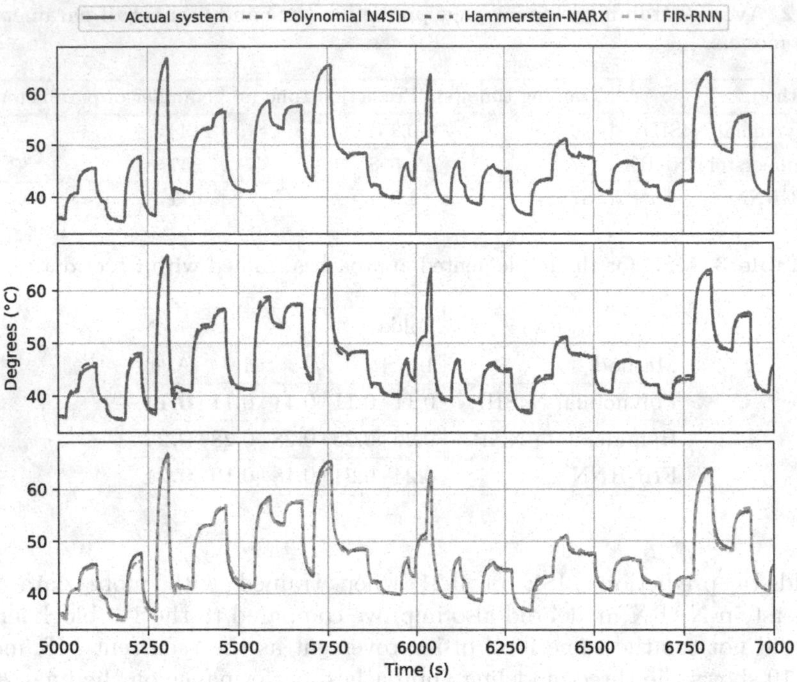

Fig. 10. 6-h model predictions on the last 2000 s of the test data.

6 Conclusion

The results of this study show that several types of modeling approaches can be utilized to predict the temperature dissipation of a heterogeneous SoC. However, Polynomial N4SID outperforms the others in its ability to learn the dynamics of a system from a limited amount of data and to predict with higher accuracy the thermal dissipation. We consider that this is because the non-linear regressors are able to better estimate the quadratic relationship between frequency and power consumption.

Future work is intended to address some of the limitations of the current study, for instance to consider several types of SoCs and workloads, to take into account the ambient temperature and humidity, and to investigate the accuracy of our models in a real-world setup without removing the heat sink and providing constant active cooling.

References

1. Balsini, A., Pannocchi, L., Cucinotta, T.: Modeling and simulation of power consumption and execution times for real-time tasks on embedded heterogeneous architectures. ACM SIGBED Rev. **16**, 51–56 (2019)

2. Beneventi, B., Tilli, B.: An effective gray-box identification procedure for multicore thermal modeling. IEEE Trans. Comput. **63**(5), 1097–1110 (2014)
3. Eguia, T.J.A., et al.: General behavioral thermal modeling and characterization for multi-core microprocessor design. In: 2010 Design, Automation Test in Europe Conference Exhibition (DATE 2010), pp. 1136–1141 (2010)
4. Öhrling, J., Truscan, D., Lafond, S.: Enabling fast exploration and validation of thermal dissipation requirements for heterogeneous CPU platforms. In: 2021 IEEE International Conference on Software Testing, Verification and Validation Workshops (ICSTW) (2021)
5. Huang, W., et al.: Accurate, Pre-RTL temperature-aware design using a parameterized, geometric thermal model. IEEE Trans. Comput. **57**(9), 1277–1288 (2008)
6. Janczak, A.: Identification of Nonlinear Systems Using Neural Networks and Polynomial Models: A Block-oriented Approach. Springer, Heidelberg (2005). https://doi.org/10.1007/b98334
7. Lee, S., et al.: Thermoelectric-based sustainable self-cooling for fine-grained processor hot spots. In: 15th IEEE Intersociety Conference on Thermal and Thermomechanical Phenomena in Electronic Systems (ITherm), pp. 847–856, May 2016
8. Liu, W., Calimera, A., Nannarelli, A., Macii, E., Poncino, M.: On-chip thermal modeling based on SPICE simulation. In: Monteiro, J., van Leuken, R. (eds.) PATMOS 2009. LNCS, vol. 5953, pp. 66–75. Springer, Heidelberg (2010). https://doi.org/10.1007/978-3-642-11802-9_11
9. Liu, Z., et al.: Compact thermal modeling for packaged microprocessor design with practical power maps. Integration **47**(1), 71–85 (2014)
10. Ljung, L.: System Identification: Theory for the User. Prentice Hall PTR, Upper Saddle River (1999)
11. McGuinness, P.: What's next for mobile? Heterogeneous processing evolves. Online at www.embedded-computing.com, https://www.embedded-computing.com/embedded-computing-design/whats-next-for-mobile-heterogeneous-processing-evolves, August 2014
12. Paci, G., et al.: Exploring temperature-aware design in low-power MPSocS. Int. J. Embedded Syst. **3**(1–2), 43–51 (2007)
13. Pérez, J., Pérez, S., Moya, J.M., Arroba, P.: Thermal prediction for immersion cooling data centers based on recurrent neural networks. In: Yin, H., Camacho, D., Novais, P., Tallón-Ballesteros, A.J. (eds.) IDEAL 2018. LNCS, vol. 11314, pp. 491–498. Springer, Cham (2018). https://doi.org/10.1007/978-3-030-03493-1_51
14. Shetu, R.A., et al.: Workload-based prediction of CPU temperature and usage for small-scale distributed systems. In: 2015 4th International Conference on Computer Science and Network Technology (ICCSNT), vol. 01, pp. 1090–1093 (2015)
15. Sridhar, A., et al.: Neural network-based thermal simulation of integrated circuits on GPUs. IEEE Trans. Comput. Aided Des. Integr. Circuits Syst. **31**(1), 23–36 (2012)
16. Ullman, B.: Designing an ARM-based Cloud RAN cellular/wireless base station, December 2013. https://www.embedded.com/designing-an-arm-based-cloud-ran-cellular-wireless-base-station/. Accessed 28 May 2021
17. Vincenzi, A., et al.: Fast thermal simulation of 2D/3D integrated circuits exploiting neural networks and GPUs. In: IEEE/ACM International Symposium on Low Power Electronics and Design, pp. 151–156 (2011)
18. Walker, M., et al.: Accurate and stable empirical CPU power modelling for multi- and many-core systems. In: Adaptive Many-Core Architectures and Systems Workshop, 15 June 18, June 2018. https://eprints.soton.ac.uk/421995/

19. Huang, W., et al.: HotSpot: a compact thermal modeling methodology for early-stage VLSI design. IEEE Trans. Very Large Scale Integr. (VLSI) Syst. **14**(5), 501–513 (2006)
20. Zhang, K., et al.: Machine learning-based temperature prediction for runtime thermal management across system components. IEEE Trans. Parallel Distrib. Syst. **29**(2), 405–419 (2018)
21. Zhang, Y., et al.: Towards better CPU power management on multicore smartphones. In: Proceedings of the Workshop on Power-Aware Computing and Systems. In: HotPower 2013 (2013)

Embeddings of Task Mappings to Multicore Systems

Andrés Goens(✉) and Jeronimo Castrillon

Chair for Compiler Construction, Center for Advancing Electronics Dresden (cfaed), TU Dresden, Dresden, Germany
{andres.goens,jeronimo.castrillon}@tu-dresden.de

Abstract. The problem of finding good mappings is central to designing and executing applications efficiently in embedded systems. In heterogeneous multicores, which are ubiquitous today, this problem yields an intractably large design space of possible mappings. Most methods explore this space using heuristics, many of which implicitly use geometric notions in mappings. In this paper we explore the geometry of the mapping problem explicitly, for finding embeddings of the mapping space that capture its structure. This allows us to formulate new mapping strategies by leveraging the geometry of the mapping space, as well as improving existing heuristics that do so implicitly. We evaluate our approach on a novel mapping heuristic based on gradient descent, as well as multiple existing meta-heuristics. For complex architectures, our methods improved the results of established exploration meta-heuristics by about an order of magnitude in average.

1 Introduction

As the complexity of hardware systems increases, the problem of efficiently programming them not only becomes harder but also more crucial. For Cyber-Physical System (CPS) and embedded systems in general, there is a family of methods called software synthesis [3,6]. Inspired by hardware design flows, it aims to bridge the ensuing software productivity gap by integrating knowledge of the application and target multicore architecture into the compilation process.

A central concept in software synthesis is that of mappings, which divide the tasks in an application between the different processing elements (PEs) of the target architecture. Using mappings allow the compiler to produce code for heterogeneous Instruction-Set Architectures (ISAs), find especially efficient configurations and even increase the predictability in systems with homogeneous ISAs like ARM big.LITTLE [11]. The *mapping problem*, of finding such efficient mappings, is a difficult yet crucial step in this process. Because of the sheer size of the mapping space, which grows prohibitively large with increasing architecture

This work has been funded in part by the German Research Council (DFG) through the TraceSymm project (number 366764507) and the Studienstiftung des deutschen Volkes.

© Springer Nature Switzerland AG 2022
A. Orailoglu et al. (Eds.): SAMOS 2021, LNCS 13227, pp. 161–176, 2022.
https://doi.org/10.1007/978-3-031-04580-6_11

and application complexities, exploring it exhaustively is intractable. Moreover, there is a complex relationship between a mapping and its performance, which in general cannot be modeled well analytically, which is why we need simulation to estimate it.

A great deal of research has focused on the mapping problem, spawning many sophisticated heuristics and meta-heuristics to find mappings with different characteristics. A survey of mapping approaches can be found in [29]. Many of these mapping meta-heuristics are based on an intuitive notion of a geometry of the mapping space. For example, the Tabu Search algorithm proposed in [18] relies on exploring neighboring mappings in order to improve their performance. Other similar principles underly methods like Simulated Annealing [22], L_p-adaptation [15] or genetic algorithms [9,24]. This is usually done in an ad-hoc fashion, without explicitly considering how to best endow the mapping space with such a geometric notion. Mappings are simply considered as integer vectors where the components represent the tasks, and the values represent the PEs these tasks are mapped to.

Fig. 1. A visualization of the mapping space. The axes are random proyections in the multi-dimensional space and have no direct interpretation.

Figure 1 shows a rendering of the design space of mappings for an audio filter C for Process Networks (CPN) benchmark onto the MPPA3 Coolidge architecture [16]. We generate this rendering using the methods of [17], generating a smoothening from a triangulation of a random projection of 1000 random mappings as an artistic interpretation that we can visualize with ParaView [1]. The height of the mountains and valleys in this landscape, as well as their coloring, represent the value of the execution time for the mappings being visualized. We see how the mapping space has multiple local minima and maxima, and generally a complex structure. The complexity of this structure is a direct consequence of the geometry we endow it.

In this paper we argue that we can find better geometries for the mapping space, simplifying the mapping problem by construction. We do this by considering a systematic approach to reason about the geometry of the mapping space. We also present some concrete alternative geometric structures for the mapping space, and discuss methods to find embeddings of these geometries to real vector spaces for computation. Since these embeddings can have a very high dimension, we also discuss and evaluate methods to reduce their dimension.

We show how this geometric structure can be leveraged by proposing a mapping algorithm based on the simple and well-known gradient descent method. Other algorithms which implicitly assume an underlying geometric structure also benefit from our approach, and we show how we can improve them as well. Finally, we evaluate these methods on their effect on multiple benchmarks, showing how the geometric structure plays an important role in the mapping problem and can be used to find novel mapping methods as well as improving established ones.

2 Related Work

Many flows exist that enable model-based design in a software synthesis flow [5,10,23,30,31]. In this paper we focus on the mapping problem addressed in these systems. As mentioned in the introduction, many such mapping algorithms implicitly use geometric structures of the mapping space [9,15,18,22,24]. These approaches do not explicitly model and reason about the geometry of the mapping space, this is done in an ad-hoc fashion.

In [32], Thompson and Pimentel exploit the mapping space structure explicitly, making explicit considerations of the geometry for defining operators in a genetic algorithm. These can both be seen as special cases of the methods presented in this paper, albeit for a simpler case with homogeneous architectures. In a related idea, in [33] they also introduce the concept of "shapes", which is also an explicit consideration of some geometric aspects.

The work from Richthammer and others [25–27] is very similar in nature to the applications discussed in this paper. They also aim to improve Design-Space Exploration (DSE) methods by statically exploiting the architectural structure, although the concrete structure they exploit is different. They leverage the concrete structure of NoC meshes, by considering sub-structures in the architecture.

In previous work we have considered the geometry explicitly [12] but did not apply it to design-space exploration. Similarly, in [13] we discussed some geometric aspects of Network on Chip (NoC)-based architectures. This paper can be seen as an extension on the geometric considerations in these previous works.

3 Mapping Tasks to Multicores

As motivated in the introduction, the mapping problem [19] is the decision problem of assigning physical resources (hardware) to the logical tasks and data (software) of an application. We formulate this problem mathematically as finding graph morphisms. We model the architecture as a graph $A = (V_A, E_A)$. Here, the nodes V_A represent the PEs in the architecture and annotated with core types. The edges E_A represent communication primitives [7], an abstraction that models any method for communicating between PE, like caches, scratchpad memories or Direct Memory Access (DMA). The application we model as a graph $K = (V_K, E_K)$, where the nodes represent computation tasks (actors, processes) and the edges E_K represent data flow or dependencies. We model mappings as functions $m : K \to A$, i.e. assigning physical resources to the logical ones. A mapping also needs to be consistent. If it assigns two tasks $t_1, t_2 \in V_K$ to different PEs, when these tasks exchange data (i.e., $(t_1, t_2) \in E_K$), the data communication channel needs to be mapped to a physical channel that respects the task assignment: we require that $m((t_1, t_2)) = (m(t_1), m(t_2)) \in E_A$. This condition, mathematically, means precisely that a mapping respects the graph structure of K and A. In other words, a mapping is a *morphism of graphs* $m : K \to A$.

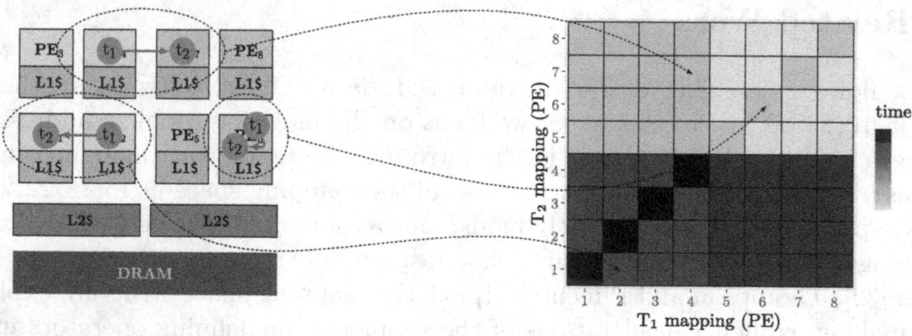

Fig. 2. An example of the mapping space for a simple two-task application.

Figure 2 depicts the mapping problem on a very simple example. The example is based on a telecom application of the E3S benchmark suite [8], chosen specifically because it consists of exactly two tasks, which allows the mapping space to be visualized in two dimensions. The mappings are plotted by encoding the mapping of each of the two tasks as the x and y coordinates of the grid, and the color of the squares in the grid encodes the (simulated) execution time on an Odroid-XU4 architecture. The actual values of the execution time are irrelevant here and have been deliberately omitted. In the figure it is clear that the minimal execution time is obtained by mapping the two tasks to two distinct Cortex-A15 (big) cores.

The example in Fig. 2 is chosen deliberately to be so simple that it can be depicted in a figure. There are exactly $8^2 = 64$ mappings in the mapping space. For the audio filter application from the introduction, this space has already $8^8 = 16777216$ mappings and finding the minimal execution time is much less tractable. In general, the mapping space has cardinality $|V_A|^{|V_K|}$, and thus grows exponentially with the number of tasks $|V_K|$. For an 85-core architecture like the

MPPA3 Coolidge [16], the mapping space of a moderately-large application with 42 tasks has more than 10^{81} possible mappings, more than there are atoms in the observable universe.

4 Metric Spaces

We endow the mapping space with a geometric structure by using the concept of metric spaces. In mathematics, metric spaces are an abstract structure that describes a space where distances can be measured. As such, it is described as a tuple (M, d), with a set M, the space, and a (non-negative) "distance" function $d : M \times M \to \mathbb{R}_{\geq 0}$, called the *metric*. To be a metric space, this distance function d has to follow the following axioms:

1. The distance of any object to itself is 0:
$$d(x, x) = 0, \text{ for all } x \in M.$$
2. The distance metric is symmetric:
$$d(x, y) = d(y, x), \text{ for all } x, y \in M.$$
3. A version of the triangle inequality:
$$d(x, z) \leq d(x, y) + d(y, z), \text{ for all } x, y, z \in M.$$

Traditionally, we encode mappings as vectors $m = \left(a_1, \dots, a_{|V_K|}\right)$ where $a_i \in V_A$ are the PEs where task i is mapped. If we interpret these vectors as being (real) vectors in $\mathbb{R}^{|V_K|}$, we can endow them with a vector distance, like the Euclidean distance $d_{\text{Euclidean}}(v, w) = \sqrt{\sum_i (v_i - w_i)^2}$. This can be generalized to other p-norms, as $d_{L_p}(v, w) = \sum_i ((|v_i - w_i|)^p)^{1/p}$, which is a norm for $p \geq 1$. For $p = 1$, this norm is also known as the Mathattan distance, in allusion to the distance between buildings in a regular mesh like the streets of Manhattan. We can endow the space of mappings with a metric also by using the Hamming distance, which counts only the number of differing entries in the vector. However, none of these metrics are ideal for the mapping space, as we will now explain.

4.1 Metrics

In the example illustrated in Fig. 3 we saw intuitively how mappings can be more or less similar. This intuitive notion clearly depends on the underlying architecture. It is the hardware architecture that determines the cost of communicating data between processes. In order to endow the space of mappings with a metric space structure, we should first do so with the architecture.

We can use the intuition behind the example to define a metric that takes latency into account this way [12]. The fundamental observation here is that in a multicore architecture, communication between different PEs takes different amounts of time. There are multiple problems with using the communication

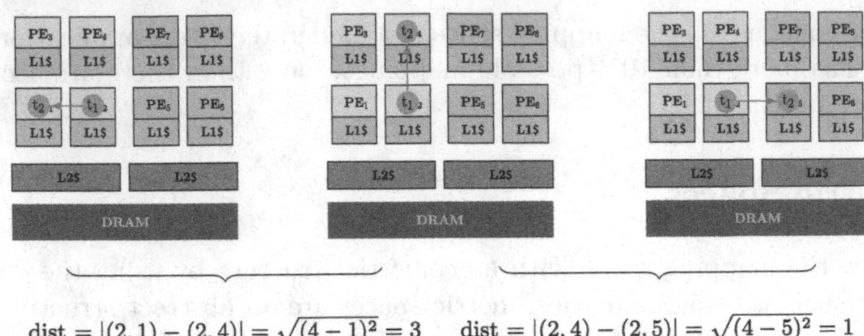

$$\text{dist} = |(2,1) - (2,4)| = \sqrt{(4-1)^2} = 3 \quad \text{dist} = |(2,4) - (2,5)| = \sqrt{(4-5)^2} = 1$$

Fig. 3. An intuitive example of distance between mappings.

time between PEs directly as a distance between PEs. Firstly, communication times depend on multiple factors: the latency and bandwidth of the communication resources used, the amount of data being sent, the (software) communication protocol, clock synchronization between hardware resources like the PEs and buses, arbitration or other contention issues, etc. Of course, we can model these to various degrees. However, the distance between PEs needs to be a fixed number and not a function of all these factors. As an approximation, however, we can use the expected latency for a package of a standardized size (e.g. 8 bytes). As an expected value, this is a fixed number, but through its statistical nature it can include as much complexity in the model as required[1].

The second issue we run into when using communication times for defining a distance is that, by definition, the distance between a point and itself has to be 0, but usually a PE has to communicate with itself using an $L1$ cache, scratchpad memory or similar, which has a small but non-zero latency. In this sense, the expected communication latency between cores is **not** a metric space distance, but it approximates one well. We propose thus to ignore this latency and set the distance to 0, to obtain the mathematical metric space structure.

Finally, this metric space structure depends strongly on the unit used to measure latency (e.g. cycles, milliseconds, etc.), as well as on the absolute speed of the communication sub-architecture. Since the goal of exposing this structure is to leverage it for algorithmic decisions like finding good mappings, it is useful to have comparable distances between different architectures. For this, we propose to norm the metric distance function such that the average distance between PEs is 1.

Put together, these principles yield the following definition:

Definition 1 (Architecture Metric Space). *Let* $A = (V_A, E_A)$ *be an architecture graph and* $\text{lat} : V_A \to V_A$ *be the expected latency between PEs. Then we set*

[1] If communication in the architecture is asymmetric, this will not define a metric. We can average the communication from p to q and from q to p to fix this, but we should probably consider this case separately.

$$d_A : V_A \times V_A, (p,q) \mapsto \begin{cases} \text{lat}(p,q), & \text{if } p \neq q \\ 0, & \text{otherwise} \end{cases} \tag{1}$$

Remark 1. For an architecture graph $A = (V_A, E_A)$, the tuple (V_A, d_A) is a metric space.

Proof. Obviously $d_A(p,p) = 0$ for all $p \in V_A$, by definition, and $d_A(p,q) > 0$ for $p \neq q$ since the expected latency between PEs is always greater than 0. For $p, q, r \in P$ we have $d_A(p,q) + d_A(q,r) \geq d_A(p,r)$ since the expected latency of moving data from p to q and then to r will always be at least as much as moving it from p to r directly.

In this way we endow M with a discrete metric space structure, with a metric that reflects the memory subsystem of the architecture, or more generally, its communication. This is the metric introduced in [12], which has some issues. In particular, it does not distinguish between core types on heterogeneous systems. To fix this, we propose an alternative metric space structure on M, by adding extra dimensions for the communication and the computation. This is fundamentally very similar to adding channels in the mapping vectors. We thus define a metric on the channels, based on the metric defined by Definition 1. The distance between two channels $c, c' \in E_A$ is defined as $|\,\text{lat}(c_1) - \text{lat}(c_2)|$ for the communication channel between the cores. We then apply a similar concept for the cores, and take relative values of the expected runtime. Disregarding the ISA or micro-architecture, we can use the frequencies as a first estimation, which is what we do here. Thus, we set the distance between two cores p, p' as $|\,\text{freq}(p) - \text{freq}(p')|$. Obviously the frequency is not the best estimation of the expected differences in execution times between PEs, but we restrict our consideration to this for the scope of this paper. Future work should focus on finding better metrics for the mapping space.

This definition would not produce a metric, since distinct cores with the same frequency will have a distance of 0, and similarly channels with the same latency. To deal with this, we add a minimal distance between distinct cores and channels (e.g. 0.1 times the distance between the next two core types).

Application Distances. To go from A to M, we can use the same principle as the L_p norms and define $d(m, m') = (\sum_i d(m_i, m'_i)^p)^{1/p}$, which can immediately be checked to be a metric on M. This way we can consider, as a metric space (embedding), the structure of A to be

$$M \underbrace{\perp \ldots \perp}_{\times |V_K|} M, \text{ i.e. } M \underbrace{\times \ldots \times}_{\times |V_K|} \times M \text{ with } d(M_i, M_j) = \{0\} \text{ for all } i \neq j. \tag{2}$$

There are multiple issues with this as well. A very crucial problem with it is that this does not consider the dependencies between tasks in the application graph A, nor does it consider how multiple tasks might be more or less relevant. Many methods can be considered to account for this fact, like having factors for the dimensions of the copies of M in the orthogonal sum.

5 Low-Distortion Embeddings

We have seen so far how we can endow the mapping space with multiple metrics $d_M : M \times M \to \mathbb{R}_{\geq 0}$ to define distances between mappings. A problem with this is that the mapping space is a discrete space, with a very large cardinality. To algorithmically do any computation in this space, e.g. in DSE, we need to iterate through the whole space. For example, we might have a mapping m_0, for which we want to find all mappings that are within a radius r of it, i.e. compute the ball $B_r(m_0)$ with radius r around m_0. For this we need to iterate over all $m \in M$ and calculate if $d_M(m_0, m) \leq r$, which is intractable for all but the simplest examples.

To deal with this, we use established methods from discrete geometry to calculate *low-distortion embeddings*. A mapping $\iota : M \hookrightarrow \mathbb{R}^n$ such that there exists a $D > 0$ with

$$D^{-1} d(x,y) \leq \|\iota(x) - \iota(y)\| \leq d(x,y) \tag{3}$$

is called an embedding with distortion D. In other words, the *relative error* of the distances is at most D. Using convex optimization [20], we can calculate a low-distortion embedding for a finite metric space. This allows us to work with vectors of real numbers which make many algorithmic tasks scalable, e.g. computing random points in a ball.

Since the size of the mapping space grows exponentially with the number of tasks and changes for every application, computing such an embedding for a large mapping space every time we want to do DSE would also be intractable. We can avoid this by using the orthogonal sum construction from Eq. 2. Given an embedding $\iota : A \hookrightarrow \mathbb{R}^k$ with distortion D for the architecture with a given metric d_A, we can construct an embedding ι^k of the mapping space defined as in Eq. 2 with distortion D [12].

The mapping space can still have a very high dimension, a problem usually called the *curse of dimensionality.* With this construction, for the metric without the extra dimensions, the dimension of the embedding ι^k is $k|V_A| = |V_K||V_A|$. The Johnson-Lindenstrauss lemma can be used to reduce the dimension with a projection [20]. We do this with an iterative method, described in Algorithm 1

Algorithm 1 exponentially increases the dimension, running `numIterationPerDim` iterations of a Johnson-Lindenstrauss transform and testing the distortion to see if a target distortion has been reached. Using this algorithm, or variants thereof, we can control the trade-off between the distance and the dimension of the embedding.

To compare the different metrics and embeddings, for each of them we calculated 1000 mappings of an audio filter benchmark from the MAPS framework [5] on the Odroid XU4 platform. For a random subset of the $1000^2 = 10^6$ pairs of mappings we calculated the (relative) distance between two mappings and the relative runtime of the simulation on these two mappings.

There is basically no correlation between mappings distance and the (relative) runtimes. Two mappings can be very far apart and have (almost) the same

Algorithm 1. Iterative dimensionality reduction via the Johnson-Lindenstrauss lemma.

input: A discrete metric space M, a low-distortion embedding $\iota : M \hookrightarrow \mathbb{R}^n$ and a target distortion D.
output: An embedding with dimension $\leq n$ and distortion at most D.

dim $\leftarrow$ 1
while **do**dim $\leq n$
  for $\_ \in$ numIterationsPerDim **do**
    $\tilde{\iota} \leftarrow$ JLReduction(ι, dim)
    $\tilde{D} \leftarrow$ CalculateDistortion($\tilde{\iota}$)
    if $\tilde{D} \leq D$ **then return** $\tilde{\iota}$
  dim $\leftarrow$ 2dim
return ι

execution time. This seems very plausible if we consider the symmetries of the problem [14], where multiple mappings are equivalent yet distinct. There are also other similarities in mappings. For example, audio filter benchmark computes an Fast Fourier Transform (FFT) and inverse FFT (IFFT) which are virtually identical, yet not precisely so.

A perhaps better assessment of the metrics is to ask what is the *maximal* relative execution time possible for a given distance. While we understand why two similar mappings that are far apart will have similar results, we would expect two mappings that are close to each other to have similar execution times with a good metric. To test this, we just consider the maximal relative execution time for two mappings which are (at most) the given distance apart. In the figure, the metrics described in this section are labeled as follows: We call `SimpleVector` the Euclidean norm on the mappings described as simple vectors. The metric based on the latencies as motivated from Fig. 3 we denote as `Embedding`, whereas we add the annotation `ED` for the metric with extra dimensions which accounts for heterogeneous PEs.

Figure 4 shows this maximal relative execution times for the data of the Odroid XU4. It also includes a linear regression of the points for each metric and embedding. We can see that indeed, most of the metrics are pretty good as an *upper bound* on the relative runtime, as seen by the linear behavior on the figure.

The Odroid XU4 architecture is comparatively small, which obviously has consequences for the mapping space. The smaller (discrete) space results in an embedding space that is not as high-dimensional. Figure 5 shows how this situation changes for the MPPA3 Coolidge.

Similar to the case for the Odroid XU4, Fig. 6 shows the same comparison with the maximal run-time difference for the MPPA3 Coolidge. Again we see that many metrics seem to be a decent bound for the difference in execution time, although less so than for the simple Odroid XU4 platform. The Euclidean norm on the simple vector mappings, for example, is considerably worse than in this case than in the Odroid XU4. We can quantify more precisely how good

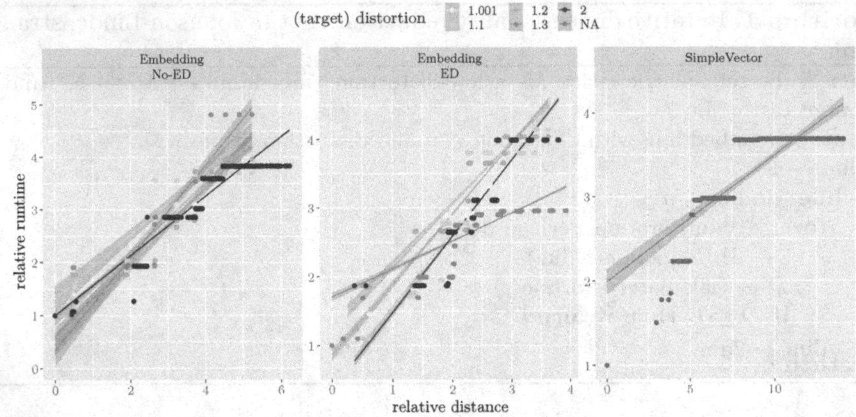

Fig. 4. Comparison of multiple distance metrics as predictors of the *maximal* run-time difference on the Odroid XU4 platform.

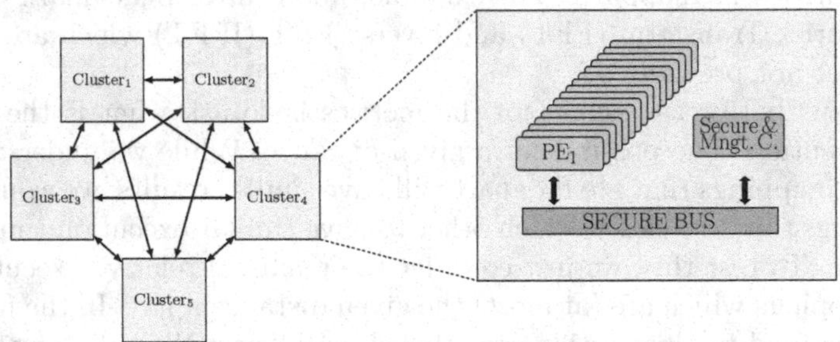

Fig. 5. The topology of the MPPA3 Coolidge platform, which consists of five clusters fully connected with a NoC, each cluster consisting of 16 identical general-purpose cores, as well as a secure and management core.

metrics are as a bound for the execution time by comparing the R^2 value as goodness of fit assessment of the depicted linear regressions.

Figure 7 shows the R^2 value, comparing the predictive power of the different distance metrics and their embeddings. Here it is also very clear that the Euclidean norm on simple vectors is not so good for the MPPA3 Cooldige, while it is comparable to other metrics in the Odroid XU4. We also see how the curse of dimensionality yields a trade-off not only in the computation time (for larger-dimensional spaces), but also in the predictive quality of the different norms. This is more visible on the MPPA3 Coolidge. We see that the trade-off between the predictive power and the distortion is not very clear from this preliminary results. Future work should investigate this trade-off more in-depth.

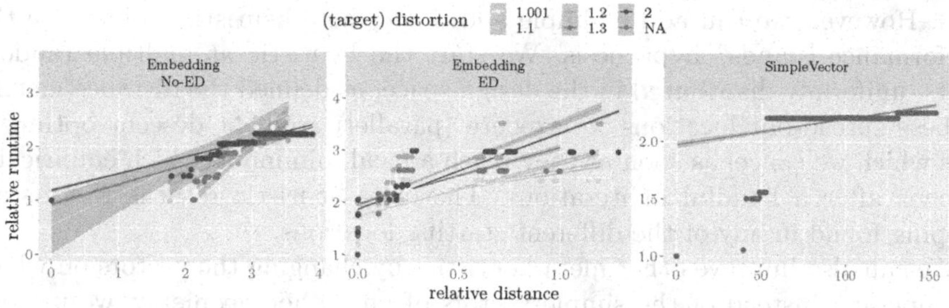

Fig. 6. Comparison of multiple distance metrics as predictors of the *maximal* run-time difference on the MPPA3 Coolidge platform.

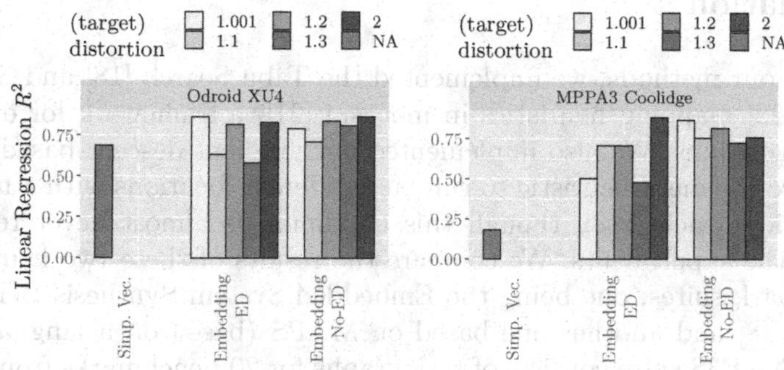

Fig. 7. Comparison of the predictive power of multiple distance metrics.

6 A Heuristic for Design-Space Exploration

Having defined a geometric interpretation for the mapping space, we show how we can leverage this in DSE. For this, we proposed a simple mapping algorithm based on the geometric structure of the mapping space. We discuss and evaluate our methods on the example objective of execution time, but do not use its structure directly. As such, we expect them to generalize to other objectives, like energy consumption.

Our algorithm is based on an observation of the geometry mapping space. The design spaces of mappings seem to consist of multiple islands of performance with similar properties, separated by poorly-performing mappings. Our "performance islands" hypothesis implies the mapping space is full of local minima. Guiding a local search towards an optimum should thus not be as conducive to good results. Instead, we can use a simple and fast meta-heuristic to find a local minimum quickly and apply it to multiple points spread around the design space's geometry. As meta-heuristic for finding local minima we use the well-known gradient descent optimization algorithm with the momentum method [28]. For the step-size we use the Barzilai-Borwein [2] method.

In its regular form, this heuristic will quickly get stuck in a local minimum and produce poor mapping results, as confirmed by experiments (which we omit here). However, we can add a simple additional meta-heuristic to leverage the "performance islands" hypothesis. We start the heuristic at multiple random points, uniformly distributed in the design space, as defined the distance metric. In these spread-out locations we execute (parallel) gradient descent optimizations which we cancel as soon as they reach a local minimum, which empirically happens after a handful of iterations. The meta-heuristic returns the fastest mapping found in any of the different starting locations.

We can also improve other meta-heuristics by changing the vectors on which they operate, instead of the simple vectors of an ad-hoc geometry, we use our embeddings [12].

7 Evaluation

To evaluate our methods, we implemented the Tabu Search [18] and Simulated Annealing [22] mapping heuristics in mocasin [21], a framework for evaluating mapping algorithms. We also implemented our gradient-descent-based mapper. We configure the meta-heuristic to run on 5 different locations with a maximum of 20 iterations each, even though this maximum is almost never reached in practice in the experiments. We compare the results of these two heuristics on two benchmark suites, one being the Embedded System Synthesis Benchmarks Suite (E3S) [8] and another one based on MAPS (based on a language called CPN) [5]. The E3S suite consists of task graphs for 20 benchmarks from 5 different domains: auto-indust., networking, telecom, consumer and office-automation. The CPN benchmarks, on the other hand, are three benchmarks: a two-channel audio filter, a Histogram of Oriented Gradients (HOG)-based pedestrian recognition application and speaker recognition application [4]. For each meta-heuristic, each representation and each benchmark application, we measure the results of 10 runs with different random seeds.

Figure 8 shows the results of these experiments for the Odroid XU4 platform. The columns labeled as `SimpleVector` correspond to the Euclidean norm on the simple mapping vectors used commonly in most mapping scenarios. On the other hand, the label `MetricSpaceEmbedding` corresponds to the algorithms using the embedding as discussed here. Concretely, the embedding of the metric with the extra dimensions, without dimensionality reduction.

The logarithmic scale of the figure shows two different comparison criteria, the relative results of the mapping and the relative exploration time of the DSE. Both are normed to the results of the simulated annealing heuristic with the `SimpleVector` representation. For the DSE results, we summarize execution time as the geometric mean of the relative times of the benchmark, as simulated. The other metric is the relative exploration time. This is the time that the DSE needed to explore the design space. The error bars show the variance between the different benchmarks and the 10 different runs with different random seeds.

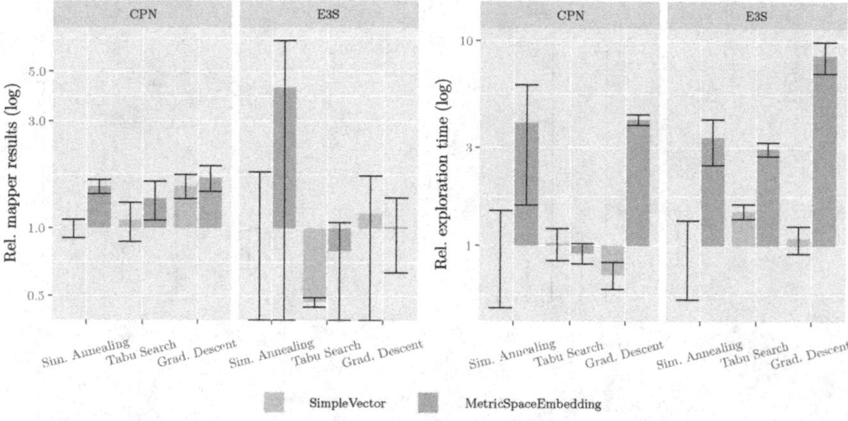

Fig. 8. The effect of embedding-based representations on the Odroid XU4 platform.

We see that changing geometry of the design space is not very effective for this simple architecture, although it does show more improvement for the E3S benchmarks. The gradient descent meta-heuristic with our performance island hypothesis is on par with the other meta-heuristics, which is already a strong result given the simplicity of the algorithm. As was seen before on the comparison of the metrics, the Euclidean norm on the simple vector representation is a decent metric for this space, which explains the results. On the other hand, using embeddings increases the execution time. This is because of the large dimension, and the necessity to do a nearest-neighbor approximation. In future work, applying methods for improving nearest-neighbor algorithms like in the Annoy library[2] could improve this time. We also did not reduce the dimension for this evaluation, to see the effects on the algorithm. In future work this trade-off could be exploited to improve the execution time.

Figure 9 summarizes the results of this experiments for the MPPA3 Coolidge platform, for which we showed that the metric space structure of our embedding-based representations is better than the canonical metric in the `SimpleVector` representation. We see that the results of the exploration are significantly better for both meta-heuristics with the representations based on this better distance metric. More importantly, the gradient-descent-based heuristic performs considerably better even. In some cases, the results of this simple heuristic are *on average* over an order of magnitude better than the other unmodified meta-heuristics. This is perhaps a statement about how poorly established meta-heuristics perform on a very complex design space, more so than a testament in favor of our gradient-descent-based heuristic. It shows thus, that our geometric representations are particularly useful in more complex architectures. Additionally, the effect on the exploration time is much less pronounced in this case, since the overhead of the linear algebra involved becomes a smaller portion of the total exploration time.

[2] https://github.com/spotify/annoy.

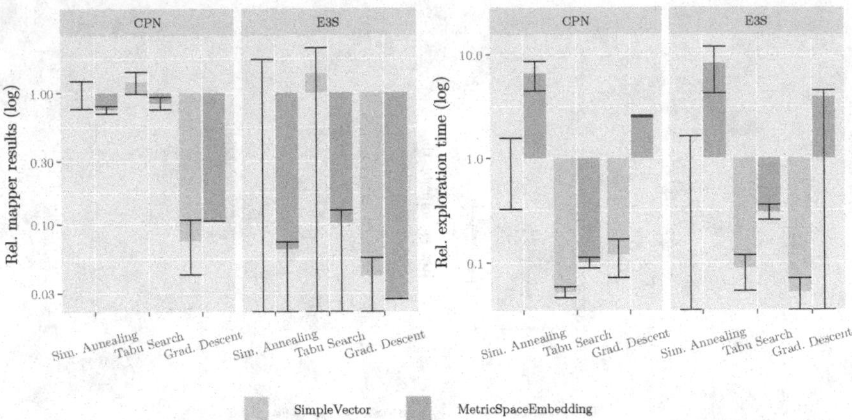

Fig. 9. The effect of embedding-based representations on the MPPA3 Coolidge platform.

8 Conclusions

In this paper we have seen how to endow the space of mappings to multicores with a geometric interpretation, and defined some metrics that might be better suited to describe the space than the ad-hoc simple vector structure used commonly. We have seen from experiments that this structure helps especially well in the DSE of more complex architectures. Importantly, it allows us to use simple algorithms like gradient descent for mapping, which otherwise was infeasible. For two different sets of benchmark suites, our heuristic armed with this geometric interpretation managed to find good mappings much more reliably than established heuristics on the complex architecture topology of the MPPA3 Coolidge. Mapping heuristics based on tabu search and simulated annealing produced mappings about an order of magnitude worse *on average* for this architecture.

We believe the main contribution of this paper is the geometric view of the mapping space, not the metrics themselves. Future work should focus on finding better metrics. This might be especially conducive to machine learning algorithms for mapping, which usually work with embeddings as the ones described in this paper.

References

1. Ahrens, J., Geveci, B., Law, C.: ParaView: an end-user tool for large data visualization. Vis. Handbook **717**(8) (2005)
2. Barzilai, J., Borwein, J.M.: Two-point step size gradient methods. IMA J. Numer. Anal. **8**(1), 141–148 (1988)
3. Bhattacharyya, S.S., Murthy, P.K., Lee, E.A.: Software Synthesis from Dataflow Graphs, vol. 360. Springer, Heidelberg (2012)
4. Bouraoui, H., Castrillon, J., Jerad, C.: Comparing dataflow and OpenMP programming for speaker recognition applications. In: Proceedings of PARMA-DITAM 2019, pp. 1–6 (2019)

5. Castrillon, J., Leupers, R., Ascheid, G.: MAPS: mapping concurrent dataflow applications to heterogeneous MPSoCs. IEEE Trans. Industr. Inf. **9**(1), 527–545 (2011)
6. Castrillon, J., Sheng, W., Leupers, R.: Trends in embedded software synthesis. In: 2011 International Conference on Embedded Computer Systems: Architectures, Modeling and Simulation, pp. 347–354. IEEE (2011)
7. Castrillon, J., Tretter, A., Leupers, R., Ascheid, G.: Communication-aware mapping of KPN applications onto heterogeneous MPSoCs. In: DAC Design Automation Conference 2012, pp. 1262–1267. IEEE (2012)
8. Dick, R.: Embedded systems synthesis benchmark suite (e3s) (2008). http://ziyang.eecs.umich.edu/~dickrp/e3s/
9. Erbas, C., Cerav-Erbas, S., Pimentel, A.D.: Multiobjective optimization and evolutionary algorithms for the application mapping problem in multiprocessor system-on-chip design. IEEE Trans. Evol. Comput. **10**(3), 358–374 (2006)
10. Erbas, C., Pimentel, A.D., Thompson, M., Polstra, S.: A framework for system-level modeling and simulation of embedded systems architectures. EURASIP J. Embed. Syst. **2007**, 1–11 (2007)
11. Goens, A., Khasanov, R., Hähnel, M., Smejkal, T., Härtig, H., Castrillon, J.: Tetris: a multi-application run-time system for predictable execution of static mappings. In: Proceedings of the 20th International Workshop on Software and Compilers for Embedded Systems (SCOPES 2017). SCOPES 2017 (2017)
12. Goens, A., Menard, C., Castrillon, J.: On the representation of mappings to multicores. In: Proceedings of the IEEE 12th International Symposium on Embedded Multicore/Many-Core Systems-on-Chip (MCSoC 2018) (2018)
13. Goens, A., Menard, C., Castrillon, J.: On compact mappings for multicore systems. In: Pnevmatikatos, D.N., Pelcat, M., Jung, M. (eds.) SAMOS 2019. LNCS, vol. 11733, pp. 325–335. Springer, Cham (2019). https://doi.org/10.1007/978-3-030-27562-4_23
14. Goens, A., Siccha, S., Castrillon, J.: Symmetry in software synthesis. ACM Trans. Archit. Code Optim. (TACO)
15. Hempel, G., Goens, A., Asmus, J., Castrillon, J., Sbalzarini, I.F.: Robust mapping of process networks to many-core systems using bio-inspired design centering. In: Proceedings of the 20th International Workshop on Software and Compilers for Embedded Systems (SCOPES 2017). SCOPES 2017 (2017)
16. inc, K.: Kalray mppa3 coolidge anouncement (2020). https://www.kalrayinc.com/release-of-third-generation-mppa-processor-coolidge/
17. Li, H., Xu, Z., Taylor, G., Studer, C., Goldstein, T.: Visualizing the loss landscape of neural nets. In: Neural Information Processing Systems (2018)
18. Manolache, S., Eles, P., Peng, Z.: Task mapping and priority assignment for soft real-time applications under deadline miss ratio constraints. ACM Trans. Embedded Comput. Syst. (TECS) **7**(2), 1–35 (2008)
19. Marwedel, P., et al.: Mapping of applications to MPSoCs. In: 2011 Proceedings of the Ninth IEEE/ACM/IFIP International Conference on Hardware/Software Codesign and System Synthesis (CODES+ ISSS), pp. 109–118. IEEE (2011)
20. Matoušek, J.: Lectures on Discrete Geometry. GTM, vol. 212. Springer, New York (2002). https://doi.org/10.1007/978-1-4613-0039-7
21. Menard, C., et al.: Mocasin - rapid prototyping of rapid prototyping tools: a framework for exploring new approaches in mapping software to heterogeneous multi-cores. In: Proceedings of the 13th RAPIDO Workshop on Rapid Simulation and Performance Evaluation: Methods and Tools, Co-located with 16th International Conference on High-Performance and Embedded Architectures and Compilers (HiPEAC). RAPIDO 2021. ACM, New York, January 2021

22. Orsila, H., Kangas, T., Salminen, E., Hämäläinen, T.D., Hännikäinen, M.: Automated memory-aware application distribution for multi-processor system-on-chips. J. Syst. Archit. **53**(11), 795–815 (2007)
23. Pelcat, M., Desnos, K., Heulot, J., Guy, C., Nezan, J.F., Aridhi, S.: Preesm: a dataflow-based rapid prototyping framework for simplifying multicore DSP programming. In: 2014 6th European Embedded Design in Education and Research Conference (EDERC), pp. 36–40. IEEE (2014)
24. Quan, W., Pimentel, A.D.: Towards exploring vast MPSoC mapping design spaces using a bias-elitist evolutionary approach. In: 2014 17th Euromicro Conference on Digital System Design. IEEE (2014)
25. Richthammer, V., Fassnacht, F., Glaß, M.: Search-space decomposition for system-level design space exploration of embedded systems. ACM Trans. Des. Autom. Electron. Syst. (TODAES) **25**(2), 1–32 (2020)
26. Richthammer, V., Glaß, M.: On search-space restriction for design space exploration of multi-/many-core systems. In: MBMV (2018)
27. Richthammer, V., Glaß, M.: Efficient search-space encoding for system-level design space exploration of embedded systems. In: 2019 IEEE 13th International Symposium on Embedded Multicore/Many-Core Systems-on-Chip (MCSoC), pp. 273–280. IEEE (2019)
28. Rumelhart, D.E., Hinton, G.E., Williams, R.J.: Learning representations by back-propagating errors. Nature **323**(6088), 533–536 (1986)
29. Singh, A.K., Shafique, M., Kumar, A., Henkel, J.: Mapping on multi/many-core systems: survey of current and emerging trends. In: 2013 50th ACM/EDAC/IEEE Design Automation Conference (DAC), pp. 1–10. IEEE (2013)
30. Stuijk, S., Geilen, M., Basten, T.: A predictable multiprocessor design flow for streaming applications with dynamic behaviour. In: 2010 13th Euromicro Conference on Digital System Design: Architectures, Methods and Tools. IEEE (2010)
31. Thiele, L., Bacivarov, I., Haid, W., Huang, K.: Mapping applications to tiled multiprocessor embedded systems. In: Seventh International Conference on Application of Concurrency to System Design (ACSD 2007), pp. 29–40. IEEE (2007)
32. Thompson, M., Pimentel, A.D.: Exploiting domain knowledge in system-level MPSoC design space exploration. J. Syst. Archit. **59**, 351–360 (2013)
33. Weichslgartner, A., Wildermann, S., Götzfried, J., Freiling, F., Glaß, M., Teich, J.: Design-time/run-time mapping of security-critical applications in heterogeneous MPSoCs. In: Proceedings of the 19th International Workshop on Software and Compilers for Embedded Systems, pp. 153–162 (2016)

Novel CPU Architectures and Applications

RT-LIFE: Portable RISC-V Interface for Real-Time Lightweight Security Enforcement

Christoph Spang(✉), Florian Meisel, and Andreas Koch

Embedded Systems and Applications Group, TU Darmstadt, Darmstadt, Germany
{spang,koch}@esa.tu-darmstadt.de
https://www.esa.informatik.tu-darmstadt.de

Abstract. With the ever-expanding attack surface of low-cost processors in IoT applications, the interest in lightweight hardware support for improving their security is growing. While industry has already adopted mostly static low-overhead mitigation approaches against code-*injection* attacks, the race against code-*reuse* attacks is not yet over. One commonly proposed measure against code-reuse attacks aims to enforce runtime-dynamic integrity. In contrast to runtime-dynamic remote attestation, which is limited by its periodic attestation interval (possibly hours or weeks), runtime-dynamic integrity enforcement performs runtime-integrity checking in parallel to the actual execution. This allows very short attack response times, ideally stopping all evil instructions in flight from actually taking effect. To guarantee a prevention-in-time, one requirement is a low latency trace of uncommitted instructions. This typically would require a deep and core-specific integration. As an abstraction layer, we present our highly portable Real-Time Lightweight Integrity enForcement intErface (RT-LIFE), which is optimized to provide the core's state (uncommitted instructions) to an arbitrary runtime-dynamic low-latency Security Enforcement Unit (SecEU) as early as possible, while minimizing the interface's area and clock frequency penalties. We demonstrate RT-LIFE for six very different RISC-V cores together with our initial control-flow-integrity-enforcing SecEU DExIE, discuss the hardware architecture and its timing in detail, and finally provide an open-source release of RT-LIFE.

Keywords: Hardware security · Security monitoring · Portable uncommitted instruction tracing · Runtime-dynamic integrity · Real-time · IoT · RISC-V · Attack prevention · Code-reuse attacks · Open-source

1 Introduction

General-purpose processors are vulnerable to different types of runtime attacks. One sub-class of these are sophisticated and at the same time practical code-reuse attacks, which cannot be mitigated by traditional techniques such as read-only

© Springer Nature Switzerland AG 2022
A. Orailoglu et al. (Eds.): SAMOS 2021, LNCS 13227, pp. 179–194, 2022.
https://doi.org/10.1007/978-3-031-04580-6_12

memory, Write ⊕ Execute, or Address Space Layout Randomization [27]. Code-reuse attacks do not inject malicious code, but execute existing code gadgets in a sequence not intended by the developer. This includes Return-into-libc, Return- and Jump-Oriented Programming (RoP, JoP) Control Flow attacks [1,9,29].

Without injecting new code instructions, Return-into-libc attacks exploit memory errors such as buffer overflows to replace the return address on a call stack to target on another subroutine [9]. RoP attacks extend this concept, and collect a potentially large number of code snippets, which are then concatenated and executed in an unintended order via manipulated return addresses [29]. Besides memory-safe programming languages, which trade performance for security [25], Return-into-libc and RoP attacks can be mitigated by storing a duplicate of the original return address on a shadow call stack, to be validated at return time [5,7,23,30].

JoP attacks further extend the concept of RoP, but place their dispatcher gadget in heap memory [1]. By manipulating forward edges, JoP attacks bypass RoP countermeasures such as a shadow call stack. Beyond software solutions [33], one common mitigation approach is using a hardware monitor to safeguard inter- and intra-function Control Flow Integrity at runtime [7,21,24,28,32]. Depending on the attacker, this includes direct and indirect Control Flow (CF) [17,20,26].

Such a hardware monitor's [3] main functionality can be either deeply integrated into a core's pipeline [5,6,24], or in an on-chip module [7,23,32], or in a separate off-chip device, e.g. connected via a debug interface [4,18].

In-pipeline monitors offer low-latency, but impose invasive changes to the pipeline, caches, memory, and executable binary [5,6,24]. On-chip and off-chip solutions are typically trace-based, and require only minimally-invasive changes (signal taps, stall, reset, interrupt). Off-chip monitors leave the entire SoC unchanged, but suffer from limited transmission data rates, data drops, and longer latency [4,18]. Despite their tighter integration, many on-chip monitors cannot fully achieve short detection latencies. E.g. PHMon [7] evaluates only *fully-committed* instructions, which potentially cannot be reverted or aborted after detection. Additionally, PHMon relies on queues (2048 entries) and has multiple stages itself, thus no short detection is possible. This is potentially insecure, as an attack's impact may occur earlier than the monitor's delayed reaction, thereby circumventing the attack prevention capability. PHMon's design choice is a trade-off between low-invasiveness (tapping only the final stage) and performance (high F_{max}, no stalls) at the cost of latency-related security. However, PHMon gives an example (Heartbleed) where its detection latency is sufficient and network information leakage still *can* be prevented.

As an alternative, our prior work Dynamic Execution and Integrity Engine (DExIE) is an on-chip real-time SecEU for global and local control flow integrity enforcement [31] that is capable of stopping ongoing attacks early within short and guaranteed latency. To fulfill this guarantee, it must be supplied with a low-latency trace of early uncommitted instructions.

This trace is realized by RT-LIFE (in this work and in [31]). As a security monitoring interface built for attack prevention, RT-LIFE is the first portable interface providing an attached Security Enforcement Unit (SecEU) such as

DExIE sufficient time to reliably make its decision **(Decision Latency, DL)** to actually prevent illegal instructions from having any externally visible effects (Fig. 1). To this end, RT-LIFE retrieves the relevant signals of *uncommitted instructions* from the pipeline as early as possible and forwards them with low **Capture Latency (CL)** to the SecEU. The feedback loop (CL+DL) including the SecEU should be faster than the processor. No or only very few extra stall cycles are introduced into the regular pipeline, when the SecEU is operating (Sec. 8). If a SecEU introduces stall cycles, they can be fully-predictable at compile time, as this allows the tight Worst Case Execution Time (WCET) computations that are crucial for real-time applications.

After focusing on existing related interfaces (Sect. 2), Sect. 3 introduces RT-LIFE's security model and timings. In order to discuss requirements, Sect. 4 presents a case-study using our SecEU (DExIE). Section 5 explains RT-LIFE's behavior. The next section sets the design considerations (Sect. 6) which are followed by the concrete RT-LIFE implementations (Sect. 7). The final sections contain the evaluation (Sect. 8) and conclusion (Sect. 9).

Key Contributions

- Whereas existing portable tracing interfaces forward only fully-committed instructions, RT-LIFE reduces the latency by tracing *uncommitted* instructions in early pipeline states. Ideally, and also depending on the attached SecEU, this would allow to catch any malicious instruction in flight (and prevent it from being committed) without any extra stall cycles.
- We re-use our prior work DExIE to provide a practical use-case for RT-LIFE. As a trade-off between latency-related security, performance and portability, DExIE guarantees to stop any illegal CF in time and before any (directly) subsequent malicious and potentially irreversible Memory-Mapped I/O (MMIO) write access will be committed (take effect).
- We explain our hardware architecture and the given RISC-V cores in detail to facilitate reproducibility. We also publish our work in an open source repository [8]. This is an initial step to flexibly combine a variety of future attack-prevention SecEUs with different cores.

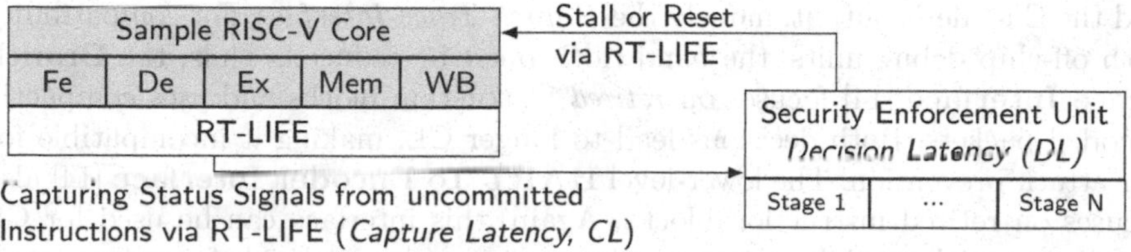

Fig. 1. Feedback loop for a generic RT-LIFE-enhanced *RISC-V* core and a generic SecEU. If the loop's accumulated latency (CL+DL) is *longer* than the core's latency to fully execute the first harmful instruction, stalls can be issued to halt the core, increasing the time interval available for detection and thus preventing an attack in time.

2 Related Work

We differentiate between open-loop *monitoring* for debugging and tracing purposes, and closed-loop security *enforcement* for attack prevention. Whereas the latter requires tight timing, monitoring does not. All interfaces discussed below are designed for monitoring only. As both use-cases require similar signals, we discuss which available standard RISC-V interfaces could be suitable for enforcement as well.

The **RISC-V Formal Interface (RVFI)** [13] contains a number of signals intended for formal verification. We used RVFI for an early draft monitoring unit. However, the RVFI focuses on *retired instructions* and only provides one global valid (*rvfi_valid*) signal for all captured data. Instead of directly forwarding captured data, earlier stages's signal values need to be delayed until the instruction reaches the pipeline's final stage. An earlier capture would require individual valid signals, which are not covered by the standard. Thus enforcement and attack prevention of an instruction is impossible. Stalling any pipeline stage would not solve the issue, as it equally delays an instruction and its CL, thus cannot increase the available DL. With RFVI, an attack would only be detected *after* occurring, but could not be prevented in time. Additionally, RVFI does not integrate stall control signals, which are, under some conditions, necessary to fulfill our security guarantees.

The **RISC-V Debug Specification** [12] describes debugging interfaces for RISC-V processors. The execution of a Hardware Thread (HART) can be paused via explicit breakpoint instructions or debugger triggers. The debugger then has access to the state of the HART, including the Program Counter (PC) and registers. The interface would support our intended security guarantees for enforcement. However, continuous single-stepping would be necessary for capturing the instruction before execution, resulting in a massive performance drop. Therefore, we do not see this as a reasonable choice for SecEUs, except for very lightweight applications *without* real-time requirements.

In contrast to the RISC-V Debug Specification, the **RISC-V Trace Specification** [14] is designed for execution tracing without the externally induced stalls of single-stepping. However, compared to RT-LIFE, it focuses exclusively on CF. The specification differentiates between the *HART to Encoder Interface* and the Encoder's output, namely the *Branch Trace Interface.* For compatibility with off-chip debug units, the bandwidth must be reduced. Thus, the **Branch Trace Interface** [14] focuses on *retired* instruction blocks and uses compactly encoded packets. Both decisions lead to longer CL, making it incompatible for our attack prevention. The lower-level **HART To Encoder Interface** [14] also focuses on retired instruction blocks. Again, this interface can be used for CF *monitoring* without tight timing requirements, but is unsuitable for *enforcement.*

Although one could use other interfaces for monitoring, there is no other option, which forwards *uncommitted* instructions. Hence, none of the existing interfaces is suitable for analyzing and eventually stopping the currently ongoing (possibly malicious) instruction before it will be committed.

3 Fundamentals

3.1 RT-LIFE's Security Model

Attacker Model: Whereas the specific *Threat Model* defended against depends on the attached SecEU unit, RT-LIFE is designed to thwart an attacker who has access to the core's state and can arbitrarily alter CF, register write instructions, and memory store instructions [1,9,20,29].

Guarantees: With constant and short CL, RT-LIFE provides the core's current state early and thus allows a long DL to the SecEU attached to the core. RT-LIFE's signals provide support for trace-based SecEUs [3] that require the core's current status. This includes SecEUs that support a broad range of security policies, including Control Flow (CF), Data Flow (DF), Memory Security, and Value Invariant Enforcement [3,7]. With the information captured by RT-LIFE, attached SecEUs can guarantee to *prevent* illegal instructions from execution, often without incurring additional pipeline stalls.

Assumptions: RT-LIFE is intended to support mitigating code-reuse attacks, it thus monitors the dynamic execution of instructions in the core. As we assume read-only memory (enforced via a Memory Protection Unit - MPU, or static partitioning), RT-LIFE does not perform static (memory) integrity attestation (against code injection attacks).

3.2 Decision Latency for CF, DF and Memory Attack Prevention

To our current knowledge, all existing interfaces (Sect. 2) have CLs that are too long, leading to the remaining DL between capture and an attack with real-world impact to be too short to make a decision (Fig. 1). Stalling each instruction to meet DL requirements is possible, but this would slow down code execution. Instead, we optimize the interface as well as the SecEU for a *reduced* latency, where additional stalls are avoided, and will only be introduced for handling edge cases.

We define a **successful attack** by its immediate real-world impact, which can be caused by **(A)** MMIO write instructions, or **(B)** tampering with Control and Status Registers (CSR). These attacks should be stopped before they take effect. Other scenarios without immediate real-world impact, e.g., combinatorial General Purpose Register (GPR) writes, are categorized as less harmful, and can be safely stopped just *after* the manipulation occurred. In closer detail, four latency guarantees, grouped by **MMIO (A)** and **CSR (B)** tampering, have been implemented:

(A1) If a manipulated CF Instruction (CFI) is followed by a memory instruction potentially writing to an attached MMIO device, RT-LIFE guarantees to provide a DL of at least one clock cycle to the SecEU to make its decision. **(B1)** If a manipulated CFI is followed by a malicious CSR register write, RT-LIFE guarantees to provide a DL of one cycle to the SecEU. **(A2)** For a malicious memory write access, RT-LIFE can guarantee to capture its value and address, such that a SecEU can combinatorially (DL = 0) decide and prevent the write from taking effect. **(B2)** In the RISC-V ISA, a CSR cannot be directly written. Instead, its new value is *moved* from a GPR. Therefore, we are focusing on GPR integrity. At the latest safe moment, RT-LIFE allows stopping code execution directly *after* a GPR is maliciously written, with a guaranteed combinatorial DL. But this is still sufficiently early to *prevent* a subsequent CSR write from actually taking effect.

4 DExIE - A Sample Security Enforcement Unit

Before further elaborating on RT-LIFE's details, this section introduces our sample implementation of a SecEU, which itself is called DExIE - Dynamic Execution Integrity Engine [31]. It requires RT-LIFE's low latency, and already uses the CF-focused subset of RT-LIFE's functionality for a low-overhead fine-grained Control Flow Enforcement. A forward edge in a Control Flow Graph's (CFG) corresponds either to a jump, branch or call instruction. Backward edges always correspond to return instructions. DExIE enforces forward edges via auto-generated CFG- or profiling-based (for increased granularity) Enforcement FSMs (EFSM). In contrast, backward edges are safeguarded by an EFSM-state-agnostic Shadow Stack. Each subroutine corresponds to one EFSM at a time. Branches and jumps correspond to the current function's EFSM-internal transitions. For calls and returns, that function's EFSM becomes active. Per call, the Shadow Stack holds return address, return EFSM, and return EFSM state.

After discussing DExIE's security model, which employs a subset of RT-LIFE's features, the DExIE tool-chain and architecture are explained, and the realization of security guarantees as well as DExIE's behavior is presented.

4.1 DExIE's Security Model

Threat Model: DExIE is fitted for (industrial) real-time IoT devices with MMIO peripherals. The device's firmware includes memory unsafe languages such as C with possible vulnerabilities that are (remotely) exploitable.

Attacker Model: The attacker (in)directly and arbitrarily tampers with control flow instructions [1,9,29].

Guarantees: For any illegal CFI, DExIE immediately resets the core, thus prevents it from executing any subsequent memory write instruction, which might have a potentially irreversible real-world impact. As EFSMs are stored and protected in on-chip SRAM and no caching is used, DExIE guarantees to react in *constant* time. DExIE and RT-LIFE operate faster than the attached core can fully execute a memory write instruction following an illegal CF.

Assumptions: By exploiting a software weakness (e.g., a huge overflow), an attacker could potentially overwrite a function's code with new instructions which do not include *any* CF, or have *identical* CF, and thus would not violate any EFSM imposed by DExIE. Therefore, we assume read-only program memory (e.g., enforced via a MPU).

4.2 DExIE's Fundamentals

Figure 2, shows DExIE's key idea. First, the sample application C-Code (a) is compiled into RISC-V assembly code (b). The DExIE [31] compiler reconstructs the program structure, to build and interconnect the CFG-based function-individual EFSMs (c), that are actually being used for enforcement [2].

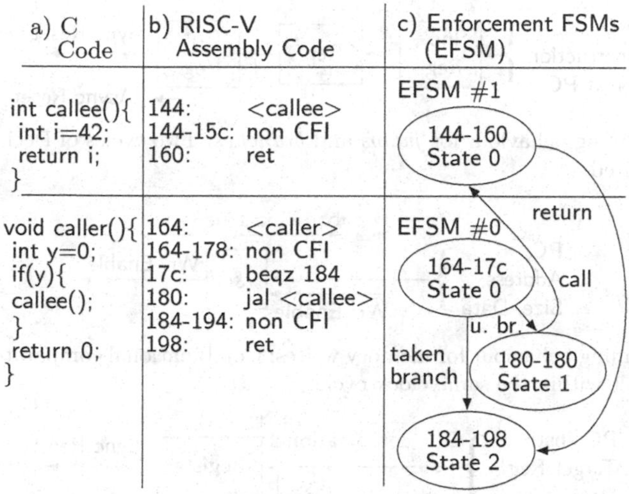

a) C Code	b) RISC-V Assembly Code	c) Enforcement FSMs (EFSM)

int callee(){
int i=42;
return i;
}
	144: <callee>
	144-15c: non CFI
	160: ret
		EFSM #1
		144-160 State 0

void caller(){
int y=0;
if(y){
callee();
}
return 0;
}
	164: <caller>
	164-178: non CFI
	17c: beqz 184
	180: jal <callee>
	184-194: non CFI
	198: ret
		EFSM #0
		164-17c State 0
		180-180 State 1
		184-198 State 2
		return
		call
		u. br.
		taken branch

Fig. 2. A standard compiler compiles C-code (a) into Assembly code (b), which gets automatically converted into interconnected enforcement FSMs (c)

4.3 DExIE's Behavior and Interface Requirements

CF monitoring is limited by the frequency of CFI in the executable. We call the number of CFI per clock cycle the *CFRate*. DExIE's microarchitecture can cope with a CFRate of one CFI per cycle for calls and returns, and still achieves a single clock cycle of DL (Fig. 3a). For branches and jumps, the required DL is two cycles, thus dropping the maximum CFRate that can be handled without stalling to 1/2 (Fig. 3b). Stalls are only needed for chained branches and jumps in combination with a successful branch prediction. For DExIE, the ideal interface to the core would collect all required CF-related data (PC, Instruction, Next PC), write it into a register, and ideally leave two (or more) cycles of DL headroom. For memory writes, combinational comparators will validate values and addresses against DExIE's statefully loaded constraints (Fig. 3c). For GPR writes, DExIE will stop execution directly *after* the write occurred (Fig. 3d).

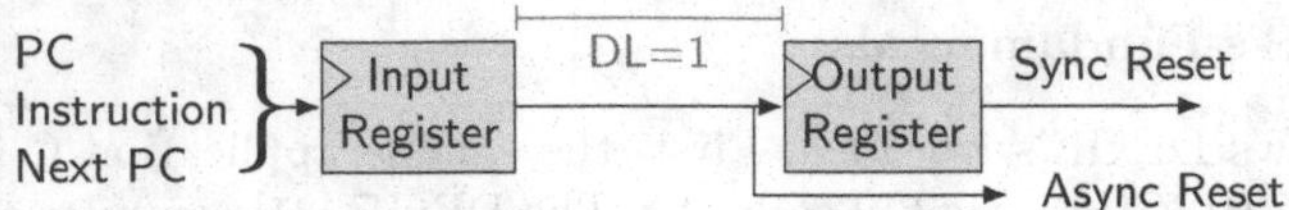

(a) DExIE's timing behaviour for *calls* and *returns*: After RT-LIFE's signal capture, which happens before the input register, DExIE needs one clock cycle of DL for its decision to reach the output register.

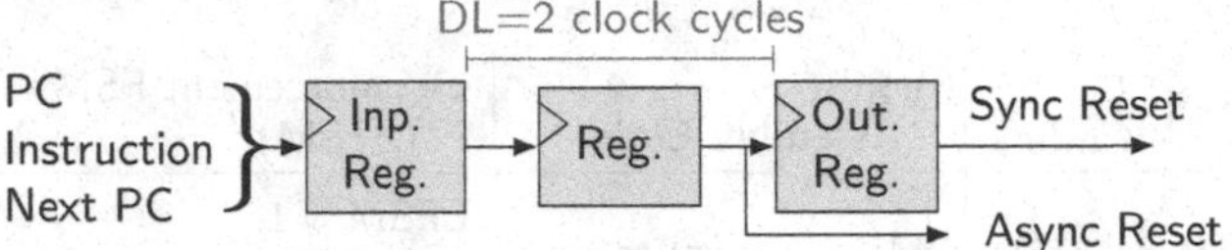

(b) DExIE's timing behaviour for *jumps* and *branches*: Two cycles of Decision Latency (DL) are required.

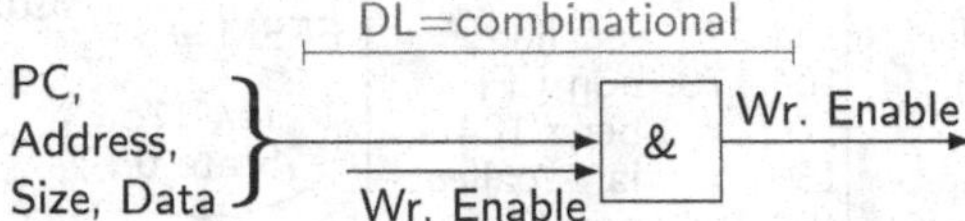

(c) DExIE's timing behaviour for memory writes: Combinational comparators for memory writes react within the same clock cycle.

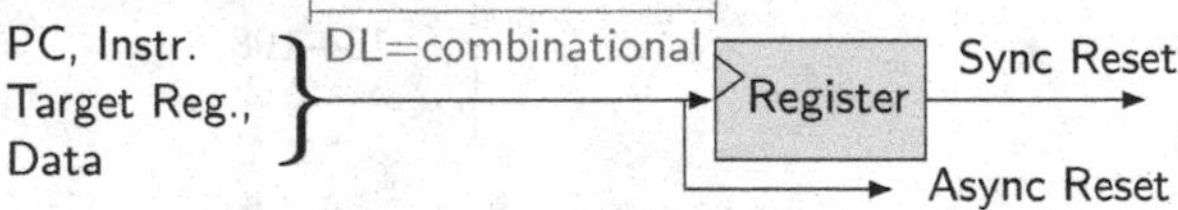

(d) DExIE's timing behaviour for general purpose register (GPR) writes: Combinational logic stops a core directly after an illegal GPR write.

Fig. 3. DExIE's timing behaviour under different conditions

5 RT-LIFE: Signals and Behavior

After the discussion of DExIE as a sample SecEU to motivate the design of RT-LIFE, this section focuses on RT-LIFE's actual implementation.

Table 1 gives an overview of the signals used in RT-LIFE, grouped by their corresponding type of enforcement function. Columns (a) to (c) contain CF and DF signals, which are captured from the processor. Column (d) provides the control signals from SecEU to the core, closing the feedback loop.

In case the core processes a CF instruction (a), RT-LIFE provides the PC, instruction and the Next PC together with a valid signal. For memory store instructions (b), the instruction's PC, the target address, the access size, the data to be written, and a valid signal are captured. For a register write instruction (c), the interface provides the PC, the target register ID, and the corresponding data.

Table 1. RT-LIFE's signals

(a) CF	(b) Mem. Store	(c) Reg. Write	(d) SecEU control
To SecEU			From SecEU
Valid,	Valid,		CF-Stall (CFS),
PC,	PC,	PC	Stall-on-Store (SoS),
Instruction,	Address,	Target Register	Continue-Store (CS)
Next PC	Size, Data	(0: invalid), Data	Reset

If a SecEU's decision latency is too long to prevent real-world impact of an instruction, it can request additional time by asserting the stall signals (d) CF-Stall (CFS), Stall-on-Store (SoS), and Continue-Store (CS). The CFS signal is used if a CF instruction decision takes too long, and the following instruction with potential real-world impact could not be stopped otherwise. In case the signal is set, the following instruction is to be stalled *before* it reaches the WB and MEM stages, gaining additional DL clock cycles for the SecEU. For memory writes, the SoS signal allows a SecEU to combinatorially validate the data to be written, and combinatorially stall a memory write operation before the validation is complete. To prevent combinatorial loops, which can be caused by RT-LIFE's constantly captured signals, the SecEU then asserts a *separate* combinatorial CS signal, if the write operation is deemed valid.

6 RT-LIFE Design and Behavior Considerations

For reduced logic overhead, RT-LIFE by default does not compute the next PC itself, but utilizes the core's computation. We decided against branch prediction awareness, as it would increase RT-LIFE's complexity and potentially degrade portability. Per group of signals (each column in Table 1), DExIE captures *all* signals in the same cycle, and thus would not benefit if only a subset of a group's signals were valid. Thus, we capture the signals as soon as *all* of them are valid.

7 RT-LIFE Implementation

To achieve portability for SecEUs and maintain compliance with the specified behaviour (Sect. 5), the microarchitecture of RT-LIFE is adapted individually to each core. We show six examples here for different cores.

With the exception of their pipeline depth, which is 3 and 5 stages respectively, **Piccolo** (Fig. 4) and **Flute** are closely related RISC-V cores [10]. Figure 4 shows Piccolo and draws vertical separation lines between its pipeline stages. As Flute adds additional separators between FE, DE and EX, and RT-LIFE only interacts with EX and later stages, the *same* RT-LIFE microarchitecture can be used for both cores.

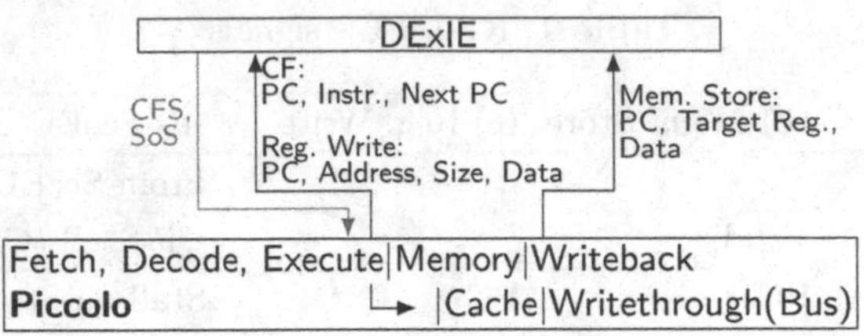

Fig. 4. RT-LIFE microarchitecture for the Piccolo RISC-V core. Vertical lines separate the three pipeline stages and the dedicated memory write stages (Cache, Writethrough (Bus)). Flute is similar, with FE, DE, EX being separated.

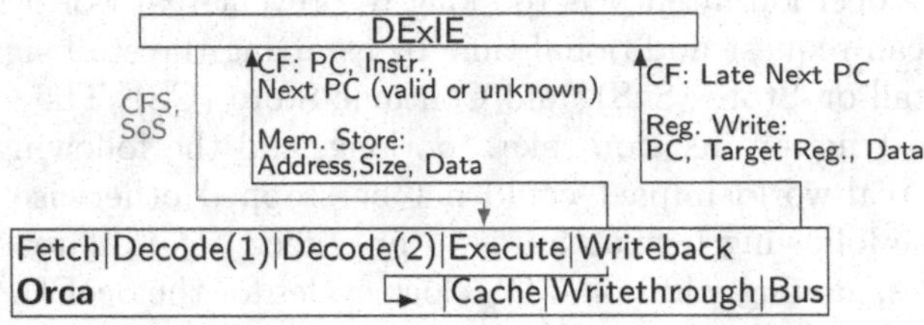

Fig. 5. RT-LIFE microarchitecture for Orca RISC-V core. Vertical lines separate pipeline stages. Note the increased memory write latency.

VectorBlox' **Orca** (Fig. 5) is a 5-stage core. One interface difference to Piccolo and Flute is the possibility of an *unknown* Next PC in the EX stage, which becomes only known later in the WB stage. Another difference is the additional clock cycle for memory write accesses after the Execute stage (Cache, Writethrough, Bus), increasing DL headrom for memory writes.

PicoRV32 (Fig. 6) [11] is a fast-clocked *non-pipelined* multicycle core, which already implements the RVFI. PicoRV32 uses an FSM to control the current instruction's execution. Figure 6 shows the control FSM extended with RT-LIFE. A CF-stall blocks *all* FSM transitions towards the `fetch` FSM state, which are also marked as red crosses in Fig. 6. The SoS signal only stalls the `stmem` FSM state.

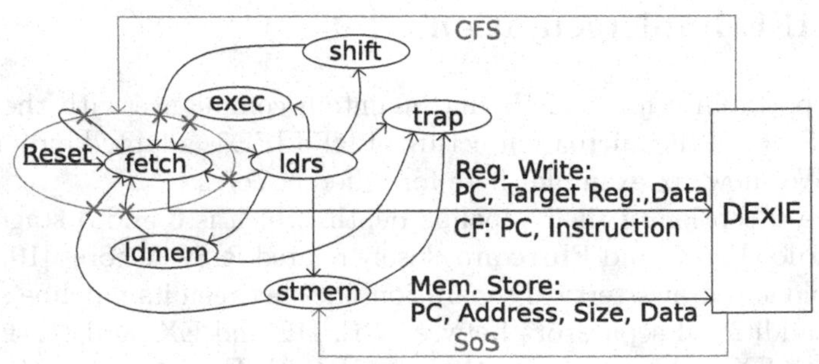

Fig. 6. RT-LIFE microarchitecture for PicoRV32 RISC-V core.

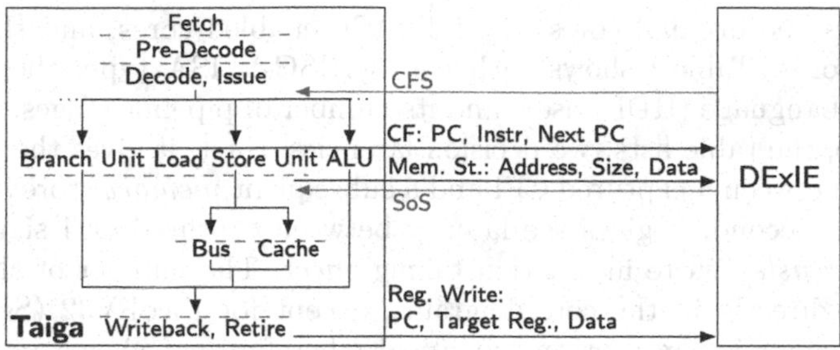

Fig. 7. RT-LIFE microarchitecture for Taiga RISC-V core. Dashed blue horizontal lines separate pipeline stages.

Taiga's (Fig. 7) [15] execution units work partly independently and in parallel. The elastic pipeline also causes instructions to reach the WB stage possibly out-of-order, and bypassing of values can happen even earlier. However, the final WB always happens in-order at retirement time. Our interface's SoS affects the Load Store Unit (LSU), which is only stalled if a subsequent *write* instruction enters the LSU. Compared to other cores with intermediary AXI busses, Taiga employs *directly* attached BRAMs, resulting in a shorter latency for memory accesses.

VexRiscv (Fig. 8) [16] is a modular core of adaptable pipeline depth with a plugin-based implementation. It supports RVFI via its FormalPlugin. We implemented a new plugin to externally stall the execute stage. The DBusSimplePlugin is extended to autonomously stall one cycle, if a CF instruction is *directly* followed by a memory write operation (DL = DL + 1).

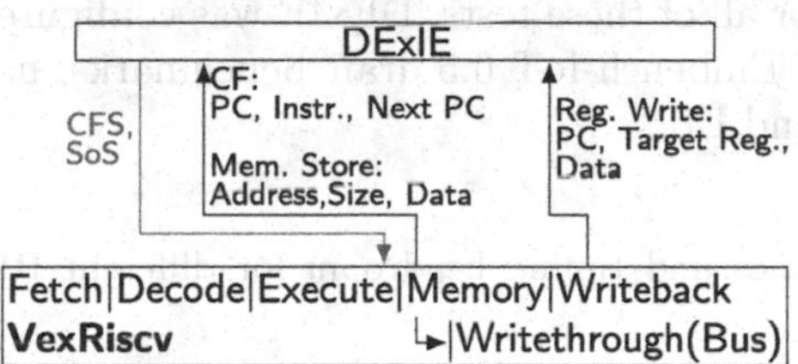

Fig. 8. RT-LIFE microarchitecture for VexRiscv RISC-V core. Vertical lines separate pipeline stages.

8 Evaluation

We implemented all designs as Processing Elements (PE) in the FPGA SoC framework Task Parallel System Composer (TaPaSCo) [19,22] on the VC709 Xilinx Virtex 7 device prototyping board using Vivado 2018.3 (in this particular use case 2018.3 reached higher clock frequencies than more recent versions).

This includes the original cores, the RT-LIFE-enabled cores, and the DExIE-monitored cores. Table 2 shows each core's RISC-V ISA type, the Hardware Description Language (HDL) used, and its number of pipeline stages. Regarding the interface, the table lists two decision latencies. First, it gives the number of clock cycles between a captured CFI and a subsequent *memory* store instruction taking effect. Second, it gives the latency between captured CFI signals and a subsequent *register* write instruction taking effect. The number of clock cycles can be seen directly in the core diagrams, except for PicoRV32 (Sect. 7). For all cores behavior is constant and identical (therefore not shown in the table) for plain memory stores (combinatorial DL, can be blocked in time) and GPR writes (comb. DL, safe to stop directly *after* malicious GPR write).

The following diagrams (Fig. 9a to 9d) show the f_{max}, LUTs, register and BRAM usage for all cores. By comparing each core's implementation against the corresponding RT-LIFE-augmented implementation, we show that RT-LIFE itself has *no* or only *minimal* overheads. In some cases, RT-LIFE seems to even improve the performance. This is an artifact and *unrelated* to RT-LIFE. It is caused by the Xilinx Vivado proprietary logic synthesis flow, which also includes heuristic algorithms, which may produce slightly better or worse results in different runs, even on the same design. Compared to the other cores, RT-LIFE shows somewhat higher overheads for PicoRV32 (due to our FSM modifications, see Fig. 6). Only when combined with a full-blown SecEU like DExIE do the overheads increase. This is expected, as enforcing fine-grained Control Flow Integrity within only 1–2 clock cycles is quite challenging. The critical path lies within DExIE for four out of the six cores. With DExIE being attached, the number of additional stalls introduced ranges from 0% for the higher clocking, but longer latency PicoRV32, to 10.4% for Taiga, which employs partially parallelized execution units. The wall-clock performance penalty with DExIE ranges from 0% for Piccolo, to 134 % for PicoRV32. The latter is the worst-case scenario, as its f_{max} suffers most. For all of these tests, DExIE was configured identical to monitor the execution of Embench-IoT 0.5 draft benchmarks, namely Aha-Mont64, Edn, Matmult-Int, and Ud.

Table 2. Characteristics and timing headroom for different RISC-V cores and CF scenarios

Core	ISA RV32	HDL	Pipeline Stages	Cycles betw. CF & subseq. memory store	Cycles betw. CF & subseq. reg. WB
Flute	ACIMU	BlueSpec	5	2	2
Orca	IM	VHDL	5	3	1
Piccolo	ACIMU	BlueSpec	3	2	2
PicoRV32	IM	Verilog	Multicycle Core	4	0
Taiga	IMA	SystemVerilog	3 (var.)	3	2
VexRiscv	IM	SpinalHDL	5	2	2

As we have described in our related work (Sect. 2), we are not aware of any other *portable* interface for tracing *uncommitted* instructions. Thus, we cannot directly compare RT-LIFE to any similar implementation. Also, attaching DExIE [31] to one of the many interfaces tracing *committed* instructions would be insecure, as the SecEU would no longer be able to stop evil instructions *before* taking effect.

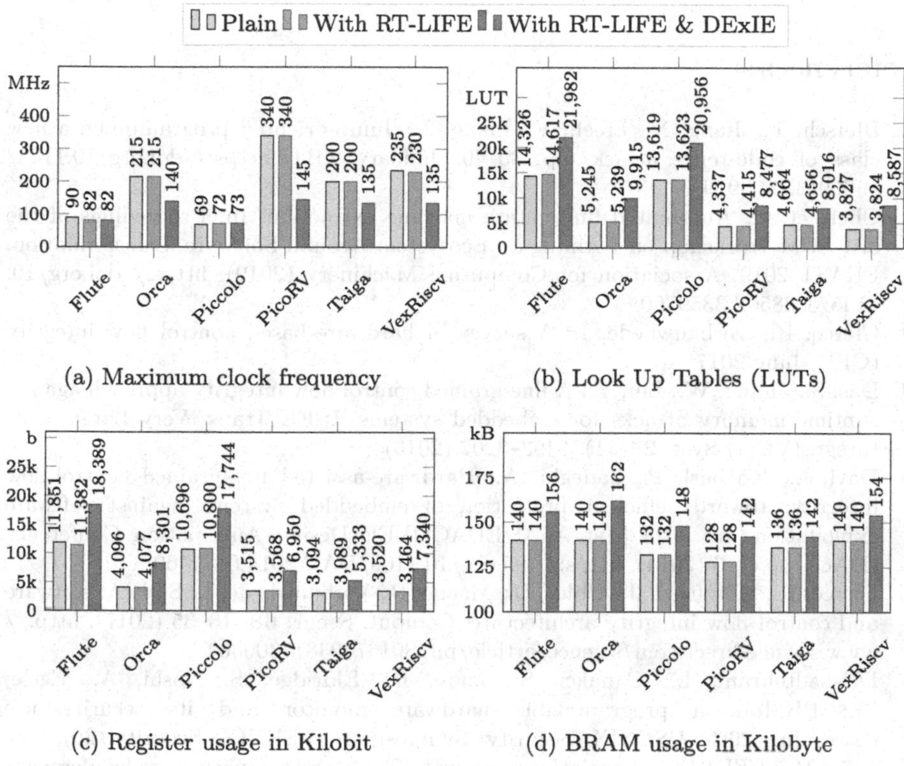

(a) Maximum clock frequency
(b) Look Up Tables (LUTs)
(c) Register usage in Kilobit
(d) BRAM usage in Kilobyte

Fig. 9. Maximum frequency in MHz, number of look up tables and registers, BRAM in kB

9 Conclusion

To the best of our knowledge, RT-LIFE is the first approach for building a *portable* security monitoring interface, aiming for reduced *latency*, *guaranteed timing*, and *low overhead* that captures *uncommitted* instructions. We identified and demonstrated these attributes as key requirements for SecEUs with *guaranteed* attack prevention, with *no* or only limited performance overhead.

With its inter-core portability, RT-LIFE can ease future research in the area of real-time low-overhead SecEUs, with our SecEU DExIE serving as an initial use-case. Future work will further reduce DExIE's overhead, and add Data

Flow and Invariant Enforcement to DExIE. The RT-LIFE specifications, the RT-LIFE-extended RISC-V cores, and a simple demonstration SecEU have been released as open-source [8].

Acknowledgement. This research work has been funded by the German Federal Ministry of Education and Research and the Hessian Ministry of Higher Education, Research, Science and the Arts within their joint support of the National Research Center for Applied Cybersecurity *ATHENE*.

References

1. Bletsch, T., Jiang, X., Freeh, V., Liang, Z.: Jump-oriented programming: a new class of code-reuse attack, pp. 30–40, January 2011. https://doi.org/10.1145/1966913.1966919
2. Chen, et al.: Automated finite state machine extraction. In: Proceedings of the 3rd ACM Workshop on Forming an Ecosystem Around Software Transformation. FEAST 2019. Association for Computing Machinery (2019). https://doi.org/10.1145/3338502.3359760
3. Clercq, R., Verbauwhede, I.: A survey of hardware-based control flow integrity (CFI), June 2017
4. Das, S., Zhang, W., Liu, Y.: A fine-grained control flow integrity approach against runtime memory attacks for embedded systems. IEEE Trans. Very Large Scale Integr. (VLSI) Syst. **24**(11), 3193–3207 (2016)
5. Davi, L., Koeberl, P., Sadeghi, A.: Hardware-assisted fine-grained control-flow integrity: towards efficient protection of embedded systems against software exploitation. In: 2014 51st ACM/EDAC/IEEE Design Automation Conference (DAC), pp. 1–6 (2014). https://doi.org/10.1109/DAC.2014.6881460
6. Clercq, R., Götzfried, J., Übler, D., Maene, P., Verbauwhede, I.: SOFIA: software and control flow integrity architecture. Comput. Secur. **68**, 16–35 (2017). http://www.sciencedirect.com/science/article/pii/S0167404817300664
7. Delshadtehrani, L., Canakci, S., Zhou, B., Eldridge, S., Joshi, A., Egele, M.: PHMon: a programmable hardware monitor and its security use cases. In: 29th USENIX Security Symposium (USENIX Security 20), pp. 807–824. USENIX Association, August 2020. http://usenix.org/conference/usenixsecurity20/presentation/delshadtehrani
8. Div.: RT-LIFE: An interface to easily attach integrity monitors to IoT-class processors. https://github.com/esa-tu-darmstadt/RT-LIFE
9. Div.: Getting around non-executable stack (and fix) (1997). https://seclists.org/bugtraq/1997/Aug/63
10. Div.: Open-source RISC-V CPUs from Bluespec, Inc. (2020). https://github.com/bluespec/Flute
11. Div.: PicoRV32 - a size-optimized RISC-V CPU (2020). https://github.com/cliffordwolf/picorv32
12. Div.: RISC-V debug specification (2020). https://github.com/riscv/riscv-debug-spec
13. Div.: RISC-V Formal verification framework (2020). https://github.com/SymbioticEDA/riscv-formal
14. Div.: RISC-V trace specification (2020). https://github.com/riscv/riscv-trace-spec
15. Div.: Taiga GitLab repository (2020). https://gitlab.com/sfu-rcl/Taiga

16. Div.: VexRiscv github repository (2020). https://github.com/SpinalHDL/VexRiscv
17. Evans, et al.: Control jujutsu: on the weaknesses of fine-grained control flow integrity. In: Proceedings of the 22nd ACM SIGSAC Conference on Computer and Communications Security, CCS 2015, pp. 901–913. Association for Computing Machinery, New York (2015). https://doi.org/10.1145/2810103.2813646
18. Guo, Z., Bhakta, R., Harris, I.G.: Control-flow checking for intrusion detection via a real-time debug interface. In: 2014 SMARTCOMP Workshops. IEEE Computer Society (2014). https://doi.org/10.1109/SMARTCOMP-W.2014.7046672. https://doi.ieeecomputersociety.org/10.1109/SMARTCOMP-W.2014.7046672
19. Heinz, C., Lavan, Y., Hofmann, J., Koch, A.: A catalog and in-hardware evaluation of open-source drop-in compatible RISC-V softcore processors. In: IEEE Proceedings of the International Conference on ReConFigurable Computing and FPGAs (ReConFig). IEEE (2019)
20. Hu, H., Shinde, S., Adrian, S., Chua, Z.L., Saxena, P., Liang, Z.: Data-oriented programming: on the expressiveness of non-control data attacks. In: 2016 IEEE Symposium on Security and Privacy (SP), pp. 969–986 (2016)
21. Intel: Control-flow Enforcement Technology specification, rev. 3.0 (2020). https://software.intel.com/sites/default/files/managed/4d/2a/control-flow-enforcement-technology-preview.pdf
22. Korinth, J., Hofmann, J., Heinz, C., Koch, A.: The TaPaSCo open-source toolflow for the automated composition of task-based parallel reconfigurable computing systems. In: Hochberger, C., Nelson, B., Koch, A., Woods, R., Diniz, P. (eds.) ARC 2019. LNCS, vol. 11444, pp. 214–229. Springer, Cham (2019). https://doi.org/10.1007/978-3-030-17227-5_16
23. Li, J., Chen, L., Xu, Q., et al.: Zipper stack: shadow stacks without shadow. arXiv (2019)
24. Li, Y., Li, J.w.: A technique preventing code reuse attacks based on RISC processor. DEStech Trans. Comput. Sci. Eng. (2018). https://doi.org/10.12783/dtcse/CCNT2018/24682
25. Nagarakatte, S.: Practical low-overhead enforcement of memory safety for c programs, January 2012
26. Palmiero, C., Di Guglielmo, G., Lavagno, L., Carloni, L.P.: Design and implementation of a dynamic information flow tracking architecture to secure a RISC-V core for IoT applications. In: 2018 IEEE High Performance Extreme Computing Conference (HPEC), pp. 1–7 (2018)
27. Prandini, M., Ramilli, M.: Return-oriented programming. IEEE Secur. Priv. **10**(6), 84–87 (2012)
28. Qualcomm: Pointer Authentication on armv8.3 (2017). https://www.qualcomm.com/media/documents/files/whitepaper-pointer-authentication-on-armv8-3.pdf
29. Roemer, R., Buchanan, E., Shacham, H., Savage, S.: Return-oriented programming: systems, languages, and applications. ACM Trans. Inf. Syst. Secur. **15**(1) (2012). https://doi.org/10.1145/2133375.2133377
30. Sinnadurai, S., Zhao, Q., Wong, W.F.: Transparent runtime shadow stack: protection against malicious return address modifications (2008)
31. Spang, C., Lavan, Y., Hartmann, M., Meisel, F., Koch, A.: DExIE - an IoT-class hardware monitor for real-time fine-grained control-flow integrity. In: Workshop on Design and Architectures for Signal and Image Processing, DASIP 2021, 14th edn., pp. 26–34. Association for Computing Machinery, New York (2021). https://doi.org/10.1145/3441110.3441146

32. Sullivan, G.T., et al.: The dover inherently secure processor. In: 2017 IEEE International Symposium on Technologies for Homeland Security (HST), pp. 1–5 (2017)
33. Yuan, P., Zeng, Q., Ding, X.: Hardware-assisted fine-grained code-reuse attack detection. In: Bos, H., Monrose, F., Blanc, G. (eds.) RAID 2015. LNCS, vol. 9404, pp. 66–85. Springer, Cham (2015). https://doi.org/10.1007/978-3-319-26362-5_4

Phase-Aware CPU Workload Forecasting

Erika S. Alcorta[1(✉)], Pranav Rama[1(✉)], Aswin Ramachandran[2(✉)], and Andreas Gerstlauer[1(✉)]

[1] The University of Texas at Austin, Austin, TX, USA
{esalcort,pranavrama9999,gerstl}@utexas.edu
[2] Intel Corporation, Austin, TX, USA
aswin.ramachandran@intel.com

Abstract. Predicting workload behavior during execution is essential for dynamic resource optimization of processor systems. Early studies used simple prediction algorithms such as a history tables. More recently, researchers have applied advanced machine learning regression techniques. Workload prediction can be cast as a time series forecasting problem. Time series forecasting is an active research area with recent advances that have not been studied in the context of workload prediction. In this paper, we first perform a comparative study of representative time series forecasting techniques to predict the dynamic workload of applications running on a CPU. We adapt state-of-the-art matrix profile and dynamic linear models (DLMs) not previously applied to workload prediction and compare them against traditional SVM and LSTM models that have been popular for handling non-stationary data. We find that all time series forecasting models struggle to predict abrupt workload changes. These changes occur because workloads go through phases, where prior work has studied workload phase detection, classification and prediction. We propose a novel approach that combines time series forecasting with phase prediction. We process each phase as a separate time series and train one forecasting model per phase. At runtime, forecasts from phase-specific models are selected and combined based on the predicted phase behavior. We apply our approach to forecasting of SPEC workloads running on a state-of-the-art Intel machine. Our results show that an LSTM-based phase-aware predictor can forecast workload CPI with less than 8% mean absolute error while reducing CPI error by more than 12% on average compared to a non-phase-aware approach.

Keywords: Run time workload prediction · Time series forecasting

1 Introduction

Predicting dynamic workload behaviors has become an essential step in optimizing hardware resources at runtime. For example, anticipating an application's memory intense period can result in power savings if the power management module switches the core frequency promptly. In addition to power management, prediction of workload metrics such as CPI has also been exploited in a

© Springer Nature Switzerland AG 2022
A. Orailoglu et al. (Eds.): SAMOS 2021, LNCS 13227, pp. 195–209, 2022.
https://doi.org/10.1007/978-3-031-04580-6_13

variety of applications including reduction of task interference in multi-tenant systems [13], task migration and scheduling [19], and defending against side-channel attacks [17]. Predictions allow systems to behave proactively instead of reactively. It has been previously shown that proactive decisions yield better optimization results [1]. However, proactive approaches are challenging because they require predicting the future.

Looking at the past is often a reliable way of estimating the future. Program applications specifically present variable workload behaviors throughout their execution and many of them exhibit periodic trends or patterns. Workload prediction techniques exploit these characteristics to estimate future behaviors. Early work in dynamic workload forecasting investigated basic methods such as exponential averaging and history tables [7]. Later studies proposed more advanced approaches, ranging from linear regression [20] to, more recently, recurrent neural networks (RNNs) [13]. Their objective is to minimize the forecasting error of periodically measured CPU workload metrics, such as CPI. This periodic collection of metrics forms a time series; hence, runtime workload behavior forecasting is formally a time series forecasting problem [6,7,20,26].

Time series analysis has been studied for numerous applications, such as stock price prediction, earthquake detection and traffic forecasting [15]. Researchers have proposed many recent advances in these fields that have not been studied in the context of dynamic workload forecasting. In this paper, we first perform a comparative study of representative time series forecasting models applied to predicting CPU workload metrics on a single core. We focus on models that can handle non-stationary program behaviors. We compare classic support vector machine (SVM) [21] and RNN-based long-short term memory (LSTM) [8] regressors against auto-regressive dynamic linear models (DLMs) [11] from the controls domain as well as predictors based on state-of-the-art matrix profile (MP) [27] time series data mining models.

Our results show that all time series forecasting techniques struggle to predict abrupt workload changes. Such changes occur because workloads go through phases. Program phases and their detection, classification and prediction at runtime have been extensively studied [4]. Phase predictors excel at predicting abrupt workload changes since, by definition, a phase is composed of intervals of execution with similar behaviors. A change of phase is thus a change in average workload behavior. We propose to complement time series forecasting with phase classification and prediction. Our approach trains multiple regression models, one per program phase. At runtime, sampled workload traces are fed into the appropriate phase-specific model and forecasted workload metrics are selected and concatenated based on the output of a phase classifier and predictor. Our results show that complementing time series forecasting with phase prediction consistently decreases the forecasting error of all forecasting techniques and programs that go through phases.

We summarize the contributions of this paper as follows:

1. We perform a comparative study of representative time series forecasting techniques to predict application workload behavior at run time. Our com-

parative study includes state-of-the-art time series techniques that, to the best of our knowledge, have not previously been adopted for time series forecasting before.
2. We propose to complement time series forecasting techniques with phase prediction by implementing a separate forecaster per workload phase, which results in significant reductions of forecasting errors for all benchmarks.
3. We perform our study and evaluate our approach for prediction of large-scale SPEC benchmark behavior running on state-of-the-art CPUs for up to 20 time steps into the future. Results show that a phase-aware LSTM provides the best predictions, where a phase-aware approach improves prediction accuracy by more than 12% compared to a non-phase-aware setup.

The remainder of this paper is organized as follows. We review the related work in the next section. In Sect. 3, we provide background about the forecasting models that we evaluate. We summarize the workload forecasting formulation and explain how we complement it with phase prediction in Sect. 4. Section 5 presents the experimental methodology and Sect. 6 shows our results. Finally, we present our conclusions in Sect. 7.

2 Related Work

Time series analysis applications are prevalent in economics, demography, industrial process control, etc. [15]. Time series forecasting has been used in a wide range of computing applications as well. In [3], the auto-regressive moving average (ARMA) model was compared against exponential averaging, history table predictor, and least squares regression for thermal prediction in multiprocessor SoCs. In data centers, forecasting has been used to predict cluster utilization [24]. Nikravesh et al. [16] noticed that SVMs and MLPs have comparative accuracies in predicting data center user requests over time. Matrix profile is a state-of-the-art technique used for time series motif discovery and analysis [27]. It has been applied in detecting anomalies in CPU utilization traces of various workloads [5]. However, existing work has not studied matrix profile for time series prediction. In our work, we specifically demonstrate its adoption for workload forecasting.

Early studies in forecasting dynamic workload metrics proposed basic statistical and table-based predictors. Duesterwald et al. [7] compared a last-value predictor with exponentially weighted moving average (EWMA) and history predictors to forecast instructions per cycle (IPC) and L1D cache misses. The history table predictor resulted in the lowest mean absolute error (MAE). Another study [20] evaluated linear regression to forecast IPC. The results show that they have a lower MAE than the last-value predictor. Kalman filters have been recently used in the context of CPU workload prediction [14]. They are used to predict cycles per instruction (CPI) to optimize dynamic energy management. One of the forecasting models that we study in this work is DLM [11], which uses a state-space representation similar to Kalman filters. It additionally can capture short-term periodicity and trends in time series, but has not been applied to workload prediction before. Advanced machine learning techniques have shown to be more accurate than traditional predictors. Zaman et al. [26]

found that a SVM regressor results in the lowest MAE when forecasting various performance counters. They compared an SVM against last-value, history table, and ARMA predictors. ARMA is an auto-regressive predictor that assumes that the time series is stationary. Since workload behaviors are not stationary, we include DLM as representative auto-regressive technique that does not assume stationarity. With recent popularity of RNNs, a later study [13] investigated the design space of LSTMs to forecast IPC and other metrics of workloads when they are co-allocated with other tasks in data centers. They compared LSTMs against linear regression and MLPs, concluding that LSTMs result in the highest coefficient of determination (R^2) scores.

Multiple studies have proposed to detect and classify workload phases using hardware counters. Early work [9] categorized the memory-boundedness of a workload into phases. A more recent study [10] uses unsupervised learning to cluster samples of hardware counters. In addition to detection and classification, studies in phase prediction focus on predicting discrete workload transitions, i.e., its phase changes. In [9], a global phase history table was proposed. In [10] a genetic algorithm uses phase labels and other parameters for thermal prediction, where changes occur at a slower pace as opposed to CPU workload prediction, where changes can be abrupt. Laun et al. [12] compared Markov tables with last-value predictors. They observed that the same phase is detected in consecutive sampling periods and proposed to use run-length encoding to predict phase changes and estimate phase duration interval ranges. This observation has been made in more recent studies as well. Srinivasan et al. [23] proposed a linear adaptive filter to predict the duration of classified phases. To the best of our knowledge, however, there is no existing work that has short-term workload time series forecasting with phase prediction to capture long-term patterns. In this work, we aim to evaluate how the notion of phases impacts forecasting accuracy orthogonal to any specific phase prediction approach. As such, we implement an oracle predictor and leave research into phase predictors for forecasting to future work.

3 Background

This section describes in further detail the models that we evaluate in this study.

Support Vector Machines (SVMs). An SVM is a supervised learning model whose objective is to minimize an error bound instead of minimizing residuals. This objective has the purpose of generalizing unseen data [21]. We use SVMs for regression, which is commonly referred to as support vector regression (SVR). It is common to apply non-linear transformations, called kernels, to the SVM's input space. In this work, we show the performance of both linear and kernel SVRs. We use a radial-basis function (RBF) as kernel, which is expected to improve accuracy compared to a linear SVR at the expense of computational cost. SVMs take a vector of features as their input. Thus, we convert the multivariate history window to a single-dimensional space. In our study, when the forecast horizon, k, is greater than 1, multiple SVM models are learned independently.

Dynamic Linear Models (DLMs). Dynamic linear models (DLMs) [11] are recursive models formulated as state space models with state parameters corresponding to the structure of the time series. We include DLM components for the general trend of the time series, seasonality of a given size (to capture periodicity) and dynamic regression with predictor variables. These components are combined into state space form to iteratively estimate the next step in time series given the previous inputs of a certain window size. Due to the iterative nature, the model can only consider the previous input window to make a prediction. Making the window size and seasonality too large might result in infeasible computation time. As such, this model is suitable for short term but not long term periodicity.

Long-Short Term Memory (LSTM). LSTM networks are a type of RNN whose structure is characterized by having a memory unit that holds long-term information. The architectures used in this work is composed out of one or more stacked LSTM layers and one fully connected layer. The LSTM layers process the inputs in the time domain to encode a feature vector that the fully connected layer uses to output the forecasts. This architecture is formally classified as an acceptor LSTM. The fully connected layer has k output neurons, which simultaneously predict each value of the forecast horizon.

Matrix Profile (MP). Matrix profile is a recent and fast algorithm for uni-variate time series motif discovery [27]. Motifs are defined as pairs of subsequences of the same time series that are very similar to each other. We propose to adopt matrix profile for workload forecasting by finding a window in a workload time series y_t that is most similar to the most recent window of size h, $(y_{t-h+1}, ..., y_t)$. The samples that follow the most similar window are then used as the forecast values at time t. In other words, there is a subsequence $(y_{v-h+1}, ..., y_v)$, $v + h < t$, that matrix profile finds to be the most similar to $(y_{t-h+1}, ..., y_t)$. The k samples that follow v are then used as the forecast at time t, i.e. $(\hat{y}_{t+1}, ..., \hat{y}_{t+k}) = (y_{v+1}, ...y_{v+k})$.

4 CPU Workload Forecasting

In the following, we first summarize the task of forecasting CPU workload metrics as used in this work. We then describe our proposal to combine forecasting with phase detection and prediction.

4.1 Basic Forecasting

Workload time series are formed from hardware counter data collected using the CPU's performance monitoring units (PMU). Multiple PMU counters are collected each period, resulting in a multivariate time series. The forecasting techniques focus on predicting one of the counters and may use the rest of them as inputs for additional information. We run different programs and consider the execution of each program as a separate time series forecasting task.

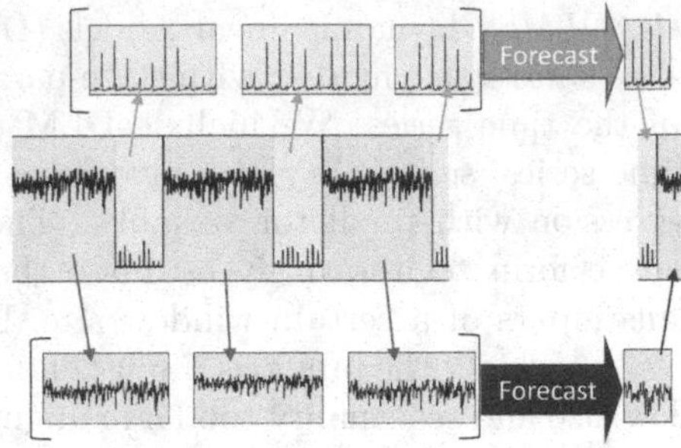

Fig. 1. Example of forecasting executions of two different phases of *nab* (Color figure online)

Formally, each multivariate time series $U \in \mathbb{R}^{n \times m}$ is composed out of n observations of m variables. In the case of workload metric forecasting, the value of m depends on the maximum number of PMU counters that can be collected at the same time. We are interested in predicting one of the m variables, $y \in U$. The observation of this variable at time t, $1 \leq t \leq n$, is denoted as y_t. We are interested in predicting k future values of y at time t, $(\hat{y}_t + 1, ..., \hat{y}_{t+k})$, using only past observations $U_i, i \leq t$. k is known as the forecast horizon. At each step t, a predictor generally takes as input a history window of size h, $(U_{t-h+1}, ..., U_t)$. In summary, the time series forecasting problem can be formalized as follows:

$$(\hat{y}_{t+1}, ..., \hat{y}_{t+k}) = m_{p,w}\big((U_{t-h+1}, ..., U_t)\big), \tag{1}$$

where $m_{p,w}$ represents the trained model function of predictor p with its set of trainable parameters w.

Finding model parameters w is a supervised learning problem. We use a subset of observations t in U with known true values $\hat{y}$ to create a training data set. During prediction at runtime, we use sliding windows of h history values for every new time step t in the test set to predict k future values rooted at t.

4.2 Phase-Aware Forecasting

As our results will show, basic forecasting techniques show low prediction accuracy for workloads that exhibit distinct long-term phase behavior, even when those phases repeat over time. We propose to alleviate this problem by expanding the scope of time series forecasting using phase detection and prediction. Figure 1 shows the intuition behind our approach. The center of the figure shows a snippet of the *nab* workload going through two different phases, highlighted as red and green regions. We partition the trace based on phases, concatenate the sub-traces, and train a predictor specific to each phase. The forecasts belonging to a phase are thus only dependent on the history of that phase, and phase-specific predictors can be specialized to a single phase to increase accuracy.

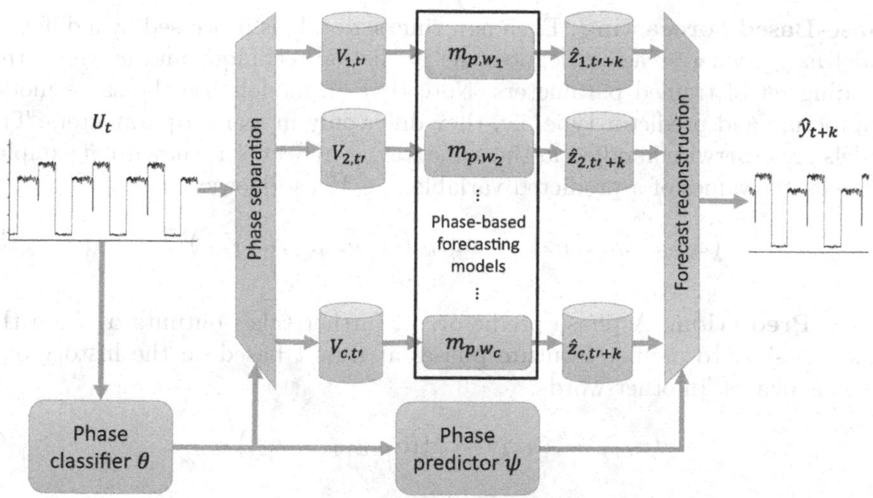

Fig. 2. Phase-aware workload forecasting.

Finally, with knowledge of the future phase behavior, phase-specific forecasts are concatenated and assembled to reconstruct the forecast for the overall time series.

Formally, we use c to denote the total number of distinct phases that a workload cycles through. An overview of our phase-aware forecasting approach is shown in Fig. 2. Our approach consists of four high-level stages: (1) phase classification and separation, (2) phase-based forecasting, (3) phase prediction, and (4) forecast reconstruction. In the following, we formalize each step in detail.

Phase Classification and Separation. A phase classifier, Θ, maps each sample, U_t, to a phase, α_t, $1 \leq \alpha_t \leq c$:

$$\alpha_t = \Theta(U_t). \tag{2}$$

The samples of U that share the same phase, i, are concatenated into a single vector. In total, there are c disjoint time series V_i, defined as follows:

$$V_i = (U_t | \alpha_t = i), 1 \leq i \leq c \tag{3}$$

with observations $V_{i,t'}$, where t' represents the mapping of original observations U_t into a new time dimension t' for each series. Note that the following conditions must be true:

$$U = \bigcup_{i=1}^{c} V_i, \text{ and} \bigcap_{i=1}^{c} V_i = \emptyset. \tag{4}$$

Phase-Based Forecasting. Each new time series, V_i is processed by a different model m_{p,w_i}, where p again denotes the prediction technique and w_i the corresponding set of trained parameters. Note that all models use the same model architecture and predictor type, i.e. they differ only in trained parameters. The models are otherwise handled in the same way as in Sect. 4.1; they use h samples to forecast k values of a predicted variable $z_i \in V_i$ as follows:

$$(\hat{z}_{i,t'+1}, ..., \hat{z}_{i,t'+k}) = m_{p,w_i}\big((V_{i,t'-h+1}, ..., V_{i,t'})\big). \tag{5}$$

Phase Prediction. A phase predictor, ψ, further takes outputs α_t from the phase classifier to predict k future phases at time t based on the history of d previous phases. In other words:

$$(\hat{\alpha}_{t+1}, ..., \hat{\alpha}_{t+k}) = \psi\big((\alpha_{t-d+1}, ..., \alpha_t)\big). \tag{6}$$

Forecast Reconstruction. Finally, since the forecasting models m_{p,w_i} are unaware of their interactions and relationships to the original time series, we use the outputs $\hat{\alpha}_t$ from the phase predictor to select those values of $\hat{z}_{i,t'}$ that should be output as overall forecast $\hat{y}_t$. Formally:

$$(\hat{y}_{t+1}, ..., \hat{y}_{t+k}) = (\hat{z}_{\hat{\alpha}_{t+1},t'+1}, ..., \hat{z}_{\hat{\alpha}_{t+k},t'+k}). \tag{7}$$

5 Experimental Methodology

To generate the workload traces, we use a subset of programs from the SPEC CPU 2017 benchmark suite [22]. The subset was chosen to represent different representative workload phase behaviors: a uniform pattern (*nab*), abrupt transitions (*cactuBSSN*), hard to predict non-stationary patterns (*mcf*), long phase durations (*xz*), and workloads with only a single phase (*perlbench*). We used the *ref* inputs given by the benchmark suite. The execution time of all workloads is more than one minute, which provides enough data to train the forecasting models. Table 1 summarizes the workloads and their phase characteristics.

Our target platform is an Intel Xeon-SP running Ubuntu 18.04. We collect PMU counters every 10 ms using Intel's EMON command-line tool. We constrained our data features to the number of PMU events that can be accessed simultaneously. In the case of the Intel Xeon-SP platform, 4 fixed counters and up to 8 variable counters can be sampled per core (or uncore) simultaneously. In addition to fixed instruction and cycle counters, we selected 8 counters for prediction that can characterize the workload behaviors by their memory boundedness (L2 accesses, L2 hits and L3 misses, i.e. main memory accesses), control flow predictability (retired total and mispredicted branch instructions), and operation mix (retired floating point operations). We also use executed μOps and stall cycles to account for other resources stalling the CPU pipeline execution. Normalizing the PMU counters to the number of instructions yielded more accurate results for all multi-variate models. We also found that reducing dimensionality

Table 1. Benchmark summary.

Benchmark	Samples	No. of phases	Avg. phase length
cactuBSSN	202,179	5	167
mcf	52,673	5	599
nab	170,251	5	231
perlbench	16,462	1	–
xz	126,669	4	7,037

with principal component analysis (PCA) improves the performance of SVR and LSTM models. Finally, we applied a median filter to the data to eliminate noise. A median filter was preferred over other smoothing techniques for its ability to preserve workload behavior changes.

CPI is used as the variable of interest, y, to compare our models. The rest of the collected performance counters are used by some of the models as inputs. The matrix profile algorithm is designed for uni-variate time series; therefore, we only use CPI as input. The rest of the models use the other counters in a multi-variate fashion as described in Eq. (1).

We split each time series into 70% of samples used for training, hyperparameter tuning and model selection, and 30% of samples for testing. We use the mean absolute percentage error (MAPE) between measured and predicted CPI to evaluate our forecasting models. We set a fixed forecast horizon of all models of $k = 20$. With this, we compute a separate $MAPE_i$ for every step $1 \leq i \leq k$ in the forecast horizon as follows:

$$MAPE_i = \frac{100\%}{n} \sum_{t=1}^{n-k} \left(\frac{|y_{t+i} - \hat{y}_{t+i}|}{y_{t+i}} \right) \tag{8}$$

When comparing different models, we look at the average MAPE ($AMAPE$) of all 20 predictions: $AMAPE = \frac{1}{k} \sum_{i=1}^{k} MAPE_i$.

In addition to evaluating forecast errors, we measured the inference time corresponding to one prediction step. To perform a fair comparative study, we run the inference of all forecasting models on the same machine, an Intel Core i9-9900K running Debian 9.13. We use Python's *time* standard library to measure the inference time. The frameworks that we use to implement and train our forecasting models are *PyDLM* [25] for DLM, *scikit-learn* [18] for SVM, *Keras* [2] for LSTM, and *PySCAMP* [28] for matrix profile.

To evaluate the benefits of phase-aware forecasting independent of a specific phase prediction approach that comes with its own inaccuracies, we use an oracle phase predictor. We focus our work on the study of forecasting models in phase-aware versus -unaware settings, and leave the selection of phase predictors to future work.

6 Experimental Results

We first discuss tuning of hyperparameters and selection of forecasting model architectures. We then evaluate and compare accuracy of different phase-aware versus -unaware variants of each model. As described above, we use 70% of the trace of each benchmark for training and 30% for testing. For hyperparameter tuning and model selection, we further split the training set into 50% of samples used for exploration, i.e. to train the models with different hyperparameters, and 20% used for validation, i.e. to select the best parameters based on the average performance across benchmarks. We then train the final models with the complete 70% of samples and use the remaining 30% in the test set to evaluate accuracy of each forecasting technique.

6.1 Hyperparameter Tuning and Model Selection

We evaluate each technique's sensitivity to history window size, h, and other relevant model parameters to select the best overall architecture for each model. Figure 3 shows the exploration of all forecasting models. We plot the tradeoff between the mean AMAPE across all benchmarks on the y-axis and the inference time on the x-axis. We also show the finally selected hyperparameters of each model with a dotted green circle on each figure.

For SVMs (Fig. 3a), we explored both linear and RBF kernels. Given inherently non-linear workload behavior, RBF kernels show significantly better accuracy, but come at the expense of higher computational cost. Window size impacts inference time with an RBF kernel, where more complex models with larger input features increase computation time. By contrast, the forecast error is very similar across window sizes. In general, a window size that is too small to capture workload periodicity will result in larger errors. At the same time, very long window sizes result in a model that averages samples instead of learning their interactions. The optimal window size strongly depends on the workload, however. The mean AMAPE is lowest for a window size of 70, but smaller window sizes have better accuracy for *nab* while larger window sizes are better for *xz*. We chose a window size of $h = 50$ due to its faster inference time and mean AMAPE that is very close to $h = 70$ (less than 1% difference).

For DLM (Fig. 3b), in addition to history window sizes, we selected seasonality (periodicity) through validation. Larger periodicity improves accuracy regardless of the window size, albeit at the cost of a significant increase in computation time. Window sizes show similar accuracy and inference time trends than in SVMs, but they have a stronger impact on accuracy for DLMs. Medium window sizes show best accuracy at intermediate computation costs. These trends in window sizes and periodicity were consistent in all benchmarks. The best mean AMPAE with reasonable computation time was found to be for a window size of $h = 80$ with periodicity of 100. Our DLM model also includes a degree 2 trend component and a multivariate dynamic regression component with 8 predictor variables. The DLM was found to do better with the multivariate predictor variable component compared to without it.

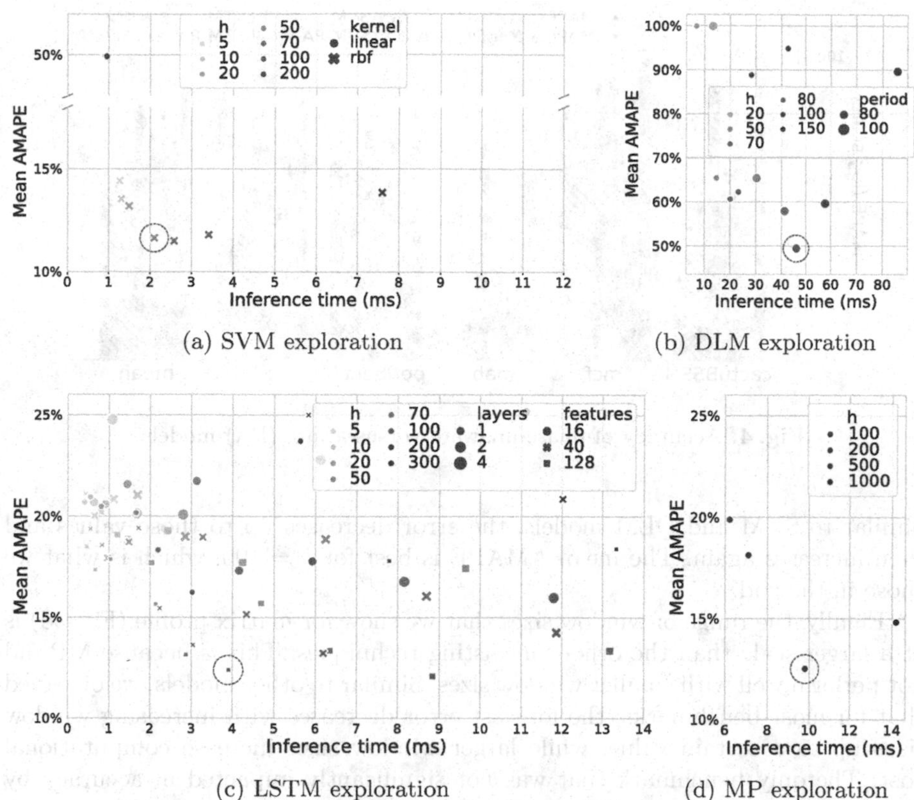

Fig. 3. Exploration of the forecasting techniques hyperparameter space. (Color figure online)

The exploration of LSTM hyperparameters (Fig. 3c) included the number of LSTM layers and the number of features per layer in addition to input window size h. They all impact the computational costs, with fewer features, fewer layers and smaller window sizes being faster. Having more features reduces the forecasting error. This is a trend we observed across all benchmarks except *perlbench*, which showed an opposite trend. We thus selected 128 as the number of features. A smaller number of layers generally decreases mean AMAPE, but the impact on forecasting error is dependent on the number of features and the workload. For example, for *nab*, increasing the number of layers with 16 features reduces AMAPE, but the trend is opposite with 40 features. The models with lowest mean AMAPE, however, all have 1 and 2 layers. As such, we chose 1 layer for our final model as the inference time is faster and the mean AMPE difference is not significant. The window sizes with lowest mean AMAPE were 70 and 100. The best performing window, however, was different for each benchmark. The best window size was 100 for *cactuBBSN*, 70 for *mcf*, 50 for *nab* and 10 for *xz*.

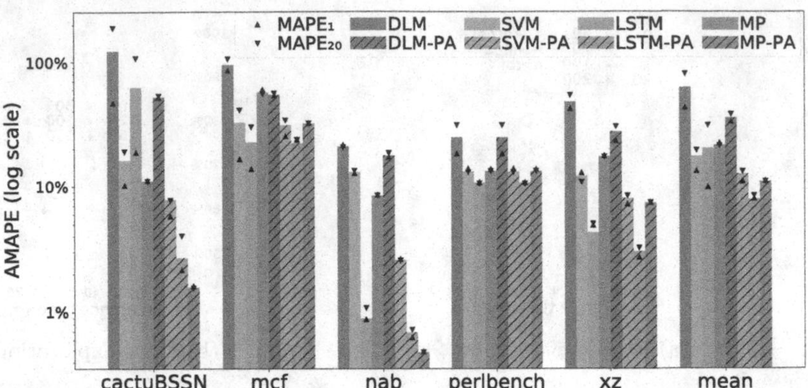

Fig. 4. Accuracy of phase-unaware versus-aware (PA) models.

Similar to SVM and DLM models, the error decreases up to those values and then increases again. The mean AMAPE is best for $h = 100$, which is what we chose in the end.

Finally, the range of window sizes that we show for matrix profile (Fig. 3d) is at a larger scale than the other forecasting techniques. This is because MP did not perform well with smaller window sizes. Similar to other models, we observed that for most benchmarks, the forecast error decreases with increasing window sizes up to a certain value, while larger window sizes increase computational cost. The only benchmark that was not significantly impacted in accuracy by the window size was *xz*. The best mean AMAPE for matrix profile was for $h = 500$, which we chose for this model.

Overall, with the exception of DLM, all models show similar validation accuracies and inference times. DLM, however, is both significantly more inaccurate and slower than other approaches. The technique with the fastest inference time is SVM with 2.1 ms, followed by LSTM with 3.9 ms, matrix profile with 9.8 ms and lastly, DLM with 46 ms. These time measurements were taken with the purposes of comparing the inference times of different models relative to each other in their base software implementation. Further investigation is required to optimize their implementations and reduce overhead for actual deployment, e.g., by pruning or hardware acceleration. We evaluate final model accuracy for the test set in the next section.

6.2 Accuracy Evaluation

Figure 4 shows the accuracy comparison of all four forecasting techniques using a basic and our proposed phase-aware (PA) setup. In addition to $AMAPE$, the graph also shows the range of $MAPE_1$ and $MAPE_{20}$ across the nearest and farthest prediction in the forecast horizon for each model and benchmark. Most benchmarks and models show that the closest forecast is more accurate than the farthest, with the mean between them.

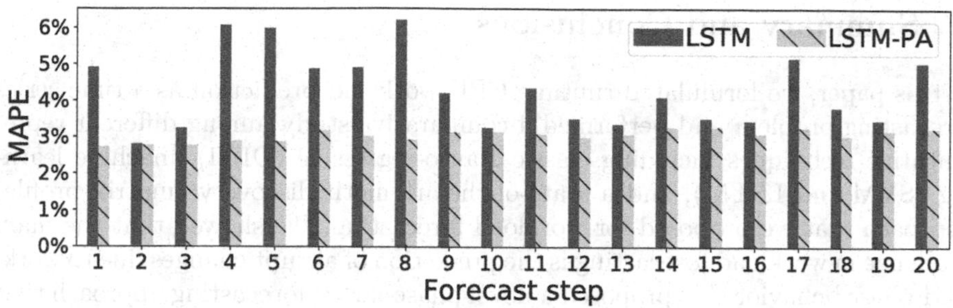

Fig. 5. Accuracy per forecast steps of phase-aware and -unaware LSTM for *xz*.

When comparing traditional models with phase-aware approaches, results show that using phase-specific models consistently decreases the forecasting error of all techniques for all benchmarks except *perlbench*. The workload traces of *perlbench* do not go through phases and there is no room of improvement for phase-aware forecasting.

We observe that *cactuBSSN* exhibits the most impact in forecasting error reduction with a phase-aware approach. Some of its transitions between phases have very abrupt changes where the CPI value increases by 500%. Any mispredictions of these transitions result in very large error penalization. This is also reflected in the large variation in errors between the first and last prediction in the forecast horizon. A phase-unaware LSTM in particular struggles to predict those changes and benefits significantly from a phase-aware approach. By contrast, *mcf* is impacted the least from phase-aware models and generally exhibits poor accuracy and larger error variations. This is because its phases continuously change and reduce in length over time, which makes the workload hard to predict overall. Note that matrix profile in particular cannot accurately predict this trend since its predictions are purely based on recalling past behavior unchanged. As opposed to *mcf*, the phases of *nab* have repetitive uniform patterns, where phase-aware models have a significant impact in decreasing forecast error. A basic LSTM is able to accurately learn both short-term and long-term phase patterns for this workload, but its phase-aware counterpart still had room for improvement.

Finally, Fig. 5 shows the MAPE of all steps in the forecast horizon of a phase-aware and -unaware LSTM when predicting *xz*. While a phase-unaware LSTM provides good AMAPE across all steps, it shows high maximum errors due to its inability to predict phase changes with larger CPI jumps for this workload. The phase-unaware LSTM will sometimes predict a phase change when there is none or will fail to predict a change at the right time, which results in large errors for certain forecast steps. By contrast, the phase-aware LSMT shows small variations in errors across steps with a general trend of slightly increasing errors the further the predictions are made into the future.

7 Summary and Conclusions

In this paper, we formulated runtime CPU workload prediction as a time series forecasting problem and performed a comparative study among different representative techniques including classical auto-regressive (DLM), machine learning (SVM and LSTM), and a state-of-the-art motif discovery (matrix profile) approach that we proposed for workload forecasting. We showed that the main challenge in workload forecasting is the prediction of abrupt changes due to workload phase behavior. We proposed a novel phase-aware forecasting approach that leverages phase classification and prediction to separate time series into phases and train a separate, specialized prediction model for each phase. Results on a subset of SPEC 2017 benchmarks running on a state-of-the-art workstation show that phase-aware forecasting improves MAPE by 14% on average across different models and benchmarks. A phase-aware LSTM was the best performing predictor with less than 8% average MAPE across benchmarks and a forecast horizon of 20 steps. By contrast, a phase-aware SVM is almost twice as fast but at decreased accuracy of 13% MAPE. A phase-aware matrix profile predictor can in some cases outperform an LSTM, but at much higher computational cost.

Future work includes investigating phase-aware forecasting for a wider range of workloads, integrating phase predictors to complement phase-aware models, approaches for online training of predictors, efficient hardware or software deployment of predictors, application of phase-aware workload forecasting to various use cases such as power management or system scheduling, as well as workload forecasting for multi-threaded workloads running in multi-core settings, where task interference effects are considered in phase classification, detection and forecasting.

Acknowledgments. We thank the anonymous reviewers for their valuable feedback. This work was supported in part by Intel and NSF grant CCF-1763848.

References

1. Ababei, C., Moghaddam, M.G.: A survey of prediction and classification techniques in multicore processor systems. IEEE TPDS **30**(5), 1184–1200 (2018)
2. Chollet, F., et al.: Keras (2015). https://keras.io
3. Coskun, A.K., Rosing, T.S., Gross, K.C.: Utilizing predictors for efficient thermal management in multiprocessor SoCs. IEEE TCAD **28**(10), 1503–1516 (2009)
4. Criswell, K., Adegbija, T.: A survey of phase classification techniques for characterizing variable application behavior. IEEE TPDS **31**(1), 224–236 (2019)
5. Dieter De Paepe, O.J., Hoecke, S.V.: Eliminating noise in the matrix profile. In: ICPRAM (2019)
6. Dietrich, B., et al.: Time series characterization of gaming workload for runtime power management. IEEE TC **64**(1), 260–273 (2015)
7. Duesterwald, E., Cascaval, C., Dwarkadas, S.: Characterizing and predicting program behavior and its variability. In: PACT (2003)
8. Hochreiter, S., Schmidhuber, J.: Long short-term memory. Neural Comput. **9**(8), 1735–1780 (1997)

9. Isci, C., Contreras, G., Martonosi, M.: Live, runtime phase monitoring and prediction on real systems with application to dynamic power management. In: MICRO (2006)
10. Khanna, R., John, J., Rangarajan, T.: Phase-aware predictive thermal modeling for proactive load-balancing of compute clusters. In: ICEAC (2012)
11. Laine, M.: Introduction to dynamic linear models for time series analysis. In: Montillet, J.-P., Bos, M.S. (eds.) Geodetic Time Series Analysis in Earth Sciences. SG, pp. 139–156. Springer, Cham (2020). https://doi.org/10.1007/978-3-030-21718-1_4
12. Lau, J., Schoenmackers, S., Calder, B.: Transition phase classification and prediction. In: HPCA (2005)
13. Masouros, D., Xydis, S., Soudris, D.: Rusty: runtime system predictability leveraging LSTM neural networks. IEEE CAL **18**(2), 103–106 (2019)
14. Moghaddam, M.G., Ababei, C.: Dynamic energy management for chip multiprocessors under performance constraints. Microprocess. Microsyst. **54**, 1–13 (2017)
15. Montgomery, D.C.: Introduction to Time Series Analysis and Forecasting. Wiley, Hoboken (2015)
16. Nikravesh, A.Y., Ajila, S.A., Lung, C.: Towards an autonomic auto-scaling prediction system for cloud resource provisioning. In: SEAMS (2015)
17. Nomani, J., Szefer, J.: Predicting program phases and defending against side-channel attacks using hardware performance counters. In: HASP (2015)
18. Pedregosa, F., et al.: Scikit-learn: machine learning in Python. JMLR **12**, 2825–2830 (2011)
19. Rapp, M., Pathania, A., Mitra, T., Henkel, J.: Prediction-based task migration on S-NUCA many-cores. In: DATE (2019)
20. Sarikaya, R., Buyuktosunoglu, A.: Predicting program behavior based on objective function minimization. In: IISWC (2007)
21. Smola, A.J., Schölkopf, B.: A tutorial on support vector regression. Stat. Comput. **14**(3), 199–222 (2004)
22. SPEC CPU® (2017). https://www.spec.org/cpu2017/index.html
23. Srinivasan, S., Kumar, R., Kundu, S.: Program phase duration prediction and its application to fine-grain power management. In: IEEE Computer Society Annual Symposium on VLSI, pp. 127–132 (2013)
24. Vashistha, A., Verma, P.: A literature review and taxonomy on workload prediction in cloud data center. In: Confluence (2020)
25. Wang, X.: Pydlm user manual (2016). https://pydlm.github.io/
26. Zaman, M., Ahmadi, A., Makris, Y.: Workload characterization and prediction: a pathway to reliable multi-core systems. In: IOLTS (2015)
27. Zhu, Y., et al.: The swiss army knife of time series data mining: ten useful things you can do with the matrix profile and ten lines of code. Data Min. Knowl. Disc. **34**(4), 949–979 (2020)
28. Zimmerman, Z., et al.: Matrix profile XIV: scaling time series motif discovery with GPUs to break a quintillion pairwise comparisons a day and beyond. In: SoCC (2019)

WhiskEras 2.0: Fast and Accurate Whisker Tracking in Rodents

Petros Arvanitis[1,2], Jan-Harm L.F. Betting[1], Laurens W.J. Bosman[1], Zaid Al-Ars[2], and Christos Strydis[1(✉)]

[1] Department of Neuroscience, Erasmus Medical Centre, Rotterdam, The Netherlands
c.strydis@erasmusmc.nl

[2] Department of Quantum and Computer Engineering, Delft University of Technology, Delft, The Netherlands

Abstract. Mice and rats can rapidly move their whiskers when exploring the environment. Accurate description of these movements is important for behavioral studies in neuroscience. Whisker tracking is, however, a notoriously difficult task due to the fast movements and frequent crossings and juxtapositionings among whiskers. We have recently developed WhiskEras, a computer-vision-based algorithm for whisker tracking in untrimmed, head-restrained mice. Although WhiskEras excels in tracking the movements of individual unmarked whiskers over time based on high-speed videos, the initial version of WhiskEras still had two issues preventing its widespread use: it involved tuning a great number of parameters manually to adjust for different experimental setups, and it was slow, processing less than 1 frame per second. To overcome these problems, we present here WhiskEras 2.0, in which the unwieldy stages of the initial algorithm were improved. The enhanced algorithm is more robust, not requiring intense parameter tuning. Furthermore, it was accelerated by first porting the code from MATLAB to C++ and then using advanced parallelization techniques with CUDA and OpenMP to achieve a speedup of at least 75x when processing a challenging whisker video. The improved WhiskEras 2.0 is made publicly available and is ready for processing high-speed videos, thus propelling behavioral research in neuroscience, in particular on sensorimotor integration.

Keywords: Whisker tracking · Algorithmic improvement · Acceleration

1 Introduction

Whiskers, or vibrissae, are tactile hairs found in most mammals [3]. Some rodents, like mice and rats, engage in active touch behavior during which they make fast rhythmic movements with their facial whiskers [10]. The facial whiskers are arranged in a conserved geometric pattern in the skin, which is reflected in

© Springer Nature Switzerland AG 2022
A. Orailoglu et al. (Eds.): SAMOS 2021, LNCS 13227, pp. 210–225, 2022.
https://doi.org/10.1007/978-3-031-04580-6_14

the organization of the primary somatosensory cortex [23]. The behavioral relevance of whisker use and the well-defined anatomy of whisker representation in the brain have made them particularly interesting for neuroscience.

Whisker movements are typically recorded using high-speed cameras with up to 1,000 frames per second, required to faithfully capture whisker movements during *whisking*, back-and-forth movements with frequencies of up to >25 Hz at speeds up to ~1000 deg./s [5,21]. Whisker movements can be described by the angle of the whisker root relative to the snout. Keeping track of the angle of each whisker over time, however, is challenging. Most current whisker trackers make compromises to provide accurate tracking, like clipping of most of the whiskers (e.g., see [7]), or attaching markers to individual whiskers [13].

Recently developed, WhiskEras [2] is a promising framework for collecting accurate tracking data from untrimmed head-restrained mice, without the need for attaching markers to the whiskers. It was built to increase the performance of the BIOTACT Whisker-Tracking Tool (BWTT) [18]. In particular, BWTT can only *detect* whiskers frame by frame, but does not *track* them through time. For this reason, WhiskEras introduced a tracking module. WhiskEras, however, involves tuning a great number of parameters, owing to the various algorithmic steps it involves. It is expected that, in order to maximize the quality of results, many of these parameters need to be re-tuned for different videos, which is cumbersome and tough to automate. Furthermore, it is slow, processing less than 1 frame per second, which makes it ill-suited for long videos.

This work focuses on studying WhiskEras, identifying and extending its potential and accelerating it. For a complete, detailed description of this work, refer to [1]. The contributions of this paper are summarized as follows:

- Deliver WhiskEras 2.0, an improved version of the original framework which is more robust and easier to tune.
- Accelerate WhiskEras 2.0 by 74.96x by porting the code from MATLAB to C++, exploiting parallel execution on the CPU and GPU and performing several optimizations. The code is available online.[1]
- Pinpoint the limitations of computer-vision based approaches in whisker tracking, steering future endeavors in the field.

This paper is organized as follows: In Sect. 2, related works on whisker tracking are presented. Section 3 outlines the algorithmic stages of WhiskEras. In Sect. 4, the shortcomings of WhiskEras are pinpointed and its performance is analyzed. Then, Sect. 5 contains the implementation details of this work. In Sect. 6, WhiskEras 2.0 is compared to the original WhiskEras in terms of quality and performance, using two benchmark videos. Finally, conclusions of this work and some recommendations for future work are given in Sect. 7.

2 Related Work

In theory, high-speed videography allows accurate and non-invasive detection of whisker movements, but, for instance, crossings and juxtapositions complicate

[1] https://gitlab.com/neurocomputing-lab/whisker/whiskeras-2.0.

tracking. There are two common solutions to this problem. One way is reducing complexity by clipping all but one or a few whiskers, e.g. as is the case with Janelia Whisk [7]. This algorithm uses complex image-processing, statistical and machine-learning methods to follow whisker trajectories. However, it is not very accurate when tracking many whiskers [2]. Also, studies using the DeepLabCut framework, based on modern deep-learning methods, to track whiskers still used whisker clipping [8]. The clipping of whiskers, however, affects animal behaviour and neural processing [15], and should therefore ideally be avoided.

Alternatively, one can detect all whiskers, but without attempting to track individual whiskers over time, as does BWTT [18]. The original version of BWTT was slow, but was accelerated previously to achieve almost real-time processing [17]. A post-processing script, also developed previously, was deployed to track whiskers over time, but it does so with low accuracy [21].

WhiskEras is more promising in terms of tracking whisker movement of unmarked and untrimmed mice [2]. It is an unsupervised algorithm, which uses computer-vision algorithms to detect whiskers, and a machine-learning method to track them. Hence, there is no need for collecting labelled data to feed to a neural network for training, as necessary for (most) deep-learning techniques. In this sense, WhiskEras can be more convenient as it is ready to use on various experimental setups, particularly after the improvements described in this work.

3 WhiskEras Algorithm

WhiskEras comprises two main modules: Detection and Tracking, responsible for *detecting* whiskers and fitting them into a compact representation of several parameters, and for *following* these whiskers, frame-by-frame, respectively (Fig. 1). The system can also be organized into three components:

1. **Whisker-Point Detection** involves preprocessing of each frame in order to remove the background, silhouette and fur of the animal. Its result is an image of bright whiskers on a dark background. Then, Centerline Extraction is used to locate the whisker points on the centerline of each whisker, using Steger's Curvilinear Detector algorithm [22].
2. **Whisker Forming** takes as input the centerline positions of the whisker points in the image and performs Local Clustering to form groups of points which belong to the same whisker. This clustering, however, does not yet result in complete grouping, so that Cluster Stitching is required to unify clusters belonging to the same whisker. Afterwards, Parameter Fitting takes place, where each whisker representation is encoded as a set of four parameters.
3. **Tracking over time** matches whiskers found in the current frame with whiskers found in previous frames. The Tracking - Learning - Detection (TLD) technique [14] was adopted, to achieve consistency across a long sequence of frames. Tracking whiskers, from frame $n-1$ to n is performed using either a Kalman filter or by fitting whisker points to previously detected whiskers.

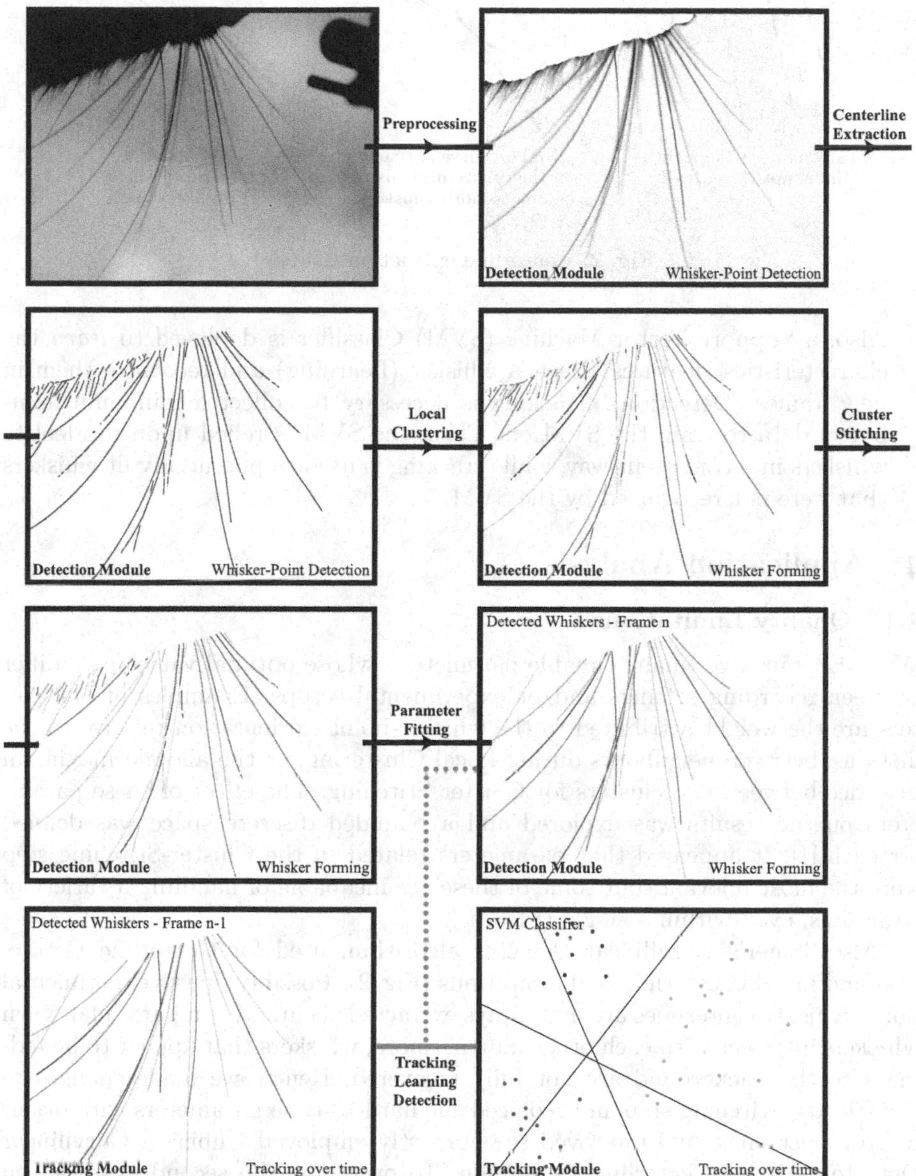

Fig. 1. WhiskEras pipeline overview: algorithmic steps are illustrated between the processing states of a whisker video frame, in the Detection module. The Tracking module makes use of the results from the current and previous frames, as well as an SVM Classifier to track whiskers over time.

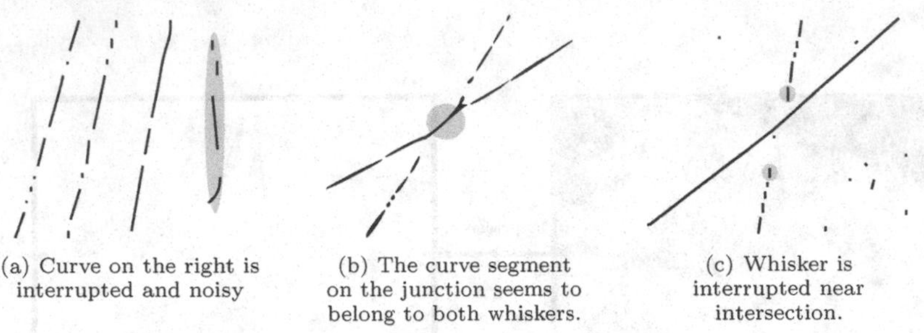

(a) Curve on the right is interrupted and noisy

(b) The curve segment on the junction seems to belong to both whiskers.

(c) Whisker is interrupted near intersection.

Fig. 2. Centerline extraction issues

Also, a Support Vector Machine (SVM) Classifier is deployed to *learn* the characteristics (features) of each whisker (Learning) and recognize them in new frames (Detection). Tracking is necessary to collect a minimum number of data to train the SVM on. Then, the SVM is relied upon to identify whiskers in a consistent way, while tracking is used to potentially fit whiskers that were not recognized by the SVM.

4 Application Analysis

4.1 Quality Limitations

WhiskEras involves many tunable parameters, whose optimal values may differ between recording settings and/or experimental setups. Examples of parameters are the weight attributed to the whisker-point's orientation relative to the distance between neighbours during Local Clustering, or the allowed maximum distance between two clusters for Cluster Stitching. The effect of these parameters on the results was explored and a bounded discrete space was defined for each [1]. It appeared that parameters related to the Cluster-Stitching step were the most relevant, but some of these are incapable of handling a variety of situations, even within a single video.

Also Steger's Curvilinear Detector algorithm, used for Centerline Extraction and Local Clustering, had limitations (Fig. 2). Possibly due to experimental noise, whisker centerlines are not always extracted accurately, in particular when whiskers intersect with each other. Furthermore, whiskers that appear to be fading into the background are not fully recovered. Hence, we made changes to the Cluster-Stitching step and replaced the hard-to-tune parameters with other, more robust ones, and improved the currently employed Unbiased Curvilinear Detector [22] for Centerline Extraction. To overcome the second obstacle, an adaptation of Improved Curve Tracing [20], an expansion on the Curvilinear Detector algorithm, was materialized.

4.2 Performance Profiling

WhiskEras is coded in MATLAB, a high-level programming language, which is generally inefficient for applications that demand large processing power. The

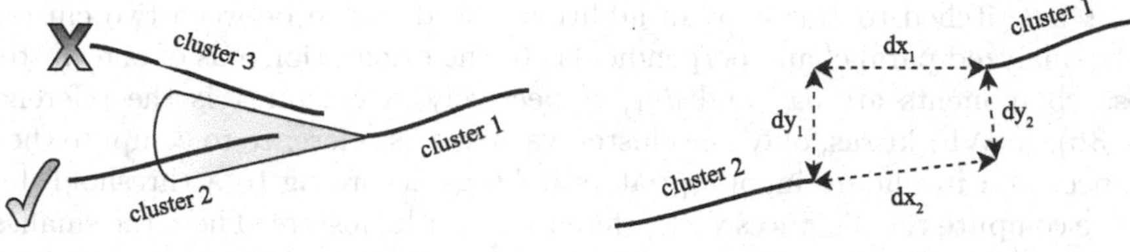

(a) Cluster 2 can be stitched to cluster 1, while cluster 3 cannot.

(b) The parallel and perpendicular distances between two clusters. Depending on the reference cluster, these are different.

Fig. 3. Cluster stitching: maximum angle condition and distance between clusters

implementation of WhiskEras was done nearly optimally, taking advantage of any inherent parallelization present in its algorithmic stages. Centerline Extraction is performed on the GPU, exploiting the massive data-level parallelism (DLP), while some costly steps during Cluster Stitching and Learning are also parallelized, using multiple threads on the CPU. Despite these optimizations, the application takes about 1.3 s to process a single frame. For context, a 50-second-long high-speed video (1,000 fps) would require ~18 h of processing on a powerful machine.

For acceleration, the code was ported to C++, a high-level language incorporating also low-level features in C, such as efficient memory management, optimized compiler support, and the availability of many fast libraries. Furthermore, the parallelizable portions had to retain multithreading, following the MATLAB implementation. To this end, the OpenMP API and CUDA API were used, respectively for CPUs and GPUs. After this initial acceleration, an iterative process was performed where the code's most expensive portions were pinpointed through profiling, and optimizations were carried out accordingly.

5 Implementation

5.1 Quality Improvements

Pairs of clusters belonging to the same whisker are stitched together based on the distance between the edges of these clusters, and their orientation proximity. Originally, the maximal distance between clusters to allow stitching was a fixed value, as specified a priori by the user, limiting the flexibility to stitch more distant clusters, e.g. of disappearing and re-emerging whiskers (Fig. 2c). Instead, to guard against invalid stitchings, Radon Transform, a technique usually used in tomographic reconstruction in medical imaging [19], was deployed. We implemented first-order, Localized Radon Transform to detect lines between the edges of two clusters. If a line in between them is not found in the unprocessed frame of whiskers, then stitching of this pair is aborted.

In addition, a maximum-angle condition was utilized (Fig. 3a). Clusters that are not rooted within the angle margin, derived from cluster 1's orientation, cannot be stitched to cluster 1. In addition, the distance between two clusters can be analyzed parallel and perpendicular to the orientation axis of one cluster. These components are dx_1 and dy_1, respectively, if cluster 1 is the reference (Fig. 3b). In WhiskEras, only one cluster was used as reference to compute these distances and invalidate inappropriate stitchings according to a threshold, but now we compute the distances with reference to both clusters. Then, the smallest ones are used to determine if a stitching is valid. This proved to be favorable, as the edge of one of the two clusters belonging to the same whisker is often noisy, not pointing towards the other edge.

In WhiskEras, the stitching score was given by

$$score = \sqrt{dx^2 + dy^2} + c \cdot \beta$$

where β is the angle difference of the edges of the two clusters and c is its weight. However, dy and β should be weighted more heavily than dx, especially as dx grows larger, but dy and β should be allowed to be a bit larger when two clusters are really close to each other, since they are disconnected in the first place due to noise. Taking all these into consideration, the new score is

$$score = \begin{cases} dx + dy + \beta, & \text{if } d \leq d_0 \\ dx + \frac{c}{dx} \cdot dy + c \cdot \beta, & \text{if } d > d_0 \end{cases}$$

Notice that dy and β are weighted as much as dx for small distances, up to d_0 (e.g. $d_0 = 5$ px). When the distance indicates that the clusters are not proximal whisker segments, dy and β should be the prime factors. This necessitates the use of a large value for c (e.g., $c = 200$).

In contrast to the original version of WhiskEras, we consistently opt for Steger's Curvilinear Detector for Centerline Extraction and Local Clustering. Steger's algorithm works as follows: it uses a characteristic 1D line profile to model curves in 2D images by computing the Hessian Matrix of the image and then the first- and second-order derivatives of the image in the direction perpendicular to the curves. A pixel point potentially contains a curve point if the first directional derivative vanishes in its vicinity. The lower the second directional derivative value, the more likely it is that a pixel indeed contains a curve point. This concludes the curve-point detection part of the algorithm. This step is completely retained in Improved Curve Tracing.

The rest of the algorithm finalizes the curve points, while forming clusters, which constitute curves, at the same time. For this purpose, a threshold $tr2$ is used. Pixels with second directional derivative less than $-tr2$, whose first directional derivative vanishes, are marked as curve points. The rest of the curve points are found by extending the curves, starting from these points. A curve is extended neighbour-by-neighbour as long as there is a valid curve point near the last curve point detected, in the curvilinear direction. This part is referred to as *Steger Clustering* in [2].

Improved Curve Tracing enhances Steger Clustering by expanding on how a new neighbour can be discovered by considering the following problematic cases:

multiple and possibly intersecting curves, disappearance and re-emergence of a curve, and tracing curves that fade out. Even though the intuition should be similar in improving the Curvilinear Detector algorithm in whisker tracking, WhiskEras already partially deals with some of these issues by using Cluster Stitching. Improved Curve Tracing was not found to work well with Cluster Stitching. On the other hand, using Improved Curve Tracing and completely eliminating the Cluster Stitching step was also disadvantageous. Thus, an alternative implementation was adopted, that is largely inspired by the Improved Curve Tracing method. In this work, we call it Improved Whisker Tracing.

During Steger Clustering, a neighbour curve point is located by searching in the orientation of the current curve point, which is computed by the Curvilinear Detector algorithm, in a 1-pixel radius (*Steger linking*). In Improved Whisker Tracing, this radius can be >1, as sometimes there is an apparent gap between neighbour whisker points. This is now named *pixel peeking.* Additionally, *beam scanning*, a new neighbour-detecting step was added. If no neighbour is found during pixel peeking, beam scanning is used to search for a neighbour some pixels further, in the orientation of the last whisker point found. A $K = 15$ distance -in pixels- is used but this can also be configured. The addition of these two steps is not trivial, as there is some back-and-forth of extending each whisker cluster from both sides and using pixel peeking and beam scanning interchangeably. Although noisy videos pose challenges to the algorithm, the new methods generally result in larger and fewer initial clusters than using Steger Clustering. This significantly reduces the workload of Cluster Stitching, improving the quality of the final results.

5.2 Acceleration

Accelerating WhiskEras 2.0 was no trivial task due to complex algorithmic stages which required careful implementation to eliminate redundant operations and reduce computational cost. First, the code was ported from MATLAB to C++. This required analyzing many high-level MATLAB functions and writing them in C++, top-down, using imperative statements in an efficient way. Then, the parallelizeable sections were located. Both Preprocessing and Centerline Extraction are performed on an NVidia GPU, using CUDA, exploiting pixel-level parallelism. Furthermore, Parameter Fitting is done using multiple threads on the CPU, one for each whisker to be fitted. The same was done for each pair of whisker classes during the SVM Classifier's one-vs-one training. Finally, properties of the clusters, such as rotation data, necessary in Cluster Stitching, are also computed in parallel using CPU multithreading. After this initial phase of acceleration, several optimizations per algorithmic stage were pursued:

1) **Separable convolution:** Centerline Extraction was a particularly expensive step. Specifically, during this step, five convolutions between the image and Guassian derivative kernels are performed. Initially, this step was the bottleneck, yielding a computational complexity of $\mathcal{O}(n \cdot m^2)$, where n are the image dimensions and m is the kernel's width ($m = 20$). It was found that

the kernels used to convolve the image were separable: instead of carrying out normal convolutions, we can perform spatially separable convolutions and obtain the exact same results. The total complexity is now reduced to $\mathcal{O}(n \cdot 2m)$. This implementation is extremely efficient, making use of the GPU's shared memory to minimize memory access latency between consecutive accesses to the same image pixels.

2) **GPU-based sorting:** In the Local-Clustering step, the whisker points with the second directional derivatives are accessed from the lowest to the highest values. Initially, before extending every new curve, an unvisited whisker point with the minimum value of this array was located. This proved to be slow. Thus, this array was sorted before entering the loop, instead. This optimization was even taken one step further by performing the sorting on the GPU, using the highly optimized CUB library.
3) **CPU-GPU-transfer reduction:** Costly data transfers between the host (CPU) and the device (GPU) were minimized in two ways:
   - Constant-sized structures that accommodated variable data per frame are allocated once at the start of processing in the host's pinned memory. This alleviates the need to first transfer the data from the host's pageable memory to pinned memory and then to the GPU, thus maximizing transfer bandwidth [12].
   - The whisker points' orientations and second directional derivative values were originally transferred to the host in arrays with as many entries as image pixels, to be used in the Local Clustering step. This was a naive approach. Instead, another image-sized array was allocated on the device to indicate the presence of whisker points. Then, the CUB library's *DeviceSelect* class was used to discard non-whisker points from the arrays of interest and keep whisker points only. Consequently, the size of these arrays, which are transferred from the GPU to the CPU, decreased dramatically.
4) **Optimal SVM-library selection:** Different libraries were tested on their performance in the demanding SVM training, which can occur e.g. every five frames (user-selectable): a commonly-used SVM library in *libSVM* [6], a GPU SVM library in *gpuSVM* [16], a library using Stochastic Gradient Descent for SVM training in *sgdSVM* [4], with the best choice being an SVM library specialized in linear kernels in *libLinear* [9].

6 Evaluation

The quality and performance of WhiskEras 2.0 is demonstrated in this section by utilizing only two videos (Fig. 4), due to paper space restrictions. However, the videos are markedly different, originating from different experimental setups, thus showcasing the robustness of the WhiskEras 2.0 approach. Video A is focused on one side of the animal's snout, while the whole snout is visible in Video B. The whole Video A (34,133 frames) and a segment from Video B (frames 5,000–30,000) were evaluated qualitatively. The processing power was

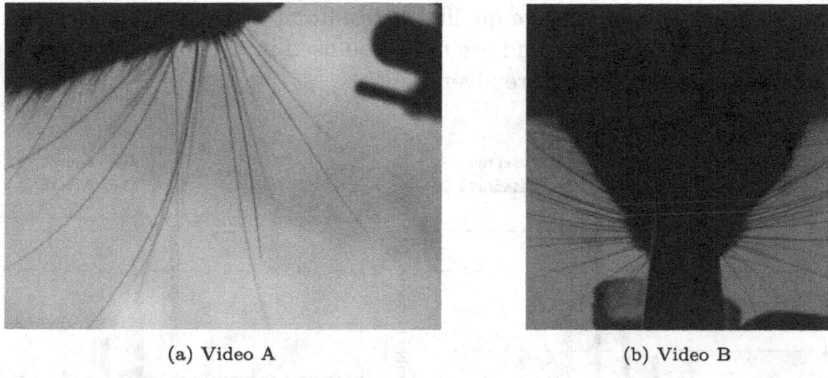

(a) Video A (b) Video B

Fig. 4. Representative frames from videos used for evaluation

Table 1. Metrics to compare the quality of WhiskEras vs WhiskEras 2.0

Evaluation metric	Description
Detected whiskers per frame	Number of whiskers detected per frame
Detection ratio	Fraction of the video in which whiskers were detected
Tracking quality	Trajectory of whiskers' angles in time
Signal-to-noise ratio	Ratio of smoothened whisker angle trajectory to (subtracted) noisy whisker angle trajectory (in dB)

measured by taking the average execution time per frame, over 1,000 frames. The hardware used to assess performance included an AMD EPYC 7551 32-Core Processor @ 2.0 GHz with 64 threads and an NVidia Tesla V100-PCIE GPU. The C++ 17 standard was used, compiled with g++ 4.8.5 using the *-O3* flag to perform aggressive optimizations such as loop unrolling and vectorized operations. OpenMP 3.1 and CUDA 11.1 were used for multithreading on the CPU and the GPU, respectively. The OpenCV 4.2 library was used to read video frames and perform out-of-the-box, image-processing functions, while Eigen 3.3 [11] was used to perform fast linear algebra operations.

6.1 Quality Improvements

To evaluate the effect of the improvements, WhiskEras and WhiskEras 2.0 were run on the same video segments, after manually tuning parameters for both versions. In addition, both were configured to follow the same whisker *tracks*, i.e., have the same starting point to measure how well they can follow their trajectories. Video A contains numerous whiskers, which also intersect and often hide behind each other. On the other hand, we only track the whiskers on the right side of the snout in Video B. Thus, Video A poses more challenges which WhiskEras 2.0 is expected to deal with more consistently than WhiskEras. Evaluating quality is no trivial task, since there is no ground truth. Consequently, the metrics used to compare the quality of results attempt to quantify tracking quality in an automated way and are the same used in [2], presented in Table 1. The results for each criterion are given below.

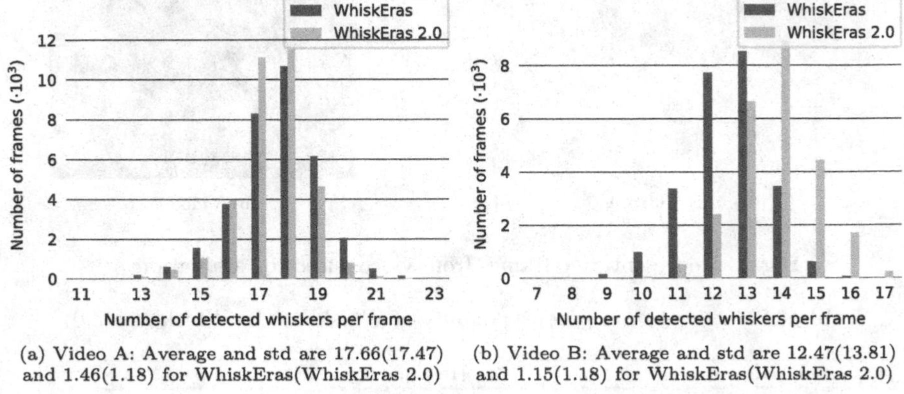

(a) Video A: Average and std are 17.66(17.47) and 1.46(1.18) for WhiskEras(WhiskEras 2.0)

(b) Video B: Average and std are 12.47(13.81) and 1.15(1.18) for WhiskEras(WhiskEras 2.0)

Fig. 5. Histogram of detected whiskers per frame

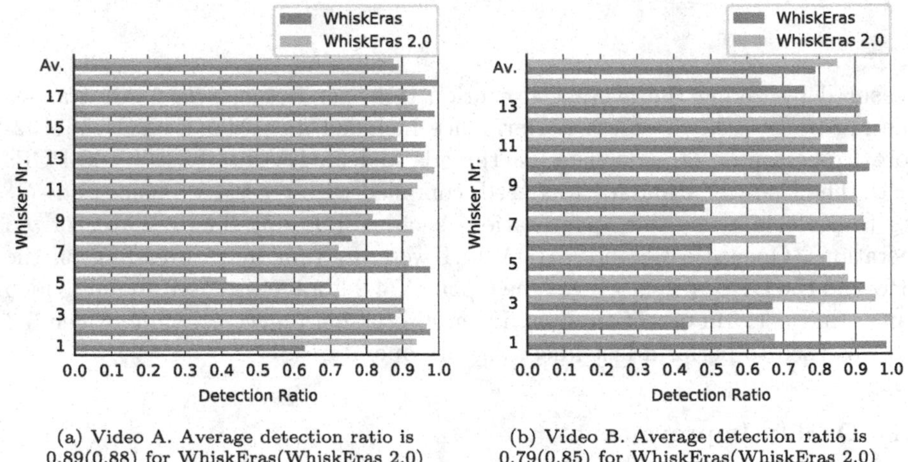

(a) Video A. Average detection ratio is 0.89(0.88) for WhiskEras(WhiskEras 2.0)

(b) Video B. Average detection ratio is 0.79(0.85) for WhiskEras(WhiskEras 2.0)

Fig. 6. Detection ratios

1. **Detected whiskers per frame:** This metric should be fairly stable, meaning a constant number of whiskers is detected throughout a video. Although, whiskers are often hidden, the variance of this metric should be kept to a minimum, indicating algorithmic robustness to whisker movement. A second point of interest is the average number of whiskers detected per frame,

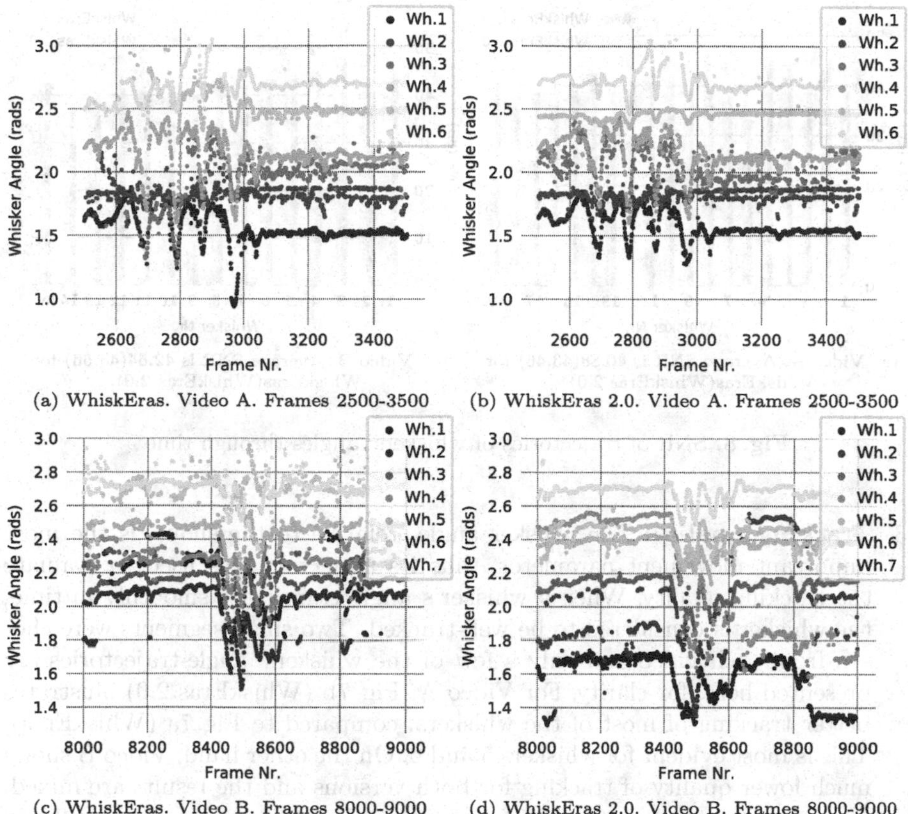

(a) WhiskEras. Video A. Frames 2500-3500 (b) WhiskEras 2.0. Video A. Frames 2500-3500

(c) WhiskEras. Video B. Frames 8000-9000 (d) WhiskEras 2.0. Video B. Frames 8000-9000

Fig. 7. Angle tracking

reflecting false positives as well as false negatives. For Video A, Fig. 5a shows a 19% decrease in standard deviation over the number of detected whiskers per frame, which is positive. Yet, the average number of whiskers detected per frame is marginally smaller. The results were quite different for Video B: a higher average and an almost identical standard deviation (Fig. 5b).

2. **Detection ratio:** The detection ratio of each whisker indicates the percentage of the frames wherein a whisker was successfully tracked. Some whiskers have different detection ratios in the two WhiskEras versions, in both videos. It should be mentioned that whisker indexing refers to the starting point of each whisker (first frame), which is identical for both versions. The same whisker indices do not necessarily represent the same whiskers, as these starting points may have evolved to a different trajectory. Overall, however, the average detection ratios are similar in Video A, while Video B shows a 5% increase for WhiskEras 2.0, compared to WhiskEras (Fig. 6). This also aligns with the increased number of detected whiskers, which translates to more successfully tracked whiskers.

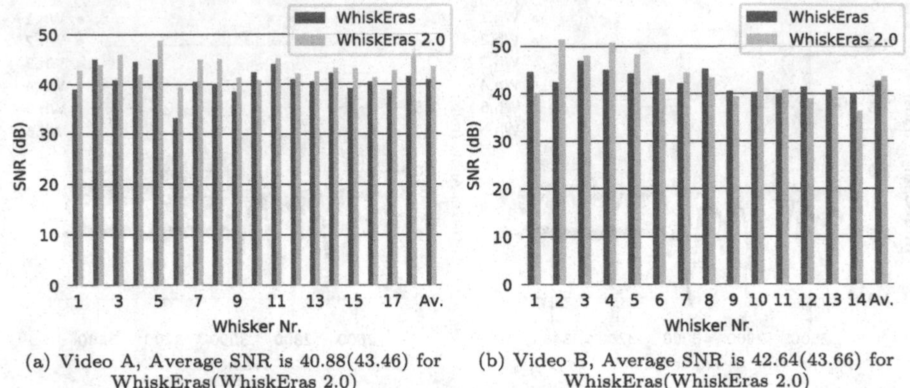

(a) Video A, Average SNR is 40.88(43.46) for WhiskEras(WhiskEras 2.0)

(b) Video B, Average SNR is 42.64(43.66) for WhiskEras(WhiskEras 2.0)

Fig. 8. SNR of trajectories of whiskers' angles through time

3. **Tracking quality:** The whisker angle, relative to the snout, is the most important movement parameter, thus its trajectory was used to evaluate the tracking quality. When a whisker's angle transitions smoothly in time, the whisker is considered to be well-tracked. Two small segments were chosen from each video and only a few of the whiskers' angle-trajectories are presented here, for clarity. For Video A, Fig. 7b (WhiskEras 2.0) illustrates better tracking of most of the whiskers, compared to Fig. 7a (WhiskEras). This is most evident for whiskers 5 and 6. On the other hand, Video B shows much lower quality of tracking for both versions and the results are mixed. For example, whiskers 6 and 7 favour WhiskEras 2.0, while whiskers 2 and 4 show better quality in WhiskEras. Importantly, some of these whiskers do not have a one-to-one correspondence between the two versions, as already stated, thus it is hard to draw any conclusions about which version has the edge in Video B from this metric.
4. **Signal-to-noise ratio (SNR)** represents the quantitative evaluation of the angular change. As in [2], this signal was computed by smoothing the calculated angle of each whisker over time using a Savitzky-Golay filter, which is appropriate for quick variations. A window size of 9 was chosen and the data was fit quadratically. The noise was extracted by subtracting the smoothed data from the actual data. Then, the SNR of each whisker was computed as the ratio of the squared magnitudes of the signal over the noise, in dB. For Video A, WhiskEras 2.0 exhibits a larger SNR for most of the whiskers (Fig. 8a), which was less consistent in Video B (Fig. 8b). Overall, the algorithmic improvements benefited good-quality videos (Video A) more than poor-quality ones (Video B), but even for the latter, gains could be made.

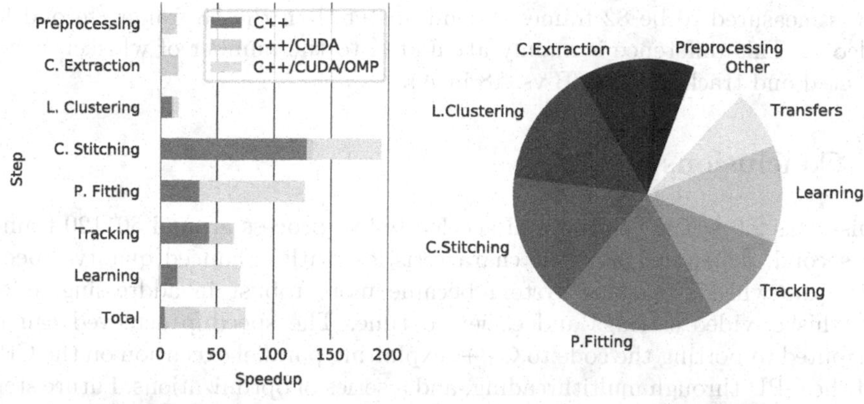

(a) Bar diagram of the accelerated versions' cumulative speedups over MATLAB. Each algorithmic step is shown.

(b) Execution time percentage of each WhiskEras 2.0 accelerated step

Fig. 9. Speedup and execution-time profiling when processing Video A

6.2 Acceleration

The performance of WhiskEras 2.0 was tested in both videos, but here we present the analysis of Video A (see Table 2), due to page limitations. Note that *Other* refers to overhead in between algorithmic steps and OpenCV reading video frames. The speedups obtained are illustrated in Fig. 9a. Simply porting the code to C++ did not provide a massive speedup, due to the lack of execution parallelism in this purely sequential implementation. MATLAB, on the other hand, already made use of CPU and GPU multithreading. The Preprocessing and Centerline Extraction steps, in particular, are much slower in pure C++ than in MATLAB because of the lack of GPU execution, but the C++/CUDA version surpasses both. The optimization involving separable convolution reduced the Centerline Extraction's execution time even more, by a factor of 10x. Furthermore, using OpenMP to take advantage of multiple CPU threads contributed to the final speedup of 74.96x. The execution time per algorithmic step is fairly balanced (Fig. 9b). Further acceleration is *not* achievable without major investments. The processing power of the final version of WhiskEras 2.0 for Video

Table 2. Execution time (in milliseconds) per frame for various development stages of WhiskEras 2.0, as measured when processing Video A

	Pre-process	Centerline extraction	Local cluster	Cluster stitch	Param. fitting	Track	Learn	Trans-fers	Other	Total
MATLAB	12.3	23.0	39.7	520.2	421.3	123.0	140.6	–	4.6	**1284.7**
C++	23.4	232.1	3.9	4.0	12.1	2.9	9.1	0	20.6	**308.1**
C++/CUDA	0.9	1.5	3.2	3.9	12.0	1.9	9.9	2.1	1.2	**36.6**
C++/CUDA/OMP	0.9	1.5	2.5	2.7	3.3	1.9	2.0	1.2	1.1	**17.1**

B was measured to be 82 frames/second, faster than the 58 frames/second for Video A. This difference is mainly attributed to the number of whiskers being detected and tracked (14 in B vs. 18 in A).

7 Conclusions

WhiskEras 2.0 was developed and accelerated to process around 50–120 frames per second, depending on their characteristics, with enhanced quality. Specifically, the whisker-tracking system became more robust in addressing different whisker-video settings and easier to tune. The speedup achieved can be attributed to porting the code to C++, exploiting parallel execution on the CPU and the GPU through multithreading, and a series of optimizations. Future steps include further algorithmic improvements to the Centerline-Extraction step now that the Unbiased Curvilinear Detector's [22] inherent limitations are exposed. Finally, in order to make WhiskEras 2.0 capable of performing online tracking – a desired feature which enables neuroscientists to process whisker videos as they are recorded – more acceleration routes should be explored, such as different/more hardware accelerators.

References

1. Arvanitis, P.: Towards automated and fast whisker tracking in rodents. Master's thesis, Delft University of Technology, January 2021
2. Betting, J.-H.L.F., Romano, V., Al-Ars, Z., Bosman, L.W.J., Strydis, C., De Zeeuw C.I.: WhiskEras: a new algorithm for accurate whisker tracking. Fron. Cell. Neurosci. **14** (2020). https://doi.org/10.3389/fncel.2020.588445. https://www.ncbi.nlm.nih.gov/pmc/issues/351366/. ISSN 1662-5102
3. Bosman, L., Houweling, A., Owens, C., Tanke, N., Shevchouk, O., Rahmati, N., Teunissen, W., Ju, C., Gong, W., Koekkoek, S., De Zeeuw, C.: Anatomical pathways involved in generating and sensing rhythmic whisker movements. Front. Integr. Neurosci. **5**, 53 (2011)
4. Bottou, L.: Stochastic gradient SVM (2007). https://leon.bottou.org/projects/sgd. Accessed 10 Mar 2021
5. Carvell, G., Simons, D.: Biometric analyses of vibrissal tactile discrimination in the rat. J. Neurosci. **10**(8), 2638–2648 (1990)
6. Chang, C.C., Lin, C.J.: LIBSVM: a library for support vector machines. ACM TIST **2**, 27:1–27:27 (2011). http://www.csie.ntu.edu.tw/~cjlin/libsvm
7. Clack, N.G., et al.: Automated tracking of whiskers in videos of head fixed rodents. PLoS Comput. Biol. **8**(7), e1002591 (2012)
8. Dooley, J.C., Glanz, R.M., Sokoloff, G., Blumberg, M.S.: Self-generated whisker movements drive state-dependent sensory input to developing barrel cortex. Curr. Biol. **30**(12), 2404–2410.e4 (2020)
9. Fan, R.E., Chang, K.W., Hsieh, C.J., Wang, X.R., Lin, C.J.: LIBLINEAR: a library for large linear classification. JMLR **9**, 1871–1874 (2008)
10. Grant, R.A., Mitchinson, B., Fox, C.W., Prescott, T.J.: Active touch sensing in the rat: anticipatory and regulatory control of whisker movements during surface exploration. JNP **101**(2), 862–874 (2009)

11. Guennebaud, G., Jacob, B., et al.: Eigen v3 (2010). http://eigen.tuxfamily.org. Accessed 10 Mar 2021
12. Harris, M.: How to optimize data transfers in CUDA C/C++ (2012). https://developer.nvidia.com/blog/how-optimize-data-transfers-cuda-cc/. Accessed 5 Mar 2021
13. Herfst, L.J., Brecht, M.: Whisker movements evoked by stimulation of single motor neurons in the facial nucleus of the rat. JNP **99**(6), 2821–2832 (2008)
14. Kalal, Z., Mikolajczyk, K., Matas, J.: Tracking-learning-detection. IEEE TPAMI **34**(7), 1409–1422 (2012)
15. Kelly, M.K., Carvell, G.E., Kodger, J.M., Simons, D.J.: Sensory loss by selected whisker removal produces immediate disinhibition in the somatosensory cortex of behaving rats. J. Neurosci. **19**(20), 9117–9125 (1999)
16. Li, Q., Salman, R., Test, E., Strack, R., Kecman, V.: GPUSVM: a comprehensive CUDA based support vector machine package. OCS **1**(4), 387–405 (2011)
17. Ma, Y., et al.: Towards real-time whisker tracking in rodents for studying sensorimotor disorders, July 2017
18. Perkon, I., Košir, A., Itskov, P.M., Tasič, J., Diamond, M.E.: Unsupervised quantification of whisking and head movement in freely moving rodents. JNP **105**(4), 1950–1962 (2011)
19. Radon, J.: On the determination of functions from their integral values along certain manifolds. IEEE T-MI **5**(4), 170–176 (1986)
20. Raghupathy, K., Parks, T.: Improved curve tracing in images. In: 2004 ICASSP. IEEE (2004)
21. Rahmati, N., et al.: Cerebellar potentiation and learning a whisker-based object localization task with a time response window. J. Neurosci. **34**(5), 1949–1962 (2014)
22. Steger, C.: An unbiased detector of curvilinear structures. IEEE TPAMI **20**(2), 113–125 (1998)
23. Woolsey, T.A., Welker, C., Schwartz, R.H.: Comparative anatomical studies of the SmL face cortex with special reference to the occurrence of "barrels" in layer IV. JCN **164**(1), 79–94 (1975)

11. [illegible]
12. [illegible]
13. [illegible]
14. [illegible]
15. [illegible]
16. [illegible]
17. [illegible]
18. [illegible]
19. [illegible]
20. [illegible]
21. [illegible]
22. [illegible]
23. [illegible]

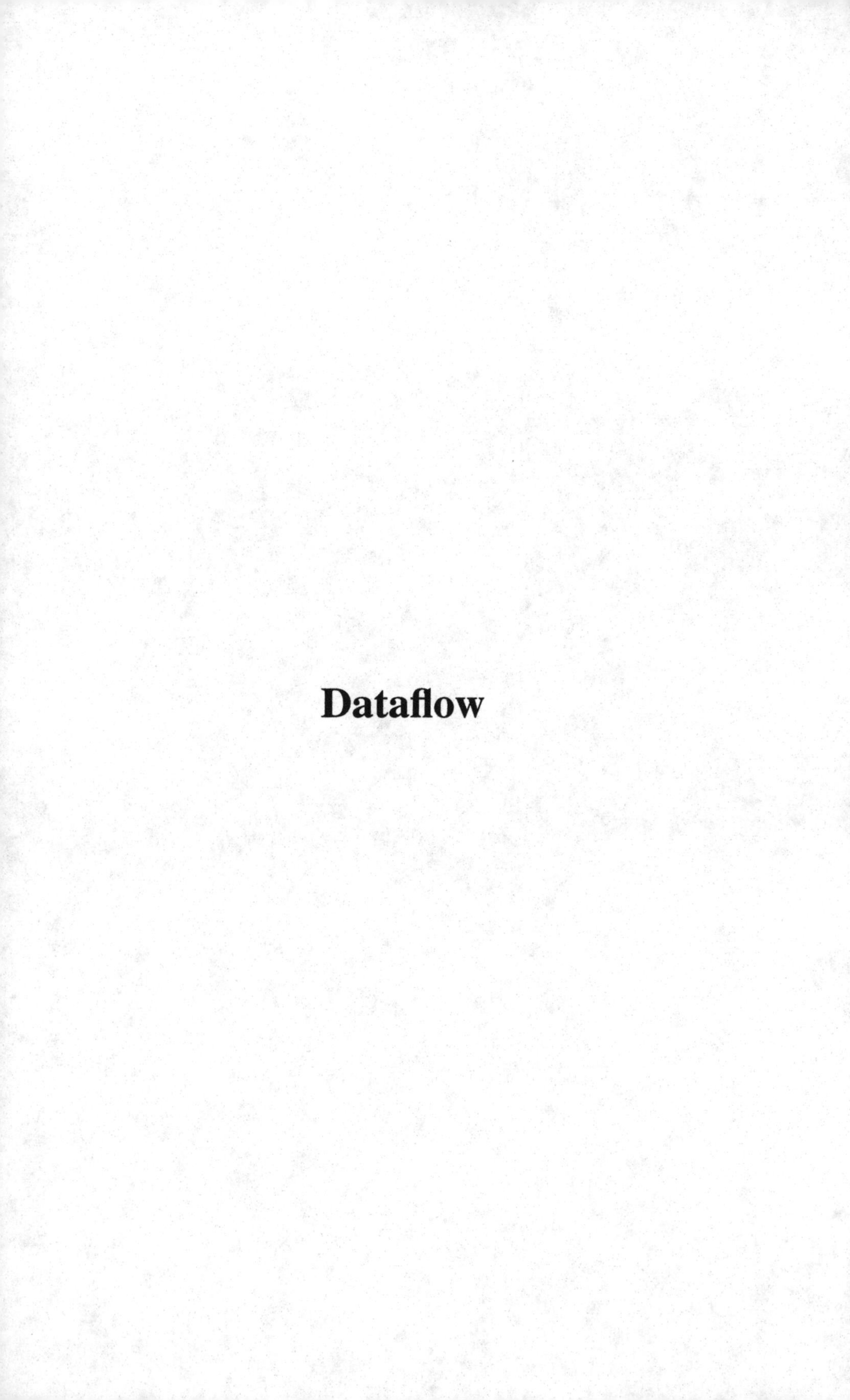

Dataflow

Strictly Periodic Scheduling of Cyclo-Static Dataflow Models

Sam Nicholas Kouteili[1], Francesca Spagnuolo[1], and Bruno Bodin[1,2(✉)]

[1] Yale-NUS College, Singapore, Singapore
bruno.bodin@yale-nus.edu.sg
[2] School of Computing, National University of Singapore, Singapore, Singapore

Abstract. This paper considers *strictly periodic* schedules for Cyclo-Static Dataflow Graphs (CSDFGs) where, for every task, only the start time of the first phase of the first iteration is fixed. This alternative CSDFG scheduling paradigm presents further computational optimization for throughput computations and buffer sizing. It also allows us to consider a wider range of DSP applications and real-time devices, such as time triggered architectures and bufferless software-defined Network-on-chips (NoCs), where the number of periodic executions could be limited. We propose a new framework that defines a necessary and sufficient condition for the existence of such schedules, and present throughput evaluation and buffer sizing use cases.

Keywords: Dataflow models · Scheduling · Throughput · Buffer sizing

1 Introduction

Digital Signal Processors (DSPs) take real-world signals and computationally manipulate them [1]. The Synchronous Data-flow Graph (SDFG) is a formalism method that is commonly used in the field of DSP. SDFGs are a class of dataflow graphs, which are directed multi-graphs where the vertices (tasks) represent computations, and the edges (arcs) represent buffers [2]. The buffers act as queues that direct the data output of one task to the input of another [1]. SDFGs by design possess a constraint: the amount of data produced (and consumed) by a task on each output (input) edge is a fixed number determined at compile time [2]. This presents us with the ability to schedule task firing sequences at compile time, which greatly reduces run-time overheads associated with data-flow graphs [2].

SDFGs, by nature, are mono-phased: each task produces (and consumes) a constant unchanging amount of data per execution. This proves to be limiting for some applications, which require greater granularity and variation in the amount of data produced (and consumed) at each task execution. As such, *Bilsen et al.* introduced Cyclo-Static Data-flow Graphs (CSDFGs), a generalization of SDFGs [3]. CSDFG tasks iterate through a set of periodically repeating predefined sequence of phases. The production (and consumption) associated

© Springer Nature Switzerland AG 2022
A. Orailoglu et al. (Eds.): SAMOS 2021, LNCS 13227, pp. 229–241, 2022.
https://doi.org/10.1007/978-3-031-04580-6_15

with a task is constant at different iterations of a given phase, but may vary between phases [3]. CSDFGs, similarly to SDFGs, are deterministic – the production (and consumption) of data at different phases of each task is statically determined at compile time.

The scheduling of SDFGs and CSDFGs remains a complex problem for which there are no ubiquitous ideal solutions. Previous works [4,5] have attempted to create exact *as-soon-as-possible* solutions, however, such solutions maintain exponential computation time. Another class of solutions considers *periodic* schedules [6] which order the execution of tasks in a consistent periodic manner. Applying a periodic constraint allows for the construction of schedules with polynomial sets of linear equations [7]. Moreover, the implementation of periodic schedules enables the use of linear programming to model the optimization of the total buffer size problem under a minimum throughput requirement [7–10]. This is especially pertinent to certain applications with dynamic overhead limitations such as time triggered hardware. The design of more complex real-time hardware such as time triggered architectures [11] and software-defined Network-on-Chip (NoC) with programmable routers [12] presents a new constraint to dataflow scheduling techniques.

With dynamic software schedulers [13] and dynamically routed Network-on-Chips [14], the schedule of dataflow applications is implicitly expressed by data-driven constraints (such as the buffer sizes) at run-time. Conversely, statically scheduled real-time devices require explicit definition of the application schedule [15]. More importantly, this schedule definition must fit in the hardware. For example, the SPECTRUM architecture [12] has been designed to support the Long Term Evolution (LTE) 4G/5G communication protocol. This architecture is made of programmable routers, each containing only four scheduling entries. Supporting such hardware requires scheduling techniques that trade-off the size of schedule definition versus its performance. In some cases (such as SPECTRUM), this necessitates the introduction of different classes of periodic schedules.

This paper specifically considers strictly periodic schedules, as introduced in [15]. We present a novel mathematical framework that formalizes strictly periodic schedules, adding a rudimentary layer to prune through existing periodic methods. Our mathematical formalism of strictly periodic schedules differs from [15] in that we present not only necessary, but also sufficient bounds for the formation of strictly periodic schedules; this allows us to construct and confirm exact solutions for strictly periodic schedules. We present two practical applications of the framework for throughput evaluation and buffer sizing. In addition, we study the size of schedule definition. The paper first develops relevant terminology, before exploring related works. It then presents our novel mathematical constraints and theorems, which are integrated in the respective algorithms. The paper concludes by comparing the performance of existing scheduling strategies, including the strictly periodic schedules.

2 Syntax and Problem Definition

2.1 Model Definition

A Cyclo-Static Dataflow Graph (CSDFG) is denoted by $G = (T, A)$ where T (*resp.* A) is the set of tasks (*resp.* arcs).

Tasks: Every *task* $t \in T$ is composed of $\varphi(t) \in \mathbb{N} - \{0\}$ phases - these can be interpreted as incremental sub-tasks. An iteration of the task $t \in T$ corresponds to the ordered executions of the phases $(t_1, ..., t_{\varphi(t)})$. The firing of the kth phase, $k \in \{1, ..., \varphi(t)\}$, of t is denoted t_k, and has a duration time $d(t_k) \in \mathbb{R}$. Entire tasks can be iterated over several times. The nth firing, $n \in \mathbb{N} - \{0\}$ of the kth phase of t is denoted $\langle t_k, n \rangle$. At $\langle t_k, n \rangle$, all phases have been iterated through $n-1$ times, with the phases up to and including the kth one iterating one more time. A Synchronous Data-Flow Graph can be viewed as an instance of a CSDFG, where each task only has one phase.

Buffers: Every arc $a = (t, t') \in A$ represents a buffer $b(a)$ from t to t' that stores data. We suppose that $\forall k \in \{1, ..., \varphi(t)\}$, $in_a(k)$ data is written in $b(a)$ at the end of the execution t_k. Similarly, $\forall k' \in \{1, ..., \varphi(t')\}$, $out_a(k')$ data is read from $b(a)$ before the execution $t'_{k'}$. Buffers may have initial stored data, denoted $M_0(a)$.

Figure 1a shows a CSDFG with 5 arcs. Arc h is an example of a buffer between the two tasks A and B. The number of phases associated to the tasks A and B is $\varphi(A) = 2$ and $\varphi(B) = 3$. The associated rate vectors of h and its initial amounts of data are $in_h = [3, 5]$, $out_h = [1, 1, 4]$, and $M_0(h) = 0$.

For an arc $a \in A$, we define $I_a\langle t_k, n \rangle$ to be the total amount of data produced by t in $b(a)$ at the completion of $\langle t_k, n \rangle$ [7]. Similarly, $O_a\langle t'_{k'}, n' \rangle$ is defined to be the total amount of data consumed by t' in $b(a)$ at the completion of $\langle t'_{k'}, n' \rangle$. Given the constant nature of phase sequences, we can formalize the following;

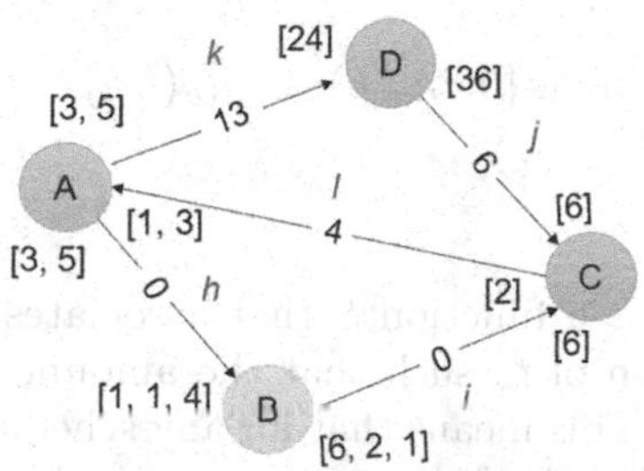

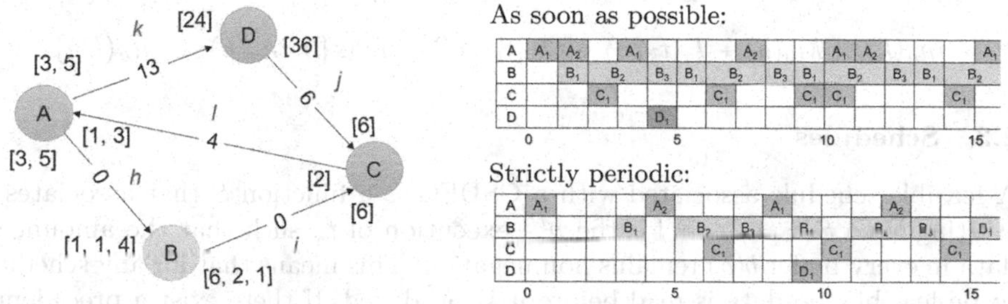

(a) CSDFG application with 4 tasks. Execution times are $d(A) = [1, 1]$, $d(B) = [1, 2, 1]$, $d(C) = [1]$, and $d(D) = [1]$.

As soon as possible:

Strictly periodic:

(b) The *as-soon-as-possible* schedule hyper-period is $\Omega^S_G = 16.0$, the *strictly periodic* hyper-period is $\Omega^S_G = 24.0$.

Fig. 1. Example of a CSDFG and corresponding schedules.

$$I_a\langle t_k, n\rangle = (n-1) \times \sum_{i=1}^{\varphi(t)} in_a(i) + \sum_{i=1}^{k} in_a(i)$$

$$O_a\langle t'_{k'}, n'\rangle = (n'-1) \times \sum_{j=1}^{\varphi(t')} out_a(j) + \sum_{j=1}^{k'} out_a(j)$$

As a shorthand notation, we set $i_a = I_a\langle t_{\varphi(t)}, 1\rangle$ and $o_a = O_a\langle t_{\varphi(t')}, 1\rangle$. These values represent the amount of data, respectively, produced and consumed by one complete iteration of tasks t and t' respectively in some buffer $b(a)$. For example, in Fig. 1a, $i_h = I_h\langle A_2, 1\rangle = 8$ and $o_h = O_h\langle B_3, 1\rangle = 6$. Finally, we note a constraint on all buffers, which states that the amount of data in every buffer $b(a)$ must remain non negative - this implies a precedence constraint between the executions of tasks.

2.2 Precedence Constraints

There exist a precedence constraint between two task executions when the latter execution requires data produced from the former. More formally, supposing an arc $a = (t, t') \in A$, there exists a precedence constraint between $\langle t_k, n\rangle$ and $\langle t'_{k'}, n'\rangle$ if the following conditions hold:

1. $\langle t'_{k'}, n'\rangle$ can only be executed after the completion of $\langle t_k, n\rangle$.
2. The phase firing preceding $\langle t'_{k'}, n'\rangle$, denoted $Pr\langle t'_{k'}, n'\rangle$, can be executed before the completion of $\langle t_k, n\rangle$.

These are self-evident formalisations of classical notions of precedence constraints. In their paper, Benazouz *et al.* [9] built on these principles to prove Lemma 1:

Lemma 1 [9]. *Let* $a = (t, t') \in A$, *a couple* $(k, k') \in (\{1, ..., \varphi(t)\} \times \{1, ..., \varphi(t')\})$. *For any couple* $(n, n') \in \mathbb{N}^2$, *there exists a precedence relation from* $\langle t_k, n\rangle$ *to* $\langle t'_{k'}, n'\rangle$, *iff*

$$in_a(k) > M_0(a) + I_a\langle t_k, n\rangle - O_a\langle t'_{k'}, n'\rangle \geq \max\{0, in_a(k) - out_a(k')\}$$

2.3 Schedules

A feasible schedule associated with a CSDFG is a function S that associates a starting time $S\langle t_k, n\rangle \in \mathbb{R}$ for the nth execution of t_k such that the amount of data in every buffer $b(a)$ remains non negative. This means that for any schedule to be feasible, no data is read before it is produced. If there exist a precedence constraint between two executions $\langle t_k, n\rangle$ and $\langle t'_{k'}, n'\rangle$ then the following holds:

$$S\langle t_k, n\rangle + d(t_k) \leq S\langle t'_{k'}, n'\rangle.$$

This effectively implies that the latter execution must start after the prior has fully completed execution.

2.4 Consistency and Liveness

The existence of a feasible schedule is partially dependent on the *consistency* of a CSDFG [1]. A CSDFG is said to be *consistent* if it admits a repetition vector $q \in \mathbb{N}^{|T|}$, with q_t the repetition factor of any task $t \in T$, such that

$$\forall a = (t, t') \in A, q_t \times i_a = q_{t'} \times o_a.$$

This constraint result from the fact that the amount of data consumed should ultimately be equal to the amount of data produced.

The repetition vector defines the number of times each task need to be executed in a scheduling sequence that preserves data quantities [2]. The repetition vector of Fig. 1a is $q = [3, 4, 6, 1]$.

In order to admit a valid schedule, an application also needs to be deadlock-free. A CSDFG is *alive* if every task in the application can be executed infinitely often. This is the *liveness* property.

2.5 Throughput and Hyper-period

For any given schedule S, the throughput of a task $t \in T$ with a start time for the nth iteration $S\langle t_1, n\rangle$ is defined as

$$Th_t^S = \lim_{n \to \infty} \frac{n}{S\langle t_1, n\rangle}.$$

Stuijk *et al.* prove that for any couple $(t, t') \in T^2$, $\frac{Th_t^S}{q_t} = \frac{Th_{t'}^S}{q_{t'}}$ [16]. By extension, we define the hyper-period of schedule S for a graph G,

$$\Omega_G^S = \frac{q_t}{Th_t^S}.$$

3 Related Works

This paper builds a new mathematical framework to reflect upon and analyze cyclo-static dataflow schedules. We can use this framework to conduct both throughput analysis and buffer sizing.

The question of throughput evaluation of a CSDFG in a given time constraint remains open. A complete solution for throughput evaluation of HSDFGs (where for any task t and arc $a = (t, t')$, $\varphi(t) = 1, i_a = 1, o_a = 1$) has existed for some time [17]. However, translation of such solutions to SDFGs and CSDFGs have been limited. *Lee & Messerschmitt* proved that any SDFG can be translated into an HSDFG; however this operation leads to graphs of exponential size [2]. Several works, such as [18], have since employed and improved this SDF to HSDF translation model, developing exact approaches that remain constrained by being in exponential time.

Other approaches to throughput analysis have been presented using symbolic execution [4], but the exponential execution time issue remained for most case.

de Groote [5] presents Max-plus algebra as an exact approach and near exact application to CSDFGs using single-rate approximations, unfolding transformations, and execution state. Interestingly, single-rate approximations for CSDFG are very close to the definition of strictly periodic schedules. However the number of constraints to consider is different (execution time of phases can vary), thus it does not exactly match the performance of strictly periodic schedules.

Some authors have attempted to circumvent exponentiation by incorporating elements of periodic scheduling into their throughput analysis. [19] introduces periodic static-order schedule (PSOS), which looks at the firing order of tasks, but not task start times, to examine task firing order sequences. [20] conducts throughput analysis and analyzes the scheduling of Cyber-Physical Systems (CPSs), composed of periodic and aperiodic components.

The present paper considers and builds upon scholarship conducting throughput analysis of fully periodic schedules. *Benabid et al.* [6] proved that any periodic schedule of an SDFG may be characterized using linear equations on the starting times of the first execution of the tasks. The paper importantly showed that the throughput achieved with this scheduling policy will remain a lower bound of the maximum throughput. *Bodin et al.* [7] built on [6] to construct periodic schedules for all CSDFGs. These periodic schedules present a lower bound on throughput, and allow for buffer size analysis.

Buffer sizing was initially defined to be NP-hard for all classes of dataflow graphs, including HSDFGs [1]. Albeit this, *Stuijk et al.* [16] developed the first exact method exploring all buffer sizes for SDFGs, eventually generalizing to CSDFGs [21]. Performance of this method is limited by the fact that throughput evaluation is itself in exponential time. Throughput-buffer sizing is leveraged in [22] to present an algorithm that minimizes total buffer sizing given different throughput constraints.

One approach to measuring buffer sizing is to consider only periodic schedules, which allows us to obtain buffer sizing linear constraints. It is shown that buffer sizes can be computed given a periodic sequence of tasks in polynomial time, defined by a set of linear equations [8]. *Benazouz et al.* [10] then showed that the execution policy of such phases may also be modelled with linear programs.

This paper deviates from these proposed solutions, as we tackle throughput evaluation and buffer sizing under a strictly periodic scheduling constraint. The closest work we can see is certainly from *Niknam et al.* [15]: they propose a sufficient condition for the existence of a strictly periodic schedule for a CSDF while focusing on real-time applications. However, similarly to the single-rate approximation [5], their method is an over-approximation. Our framework is intended to be more general and includes a necessary and sufficient condition of existence, leading to exact solutions for strictly periodic schedules.

4 Strictly Periodic Scheduling

In this section we define strictly periodic schedules and present our main contribution - the formalization of linear constraints to compute any strictly periodic schedules.

Definition 2. *Given a CSDFG $G = (T, A)$, a schedule S of hyper-period Ω_G^S is strictly periodic if it verifies, for any task $t \in T$:*

$$S\langle t_k, n\rangle = S\langle t_1, 1\rangle + (k-1)\frac{\Omega_G^S}{\varphi(t)q_t} + (n-1)\frac{\Omega_G^S}{q_t}.$$

Given such mathematical paradigms, Fig. 1b is a *strictly periodic* schedule, specifically scheduling the CSDF in Fig. 1a. The schedule period is in general not optimal. However, we recognize the considered benefits of applying a *strictly periodic* schedule as described in Sect. 5.3.

To prove a necessary and sufficient condition for the linear constraint formulation of a feasible strictly periodic schedule, we make use of the existing work from *Bodin et al.* [7].

Given an arc $a = (t, t') \in A$ and a couple $(k, k') \in \{1, \dots, \varphi(t)\} \times \{1, \dots, \varphi(t')\}$, define

$$\alpha_a^{min}(k, k') = \lceil O_a\langle t'_{k'}, 1\rangle - I_a\langle t_k, 1\rangle - M_o(a) + \max\{in_a(k) - out_a(k'), 0\}\rceil^{gcd_a}$$
$$\alpha_a^{max}(k, k') = \lfloor O_a\langle t'_{k'}, 1\rangle - I_a Pr\langle t_k, 1\rangle - M_o(a) - 1\rfloor^{gcd_a}$$

with $gcd_a = gcd(i_a, o_a)$, and the operators $\lfloor\alpha\rfloor^\gamma = \lfloor\frac{\alpha}{\gamma}\rfloor \times \gamma$ and $\lceil\alpha\rceil^\gamma = \lceil\frac{\alpha}{\gamma}\rceil \times \gamma$ defined for any pair $(\alpha, \gamma) \in \mathbb{Z} \times \mathbb{N} - \{0\}$.

For any pair (k, k'), $\alpha_a^{min}(k, k')$ and $\alpha_a^{max}(k, k')$ represent the lower and upper bound, respectively, of the amount of data needed for the existence of a precedence constraint from the execution of $\langle t_k, n\rangle$ to the execution of $\langle t'_{k'}, n'\rangle$ for any $(n, n') \in (\mathbb{N} - \{0\})^2$. In other words, if $\alpha_a^{min}(k, k') > \alpha_a^{max}(k, k')$ then there is no couple $(n, n') \in (\mathbb{N} - \{0\})^2$ such that a induces a precedence constraint from $\langle t_k, n\rangle$ to $\langle t'_{k'}, n'\rangle$.

The following theorem provides the basis for the proof of our main result.

Theorem 3 *([7]). Let $G = (T, A)$ be a strongly connected CSDFG. For any feasible periodic schedule S, precedence constraints associated with an arc $a = (t, t') \in A$ are fulfilled if and only if, for every couple $(k, k') \in \{1, \dots, \varphi(t)\} \times \{1, \dots, \varphi(t')\}$ with $\alpha_a^{min}(k, k') \le \alpha_a^{max}(k, k')$*

$$S\langle t'_{k'}, 1\rangle - S\langle t_k, 1\rangle \ge d(t_k) + \Omega_G^S \frac{\alpha_a^{max}(k, k')}{i_a q_t}.$$

Given a duration time l and an arc $a = (t, t') \in A$, define δ_a^l to be the set of phases k of t with duration time l such that there is a $k' \in \{1, \dots, \varphi(t')\}$ for which $\alpha_a^{min}(k, k') \le \alpha_a^{max}(k, k')$:

$$\delta_a^l = \{k \in \{1, \dots, \varphi(t)\} | d(t_k) = l \ \& \ \exists k' \in \{1, \dots, \varphi(t')\}, \alpha_a^{min}(k, k') \le \alpha_a^{max}(k, k')\}.$$

Then for any $l \in \mathbb{R}$ and task $t \in T$, define

$$\beta_a^{max}(\delta_a^l) = \max\{\beta_a(k,k') | k \in \delta_a^l \;\&\; k' \in \{1,\ldots,\varphi(t')\}, \alpha_a^{min}(k,k') \leq \alpha_a^{max}(k,k')\},$$

where $\beta_a(k,k') = \alpha_a^{max}(k,k') - \frac{(k'-1)o_a}{\varphi(t')} + \frac{(k-1)i_a}{\varphi(t)}$.

The next theorem presents a necessary and sufficient condition for the existence of a feasible strictly periodic schedule.

Theorem 4. *Let $G = (T, A)$ be a strongly connected CSDFG. For any feasible strictly periodic schedule S, precedence constraints associated with an arc $a = (t, t') \in A$ are fulfilled iff*

$$S\langle t'_1, 1\rangle - S\langle t_1, 1\rangle \geq l + \frac{\Omega_G^S}{i_a q_t}\beta_a^{max}(\delta_a^l)$$

for every l such that $\delta_a^l \neq \emptyset$

Proof. Let $k \in \delta_a^l$ and suppose that the arc a induces a precedence constraint from $\langle t_k, n\rangle$ to $\langle t'_{k'}, n'\rangle$.

From Theorem 3 (Theorem 2 of [7]) we know that every precedence constraint is verified for any periodic schedule iff

$$S\langle t'_{k'}, 1\rangle - S\langle t_k, 1\rangle \geq l + \Omega_G^S \frac{\alpha_a^{max}(k,k')}{q_t i_a} \tag{1}$$

for every pair $(k, k') \in \{1,\ldots,\varphi(t)\} \times \{1,\ldots,\varphi(t')\}$, with $\alpha_a^{min}(k,k') \leq \alpha_a^{max}(k,k')$. Furthermore from Definition 2

$$S\langle t_k, n\rangle = S\langle t_1, 1\rangle + (k-1)\frac{\Omega_G^S}{\varphi(t) q_t} + (n-1)\frac{\Omega_G^S}{q_t}.$$

Therefore

$$S\langle t'_{k'}, 1\rangle - S\langle t_k, 1\rangle = S\langle t'_1, 1\rangle + (k'-1)\frac{\Omega_G^S}{\varphi(t') q_{t'}} - S\langle t_1, 1\rangle - (k-1)\frac{\Omega_G^S}{\varphi(t) q_t}. \tag{2}$$

Combining (1) and (2)

$$S\langle t'_1, 1\rangle - S\langle t_1, 1\rangle \geq l + \Omega_G^S \frac{\alpha_a^{max}(k,k')}{q_t i_a} - (k'-1)\frac{\Omega_G^S}{\varphi(t') q_{t'}} + (k-1)\frac{\Omega_G^S}{\varphi(t) q_t}$$

Recalling that $q_t \times i_a = q_{t'} \times o_a$,

$$S\langle t'_1, 1\rangle - S\langle t_1, 1\rangle \geq l + \frac{\Omega_G^S}{q_t i_a}\left(\alpha_a^{max}(k,k') - \frac{(k'-1)o_a}{\varphi(t')} + \frac{(k-1)i_a}{\varphi(t)}\right).$$

As $k \in \delta_a^l$, by definition of $\beta_a^{max}(\delta_a^l)$,

$$\alpha_a^{max}(k,k') - \frac{(k'-1)o_a}{\varphi(t')} + \frac{(k-1)i_a}{\varphi(t)} = \beta_a(k,k') \leq \beta_a^{max}(\delta_a^l)$$

thus the theorem condition holds. ∎

Theorem 4 can be directly used to express linear problems that maximize throughput or minimize buffer size. This is demonstrated in Sect. 5.

5 Applications

In this section, we present three possible uses of the devised strictly periodic scheduling framework. First, we compare strictly periodic scheduling (S-Periodic) with 1-Periodic and K-Periodic solutions in the context of throughput evaluation. We then consider these techniques in the context of buffer sizing. Lastly, we consider the problem of scheduling definition size.

While results in terms of throughput and buffer size are expected to be notably lower than traditional techniques, it is important to note that such traditional techniques are not realistic solutions for recently proposed time triggered hardware such as real-time systems [15]. Furthermore, strictly periodic schedules fit very small programmable areas such as programmable NoC routers [12].

Experiments[1] are performed on a 3.7 GHz Intel Xeon processor and consider real-life and synthetic CSDFG benchmarks from [23] - we recall them on Table 1. Graphs marked with the `_sized` suffix are graphs where a particular buffer size has been used to constraint the schedule.

5.1 Throughput Evaluation

The proposed framework is directly applicable to the maximum throughput evaluation of a strictly periodic schedule for CSDFGs. Using linear programming, we minimize the hyper-period with the given framework constraints.

Table 1 summarizes the performance of different scheduling strategies in terms of maximal reachable throughput. The S-Periodic approach is compared to a 1-Periodic strategy (as defined from [7]) that sets one starting time per phase of each task, and the K-Periodic strategy that may set several start times per phase in order to reach optimality [23].

These experiments confirm the expected results. Because S-Periodic scheduling is more constrained than the 1-Periodic and K-Periodic counterparts, its maximal throughput performance will necessarily be lower.

In the case of an acyclic CSDFG (such as Black-Scholes), the 1-Periodic paradigm was proven to produce optimal schedules [7]. We observe from these experiments that this is not the case with S-Periodic schedules. We can explain this interesting finding by considering a single-task example. If a task has two phases with different execution times, a 1-Periodic solution can execute each phase one after the other, producing an optimal solution. Conversely, an S-Periodic schedule will be constrained by the shortest phase having to wait as long as the duration of the longest phase. As a result, while 1-Periodic schedules can often be optimal or near-optimal, S-Periodic schedules may be much slower.

From these results, even if strictly periodic schedules are necessary for certain real-time devices, this demonstrates the limitations of hardware on application performance. From a model point of view, we note that strictly periodic schedules are more appropriate when applications have uniform execution time across task phases.

[1] Available online: https://github.com/bbodin/kiter.

Table 1. Throughput Evaluation of Benchmark Applications. (higher is better). A "-" indicates there was no possible solution or, in the case of the optimal solution, the computation time exceeded 24 h. Complexity is defined as the size of a repetition pattern ($\sum q_t \times \varphi(t)$). The optimal value is the maximal reachable throughput of the application.

Graph	#tasks	#buffers	Complexity	S-Periodic	1-Periodic	Optimal
autogen1	90	617	250992	–	4.85E−08	**3.84E−05**
autogen2	70	473	41331062	–	1.56E−11	–
autogen3	154	671	308818852	–	4.76E−13	–
autogen4	2426	2900	51301	2.08E−02	2.68E−02	**2.78E−02**
autogen5	2767	4894	312485	5.25E−05	5.25E−05	**2.44E−03**
BlackScholes	41	40	2379	1.79E−08	**2.38E−08**	**2.38E−08**
BlackScholes_sized	41	80	2379	6.22E-09	1.53E−08	**1.55E−08**
Echo	38	82	42003	4.06E-11	**1.96E−10**	**1.96E−10**
Echo_sized	38	164	42003	4.06E−11	5.47E−11	**1.67E−10**
H264	666	3128	1471	–	**4.20E−06**	**4.20E−06**
H264_sized	666	6256	1471	–	**3.92E−06**	**3.92E−06**
JPEG2000	240	703	29595	**4.11E−07**	**4.11E−07**	**4.11E−07**
JPEG2000_sized	240	1406	29595	–	–	**2.05E−07**
PDectect	58	76	4045	**4.92E−07**	**4.92E−07**	**4.92E−07**
PDectect_sized	58	152	4045	2.54E−09	**2.46E−07**	**2.46E−07**

5.2 Buffer Sizing

Buffer sizing can be a major constraint in the context of embedded systems, particularly DSPs that need to manipulate extensive amounts of data while keeping the memory footprint as low as possible. Even if an application could be supported by an S-Periodic schedule, it is important to verify that the amount of memory required remains realistically feasible.

Table 2 presents our experimental results comparing S-Periodic and 1-Periodic based buffer sizing techniques for instances where an S-Periodic solution is supported. While we intend to primarily focus on comparing the buffer sizes obtained with 1-Periodic and S-Periodic schedules, we also present optimal results if they were computed in a reasonable amount of time (>24 h).

The experiments show that the buffer sizes required to admit a strictly periodic solution may be significantly higher than alternative periodic methods, presenting up to a 20% overhead with certain applications (autogen4). Comparing to optimal buffer sizing – when it was possible to compute it – the overhead remained acceptable, only citing a 7% overhead for Pdetect.

Table 2. Minimal buffer size estimation of Benchmark Applications for applications that admit a S-Periodic solution. (lower is better). Absence of result implies the computation time was greater than 24 h.

Graph	S-Periodic	1-Periodic	Optimal
BlackScholes	**16250**	**16250**	**16250**
Echo	30206	30206	**28022**
JPEG2000	3865869	3608503	–
Pdetect	4263895	4187155	**3958195**
autogen4	36412	29294	–
autogen5	1464710	1442122	–

5.3 Scheduling Definition

The main motivation for considering strictly periodic scheduling was to find a way to reduce the size of the application schedule. This is a crucial problem for real-time devices that support a limited number of start times per task [12,15].

In Table 3, we compare the size of different schedules in terms of the number of start times required to define them. In order to better contextualize the gain, we also present K-Periodic and HSDFG expansion [18], two methods that present optimal throughput.

Table 3. Size of the schedule definition (in number of starting time) for several strategies.

Graph	S-Periodic	1-Periodic	K-Periodic	MCM
autogen1	–	126 (1.4)	250992 (2788.8)	250992 (2788.8)
autogen2	–	196 (2.8)	–	41331062 (590443.7)
autogen3	–	368 (2.4)	–	308818852 (2005317.2)
autogen4	2426 (1.0)	5422 (2.2)	5449 (2.2)	51301 (21.1)
autogen5	2767 (1.0)	4167 (1.5)	60009 (21.7)	312485 (112.9)
BlackScholes	41 (1.0)	261 (6.4)	261 (6.4)	2379 (58.0)
BlackScholes_sized	41 (1.0)	261 (6.4)	264 (6.4)	2379 (58.0)
Echo	38 (1.0)	45 (1.2)	45 (1.2)	42003 (1105.3)
Echo_sized	38 (1.0)	45 (1.2)	42003 (1105.3)	42003 (1105.3)
H264	–	1375 (2.1)	1375 (2.1)	1471 (2.2)
H264_sized	–	1375 (2.1)	1375 (2.1)	1471 (2.2)
JPEG2000	240 (1.0)	639 (2.7)	639 (2.7)	29595 (123.3)
JPEG2000_sized	–	–	9934 (41.4)	29595 (123.3)
PDectect	58 (1.0)	4045 (69.7)	4045 (69.7)	4045 (69.7)
PDectect_sized	58 (1.0)	4045 (69.7)	4045 (69.7)	4045 (69.7)

As the objective is to reduce the number of starting times per task, we also include in parenthesis the ratio of starting time per task. By definition, the strictly periodic schedule always has a single start time per task.

From these results, we note that when there exists a strictly periodic schedule, the size of these schedules are on average 142 times smaller than any optimal scheduling solution, and 15 times smaller than 1-Periodic results.

6 Conclusion

This paper presents a necessary and sufficient condition for the existence of *strictly-periodic* schedules of CSDFGs. Application tests are presented to display both the strengths and drawbacks of strictly-periodic schedule generation relative to different *state-of-the-art* techniques. In certain cases, *strictly-periodic* schedules performed similarly to more computationally expensive counterparts (which is to be expected in cases where the optimal schedule happens to be strictly-periodic), however in most cases the generated schedule throughput is smaller. Generation of *strictly-periodic* schedules under bounded buffers is more noticeably limited. Keeping this in mind, in many cases the generated schedules are still sufficient such that the applications in question run for real-life systems.

A potential extension of this work would be to create an algorithm that combines *strictly-periodic* schedules with other defined periodic scheduling methods, effectively extending upon the methods presented in [23]. Integrating *strictly-periodic* schedules would further optimize the work done in [23], such that in cases where a *strictly-periodic* schedule is optimal, there would be no need to consider more computationally expensive alternatives.

Acknowledgements. The authors wish to express their thanks for the financial support of the Yale-NUS College Summer Research Programme. This work was also supported by a grant awarded to Dr. Bruno Bodin by the Singapore Ministry of Education (AcRF Tier 1/Yale-NUS Internal Grant IG19-SG102).

References

1. Sriram, S., Bhattacharyya, S.S.: Embedded Multiprocessors: Scheduling and Synchronization. CRC, Boca Raton, second edition (2009)
2. Lee, E.A., Messerschmitt, D.G.: Synchronous data flow. Proc. IEEE **75**(9), 1235–1245 (1987)
3. Bilsen, G., Engels, M., Lauwereins, R., Peperstraete, J.A.: Cyclo-static data flow. IEEE Trans. Sign. Process. 3255–3258 (1995)
4. Mousavi, M.R., et al.: Throughput analysis of synchronous data flow graphs. In: Application of Concurrency to System Design (2006)
5. de Groote, R.: Throughput analysis of dataflow graphs. In: Handbook of Signal Processing Systems, pp. 751–786. Springer (2018)
6. Benabid, A., Hanen, C., Marchetti, O., Munier-Kordon, A.: Periodic schedules for bounded timed weighted event graphs. IEEE Trans. Autom. Control **57**(5), 1222–1232 (2012)

7. Bodin, B., Munier-Kordon, A., De Dinechin, B.D.: Periodic schedules for cyclo-static dataflow. In: ESTIMedia 2013–11th IEEE Symposium on Embedded Systems for Real-Time Multimedia, pp. 105–114 (2013)
8. Wiggers, M.H., Bekooij, M.J.G., Smit, G.J.M.: Efficient computation of buffer capacities for cyclo-static dataflow graphs. In: Design Automation Conference, pp. 658–663 (2007)
9. Benazouz, M., Marchetti, O., Munier-Kordon, A., Michel, T.: A new method for minimizing buffer sizes for cyclo-static dataflow graphs. In: IEEE Workshop on Embedded Systems for Real-Time Multimedia, pp. 11–20 (2010)
10. Benazouz, M., Munier-Kordon, A.: Cyclo-static dataflow phases scheduling optimization for buffer sizes minimization, pp. 3–12. International Workshop on Software and Compilers for Embedded Systems, M-SCOPES (2013)
11. Gendy, A.K., Pont, M.J.: Automatically configuring time-triggered schedulers for use with resource-constrained, single-processor embedded systems. IEEE Trans. Ind. Inform. **4**(1), 37–46 (2008)
12. Venkataramani, V., Kulkarni, A., Mitra, T., Peh, L.S.: Spectrum: a software-defined predictable many-core architecture for LTE/5g baseband processing. ACM Trans. Embed. Comput. Syst. **19**(5), 1–28 (2020)
13. Aubry, P., et al.: Extended cyclostatic dataflow program compilation and execution for an integrated manycore processor. Proc. Comput. Sci. **18**, 1624–1633 (2013)
14. Bell, S., et al.: TILE64^{TM}processor: a 64-core SoC with mesh interconnect. In: Digest of Technical Papers - IEEE International Solid-State Circuits Conference (2008)
15. Niknam, S., Wang, P., Stefanov, T.: Hard Real-Time Scheduling of Streaming Applications Modeled as Cyclic CSDF Graphs. Design, Automation and Test in Europe, pp. 1549–1554 (2019)
16. Stuijk, S., Geilen, M., Basten, T.: Exploring trade-offs in buffer requirements and throughput constraints for synchronous dataflow graphs. In: Proceedings - Design Automation Conference, pp. 899–904 (2006)
17. Reiter, R.: Scheduling parallel computations. JACM **15**(4), 590–599 (1968)
18. De Groote, R., Hölzenspies, P.K.F., Kuper, J., Broersma, H.: Back to basics: homogeneous representations of multi-rate synchronous dataflow graphs. In: International Conference on Formal Methods and Models for Codesign (2013)
19. Damavandpeyma, M., Stuijk, S., Basten, T., Geilen, M., Corporaal, H.: Schedule-extended synchronous dataflow graphs. IEEE Trans. Comput. Aided Des. Integr. Circ. Syst. **32**(10) (2013)
20. Honorat, A., Desnos, K., Bhattacharyya, S.S., Nezan, J.-F.: Scheduling of synchronous dataflow graphs with partially periodic real-time constraints. In: RTNS 2020: Proceedings of the 28th International Conference on Real-Time Networks and Systems, pp. 22–33 (2020)
21. Stuijk, S., Geilen, M., Basten, T.: Throughput-buffering trade-off exploration for cyclo-static and synchronous dataflow graphs. IEEE Trans. Comput. **57**(10), 1331–1345 (2008)
22. Hendriks, M., et al.: Monotonic optimization of dataflow buffer sizes. J. Sign. Process. Syst. **91**(1), 21–32 (2019)
23. Bodin, B., Munier-Kordon, A., De Dinechin, B.D.: Optimal and fast throughput evaluation of CSDF. In: Design Automation Conference (2016)

Efficient Operator Sharing Modulo Scheduling for Sum-Product Network Inference on FPGAs

Hanna Kruppe[1(✉)], Lukas Sommer[1], Lukas Weber[1], Julian Oppermann[1], Cristian Axenie[2], and Andreas Koch[1]

[1] Embedded Systems and Applications Group, Technical University Darmstadt, Darmstadt, Germany
{kruppe,sommer,weber,oppermann,koch}@esa.tu-darmstadt.de

[2] Intelligent Cloud Technologies Laboratory, Huawei Munich Research Center, Munich, Germany
cristian.axenie@huawei.com

Abstract. Probabilistic models are receiving increasing attention as a complementary alternative to more widespread machine learning approaches such as neural networks. One particularly interesting class of models, so-called *Sum-Product Networks* (SPNs), combine the expressiveness of probabilistic models with tractable inference, making them an interesting candidate for use in real-world applications.

Previously, inference in SPNs has successfully been accelerated by fully pipelined FPGA-based hardware. However, with these approaches, the maximum size of the SPN for FPGA acceleration has effectively been limited by the fully spatial mapping of arithmetic operations into hardware and the number of available resources in the FPGA.

In this work, we present an extended and specialized modulo scheduling algorithm based on Integer Linear Programming (ILP) for time-multiplexed sharing of hardware arithmetic operators in the SPN inference accelerator. In addition and in order to scale the scheduling to large SPN graphs, we combine the scheduling algorithm with a graph-partitioning heuristic, exploiting the graph structure of SPNs.

The combination of heuristic graph partitioning and ILP-based scheduling allows generating pipelined accelerators with the best possible initiation interval, while limiting the resource utilization to pre-set bounds. The evaluation discusses the effect different parameters have on convergence time and solution quality. A performance comparison shows that the FPGA improves the inference throughput over a comparable CPU- and GPU platform by a factor (geo.-mean) of 4.4x and 1.7x, respectively.

The authors would like to thank Xilinx Inc. for supporting their work by donations of hard- and software. Calculations for this research were conducted on the Lichtenberg high performance computer of TU Darmstadt. This research was partially funded by the German Federal Ministry for Education and Research (BMBF) with the funding ID ZN 01|S17050.

© Springer Nature Switzerland AG 2022
A. Orailoglu et al. (Eds.): SAMOS 2021, LNCS 13227, pp. 242–258, 2022.
https://doi.org/10.1007/978-3-031-04580-6_16

Keywords: FPGA · Machine learning · Probabilistic model · Sum-product network · Modulo scheduling · Graph partitioning

1 Introduction

Probabilistic models are receiving increasing attention from both academia and industry, as a complementary alternative to more widespread machine learning approaches such as (deep) neural networks (NNs). Probabilistic models can handle the uncertainty found in real-world scenarios better [17] and are also, in contrast to NNs, able to express uncertainty over their output.

While many probabilistic models quickly become intractable for larger use cases, so-called *Sum-Product Networks* (SPNs) provide efficient inference for a wide range of probabilistic queries in different real-world use cases. Similar to neural networks, for which both accelerated inference and training have been implemented on reconfigurable architectures, SPNs lend themselves to accelerated inference on FPGAs [11,19]. Key to the efficient computation of probabilistic queries in prior work was the pipelining of batches of queries. This task is further complicated by the fact that the probability values computed in the SPN require expensive floating-point arithmetic and in general cannot be quantized to integer values as it is done for neural network inference. So, despite successful efforts to realize the necessary probabilistic arithmetic efficiently with specialized hardware operators [20,23], prior approaches are constrained by the fully spatial mapping of operations and the available FPGA resources, effectively limiting the maximum size of the SPN that can be mapped to the physical resources on the target FPGA. A possible solution to overcome this limitation is to map multiple *operations* to the same hardware arithmetic *operator*, so that operators are time-shared. In order to retain as much performance as possible, this time-sharing of operators needs to be combined with efficient pipelining, requiring a resource-aware modulo scheduler [12].

Our main contribution is a scheduling algorithm specialized for the automatic mapping of SPNs to a pipelined FPGA accelerator. Our approach extends an existing Integer Linear Programming (ILP) formulation [21] to also optimize the size of the multiplexers used to realize the time-sharing of operators, a crucial factor for the operating frequency of the whole accelerator. Beyond that and in order to be able to handle large SPN graphs during scheduling, a divide-and-conquer heuristic leveraging the special graph structure of SPNs is presented.

2 Background

SPNs [15,17] are a relatively young class of probabilistic models. Similar to other probabilistic graphical models (PGM), SPNs are able to efficiently handle real-world uncertainties, such as missing feature values, and express uncertainty over their output. They are used in several domains [17] including, but not limited to, image classification and reconstruction, image segmentation, robotics, and natural language processing.

Sum-Product Networks capture the joint probability distribution over a number of variables as a directed acyclic graph. As shown in the example in Fig. 1, the graph consists of three different types of nodes, namely weighted sum-nodes (red), product nodes (green) and nodes representing univariate distributions (orange), where the latter can only occur as leaf nodes.

The graph structure of Sum-Product Networks, including the parameters such as weights and distribution parameters, can either be hand-crafted, completely learned from data (e.g., [10]) or can be generated and refined through learning of parameters (e.g., [14]).

Semantically, the product nodes in the graph correspond to factorizations of independent variables. As variables in a joint probability distribution are not independent in general, the weighted sum nodes come into play. They represent mixtures of distributions and, through clustering, expose independencies for factorization. If, after repeated mixture and factorization, only a single variable remains, the univariate distributions of these variables are captured by the leaf nodes. In this work, based on the approach for Mixed Sum-Product Networks by Molina et al. [10], univariate distributions of discrete variables are represented as histograms.

In contrast to many other probabilistic graphical models, inference in Sum-Product Networks is tractable, even for large graphs with many variables [13]. Enabled by the graph structure capturing the joint probability, a wide range of probabilistic queries, including conditional probability and most-probable explanation (MPE), can be computed efficiently by evaluating the SPN graph bottom-up (starting at the univariate distributions at the leaf nodes) one or multiple times (linear w.r.t. to the graph size). This work focuses on the efficient evaluation of a batch of queries and generation of pipelined FPGA accelerators under resource constraints.

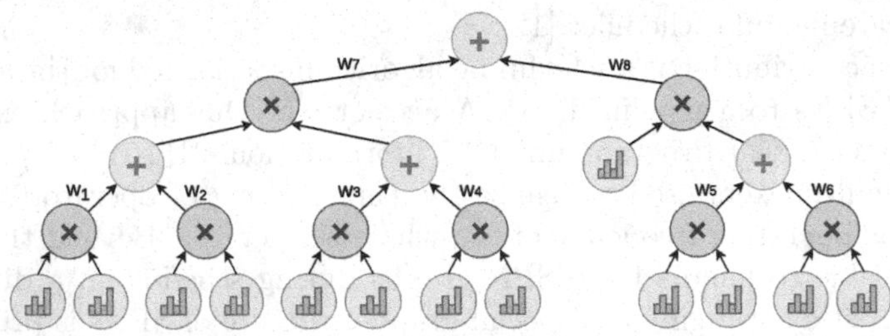

Fig. 1. Example of a Sum-Product Network graph.

3 Modulo Scheduling of SPN Inference

The core of our work is a resource-aware modulo scheduler tailored for SPN inference computations, which are described as acyclic data-flow graphs (DFGs).

Operations in these data flow graphs include additions, multiplications, histogram evaluations, and constant weights. Among the operators realizing these operations, only adders and multipliers are subject to operator sharing. Other operations require only very few resources to realize in hardware and there are few opportunities to share these operators.

The throughput of a shared, modulo-scheduled datapath is chiefly determined by the initiation interval (II), the duration between starting successive overlapped computations in the datapath. As recurrences in the DFG significantly constrain the achievable II, the fact that we only need to support acyclic DFGs simplifies some typical challenges of modulo scheduling: without recurrences, the resource-constrained minimum II [16] is not just a lower bound on feasible IIs, but always equals the minimal feasible II. This allows us to determine the smallest II and smallest number of operators for a given hardware resource budget and SPN up-front before scheduling begins, rather than repeatedly attempting scheduling with different candidate IIs, as in most other applications of modulo scheduling.

To illustrate why the resource-constrained minimum II is always feasible, consider a variant of ASAP scheduling that starts operations once all their inputs are ready, but delays these start times as necessary to avoid over-subscription of operators. The resulting schedule will most likely be sub-optimal, but without recurrences that would impose additional *upper* limits on the start times of operations, such a schedule will always exist.

Based on similar considerations, we developed a divide-and-conquer heuristic for scheduling and binding, detailed in Sect. 3.2. Once II and available operators have been determined, this heuristic partitions the DFG and the available operators to produce a set of smaller scheduling and binding problems, whose solutions can be combined into a solution for the whole problem.

These sub-problems are then translated to ILP instances with an objective that attempts to reduce multiplexing overhead, detailed in Sect. 3.1. The bindings – the mapping of each DFG operation to a specific physical operator – heavily influence the amount of multiplexing necessary to realize the sharing of the operators, and this multiplexing can, in turn, limit the maximum operating frequency of the accelerator. As schedule and bindings influence and constrain each other, we consider them together in a joint optimization problem, rather than computing one before the other. After schedules and bindings for each subproblem have been found by an off-the-shelf ILP solver, the results are combined into overall schedule and bindings by the heuristic component.

The heuristic combination of solutions for sub-graphs obtained by expensive, high quality scheduling algorithms has been proposed before [5,6]. In our context, it provides a simple way to trade scheduling effort for solution quality, and offers a practical way of optimizing for a different objective than usual (reducing multiplexing overhead) without having to develop new heuristics specifically for this purpose.

3.1 ILP Extension for Multiplexer Reduction

We extended an ILP formulation of modulo scheduling and binding proposed by Šůcha and Hanzálek [21]. Out of the several variants presented there, we use the formulation for general processing time and multiple operator types (see Sects. 4 and 5 there). This formulation prohibits over-subscription of shared operators by encoding the bindings in binary decision variables $\hat{z}_{iv}$ which are constrained such that $\hat{z}_{iv} = 1$ if and only if the operation identified by i should be bound to the vth suitable operator (assuming some arbitrary but consistent numbering of the operator instances). We reuse these decision variables to also model connections between operators, as a proxy for multiplexing overhead.

Formally, each operation $i \in O$ is associated with a type of operator q such as adders, multipliers, histograms, and constant weights. For those operator types subject to sharing (in our case, adders and multipliers), there is a limited number m_q of operator instances, while the other types are *unlimited* – they are instantiated once per operation requiring them.

The baseline ILP formulation as presented by Šůcha and Hanzálek assumes all operator types are subject to sharing. It is simple to adapt the formulation to support unlimited operators: we can just omit decision variables and constraints related to bindings of operations implemented by unlimited operators[1] and leave only start time constraints in place. Due to space limitations, we do not show the ILP formulation here with these minor modifications applied.

The multiplexer at input port p of a shared operator v needs to select among all the physical locations in the datapath which produce the pth input operand to any of the operations bound to v. In our accelerator's datapath, these values can be sourced from the output ports of other operators – whether they are themselves shared or not – as well as from shift registers inserted to buffer intermediate results for several cycles between being produced and consumed. Modeling the latter in the ILP formulation requires significant additional complexity: Sittel et al. [18] measured the register area by the maximum lifetime of intermediate results that can share registers, while multiplexer width is determined by the number of *distinct* lifetimes among intermediate results that could share a connection, which is far more difficult to linearize. This extra complexity is likely not justified in our context, as we combine the ILP formulation with a heuristic and thus will not obtain globally optimal solutions in any case.

Instead, we model only the presence or absence of connections between operator output ports and the input ports of shared operators. These connections are induced by the data flow edges $(i \to j) \in E$ and the bindings, encoded in the ILP by binary decision variables $\hat{z}_{iv}$ and $\hat{z}_{jv}$. The shared operators are identified by their type q and an index v from 1 to m_q. We also need to distinguish the different input ports p of the operators (typically, the operators are binary and thus $p \in \{1, 2\}$). Thus, for all q', v', p identifying a shared operator input port, there are binary variables $c^r_{q'v'p}$ for r ranging over the possible sources of a connection. These sources are the shared operator instances (q, v) as well as

[1] Specifically, variables $\hat{x}_{ij}, \hat{y}_{ij}, \hat{z}_{iv}$ and all constraints mentioning them.

the operations $i \in O$ which are unlimited, i.e., *not* subject to operator sharing. Each such variable should be 1 if the result of operator r needs to be connected to port p of the shared operator (q', v').

Note that a single connection suffices for multiple edges $(i_1 \rightarrow j_1), \ldots, (i_n \rightarrow j_n) \in E$ if all the $i_1 \ldots i_n$ are mapped to the same shared operator, all the $j_1 \ldots j_n$ are mapped to the same shared operator, and each value is routed to the same input port of that shared operator. This is shown in Fig. 2(b), while (c) shows different bindings that prevent sharing. When the sources of the data flow edges are not subject to operator sharing (d), separate connections are always required.

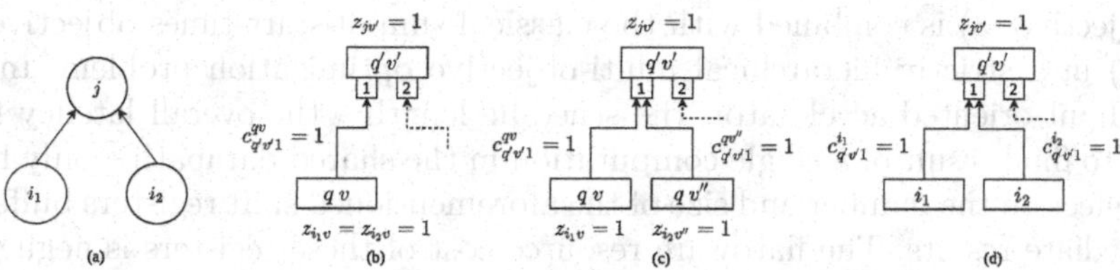

Fig. 2. Dataflow graph (a) and the impact of binding two operations to the same (b) or different (c) shared operator. When operations are not subject to operator sharing (d), multiple connections are necessary regardless of bindings.

To encode these considerations into the ILP, we add constraints for every data flow edge $(i \rightarrow j) \in E$ whose destination j is subject to operator sharing, as those edges are the cause of the connections we model. Let q be the operator type of i and q' of j. When i is also subject to operator sharing, then it is bound to some shared operator (q, v) which will be connected to the input port p of the operator (q', v') which j is bound to. Hence, we add the following set of constraints:

$$c_{q'v'p}^{qv} \geq \hat{z}_{iv} + \hat{z}_{jv'} - 1 \qquad \begin{array}{l} \forall v = 1, \ldots, m_q \\ \forall v' = 1, \ldots, m_{q'} \end{array} \tag{1}$$

Otherwise, if j requires an unlimited operator type, we simply have a connection from i to whatever operator (q', v') the operation j is bound to. In that case, we add the following set of constraints:

$$c_{q'v'p}^{i} \geq \hat{z}_{jv'} \qquad \forall v' = 1, \ldots, m_{q'} \tag{2}$$

Constraints (1) and (2) only ensure that a connection indicator is set to 1 if the corresponding connection is required, but not the inverse implication. This modeling is correct within our formulation: we only use the values of these decision variables for the objective function (unlike other decision variables, which yield the schedule and bindings), and objective functions suitable for our purpose (reducing multiplexers or connection density) cannot be improved by setting more $c_{q'v'p}^{r}$ to 1 than necessary.

For the objective function, we first and foremost minimize the total connections between operators:

$$\min \sum_{r,q',v',p} c^r_{q'v'p} \quad (3)$$

This objective was proposed by Cong and Xu [4] in the context of choosing operator and register bindings for an already-determined schedule. As they noted, this objective is only an approximation of the real (non-linear) hardware cost, but minimizing it correlates with minimizing the number of multiplexer inputs, so it is a reasonable way to address the need for a linear objective function. They could only evaluate it on relatively small examples, but found it to be effective at least in those cases.

Objective (3) is combined with the classical sum-of-start-times objective (as in [21]) in a strictly hierarchical multi-objective optimization problem. In our throughput-oriented accelerator, the schedule length – the overall latency from inputs to final result of a single computation in the shared datapath – only has a small effect on the number and size of the aforementioned shift registers buffering intermediate results. The hardware resource cost of these registers is negligible, while large multiplexers can negatively affect the maximum frequency, so we prioritize multiplexer reduction over schedule length reduction.

Overall, our proposed ILP formulation consists of these two objectives and the constraints of the formulation by Šůcha and Hanzálek [21] – not repeated here due to the page limit – plus our constraints (1) and (2).

3.2 Divide-and-Conquer Heuristic

In this section, we present an algorithm for decomposing a modulo scheduling and binding problem on an acyclic DFG into smaller sub-problems whose solutions can be combined into a solution for the original problem. As presented here, the algorithm works for any acyclic DFG and any partitioning, although our implementation (Sect. 4) and evaluation is limited to DFGs that are trees, since most SPN learning algorithms only produce trees.

For now, assume some arbitrary partitioning of the DFG is given. We first partition the modulo reservation table (MRT) [8] – a data structure organizing the operations by the operator they are bound to and the time step modulo II in which they are scheduled – to match the DFG partitioning. Each available time step (modulo the II) on each available operator is exclusively assigned to one of the DFG partitions: only operations from that part of the DFG will be permitted to use that operator in that time step. By assigning each partition at least as many operator time slices as there are operations requiring such an operator in the partition, we ensure that each of the sub-problems is feasible in isolation. In addition, the exclusive assignment avoids conflicting bindings between the solutions of each sub-problem: no two operations from different partitions can use the same operator at the same time.

Figure 3 shows such a partitioning of DFG and MRT, along with a solution for each partition. Note that the two available adders are each fully assigned to one or the other partition, while the multiplier is split up: node C can only be scheduled in even cycles while node D can only be scheduled in odd cycles. Although the schedules are correct with respect to each partition, the data flow edge C → E was ignored: the result of C is only available by cycle 10 (start time six plus latency of four), while E was scheduled to start in cycle five.

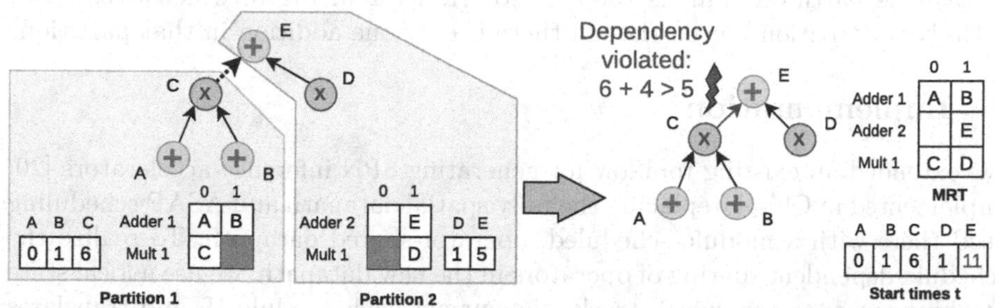

Fig. 3. Example of scheduling with graph partitioning ($II = 2$, all operators have a latency of four cycles). Left: partitioning and partial solutions (MRT, operation start times). Right: overall solution after merging the partial solutions, including the adaptation of E's schedule to preserve dependencies.

To repair such inconsistencies arising from data flow between partitions, we delay the start time of affected operations when we combine partial schedules. Specifically, we inspect all edges between the different partitions, and if the destination operation starts before the source operation finishes, we increase the start time of the destination operation by the smallest multiple of the II that fixes this problem. After the adjustment has been made, successors of the delayed operation may face a similar problem and we also delay their start times as necessary until all start time constraints are satisfied.

Note that a smaller delay may work sometimes, but would place the operation in a different MRT cell, which may not be available. For simplicity, we always use a multiple of the II, as shown in Fig. 3: while all inputs to operation E are ready by cycle 10, our algorithm schedules it for time step 11 since that is the earliest start time compatible with the MRT chosen previously.

After repairing the start time constraints, the start times and bindings of each partial solutions can be combined without further changes to produce a valid schedule and bindings for the entire DFG. As each operation belongs to exactly one partition, the start time and binding of each operation is uniquely determined, start time constraints are now satisfied, and the up-front partitioning of the MRT ensures no operator is over-subscribed in the combined solution. As the bindings are combined without changes, the effort expended by the ILP solver trying to optimize the bindings within each partition carries over into the overall solution.

To ensure that each partition only uses the parts of the MRT assigned to it, we need to modify the ILP construction slightly. We create *virtual* operations that occupy partially-available operators in the time steps assigned to other partitions, substituting constants for the ILP decision variables relating to the virtual operations. This increases the size of the ILP, which is quadratic in the number of operations even without our extensions. We limit this increase by partitioning the MRT such that every partition has at most two operators partially assigned to it, and where possible prefer to exclusively assign operators to a single partition. This is the case for Adder 2 in Fig. 3, which is assigned entirely to Partition 2 even though there is only one addition in that partition.

4 Implementation

We extended an existing toolflow for generating SPN inference accelerators [20] implemented in Chisel, replacing the fully spatial datapath and ASAP scheduling used there with a modulo-scheduled, operator-shared datapath. To realize the schedule-dependent sharing of operators in the new datapath, we use a local state machine per operator, which tracks the current cycle modulo II, and translates this local state to the control signals of multiplexers for selecting the current inputs to the operator. Due to space constraints, we must leave the presentation of the overall accelerator architecture to the prior work [20].

During scheduling, the multiple sub-problems generated by the divide-and-conquer approach are solved in parallel by launching multiple single-threaded ILP solver instances in a thread pool.

Graph partitioning is performed recursively, applying balanced 1-cuts repeatedly until the number of operations subject to operator sharing (which influences the size and difficulty of the ILP) falls below a user-specified threshold. We call this parameter the *split threshold* S and will evaluate its impact in Sect. 5. This approach works well in our domain, because most algorithms for learning SPNs produce trees rather than general directed acyclic graphs, but the latter could also be supported by using a more general graph partitioning method.

As in prior work, the open-source TaPaSCo framework [7] is used to integrate the core accelerator (load unit, store unit, data path, and controller) into a platform-specific SoC design, and provides a software API for interacting with the accelerator from the host CPU. In contrast to prior work [20], we also target MPSoC systems with *shared* memory between the host CPU and FPGA. However, the current version of TaPaSCo does not yet support *cache-coherent* shared memory between host and accelerator. To avoid the costs of copying input and output buffers, we use a custom user-space mappable memory buffer to make the input and output data available to both CPU and FPGA, rather than using the TaPaSCo-provided APIs for host-accelerator data transfers. This buffer is marked as cacheable, and the CPU cache is flushed explicitly and invalidated before launching inference jobs on the accelerator.

5 Evaluation

Our evaluation comprises two parts: an evaluation of the proposed ILP formulation and graph partitioning-based heuristic on a range of SPNs, FPGA platforms, IIs and resource constraints; and a case study on real hardware platforms suitable for embedded computing, comparing operator-shared accelerators on a Xilinx UltraScale+ MPSoC device to an Nvidia Jetson Xavier device.

In both parts of the evaluation, we use the customized floating-point formats and operators developed for SPN inference in prior work [20], which represent the probabilities on a linear scale, and were found to be more resource-efficient than a log-scale representation of probabilities in most cases. For the SPNs already investigated in the prior work, we use the format parameters as reported there. For the other SPNs, we use a format with 10 exponent bits and 26 mantissa bits, as it has the largest exponent range, and therefore is least vulnerable to overflow and underflow out of the currently implemented formats.

5.1 Scheduler Evaluation

For the scheduler evaluation, we target Digilent PYNQ-Z1, AVNET Ultra96-V2, and Xilinx VC709 boards. We used 14 out of 16 SPNs used in prior work [20], excluding NIPS5 and MSNBC 300 for being too small to benefit from operator sharing on any of the target platforms. To these, we add another SPN over binary data (DNA) and three large-scale artificial examples that were randomly generated to serve as stress tests: fully spatial realizations of these SPNs would require 1499, 2249 and 2699 floating-point adders and multipliers respectively, far larger than practical for ILP-based modulo scheduling.

Experimental Setup. Each of these 18 SPNs is tested against the resource model of each target platform to determine the resource-constrained minimum II. In many cases, this results in an accelerator design that would be severely memory-bound and could use a larger II – allowing more sharing and thus requiring fewer FPGA resources – without loss of performance. Thus, we also compute an alternative II (per SPN and platform) that would balance computational throughput with memory bandwidth requirement. Out of these $18 \times 3 \times 2$ candidate {SPN, Platform, II} triples, the 35 unique combinations with II from two to seven (inclusive) are used.

For each of the 35 {SPN, Platform, II} combinations, we perform scheduling and binding for three different resource constraints: the minimum number of operators possible, that minimum scaled up by a factor of 1.25 (rounded), and the largest number of operators that will fit on the device. These 105 scheduling tasks capture a wide range of DFG sizes and available number of operators.

Each scheduling task is solved by constructing a single large ILP instance as well as by our proposed divide-and-conquer heuristic with varying granularity for the graph partitioning step. In each case, we compare the baseline ILP formulation [21] to our proposed extension (Sect. 3.1).

Experiments were performed with Gurobi 8.1 as ILP solver, on systems equipped with two 12-core Intel Xeon E5-2680 v3 CPUs and 64 GiB of RAM. Each scheduler run was given access to four cores and 16 GiB of RAM, and wall clock running time was limited to two hours each. For each individual sub-problem generated by graph partitioning, the ILP solver was given a time limit of 15 min.

For the split threshold S controlling the granularity of the graph partitioning, we evaluate $S \in \{1, 5, 10, 14, 18, 22, 26, 30\}$ – using 1 as naive baseline, 5 and 10 as very fast but low-quality variants, and equidistant values from 10 to 30 to explore the trade off between running time and solution quality as sub-graphs become more complex.

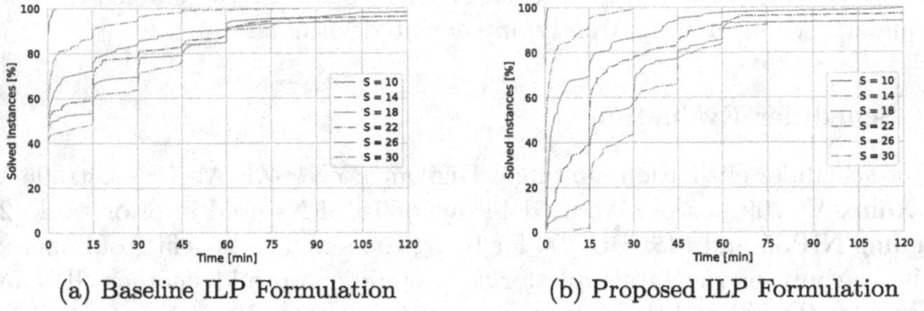

(a) Baseline ILP Formulation (b) Proposed ILP Formulation

Fig. 4. Scheduler runtime profile for different split thresholds (S) with the baseline and proposed ILP formulation, plotting scheduler run time against the cumulative percentage of instances solved within that time frame.

Scheduler Runtime. Attempting to schedule the entire DFG by a single ILP is impractical on many of the instances in our benchmark suite. With the baseline ILP formulation, the solver finds a solution for just 57 out of 105 instances, of which only 30 are proven to be optimal solutions, while the other instances run out of time or memory while solving the ILP, or already while creating the constraints. Results are even worse with our proposed extension of the ILP: only 31 solutions are found, and none of them could be proven optimal.

In contrast, fine-granular graph partitioning ($S \leq 10$) enables heuristic scheduling within a minute on almost all examples, with only a few exceptions taking slightly longer. As Fig. 4 shows, run times rapidly increase as the graph partition gets more coarse. Curiously, although a significant number of instances are solved almost instantaneously with the baseline ILP formulation, with the extended ILP formulation, we observe fewer outliers that take exceptionally long to schedule. With the extended ILP formulation, the configuration $S = 14$ schedules most examples in 15 min, and all within 30 min. Even with $S = 30$, the majority of instances are successfully scheduled within one hour, but too many exceed the two hour time limit (especially with the baseline ILP formulation) to claim that larger values of S are always beneficial.

Solution Quality. For lack of a clear baseline to compare the scheduling algorithms against, we resort to scoring the different scheduler variants by how well their solutions for each instance score relative to the best solution found by all of the variants evaluated. We compare both the schedule length (datapath latency) achieved and the multiplexer size (as encoded in the ILP objective) achieved by each variant. We record this ratio for every instance and report the distribution of these ratios in Fig. 5a and Fig. 5b (standard box plots with whiskers at $Q_1 - 1.5 \cdot \text{IQR}$ and $Q_3 + 1.5 \cdot \text{IQR}$).

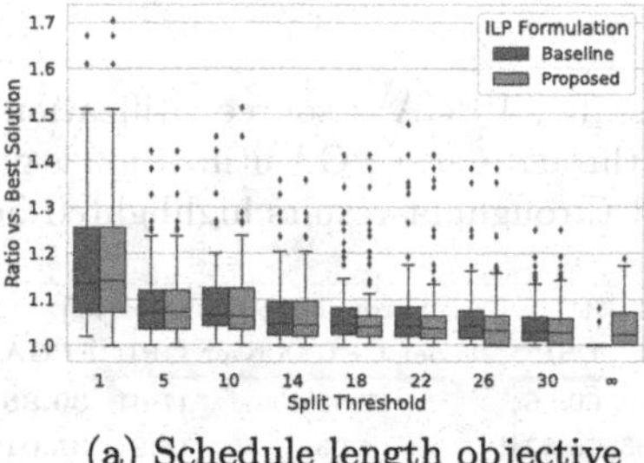

(a) Schedule length objective

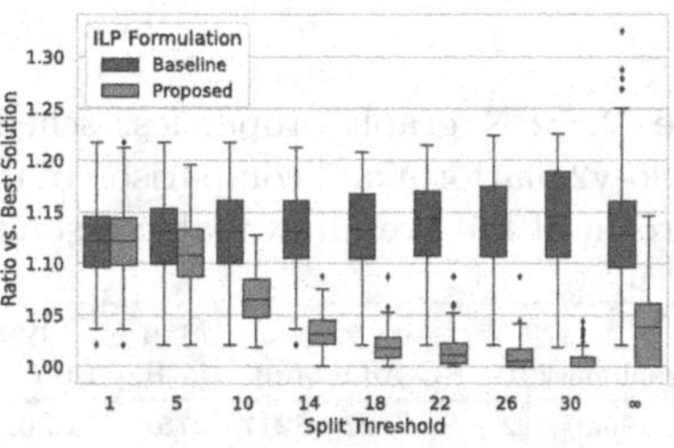

(b) Multiplexer size objective

Fig. 5. Solution quality of different scheduler variants w.r.t. to schedule length (5a) and multiplexer size (5b) objective. Split threshold = ∞ is the case of a single ILP for the whole graph. Values closer to 1 are better.

Note that many variants, especially those with a single large ILP for the entire problem, did not find solutions for all of the 105 scheduling tasks. The number of solutions found within two hours is listed in Table 1.

Table 1. Number of solutions found by each scheduler variant.

ILP-Form.	Split threshold								
	1	5	10	14	18	22	26	30	∞
Baseline	105	105	105	105	103	101	99	99	57
Proposed	105	105	105	105	104	101	98	98	31

Generally, coarser partitioning (larger S) yields better results – at the cost of longer running time, as seen above. The divide-and-conquer heuristic combined with our proposed ILP formulation improves multiplexer sizes, and prioritizing this objective does not have a negative impact on the schedule length. However, the improvements beyond $S = 14$ are marginal and may not justify the significantly longer running times.

While the baseline ILP without graph partitioning ($S = \infty$) achieves best-in-class schedule lengths on most instances where the ILP solver finds any solution, the third quartiles show that the heuristic schedulers with $S \geq 14$ get within 10% of the schedule length achieved by the ILP solver in the majority of cases, and occasionally obtain even better results.

5.2 Hardware Evaluation

Out of the 35 {SPN, Platform, II} combinations used in the scheduler evaluation, 13 target the AVNET Ultra96-V2 device. We generate accelerators for these configurations, using the heuristic scheduler with our proposed ILP formulation and $S = 14$. This configuration gives acceptable results, while also reliably finishing in half an hour, which is a typical time frame for FPGA implementation of the entire accelerator for the target device.

Table 2. SPN graph properties, scheduling results, FPGA resource utilization on Ultra96-v2 platform and comparison of inference throughput. FPGA utilization is given as percent of the overall available resources. Best throughput results highlighted bold.

					Freq.	Resource Util. [%]				Throughput [samples/µs]		
Benchmark	II	SL	Add	Mult.	[MHz]	LUT	Reg.	CLB	DSP	Xavier CPU	Xavier GPU	FPGA
Accidents	2	81	27	217	275	61.30	38.04	92.23	60.56	7.53	17.61	**39.85**
Audio	4	88	12	275	280	51.94	30.91	77.65	76.67	4.05	16.82	**35.01**
DNA	3	73	2	363	260	66.09	38.49	96.92	67.22	1.51	15.22	**25.95**
Netflix	2	73	11	231	260	62.07	37.82	92.85	64.44	3.44	26.63	**44.31**
Plants	3	140	14	256	280	53.58	35.85	86.63	95.56	4.21	30.23	**48.98**
NIPS20	2	47	7	56	350	38.00	20.33	57.03	15.56	27.55	19.42	**30.01**
NIPS30	2	65	10	87	345	49.57	24.94	71.52	24.44	15.95	15.82	**24.67**
NIPS40	3	74	16	122	350	51.52	26.62	76.17	22.78	10.27	12.61	**21.39**
NIPS50	4	80	16	143	340	57.95	26.29	78.72	20.00	7.79	11.59	**17.74**
NIPS60	4	77	13	156	350	57.85	27.74	81.89	21.67	5.23	10.28	**14.86**
NIPS70	5	88	14	180	205	62.52	28.36	84.17	20.83	3.09	9.36	**14.00**
NIPS80	2	85	32	265	245	83.16	43.53	99.34	74.72	3.20	6.41	**12.48**
NIPS80	5	93	32	265	245	68.49	34.18	93.84	30.28	3.20	6.41	**12.39**

We performed a design space exploration using the development version of the open-source framework TaPaSCo[2] and Vivado version 2019.2 to determine the highest possible frequency and corresponding FPGA resource utilization. Results are reported in Table 2, with resource utilization given as percentage of the total number of available resources (70,560 LUT, 141,120 Reg., 8,820 CLB, 360 DSP).

With these maximum frequencies, we compare the performance of the FPGA accelerators with the CPU and GPU implementations of the same inference computations running on another SoC suitable for embedded and edge AI computation, namely an Nvidia Jetson AGX Xavier SoC, having ARM CPU cores and an integrated 512-core Volta-class GPU. Similar to prior work [20], optimized C++ (single-threaded) or CUDA code is generated from the SPN description using an automated toolflow and then compiled by the respective compiler available on the Jetson Xavier System (NVCC version 10.0, GCC version 7.5.0). Just as in the Ultra96 used for FPGA performance measurements, CPU and GPU on the Jetson AGX Xavier share the same physical memory, which removes the need for expensive host-accelerator data transfers.

[2] https://github.com/esa-tu-darmstadt/tapasco.

Table 2 lists the throughput achieved by the CPU, GPU and FPGA implementations. Each measurement is averaged over five runs. Our accelerators achieve better throughput than the implementations on CPU (geo.-mean speedup 4.4x) and GPU (geo.-mean speedup 1.7x) on the Xavier device.

Avoiding data transfers between CPU and GPU, respectively CPU and FPGA, has significant impact: it allows these embedded SoCs to achieve performance much closer to the more powerful workstations evaluated in prior work [20] than one would expect from comparing hardware specifications. On several benchmarks, the Xavier GPU implementation even achieves significantly higher throughput than the discrete Nvidia 1080Ti GPU used in prior work, primarily because the latter needs to transfer all input data and results over PCIe.

Note that the two FPGA accelerators for NIPS80 have vastly different datapath throughput (II = 2 versus 5) and resource (DSP) requirements. They achieve essentially the same end-to-end performance because the larger II = 2 configuration is limited by memory bandwidth, while the smaller II = 5 configuration was selected to match the memory bandwidth.

6 Related Work

Two key components of our work are the use of graph partitioning to accelerate modulo scheduling and the optimization of operator bindings. The discussion in this section focuses on works related to these aspects. Please note that many other approaches to heuristic modulo scheduling exist [1,3,24].

Compared to scheduling in compilation flows for neural networks on FPGAs, our approach works on a much finer level of granularity. As outlined in the survey by Venieris et al. [22], scheduling in compilation flows for neural networks typically happens on the granularity of coarse-grained neural network operations, such as matrix multiplication, convolution, or even entire layers, whereas our scheduler operates on individual arithmetic operations.

6.1 Graph Transformations for Modulo Scheduling

Fan et al. [6] previously used graph partitioning to decompose large modulo scheduling tasks into multiple sub-problems. Due to recurrences, solutions to the sub-problems can not necessarily be combined into a valid solution to the whole problem. To address this, they perform scheduling of sub-graphs sequentially and back-track when later sub-graphs cannot be scheduled due to conflicts arising from previous decisions. As a consequence, this approach fails to schedule some examples even with a relatively fine-grained partitioning (ca. eight operations per sub-graph).

Dai and Zhang [5] used strongly connected components (SCCs) to partition the graph. As this partitioning does not split recurrences, partial solutions can always be combined into a full schedule. They demonstrate that this often accelerates scheduling significantly, though it is less effective when a single SCC encompasses most of the graph.

6.2 Optimization of Bindings

There are numerous works optimizing the bindings alongside the schedule as one of the key factors affecting the physical realization of operator sharing. Cong and Xu [4] perform this in a separate step after scheduling using a heuristic based on min-cost network flows. LegUp [2] is a more recent example of binding as a separate phase after scheduling, focusing on balancing multiplexer sizes.

Other works are more closely related to our approach of integrated scheduling and binding. The aforementioned work by Fan et al. [6] focuses on ASIC implementations, while Memik et al. [9] target FPGA architectures. More recently and most closely related to our ILP formulation, Sittel et al. [18] incorporated the operator bindings into an ILP-based modulo scheduler to optimize the area required for registers holding intermediate values.

7 Conclusion and Outlook

In this paper, we presented an ILP formulation for modulo scheduling and binding of SPN inference computations, and a divide-and-conquer heuristic that makes the ILP-based approach practical for use on large SPNs by graph partitioning and combination of partial solutions.

This heuristic can schedule very large examples in minutes, while finding the optimal II by construction and making only minor sacrifices in schedule length – within 10% of the best known solution for most instances. In addition, our extended ILP formulation also reduces datapath multiplexing significantly, compared to scheduling approaches that only target the schedule length.

Using this scheduling algorithm, we generate SPN inference accelerators on an embedded FPGA-CPU hybrid SoC, where a fully spatial realization of the datapath would exceed the available hardware resources. These FPGA accelerators achieve higher throughput than CPU and GPU implementations on an Nvidia Jetson Xavier SoC in our benchmarks, with geometric mean speed-up of 4.4x over CPU and 1.7x over GPU.

The properties of acyclic data flow graphs that enable our divide-and-conquer heuristic also suggest other approaches to heuristic scheduling that hold promise for improving the running time and/or solution quality further. Since a feasible suboptimal solution is easy to find, local search approaches such as simulated annealing could be used as well, which allow specifying non-linear constraints and objectives directly.

References

1. Canis, A., Brown, S.D., Anderson, J.H.: Modulo SDC scheduling with recurrence minimization in high-level synthesis. In: International Conference on Field Programmable Logic and Applications (FPL) (2014)
2. Canis, A., et al.: LegUp: an open-source high-level synthesis tool for FPGA-based processor/accelerator systems. ACM Trans. Embedded Comput. Syst. (TECS) 13(2), 1–27 (2013)

3. Codina, J.M., Llosa, J., González, A.: A comparative study of modulo scheduling techniques. In: International Conference on Supercomputing (ICS 2002) (2002)
4. Cong, J., Xu, J.: Simultaneous FU and register binding based on network flow method. In: Design, Automation and Test in Europe (2008)
5. Dai, S., Zhang, Z.: Improving scalability of exact modulo scheduling with specialized conflict-driven learning. In: Design Automation Conference (2019)
6. Fan, K., Kudlur, M., Park, H., Mahlke, S.: Cost sensitive modulo scheduling in a loop accelerator synthesis system. In: IEEE/ACM International Symposium on Microarchitecture (MICRO2005) (2005)
7. Heinz, C., Hofmann, J., Korinth, J., Sommer, L., Weber, L., Koch, A.: The TaPaSCo open-source Toolflow. J. Sign. Process. Syst. **93**(5), 545–563 (2021). https://doi.org/10.1007/s11265-021-01640-8
8. Lam, M.: Software pipelining: an effective scheduling technique for VLIW machines. In: Programming Language Design and Implementation (PLDI) (1988)
9. Memik, S.O., Memik, G., Jafari, R., Kursun, E.: Global resource sharing for synthesis of control data flow graphs on FPGAs. In: Design Automation Conference (2003)
10. Molina, A., Vergari, A., Di Mauro, N., Natarajan, S., Esposito, F., Kersting, K.: Mixed sum-product networks: a deep architecture for hybrid domains. In: Thirty-Second AAAI Conference on artificial intelligence (2018)
11. Ober, M., Hofmann, J., Sommer, L., Weber, L., Koch, A.: High-throughput multi-threaded sum-product network inference in the reconfigurable cloud. In: Workshop on Heterogeneous High-performance Reconfigurable Computing (2019)
12. Oppermann, J., Sittel, P., Kumm, M., Reuter-Oppermann, M., Koch, A., Sinnen, O.: Design-space exploration with multi-objective resource-aware modulo scheduling. In: Conference on Parallel and Distributed Computing (Euro-Par) (2019)
13. Peharz, R., Tschiatschek, S., Pernkopf, F., Domingos, P.: On theoretical properties of sum-product networks. In: Artificial Intelligence and Statistics (2015)
14. Peharz, R., et al.: Random sum-product networks: a simple but effective approach to probabilistic deep learning. In: Proceedings of UAI (2019)
15. Poon, H., Domingos, P.: Sum-product networks: a new deep architecture. In: IEEE International Conference on Computer Vision Workshops (2011)
16. Rau, B.R.: Iterative modulo scheduling. Int. J. Parall. Programm. **24**(1), 3–64 (1996). https://doi.org/10.1007/BF03356742
17. Sánchez-Cauce, R., París, I., Díez, F.J.: Sum-product networks: a survey. IEEE Trans. Patt. Anal. Mach. Intell. (2021)
18. Sittel, P., Kumm, M., Oppermann, J., Möller, K., Zipf, P., Koch, A.: ILP-based modulo scheduling and binding for register minimization. In: International Conference on Field Programmable Logic and Applications (FPL) (2018)
19. Sommer, L., Oppermann, J., Molina, A., Binnig, C., Kersting, K., Koch, A.: Automatic mapping of the sum-product network inference problem to FPGA-based accelerators. In: IEEE International Conference on Computer Design (ICCD) (2018)
20. Sommer, L., Weber, L., Kumm, M., Koch, A.: Comparison of arithmetic number formats for inference in sum-product networks on FPGAs. In: International Symposium on Field-Programmable Custom Computing Machines (FCCM) (2020)
21. Šůcha, P., Hanzálek, Z.: A cyclic scheduling problem with an undetermined number of parallel identical processors. Comput. Optim. Appl. (2011). https://doi.org/10.1007/s10589-009-9239-4

22. Venieris, S.I., Kouris, A., Bouganis, C.S.: Toolflows for mapping convolutional neural networks on FPGAs: a survey and future directions. ACM Comput. Surv. **51**(3) (2018)
23. Weber, L., Sommer, L., Oppermann, J., Molina, A., Kersting, K., Koch, A.: Resource-efficient logarithmic number scale arithmetic for SPN inference on FPGAs. In: International Conference on Field-Programmable Technology (FPT) (2019)
24. Zhang, Z., Liu, B.: SDC-based modulo scheduling for pipeline synthesis. In: IEEE/ACM International Conference on Computer-Aided Design (2013)

A Framework for Fixed Priority Periodic Scheduling Synthesis from Synchronous Data-Flow Graphs

Hai Nam Tran[1(✉)], Alexandre Honorat[2], Shuvra S. Bhattacharyya[2,3], Jean-Pierre Talpin[4], Thierry Gautier[4], and Loïc Besnard[4]

[1] Lab STICC, CNRS, UMR 6285, University of Brest, Brest, France
hai-nam.tran@univ-brest.fr

[2] Univ Rennes, INSA Rennes, CNRS, IETR - UMR 6164, 35000 Rennes, France
ahonorat@insa-rennes.fr

[3] University of Maryland, Maryland, USA
ssb@umd.edu

[4] Inria, CNRS, IRISA, UMR 6074, Univ. Rennes, Rennes, France
{jean-pierre.talpin,thierry.gautier,loic.besnard}@inria.fr

Abstract. Synchronous data-flow graphs (SDF) are widely used in the design of concurrent real-time digital signal processing applications on multiprocessor system-on-chip. The increasing complexity of these hardware platforms advocates the use of real-time operating systems and fixed-priority scheduling to manage applications and resources. This trend calls for new methods to synthesize and implement actors in SDF graphs as real-time tasks with computed scheduling parameters (periods, priorities, processor mapping, etc.). This article presents a framework supporting scheduling synthesis, scheduling simulation, and code generation of these graphs. The scheduling synthesis maps each actor to a periodic real-time task and computes the appropriate buffer sizes and scheduling parameters. The results are verified by a scheduling simulator and instantiated by a code generator targeting the RTEMS (Real-Time Executive for Multiprocessor Systems) operating system. Experiments are conducted to evaluate the framework's performance and scalability as well as the overhead induced by the code generator.

1 Introduction

Data-flow models of computation are commonly used in embedded system design to describe stream processing or control applications. Their simplicity allows the adaptation of automated code generation techniques to limit the problematic and error-prone task of programming real-time parallel applications. Among data-flow models, synchronous data-flow (SDF) [6] is one of the most popular in the embedded community.

Multiprocessor system-on-chips, which are used to host real-time applications, are so complex that real-time operating systems (RTOS) with fixed-priority preemptive scheduling are used to manage resources and host real-time

© Springer Nature Switzerland AG 2022
A. Orailoglu et al. (Eds.): SAMOS 2021, LNCS 13227, pp. 259–271, 2022.
https://doi.org/10.1007/978-3-031-04580-6_17

tasks. The implementation of a data-flow application on an RTOS calls for methods to efficiently synthesize periodic real-time tasks from a data-flow model.

The work in [8] has established a strong theoretical background on scheduling synthesis of SDF graphs. The tool Affine Data-Flow Graph (ADFG) [8,15] was developed to support a large number of scheduling synthesis algorithms. From an input SDF graph, ADFG synthesizes a fixed priority periodic task set preserving the consistency of the SDF graph with the objective of maximizing the throughput and minimizing the buffer size requirement. Nevertheless, some important elements are not covered in the scope of ADFG. First, scheduling in multiprocessor platforms can be highly impacted by extra parameters such as interference due to resource sharing (bus and memory) and preemption costs. To take these elements into account, a viable solution is to apply either dedicated feasibility tests or scheduling simulation to verify schedulability. Second, when the computed schedule is verified to be schedulable, one must take advantage of the SDF model to quickly and reliably generate the corresponding scheduler code. This requires knowledge of the implementation of a specific scheduler by using the APIs provided by an RTOS.

Problem Statement and Contribution: Motivated by these observations, the problem addressed in this paper is the lack of integration of the results synthesized by ADFG in a real-time scheduling simulator and a code generator.

This article presents a framework to integrate the scheduling synthesized by ADFG into a scheduling simulator and a code generator targeting the RTEMS (Real-Time Executive for Multiprocessor Systems) [1] RTOS. Scheduling simulation is achieved by Cheddar [22], which is interoperable with ADFG. Automated scheduler code generation is achieved by exploiting the lightweight data-flow environment (LIDE) [16] to implement the core functionality of actors and then instantiate them as POSIX threads. Our framework provides novel capabilities for design space exploration and iterative tuning of real-time, SDF-based signal processing systems.

The rest of this article is organized as follows. Section 2 describes the background of our work. Section 3 provides a brief summary of scheduling synthesis and focuses on our approach to achieve scheduling simulation and code generation. Section 4 shows two experiments conducted to evaluate the performance of the framework. Finally, Sect. 5 presents related work and Sect. 6 concludes the article and discusses future work.

2 Background and Terminology

In this section, we present the SDF graph model, the periodic real-time task model, and the notations used in the article. In addition, we briefly introduce our usage of scheduling simulation and code generation.

An SDF graph is a directed graph $G = (V, E)$ consisting of a finite set of *actors* $V = \{v_1, ..., v_N\}$ and a finite set of one-to-one *channels* E. A channel $e_{ab} = (v_a, v_b, p, q) \in E$ connects the producer v_a to the consumer v_b such that

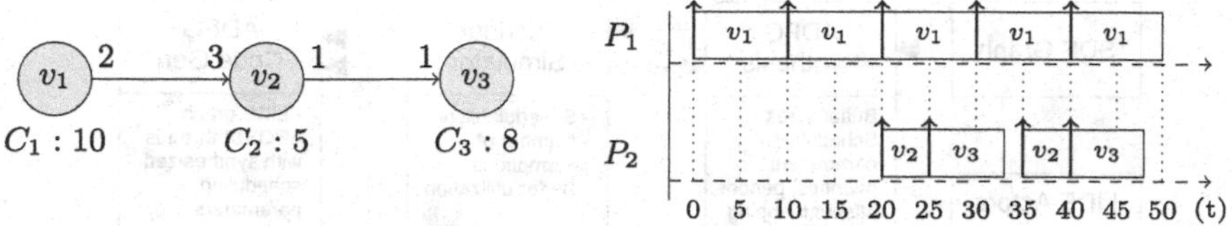

Fig. 1. An SDF graph of 3 actors, 2 channels and its FPP scheduling

the production (resp., consumption) rate is given by an integer $p \in \mathbb{N}$ (resp., $q \in \mathbb{N}$). A channel e_{ab} has a bounded *buffer size* δ_{ab} and can have a number of *initial tokens*. Every time an actor fires, it consumes q tokens from an input channel and produces p tokens to an output channel.

On the scheduling analysis front, we assume the classic *fixed priority periodic* (FPP) scheduling on a multiprocessor platform. A task τ_i is defined by a sextuple: $(C_i, T_i, D_i, \Pi_i, O_i, P_i)$. The parameter C_i, called the *capacity*, denotes the worst-case execution time (WCET) of task τ_i when it executes non-preemptively. T_i, called the *period*, denotes the fixed interval between two successive releases of τ_i. D_i is the *deadline* of τ_i. In this article, we assume that tasks have implicit deadlines (i.e., $\forall i : D_i = T_i$). A task is assigned a *priority level* Π_i and makes its initial request at time O_i, called the *offset*. The last parameter P_i, called the *mapping*, denotes the processing unit that the task is assigned to.

Figure 1 shows a simple SDF graph consisting of three actors and two channels. The notation C_i below an actor represents its WCET. For a channel $v_a \xrightarrow{p \quad q} v_b$, the production rate and consumption rate are provided. The channel sizes are not set here because these values depend on the computed schedule. An *iteration* [6] of an SDF graph is a non-empty sequence of firings that returns the graph to its initial state. For the graph in Fig. 1, firing actor v_1 3 times, actor v_2 2 times and actor v_3 2 times forms an iteration.

FPP scheduling of an SDF graph requires the mapping of each actor to a periodic real-time task. The tasks must allow a *consistent* schedule for one iteration of the graph. By definition, a schedule is consistent if it has bounded buffer sizes, and if there is no deadlock, overflow, nor underflow. For a given actor v_i, we need to synthesize a periodic task τ_i and its scheduling parameters. Amongst those presented parameters, only the capacity is available in the SDF model. Other scheduling parameters must be computed to guarantee the consistency. In the next section, we introduce our approach and elaborate on how the approach supports consistent, real-time scheduling of SDF graphs.

3 Approach

Our framework consists of three main steps illustrated in Fig. 2. First, from an input SDF graph, ADFG computes the required buffer sizes and synthesizes periodic scheduling parameters. The objective is to guarantee the consistency of the SDF graph while maximizing the throughput and minimizing the buffer size

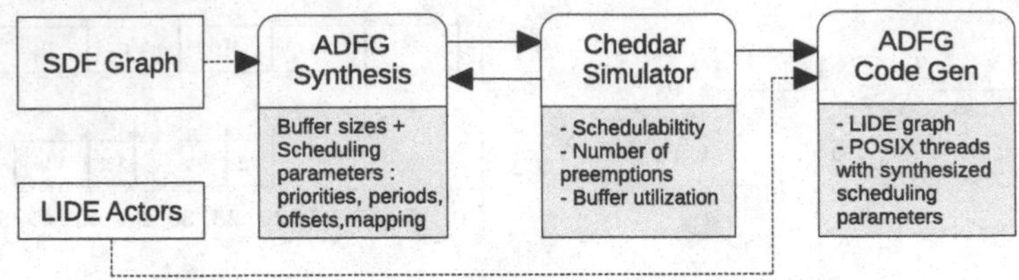

Fig. 2. Framework

requirement. Second, a scheduling simulation is run by the Cheddar scheduling analyzer [22] to verify the schedulability and to give a thorough analysis of the synthesized schedule. Finally, after the schedule is verified, ADFG generates a real-time implementation of the computed schedule. We assume that actors are implemented in the lightweight data-flow environment (LIDE) [16] and we target the RTEMS RTOS. In the generated code, the input SDF graph is instantiated as a graph of LIDE actors and channels. Scheduling parameters are taken into account by using the POSIX thread API.

3.1 Scheduling Synthesis with ADFG

In this section, we present the ADFG tool and give a brief summary of the constraints and the objectives that we need to take into account in the scheduling synthesis step. ADFG [8,15] is a free real-time scheduling synthesis tool for data-flow graphs. Periodic scheduling synthesis in ADFG takes into account the following two constraints to guarantee SDF graph consistency.

Underflow Constraint: we have an underflow when an actor attempts to read and there are not enough tokens on the channel. Thus, we need to compute the firing dependencies that guarantee no underflow. For a channel $v_a \xrightarrow{p \quad q} v_b$, the nth firing of v_b is enabled if and only if the number of produced tokens is larger than $q \cdot n$. Hence, v_b has to wait for the lth firing of v_a such that: $l \cdot p - n \cdot q \geq 0$.

Overflow Constraint: we have an overflow when an actor attempts to write and there are not enough empty spaces on the channel. For a channel $v_a \xrightarrow{p \quad q} v_b$ of size δ_{ab}, the lth firing of v_a is enabled if and only if the number of produced tokens is smaller than or equal to the number of empty spaces. Hence, v_a has to wait for the nth firing of v_b such that: $l \cdot p - n \cdot q \leq \delta_{ab}$.

In addition, ADFG accounts for two objectives in order to optimize the synthesized schedule. Scheduling requires computing the task periods and buffer sizes such that there is no buffer underflow or overflow, while maximizing the throughput and minimizing the total buffer size. Then the total buffer size and the throughput are the main metrics to compare different scheduling parameter valuations. In [8], Bouakaz proved that the maximum throughput problem can be translated to a maximum processor utilization one.

Considering the SDF graph in Fig. 1, ADFG computes the smallest possible actor periods to ensure the consistency. For example, if the targeted system has 2 processing units, ADFG finds the periods $T_1 = 10$, $T_2 = 15$, $T_3 = 15$ and offsets $O_1 = 0$, $O_2 = 20$, $O_3 = 20$. Actor v_1 is mapped alone on the first core, for a total processor utilization factor of $U = 1.87$ for two cores. Part of the resulting schedule is depicted in Fig. 1. Actors v_2 and v_3 are released at the same time but ADFG sets a higher priority to v_2 and thus v_2 is executed first.

3.2 Scheduling Simulation with Cheddar

In our approach, scheduling simulation is used to provide a thorough analysis of the schedule synthesized by ADFG. It allows us to verify not only the correctness of the results but also obtain additional information including the number of preemptions and the buffer utilization. The second advantage of scheduling simulation is that it allows a thorough analysis of interference due to shared resources such as caches and memory bus. While this data is not directly given by ADFG, we have the possibility of using an external static analysis tool to obtain a richer execution profile of an actor. In [25], a preliminary work has been implemented in ADFG to support time-triggered schedules with memory interference but not yet FPP schedules.

In the development of our proposed framework, we have extended ADFG with capabilities that enable interoperability with Cheddar [22]—an open-source real-time scheduling analyzer. Classical feasibility tests, scheduling algorithms and a simulator are implemented in Cheddar. System architectures are defined with the Cheddar Architecture Description Language (Cheddar-ADL). The periodic scheduling of periodic tasks with buffer communication is supported by the simulator and used to evaluate the results of ADFG in [15]. ADFG generates the scheduling synthesized to an XML file compliant to Cheddar-ADL.

If the schedule synthesized by ADFG is shown to be not schedulable with Cheddar due to interference, some adjustments must be made. For example, the cache related preemption delay [2], which is a well-studied source of interference in preemptive scheduling, can make a schedulable task set become unschedulable. A solution is to incorporate this delay in the WCET of actors and rerun the scheduling synthesis with ADFG. This is an example of the important kinds of design iteration that are facilitated by the proposed framework.

3.3 Code Generation with LIDE

The final step is to generate the implementation of the graph with computed scheduling parameters. It consists of generating the graph implementation from a set of pre-implemented actors and instantiating them with scheduling parameters by using the APIs supported by an RTOS.

ADFG supports automated code generation of the computed buffer sizes and scheduling parameters for data-flow applications that are implemented in the Lightweight Data-flow Environment (LIDE) [16]. LIDE is a flexible, lightweight design environment that allows designers to experiment with data-flow-based

LIDE Prototype 1: Actor and FIFO functions

```
lide_c_<actor name>_context_type *lide_c_<actor name>_new(<FIFO pointer list>, [parameter list])
boolean lide_c_<actor name>_enable (lide_c_<actor name>_context_type *context);
void lide_c_<actor name>_invoke (lide_c_<actor name>_context_type *context);
void lide_c_<actor name>_terminate (lide_c_<actor name>_context_type *context);
lide_c_fifo_pointer lide_c_fifo_new (int capacity, int token_size)
```

implementations directly. A data-flow graph consists of LIDE actors that can be initialized with parameters including channels and buffer sizes. The usage of LIDE allows a systematic way to instantiate data-flow graphs with the buffer size parameters computed by ADFG. In addition, it also allows us to separate concerns involving the implementation of actors and schedulers.

RTEMS [1] is an open-source real-time operating system that supports open standard application programming interfaces such as POSIX. We consider the usage of the RTEMS to generate the computed scheduling parameters. Actor invocations and fixed-priority periodic scheduling are achieved by the usage of the POSIX thread library.

The code generator's inputs are the results computed by ADFG, including: buffer sizes, periods, offsets, priorities and mapping. The generated code is cross-compiled and tested by using the QEMU tool to emulate an ARM platform with RTEMS. Next, we introduce LIDE and demonstrate our method of taking into account the computed results in the code generation process.

Actors and Channels. Graph elements in LIDE are designed and implemented as abstract data types (ADTs) that provide C based, object-oriented implementation of actors and channels [16]. Each actor has an associated `context`, which encapsulates pointers to the FIFO channels that are associated with the edges incident to the actor. Four interface functions, namely `new`, `enable`, `invoke` and `terminate` presented in the LIDE Prototype 1, are required to create an actor. Designers can develop their own actors by appropriately specializing the prototype function templates.

To implement a data-flow application we need to instantiate predefined actors, allocating channels and connecting them together. A channel is instantiated with the function `lide_c_fifo_new` which takes two input parameters: `capacity` and `token_size`. It allows us to apply buffer size results computed by ADFG in the code generation step.

- Capacity: the computed buffer size for a channel is given as an input parameter of the function `lide_c_fifo_new`. It is the number of tokens of which sizes are given as the second input parameter to the function.
- Token size: this information is given in the specification of the graph and passed directly to the code generator. In case of complex types, we assume that their specifications in C are also provided.

An actor is instantiated with the interface function `lide_c_<actor_name>_new`. The input parameters are FIFO channels that are connected to the actor. An exam-

```
lide_c_fifo_pointer v2_in = lide_c_fifo_new(6, sizeof(int));
lide_c_fifo_pointer v2_out = lide_c_fifo_new(1, sizeof(int));
lide_c_actor_context_type* actors[ACTOR_COUNT]; /* LIDE-C Actors */
actors[0] = (lide_c_actor_context_type*) (lide_c_v1_new (v2_in));
actors[1] = (lide_c_actor_context_type*) (lide_c_v2_new (v2_in, v2_out));
actors[2] = (lide_c_actor_context_type*) (lide_c_v3_new (v2_out));
```

Fig. 3. Actors and channels declaration with LIDE

```
rtems_actors[0].context = actors[0];
rtems_actors[0].name = "v1"
rtems_actors[0].priority = 1;
rtems_actors[0].period.tv_nsec = 10;
rtems_actors[0].processor = 1;
param.sched_priority=rtems_actors[0].priority; ;
pthread_attr_setschedparam(&attr,&param);
pthread_create(&id,&attr,lide_c_actor_start_routine,&rtems_actors[0]);
CPU_ZERO(&cpuset);
CPU_SET(processors[0], &cpuset);
pthread_setaffinity_np(id, sizeof(cpu_set_t), &cpuset);
```

Fig. 4. Generated code configuring the scheduling parameters in RTEMS

ple of the generated code is given in Fig. 3. We generate a graph of two channels and three actors corresponding to the SDF graph in Fig. 1.

Scheduling Parameters. Actor firings are managed by a scheduler with scheduling parameters computed by ADFG. Four scheduling parameters are computed, namely: `priority`, `mapping`, `period` and `offset`. Code generation for these parameters is done by exploiting the POSIX thread API supported by RTEMS. The `priority` and `mapping` parameters are natively supported. The `period` and `offset` are taken into account by implementing a FPP scheduler.

- Priority: POSIX `set_affinity` function is used to set thread priorities.
- Mapping: POSIX provides the `cpu_set` property that allows us to choose the set of cores that a thread can execute on.
- Period: is implemented by exploiting the `nanosleep` function. The sleep duration is equal to the period minus the execution time of a thread.
- Offset: is generated by adding an idle period to the first execution of a thread.

An example of the generated code is given in Fig. 4. We create a data structure named `rtems_actor` that encapsulates a `lide_c_actor_context` and its scheduling parameters. Then, these parameters are passed to the attributes of a pthread accordingly. This example and its code can be duplicated systematically for all the actors in the graph and their corresponding threads in order to apply scheduling parameters computed by ADFG.

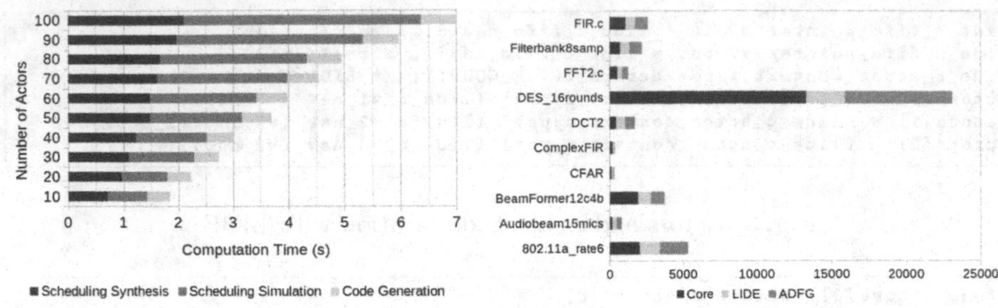

(a) Computation time of the three steps (b) LoC added by the code generator

Fig. 5. Performance, scalability and code generation overhead

4 Evaluation

Experiments are conducted to evaluate our framework by three criteria. First, we show the time taken by each analysis step with SDF graphs of various sizes. Second, we present the overhead induced by the code generator in terms of lines of code (LoC) added to a data-flow application. Then, we discuss the run-time overhead introduced by the usage of our framework. In summary, our experiments show that with scalable compile-time cost, and relatively low run-time overhead, our framework is capable of deploying FPP scheduling based on ADFG theory that are automatically generated, correct by construction, and jointly optimized for throughput and memory requirements.

4.1 Framework Performance and Scalability

We evaluate the framework with synthetic SDF graphs generated by the SDF3 tool [23]. The number of actors varies from 10 to 100 in steps of 10. We generate 100 graphs per number of actors. SDF3 takes many parameters besides number of actors; however, their values are chosen arbitrarily as they do not have a significant impact on the performance of our toolchain. The number of processing units is fixed at 4. This experiment is conducted on a PC with an Intel Core i7-8650U (1.90 GHz $\times$ 8) processor, having 16 GBs of memory, and running Ubuntu 18.04.4.

Figure 5a shows the average computation time of each analysis step. It takes from 1.85 s to 7.01 s to synthesize, simulate, and generate FPP scheduling for the tested SDF graphs. We observe that the computation time grows linearly with the number of actors so the framework has an acceptable scalability. If we analyse each analysis step, scheduling synthesis and code generation have a better scalability than scheduling simulation. The differences between the maximum and minimum computation time of each step are 1.4 s, 3.54 s, and 0.22 s. Scheduling simulation is also the analysis step taking the most time with up to 60% of the total computation time.

4.2 Code Generation Overhead

The code generator is evaluated by comparing the number of lines of code (LoC) added to a data-flow application. As our targets of hardware platforms are embedded systems, code size is an important metric to evaluate.

For a given application, we count the LoC of its core functionality. Then we count the LoC added in order to implement each actor with LIDE interface functions. Next, we count the LoC generated for the parameters computed by ADFG. We have selected a subset of applications in the STR2RTS benchmark [21], which is a refactored version of the StreamIT benchmark.

The LoC added to support LIDE interface functions are 30 LoC per unique actor. In an SDF graph, we often observe that some actors are duplicated to exploit the parallelism. In other words, they are copies of an actor and they have identical functionalities As a result, they only need to be implemented once. The LoC added to support the POSIX thread API are 14 LoC per actor and 3 LoC per buffer. On the contrary to the first category, we always need to generate the code for an actor, even if it is a duplication of another actor.

The result of the evaluation is given in Fig. 5b. On average, the LoC generated are about 60% of the complete application. As actors in the benchmark have simple functionality and do not support the implementation of multi-threaded execution, this proportion is expected. This number is lower for SDF graphs with a high number of actors but a low number of unique ones such as DES_16round.

4.3 Run-Time Overhead

In this section, we discuss and evaluate the run-time overhead introduced by the usage of our framework. This overhead can be categorized in three sources: (1) RTOS overhead, (2) FPP scheduling overhead, and (3) LIDE overhead.

RTOS overhead is due to the usage of an operating system such as RTEMS and its services instead of a bare-metal implementation. In [18], the authors provided an evaluation of RTEMS core characteristics. RTOS overhead depends on the choice of system designers and the evaluation of different embedded RTOS is not in the scope of our work. FPP scheduling overhead is due-to the usage of a FPP scheduler instead of a rate optimal one. A comparison between the two schedulers in ADFG has been presented in [8].

LIDE overhead is due to the code added when refactoring SDF actors and the usage of LIDE functions to read/write data in the channels. We present in Table 1 the WCET of the added functions. WCET analysis is done by the tool OTAWA [4] and the compiler used is arm-linux-gnueabi-gcc version 9.3.0. The token size, which is used to determine the loop bound when using the `memcpy` function to read/write data in the channels, is set to 8 bytes (integer token).

WCET analysis cannot be done for the functions 5, 6, 7 in Table 1 because the usage of the system calls `free` and `malloc`, which cannot be analyzed by the WCET analyzer. These functions are only called once at the initialisation/termination step and are not used when the system enters the steady-state.

Table 1. WCET analysis of LIDE functions

	LIDE C functions	WCET analysis
1	`lide_c_<actor name>_enable`	165 cycles
2	`lide_c_fifo_write`	825 cycles (token size = 8)
3	`lide_c_fifo_read`	815 cycles (token size = 8)
4	`lide_c_<actor name>_invoke`	1640 cycles (token size = 8)
5	`lide_c_<actor name>_terminate`	System call: free()
6	`lide_c_<actor name>_new`	System call: malloc()
7	`lide_c_fifo_new`	System call: malloc()

We compare the obtained results with the average WCETs of actors found in the StreamIT [24] benchmark to have a quantitative evaluation. As presented in [21], the average WCETs in the benchmark ranges from 273 to 2.94e5 cycles. Compared to this result, the overhead of the LIDE functions varies between 12.6 and 0.01 times the WCET of the actors. This high variation exists because in the benchmark, there are both fine-grained actors with only few lines of code and coarse-grained ones, which contain more complex actors. Coarse-grained SDF graphs are the main targets of our framework as we consider the usage of RTOS and FPP scheduling.

5 Related Work

In this section, we position our contribution by providing discussions on SDF graph analysis tools. Many tools are able to analyze SDF graphs, to derive various properties (e.g. mapping and buffer size), and finally to generate the glue code of the schedule automatically: for example, DIF-GPU [17], PREESM [20], MAPS [9], Diplomat [7], Gaspard [12], PeaCE [14], and Ptolemy [13]. But these tools either do not jointly consider real-time execution and FPP scheduling, or do not perform all syntheses automatically.

Another line of work is to build a complete data-flow compilation toolchain. In [24] and [3], the authors both introduce their own programming languages, namely, StreamIT and ΣC. Many analysis steps are applied to compute a static time-triggered schedule and generate an executable. Our approach differs from the two in terms of the choice of programming language and scheduling strategy. First, we refactor programs written in the C programming language to facilitate the generation of scheduling parameters. Second, we aim to generate a FPP scheduling instead of static time-triggered ones as described in [19,27].

The most related work to ADFG is the DARTS tool [5]. It allows to compute the strictly periodic scheduling parameters achieving the best throughput under earliest deadline first or rate monotonic scheduling policies. The main difference is that DARTS considers a non-constrained number of available processors on the target system and requires a constraint on the maximum total buffer size.

Compared to prior work on data-flow analysis tools, such as those summarized above, and to prior work on tools for real-time embedded systems (e.g., [10,11], and [26]), our proposed framework provides a novel integration of real-time execution, periodic scheduling, resource-constrained mapping, and capabilities for iterative tuning and optimization of scheduling parameters.

6 Conclusions

In this article, we present a framework for periodic scheduling synthesis of SDF graphs. The framework is built from three open-source tools: ADFG [15], Cheddar [22], and LIDE [16]. Starting from an SDF graph, we synthesize its FPP scheduling with ADFG and then verify the result with Cheddar. We assume that actors are implemented in LIDE and generate the implementation of the graph and the computed schedule by targeting the RTEMS RTOS. Our experiments have shown that the proposed framework has an acceptable performance, thus it can be used in the early stage of system design when changes occur quite frequently. For future works, we want to extend the scheduling synthesis in ADFG to take into account interference in order to provide more precise results. In addition, we aim to extend the framework with the integration of static resource analysis tools to directly obtain the timing and memory footprint of actors instead of relying on external sources of information.

Engineering effort has been put in this framework to assure that tool interoperability is achieved by data file export/import and a set of scripts. Nevertheless, the process of installing and configuring all the tools presented can be complex and time-consuming. We are investigating options to make a ready-to-use setup of the framework such as a pre-configured virtual machine.

References

1. RTEMS real time operating system (RTOS). https://www.rtems.org/
2. Altmeyer, S., Maiza Burguière, C.: Cache-related preemption delay via useful cache blocks: survey and redefinition. J. Syst. Architect. **57**(7), 707–719 (2011)
3. Aubry, P., et al.: Extended cyclostatic dataflow program compilation and execution for an integrated manycore processor. Procedia Comput. Sci. **18**, 1624–1633 (2013)
4. Ballabriga, C., Cassé, H., Rochange, C., Sainrat, P.: OTAWA: an open toolbox for adaptive WCET analysis. In: Min, S.L., Pettit, R., Puschner, P., Ungerer, T. (eds.) SEUS 2010. LNCS, vol. 6399, pp. 35–46. Springer, Heidelberg (2010). https://doi.org/10.1007/978-3-642-16256-5_6
5. Bamakhrama, M., Stefanov, T.: Hard-real time scheduling of data-dependent tasks in embedded streaming applications. In: International Conference on Embedded Software (EMSOFT) (2011)
6. Bhattacharyya, S.S., Lee, E.A., Murthy, P.K.: Software Synthesis from Dataflow Graphs. Kluwer Academic Publishers, Norwell (1996)
7. Bodin, B., Nardi, L., Kelly, P.H.J., O'Boyle, M.F.P.: Diplomat: mapping of multi-kernel applications using a static dataflow abstraction. In: 2016 IEEE 24th International Symposium on Modeling, Analysis and Simulation of Computer and Telecommunication Systems (MASCOTS), pp. 241–250, September 2016

8. Bouakaz, A.: Real-time scheduling of dataflow graphs. (Ordonnancement temps-réel des graphes flots de données). Ph.D. thesis, University of Rennes 1, France (2013). https://tel.archives-ouvertes.fr/tel-00945453
9. Castrillon, J., Leupers, R., Ascheid, G.: MAPS: mapping concurrent dataflow applications to heterogeneous MPSoCs. IEEE Trans. Industr. Inf. **9**(1), 527–545 (2013)
10. Chandarli, Y., Fauberteau, F., Masson, D., Midonnet, S., Qamhieh, M., et al.: YARTISS: a tool to visualize, test, compare and evaluate real-time scheduling algorithms. In: Proceedings of the 3rd International Workshop on Analysis Tools and Methodologies for Embedded and Real-Time Systems, pp. 21–26 (2012)
11. Chéramy, M., Déplanche, A.M., Hladik, P.E., et al.: Simulation of real-time multiprocessor scheduling with overheads. In: International Conference on Simulation and Modeling Methodologies, Technologies and Applications (SIMULTECH) (2013)
12. Gamatié, A., et al.: A model-driven design framework for massively parallel embedded systems. ACM Trans. Embed. Comput. Syst. **10**(4), 1–36 (2011)
13. Guo, L., Zhu, Q., Nuzzo, P., Passerone, R., Sangiovanni-Vincentelli, A., Lee, E.A.: Metronomy: a function-architecture co-simulation framework for timing verification of cyber-physical systems. In: 2014 International Conference on Hardware/Software Codesign and System Synthesis (CODES+ISSS), pp. 1–10, October 2014
14. Ha, S., Kim, S., Lee, C., Yi, Y., Kwon, S., Joo, Y.P.: PeaCE: a hardware-software codesign environment for multimedia embedded systems. ACM Trans. Des. Autom. Electron. Syst. **12**(3), 24:1-24:25 (2008)
15. Honorat, A., Tran, H.N., Besnard, L., Gautier, T., Talpin, J.P., Bouakaz, A.: ADFG: a scheduling synthesis tool for dataflow graphs in real-time systems. In: 25th International Conference on Real-Time Networks and Systems (2017)
16. Lin, S., Liu, Y., Lee, K., Li, L., Plishker, W., Bhattacharyya, S.S.: The DSPCAD framework for modeling and synthesis of signal processing systems. In: Handbook of Hardware/Software Codesign, pp. 1185–1219 (2017)
17. Lin, S., Wu, J., Bhattacharyya, S.S.: Memory-constrained vectorization and scheduling of dataflow graphs for hybrid CPU-GPU platforms. ACM Trans. Embedded Comput. Syst. **17**(2), 50:1-50:25 (2018)
18. Nicodemos, F.G., Saotome, O., Lima, G., Sato, S.S.: A minimally intrusive method for analysing the timing of RTEMS core characteristics. Int. J. Embedded Syst. **8**(5–6), 391–411 (2016)
19. Parhi, K.K., Messerschmitt, D.G.: Static rate-optimal scheduling of iterative dataflow programs via optimum unfolding. IEEE Trans. Comput. **40**(2), 178–195 (1991). https://doi.org/10.1109/12.73588
20. Pelcat, M., Desnos, K., Heulot, J., Guy, C., Nezan, J.F., Aridhi, S.: Preesm: a dataflow-based rapid prototyping framework for simplifying multicore DSP programming. In: 2014 6th European Embedded Design in Education and Research Conference (EDERC), pp. 36–40, September 2014
21. Rouxel, B., Puaut, I.: STR2RTS: Refactored StreamIT benchmarks into statically analysable parallel benchmarks for WCET estimation & real-time scheduling. In: OASIcs-OpenAccess Series in Informatics, vol. 57. Schloss Dagstuhl-Leibniz-Zentrum fuer Informatik (2017)
22. Singhoff, F., Legrand, J., Nana, L., Marcé, L.: Cheddar: a flexible real time scheduling framework. ACM SIGAda Ada Lett. **24**, 1–8 (2004)
23. Stuijk, S., Geilen, M., Basten, T.: SDF^3: SDF for free. In: Sixth International Conference on Application of Concurrency to System Design (ACSD 2006), pp. 276–278. IEEE (2006)

24. Thies, W., Karczmarek, M., Amarasinghe, S.: StreamIt: A language for streaming applications. In: International Conference on Compiler Construction. pp. 179–196. Springer (2002)
25. Tran, H.N., Honorat, A., Talpin, J.P., Gautier, T., Besnard, L.: Efficient contention-aware scheduling of SDF graphs on shared multi-bank memory. In: 2019 24th International Conference on Engineering of Complex Computer Systems (ICECCS), pp. 114–123. IEEE (2019)
26. Urunuela, R., Déplanche, A.M., Trinquet, Y.: STORM: a simulation tool for real-time multiprocessor scheduling evaluation. In: 2010 IEEE Conference on Emerging Technologies and Factory Automation (ETFA), pp. 1–8. IEEE (2010)
27. Wang, C.Y., Parhi, K.K.: High-level DSP synthesis using concurrent transformations, scheduling, and allocation. IEEE Trans. Comput. Aided Des. Integr. Circuits Syst. **14**(3), 274–295 (1995). https://doi.org/10.1109/43.365120

Special Session on Innovative Architectures and Tools for Security

Hard Edges: Hardware-Based Control-Flow Integrity for Embedded Devices

George Christou[1(✉)], Giorgos Vasiliadis[1], Elias Athanasopoulos[2], and Sotiris Ioannidis[3]

[1] Foundation for Research and Technology Hellas (FORTH-ICS), Heraklion, Greece
{gchri,gvasil}@ics.forth.gr

[2] University Of Cyprus, Nicosia, Cyprus
athanasopoulos.elias@cs.ucy.ac.cy

[3] Technical University of Crete (TUC-ECE), Chania, Greece
sotiris@ece.tuc.gr

Abstract. Control-Flow Integrity (CFI) is a popular technique to defend against State-of-the-Art exploits, by ensuring that every (indirect) control-flow transfer points to a legitimate address and it is part of the Control-flow Graph (CFG) of a program. Enabling CFI in real systems is not straightforward, since in many cases the actual CFG of a program can only be approximated. Even in the case where there is perfect knowledge of the CFG, ensuring that all return instructions will return to their actual call sites, without employing a shadow stack, is questionable.

In this work, we explore the implementation of a full-featured CFI-enabled Instruction Set Architecture (ISA) on actual hardware. Our new instructions provide the finest possible granularity for both intra-function and inter-function Control-Flow Integrity. We implement hardware-based CFI (HCFI) by modifying a SPARC SoC and evaluate the prototype on an FPGA board by running SPECInt benchmarks instrumented with a fine-grained CFI policy. HCFI can effectively protect applications from code-reuse attacks, while adding less than 1% average runtime and 2% power consumption overhead, making it particularly suitable for embedded systems.

1 Introduction

The diversification of computing systems and the wide adoption of IoT devices that pervade our lives has grown the security and safety concerns in home appliances, enterprise infrastructure and control systems. Typical examples range from traditional IoT environments where data are collected and processed in back-end cloud systems, to more sophisticated, edge-based scenarios where part of processing also occurs in end-devices. Protecting against such cases using software-only solutions is not sufficient, since advanced attacks can modify even the security software itself, thus bypassing any restrictions posed. In addition,

© Springer Nature Switzerland AG 2022
A. Orailoglu et al. (Eds.): SAMOS 2021, LNCS 13227, pp. 275–287, 2022.
https://doi.org/10.1007/978-3-031-04580-6_18

the performance overheads of software-based solutions is non-negligible in certain cases. The use of hardware-backed solutions can vitally improve the security of embedded devices, even though this is still challenging due to their limited resources and their intrinsic budget of performance and memory.

At the same time, the exploitation threats are constantly evolving. More than a decade ago, exploiting software was as easy as just simply smashing the stack [16]. An attacker could simply inject code into a vulnerable buffer in the stack and overwrite the return address (of the current stack frame) to point back to their code. Today, this is not possible due to data execution prevention (DEP) mechanisms, however attackers can still exploit software in other ways. For instance, code-reuse attacks, such as Return-Oriented Programming (ROP) [19] and Jump-Oriented Programming (JOP) [6] can potentially take advantage of any vulnerability and transform it to a functional exploit. These techniques do not require any code injections; instead, they re-use existing parts of the program to build the necessary functionality without violating DEP. According to a recent report, more than 80% of the vulnerabilities are exploited using code-reuse attacks [18].

Code randomization techniques [17] are shuffling the location of the code, in order to make code reuse attacks harder to achieve. Still, even a small information leak can reveal all of the process code and bypass any randomization scheme [20]. Instead of hiding the code, another way for stopping exploits is to prevent the execution of any new functionality, by employing Control-Flow Integrity (CFI) techniques [3]. An attacker cannot inject code or introduce any new functionality that is not part of the *legitimate* control-flow graph (CFG). Unfortunately, the majority of existing CFI proposals have still many open issues (related to *accuracy* and *performance*), that hinder its applicability [5].

In this work, we extend our previous hardware-assisted CFI (HCFI) [8] in order to enhance its granularity and flexibility. The implementation of new hardware instructions dedicated for CFI, and the deployment of shadow memory within the processor core, increase the granularity of CFI (especially in forward-edge situations); moreover they cover a couple of intrinsic situations (including the instrumentation of fall-through functions and indirect jumps, such as `switch` statements, within functions). Performance-wise, the implementation in hardware is the optimal choise; our approach adds less than 1% average runtime and 2% power overhead, making it suitable for embedded systems.

Overall, HCFI is a hardware design that offers a CFI solution that is (*i*) *complete*, since it protects both forward and backward edges, (*ii*) *fast*, since the experienced overhead is, on average, less than 1%, and (*iii*) *more accurate*, since it employs a full-functional shadow stack implemented inside the processor core. Furthermore, we argue that HCFI is the most complete hardware implementation of CFI so far, supporting many problematic cases (such as `setjmp`/`longjmp`, recursion, fall-through functions and indirect jumps within functions).

2 Background

Control-Flow Integrity (CFI) [3] constraints all indirect branches in a control-flow graph (CFG), which is determined statically before the program execution. In essence, this is achieved by setting a simple set of rules that a program execution flow must adhere to:

1. A call-site "A" can call a function "B" only if the edge (the call itself) is part of the Control-Flow Graph (CFG). This is called Forward-Edge CFI and can easily applied to direct calls, as the only way to modify a direct call is to overwrite the code itself. This is not the case for indirect calls though, where function pointers are typically stored in data regions.
2. A function "B" can only return to the call-site "A" that actually called it, and no other place in the code. This is called Backward-Edge CFI. Backward-edges are, in essence, indirect calls, since they rely on a pointer (return address) to jump to their target.

An attacker cannot inject code or introduce any new functionality that is not part of the *legitimate* control-flow graph (CFG). The majority of existing CFI proposals have still many open issues (related to *accuracy* and *performance overhead*), that hinder its applicability, especially, to embedded devices [5,22]. For instance, it is not always easy to compute the program's CFG. This is mainly because the source code might not always be available, while even if it does, dynamic code that might be introduced at run-time or the heavy use of function pointers can lead to inconclusive target resolution [5]. This problem has led researchers to develop CFI techniques that are based on a relaxed approximation of the CFG [22], also known as coarse-grained CFI.

Unfortunately, coarse-grained CFI has been demonstrated to exhibit weak security guarantees and it is today well established that it can be bypassed [12]. Approximation of the ideal CFG through code analysis is not always sound, therefore, at least for protecting backward edges, the community has suggested *shadow stacks* [9] - secure memory that stores all return address during function calls. Many research efforts have stressed that shadow stacks are important for securing programs, even when we know the program's CFG with high accuracy [11]. A trivial case is when a function is called by multiple places in the program. According to the CFG, all return locations are legitimate, however only one is actually correct. Moreover, implementing fine grained CFI solely on software, introduces prohibitive performance impact. In the original CFI proposal by Abadi [3], the average performance was 21%. More recent approaches like SafeStack [15], are designed to offer fine grained backward edge protection with minimal overhead. The applications are instrumented during compilation in order to use a different, protected stack for storing control flow variables used in backward edges. However, protecting memory regions using software techniques has been proven ineffective against sophisticated attacks [7,13].

To overcome there restrictions, hardware-assisted CFI implementations can provide architecturally protected memory regions for storing control-flow variables, while at the same time accelerate significantly any checks required during control-flow transitions; this enables the use of fine-grained CFI even in low-powered devices.

3 Threat Model

Our threat model assumes an attacker that can exploit a vulnerability, either a stack or heap overflow, or use-after-free. This vulnerability can be further used to overwrite key components of the running process like return addresses, function pointers, or VTable pointers. We also consider that the attacker has successfully bypassed ASLR or fine-grained randomization [20], and has full knowledge of the process' memory layout. Nevertheless, the system enforces that (*i*) the `.text` segment is non-writable preventing the application's code from being overwritten, and (*ii*) the `.data` segment is non-executable blocking the attacker from executing directly data with proper CFI annotation. Both of these are commonplace in today's systems preventing software exploitation.

4 Hardware-Enforced Control-Flow Integrity

HCFI enforces the set of CFI rules (described in Sect. 2) in hardware, while also provide workarounds for certain corner cases. More specifically, a valid call requires that the call site and the destination have been previously acknowledged to be a valid pair in the CFG. A simple way to avoid checking a list of valid pairs for every indirect call, is to group valid pairs with a label. If the label of the source and the destination match, then the edge is legal.

On the contrary, a valid return is typically simpler to validate. Whenever a call takes place, the return address is pushed to the stack. If the address reached after a return, matches the *top* of the stack, the return is valid. This is achieved by also pushing the return address to a new, hidden, stack (namely *shadow stack*), and comparing the return's target to the one stored at the top of the shadow stack. However, this is not the case for the `setjmp`/`longjmp` case, in which a function does not necessarily return to its caller. In particular, `longjmp` never returns to its caller but to its matching `setjmp` (Fig. 1).

To support this functionality, the ISA is extended with new instructions (shown in Table 1): two for the instrumentation of the backward edges, two for the forward edges, and two for handling `setjmp`/`longjmp` cases. The instructions are strategically placed, so as to wrap the Control-Flow edges. `SetPC` and `SetPCLabel` are paired with direct and indirect calls respectively, while `CheckPC` is paired with return instructions, and `CheckLabel` is placed in function entry points, if the function is an indirect call target. Finally, `SJCFI` and `LJCFI` are paired with the calls to `setjmp` and `longjmp` themselves. `LJCFI` is placed immediately before the call to longjmp, while `SJCFI` is placed immediately after the call to `setjmp`, so that it will be the first instruction executed after a return from `setjmp`, no matter if `setjmp` or `longjmp` was called.

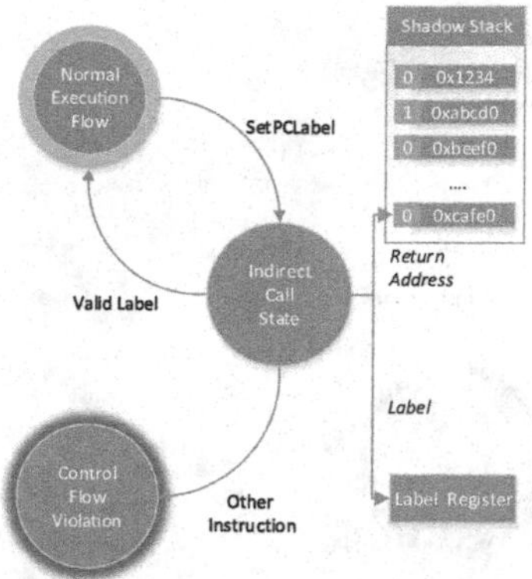

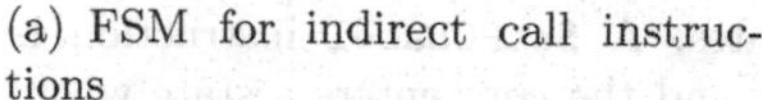
(a) FSM for indirect call instructions

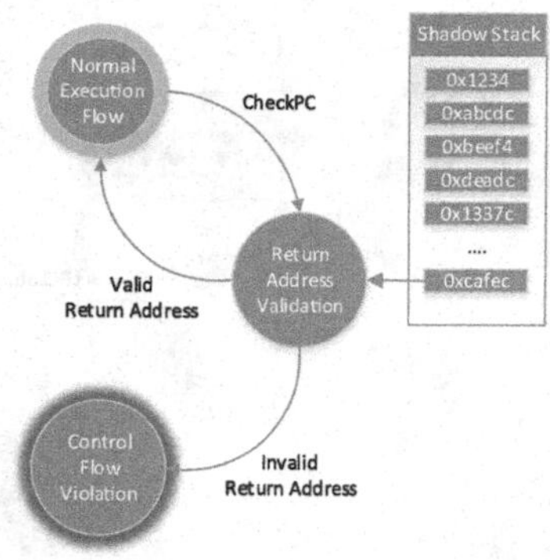

(b) FSM for return instructions

Fig. 1. The basic FSMs for the hardware-based CFI. For return instructions, the target Program Counter is compared with the top value of the stack everytime a `CheckPC` instruction is received and the execution continues normally.

Finally, given that the design of HCFI does not track stack frames, but specific addresses instead, recursion may result in the same address being pushed to the shadow stack multiple times. From this observation, a very simple optimization can be implemented; namely, not storing the address when it equals the top of the stack, but instead marking the address at the top as recursive. This effectively negates the spacial requirements of immediate recursion. During `CheckPC` execution, if the top address in the shadow stack is marked as recursive and is the same as the target of the return instruction it will not be popped. If not, the top address will be popped and the target address will be compared with the next top address in the shadow stack. If the two addresses are equal, the execution will continue normally and the top of the shadow stack will be popped (if the address was not marked as recursive). If the addesses are not equal, CheckPC will result in a CFI violation.

Table 1. Instructions needed to support HCFI.

`SetPC`	Pushes the current program counter (PC) in the shadow stack
`CheckPC`	Pops the shadow stack and compares the result with the next PC
`SetPCLabel`	Can push the PC onto the shadow stack and carries a label used to verify forward edges which is stored in a dedicated register (Label Register). Finally, it sets the requirement the next instruction must be a CheckLabel
`CheckLabel`	Carries a label that is compared to the one in the Label Register
`SJCFI`	Sets the environment for a future longjmp and acts as a landing point for an executing one
`LJCFI`	Signifies that a longjmp is underway

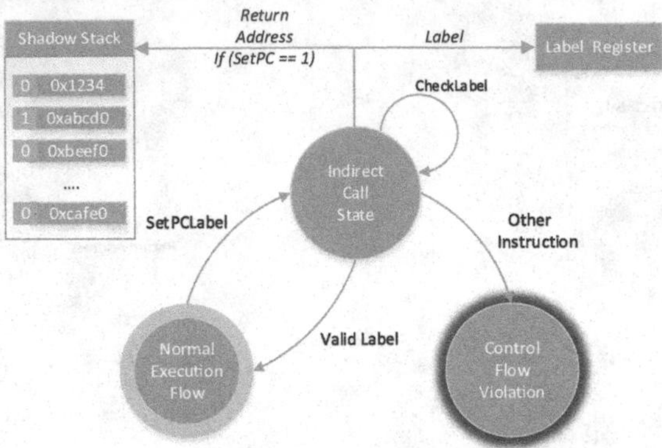

Fig. 2. The extended FSM for Indirect Call States. A `SetPCLabel` instruction is received, the appropriate memory modules are set, and the core enters a state where only `CheckLabel` instructions are accepted. Once a `CheckLabel` instruction with the appropriate label is received, the execution returns to its normal flow.

5 Fine-Grained CFI Instrumentation

The instructions presented in Sect. 4 are created in order to enable a policy agnostic CFI mechanism. Especially for the backward edges, they can easily support the finest possible granularity: by using an architecturally protected shadow stack where only the CFI instructions can modify values, we can ensure that a function will always return to the original call site. However, for forward edges, the granularity is proportional to the effort of analysis performed on the code of the executable. Ideally, every function in the binary will be reachable by a minimum set of indirect call sites. We note that our design can even support more relaxed forward-edge schemes, where indirect call sites can target every function entry point, i.e. by using only one label in the whole binary—this can be practical in cases, where extensive control flow analysis is not feasible.

To allow for finer granularity and flexibility, we make the following modifications to our initial design. Previously, every `CheckLabel` instruction was requiring the Label Register to be set, and hold the correct label. Under the new design, an unset Label Register, or one carrying an incorrect label, does not lead to a violation, as long as the next instruction is also a `CheckLabel`. Also, the `SetPCLabel` instruction can now ommit pushing the PC to the shadow stack, depending on its arguments. Moreover, we allow the instrumentation of indirect branching within the same function. Ignoring `CheckLabel` instructions does not raise security concerns, if the whole binary is instrumented properly. Forward-edge transitions should only be checked during indirect call and branch instructions—during normal execution, the `CheckLabel` instructions do not need to make any checks, since the control-flow is not influenced by data.

5.1 Finer Forward-Edge Granularity

When Control Flow Integrity was first introduced by Abadi et al. [3], indirect call targets with a common source had to be grouped together. For example, if a call site "A" indirectly called a call target "B", and a call site "C" could indirectly call "D" *and* "B", then both call sites "A" and "C", as well as the call targets "B" and "D", would have to share the same label. This is a usual case in C++ applications where indirect calls, dereference virtual table pointers. Target functions that are common between indirect call sites, will force the use of the same label across a large portion of the application. Thus, the granularity of forward-edge protections become significantly coarser.

In this work, we offer the option to set a unique label for each indirect call site, and add as many `CheckLabels` in the call target as needed. The previous example can now be instrumented with 2 labels in the "B" entry point (one for each indirect call-site). Call site "A" and "C" will carry different labels in their CheckLabel instructions. This has the effect of not allowing call site "A" to jump to "D", which was previously possible. This allows for much finer forward-edge CFI on top of an already powerful design. Figure 2 presents the operation of `CheckLabel` instruction.

Fall-Through Functions. In many popular libraries, such as GNU libc, there are functions with overlapping code sections [4]. In such cases, the execution of a function falls-through into another function's entry point (without using branch instructions). If these functions are possible targets of indirect call instructions, they should be instrumented with `CheckLabel` instructions, otherwise even if the indirect transition is valid it will result to a CFI violation. Since `CheckLabels` do not cause a CFI violation when the processor is not in indirect jump state, they are just ignored during execution. Thus, when a function falls through, the execution of the inner function's `CheckLabel` instructions will not result in a CFI violation. This allows for fall-through functions to be instrumented like regular functions.

Intra-Function Forward-Edges. Most CFI schemes do not take into account indirect branches, targeting addresses within the same function. For example, large `switch` statements are usually compiled to jump tables in order to reduce the code size of the binary. In these cases the address of each case is stored in a jump table. At runtime, the result of the `switch` statement is used in an indirect jump in order to dereference the jump table at the appropriate index. Thus, instead of emitting absolute jumps for every possible statement result, the compiler emits a single indirect jump that uses the statement result as an index in the jump table. In our design we offer the capability to instrument those indirect jumps in order to ensure that the target address is the entry point of one of the cases. Each indirect jump will be instrumented with a `SetPCLabel` instruction that will not push a return address in the shadow stack (i.e. `SetPC` bit is '0'), and the entry points of each *case* basic block will be instrumented with the appropriate CheckLabel instruction. Every switch statement in the binary should use a different label for better granularity.

6 Prototype Implementation

To implement the hardware-based CFI described in the previous sections, we extended the Leon3 SPARC V8 processor, which is a 32-bit open-source synthesizable processor. Overall, the additions to the core can be grouped in the following two categories: (*i*) Memory Components and (*ii*) CFI Pipeline.

6.1 Memory Components

The following new memory components are deployed in the Register File of the core:

- A 256 * 32 bit dual-port Block RAM was used for the Shadow Stack.
- A 256 * 8 bit single-port Block RAM was used for the setjmp and longjmp support (SJLJRAM).
- A 18 bit register was used to store the label for forward edge validation (Label Register).
- A 256 * 1 bit array helped us optimize recursive calls (Recursion Array).

6.2 CFI Pipeline

Our instructions enter the Integer Unit's (IU) pipeline as usual, however they do not interfere with it. We have developed a new pipeline within the IU (CFI Pipeline) that operates in parallel and provides the functionality required everytime the instructions are decoded.

- SetPC first tops the Shadow Stack and compares it to the current Program Counter (PC). If the memory addresses match, the Recursion Array is set; otherwise, the address is pushed onto the shadow stack. In case the Shadow Stack is full a *Full* violation is raised.
- SetPCLabel is in essence two instructions, meaning that it acts exactly as a SetPC and what could be described as a SetLabel. The SetPC functionality works only if the 25th LS bit of the instruction is set. Regardless of the SetPC functionality, the Label carried in its 18 LS bits is written to the Label Register, and the CFI Pipeline transitions to the SetLabel state. This mandates that only CheckLabel instructions can be executed, until one with the correct label is issued. If any other instruction is issued, a *Control Flow* violation is raised.
- CheckLabel compares the Label carried in its 18 LS bits to the label stored in the Label Register, if the CFI Pipeline is in the SetLabel state. Otherwise, it is ignored and acts as a nop. If the comparison holds, the Label Register is reset and the pipeline transists from SetLabel state to normal execution. If not, the execution continues, but if an instruction other than checklabel is issued, a *Control Flow* violation will be raised.

- `CheckPC` first checks the Shadow Stack; if it is empty, an *Empty* violation is raised. Otherwise, it tops the Shadow Stack, increments the value by four (one instruction) and compares it to the next PC. If the addresses match and the equivalent recursion bit is not set, the Shadow Stack is popped. If the addresses did not match but the recursion bit is set, the address is popped and another comparison is performed with the next value. Again, if they match and the top value is not recursive, it is popped. If the first comparison failed and the top address was not recursive, or if both comparisons failed, a *PC Mismatch* violation is raised.
- `SJCFI` changes its functionality depending on whether the CFI Pipeline is in the `longjmp` state. If it is not, it writes the current depth of the Shadow Stack to the SJLJRAM. The address is provided by a label it carries on its 8 LS bits. Otherwise, it uses the same label to read the address from the SJLJRAM and set the Shadow Stack to that depth. The Shadow Stack will not allow an index higher than the current, so that previously popped addresses cannot be abused. The CFI Pipeline returns to its default state.
- `LJCFI` sets the pipeline in the `longjmp` state until an `SJCFI` instruction is executed.

7 Performance Evaluation

We synthesize and program our new design, based on the Leon3 softcore, on a Xilinx ml605-rev.e FPGA board. The FPGA has 1024 MB DDR3 SO-DIMM memory and the design operates at 120 MHz clock frequency. Since we are targeting embedded systems, we run all tests without an operating system present. We instrumented most of the SpecInt2000 suite and a few microprocessor benchmarks, namely Coremark, Dhrystone, and Matmul.

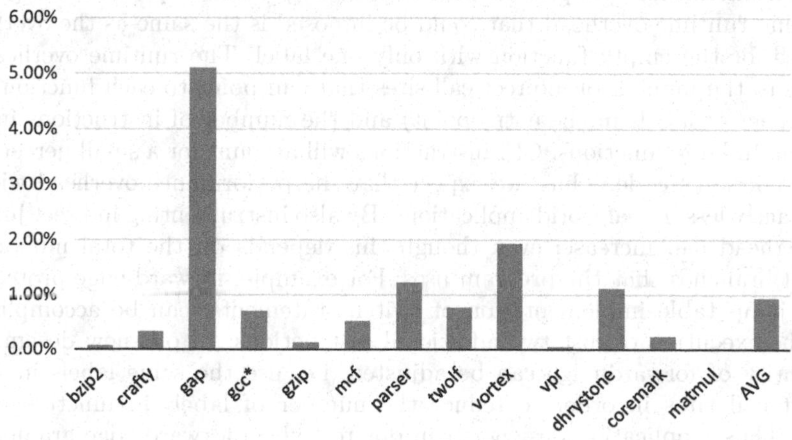

Fig. 3. The runtime overhead measured with our implementation.

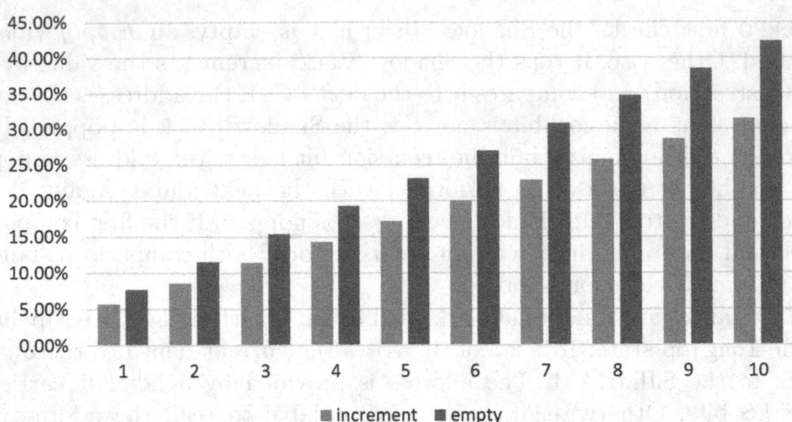

Fig. 4. The runtime overhead added by using 1–10 labels on an empty function or a function that increments a value.

Runtime Overhead. When instrumenting only calls (both direct and indirect) and returns, the average overhead lies at a little under 1% as shown in Fig. 3. In the case of gap benchmark, the reported overhead is the result of a tight loop executing a multitude of indirect calls to relatively small functions.

We also run two series of microbenchmarks to see the effect of adding multiple labels to a function. We did this by executing a tight loop with an indirect call to one of two functions. The first was an empty function, which results in three assembly instructions. The second was a function that incremented a global variable, this has a body of ten instructions. We added one to ten labels on the function entry points. With these benchmarks we can find the maximum percentage of runtime overhead imposed when a function is called indirectly with CFI instrumentation. We present our results in Fig. 4. In our previous design the maximum runtime overhead that could be imposed is the same as the overhead reported for the empty function with only one label. The runtime overhead is relative to the number of indirect call sites that can point to each function (i.e. the number of labels in the entry point) and the number of instructions in the function. In large functions, CFI instructions will account for a small percentage of the function's code. Thus, we expect that the performance overhead will be significantly less in real world applications. By also instrumenting indirect jumps, the overhead can increase; even though this depends on the total number of indirect branches that the program uses. For example, forward-edge protection in the jump table implementation of switch statements, can be accomplished with the execution of just two additional instructions. In our new design, the granularity of forward-edge can be adjusted, i.e. use the same labels in some indirect call sites in order to reduce the number of labels in function entry points. Thus, application designers can opt to reduce forward-edge granularity in order to favor performance.

Hardware Overhead. We implemented our design initially without `longjmp` support and the recursion optimization. The resulting area overhead, as detailed by the reports of the Xilinx tools used to synthesize the design, is very low, using an additional 0.65% registers and 0.81% LUTs (look-up tables). The area overhead increases significantly to 2.52% registers and 2.55% LUTs, when placing the `longjmp` support and the recursion optimization.

Power Consumption. We measure the power consumption of our design using the Xilinx XPower Analyzer tool. For the unmodified design the tool reported 6072.11 mW power consumption. The required modifications for the CFI instructions increase the power consumption to 6149.32 mW. The full fledged design with CFI and SJ/LJ support has a power consumption of 6176.92 mW. The results indicate that the power consumption overhead is about 1.2%, which increases to 1.7% when adding `longjump` support.

8 Related Work

CFI is the base of many proposed mitigation techniques in the literature. Most of them are software-based, although there are some attempts for delivering CFI-aware processors. In this section, we discuss a representative selection of CFI strategies proposed in the literature and the industry as well as their limitations. Davi et al. [10] proposed HAFIX, a system for protecting backward edges based on active set CFI. HAFIX deploys dedicated, hidden memory elements for storing critical information. Their implementation utilizes labels to mark functions as active call sites. Labels are used as index in a bitmap, which dictates if a function is active or inactive. A return can only point to an `active` function. However, it has been proven that this notion is very relaxed and can be circumvented [21]. In our design we use an architecturally protected shadow stack, a technique considered to be the state of the art for protecting beackward edges. Moreover, our design offers forward edge protection. HAFIX proposes the use of software techniques for protecting forward-edges.

Intel plans to include Control-flow Enforcement Technology (CET) [1] in future processors. In CET a shadow stack is defined in order to protect backward-edge control flow transfers in a manner similar to our design. With regards to forward-edge control flow transfers `ENDBRANCH` instruction is used to mark the legitimate landing points for call and indirect jump instructions within the applications code. However, an indirect jump can point to any `ENDBRANCH`. In comparison, HCFI can support multiple labels in every function entry offering per indirect call-site granularity for forward edges. ARM presented Pointer Authentication Code (PAC) [2]. This mechanism utilizes cryptographic primitives (hashing) in order to verify that the control flow pointers are not corrupted before using them. The pointer authentication code (PAC) of each control flow pointer is stored in the unused bits of the pointer (i.e. 24 MS bits of the pointer). Each process has a unique key which is used in order to calculate and authenticate the control flow pointers. The encryption algorithm used is QARMA. This technology has been already deployed in Apple products with ARMv8.3 cores.

A recent study from Googles project zero identified several vulnerabilities in this technology [14]. Pointer authentication can offer similar levels of protection with our design. However, the use of cryptographic primitives in PAC instructions imposes signifficantly more overhead in terms of performance and area compared to our design.

9 Conclusions

In this paper, we designed, implemented and evaluated a flexible and policy-agnostic Control-Flow Integrity Instruction Set Extension. Our extensions introduced less than 1% runtime overhead on average and less than 2% increase in power consumption, will only imposing very little overhead in terms of additional hardware circuitry (less than 2.55%). Our plan for the future is to extend our implementation to support multi-threading. While our forward-edge protections can be easily deployed in multi-threaded applications, for protecting backward-edges a single shadow stack is not enough. We plan to implement a new technique that allocates memory pages for each thread's shadow stack.

Acknowledgments. This work was supported by the projects CONCORDIA, C4IIoT, Cyrene and IntellIoT, funded by the European Commission under Grant Agreements No. 830927, No. 833828, No 952690 and No. 957218. This publication reflects the views only of the authors, and the Commission cannot be held responsible for any use which may be made of the information contained therein. The authors would like to thank Nikolaos Christoulakis for his contribution during the implementation of HCFI.

References

1. Control-flow Enforcement Technology Preview. https://software.intel.com/sites/default/files/managed/4d/2a/control-flow-enforcement-technology-preview.pdf (2016)
2. Pointer Authentication on ARMv8.3. https://www.qualcomm.com/media/documents/files/whitepaper-pointer-authentication-on-armv8-3.pdf (2017)
3. Abadi, M., Budiu, M., Erlingsson, U., Ligatti, J.: Control-flow integrity. In: Proceedings of the 12th ACM CCS (2005)
4. Agadakos, I., Jin, D., Williams-King, D., Kemerlis, V.P., Portokalidis, G.: Nibbler: Debloating binary shared libraries. In: Proceedings of the 35th Annual Computer Security Applications Conference, pp. 70–83 (2019)
5. Athanasakis, M., Athanasopoulos, E., Polychronakis, M., Portokalidis, G., Ioannidis, S.: The Devil is in the Constants: Bypassing Defenses in Browser JIT Engines. In: NDSS. The Internet Society (2015)
6. Bletsch, T., Jiang, X., Freeh, V.W., Liang, Z.: Jump-oriented programming: a new class of code-reuse attack. In: Proceedings of the 6th ACM Symposium on Information, Computer and Communications Security (2011)
7. Carlini, N., Barresi, A., Payer, M., Wagner, D., Gross, T.R.: Control-flow bending: on the effectiveness of control-flow integrity. In: USENIX Security (2015)

8. Christoulakis, N., Christou, G., Athanasopoulos, E., Ioannidis, S.: HCFI: hardware-enforced control-flow integrity. In: Proceedings of the 6th ACM Conference on Data and Application Security and Privacy. CODASPY 2016 (2016)
9. Dang, T.H., Maniatis, P., Wagner, D.: The performance cost of shadow stacks and stack canaries. In: ACM Symposium on Information, Computer and Communications Security, ASIACCS, vol. 15 (2015)
10. Davi, L., et al.: HAFIX: hardware-assisted flow integrity extension. In: Proceedings of the 52nd Annual Design Automation Conference, p. 74. ACM (2015)
11. Evans, I., et al.: Control jujutsu: on the weaknesses of fine-grained control flow integrity. CCS (2015)
12. Göktaş, E., Athanasopoulos, E., Bos, H., Portokalidis, G.: Out of control: overcoming control-flow integrity. In: IEEE Symposium on Security and Privacy (2014)
13. Göktaş, E., Economopoulos, A., Gawlik, R., Athanasopoulos, E., Portokalidis, G., Bos, H.: Bypassing Clang's SafeStack for fun and profit. Black Hat Europe (2016)
14. Google Project Zero: Examining Pointer Authentication on the iPhone XS. https://googleprojectzero.blogspot.com/2019/02/examining-pointer-authentication-on.html
15. Kuznetsov, V., Szekeres, L., Payer, M., Candea, G., Sekar, R., Song, D.: Code-Pointer Integrity. In: USENIX OSDI (2014)
16. One, A.: Smashing the stack for fun and profit. Phrack Mag. **7**(49), 365 (1996)
17. Pappas, V., Polychronakis, M., Keromytis, A.D.: Smashing the gadgets: hindering return-oriented programming using in-place code randomization. In: Proceedings of the IEEE Symposium on Security and Privacy (2012)
18. Rains, T., Miller, M., Weston, D.: Exploitation trends: From potential risk to actual risk. In: RSA Conference (2015)
19. Roemer, R., Buchanan, E., Shacham, H., Savage, S.: Return-oriented programming: systems, languages, and applications. ACM Trans. Inf. Syst. Secur. (TISSEC) **15**(1), 2 (2012)
20. Snow, K.Z., Davi, L., Dmitrienko, A., Liebchen, C., Monrose, F., Sadeghi, A.R.: Just-in-time code reuse: on the effectiveness of fine-grained address space layout randomization. In: Proceedings of the 34th IEEE Symposium on Security and Privacy, May 2013
21. Theodorides, M., Wagner, D.: Breaking active-set backward-edge CFI. In: IEEE International Symposium on Hardware Oriented Security and Trust (2017)
22. Zhang, M., Sekar, R.: Control flow integrity for cots binaries. In: USENIX Security (2013)

ROCKY: Rotation Countermeasure for the Protection of Keys and Other Sensitive Data

Konstantina Miteloudi[1(✉)], Lejla Batina[1], Joan Daemen[1], and Nele Mentens[2,3]

[1] Digital Security Group, Radboud University, Nijmegen, The Netherlands
{kmiteloudi,lejla,joan}@cs.ru.nl
[2] imec-COSIC - ES&S, ESAT, KU Leuven, Leuven, Belgium
nele.mentens@kuleuven.be
[3] LIACS, Leiden University, Leiden, The Netherlands
n.mentens@liacs.leidenuniv.nl

Abstract. Fault attacks exploit the possibility to inject a fault in an electronic device, during the execution of a cryptographic algorithm, leading the device to erroneous operation(s). An adversary can exploit these errors and extract valuable information, making the development of countermeasures against fault attacks necessary. In this work, we present a novel countermeasure that applies to cryptographic primitives that make use of a permutation with almost shift-invariant round functions. Our countermeasure offers protection against fault attacks that rely on the injection of a fault in multiple executions of the same algorithm. In order to demonstrate the hardware overhead of the proposed countermeasure, we implement an FPGA-oriented protected version of Xoodyak, an authenticated encryption lightweight scheme in the NIST lightweight cryptography standardization competition.

Keywords: Authenticated encryption · Fault attacks · Xoodyak

1 Introduction

Fault attacks intend to invoke erroneous computation in an electronic device by introducing a physical disturbance in the hardware or the software of the system. When fault attacks target implementations of cryptographic algorithms, the goal of the attacker is to extract information on the secret key or other internally processed data based on the faulty output generated by the device. Several types of fault attacks are based on the analysis of tens, hundreds, thousands or even more faulty input-output pairs. The countermeasure against fault analysis attacks proposed in this paper, is based on the assumption that a fault attack using multiple input-output pairs will be more difficult to mount when every execution of the algorithm processes the internal data in a different, semi-randomized representation. More specifically, we concentrate on a specific category of authenticated encryption algorithms, namely those that have round functions that are almost

© Springer Nature Switzerland AG 2022
A. Orailoglu et al. (Eds.): SAMOS 2021, LNCS 13227, pp. 288–299, 2022.
https://doi.org/10.1007/978-3-031-04580-6_19

shift-invariant. This allows us to calculate a rotated representation of the output based on a rotated representation of the input. We call our countermeasure "ROCKY: Rotation Countermeasure for the Protection of Keys and Other Sensitive Data". After giving background information on round functions that are almost shift-invariant, and fault analysis and countermeasures in Sect. 2, we present the design principles of ROCKY in Sect. 3. We implement and evaluate three proof-of-concept implementations in Sect. 4. Conclusions and future work are discussed in Sect. 5.

2 Background

In this section we analyze almost shift-invariant round functions and their properties. Also, related work on fault analysis and countermeasures is presented.

2.1 Round Functions that are Almost Shift-Invariant

Several cryptographic permutations have a round function that consists of a series of steps that are shift-invariant mappings. A mapping α is shift-invariant if it commutes with certain (cyclic) shift operations τ: $\alpha \circ \tau = \tau \circ \alpha$. If all steps of a round function R are shift-invariant, the round function itself is shift-invariant: $\mathrm{R} \circ \tau = \tau \circ \mathrm{R}$.

Shift-invariance is a symmetry property that is desired in design: symmetry tends to reduce the range of possible attack vectors. However, symmetry is a double-edged sword and can also be exploited in attacks, such as rotational cryptanalysis [2] and slide attacks [9]. For that reason, one often includes in the round function of cryptographic permutations the addition of a round constant to break the symmetry. In block ciphers with shift-invariant steps, one ensures that the key schedule does not generate round keys that are shift-invariant. We will call such permutations almost shift-invariant.

Some round functions are not strictly shift-invariant but have a symmetry property that is similar: they satisfy $\mathrm{R} \circ \tau = \tau' \circ \mathrm{R}$, with τ and τ' shifts over different, but related, offsets (Table 1).

One can apply a permutation with a shift-invariant round function to a shifted version of a state A. Let $f = \mathrm{R}^d$ with d the number of rounds, then we have:

$$f(A) = \tau^{-1}(f(\tau(A))\,.$$

hence, given a circuit or program to compute f, shifting the state A before presenting to A and shifting back the result gives the same result as just applying f on the state directly.

Table 1. Permutations with a (almost) shift-invariant round function. The range of shifts is indicated in bold. E.g., Salsa is shift-invariant with respect to shifts over 4×4 different offsets and Keccak-f with respect to 64 different offsets.

Primitive	State size	Width	Height	Depth	Round constant
Salsa [5]	512	**4**	**4**	(32)	No
Chacha	512	**4**	**4**	(32)	No
Keccak-f [6]	1600	**64**	5	5	Yes
Ascon [14]	320	**64**	5	(1)	Yes
Xoodoo	384	**32**	3	**4**	Yes
Subterranean [12]	257	**257**	(1)	(1)	Yes
AES unkeyed	128	**4**	4	(8)	No

If the round function includes the addition of a round constant, one can still apply this trick by additionally shifting the round constants. Let us denote the round constant C and assume without loss of generality that the round constant is added at the end of the round. Let $B = \mathrm{C} + \mathrm{R}(\mathrm{A})$, then clearly $B = \tau^{-1}(\tau C + \mathrm{R}(\tau(A)))$.

2.2 Fault Analysis and Countermeasures

The effects of faulty behaviour of chips caused by external disturbances have a long history. However, a possible impact that fault injection could have on cryptographic implementations was only revealed in 1997, when the first Differential Fault Attack (DFA) on the RSA cryptosystem system was introduced by Boneh et al. [10]. The authors presented the concept and outlined how a single fault on a private-key computation of RSA with Chinese Remainder Theorem (CRT) could result in breaking the scheme, i.e. factoring the RSA modulus. They also proposed a countermeasure. Later, Aumüller et al. [3] showed the feasibility of the attack on a micro-controller and they presented another countermeasure. Most of the ideas behind countermeasures were based on the concept of duplication, so to perform the same computation twice and compare the results, or to follow up on the (sensitive) private-key computation by the corresponding public-key one. Needless to say, both imply a substantial overhead in performance and resources such as memory, power and energy.

Considering other algorithms, the first differential fault attack on Elliptic Curve Cryptography (ECC) was presented by Biehl et al. in 2000 [7]. In the proposed attack scenario, the resulting elliptic curve point is not on the original curve anymore, but on another one on which the Elliptic Curve Discrete Logarithm problem is easy. Hence, to mitigate this attack, the authors propose to validate that the point is on the given elliptic curve. Many other practical attacks on real-world ECC schemes followed, such as [1,19].

Close to that time, Biham and Shamir published a DFA attack on secret-key cryptosystems [8] that was contextualized with the DES algorithm [17] but the attack itself does not apply to AES [13]. The first one to propose the DFA attack on AES was Giraud [15]. The two attacks assumed different fault models and were requiring close to 50 or 250 faulty ciphertexts respectively. Nevertheless, both were successfully demonstrated on a smartcard implementation. Later, as the attackers' capabilities and accordingly fault models improved, the DFA attacks on AES reached the requirement of only one faulty ciphertext [16]. Attacks and countermeasures on other symmetric-key ciphers followed and the topic remains active due to its impact to real-world embedded security applications.

More recently, researchers have started considering fault resistance in the algorithm design phase and as a consequence several proposals came out, such as CRAFT [4] and FRIET [20]. Nevertheless, effective and efficient (in terms of added overhead) countermeasures that are also generic and broadly applicable remain a topic of interest.

3 New Countermeasure: ROCKY

In this section we present the proposed countermeasure paired with the Xoodoo primitive and double modular redundancy.

3.1 Concept

Redundancy techniques offer high fault coverage against many types of random faults, but can be nullified by an attacker by injecting the same fault to all executions or replications of the computation. For example, Fig. 1 (left) depicts the classical scheme of Double Modular Redundancy in hardware. Assuming that the attacker can induce an error (bit-flip, byte change etc.) at the state register (type 1) or can attack in the same way both permutation functions (type 2), then the error can not be detected and the countermeasure becomes ineffective.

Figure 1 (right) shows our novel countermeasure, which we call "ROCKY: Rotation Countermeasure for the Protection of Keys and Other Sensitive Data". Instead of repeating the same computation twice, we propose to have one circuit with the regular input, and one circuit with a rotated version of the input. By applying the inverse rotation to the output, the input-output behavior of both computations is the same for (almost) shift-invariant round functions. If the number of bits over which the rotation and the inverse rotation take place is randomly chosen and unknown to the attacker, it will be much more difficult for an attacker to inject the same fault in both computations and to bypass the detection mechanism.

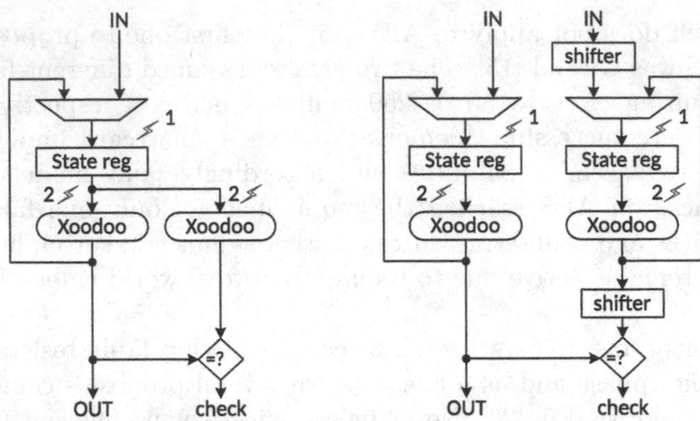

Fig. 1. Typical error detection architecture in hardware, based on Double Modular Redundancy (left) and our proposed ROCKY countermeasure (right)

3.2 Example of Error Propagation

Xoodyak. In order to analyze the countermeasure, we chose Xoodyak, one of the finalists in NIST's lightweight cryptography standardization competition [11]. The Xoodyak authenticated encryption algorithm is built on Xoodoo, a 48-byte cryptographic permutation. Xoodoo applies iteratively a round function R_i on a 384-bit, three-dimensional state A. State A is depicted in Fig. 2. On the z-axis there is a 32-bit array, the lane. On the x-axis, 4 lanes are combined to form a plane. On the y-axis, three planes form a full state. A specific bit inside the state has coordinates (y,x,z).

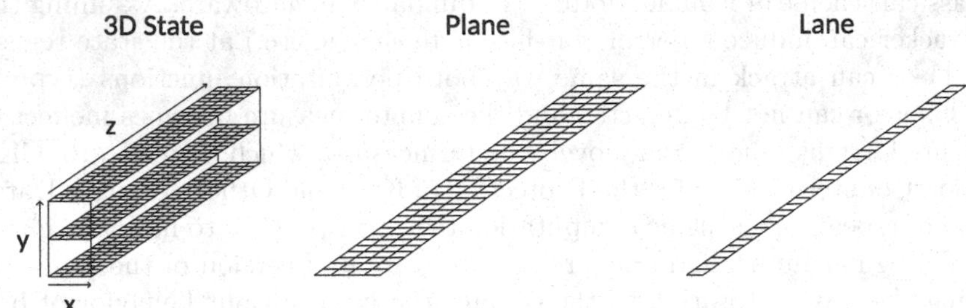

Fig. 2. State representation of Xoodoo

The round function, R_i, consists of 5 steps: a mixing layer θ, a plane shifting ρ_{west}, the addition of round constants ι, a non-linear layer χ, and another plane shifting step ρ_{east}. These steps are specified in Alg. 1. A_y refers to a plane y of state A, $A_y \lll (t, v)$ refers to a cyclic shift of Ay, moving a bit in (x, z) to position $(x + t, z + v)$ and the rest of the operations are AND, XOR and *negation*. C_i refers to the round constants, whose values can be found in [11]. We can transform the three-dimensional state (x, y, z) into an array of i bits, using the type $i = z + 32(x + 4y)$.

Algorithm 1: Definition of Xoodoo[n_r] with n_r the number of rounds

Parameters : Number of rounds n_r
for *Round index i from 1 - n_r to 0* **do**
| $A = R_i(A)$
end
Here R_i is specified by the following sequence of steps:

θ :

$$P \leftarrow A_0 \oplus A_1 \oplus A_2$$
$$E \leftarrow P \lll (1,5) \oplus P \lll (1,14)$$
$$A_y \leftarrow A_y \oplus E \quad for\ y \in \{0,1,2\}$$

ρ_{west} :

$$A_1 \leftarrow A_1 \lll (1,0)$$
$$A_2 \leftarrow A_2 \lll (0,11)$$

ι :

$$A_0 \leftarrow A_0 \oplus C_i$$

χ :

$$B_0 \leftarrow \overline{A_1} \bullet A_2$$
$$B_1 \leftarrow \overline{A_2} \bullet A_0$$
$$B_2 \leftarrow \overline{A_0} \bullet A_1$$
$$A_y \leftarrow A_y \oplus B_y \quad for\ y \in \{0,1,2\}$$

ρ_{east} :

$$A_1 \leftarrow A_1 \lll (0,1)$$
$$A_2 \leftarrow A_2 \lll (2,8)$$

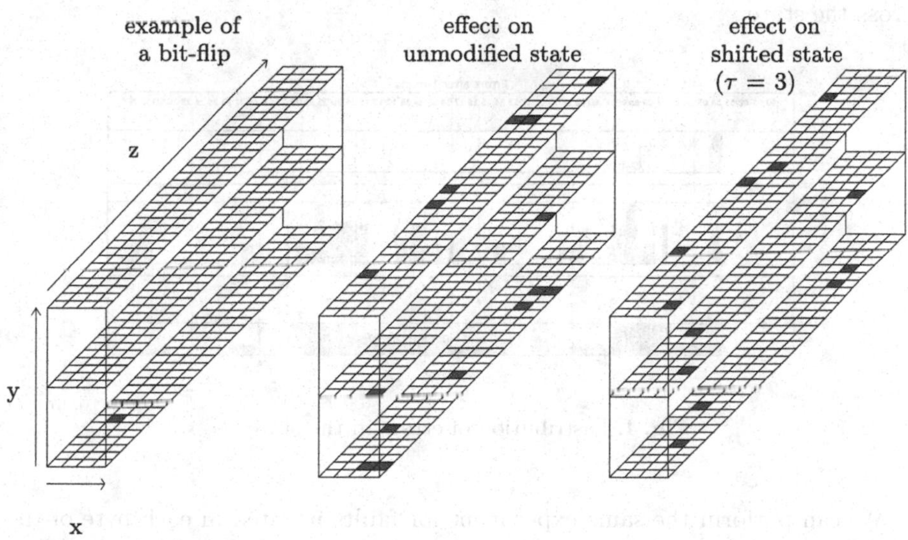

Fig. 3. Error propagation of an example bit-flip (left) after one round on the unmodified state (middle) and the shifted state (right)

Error Propagation. Figure 3 (left) shows an example of the change of one bit in the initial state of Xoodoo. After one round, the effect of the bit-flip on the unmodified state (middle) and the shifted state (right) are shown, respectively. It is clear that the effect is different.

In [18], the idea of transformation functions that change the fault space is explored as a countermeasure. The concept behind the fault space transformation is to ensure that the computations for two redundant rounds R0 and R1 are performed under different encodings, such that it is difficult to inject equivalent faults. They authors provide a classification of such functions in two categories (*'good'* or *'bad'*) based in two criteria: 1) The transformation function must ensure that a smaller fault space F_0 should be mapped onto the subspace of a larger fault space F_1. This is because a larger fault space makes it more difficult for the adversary to achieve the desired fault with the desired precision. 2) The occurrence of faults in the original and transformed fault spaces should be uncorrelated in order to reduce the fault collision probability.

The transformation we propose in ROCKY is a cyclic-shift. Figure 4 shows the results of a simulation experiment where 10000 faults are induced with a bit-flip in the state of Xoodoo at a specific group of eight bits (0×04). The bit-flip is produced randomly with a uniform distribution such that every bit will theoretically flip 10000/8bits = 1250 times (top). We examine the effect on an unmodified version of the algorithm (middle) and on a version where the state is randomly shifted before every execution (bottom). After one round of Xoodoo, for the unmodified state, the fault space is smaller than for the randomly shifted state, and the distribution of the errors is not uniform across the state. In contrast, when the state is randomly shifted for each of the 10000 executions, the fault space is much larger and the distribution of errors is more uniform across the state.

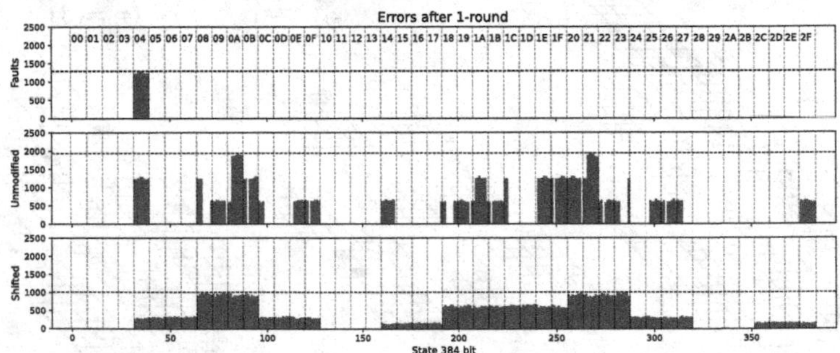

Fig. 4. Distribution of errors in the state

We can perform the same experiment for faults injected in each byte of the input state and get to a similar conclusion. This does not prove the strength of the proposed countermeasure, but it shows that, by randomly shifting the input state, the injected fault will have an effect on a larger part of the output state.

4 Proof-of-Concept Implementation

In this section, we take Xoodoo as a case study and we elaborate on the details of the implementation with the shifted input.

4.1 Architecture

Figure 5 shows the top level architecture. It consists of two cyclic shifters and the Xoodoo round function. The input is rotated before permutation, over a value τ. After 12 rounds of Xoodoo, the output is rotated over the same value, in the opposite direction.

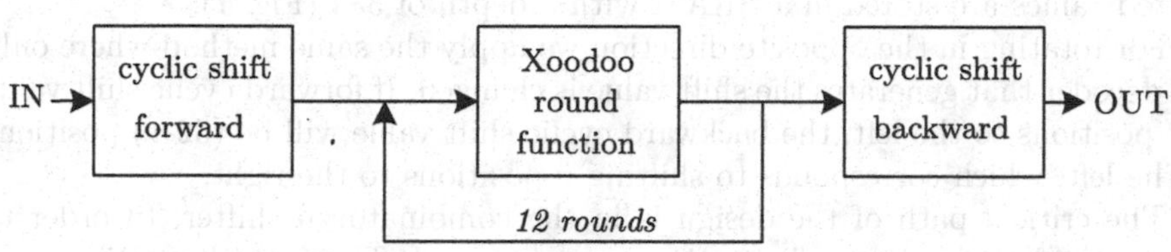

Fig. 5. Top level architecture

In each clock cycle, our design takes as input all 32-bit lanes that form the state, and the shift value τ. The parameter τ can take values from 0 to 31, hence 5 bits are needed. We treat a lane as a 32-bit integer and feed it to a multiplier circuit, where it is multiplied with a power of two number. First, the shift value is decoded into a 32-bit array, in which all bits but one, are zero. From the multiplication, we get a 64-bit product in which we add the 32 most significant bits to the 32 least significant bits. Our purpose for this approach is the use of DSP48E1 slices, taking advantage of their optimized hardware implementation and dedicated interconnection to achieve a fast and time-constant shift operation (Fig. 6).

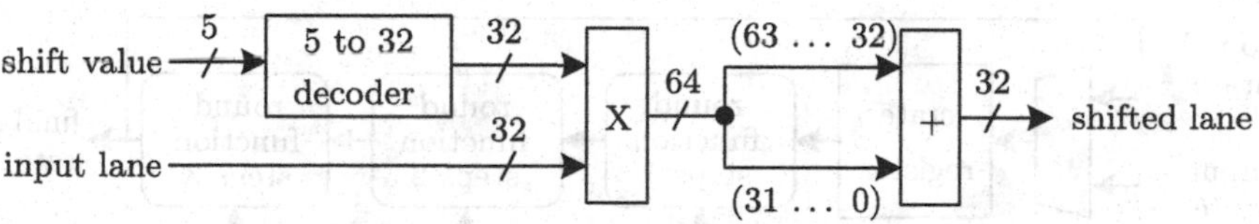

Fig. 6. Implementation of the cyclic shift

After all 12 lanes are shifted, they go into the Xoodoo round function. One round takes one clock cycle to produce a new state. A register keeps the initial state before the first round and all the intermediate ones. After 12 rounds, ρ_{east} gives the final state to the output shifter. Along with the state, Xoodoo gets the

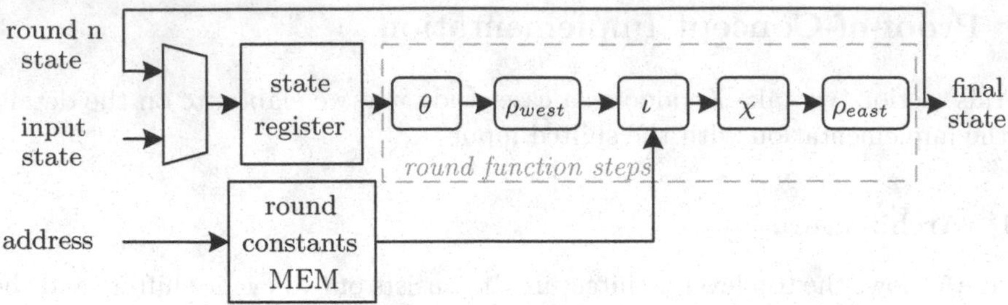

Fig. 7. Xoodoo module

round constants for the ι step. All 12 round constants, with all their possible shifted values are stored in a BRAM with a depth of 384 (Fig. 7).

For rotating in the opposite direction we apply the same method where only the decoder that generates the shift value is changed. If forward cyclic shift value is τ positions to the left, the backward cyclic shift value will be (32-τ) positions to the left, which corresponds to shifting τ positions to the right.

The critical path of the design is in the combinatorial shifter. In order to reduce total latency, two alternatives are examined. The first alternative combines more than one round of Xoodoo in one cycle and keeps the clock period almost the same. We experimented with the number of Xoodoo rounds that can be executed in one clock cycle: two, three and four rounds. In the implementation that executed three rounds in one clock cycle, the clock period is similar to the one with one round per cycle, so we use that implementation for our evaluation in Sect. 4.2.

As shown in Fig. 8, core 1 executes Xoodoo rounds 1, 4, 7 and 10, core 2 is for rounds 2, 5, 8 and 11 and core 3 is for rounds 3, 6, 9 and 12. Another modification that we do in this design is related to the reading of round constants from memory. We now need three round constants in each clock cycle. Therefore, we cannot read them one by one in every round. In order to avoid additional timing overhead, we read all constants in parallel while we read and shift the input lanes and store them into registers.

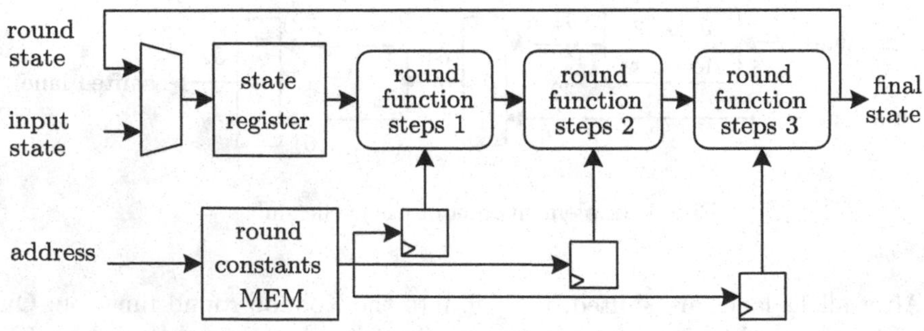

Fig. 8. Xoodoo module with 3 rounds per cycle

The second alternative we examine is to add pipeline registers to the multipliers that are responsible for the shifting. This way, critical path of the shifter becomes similar to the critical path of one round and the clock frequency is reduced. Compared to the first baseline design, the only modification we do here is the addition of pipeline registers. the feeding of the round constants does not need to be altered. Figure 9 shows the new shifter.

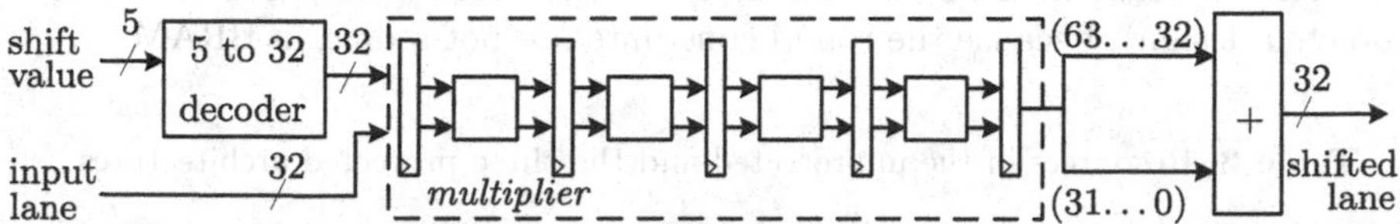

Fig. 9. Shifter with 5 pipeline stages

4.2 Implementation Results

In this section we present and compare the results of all implementations previously described with an unprotected architecture. We target a Xilinx Artix-7 FPGA (XC7A100T-FTG256) and we use Xilinx ISE 14.7. We measure one full operation, reading and shifting input lanes, followed by 12 rounds of Xoodoo, followed by shifting and writing the output lanes. The first input in the design is a 5-bit shift value, followed by the twelve 32-bit lanes that form the 384-bit state. The outputs are generated in the same way, one lane in each clock cycle. The unprotected design implements the round function without shifting. In our first protected architecture, each Xoodoo round takes one cycle and the Xoodoo round function module is occupied for 12 cycles, until all rounds are finished. For a complete operation, the first protected design takes 40 cycles with a 9.8ns clock period. As can be seen in Table 2, the second protected design takes 32 cycles with the same clock period. In this alternative, 12 rounds of Xoodoo take 4 cycles. In the third design, we need 50 cycles for the operation, but we reduced the clock period to 3.9 ns, achieving the minimum latency, compared to the first two protected architectures.

Table 2. Timing of the unprotected and the three protected architectures

Architecture	Clock cycles	Clock period	Latency
Comb. mult. & 1 round/cycle	40	9.8 ns	392 ns
Comb. mult. & 3 rounds/cycle	32	9.8 ns	313.6 ns
5-stage pipel. mult. & 1 round/cycle	50	3.9 ns	195 ns
Unprotected	38	3.3 ns	125.4 ns

Table 3 shows how many FPGA resources our designs consume. Each shifter's multiplier uses 4 DSP48E1s, while the 32×384 memory uses 1 BRAM block. If we compare the protected designs, the first one costs the least, because all changes that we did in the other two alternatives had as only criterion to reduce the latency. We can notice that the design with combinatorial multiplier and 3 rounds/cycles needs the most resources. As expected, the unprotected implementation costs less than the protected ones in timing and in resources. There is a slight increase in LUTs in the unprotected design (compared to the first protected design), because the round constants are not stored in BRAM.

Table 3. Resources of the unprotected and the three protected architectures

Architecture	LUTS	Flip-Flops	DSP48E1	BRAM
Comb. mult. & 1 round/cycle	1,083	1,335	8	1
Comb. mult. & 3 rounds/cycle	2,383	1,758	8	1
5-stage pipel. mult. & 1 round/cycle	1,452	1,544	8	1
Unprotected	1,335	1,211	0	0

5 Conclusions and Future Work

In this paper, we propose ROCKY, a new countermeasure against fault analysis attacks. By randomly rotating the input in symmetric-key ciphers that make use of a permutation with almost shift-invariant round functions, we make it more difficult for an attacker to introduce the same fault more than once in consecutive iterations or parallel executions of the same computation. The countermeasure can be used in combination with Double Modular Redundancy or in fault attacks that require the injection of a fault in multiple executions of the same algorithm. We measure the effectiveness and efficiency of ROCKY by evaluating the distribution of a single-bit error and the resources needed for an implementation on FPGA.

References

1. Ambrose, C., Bos, J.W., Fay, B., Joye, M., Lochter, M., Murray, B.: Differential attacks on deterministic signatures. In: Smart, N.P. (ed.) CT-RSA 2018. LNCS, vol. 10808, pp. 339–353. Springer, Cham (2018). https://doi.org/10.1007/978-3-319-76953-0_18
2. Ashur, T., Liu, Y.: Rotational cryptanalysis in the presence of constants. IACR Trans. Symm. Cryptol. **2016**(1), 57–70 (2016)
3. Aumüller, C., Bier, P., Fischer, W., Hofreiter, P., Seifert, J.-P.: Fault attacks on RSA with CRT: concrete results and practical countermeasures. In: Kaliski, B.S., Koç, K., Paar, C. (eds.) CHES 2002. LNCS, vol. 2523, pp. 260–275. Springer, Heidelberg (2003). https://doi.org/10.1007/3-540-36400-5_20

4. Beierle, C., Leander, G., Moradi, A., Rasoolzadeh, S.: CRAFT: lightweight tweakable block cipher with efficient protection against DFA attacks. IACR Trans. Symmetric Cryptol. **2019**(1), 5–45 (2019)
5. Bernstein, D.J.: The Salsa20 family of stream ciphers. In: Robshaw, M., Billet, O. (eds.) New Stream Cipher Designs. LNCS, vol. 4986, pp. 84–97. Springer, Heidelberg (2008). https://doi.org/10.1007/978-3-540-68351-3_8
6. Bertoni, G., Daemen, J., Peeters, M., Assche, G.V.: The making of KECCAK. Cryptologia **38**(1), 26–60 (2014)
7. Biehl, I., Meyer, B., Müller, V.: Differential fault attacks on elliptic curve cryptosystems. In: Bellare, M. (ed.) CRYPTO 2000. LNCS, vol. 1880, pp. 131–146. Springer, Heidelberg (2000). https://doi.org/10.1007/3-540-44598-6_8
8. Biham, E., Shamir, A.: Differential fault analysis of secret key cryptosystems. In: Kaliski, B.S. (ed.) CRYPTO 1997. LNCS, vol. 1294, pp. 513–525. Springer, Heidelberg (1997). https://doi.org/10.1007/BFb0052259
9. Biryukov, A., Wagner, D.: Slide attacks. In: Knudsen, L. (ed.) FSE 1999. LNCS, vol. 1636, pp. 245–259. Springer, Heidelberg (1999). https://doi.org/10.1007/3-540-48519-8_18
10. Boneh, D., Lipton, R.J.: Effect of operators on straight line complexity. In: Fifth Israel Symposium on Theory of Computing and Systems, ISTCS 1997, Ramat-Gan, Israel, 17–19 June 1997, Proceedings, pp. 1–5. IEEE Computer Society (1997)
11. Daemen, J., Hoffert, S., Peeters, M., Van Assche, G., Van Keer, R.: Xoodyak, a lightweight cryptographic scheme. IACR Trans. Symm. Cryptol. **2020**(S1), 60–87 (2020)
12. Daemen, J., Massolino, P.M.C., Mehrdad, A., Rotella, Y.: The subterranean 2.0 cipher suite. IACR Trans. Symmetric Cryptol. **2020**(S1), 262–294 (2020)
13. Daemen, J., Rijmen, V.: The Design of Rijndael - The Advanced Encryption Standard (AES), 2nd edn. Springer, Information Security and Cryptography (2020)
14. Dobraunig, C., Eichlseder, M., Mendel, F., Schläffer, M.: Ascon v1.2 submission to the caesar competition (2016)
15. Giraud, C.: DFA on AES. Cryptology ePrint Archive, Report 2003/008 (2003)
16. Mukhopadhyay, D.: A new fault attack on the advanced encryption standard hardware. In: 19th European Conference on Circuit Theory and Design, ECCTD 2009, Antalya, Turkey, 23–27 August 2009, pp. 387–390. IEEE (2009)
17. NIST: Specification for the Data Encryption Standard DES. Technical Report NIST FIPS PUB 46-3, Department of Commerce, October 1999
18. Patranabis, S., Chakraborty, A., Mukhopadhyay, D., Chakrabarti, P.P.: Fault space transformation: a generic approach to counter differential fault analysis and differential fault intensity analysis on AES-like block ciphers. IEEE Trans. Inf. Forens. Secur. **12**(5), 1092–1102 (2017)
19. Samwel, N., Batina, L.: Practical fault injection on deterministic signatures: the case of EdDSA. In: Joux, A., Nitaj, A., Rachidi, T. (eds.) AFRICACRYPT 2018. LNCS, vol. 10831, pp. 306–321. Springer, Cham (2018). https://doi.org/10.1007/978-3-319-89339-6_17
20. Simon, T., et al.: FRIET: an authenticated encryption scheme with built-in fault detection. In: Canteaut, A., Ishai, Y. (eds.) EUROCRYPT 2020. LNCS, vol. 12105, pp. 581–611. Springer, Cham (2020). https://doi.org/10.1007/978-3-030-45721-1_21

Deep Learning Techniques for Side-Channel Analysis on AES Datasets Collected from Hardware and Software Platforms

Tanu Shree Rastogi[1] and Elif Bilge Kavun[2(✉)]

[1] University of Sheffield, Sheffield S1 4DP, UK
[2] University of Passau, 94032 Passau, Germany
ebk@sec.uni-passau.de

Abstract. Side-channel analysis (SCA) is launched by exploiting the information leaking from the implementation a cryptographic algorithm, e.g., power consumption information. Recently, deep learning-based SCA techniques have also facilitated SCA against software and hardware implementations of various cryptographic algorithms. In this work, we perform SCA using various deep learning (DL) techniques such as Multi-layered Perceptron (MLP), Convolutional Neural Network (CNN), and Recurrent Neural Network (RNN) on the datasets collected from hardware and software platforms. The objective of this work is to identify the performance of DL techniques in performing SCA for secret key recovery and finding out the best settings for the model to optimize the attack performance in terms of on computation time and SCA efficiency. In our study, we have focused on two open-source AES-128 encryption algorithm databases, ASCAD and DPA contest v2 (DPAv2), where ASCAD database consists of the power traces captured from a software implementation of the AES and DPAv2 database consists of the power traces captured a hardware implementation of the AES. For the first time, we applied hyperparameter tuning with Bayesian Optimization and distributed computing on ASCAD database and we investigated the impact of MLP and RNN along with the distributed computing and hyperparameter tuning with Bayesian optimization on DPAv2 database. Our results show that the CNNs are the best models for performing the attack on software implementation while MLPs are the best for attacking hardware implementation of cryptographic algorithms.

Keywords: Deep learning · SCA · AES · ASCAD · DPA contest v2

1 Introduction

Despite the complex algorithms used for encryption in cryptography, there may still be security problems due to the difference between theoretical part and actual implementation. Information leakage caused by potential problems in physical

© Springer Nature Switzerland AG 2022
A. Orailoglu et al. (Eds.): SAMOS 2021, LNCS 13227, pp. 300–316, 2022.
https://doi.org/10.1007/978-3-031-04580-6_20

implementation can be used by an attacker for obtaining the secrets. An attacker can bypass the defense mechanisms implemented in a target device and collect the samples of data which is being processed inside the device without leaving any traces of device interactions. Obviously, such type of interactions do not necessarily mean the weaknesses in the implementation of algorithm used for encryption. For instance, if anyone is monitoring the variations in power consumed by a cryptographic device, they could observe the difference in the power consumption in idle phase and when some processing is happening inside the device. These variations can give an insight to the attacker for retrieving the data used inside the device or possibly access to the encryption key. This illustrative example presents *side-channel analysis (SCA)*, which is a type of cryptographic attack exploiting the information leaked from the physical environment to recover the secret key. The leakage from the hardware while running the algorithm can be captured as timing variations, power consumption and EM emanations.

In this work, the focus is on the profiling SCA, which is one of the most powerful physical attacks. Due to the mathematical nature of models describing the relation between plaintext, encrypted data and secret key, these attacks can be transformed into classification problem of supervised machine learning (ML). Specifically for power consumption example, traces of consumed power by the device can be collected by the attacker and they may establish the relation between those traces and label through a mathematical model which can be a powerful tool in the form of classification model. As mentioned by [20], DL techniques may help in exploring the correlation between the leaked information and secret key. DL-based SCAs enable the adversary to use little leaked information (e.g., power traces in power analysis) at the attack stage with a trained model. This makes DL-based SCA significantly more efficient. This motivated us to investigate how much SCAs can be improved in performance by using DL.

In our study, we focus on the characteristics of the traces available in various open source datasets (ASCAD [4] and DPA Contest v2 (DPAv2) datasets [2,3]) along with plain and encrypted data and which specific DL model would be the most fit for obtaining the secret key. Both datasets are based on AES-128 encryption algorithm but the power traces are collected from different implementation platforms, i.e., ASCAD datasets are collected from an AES software implementation while DPAv2 is collected from an AES hardware implementation. In this work, we investigated the DL models *Multi Layer Perceptron (MLP)*, *Convolution Neural Network (CNN)*, and *Recurrent Neural Network (RNN)*. We chose these DL models because our datasets are having time-series characteristics, the size of datasets are very large, and these models take care of the non-linearity in dataset, so better accuracy can be obtained for predicting the key.

The work in [16] focused on the effect of various parameters on the model performance and identifying the best parameters using normal grid search and random search methods which are time consuming. In our work, for this hyper-parameter tuning step, distributed computing is used with Python Libraries Hyperas and Hyperopt, which results in huge reduction in tuning time. We use the key results obtained in [16] in deciding the search space for various parameters of a model. In [16], the main focus is on profiling attacks using MLP and CNN; in our work, we also focus on RNN. Other studies exist for SCA with RNN on protected and unprotected AES [14]; however, we also apply distributed computing via Hyperas and Hyperopt as already pointed. In the case of DPAv2 datasets, most of the work has been done using non-profiling attacks using Differential Power Analysis (DPA) and Correlation Power Analysis (CPA). Only attacks based on CNN model are applied on DPAv2 so far, and our major contribution is attacking DPAv2 datasets using specifically the DL models MLP and RNN (and also CNN) and providing a comparison of these models in terms of speed and SCA efficiency. For hyperparameter tuning and model training, distributed computing is used similar to the case of ASCAD datasets.

2 Related Work

So far, several researchers have investigated the applications of DL techniques for SCA purposes on various datasets collected from hardware and software implementations. In our study, we focus on three of these previous works, [14, 16,19], which showcase the application of DL in SCA in detail.

In [14], a comparison of 7 machine learning models on DPAv2 is made by using key recovery with Autoencoder, CNN, MLP with PCA, MLP without PCA, Random Forest and Long Short Term Memory (LSTM) alongside a Template Attack, in which CNN outperformed all the attacks. This paper does not elaborate the implementation and pre-processing of the dataset, which makes it difficult for us to reproduce the results. The work in [19], extended the work performed in [14] by focusing on CNN for 4 different datasets including DPAv2. The network parameters used in this paper are presented in detail but the pre-processing part of the implementation is not sufficient to reproduce the results in our experiments. Also, CNN architecture used in this study is clearly described but other models are missing, so we focused on other models along with CNN.

For the ASCAD datasets, which contain unprotected and protected AES-128 implementation traces, a very detailed study is done by [16] with a good explanation on effect of each parameter value on model performance. They left an open question for finding the optimal configuration/training strategies in the SCA context which may lead to more accurate results by determining the most pertinent strategy for finding best parameters.

In contrast to software implementation, most of the research on the hardware implementation of AES algorithm is based on non-profiling attacks [15]. In particular, for DPAv2 datasets[1] very few studies are available based on various DL techniques. Also, the available resources are not very detailed for reproducibility of the results. As described in [9], the limitation of resources for DPAv2 is due to the noisy nature of traces acquired from AES hardware implementation. [18] gives a detailed description of attack on hardware implementation using ML techniques. In addition to these works, some other studies such as [7,8,11,13] extended the literature and helped us shaping this work.

[1] ASCAD and DPAv2 are the databases that cannot be directly used for model training so the datasets are prepared with some pre-processing to make it compatible for model training. The word database and datasets are used accordingly in the paper.

2.1 AES-128 Implementation Platforms

ASCAD database [4] is prepared using a masked AES-128 implementation on ATMega8515 microcontroller. Total 100,000 time samples (at 2 GSamples/sec) are captured for power consumption traces by a 4 MHz clock. The ATMega8515 microcontroller is not secure as it can work with an external clock and it does not have the hardware random generator. So, the information leakage is very high with no desynchronization noise and jittering, which makes it easier for an adversary to attack the algorithm and recover the key. Two types of captures are available for experimentation, one with fixed key and another with the variable key in which the variable key and fixed key are used in the ratio of 66:33.

DPAv2 dataset is collected from an unprotected AES-128 implemented on a SASEBO-GII board with a Xilinx FPGA Virtex-5 and Spartan-3A [1]. DPAv2 requires known-message and profiled attacks. Three trace databases are available in DPAv2 [3]: template database (1,000,000 traces with random keys and plain texts), public database, and private database. Public and template databases, are publicly available for designing, testing, and optimizing the attack. Due to a large number of traces in the template database, it can be used for performing template attacks that require profiling a device with a large number of inputs.

3 Approach

A very sound and detailed research is published in [16] for the ASCAD database. Following the methodology in this paper, which uses MLP and CNN DL techniques for SCA, we extended the SCA on ASCAD with RNN. In order to optimize the results obtained by [16] in terms of computation time and SCA efficiency (number of traces required to attack the database), new model parameters are evaluated for existing MLP, CNN, and newly introduced RNN models. But during the analysis, it was observed that the hyperparameter tuning step is consuming a large amount of the computation time if performed on a single machine with random search method, so distributed computing methods are identified and used in the analysis. The parameter search space for these DL models is selected with the help of analysis results obtained by [16]. For DPAv2 datasets, very few studies using DL-based methods for SCAs are published; the available literature is mostly based on non-profiling attacks and the data pre-processing is not explained in these studies. Also, due to the noisy nature of traces captured from FPGA, the authors of [14,19] could not achieve good performance for the classification task. For DPAv2, our first step was data pre-processing in which the relevant samples of the available traces are identified. This resulted in a smaller size for dataset which can easily be used by the DL models.

Then in the next step, hyperparameter tuning is done for each model. Since this task would normally have needed a lot of manual hyperparameter tuning, it would not be possible without automated distributed computing to perform this step in the time frame of this work. The system that we have built would have to compete in speed and performance with already established types of SCAs so this automated hyperparameter tuning using Hyperas library resulted as an efficient methodology. Due to the limited availability on the text related to effect of each parameter on the model performance from previous research, this step for DPAv2 dataset became very crucial. By utilizing the faster processing thanks to distributed computing, it became easier to identify the effect of each parameter on the model performance. After getting the best parameters for each model, the attacks are performed using MLP, CNN, and RNN. The steps used for analysis of both the datasets is shown in Fig. 1.

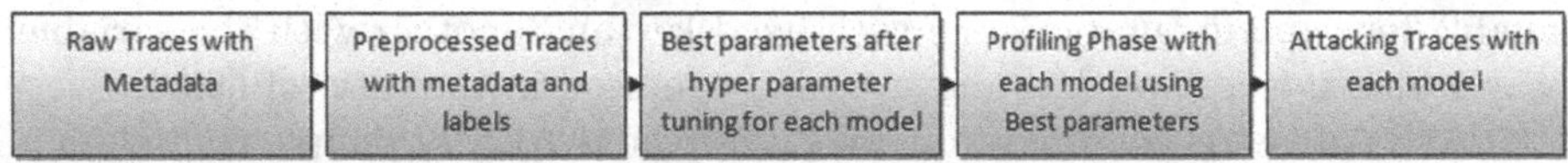

Fig. 1. Roadmap for DL-based SCA

Hardware Configuration. The training step is run on computers equipped with 13 GB of RAM with Nvidia DGX-1 (equipped with 8 T P100 GPUs connected with NVLink technology to provide super fast inter-GPU communication)[2] and on Google Colab consisting of Tesla K80 GPUs (using popular libraries such as TensorFlow, Keras, PyTorch, and OpenCV).

Model Hyperparameter Tuning. For each DL model, the first step is to perform hyperparameter tuning to extract the best parameters for the corresponding model. In [16], this step was done separately for each parameter and the effect of each parameter is analyzed on the model performance. For our case, this step is done using distributed hyperparameter tuning with the help of Python Packages "Hyperas" and "Hyperopt" [5,6]. The effect of using this package can be seen in terms of reduction in tuning time. DL models are complex models and hence each time we analyze the model performance with respect to each parameter, it adds to consumed training time. By using these packages with Bayesian optimization, this time can be reduced drastically as the best value for a set of parameters is obtained with a probabilistic approach, i.e., the best parameters selected in the previous iteration govern the most probable parameters in the next iteration whereas the parameters for the next iteration are selected randomly in the random search method. This DL library includes TPE (in other words, Bayesian optimization) which we used in our work to search the best values out of the given search space for hyperparameters. In the implementation section, the hyperspace used for each model is presented in tables with the best parameter obtained as a result after hyperparameter tuning. Note that the hyperspace for the ASCAD database is decided based on the analysis results obtained by [16] for each model parameter. For DPAv2, firstly the bigger hyperspace is chosen with some most probable random values with a broad dynamic range for each parameter. This was done to

[2] This work was done when both authors were at the University of Sheffield, and the high performance cluster at the university is used for this study.

analyze the best values selected by the model and plotting the performance of the model with respect to each value of each parameter. If the model selects the smaller values out of given hyperspace for a particular parameter, then it means a smaller value is better for that parameter and vice versa. Using this logical approach, the second step is to shrink the hyperspace with a more specific narrow dynamic range to obtain the most optimal values for the model. The first tuning task is to identify the number of traces required for the profiling phase. We cannot use all traces for the training because it enhances the computation time. After some experiments on the training set, it was observed that 1,00,000 training traces are required for getting good SCA efficiency. During the profiling of all models, early stopping is used to avoid over-fitting by monitoring the validation loss. Considering the trade-off between SCA efficiency and computation time & resources, hyperparameters are defined for all attacks and can be made public when requested.

4 Profiling Attacks on ASCAD and DPAv2

4.1 ASCAD Data Pre-processing

SCA_ASCAD.ipynb file is used to extract the profiling and attack traces dataset from the raw traces database file ATMega8515_raw_traces.h5 (raw traces without labels). In other words, this script generates ASCAD.h5 (synchronized traces, no jitters), ASCAD_desync50.h5 (similar, but has traces with a 50 samples window maximum jitter), and ASCAD_desync100.h5 (similar, but has traces with a 100 samples window maximum jitter) file system. The details of ASCAD data pre-processing for dataset extraction are explained in Fig. 2.

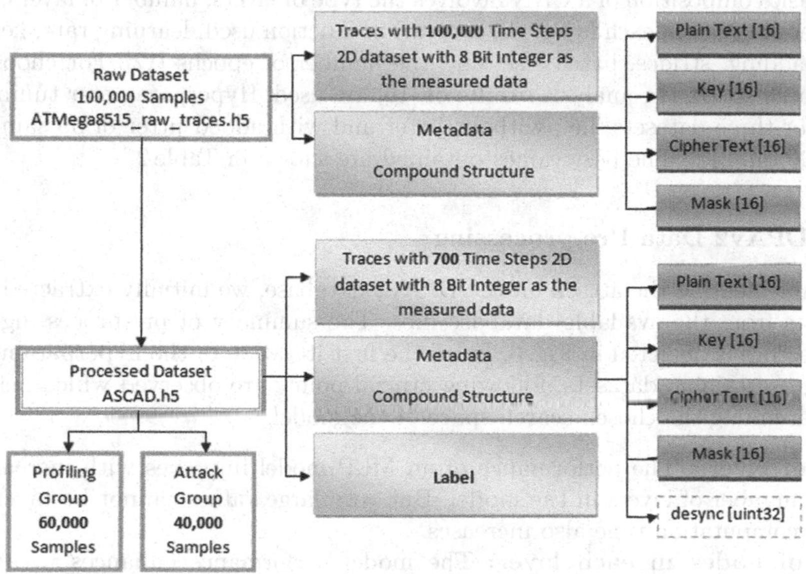

Fig. 2. ASCAD data pre-processing for dataset extraction

Data Split into Profiling/Attack Traces. As explained in the [16], out of 100,000 traces the minimum traces required for SCA are 60,000, which results in a dataset size of 60000 samples with 700 features and 256 class labels. With these specifications, the raw traces database is split into profiling and attacking set with 80:20 split. The processed dataset has two groups named the profiling group and the attacking group. The number of profiling and attacking phase are kept the same as the in [16], i.e., 50000 and 10000, respectively. [16] explain that after performing 10-fold cross-validation, by keeping all the other parameters fixed, these number of traces are sufficient for getting the optimum performance.

Based on [16], we can make the following conclusions for MLP parameters.

- **# of layers:** As the number of layers increase, the model performance improves.
- **# of nodes in each layer:** Number of nodes in a layer is proportional to the model performance; but as the nodes increase, the computation time also increases.
- **Activation function:** For most of the cases ReLU and SELU could be better choices to be chosen activation functions.
- **Learning rate:** The lower values of learning rate are better for good SCA efficiency but the smaller the value the more computation time is required to train the model.
- **Number of epochs:** As the number of epochs increases the SCA efficiency improves but computation time also increases.
- **Batch size:** As the batch size reduces the SCA efficiency improves.

Based on these points, we decided on the search space for MLP (see Table 2). The basic composition of a CNN involves the type of layers, number of layers, the number of nodes in each layer, the activation function used, learning rate, kernel size, padding, strides, batch size, and the number of epochs [12]. For choosing the search space, the analysis results of [16] are used. Hyperparameter tuning is done for three datasets, i.e., without jitter and with added jitter of 50 samples and 100 samples. The best values obtained are shown in Table 2.

4.2 DPAv2 Data Pre-processing

For implementing the attack on the DPAv2 database, we initially extracted the datasets from the available database files. The summary of pre-processing file architecture is depicted in Fig. 3. From the first iteration of the hyperparameter tuning on training datasets, following crucial points are observed which helped in determining the chosen search space of the model.

- **# of layers:** The performance of an MLP model improves with increasing the number of layers in the model. But very large values cannot be taken as the computation time also increases.
- **# of nodes in each layer:** The model performance enhances with the increasing number of nodes but in this case also computation time becomes worse.

- **Activation function:** ReLU and SELU are chosen as the best in all the iterations.
- **Learning rate:** Learning rate is an important parameter for the model as the model is very sensitive to the values chosen for the learning rate. In particular, lower values are better for good SCA efficiency, but the smaller the value the more computation time is required to train the model.
- **Number of epochs:** The number of epochs plays a very important role in model performance. As the number keeps on increasing the model may encounter overfitting. To control this parameter, the best way is to use Early Stopping criterion. In this case, the validation loss is chosen as the stopping criterion.
- **Batch size:** This parameter has an inverse relation with the model performance, i.e., as the batch size increases, the model performance deteriorates.

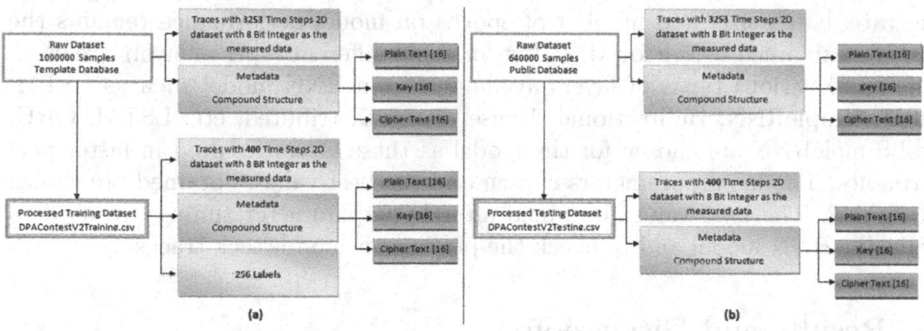

Fig. 3. Extraction of profiling dataset from DPAv2 template database (a) and extraction of attacking dataset from DPAv2 public database (b)

Considering the trade-off between SCA efficiency and computation time and resources, the search space was chosen for the MLP model in the second iteration. The best parameters obtained are mentioned in Table 2.

The best values obtained after hyperparameter tuning are used to train the MLP model which will be used to check the performance on attack traces. For all the models the input layer always has the dimensionality of 400 as we have chosen 400 samples and the output layer always has the dimensionality 256 as for 8 bits of a key total of 256 classes are possible for the classification problem.

Basic CNN is composed of layered architecture in which the number of layers in the model, type of layers, the number of nodes in each layer, the activation function used, strides, kernel size, type of padding, batch size, and the number of epochs are to be tuned [10]. Hyperparameter tuning is performed for the training dataset. Using the same approach for MLP, first the best smaller range for the hyperparameter is identified by analyzing its behaviour. The behaviour of the parameters, explained for MLP remains the same for this case as well. In addition to other CNN-specific parameters, the following points are observed:

- **# of filters:** s the number of filters increase, the performance improves with increased training time.
- **Kernel size:** Model performance is highly sensitive to this parameter but this parameter is highly dependent on the type of data available.
- **Pooling type:** Both Average and Max pooling perform well on the model.
- **Padding type:** Only three choices are available so can be tested on actual data.

Keeping these observations into consideration, the hyperspace is chosen (see Table 2). The best values obtained after hyperparameter tuning are used to train the CNN model which will be used to check the performance on attack traces.

Basic RNN is composed of layered architecture in which the number of layers in the model, type of layers, the activation function used, batch size, and the number of epochs are to be tuned [17]. Hyperparameter tuning is performed for training datasets. The effect of parameters for example number of nodes, learning rate, batch size, and number of epochs on model performance remains the same as explained before for MLP, but for RNN different types of layers are used. There are various types of layers available for an RNN model such as LSTM, GRU, SimpleRNN, Bidirectional, Dense, Time Distributed, etc. LSTM, GRU, and SimpleRNN are chosen for the model as these layers resulted in faster performance. The hyperparameters chosen and the best values obtained are shown in Table 2. The best values obtained after hyperparameter tuning are used to train the RNN model and to check the performance on attack traces.

5 Results and Discussion

5.1 Performance Evaluation of ASCAD

Testing (Attack Phase). After obtaining the best trained models using best parameters obtained using hyperas package for hyperparameter tuning, those trained models are used to test the performance on the attack dataset. For attack phase 2000 samples are used from the attack traces extracted from raw traces file. In order to check the performance, rank metric is used; hence, the trained models are tested with a single key with 2000 traces.

For the MLP model, 2000 samples are used for evaluating the rank of correct key. The model performance is checked with three variants, i.e., without jitter, with 50 sampled jitter, and with 100 sampled jitter. In Fig. 5(a), it can be seen that for detecting the correct key minimum 250 traces are required from the attack device that is the case when there is no desynchronization. In Fig. 5(b), it can be seen that with the desynchronized traces with 50 sample displacement, the performance is not as good as without jitter although the rank of the correct key lies between 40 to 10. In Fig. 5(c), with 100 sample desync, the performance is again not very well although the rank of the correct key lies between 40 to 5. The rank of the correct key is zero after 250 samples in case when there is no desynchronization. That means with the model the correct key can be extracted with 250 traces. These models depict almost similar performance as previous studies, but faster computation thanks to the tuning with Hyperas.

Also for the CNN model, 2000 samples are used for evaluating the rank of correct key. In Fig. 5(d), it can be seen that for detecting the correct key minimum 100 traces are required from the attack device that is the case when there is no desynchronization. In Fig. 5(e), it can be seen that with the desynchronized traces with 50 sample displacement, the performance is not as good as without jitter although the rank of the correct key is less than 5. In Fig. 5(f), with 100 sample desync, the performance is again not very well although the rank of the correct key is less than 5 mostly. The rank of the correct key is zero after 100 samples in case when there is no desynchronization. That means with the model the correct key can be extracted with 100 traces. The model with no jitter depicts almost similar performance as [16] while with the added jitter the performance is better than previous works.

Also for the RNN model, 2000 samples are used for evaluating the rank of correct key. In Fig. 6(a), the rank of the correct key is less than 30, which is not a good performance as was obtained in case of MLP and CNN. In Fig. 6(b), it can be seen that with the desynchronized traces with 750 sample displacement, the performance is not as good as without jitter although the rank of the correct key is less than 5. In Fig. 6(c), with 100 sample desync, a very good performance was obtained and only 300 traces are required from the attack device for extracting the correct key. The rank of the correct key is zero after 300 samples in case when there is 100 sample desynchronization. That means with the model the correct key can be extracted with 300 traces. None of the works so far used RNN for ASCAD database, so our work shows that RNN could also be a good technique for the attack, although being computationally costly.

5.2 Performance Evaluation of DPAv2

A performance comparison between various DL model is shown using the rank metric. The secondary metrics chosen for measuring the classification performance, are accuracy and loss. As per the [19], DPAv2 is one of the most difficult to classify which is also proven to be true in our case. A reason for the poor classification performance is high overlapping of traces of different classes, which makes the data highly indistinguishable by the networks. In our work, we tried to make the models achieve a better efficiency by playing with parameters and architectures of the model. The results for DL models are as follows.

Testing (Attack Phase). During the attack phase, randomly a key is selected out of 32 keys given in the dataset and the attack is launched using the corresponding 20,000 samples given in DPAv2. This is to ensure that the attack device will have only one key; and for attacking a device, one will capture samples from it to decrypt the key. In our case, to check the performance rank metric is used. Although the loss and accuracy plots are also obtained for checking the model overfitting, underfitting, but this metric did not indicate very useful results in terms of detecting the correct key which in our case is the main target of 256 class classification problem. By using the rank metric, all these classes are sorted in decreasing order of their likelihood. So the key with the maximum probability has the minimum rank, i.e., ideally the correct key should have rank zero. To check the performance of the model, the rank of the correct key is checked after sorting. If the rank curve which is plotted for rank of correct key in each trace for all 20,000 traces becomes flattened or start getting minimum values, so we can analyze the model performance. Using this approach, the trained models are tested with a single key with 20,000 traces. Here used the same byte of plaintext and key, i.e., 3rd byte to calculate the S-Box value, as in training phase.

For the MLP model initially all 20,000 samples are used for evaluating the rank of correct key. After checking the curve, it was observed that the rank curve becomes almost flattened with the less than 2500 samples of a key. In Fig. 4 (a), it can be seen that for detecting the correct key minimum 1250 traces are required from the attack device. The rank of the correct key is close to zero but not exactly zero for many traces (generally less than 5). As this model was not evaluated by any of the works before, we found this model performing satisfactorily with the hardware implementation of AES.

For the CNN model all 20,000 samples are used for evaluating the rank of correct key. In Fig. 4 (b), it can be seen that for detecting the correct key, minimum 17,500 traces are required from the attack device although with 10,000 traces the rank of the correct key becomes less than 30. The rank of the correct key is close to zero but not exactly zero for many traces (generally less than 10). This model was evaluated by [14,19], but both the works concluded with poor performance and the reason behind that was explained with the noisy nature due to parallel processing. In our work, this model performs satisfactorily, the overall plot shows that the rank of correct key is generally less than 40.

For the RNN model all 20,000 samples are used for evaluating the rank of correct key. In Fig. 4 (c), we observe that minimum 17,500 traces are required from the device for detecting the correct key, although with 10,000 traces the rank of the correct key becomes less than 30. The rank of the correct key is close to zero but not exactly zero for many traces (generally less than 10). Previous works reported poor performance as in CNN, but we observed that this model is performing satisfactorily. Looking at the plot, we may see that the rank of correct key is generally less than 40, which is an acceptable threshold for satisfactory performance (less than 5 is very good [14]). Although RNNs are good on the time-series data, noise reduction is not done. As there is noise reduction in the filtering layers of CNN, the rank reduces; but for RNN, the rank starts increasing which basically means that RNNs are not good for noisy time-series data.

5.3 Comparison

The results for DL-based SCA are summarized in Table 1. It can be observed from Table 1 that the RNN models are computationally very demanding and very slow although they can result into an efficient model for SCA. In the case of ASCAD, RNN model with 100 desync samples shows almost similar performance as MLP with no jittering. In the case of DPAv2, in fact, early stopping for the RNN models is much required for the system to run the jobs efficiently. For ASCAD, CNNs are most in the context of perfectly synchronized observations and CNN performs better than MLP in the presence of noise in the form of desynchronization/jittering. Thus CNN is a better choice for launching the SCA although the model takes long time and memory resources to train, which is similar to the results obtained in [16]. For DPAv2, MLP model is the most efficient compared to CNN and RNNs in this case as MLP requires only 1250 samples to recover the correct key, so MLP is a better choice for hardware. In our case, also the mean rank is not exactly zero; but it is less than 5, which means that better results could be achieved if the noise reduction techniques are applied in the traces captured from hardware implementation of AES-128.

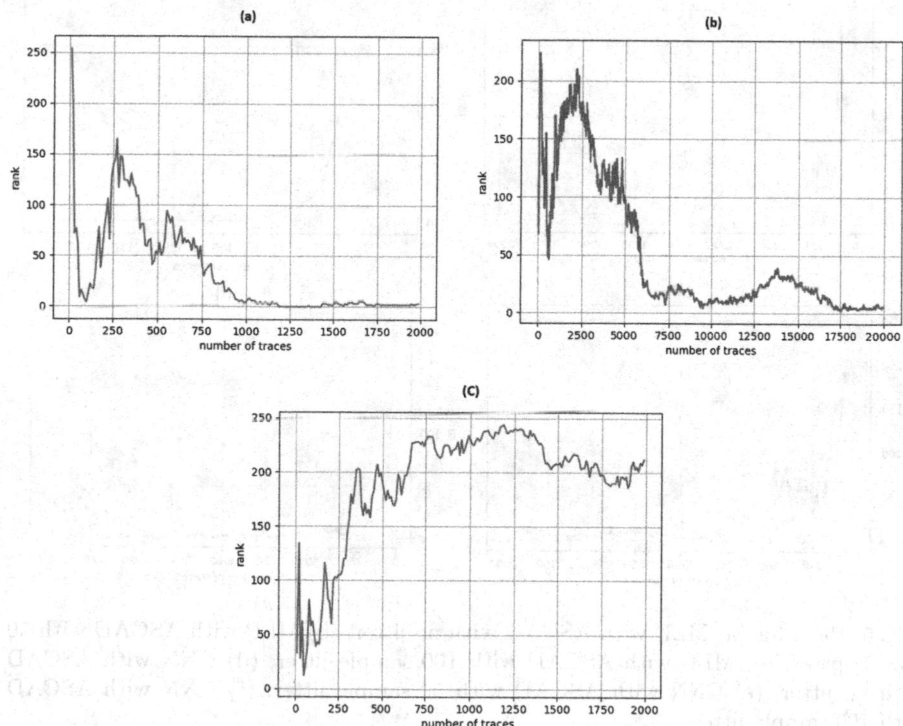

Fig. 4. Plots for (a) MLP with DPAv2 for 2000 traces, (b) CNN with DPAv2 for 20000 traces, (c) RNN with DPAv2 for 2000 traces

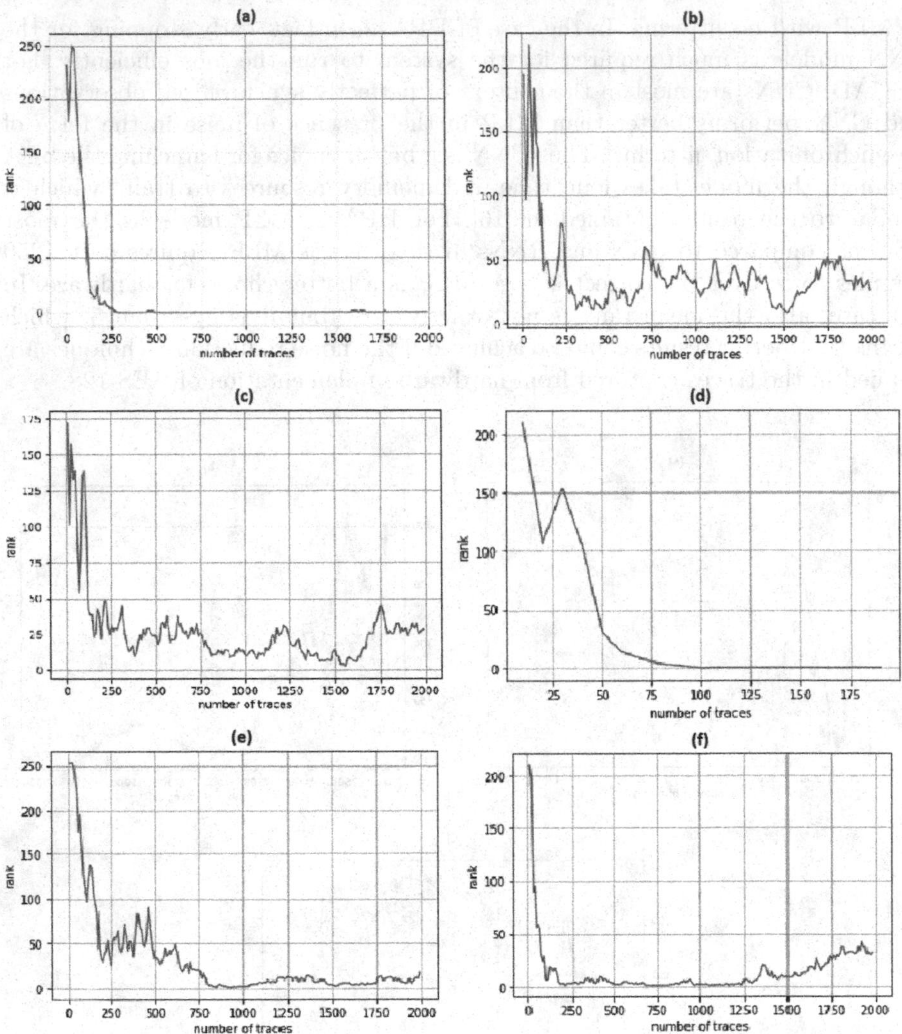

Fig. 5. Plots for (a) MLP with ASCAD with no jitter, (b) MLP with ASCAD with 50 sample jitter, (c) MLP with ASCAD with 100 sample jitter, (d) CNN with ASCAD with no jitter, (e) CNN with ASCAD with 50 sample jitter, (f) CNN with ASCAD with 100 sample jitter

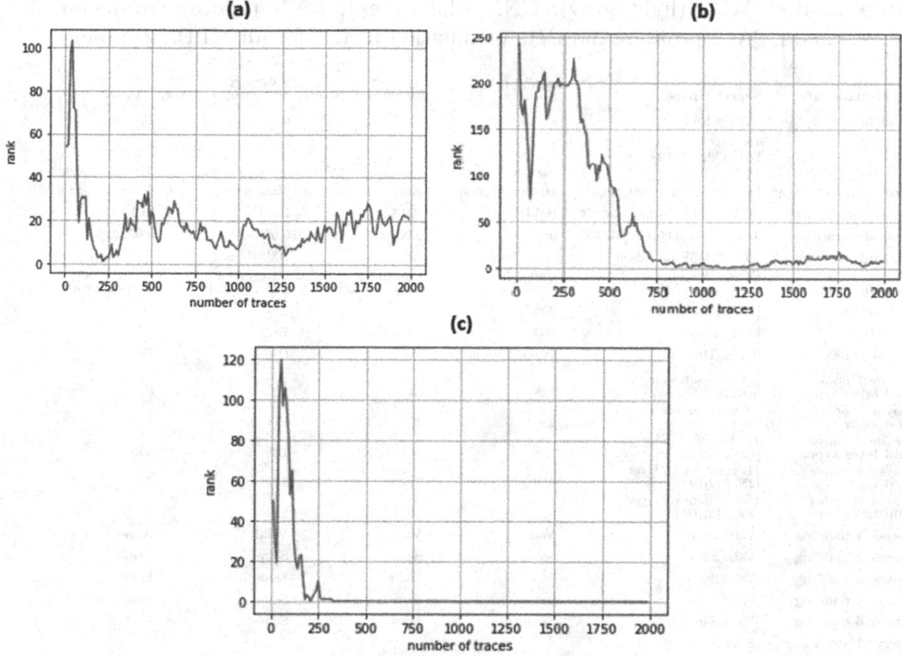

Fig. 6. Plots for (a) RNN with ASCAD with no jitter, (b) RNN with ASCAD with 50 sample jitter, (c) RNN with ASCAD with 100 sample jitter

Table 1. Performance of ASCAD (light grey) and DPAv2 (dark grey) datasets

Model	Epochs	Min Traces	Mean Rank	Computation Speed	Resources Required
MLP (no jitter)	100	250	0	25 mins	2 Cores/64GB RAM
MLP (50 sample jitter)	100	2000	Between 40 and 10	30 mins	2 Cores/64GB RAM
MLP (100 sample jitter)	75	2000	Between 40 and 5	35 mins	2 Cores/64GB RAM
CNN (no jitter)	75	75	0	75 mins	1 GPU on Google Colab
CNN (50 sample jitter)	100	1000	less than 5	75 mins	1 GPU on Google Colab
CNN (100 sample jitter)	75	250	less than 5	90 mins	1 GPU on Google Colab
RNN (no jitter)	75	2000	20-40	7 hours	1 GPU on Google Colab
RNN (50 sample jitter)	12	750	Less than 5	6 hours	1 GPU on Google Colab
RNN (100 sample jitter)	35	300	0	7 hours	1 GPU on Google Colab
MLP	75	1250	Less than 5	50 minutes	2 Cores/64GB RAM
CNN	18	10000	Between 40 and 10	130 minutes	6 Cores/64GB RAM
RNN	75	More than 20000	More than 100	72 hours	6 Cores/128GB RAM/1 GPU

Table 2. Best MLP (light grey), CNN (dark grey), RNN (white) parameters for ASCAD and DPAv2 profiling datasets (evaluation metric for all MLP: accuracy)

Hyperparameter	Search Space	ASCAD no jitter	ASCAD 50 sample jitter	ASCAD 100 sample jitter	DPAv2
# of layers	[6,7,8,9,10]	8	9	6	10
Nodes in each layer	*1st Layer*: Dense [32,64, 128,256] *Hidden Layers*: Dense [32,64,128,200,256,512]	*1st Layer*: 128 *Hidden Layers*: 512	*1st Layer*: 256 *Hidden Layers*: 256	*1st Layer*: 256 *Hidden Layers*: 256	*1st Layer*: 128 *Hidden Layers*: 128
Activation function	[SELU,ReLU,Sigmoid,tanH]	ReLU	ReLU	ReLU	SELU
Learning rate	[0.01,0.0001,0.00001,0.000001]	0.00001	0.000001	0.000001	0.00001
Optimizer	[SGD,RMSProp,Adam]	RMSProp	Adam	RMSProp	RMSProp
Loss function	[MSE,Categorical Cross Entropy]	Categorical Cross Entropy	Categorical Cross Entropy	Categorical Cross Entropy	Categorical Cross Entropy
Batch size	[100,200,300,500]	200	100	200	200
Epochs	[50,75,100]	100	100	75	75
Layer types	[Dense,Dropout]	Dense	Dense	Dense	Dense
Layer 1 nodes and layer type	1D convolution layer, [64,128,256]	128	64	128	64
Layer 2 nodes and layer type	1D convolution layer, [64,128,256]	256	128	256	128
Layer 3 nodes and layer type	1D convolution layer, [128,256,512]	128	512	128	256
Layer 4 nodes and layer type	1D convolution layer, [256,512,1024]	512	512	512	512
Layer 5 nodes and layer type	1D convolution layer, [256,512,1024]	512	1024	512	-
Layer 1 padding	[Valid,Same]	Valid	Valid	Valid	Same
Layer 2 padding	[Valid,Same]	Same	Same	Same	Same
Layer 3 padding	[Valid,Same]	Same	Same	Same	Same
Layer 4 padding	[Valid,Same]	Same	Same	Same	Same
Layer 5 padding	[Valid,Same]	Same	Same	Same	-
Layer 1 strides	[2,3,4]	4	2	4	2
Layer 2 strides	[2,3,4]	2	2	2	2
Layer 3 strides	[2,3,4]	3	2	3	2
Layer 4 strides	[2,3,4]	4	2	4	2
Layer 5 strides	[2,3,4]	2	2	2	-
Pooling type	[Max,Average]	Average	Average	Average	Average
Layer 1 kernel Size	[7,11,12,13]	11	12	11	12
Layer 2 kernel Size	[7,11,12,13]	11	12	11	12
Layer 3 kernel Size	[7,11,12,13]	11	12	11	12
Layer 4 kernel Size	[7,11,12,13]	11	12	11	12
Layer 5 kernel Size	[7,11,12,13]	11	12	11	-
Activation function	[SELU,ReLU,tanH,Sigmoid]	ReLU	ReLU	SELU	SELU
Optimizer	[RMSProp,Adam]	RMSProp	RMSProp	RMSProp	RMSProp
Learning rate	[0.01,0.0001,0.00001]	0.00001	0.00001	0.00001	0.00001
Fully connected layer 1 node	Dense, [512,1024,4096]	4096	4096	4096	1024
Fully connected layer 2 nodes	Dense, [1024,2048,4096]	1024	4096	1024	1024
Batch size	[50,100,200,300]	200	50	200	50
Epochs	[50,75,100]	100	100	100	75
Layer 1 # of nodes	[32,64,128,256,512,1024]	1024	32	1024	1024
Layer 1 type	[LSTM,Gated Recurrent Unit (GRU)]	LSTM	GRU	GRU	GRU
Layer 2 # of nodes	[64,128,200,256,512,1024,2048]	200	64	1024	2048
Layer 2 type	[SimpleRNN,LSTM,GRU]	SimpleRNN	LSTM	SimpleRNN	LSTM
Layer 2 activation function	[ReLU,tanH,SELU]	-	tanH	tanH	-
Layer 3 # of nodes	[64,128,256,512,1024,2048]	64	128	2048	-
Layer 3 type	[LSTM,GRU,Dense]	LSTM	Dense	Dense	-
Layer 3 activation function	[ReLU,tanH,SELU]	-	tanH	tanH	-
Learning rate	[0.01,0.0001,0.00001]	0.00001	0.0001	0.00001	0.00001
Optimizer	[RMSProp,Adam,SGD]	RMSProp	RMSProp	RMSProp	RMSProp
Batch size	[20,30,50,100,200,300]	200	20	20	50
Epochs	[50,75,100,150]	75	150	75	75

6 Conclusion

In this study, we empirically surveyed how SCA can be performed on data collected from software and hardware platforms and how different DL techniques and DL parameters of a model can be utilized to enhance the performance of the attack. In particular, several parametrization options and distributed computing techniques have been discussed. Our hyperparameter tuning approach using distributed computing can help researchers to make their own choice for the design of new DL models with limited computation time available. Our results matched the results available in [16] in terms of performance efficiency while the results overperformed drastically in terms of computational speed. Since CNNs have displayed almost similar performance as MLPs for perfectly synchronized traces but displayed better performance in jittering environment, similar to previous studies, this work also suggests that the CNNs are very efficient choice for SCA on software-based implementations. For SCA on hardware-based implementations, MLPs are the best choice because of reduced time-consumption.

References

1. SASEBO-GII. http://satoh.cs.uec.ac.jp/SASEBO/en/board/sasebo-g2.html
2. DPA contest v2 database (2010). www.dpacontest.org/v2/download.php
3. Results of the 2009–2010 'DPA contest v2' (2011). http://www.dpacontest.org/v2/data/dpacontest_v2_debriefing.pdf
4. ASCAD database (2018). https://github.com/ANSSI-FR/ASCAD
5. Hyperopt model optimization, July 2019. https://towardsdatascience.com/hyperparameter-optimization-in-python-part-2-hyperopt-5f661db91324
6. Hyperopt model selection (2019). https://docs.databricks.com/applications/machine-learning/automl/hyperopt/hyperopt-model-selection.html
7. Chowdhury, M.A.N.R.: Improved study of side-channel attacks using recurrent neural networks. M.Sc. thesis, Boise State University (2019)
8. Durvaux, F.: Towards fair side-channel security evaluations. UC Louvain (2015)
9. Hettwer, B., Horn, T., Gehrer, S., Güneysu, T.: Encoding power traces as images for efficient side-channel analysis. In: IEEE HOST Proceedings (2020)
10. Hou, S., Zhou, Y., Liu, H.: Convolutional neural networks for profiled side-channel analysis. Radioengineering **28**(3), 651–658 (2019)
11. Kevorkian, C., Tanenbaum, J.: Advanced cryptographic power analysis. B.Sc. thesis, WPI (2010)
12. Kim, J., Picek, S., Heuser, A., Bhasin, S., Hanjalic, A.: Make some noise: unleashing the power of convolutional neural networks for profiled side-channel analysis. IACR CHES Trans. **2019**(3), 148–170 (2019)
13. Lo, O., Buchanan, W., Carson, D.: Power analysis attacks on the AES-128 S-box using differential power analysis (DPA) and correlation power analysis (CPA). J. Cyber Secur. Technol. 1–20 (2016)
14. Maghrebi, H., Portigliatti, T., Prouff, E.: Breaking cryptographic implementations using deep learning techniques. IACR ePrint Archive, Report 2016/921 (2016)
15. Pettengil, J., Hnath, W.: Differential power analysis side-channel attacks in cryptography. B.Sc. thesis (2011)

16. Prouff, E., Strullu, R., Benadjila, R., Cagli, E., Canovas, C.: Study of deep learning techniques for side-channel analysis and introduction to ASCAD database. IACR Cryptology ePrint Archive 2018:53 (2018)
17. Ramezanpour, K., Ampadu, P., Diehl, W.: SCAUL: power side-channel analysis with unsupervised learning. arXiv 2001.05951 (2020)
18. Richmond, T.: Application of machine learning techniques to side-channel analysis on code-based cryptography [Research Report]. Univ. Rennes, Inria, CNRS, IRISA. hal-02017561 (2018)
19. Samiotis, I.P.: Side-channel attacks using CNN: a study on the performance of convolutional neural networks on side-channel data. M.Sc. thesis, TU Delft (2018)
20. Wang, H.: Side-channel analysis of AES based on deep learning. M.Sc. thesis, KTH (2019)

Special Session on Reports from Research Projects

EDRA: A Hardware-Assisted Decoupled Access/Execute Framework on the Digital Market

Invited Paper

Dimitris Theodoropoulos[1(✉)], Andreas Brokalakis[1], Nikolaos Alachiotis[2], and Dionisios Pnevmatikatos[3]

[1] Telecommunication Systems Institute, Technical University of Crete Campus - Akrotiri, 73100 Chania, Greece
{dtheodoropoulos,abrokalakis}@isc.tuc.gr

[2] Computer Architecture for Embedded Systems, Faculty of EEMCS, University of Twente, Enschede, The Netherlands
n.alachiotis@utwente.nl

[3] Institute of Communication and Computer Systems, National Technical University of Athens, Athens, Greece
pnevmati@cslab.ece.ntua.gr

Abstract. EDRA was an Horizon 2020 FET Launchpad project that focused on the commercialization of the Decoupled Access Execution Reconfigurable (DAER) framework - developed within the FET-HPC EXTRA project - on Amazon's Elastic Cloud (EC2) Compute FPGA-based infrastructure. The delivered framework encapsulates DAER into a EC2 virtual machine (VM), and uses a simple, directive-based, high-level application programming interface (API) to facilitate application mapping to the underlying hardware architecture. EDRA's Minimum Viable Product (MVP) is an accelerator for the Phylogenetic Likelihood Function (PLF), one of the cornerstone functions in most phylogenetic inference tools, achieving up to 8x performance improvement compared to optimized software implementations. Towards entering the market, research revealed that Europe is an extremely promising geographic region for focusing the project efforts on dissemination, MVP promotion and advertisement (EDRA was funded by the European Union's Horizon 2020 research and innovation programme "FET Innovation Launchpad" under grant agreement No 851631).

Keywords: Cloud computing · FPGAs · Decoupled Access-Execute

1 Introduction and Concept

Over the last years, major cloud providers (Amazon, Alibaba, Nimbix) started offering services that utilize special chips called FPGAs that enable faster

Authors alphabetically: Nikolaos, Alachiotis, Andreas Brokalakis, Dionisios Pnevmatikatos, Dimitris Theodoropoulos.

© Springer Nature Switzerland AG 2022
A. Orailoglu et al. (Eds.): SAMOS 2021, LNCS 13227, pp. 319–330, 2022.
https://doi.org/10.1007/978-3-031-04580-6_21

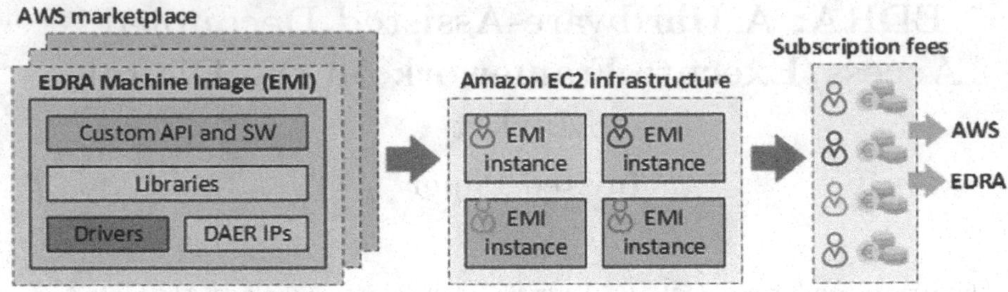

Fig. 1. Availability of the EDRA AMIs (EMIs) through the AWS marketplace to customers.

workload processing than conventional software-based configurations for a large range of high-performance applications. However, mapping applications onto FPGAs is a cumbersome process that requires extensive background on hardware development and specialized IT personnel.

To alleviate this hurdle, the FET project "EXTRA" (Exploiting eXascale Technology with Reconfigurable Architectures - GA 671653) [2] focused on devising efficient ways to deploy ultra-efficient heterogeneous compute nodes in order to meet the massive performance requirements of future exascale High Performance Computing (HPC) applications. A major outcome was the design and implementation of a novel framework that maps applications onto FPGAs employing a Decoupled Access Execute Reconfigurable (DAER) architecture for HPC platforms [1], originally based on the idea of Decoupled Access-Execute architectures [7].

During the EXTRA project, various algorithmic workloads were mapped to reconfigurable HPC platforms using the DAER approach, achieving significant performance improvements in spite of different memory access patterns and/or computational requirements. However, there are still two main obstacles for making the EXTRA results available and easily accessible to the market: (a) launching applications onto the EXTRA hardware is currently based on a semi-automatic tool flow, requiring developers to manually separate memory accesses from data processing tasks, and (b) FPGA-based acceleration requires the additional inherent cost of specialized hardware.

To this end, the EDRA framework tackles the aforementioned drawbacks as follows:

- it provides a fully-automated software workflow that automatically generates DAE-compatible application executables requiring only minor code annotation;
- it combines the EDRA workflow with Amazon's software library for taking advantage of the available reconfigurable hardware;
- it integrates the complete stack with the EXTRA DAE architecture, wrapped within a single Amazon Machine Image (AMI) dubbed EMI (EDRA AMI).

Figure 1 illustrates the EMI exploitation strategy; EDRA plans to list the EMI instance to the AWS marketplace with EDRA software, libraries/drivers (e.g., the Xilinx Runtime System for interfacing the FPGA), and domain-specific DAER IPs for accelerating application workloads. End-users can deploy an EMI instance via the AWS marketplace listing it Amazon's EC2 FPGA-supported machine instance, charged on a pay-as-you-go basis. The AWS marketplace platform is responsible for forwarding subscription fees paid by end-users to Amazon (for hosting EMI instances to its infrastructure) and the 3rd party seller (i.e., EDRA).

The rest of the paper is organized as follows: Sect. 2 presents the project achievements and impacts. Section 3 describes the EDRA framework, whereas Sect. 4 provides results on the developed MVP in terms of performance against other solutions. Section 5 elaborates on a market analysis tailored to the EDRA's MVP, and finally Sect. 6 concludes the paper.

2 Project Achievements and Impact

2.1 Project Achievements

EDRA was a FET Innovation Launchpad (GA #851631)[1], that run from May 2019 until October 2020. Interested users can follow EDRA on Twitter[2] and LinkedIn[3], as well as find more details on the project website[4].

EDRA achieved its goal on making the DAER technology ready for entering the market by reaching the following achievements:

1. EDRA framework: The project successfully updated the EXTRA IP, and developed a full-fledged framework that can (semi) automatically create DAE-compatible applications, capable to facilitate available hardware resources for faster workload processing.
2. MVP in the domain of phylogenetics: Having a strong scientific background in the domain of phylogenetics, EDRA decided to develop and deploy a first MVP using its in-house framework that accelerates phylogenetics analysis on Amazon's FPGA-supported machines.
3. MVP market analysis: Towards validating the decision of deploying the MVP to the market, the team conducted a thorough analysis on market size and opportunities with respect to the bioinformatics domain. Results suggest that an estimated market size directly fitting to the EDRA MVP is valued at approximately 7.9 M€, 10.8 M€ and 14.6 M€ for 2021, 2022 and 2023 respectively.
4. Business model formulation: EDRA developed a complete and sustainable business model. Its value proposition is based on solutions to customers who would like to execute applications faster compared to their current setup, as well as reduce IT costs related to deployment and maintenance.

---

[1] https://cordis.europa.eu/project/id/851631.
[2] https://twitter.com/ProjectEdra.
[3] https://www.linkedin.com/groups/8790812/.
[4] https://edra-project.eu/.

Due to the team expertise on hardware design and background on computational phylogenetics, EDRA plans to also provide dedicated application acceleration services on phylogenetics. Key resources required to support the EDRA value proposition are budgets related to staff support, cloud/digital resources, and facilities and IPR management. Customer segments comprise users from the HPC domain and academic institutes in the domain of Bioinformatics. As shown in Fig. 1, the revenue model is based on fixed charges for deploying customer applications to Amazon's marketplace using the EDRA framework. The EDRA's MVP revenues will be based on Amazon's pay-as-you-go charging policy.

2.2 Project Impact

- Economic and business impact: The project has delivered the EDRA framework, a novel technology for rapid and (semi) automatic hardware-accelerated deployment of applications to cloud resources. The framework essentially allows the quick launch of cloud-supported services for SMEs and corporations, thus enabling faster and better services for end users, a key aspect for economic growth.
- Increased value creation from FET projects by picking up innovation opportunities: Based on the framework developed by EDRA, the team formulated a go-to-market strategy for offering hardware-acceleration services to the cloud for demanding applications. Moreover, EDRA released an MVP that enhances research on phylogenetics, an important area that can assist on the fight against the COVID-19 outbreak and other potential pandemics.
- Improved societal and market acceptance: The COVID-19 outbreak demonstrated that scientists need access to powerful computational resources with fast turnaround times of results on drug analysis and model simulation. EDRA's MVP addresses today's important need for more computational power towards faster analyses of virus evolution.
- Contributing to the competitiveness of European industry/economy: EDRA picked up on the fact that major cloud providers, such as Amazon and Alibaba, started offering services that support FPGAs; the DAE framework allows the offer of generic low-risk hardware-acceleration services on the cloud for customers that wish to remove their application back end from their premises.
- Stimulating, supporting and rewarding an open and proactive mind-set: EDRA's ability for quick deployment of hardware-accelerated applications, allow SMEs and corporations to investigate and propose new services to end-users with minimum investment risk, strengthening even more the European industry sector.
- Scientific impact: EDRA's MVP is a novel solution that allows biologists and researchers in phylogenetics to increase their productivity while reducing IT costs. The majority of the software tools used for experiments are compute-bound, hence the additional processing power that EDRA's MVP provides

can further assist on understanding the origins of lethal viruses. This is a valuable asset for constraining the spread of potential new pandemics, should anytime happen.

3 The EDRA Framework

3.1 Source-to-Source Translation

EDRA developed a source-to-source translator infrastructure, henceforth referred to as "EDRA-gen", to facilitate code annotation and translation. Its purpose is to reduce development time and yield a correct-by-construction design for the final accelerated system. Automated hardware generation in EDRA-gen is inspired by a generic Decoupled Access-Execute (DAE) architectural paradigm.

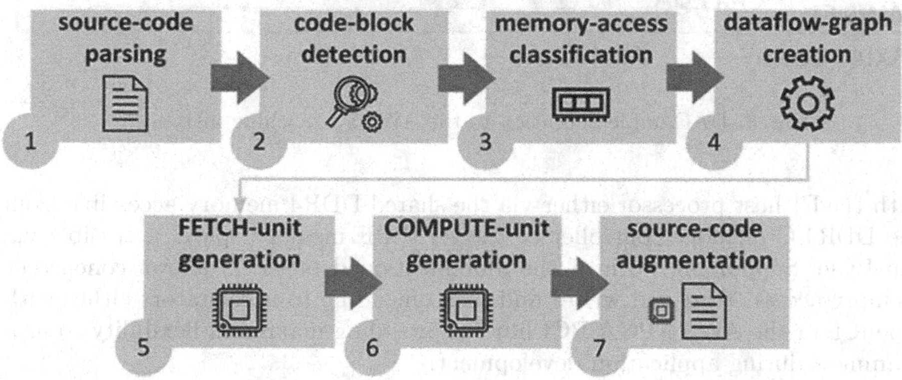

Fig. 2. Source-to-source translation stages of EDRA-gen.

EDRA-gen-based hardware generation starts with a minimally annotated user source code that indicates at least one target for-loop. The flow consists of 7 discrete steps (Fig. 2) that collectively extract the code block of interest in the user's code (the target for-loop), resolve dependencies (if exist), construct an abstract syntax tree (AST), and use it to generate all the required data-fetch (ACCESS) and process (EXECUTE) units. EDRA-gen relies on LLVM to generate token lists for the source files and implements a series of algorithms directly on the token lists to extract the AST. Once the AST is created, a series of algorithms operate on the AST to generate C code for each DAE component, driven by the available Vivado HLS directives to be used.

3.2 Hardware Support

Figure 3 shows how the EDRA hardware architecture is mapped to the AWS F1 machine instance. EDRA allows hardware accelerators to exchange data

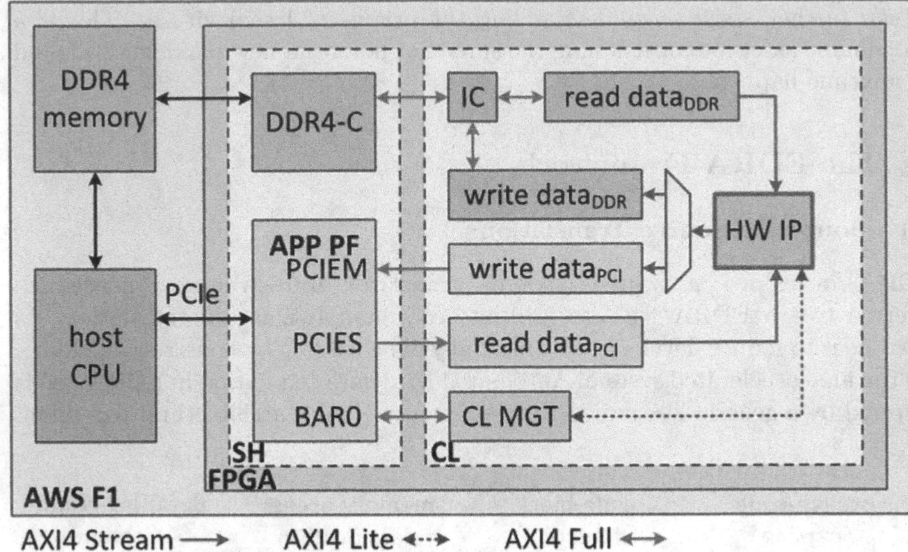

Fig. 3. DAE implementation to the AWS F1 machine instance.

with the F1 host processor either via the shared DDR4 memory accessible from the DDR4-C memory controller or the APP PF memory space, accessible via the PCIe. Supporting both of the aforementioned methods allows concurrent memory access (read and write) and task offloading to accelerators either with OpenCL or the AWS FPGA PCI library, providing maximum flexibility to programmers during application development:

- Shared data stored in the DDR4 memory: an application can share data with the accelerator via the DDR4 memory, using OpenCL functions. In this case, the "read dataDDR" module reads data via the DDR4-C memory controller over an AXI4 protocol, and then forwards it over an AXI4 Stream interface to the hardware IP (HW IP) for processing. The HW IP sends results to the "write dataDDR" also over an AXI4 Stream interface, which forwards them via an interconnect (IC) module back to the DDR4-C memory controller.
- Shared data stored in the APP PF: an application can also share data with the accelerator using the AWS FPGA PCI library. In this case, the APP PF exposes a physical address space up to 127 GiB that facilitates data transfers between the host processor and the accelerator; the "read dataPCI" module reads data via the PCIES (PCIe Slave) interface (also based on the AXI4 protocol), and then forwards it via an AXI4 Stream interface to the "HW IP". When data processing is finished, the "HW IP" sends results back to the "write dataPCI" module, which forwards them to the host CPU via the PCIEM (PCIe Master) interface.

Finally, the BAR0 (Base Address Registers) AXI4 interface space exposes the BAR0 APP PF memory space that facilitates management and monitoring (CL

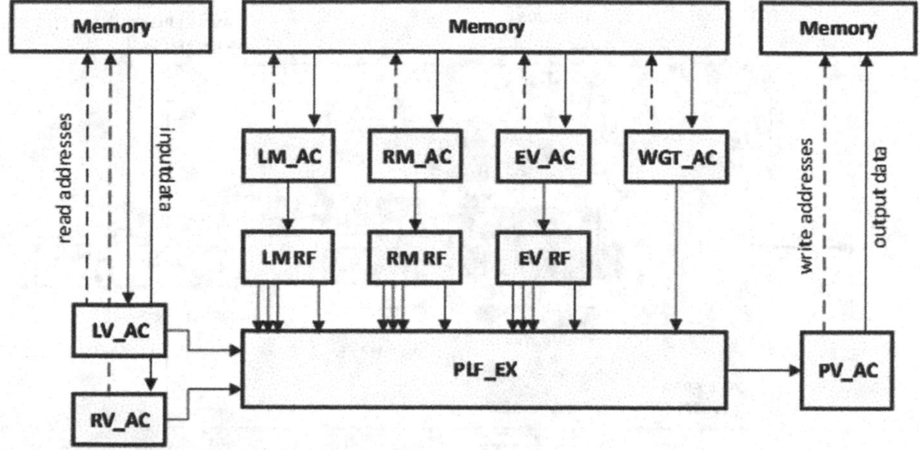

Fig. 4. Top-level decoupled access/execute architecture of the PLF accelerator core.

MGT) of the hardware accelerator (e.g., start/stop and sync barriers) by the application executed at the host CPU.

4 MVP Architecture and Performance

A detailed description of the EDRA MVP is provided by Malakonakis et al. [4]. Figure 4 illustrates the PLF accelerator based on the DAE approach. Overall, the PLF core has seven access units and a single execution unit. There are six input access units that fetch data from memory to the accelerator (Left and Right Vectors, Left and Right Matrices, EV vector and scaling vector (WGT)), and a single output access unit that writes the results of the computation back to memory.

An invocation of the accelerator consists of two steps. First, the Left- and Right-matrix access units retrieve the left and right probability matrices, and the EV access unit retrieves the inverted eigenvector (RAxML computes P(t) matrices based on eigenvector/eigenvalue decomposition) from memory and store them into register files. Then, the two FIFO-based access units fetch the Left and Right vectors that correspond to the left and right child nodes, and stream them through the PLF datapath. The output Parent vector is stored in memory through a FIFO-based access unit. The access units that prefetch data into register files do not contain FIFOs to lower resource utilization.

It should be noted that resource utilization coverage does not exceed 30% of the available resources in any of the FPGA hardware primitives (BRAMs, Logic Cells etc.). This provides a potential for further optimization of the design by adding more PLF accelerator engines. Moreover, a double-buffering mechanism was adopted to reduce data transfer overheads.

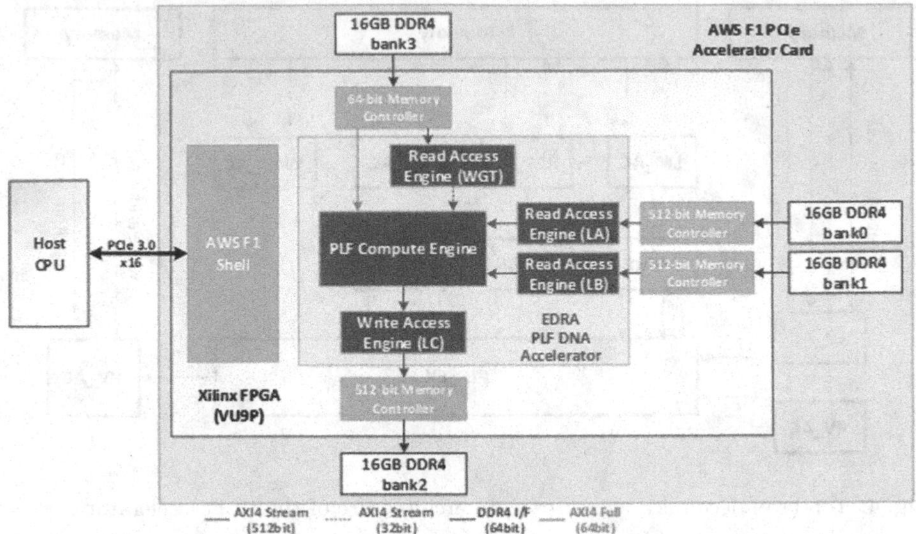

Fig. 5. PLF accelerator system architecture (AWS F1).

Figure 5 depicts the PLF integration to the AWS F1 machines. The memory controllers allow up to 512-bit-wide connections to the FPGA compute resources through an AXI stream interface. The PLF accelerator uses two such interfaces in order to transfer the two matrices from memory to the EX unit and another one to transfer the results back to memory. A fourth interface to the remaining memory channel (64 bits wide) is used for the R and L matrices and EV vector as well as the scaling factors.

N	Block Size (Double Buffering)						Single Buffering	Software PLF
	4k	8k	16k	32k	64k	128k		
1M	0,098	0,052	0,042	0,042	0,053	0,071	0,055	0,18
2M	0,3	0,11	0,079	0,076	0,085	0,11	0,11	0,36
5M	1,56	0,44	0,21	0,17	0,18	0,22	0,27	0,91
10M	3,25	0,93	0,43	0,35	0,35	0,42	0,55	1,83

Fig. 6. Execution time of the PLF function on AWS F1 instance. Software PLF is executed on the same F1 instance. N refers to the number of elements of the left and right probability vectors. All times are reported in seconds.

The PLF performance was compared against an optimized software implementation of RAxML on the same platform as the accelerated system. The underlying hardware platform is the CPU system of the AWS F1 instance, which is based on an Intel Xeon E5-2686v4 processor (8 vCPUs available). Figure 6 lists a set of experimental results that compares the software and hardware-accelerated PLF implementations. Comparing the execution time of the best accelerator case on the Amazon F1 and the time required to compute the same function in software, it can be seen that the accelerator provides 2.3x to 5.2x better performance. The performance gap widens as the input size increases. For the overall RAxML application, this translates to up to 3.2x reduction in the overall execution time for the most demanding datasets that were tested.

5 MVP Market Analysis

5.1 Market Size

EDRA's MVP accelerates the RAxML application [8], a well-established tool for phylogenetic analyses of large datasets under maximum likelihood. RAxML has more than 13K citations from its original publication (2006), and an additional 10,800 citations from researchers globally over the last 5.5 years (2014–2019) on its latest version. Based on accumulated data the estimated market size is valued at approximately 7.9 M€, 10.8 M€ and 14.6 M€ for 2021, 2022 and 2023 respectively. Knowing the market size is a valuable aspect, however a market strategy needs to reflect the target customer segments as well. Towards building the client profile for EDRA's MVP, the EDRA team used Google Scholar to collect information with respect to authors citing RAxML in their work. More specifically, starting on 2016, EDRA examined the first 100 publications each year that cite RAxML, and identified each article's leading author's affiliation and location. Figure 7 shows the analysis results from 2016 until Q2 2020. As observed, throughout each year leading authors affiliated with research institutes located in Europe and US represent 88% (2016), 72% (2017), 84% (2018), 82% (2019), and 64% (Q2 2020).

An interesting observation is that until Q2 2020 publications from authors affiliated with academic institutes in Asia raised from 6% in 2016 to 28%. One reason is that RAxML is widely used to study the evolution of viruses (among others), hence many researchers used it for analyzing the evolution of the COVID-19 virus in Asia, where the first recorded case occurred according to the World Health Organization records. This fact shows the importance of making available ample computing power to biologists, in order to speed up their analysis experiments.

Overall, the above study leads to the following conclusions:

- The potential market size for EDRA's MVP is valued at approximately 7.9 M€, 10.8 M€ and 14.6 M€ for 2021, 2022 and 2023, respectively.
- The primary client segment for EDRA's MVP is biologists and scientists working either for academic institutes or Contact Research Organizations.
- RAxML users can utilize additional processing power to conduct faster their experiments on COVID-19 evolution analysis.

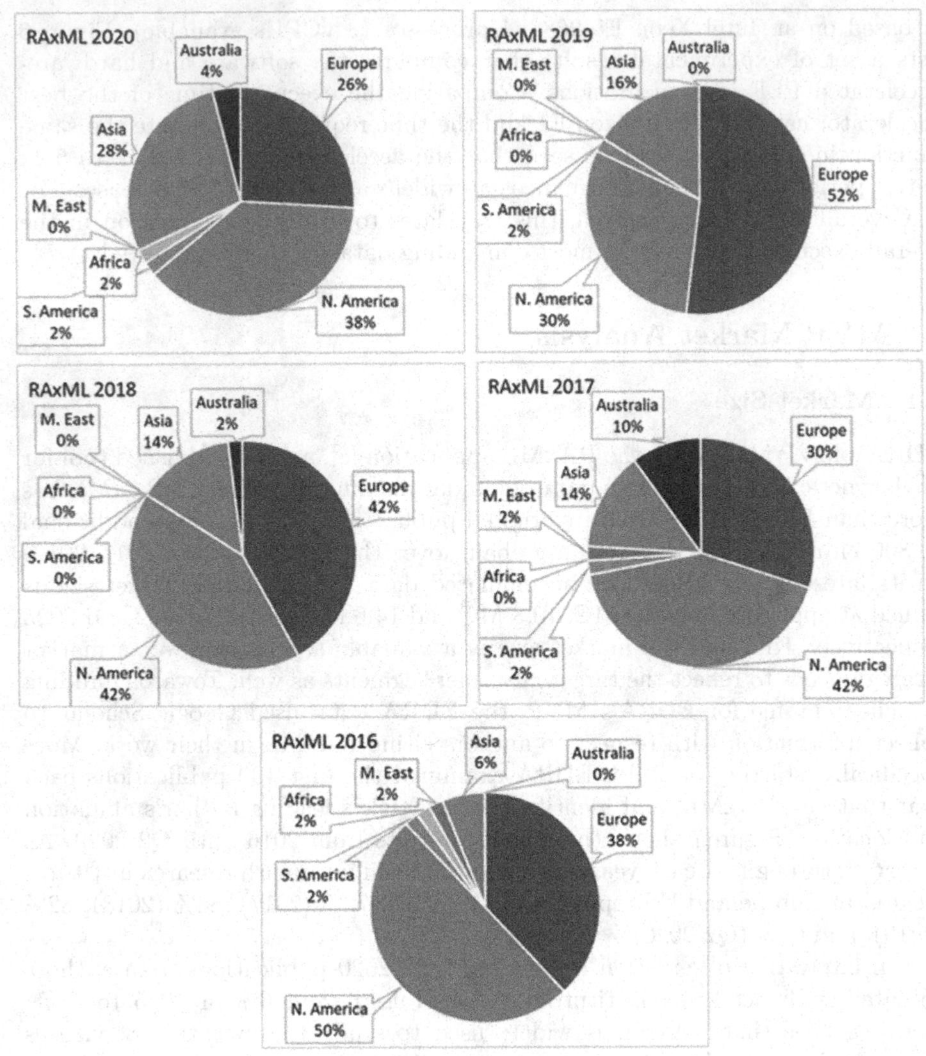

Fig. 7. Geographical breakdown of RAxML users from 2016 to Q2 2020.

5.2 Other Approaches

RAxML is made available to the community under a GNU Public License (GPL). Moreover, RAxML is already optimized for multi-threaded CPUs as well as GPUs [3,6], hence researchers clone it either on workstations or private servers to run their experiments. This approach though requires specialized IT personnel to ensure that a machine is properly configured (e.g. installing OS updates, drivers, software development tools installed, etc.), leading to increased costs related to infrastructure acquisition (e.g. buying server-class machines that cost thousands of €) and maintenance (e.g. paying electricity bills, hosting facilities for servers, salaries for extra IT personnel, etc.).

The above ad-hoc approaches are not identically configured (e.g. different OS versions, hardware resources) and usually impose significant development challenges, resulting in reduced productivity, non-optimal utilization of the available computational resources, and excessive IT costs. To partially alleviate the issue of system software variations, Informatics LLC created a virtual machine on Amazon's marketplace, called MolBioCloud [5], that contains a large set of software tools related to molecular biology. MolBioCloud offers a fully configured and tested environment in the form of a virtual machine for biologists working on different research areas. However, MolBioCloud does not support hardware acceleration.

6 Conclusions and Next Steps

EDRA successfully delivered an end-to-end framework for mapping applications onto Amazon's FPGA-supported cloud platforms based on the DAE approach. Moreover, the project delivered a pioneering MVP that enables faster processing of workloads related to phylogenetics, as well as conducted thorough research with respect to market addressable size and the MVP average customer persona.

Towards pushing the EDRA MVP to the market, the project team has already initiated the process of launching a spin-off based on the formulated business plan. The spin-off will focus on deploying the MVP to Amazon's marketplace, where biologists and researchers on phylogenetics will be able to download it on a pay-as-you-go charging policy, and instantly conduct their experiments up to 2.5x faster compared to the currently available software-optimized configurations.

References

1. Charitopoulos, G., Vatsolakis, C., Chrysos, G., Pnevmatikatos, D.: A decoupled access-execute architecture for reconfigurable accelerators. In: IEEE 18th International Conference on Computational Science and Engineering, pp. 244–247, May 2018
2. Ciobanu, C.B., et al.: Extra: towards an efficient open platform for reconfigurable high performance computing. In: 2015 IEEE 18th International Conference on Computational Science and Engineering, pp. 339–342 (2015)
3. Izquierdo-Carrasco, F., Alachiotis, N., Berger, S., Flouri, T., Pissis, S.P., Stamatakis, A.: A generic vectorization scheme and a GPU kernel for the phylogenetic likelihood library. In: 2013 IEEE International Symposium on Parallel Distributed Processing, Workshops and PhD Forum, pp. 530–538 (2013)
4. Malakonakis, P., Brokalakis, A., Alachiotis, N., Sotiriades, E., Dollas, A.: Exploring modern FPGA platforms for faster phylogeny reconstruction with RAxML. In: 2020 IEEE 20th International Conference on Bioinformatics and Bioengineering (BIBE), pp. 97–104 (2020)
5. MolBioCloud. http://molbiocloud.com/. Accessed 17 May 2021

6. Ott, M., Stamatakis, A.: Preparing RAxML for the spec MPI benchmark suite. In: High Performance Computing in Science and Engineering, pp. 757–768, January 2010
7. Smith, J.E.: Decoupled access/execute computer architectures. ACM Trans. Comput. Syst. 112–119 (1984)
8. Stamatakis, A.: RAxML version 8: a tool for phylogenetic analysis and post-analysis of large phylogenies. Bioinformatics (Oxford, England) **30** (2014)

Modeling the Scalability of the EuroExa Reconfigurable Accelerators - Preliminary Results
Invited Paper

Panagiotis Miliadis(✉), Panagiotis Mpakos, Nikela Papadopoulou, Georgios Goumas, and Dionisios Pnevmatikatos

National Technical University of Athens, Athens, Greece
{pmiliad,pmpakos,nikela,goumas,pnevmati}@cslab.ece.ntua.gr

Abstract. Current technology and application trends push for both performance and power efficiency. EuroEXA is a project that tries to achieve these goals and push its performance to exascale performance. Towards this objective, EuroEXA node integrate reconfigurable (FPGA) accelerators to offload computational intensive workloads. To fully utilize the FPGA's resource pool, multiple accelerators must be instantiated. System design and dimensioning requires an early performance estimation to evaluate different design options, including using larger FPGA devices, instantiating larger number of accelerator instances, etc.

In this paper, we present the preliminary results of modeling the scalability of EuroEXA reconfigurable accelerators in the FPGA fabric. We start by using simple equations to bound the total number of kernels that can work in parallel depending on the available memory channels and reconfigurable resources. Then, we use a 2nd degree polynomial model to predict the performance benefits of instantiating multiple replicated kernels in a FPGA. The model suggests whether the switching to another larger FPGA is advantageous choice in terms of performance. We verify our results using micro-benchmarks on two state-of-the-art FPGAs; AlveoU50 and AlveoU280.

Keywords: FPGA · FPGA modeling · EuroEXA · Reconfigurable accelerators · Performance prediction

1 Introduction

The HPC domain is well known for the gap between the theoretical peak performance of an actual platform and the achieved performance when running

[1] https://euroexa.eu/.

Georgios Goumas, Panagiotis Miliadis, Panagiotis Mpakos, Nikela Papadopoulou, Dionisios Pnevmatikatos.

© Springer Nature Switzerland AG 2022
A. Orailoglu et al. (Eds.): SAMOS 2021, LNCS 13227, pp. 331–341, 2022.
https://doi.org/10.1007/978-3-031-04580-6_22

real applications. EuroEXA[1] is a project that attempts to reduce this disparity, by enabling -through co-design- an innovative solution that achieves both extreme data processing and extreme computing. EuroEXA pushes its nodes to exaflop-level performance by implementing a new system architecture that better balances the required computing resources compared to today's systems, supporting the acceleration of key applications. A compute node in EuroEXA assembles general purpose processors, graphic processors units and reconfigurable accelerators.

Current technology and application trends push for both computational performance and power efficiency. A very promising way to achieve both prerequisites is the development of specialized hardware functions. Field-Programmable Gate Arrays (FPGAs) are strong candidates for implementing custom design circuits, as they can be programmed to easily implement a computational datapath suited for a fixed application. The fact that FPGAs are re-programmable, as compared to their ASIC counterparts, offers great flexibility for their integration to larger systems, to support emerging workloads and computational intensive kernels.

State-of-the-art FPGAs are offering a large pool of re-programmable resources, e.g. 6-port LUTs, flip flops, block memories and DSPs, as well rich interconnection between the units. Large banks of memory and processor cores are paired with FPGAs, in order to increase the overall performance of applications. A bitstream with a hardware kernel is offloaded into the FPGA, and a host application sends data and requests to it like a co-processor. In a development environment such as Vitis[2] platform from Xilinx, host applications are usually written in a high-level programming language (e.g. OpenCL), while kernels are written in C++ with HLS primitives. A toolchain converts the high-level kernel into RTL code, and then produces the bitstream with the hardware accelerated design. In EuroEXA, multiple reconfigrable accelerators are instantiated into the same FPGA fabric, to exploit the large pool of resources offered by FPGAs. However, to design the system and the application deployment, the performance benefits of this approach should be gauged. In this paper, we will try to model the scalability of reconfigurable accelerators, and predict the performance benefits acquired by adopting a larger FPGA as compared to a current smaller platform.

Roofline [4] is a model that helps an application developer to classify his computational kernel into two different classes; compute-bound or memory-bound. While a plethora of optimizations can be applied to increase the kernel's performance, it is still bound to the computational capabilities of the processor unit and to the offered memory bandwidth. After a few years, Roofline for FPGAs[2] is introduced, where the authors extended the classic Roofline approach to reconfigurable accelerators. They introduced optimization guidelines to increase the performance of the accelerator and exploit the available resources of FPGA's fabric. However, most of hardware accelerators utilize a fraction of available resources, leaving a large part of fabric unused.

---

[2] https://www.xilinx.com/products/design-tools/vitis/vitis-platform.html.

Summarizing, the primary objectives of this work are to:

1. Bound the maximum number of compute units that can be mapped on available reconfigurable resources and memory channels.
2. Create a model that can predict the performance benefits from increasing the total number of compute units.
3. Verify our model on two different FPGA accelerator cards; a smaller AlveoU50 and a larger AlveoU280.

The rest of the paper is organized as follows. In Sect. 2, we present our model for the scalability of reconfigurable accelerators. In this section we present two key parameters that strongly affects our model, FPGA area fabric and available memory channels. Furthermore, we will discuss how these parameters bound the number of kernels that can mapped in a FPGA, and how FPGA modeling can predict the performance benefits from implementing multiple instances of a kernel to a larger or newer FPGA. In Sect. 3, we present our preliminary experimental evaluation of our model, followed by Sect. 4 to finally conclude the paper.

2 FPGA Modeling

In this section, we will discuss about our model regarding the scalability of the reconfigurable accelerators in a FPGA. The two key parameters of our discussion are area and memory. The scalability of our model is strongly affected from area, as the resources of a FPGA are limited and we will provide an upper bound of maximum number of kernels that can be mapped. Furthermore, the congestion of memory bandwidth between kernels is another significant issue that may lead to performance degradation. In this section we will discuss and provide an analysis of how congested memory bandwidth can be avoided.

2.1 Scalability Limitations Due to Area Congestion

The current generation of FGPAs includes a large pool of reconfigurable resources, which include BRAM, DSPs, LUTs and FFs. The computational kernels designed for FPGAs usually bind a small fraction of the available resources. Newer FPGAs achieve to contain even more reconfigurable resources into a die region, while FPGAs with multiple die regions (SLRs) into the same package are available by the vendors [5]. So, the transition to a newer FPGA leads that the same computational kernel will bind even fewer resources. One of the most straightforward ideas to take advantage of the computational capabilities that a FPGA can offer is to create multiple instances of the same kernel. By implementing multiple instances of a kernel, a host machine can either execute multiple times an algorithm in parallel, or it can dispatch the work items of a single algorithm into the accelerated instances. The replicated instances from now on will be referred as compute units.

A computational kernel needs a fraction of the available resources to instantiate it in a FPGA. The amount of resources that a kernel binds is dependent to optimization decisions of the designer, to maximize his kernel performance.

While development decisions play a huge role on the performance capabilities of a single kernel, they are out of the scope of this paper. In our model, a kernel is considered as a "black box" so as to limit the information that our model needs to evaluate. For area scaling the only piece of information that is needed is kernel's resources which will be referred from now on as {BRAM, DSP, FF, LUT}_design.

The development platforms used by designers, such as Vitis, restrict the utilization of the FPGA area. The suggested maximum resource utilization for a design is restricted to 80% for BRAMs and DSPs resources, while the corresponding ratio for LUTs and FFs is 70%, as reported from the vendors. In our model, we decided to bound the available resources to a more optimistic approach. So the total number of compute units that a FPGA can map is given from Eq. 1.

$$\begin{aligned} \#CU_{area} = \min\Bigg(& \left\lfloor \frac{0.85 * BRAM_{total}}{BRAM_{design}} \right\rfloor, \left\lfloor \frac{0.85 * DSP_{total}}{DSP_{design}} \right\rfloor, \\ & \left\lfloor \frac{0.75 * FF_{total}}{FF_{design}} \right\rfloor, \left\lfloor \frac{0.75 * LUT_{total}}{LUT_{design}} \right\rfloor \Bigg) \end{aligned} \tag{1}$$

As shown from the equation, the total number of compute units is restricted by the most consuming resource of the computational kernel, while the floor in the equation offsets the optimistic approach that we took earlier on maximum resource utilization. If other designs occupy a fraction of the total available resources in the FPGA fabric, it is clear that the committed resources must be subtracted from each numerator in Eq. 1.

As we will discuss in Sect. 3, the scalability of reconfigurable accelerators in a FPGA platform may be restricted by HLS toolchains, especially when the number of compute units is large enough (i.e. 10–12 compute units). HLS toolchains consider each compute unit to be a distinct building block which consumes reconfigurable resources equal to the original one. So, compute resources increase linearly as more compute units are mapped into the FPGA fabric. When the number of compute units is high enough, the distinct blocks congest over the same wires into the FPGA fabric for routing. When there are not any available wires in the FPGA fabric, or timing requirements cannot be met, the toolchain rejects the design, even though there are available logic resources. This is a limitation in our current prediction model for the scalability of accelerators. In our future work, we will try to model the routing restrictions from HLS toolchains, and bound the total number of compute units in the FPGA fabric depending on the routing complexity as well available resources.

2.2 Scalability Limitations Due to Memory Congestion

Another key parameter that strongly affects the scalability of the reconfigurable accelerators is memory. Data are fetched from memory banks into compute units through memory channels. The management of memory channels from developers is the main reason for bottlenecks in a application performance. When multiple compute units try to access the same memory bank through the same memory channel, they are competing for the same memory bandwidth. The congestion of memory bandwidth and the sharing of memory channels can significantly limit the performance and can convert an algorithm from compute-bound to memory-bound, as fewer data are fetched is second to each unit. In this subsection we discuss how memory congestion can be avoided and provide guidance for better memory management between multiple kernels.

The majority of FPGA boards contain large off-chip DDR memories (e.g. 32–48 GB for state-of-the-art devices), which are used for storing large sets of data. Data are initially stored on off-chip memory and then are streamed into compute units for processing. DDR memories usually are separated in 2 to 4 banks, and a same amount of memory channels are used for communication with compute units. As discussed in the previous subsection, the FPGA fabric can fit a large number of kernels, so memory channels must serve multiple compute units concurrently, decreasing the overall performance of the system due to sharing. With the advent of High Bandwidth Memory (HBM), FPGAs are offering a much higher number of memory channels and overall memory BW at the cost of smaller storage. Xilinx states that in state-of-the-art AlveoU50 and AlveoU280, 32 HBM channels are available for communication between memory banks and compute units. As more memory channels are available for data transmission, congestion can be avoided by statically partitioning memory channels to compute units.

By partitioning the memory channels, each memory bank will serve a single compute unit. Performance bottlenecks from sharing are prevented, and a compute unit can utilize the whole available bandwidth from a memory channel. So, a "one-to-many" communication type is suggested to avoid congestion over memory bandwidth, where a compute unit is atomically served either by a single memory bank or by multiple ones concurrently. An alternative solution to prevent the sharing of memory bandwidth is to enqueue work items into compute units in different time periods, but our scope in this paper is that compute units work in parallel to provide peak performance and maximum throughput.

Given the number of memory channels that a compute unit utilizes, the total number of kernels that can work in parallel without performance degradation due to sharing, is given in Eq. 2.

$$\#CU_{mem} = \left\lfloor \frac{MemChannels_{Avail}}{MemChannels_{design}} \right\rfloor \tag{2}$$

2.3 FPGA Performance Modeling

In the previous subsections, we provided simple equations, and discussed how our model can extract the total number of compute units that a FPGA can map given a certain amount of logic and memory resources. Equation 1 provides an upper bound of compute Units due to limitation in the FPGA fabric, while Eq. 2 an upper bound due to limited memory channels. The ideal number of compute units that can work in parallel without performance loss is given by Eq. 3. However, the performance benefits from the transition to a larger or newer FPGA are still unclear.

$$\#CUs_{ideal} = \min(\#CU_{area}, \#CU_{mem}) \tag{3}$$

Our approach for modeling the scalability of the reconfigurable accelerators is to consider the computational kernel as a "black box", where the development decisions are unknown, and minimal information about the kernel is needed for modeling. During the transition to a newer or larger FPGA, the computational kernel is not subject to modifications. If no architectural changes are made from generation to generation or from FPGA to FPGA, such as LUTs or DSPs, almost the same amount of resources are needed to implement and map the same computational kernel. So, as long as more compute units can fit in a FPGA, the performance have to keep increasing linearly. However, we expect reduced performance growth, because as it was mentioned the frequency of compute units is decreased when more compute units are mapped, while an extra software overhead is introduced in order to enqueue work items into the accelerated kernels.

The performance prediction model for FPGAs can be created by following a series of small steps. At first, a scattered graph is created by extracting performance results from an initial FPGA platform. At least two performance points are needed to create a simple model, when a single kernel is mapped in the FPGA fabric and the maximum number respectively. To further increase the accuracy of the prediction model, we recommend inserting more performance points from the initial platform, for different number of compute units. From the performance points of the initial used FPGA platform, a 2nd degree polynomial model is exported. 2nd degree polynomial models have been adopted by other similar works [1], to create prediction models for general purpose processors units. With the help of the prediction model, an application developer can find out the performance benefits from the transition to another FPGA. By integrating a newer FPGA in a system, a larger pool of reconfigurable resources or more memory channels are available. By using our models' equations, the total numbers of compute units can be extracted for the new FPGA platform, and from the 2nd degree polynomial model, the performance benefits can be found out by implementing more compute units.

3 Preliminary Experimental Results

In this section, we will present our preliminary results regarding the FPGA modeling on reconfigurable accelerators. For our case study, we use two state-of-the-art FPGAs platforms: AlveoU50 and Alveo280, while their available resources are listed in Table 1. For the application development, Vitis 2020.2 unified software platform is used, the kernel was written in C++ with HLS primitives, and the host side uses OpenCL to enqueue work items to hardware kernels and to transfer data between the host machine and the FPGA. Three micro-benchmarks are used; Conv2D, MatrixMult and Sequential Read/Write. The first two are used to evaluate the performance capabilities of our platform, as compute units are keep increasing, while the latter one is used to evaluate the communication between HBM channels and kernels.

Table 1. Available resources of AlveoU50 and AlveoU280 and their maximum memory bandwidth.

FPGA	BRAM	DSP	LUTs (K)	Registers (K)	Mem BW (GB/s)
Alveo U50[a]	1344	5,952	872	1,743	316
Alveo U280[b]	2,016	9,024	1,304	2,607	460

[a] https://www.xilinx.com/products/boards-and-kits/alveo/u50.html
[b] https://www.xilinx.com/products/boards-and-kits/alveo/u280.html

3.1 Sequential Read/write

To avoid memory bandwidth congestion between multiple compute units, we assumed to statically partition memory channels to kernels. At first, we need to evaluate our decision by finding out the potential drawbacks of this choice. In Table 2, we present our results for two communication patterns, by using Sequential Read and Write. In Sequential Read/Write, data are streamed into a compute unit, and then are streamed out to off-chip memory again. One-to-all communication is when a compute unit utilizes all available memory channels, while one-to-one communication is the worst case scenario where each compute unit utilizes only one memory channel. From our results, the static partitioning of memory channels does not introduce any significant overhead in our micro-benchmarks, and almost the entire memory bandwidth can be exploited. Our results come to an agreement with a recent paper that evaluates the HBM channels of Alveo devices, [3]. Our results confirm that congestion of memory bandwidth can be easily avoided by using partition, and the number of compute units can be bounded by the available memory channels.

Table 2. Available memory channels and memory bandwidth for a) one-to-all communication and b) one-to-one communication.

FPGA	One-to-all	One-to-one	$Channels_{avail}$
AlveoU50	309.97 GB/s	307.31 GB/s	24
AlveoU280	388.82 GB/s	386.07 GB/s	30

3.2 Scalability of Accelerators

To model the scalability of reconfigurable accelerators in the FPGA fabric, we use two computational kernels with different kernel sizes, Conv2D and MatrixMmult. As the original compute units are considered "black boxes", the only pieces of information that we need for modeling are the necessary design's resources and the number of channels that utilizes. Table 3 reports the information that our model needs to find out the total number of compute units.

Table 3. Resource utilization for our micro-benchmarks when a single compute unit is mapped

Kernel	Kernel size	BRAM	DSP	LUTs	Registers	$Channels_{design}$
Conv2D	120	131	43	18,766	23,423	1
	150	227	88	13,200	14,980	1
MatrixMult	80	31	459	15,782	23,129	1
	100	47	602	51,375	58,087	1

We use two FPGA platforms, AlveoU50 as the initial FPGA where our model will be created, and AlveoU280 to verify our performance results. At first, our model exports the total number of compute units that AlveoU50 can map in its fabric based on designer's computational kernel. For Conv2D the most costly resource is BRAM while for MatrixMult is DSP. From Eq. 1, our model calculates the number of compute units and in Figs. 1 and 2 we report our results. For Conv2D the total number of compute units is 8 and 4 for kernel sizes 120 and 150 respectively, while for MatrixMult is 11 and 8 for 80 and 100 kernel sizes. The results verify our equations, as we cannot map any more compute units. Meanwhile, we report the speedup as we increase the number of compute units, by using as baseline the execution time of a single kernel in AlveoU50.

For all kernels, the speedup (Blue Triangles and Red X Marks on all Figures) does not scale linearly as more compute units are instantiated in the FPGA fabric. The loss in performance is the result of the reduced frequency. As more compute units are implemented in the FPGA, the reduction in frequency is getting bigger, until the speedup is yielded around a value. This is the result of the increased latency in data transfers, as data have to cross a larger area until their destination. Fewer data are fetched each second in the compute units, which increase the overall execution time of a kernel. Our model captures the decreasing frequency from instantiating multiple compute units, and predicts the potential drawbacks in performance from implementing a high number of computational kernels.

To export the 2nd degree polynomial model, the execution time is needed for multiple number of compute units. The minimum performance points needed are for a single compute unit and for the maximum numbers respectively. To further increase the accuracy of the model, more performance points can be included. The model for each type of kernel is printed with a light blue line in Figs. 1 and 2. The choice of the 2nd degree polynomial model is made to capture the reduced frequency on compute units as they keep increasing, and it is more adapting based on our results. By using the exported model, the potential speedup can be predicted from using a larger FPGA with either more resources in its fabric or memory channels.

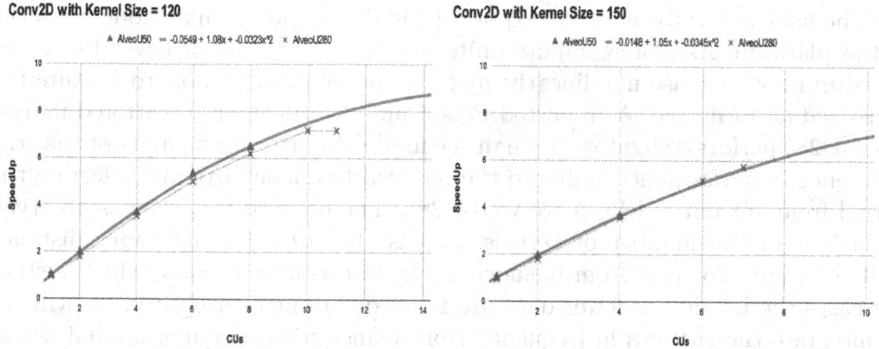

Fig. 1. Modeling the scalability of Conv2D for Kernel Size = 120 (Left) and Kernel Size = 150 (Right). From AlveoU50 performance points (Blue Triangle), we exported the performance model of the kernel (Light Blue Line) and we verified our model with AlveoU280 performance points (Red X Mark). (Color figure online)

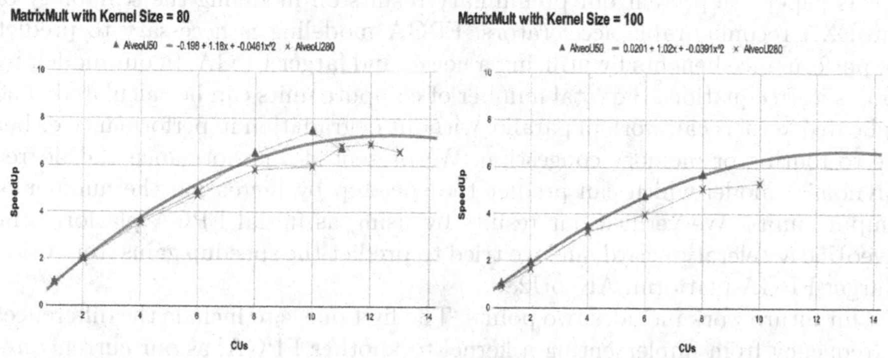

Fig. 2. Modeling the scalability of MatrixMult for Kernel Size = 80 (Left) and Kernel Size = 100 (Right). From AlveoU50 performance points (Blue Triangle), we exported the performance model of the kernel (Light Blue Line) and we verified our model with AlveoU280 performance points (Red X Mark). (Color figure online)

One of our objectives in this paper is to predict the performance benefits from implementing the same computational kernel to a larger FPGA. For this case study AlveoU280 is used, which has almost 35% more available reconfigurable resources compared to AlveoU50. As Figs. 1 and 2 reports, the maximum number of compute kernels are increased on all micro-benchmarks we used. However, the increase differs from kernel to kernel. Conv2D indeed benefits the most from the transition to a larger FPGA, as the number of compute units are capped in the FPGA fabric. However, MatrixMult cannot take full advantage of the more available resources, as the high routing complexity prevents the implementation of a high number of computational kernels due to congestion over the same wires. The wiring congestion prevents the full utilization of the FPGA fabric, and it is a limit in our current prediction model.

The final step is to verify the exported 2nd degree polynomial model from the initial platform. As more compute units can be mapped in our new FPGA, the speedup must increase non-linearly, and our model must be able to capture the increased performance. As reported Figs. 1 and 2 from the red scattered marks, AlveoU280 performs slight worse than the model reports. We figured out that the difference in performance is due to the reduced frequency from transferring the kernel from our initial FPGA to AlveoU280. The reduced frequency is observed regardless of the number of kernels, and is the result of the larger distance that data have to cross from memory banks into compute units, which further increases the latency as fewer data are fetched. In our future work, we will try to integrate the changes in frequency from transferring a computational kernel from a FPGA to a smaller or larger FPGA.

4 Conclusion and Future Work

In this paper, we present our preliminary results on modeling the scalability of EuroEXA reconfigurable accelerators. FPGA modeling is necessary to predict the performance benefits by utilizing a newer and larger FPGA. In our model, by using simple equations the total number of compute units can be calculated. The replicated kernels can work in parallel without degradation in performance either due to routing or memory congestion. We presented a performance 2nd degree polynomial model which can predict the speedup by increasing the number of compute units. We verified our results by using as initial FPGA platform the AlveoU50 acceleration card, and we tried to predict the speedup gains from using a larger FPGA platform, AlveoU280.

Our future work includes two points. The first one is to include the differences in frequency from implementing a kernel to another FPGA, as our current prediction model is proved slightly more optimistic about the performance benefits. Furthermore, high routing complexity limits toolchains to integrate a high number of compute units (i.e. 12–14) into the FPGA fabric, even though there are available logic resources. Consequently, the second point is to model the routing restrictions from congestion over FPGA wires in fabric to increase the accuracy of our equations.

Acknowledgments. This work is supported and funded by the European Commission under the H2020 Programme and the EuroEXA project (Grant Agreement no. 754337). The authors would like to thank Xilinx for their donation of FPGA Alveo development boards.

References

1. Calotoiu, A., et al.: Fast multi-parameter performance modeling. In: 2016 IEEE International Conference on Cluster Computing (CLUSTER), pp. 172–181. IEEE (2016)

2. da Silva, B., Braeken, A., D'Hollander, E.H., Touhafi, A.: Performance modeling for FPGAs: extending the roofline model with high-level synthesis tools. Int. J. Reconfig. Comput. **2013** (2013)
3. Choi, Y.K., Chi, Y., Wang, J., Guo, L., Cong, J.: Benchmarking and bandwidth optimization, when HLS meets FPGA HBM (2020)
4. Williams, S., Waterman, A., Patterson, D.: Roofline: an insightful visual performance model for multicore architectures. Commun. ACM **52**(4), 65–76 (2009)
5. Xilinx: Alveo u50 data center accelerator card data sheet. https://www.xilinx.com/support/documentation/data_sheets/ds965-u50.pdf

The Known Unknowns: Discovering Trade-Offs Between Heterogeneous Code Changes

Invited Paper

Christos P. Lamprakos(✉), Charalampos Marantos, Lazaros Papadopoulos, and Dimitrios Soudris

School of ECE, National Technical University of Athens, Athens, Greece
cplamprakos@microlab.ntua.gr

Abstract. Software projects must adhere to a variety of non-functional requirements, also known as software qualities. Automated evaluation with respect to such requirements can be conducted thanks to a wide array of available tools. Each tool usually focuses on a specific quality, since heterogeneous analyses are needed for each non-functional requirement. Apart from an overall index expressing the project's performance in terms of the software quality they specialize on, many tools recommend code changes that are expected to improve the aforementioned index. Thus, a development team that cares for more than one non-functional requirement is facing the problem of unknown trade-offs; besides improving the quality on which the tool that generated each suggestion focuses, how would this code change, if implemented, affect the rest of the non-functional requirements? We present a framework for dealing with this problem. We pick energy efficiency, technical debt and software security as our qualities of interest, and use three respective tools for the analysis of several open-source projects with regard to these qualities. We develop an extensible empirical model, based on fuzzy sets, for the characterization of each suggestion's trade-offs. Finally, we present an intuitive visualization of said trade-offs, and suggest a method of utilizing them towards reliable decision-making.

Keywords: Software quality · Trade-off analysis · Decision-making

1 Introduction

Researchers have been studying software quality for more than four decades [1–3]. Although substantial efforts of standardizing it do exist (the most notable example being ISO/IEC 25010:2011[1]), each software product most often ends up with its own, "internal" definition of quality, also known as non-functional

[1] https://www.iso.org/standard/35733.html.

© Springer Nature Switzerland AG 2022
A. Orailoglu et al. (Eds.): SAMOS 2021, LNCS 13227, pp. 342–353, 2022.
https://doi.org/10.1007/978-3-031-04580-6_23

requirements. Apart from this definition, developer teams also pick specific software metrics which are intended to *measure* the qualities defined.

This variety implies a multitude of team-dependent frameworks and methodologies with regard to measuring and improving software quality. It is also evident that a major portion of the aforementioned improvement will come in the form of changes in the source code. These changes are either products of expert knowledge and collaboration, or of automated diagnostic tools like [4], and each one of them is naturally expected to focus on a single quality.

A team that would like to improve several aspects of software quality would thus face the problem of *unknown trade-offs*; besides improving the quality on which its derivation focuses, how would each code change, if implemented, affect the rest of the non-functional requirements? We present a framework for dealing with this problem. The main contributions of this paper are:

- an empirical framework for discovering trade-offs between heterogeneous code changes with respect to arbitrary software qualities
- a suggestion as per how to utilize our framework's products towards deciding which code change to eventually implement

2 Related Work

The work presented in this paper presupposes the identification of specific non-functional requirements that are to be optimized, or at least improved, by a team of developers. Additionally, the toolsets for quality-specific analysis and code change recommendation are assumed to be known and integrated.

2.1 Software Quality Models

The definition of a non-functional requirement like energy efficiency is not identical to its quantitative evaluation. Due to this discrepancy, Bakota et al. [5] propose a probabilistic framework for measuring software quality. Driven by open-source development and its impact, Samoladas et al. [6] provide a measurement-based method for open source software evaluation. Miguel, Mauricio and Rodriguez [7] present a comprehensive review of recent work on software quality models.

2.2 Code Refactoring

In the context of this paper, refactoring is important since it is the form in which several software quality analysis tools recommend beneficial code changes. Mens and Tourwe provide an in-depth survey of refactoring until 2004 [8]. In his 2018 book, Fowler records many decades of refactoring knowledge [9]. A very recent work by Brito, Hora and Valente introduce the notion of refactoring graphs, for assessing refactoring over time [10].

2.3 Tools

The SonarQube platform exposes a plug-and-play interface for analyzing a software project's non-functional requirements [11] like security and technical debt. Customized program analysis through dynamic instrumentation, useful when profiling an application's energy efficiency, can be achieved with Pin [12].

3 Proposed Method

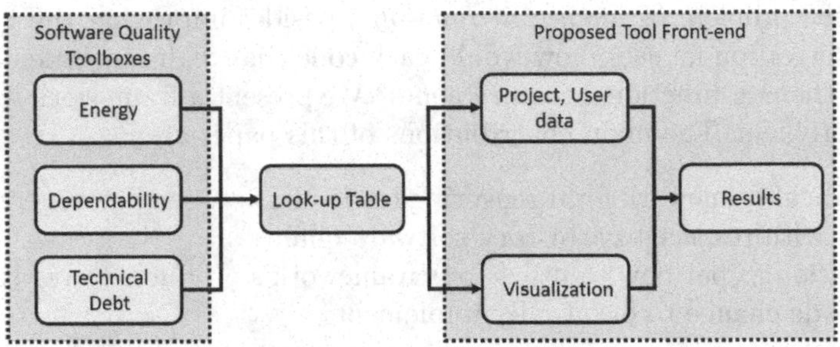

Fig. 1. A high-level description of the proposed flow

The proposed mechanism is depicted schematically in Fig. 1 with added components and interactions of its functionality. This paper focuses on derivation of the "Lookup table" component, which contains trade-offs between available decisions.

In the following subsections, work relevant to our mechanism's inputs is described on high-level terms.

3.1 Software Quality Toolboxes

Three individual Software Quality toolboxes are used [13].

Technical Debt Toolbox is responsible for monitoring and improving the application Maintainability. Its three main components include: Technical Debt Analysis, that analyses the entire projects's evolution, New Code, that analyzes the commit history and proposes quality gates and Refactorings Suggestion.

Energy Toolbox estimates the energy of a given project and suggests optimizations that can be applied. It firstly identifies the critical parts of the application and then recommends optimizations for each one of the these parts, including data-flow transformations, concurrency data accesses related optimizations, and acceleration recommendations.

Dependability Toolbox monitors the Security and Reliability level of the given software applications. More specifically, it includes three sub-components: Quantitative Security Assessment evaluates the internal security level of an application providing a high-level security indicator, Vulnerability Prediction identifies places of security issues and Optimum Checkpoint Interval suggests optimum checkpoint intervals for programs with loops [14].

3.2 Refactorings Retrieval

The user will need an overall catalogue of the suggestions proposed by each individual suggestion. As a result, upon invocation from the user interface, the Trade-off Manager back-end sends requests to all 3 of the analysis toolboxes, expecting distinct reports for the current project as responses.

3.3 Design Space Exploration

None of the individual toolboxes does take into consideration code qualities other than the one it optimizes. To take meaningful decisions, however, the user will need to evaluate all refactorings universally. Regardless of the source toolbox of a suggestion, the displayed information should include its impact on all aspects: energy, technical debt and security. From this point on, this information will be referred to as 'design space'.

Production of the design space is non-trivial, and approximate methods have to be employed. Each analysis toolbox deals with extremely dissimilar aspects of software (particularly taking energy into consideration). Moreover, it is hard to provide a fine-grained estimation of a suggestion's impact without actually applying it to the code and repeating the analysis, and this holds true even for individual toolboxes and their own suggestions and optimized qualities. Finally, the approach should be as project- and platform-agnostic as possible.

To mitigate this, a common knowledge base has been set up. Anyone with valid credentials can inspect and update this knowledge. The format chosen is that of a look-up table. Each row represents an individual code refactoring proposed by one of the analysis toolboxes (actual origin is not included for universal treatment). To ensure agnosticity as regards project and platform, the possible values of impacts are coarse-grained:

- Worsen
- No Impact
- Improve

Usage of such coarse categories is both a necessity and a valuable feature, since it can be viewed as an entry point for the introduction of uncertainty. This can be achieved, for example, with fuzzy logic. In the Trade-off Manager flow, and after gathering all proposed refactorings from all the toolboxes, the look-up table is queried for each of the suggestions. All matching entries are returned, forming the final design space of the problem with which the decision-maker is faced.

The next paragraphs present a more detailed analysis of the impact of each individual Toolbox's refactoring suggestions on the rest of the quality attributes. A systematic approach based on empirical results obtained through a number of experiments or found in the literature based on the inherent characteristics of a refactoring was followed [15].

Impact of Energy Refactorings on TD and Dependability. We selected applications from two open source benchmark suites, namely Rodinia [16] and Polybench[17], that have clearly documented test cases and execution scenarios.

The most popular energy optimization suggestions of the utilized Energy Toolbox is *Cache blocking* and *acceleration optimization*. These are both applicable in the selected applications. After analysing these applications with the Energy Toolbox, we apply the proposed refactorings for optimizing Energy Consumption. In order to evaluate the impact on the other two qualities, the following metrics are utilized: *Lines-of-Code (LOC)* and *Cyclomatic Complexity* for Maintainability and *Num. of Security issues* for Security.

Typical examples of Cache blocking (or Data-flow) optimizations are the loop transformations that aim to improve the cache performance. In cases where the Cache blocking refactoring was proposed by the Energy Toolbox, we applied the optimization manually. Most of the optimizations are Loop tiling. The Complexity increases from 10% up to 105% and LOC increases from 7% up to 50% [18].

Following the same procedure, we applied the Acceleration optimization (using CUDA). We observe that the LOC are increased from 1% up to 100% while there is an increase of 0% up to 78% for Complexity. The application sometimes needs a large number of changes (even to the algorithm itself) for applying acceleration, but on another analysed projects require simple restructuring (for example, if the for loop is already written in a way that is parallelizable and the kernel is easy to be developed). In some other cases, the first version of the application was already written with high complexity and the refactorings did not lead to more complex code.

According to these results, we might conclude that there is a clear negative impact on Maintainability.

Cache-blocking has no direct impact on security as it makes small changes in the loops. Regarding the acceleration refactoring, sometimes we observe an indirect impact on software security After comparing the CPU and GPU versions of some applications from the Rodinia benchmark suite, we observe changes in the number of the Security issues. There are a lot of applications for which we observed a negative impact on security. However, there are also cases in which the number of security issues may be reduced. It is worth mentioning that the measured impact is not due to the refactoring itself, but due to adjacent changes in the application code [19], so we might claim that the energy-related refactorings have no impact on security.

Impact of TD Refactorings on Energy and Dependability. Following the same procedure described in the previous paragraph regarding Energy optimizations impact, open source projects were selected and analysed by the TD Toolbox. The two representative TD refactorings selected to be presented in the context of this manuscript are the *extract method* that aims to solve the Long method smell and the *replace conditional with polymorphism*.

Extract Method is applied on Maven, PDFBox and SEMI software applications. The impact on Energy varies from 58% up to 500% and on Security from 74% up to 101%. In the most of the cases Energy is affected negatively but we can not have a clear conclusion, while Security level remains the same for the most cases.

Regarding the Replace Conditional with Polymorphism refactoring, we see no impact on Security and a negative impact on Energy (from 130% to 560%).

Impact of Dependability Refactorings on TD and Energy. Following the same procedure, a number of refactorings provided by the Dependability Toolbox were tested in terms of their impact on Energy and TD. In most of the cases, the security refactorings seem to have no to negative impact on the energy consumption of software programs, while we observe a positive impact on the Technical Debt [20].

Some representative Security refactorings that improve also TD are Null Pointer, Exception Handling, Misused Functionality, Synchronization, String Issues and I/O Issues (improving TD from 20% up to 60%). Their impact on Energy is neutral. Some Security refactorings like Logging and Overflow checking might slightly affect the Energy consumption negatively.

3.4 Visualization

The user would benefit greatly from an intuitive, friendly presentation of the available decisions (i.e. the design space). An appropriate method would be to treat each suggestion as a 2-dimensional vector in 3 distinct axis settings: *Energy vs. Technical Debt*, *Technical Debt vs. Security*, *Energy vs. Security*.

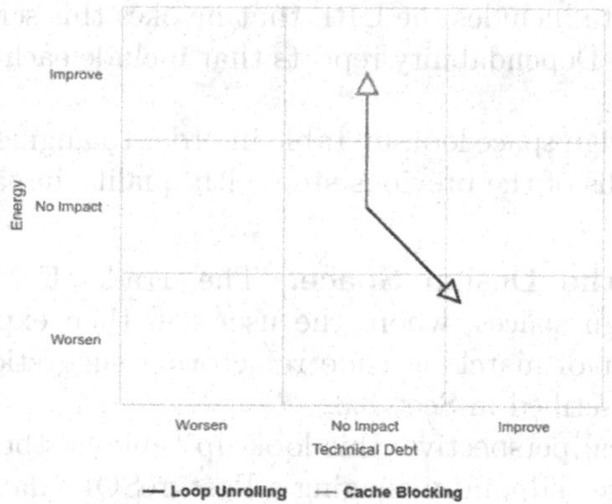

Fig. 2. A sample depiction of 2 code refactorings

Figure 2 (pulled directly from the Trade-off Manager front-end) follows the approach described above. The chart is informative and interactive. The user can select any subset of the available refactorings for depiction.

3.5 Implementation

The rest of the Section provides an overview of the user interface designed for the proposed Trade-off Manager component. The front-end has been written with use of the React[2] framework. The back-end infrastructure is described in detail. All the required information with regard to the micro-services being invoked, APIs, and databases is provided.

Docker Infrastructure. Trade-off Manager follows a dockerized architecture. Docker[3] is a platform for packaging software applications in tiny environments similar to, but better performing than, virtual machines (VMs). In the Docker lingo, these environments are called containers. The benefit of using containers is that they decouple any dependencies of the packaged projects with the platform they run on. A container developed on a Linux system can as a result be executed seamlesssly on Windows and vice-versa.

The functionality is divided in 2 sub-components:

- *RefactoringsGatherer*, which leverages existing APIs of the rest of the platform in order to get the refactoring proposals from the individual toolboxes.
- *RefactoringsVisualizer*, which is responsible for rendering the design space to the front-end. Please note the data dependency between the 2 sub-components: unless *RefactoringsGatherer* has finished constructing the design space, *RefactoringsVisualizer* has nothing to visualize

The front-end then performs the following API calls:

- The retrieval of all the information that is required to perform the subsequent call, returning an object that contains the URL of the analyzed project repo, and toolbox-specific data provided manually from the user. More specifically, the API data includes the URL that invokes this service, the Technical Debt, Energy and Dependability reports that include each quality refactoring recommendations.
- Queries to the design space look-up table in order to augment each refactoring retrieved from calls of the previous step with quality impact information

Construction of the Design Space. The Trade-off Manager constructs project-specific design spaces, whom the user can then explore. These design spaces are a product of matching code refactoring suggestions with entries in the look-up table described in Sect. 3.3.

From the technical perspective, this look-up table has been implemented as a dockerized database endpoint managing a PostgreSQL[4] database. PostgreSQL is a very popular option for production-grade applications, providing security, reliability, and an excellent community around it. A user can interact with our database through API's that inspect and/or modify it.

---

[2] https://reactjs.org/.
[3] https://www.docker.com/.
[4] https://www.postgresql.org/.

4 Potential Extensions

In the above sections we have presented a method for quantifying the trade-offs inherent between heterogeneous code changes when considering more than one non-functional requirements. Trade-offs, however, are not useful in themselves, especially as the numbers of available refactoring options as well as those of software qualities of interest increase. On top of that, trade-off magnitudes originating from defuzzified values cannot be accurate in the same degree for all possible use cases.

Thus, in this section we propose two meaningful extensions to our method.

4.1 Application-Specific Trade-Offs

As a first step, we should depart from the static nature of our refactoring impact model (lookup table), since its empirical one-off derivation most probably does not describe all potential scenarios. We should instead compute all trade-offs *per project*; our static model could or could not be used as a form of a priori knowledge, but what is certain is that the source code under inspection should be either profiled or statically analyzed in order to retrieve a concrete view of dependencies existing, for instance, between classes of objects (or between modules, libraries, etc.). The field of change impact analysis [21] could prove useful in this sense. A recent use of change impact analysis to control refactoring is that of Mongiovi et al. [22], focusing on security considerations.

The output of this imagined component should be an updated lookup table containing project-specific information.

4.2 Preference Encoding and Decision Making

We are interested in the pragmatic goal of utilizing discovered trade-offs in order to improve a project's software quality. The main problem here is that of quantifying, as was done with trade-offs, a developer team's *preferences* with respect to each of the examined non-functional requirements. If this was done, then a final ranking of available decisions (refactoring options, code changes) could be easily derived; each option's "value" would be a weighted sum of its trade-offs multiplied with a set of weights, each representing the team's degree of interest to a particular quality.

In essence, what is described above is the field of Multiple-Criteria Decision Making [23] (MCDM), which solves the central problem of encoding preferences on a set of conflicting criteria. This is an all but abandoned field, with recent published applications on energy [24], text classification [25], markets [26] and other domains.

4.3 Forecasting Quality Evolution

A team might want to decide with a deep time horizon in mind. It is true, especially for open-source collaborations, that software quality is always evolving.

A wise decision would thus take this evolutionary process into consideration. Software evolution has and is still being studied in numerous works [27–29].

Provided a set of predictors (each one treating a separate quality), a simple mechanism would then be to use its output to scale each option's value accordingly. A decision maker could then see how good or bad would each code change pay off in X versions from now, if that change were to be implemented.

4.4 Prototype

It is our strong belief that application-specific, reliable trade-off quantification coupled with a state-of-the-art MCDM algorithm and a software quality forecaster would prove extremely useful for both researchers and practitioners. One such prototype (though with a static lookup table for refactoring impacts) was developed in the context of the European H2020 projects SDK4ED and EXA2PRO. [13][5].

As an example, let us consider Fig. 3. Here we see the ranking of nine code changes produced by an array of source code analysis tools, each one of which focuses respectively on energy efficiency, technical debt and dependability[6]. This ranking is the output of a state-of-the-art MCDM algorithm [30] that we reproduced in the platform's backend. The "values" are real numbers expressing the degree to which a change's discovered trade-offs match the user's preferences[7]

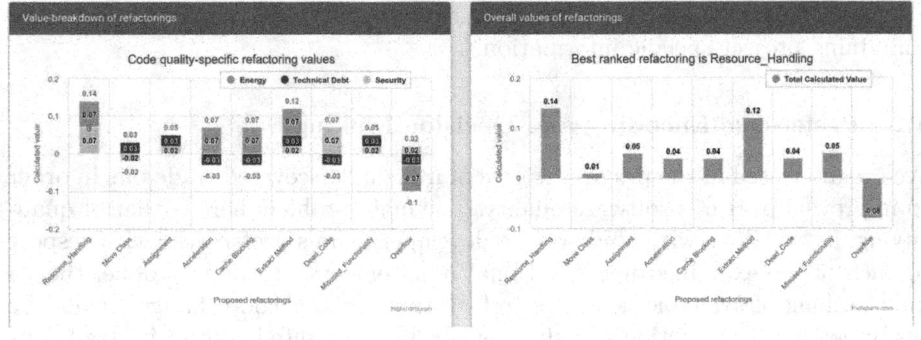

Fig. 3. Prototype code change values.

Last but not least, Fig. 4 showcases each change's value evolution based on a prototype quality forecaster's output [31]. The potential usefulness of such a projection in the future for each candidate code change is evident.

---

5 platform.sdk4ed.eu/.

6 Since this is a prototype, we do not intend to delve into further details. We use the figures in this section as assistants to the reader's intuition.

7 Preference declaration is trivial given an MCDM algorithm. The reader may study [30] for the particular case that we implemented.

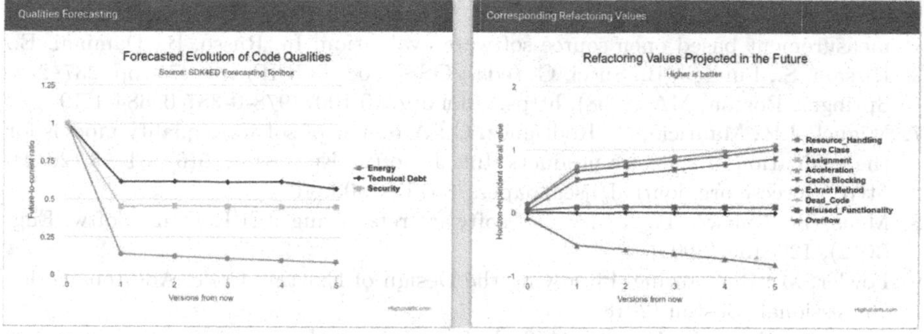

Fig. 4. Prototype future code change values evolution.

5 Conclusion

This paper treats the problem of assigning quantitative trade-offs to heterogeneous code changes. This heterogeneity stems from the fact that different developer teams construct different (i.e. dependent on their products' needs, their members' experience, etc.) descriptions of non-functional requirements.

More specifically, we demonstrated an empirical methodology for calculating the fuzzy impact of refactoring on qualities such as energy efficiency, technical debt and dependability. We showed a simple, intuitive way of visualizing this impact in two-dimensional grids. We explicitly described the technical infrastructure employed, and proposed substantial extensions to our work. Last but not least, we demonstrated some elementary, prototype implementations for said extensions.

Acknowledgments. This work has received funding by the EU H2020 research and innovation programme EXA2PRO under grant agreement No. 801015.

References

1. Boehm, B.W., Brown, J.R., Lipow, M.: Quantitative evaluation of software quality. In: Proceedings of the 2nd International Conference on Software Engineering, pp. 592–605 (1976)
2. Kan, S.H.: Metrics and Models in Software Quality Engineering. Addison-Wesley Professional, Boston (2003)
3. Kitchenham, B., Pfleeger, S.L.: Software quality: the elusive target [special issues section]. IEEE Softw. **13**(1), 12–21 (1996)
4. Tsantalis, N., Chaikalis, T., Chatzigeorgiou, A.: JDeodorant: identification and removal of type-checking bad smells. In: 2008 12th European Conference on Software Maintenance and Reengineering, pp. 329–331. IEEE (2008)
5. Bakota, T., Hegedűs, P., Körtvélyesi, P., Ferenc, R., Gyimóthy, T.: A probabilistic software quality model. In: 2011 27th IEEE International Conference on Software Maintenance (ICSM), September 2011, pp. 243–252 (2011). iSSN: 1063-6773

6. Samoladas, I., Gousios, G., Spinellis, D., Stamelos, I.: The SQO-OSS quality model: measurement based open source software evaluation. In: Russo, B., Damiani, E., Hissam, S., Lundell, B., Succi, G. (eds.) OSS 2008. ITIFIP, vol. 275, pp. 237–248. Springer, Boston, MA (2008). https://doi.org/10.1007/978-0-387-09684-1_19
7. Miguel, J.P., Mauricio, D., Rodríguez, G.: A review of software quality models for the evaluation of software products. Int. J. Softw. Eng. Appl. **5**(6), 31–53 (2014). http://airccse.org/journal/ijsea/papers/5614ijsea03.pdf
8. Mens, T., Tourwé, T.: A survey of software refactoring. IEEE Trans. Softw. Eng. **30**(2), 126–139 (2004)
9. Fowler, M.: Refactoring: Improving the Design of Existing Code. Addison-Wesley Professional, Boston (2018)
10. Brito, A., Hora, A., Valente, M.T.: Refactoring graphs: assessing refactoring over time. In: 2020 IEEE 27th International Conference on Software Analysis, Evolution and Reengineering (SANER), pp. 367–377. IEEE (2020)
11. Campbell, G.A., Papapetrou, P.P.: SonarQube in Action. Manning Publications Co. (2013)
12. Luk, C.-K., et al.: Pin: building customized program analysis tools with dynamic instrumentation. ACM SIGPLAN Not. **40**(6), 190–200 (2005)
13. Siavvas, M., et al.: The SDK4ED platform for embedded software quality improvement - preliminary overview. In: Gervasi, O., et al. (eds.) ICCSA 2020. LNCS, vol. 12252, pp. 1035–1050. Springer, Cham (2020). https://doi.org/10.1007/978-3-030-58811-3_73
14. Siavvas, M., Gelenbe, E.: Optimum checkpoints for programs with loops. Simul. Model. Pract. Theory **97**, 101951 (2019)
15. Kehagias, D., Jankovic, M., Siavvas, M., Gelenbe, E.: Investigating the interaction between energy consumption, quality of service, reliability, security, and maintainability of computer systems and networks. SN Comput. Sci. **2**(1), 1–6 (2021)
16. Che, S., et al.: Rodinia: a benchmark suite for heterogeneous computing. In: IEEE International Symposium on Workload Characterization (IISWC), pp. 44–54. IEEE (2009)
17. Pouchet, L.-N., et al.: PolyBench: The polyhedral benchmark suite (2012). http://www.cs.ucla.edu/pouchet/software/polybench
18. Papadopoulos, L., Marantos, C., Digkas, G., Ampatzoglou, A., Chatzigeorgiou, A., Soudris, D.: Interrelations between software quality metrics, performance and energy consumption in embedded applications. In: Proceedings of the 21st International Workshop on Software and Compilers for Embedded Systems, pp. 62–65 (2018)
19. Siavvas, M., Marantos, C., Papadopoulos, L., Kehagias, D., Soudris, D., Tzovaras, D.: On the relationship between software security and energy consumption. In: 15th China-Europe International Symposium on Software Engineering Education (2019)
20. Siavvas, M., et al.: An empirical evaluation of the relationship between technical debt and software security. In: 9th International Conference on Information society and technology (ICIST), vol. 2019 (2019)
21. Li, B., Sun, X., Leung, H., Zhang, S.: A survey of code-based change impact analysis techniques. Softw. Test. Verification Reliab. **23**(8), 613–646 (2013)
22. Mongiovi, M., Gheyi, R., Soares, G., Teixeira, L., Borba, P.: Making refactoring safer through impact analysis. Sci. Comput. Program. **93**, 39–64 (2014)
23. Yu, P.-L.: Multiple-Criteria Decision Making: Concepts, Techniques, and Extensions, vol. 30. Springer, Heidelberg (2013)

24. Sitorus, F., Brito-Parada, P.R.: A multiple criteria decision making method to weight the sustainability criteria of renewable energy technologies under uncertainty. Renew. Sustain. Energy Rev. **127**, 109891 (2020)
25. Kou, G., Yang, P., Peng, Y., Xiao, F., Chen, Y., Alsaadi, F.E.: Evaluation of feature selection methods for text classification with small datasets using multiple criteria decision-making methods. Appl. Soft Comput. **86**, 105836 (2020)
26. Cinelli, M., Kadziński, M., Gonzalez, M., Słowiński, R.: How to support the application of multiple criteria decision analysis? Let us start with a comprehensive taxonomy. Omega **96**, 102261 (2020)
27. Honsel, D., Herbold, V., Waack, S., Grabowski, J.: Investigation and prediction of open source software evolution using automated parameter mining for agent-based simulation. Autom. Softw. Eng. **28**(1), 1–37 (2021). https://doi.org/10.1007/s10515-021-00280-3
28. Pati, J., Kumar, B., Manjhi, D., Shukla, K.K.: A comparison among ARIMA, BP-NN, and MOGA-NN for software clone evolution prediction. IEEE Access **5**, 11841–11851 (2017)
29. Boaye Belle, A.: Estimation and prediction of technical debt: a proposal. arXiv e-prints, arXiv:1904 (2019)
30. Guo, S., Zhao, H.: Fuzzy best-worst multi-criteria decision-making method and its applications. Knowl.-Based Syst. **121**, 23–31 (2017)
31. Tsoukalas, D., Siavvas, M., Jankovic, M., Kehagias, D., Chatzigeorgiou, A., Tzovaras, D.: Methods and tools for TD estimation and forecasting: a state-of-the-art survey. In: International Conference on Intelligent Systems (IS) 2018, pp. 698–705 (2018)

Towards Efficient HW Acceleration in Edge-Cloud Infrastructures: The SERRANO Approach

Invited Paper

Aggelos Ferikoglou[1(✉)], Ioannis Oroutzoglou[1], Argyris Kokkinis[1], Dimitrios Danopoulos[1], Dimosthenis Masouros[1], Efthymios Chondrogiannis[2], Aitor Fernández Gómez[3], Aristotelis Kretsis[4], Panagiotis Kokkinos[4], Emmanouel Varvarigos[4], and Kostas Siozios[1]

[1] Aristotle University of Thessaloniki, Thessaloniki, Greece
{aferikog,ioroutzo,akokkino,ddanopou,dmasoura,ksiop}@physics.auth.gr

[2] Innovation Acts Ltd., Nicosia, Cyprus

[3] IDEKO, ICT and AUTOMATION Research Group, Elgoibar, Basque Country, Spain
afgomez@ideko.es

[4] National Technical University of Athens, Athens, Greece
{akretsis,kokkinop,vmanos}@mail.ntua.gr

Abstract. Nowadays, we witness an ever-increased number of applications deployed over Edge, Cloud and HPC infrastructures. This rapid explosion of computing devices across the computing continuum poses new challenges in terms of providing a power-efficient, secure and automatic way for deployment of different applications in such heterogeneous environments. Moreover, the need for performance efficient deployments within such environments, has introduced the presence of hardware accelerators over the entire computing stack.

In this paper, we present SERRANO's approach for providing efficient HW accelerated deployments over edge-cloud infrastructures. First, we give a brief overview of the SERRANO project, describing its goals and objectives, providing a high-level overview of SERRANO's platform architecture and presenting the use-cases involved. Then, we describe SERRANO's approach for providing efficient HW accelerators by identifying trade-offs between performance, accuracy and power consumption and also demonstrate how SERRANO aims to automate the optimization process through machine learning models in order to construct a generic optimization heuristic to fine-tune programs for both GPU and FPGA accelerators. Through some illustrative examples, we showcase that by applying approximation and optimization techniques, we are able to achieve an average decrease of 28% in power consumption for FPGA devices and trade-off between performance and power usage for GPUs, achieving up to ×1.21 speedups and 8% power improvement.

This work has been supported by the E.C. funded program SERRANO under H2020 Grant Agreement No: 101017168.

© Springer Nature Switzerland AG 2022
A. Orailoglu et al. (Eds.): SAMOS 2021, LNCS 13227, pp. 354–367, 2022.
https://doi.org/10.1007/978-3-031-04580-6_24

Keywords: Edge computing · Cloud continuum · Hardware accelerators · GPU · FPGA · Heterogeneous

1 Introduction

In recent years, emerging applications in Machine Learning, security or cloud storage have achieved great success and have been among the most responsible for the high demands in data-center or edge workloads. Different vertical sectors with diverse requirements have gained traction and induced a rise to a number of fundamental challenges that relate to the application deployment, the support of heterogeneous systems and the provided security. According to several analytical agencies, the global market for such cloud services will reach 332 billion USD in 2021 [1]. This is 50 billion USD more than 2020 and 100 billion USD more than 2019. Clouds are used in almost all high-tech industries: in software development, in projects based on IoT, for big data analysis, etc. Many organizations have already moved their workloads to the cloud. According to another research, migrations to the public cloud has grown from 89% to 92% in the last three years and over 80% of firms with more than 1000 workers use multiple cloud platforms, while, by 2024, this percentage is expected to jump up to 90% [2].

Additionally, there is a movement to define an intent-based paradigm of operating federated infrastructures consisting of edge, cloud and HPC resources that will make the process of application deployment automated across the various computing technologies and platforms. The enormous compute needs of such services and applications operating in the cloud requires joining different processing units in a networked-based system such that each task is preferably executed by the unit which is able to efficiently perform it. Heterogeneous computing represents a well established way to achieve further scalability in the computing sector, while, at the same time service assurance mechanisms are required along with a safety-critical and coordinated mechanism to adjust the required tasks.

A solution to overcome these problems and to fully align with the current trends of the cloud computing sector is to introduce various specialized hardware acceleration platforms. Such devices (e.g., GPUs, FPGAs) can achieve higher performance than typical processing systems and also significantly higher performance for the same power envelope [8]. The use of highly specialized units designed for specific workloads can greatly enhance server or edge CPUs and their power budget. Last, a cognitive orchestration of these devices can lead to a single borderless infrastructure which can shrink the existing technology gaps.

In this paper, we present an overview of the SERRANO H2020 project towards Transparent Application Deployment in a Secure, Accelerated and Cognitive Cloud Continuum. SERRANO aims to introduce a novel ecosystem of cloud-based technologies, spanning from specialized hardware resources up to software toolsets, evaluated through three well-defined use cases in cloud storage services, fintech and manufacturing. We focus on SERRANO's approach for efficient hardware acceleration in the edge-cloud computing continuum, by applying device-specific optimizations and approximation techniques on FPGA and GPU devices. We describe SERRANO's vision to apply such optimizations in an automated manner and leverage them for power-/performance-efficient application deployments within the underlying platform. By employing a set of illustrative examples, we showcase that by applying a set of optimization techniques on accelerated kernels, we are able to trade-off between power and performance efficiency both on GPU and FPGA accelerators, realizing SERRANO's ambition for dynamic, requirement-driven deployments on heterogeneous infrastructures.

2 The SERRANO Project

SERRANO[1] aims to deliver a novel ecosystem of hardware- and software-based technologies under the SERRANO platform, contributing to critical cloud related areas, including: *a)* application deployment, *b)* resource interoperability, *c)* privacy and security and *d)* cognitive and autonomous operation. SERRANO's approach is expected to reduce significantly the design and development time, through infrastructure agnostic application development, providing high quality services that utilize efficiently the available resources, thus, boosting the digital productivity. Below, we describe the project's objectives, give an overview of SERRANO's architecture and briefly present the use-cases involved.

2.1 SERRANO Goals and Objectives

In the context of its mission, SERRANO aims to satisfy 6 concrete research objectives, that are going be validated through several individual success indicators (KPIs). Initially, SERRANO **aims to define an intent-driven paradigm of federated infrastructures, with edge, cloud and HPC resources**. An abstraction layer will automate the operation and the full exploitation of the available diverse resources in order to simplify the developer's workload. The intent-driven feature of this layer will enable applications to express their high-level requirements in an infrastructure agnostic manner and translate them to infrastructure-aware configuration parameters.

On a second level, it ambitions to **develop security and privacy mechanisms for accelerated encrypted storage over heterogeneous and federated infrastructures**. SERRANO will ensure GDPR compliant distributed secure storage and data sharing, accessible at low latency with cryptographic primitives and network coding techniques. This essential capability that protects the content itself, complies with privacy implications for personal or confidential information and enables HPC applications to offload their data to edge or cloud, overcoming the local storage restrictions.

SERRANO targets to **provide workload isolation and execution trust on untrusted physical tenders** as well. It desires to deliver a secure, lightweight, and efficient framework that embraces interoperable microservices in the cloud, the fog and the edge, providing specific solutions for the low-level software stack.

[1] https://ict-serrano.eu/.

Moreover, it **focuses on providing acceleration and energy efficiency at both the edge and cloud**. SERRANO aims to introduce advanced "inline" and "online" data sampling in order to decrease the amount of data offloaded from edge/fog to cloud/HPC and therefore will develop a novel "smart sampling" technique based on approximate computing for dynamic data packing of multiple inputs into a single variable.

Furthermore, SERRANO attempts to **develop an hierarchical architecture for end-to-end cognitive orchestration and transparent application over edge/fog and cloud/HPC infrastructures**. To this end, SERRANO will develop intelligent and autonomous orchestration mechanisms that will automatically determine the most appropriate resources to be used. It will exploit multi-objective optimizations, graph theory, AI/ML techniques and heuristics to design an algorithmic toolkit, aiming to provide different trade-offs between optimality and complexity.

Finally, it visions to **demonstrate the capabilities of the secure, disaggregated and accelerated SERRANO platform in supporting highly-demanding, dynamic and safety-critical applications** with 3 use cases (UCs) across different domains with heterogeneous needs. The UCs include secure storage for data protection, secure launching of ultra-large number of fintech processing performing real-time operations, and advanced real-time anomaly detection of manufacturing machines.

2.2 SERRANO's Architecture Overview

The heterogeneity of distributed edge/cloud environments has revealed the importance of efficient resource orchestration. When multiple applications request different types of resources, meeting the requests in an optimal way becomes a challenging task, particularly when the applications have high resource demands. Heading to more complex infrastructures, the development of intelligent and self-managed orchestration mechanisms is a key factor to optimize resource utilization and meet the application requirements. SERRANO aims to contribute to the aforementioned open issue by proposing a scheme for end-to-end cognitive orchestration together with closed-loop control, based on the principles of observe, decide and act.

SERRANO targets an orchestration system that manages the underlying heterogeneous infrastructure at a more abstract and disaggregated manner compared to the current state-of-the-art solutions. This is achieved through a hierarchical architecture, consisting mainly of three components: a) the central resource orchestrator b) a set of resource-hosted local orchestrators and c) the telemetry framework. Figure 1 depicts the orchestrator's architecture.

Each application submitted to the SERRANO platform, provides a set of high-level requirements that describe the desired application state. The central resource orchestrator being aware of the underline edge, cloud and HPC resources and the current infrastructure state, decides the optimal placement of the application. Based on AI/ML algorithms, this mechanism aims to satisfy the user-defined requirements and efficiently use the underline infrastructure. When

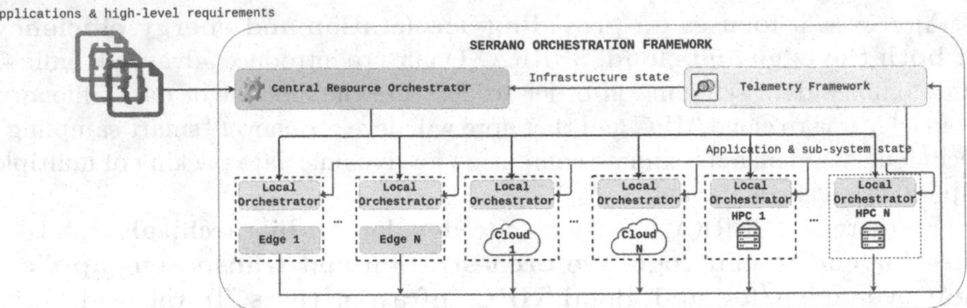

Fig. 1. SERRANO's high-level orchestration architecture

the optimal placement is decided, the central resource orchestrator assigns the workloads to the selected resources along with the desired performance state and coordinates the required data movement. Then the control is passed to local orchestrators that are responsible for the actual deployment based on the desired performance requirements.

SERRANO resource orchestrator follows a declarative approach, instead of an imperative one, for describing the workload requirements to the local orchestrator. This approach provides several degrees of freedom to the local orchestrator for serving in an optimal manner the request, satisfying both the central orchestrator and the resources' objectives (e.g. trade-off accuracy against power for inference tasks that their accuracy constraint is over-satisfied). Finally, it is evident that the service assurance provided by the central and local orchestrators would not be possible without a telemetry framework that captures information concerning the current infrastructure's and applications' state.

2.3 SERRANO's Use-Cases

The performance of the SERRANO platform will be evaluated based on three use-cases from different scientific domains. Each use case consists of challenging case studies that will be deployed and tested on the SERRANO platform, showcasing the platform's capability to address multiple computationally intensive problems, each one with varying requirements.

Use-Case 1: Secure Data Storage. The first use-case will be from the field of security and distributed data storage. Its purpose is to demonstrate the platform's capacity for high-performance, yet secure data storage across cloud and edge devices. For this case, SERRANO aims to explore network coding techniques that fragment the encoded data in multiple parts, allowing the encoded pieces to be stored in distributed locations, and thus provide a secure storage solution. For SERRANO, the computing ecosystem consists of data center and edge nodes that will perform high-performance computations for the encoding and decoding tasks and transfer the data pieces securely across heterogeneous environments without compromising data integrity and privacy.

Use-Case 2: High-Performance Fintech Analysis. The second use-case belongs to the finance sector, and more specifically in the domain of portfolio management and analysis. This use-case will underline the platform's capability for high-performance processing of various AI algorithms for investment management applications in a secure computing environment. Through the SERRANO platform, the automatic management of personalized portfolios and the market prediction mechanisms will be accelerated, scaling-up the overall efficiency by performing precise predictions and increasing the number of managed portfolios. The enhanced security will be fulfilled by the transparent execution of different tasks in multiple devices, allowing processes to switch dynamically among different cloud and edge nodes, and hence decreasing the platform dependency.

Use-Case 3: Machine Anomaly Detection in Manufacturing Environments. The third use-case belongs to the machine anomaly detection domain. Specifically, high-frequency sensors generate data that are processed in real-time in order to automatically detect anomalies in machines. However, due to the large volumes of the acquired data, edge devices have limitations for analyzing and detecting the faulty parts. Through this use-case the platform's capacity to analyze large volumes of data and perform high-performance real-time computations will be demonstrated. In the context of SERRANO project cloud devices are planned to be exploited for storing and performing anomaly detection algorithms on the acquired data. Moreover, SERRANO's orchestration mechanisms aim to move data across different platforms in order to achieve real-time anomalies detection through high-performance computations.

3 Efficient Acceleration in Heterogeneous Architectures

SERRANO hardware infrastructure exposes a wide range of acceleration devices for both edge and cloud environments. Moving towards the transparent utilization of heterogeneity, SERRANO is enabled to manage and orchestrate accelerated kernels, to optimally meet their requirements (e.g. accuracy, latency). In addition, by providing a source-to-source kernels' transformation mechanism, SERRANO aims to automatically apply device specific acceleration and resource optimizations in order to minimize developers' effort and enable efficient utilization of the underline infrastructure.

3.1 Target Hardware Infrastructure

Heterogenoous hardware architectures have increased their range of practical applications especially in the cloud and edge domains. SERRANO will introduce a novel deployment model of accelerators both in the cloud and edge sectors which will influence the use of parallel and distributed algorithms. FPGAs and GPUs as hardware platforms will be attached directly in servers or shared over the network in edge workloads. The SERRANO HW infrastructure is expected to reduce the power and execution times of the assigned tasks by extending the existing development tools and providing novel schemes for scheduling, communication, and synchronisation with the programmable accelerators.

The aim is to virtualize the available hardware accelerators such as Xilinx Alveo FPGAs or Nvidia T4 GPUs in the servers through an efficient device pass-through scheme which will limit the overheads and isolate the devices in each different guest operating system (OS). Overall, a novel VM appliance model for provisioning of data to shared accelerators will be introduced scaling intelligently, automatically and transparently from edge (local cloud) to public cloud.

3.2 Optimization Techniques for Efficient FPGA Acceleration

FPGA devices have been proven to be a promising acceleration alternative when programmed with optimal configuration [7]. Designing hardware for FPGAs can be performed at varying levels of abstraction with the commonly used being the register-transfer level (RTL) and the algorithmic level. These methodologies differ; RTL (i.e. VHDL, Verilog) is used for circuit-level programming while algorithmic level methodologies such as High Level Synthesis (HLS) are used for describing designs in a more abstract and user-friendly way [5].

Device Specific HW Optimizations: SERRANO will leverage HLS tools in order to provide accelerated kernels for the computationally intensive tasks of the use cases. Employing HLS for FPGA design, enables a faster and more flexible development process compared to RTL. By adding different directives on a C/C++ or OpenCL code, users are able to instruct the HLS compiler to synthesize kernels. In particular, the kernels will be designed by using the Xilinx Vitis framework [3] which provides a unified OpenCL interface for programming edge (e.g. MPSoC ZCU104) and cloud (e.g. Alveo U200) Xilinx FPGAs. In this manner, the kernel designing process is simplified and thus more effort can be put to the design space exploration (DSE) phase which targets the performance optimization with respect to the architecture and resources of the available FPGAs. It is evident that the kernel acceleration process is device specific, meaning that different HLS pragmas should be applied to the same application when it is targetted to different FPGAs (e.g. in loops with multiple iterations, different unrolling factors should be applied for a U200 and a ZCU104 FPGA, due to the different available resources).

Approximate Computing Techniques for FPGAs: In order to efficiently use the FPGA resources of the SERRANO infrastructure and minimize the power consumption, approximate computing techniques (ACT) will be performed on the accelerated applications. ACTs are used in computationally complex, error-resilient applications, trading-off algorithmic performance with power consumption and resource utilization. Over the years, various ACTs were presented in the literature, targeting different layers of the computing stack [18]. SERRANO mainly focuses on software based ACTs, such as precision scaling, loop perforation and approximate memoization, as they can be easily applied to kernels.

Precision scaling [9,11] is a technique that changes the bit-width of input or intermediate operands to reduce storage and computing requirements. Xilinx

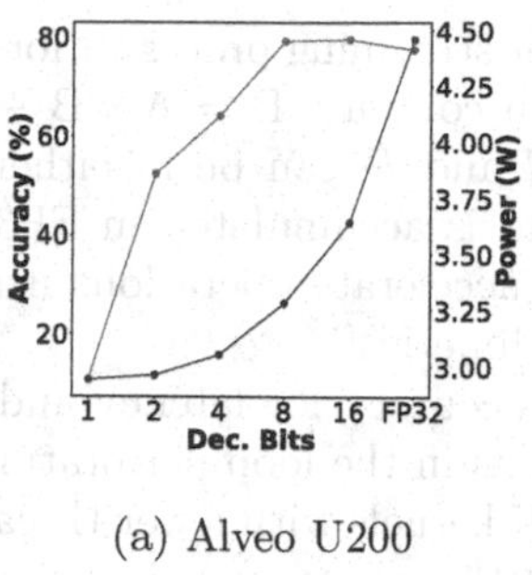

(a) Alveo U200

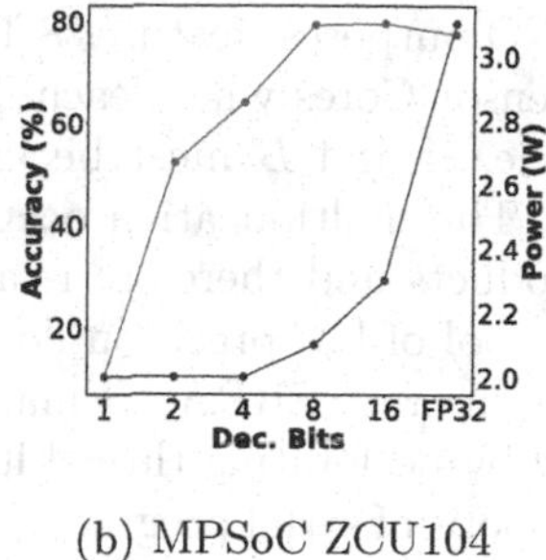

(b) MPSoC ZCU104

Fig. 2. Accuracy and power consumption vs decimal bits for Gaussian Naive Bayes algorithm in U200 (a) and ZCU104 (b) platforms

[4] provides tools and libraries that support a wide range of fixed-point precision data types, enabling the creation of power and resource efficient designs. Figure 2a and 2b show the relation between accuracy and power for different bit width approximations, for the Gaussian Naive Bayes algorithm on U200 and ZCU104 platforms. As the figures depict, for 8 bit approximation an average decrease of 28% in power consumption can be achieved without sacrificing accuracy. Loop perforation [12,16] is another ACT that selectively skips entire loop iterations to reduce computational overhead and hence resource and power consumption. Finally, approximate memoization [17,19] stores the results of expensive function calls for later use and returns the cached values when similar inputs reoccur. By replacing functions that are complex to implement on hardware with a simple look-up table, memoization leads to significant resource and power savings.

3.3 Optimization Techniques for Efficient GPU Acceleration

In order to provide acceleration and energy efficiency at both the edge and the cloud as visioned, SERRANO makes use of GPU accelerators in order to meet the desired requirements. The project aims not only to accelerate the provided use cases, but to study and apply several parallel kernels' optimizations in order to tune them in terms of both performance and power efficiency. Therefore, to achieve applications' close-to-peak efficiency, several optimization techniques are applied.

Approximate Computing Techniques for GPUs: SERRANO aims to apply approximation techniques in order to further improve its applications' efficiency. Such as the FPGA case, precision scaling will be applied by executing the kernels on after-Volta architecture featured Tensor Cores [15], instead of CUDA cores, in order to enable mixed-precision computing and provide efficient implementations. Driven primarily by the need for training in deep learning, Volta, Turing and Ampere GPU architectures provide specific programmable matrix multiply-accumulate units able to deliver a theoretical peak performance of 110 teraFLOP/s in FP16-TC. More specifically, the V100 GPU (used for the

SERRANO purposes) features 8 Tensor Cores per streaming processor for a total of 640 Tensor Cores where each Tensor Core can compute $\mathrm{D} = \mathrm{A} \times \mathrm{B} + \mathrm{C}$ per clock cycle. A and B must be in FP16, but C and D can be in either FP16 or FP32. The multiplication occurs in FP16 and is accumulated in FP32 with other products and therefore is able to further accelerate operations using the powerful tool of low-precision floating-point arithmetic.

Furthermore, SERRANO manages to trade accuracy for latency and power efficiency by perforating thread iterations. Such as in the loop perforating technique in loops of serial programs, launching GPU kernels with fewer threads and processing a part of the output result instead of the whole, promises significant gains in both performance and power consumption by loosing accuracy.

Kernel's Block Coarsening Transformation: Block coarsening is an optimization for parallel applications such as GPU programs. It refers to the kernel transformation that merges together the workload of 2 or more thread blocks and therefore reduces their total number by leaving the number of threads per block the same. Consequently, it merges multiple neighboring blocks in order to deal with the problems associated with extensive fine-grained parallelism.

Kernel's Thread Coarsening Transformation: In contrast with block, thread coarsening transformation fuses together 2 or more neighboring threads within the same block and can be proved beneficial on several parallel programs and architectures. In that case, it reduces the number of threads per block, while leaving the number of launched blocks the same. It is able to increase the amount of work performed by each kernel by replicating the instructions in its body, while it reduces the number of instantiated threads at the runtime.

Insights about Thread VS Block Coarsening Optimizations: Similar but with different impacts, both the block and thread coarsening transformations are able to improve efficiency of various parallel applications on different architectures. While they both reduce the total number of each kernel's threads, they distribute them in a different way across GPU's resources and thereupon affect kernel's execution at runtime differently. Listing 1.1 depicts a simple squared kernel written in CUDA, while Listings 1.2 and 1.3 demonstrate how it is transformed after block and thread coarsening transformation accordingly. Integer *bc* and *tc* parameters, named as BCF and TCF for the rest of the work, constitute an effective design parameter and refer to the number of blocks and threads merged together accordingly.

From an architectural perspective, GPUs map blocks to SMs (multiprocessors) and threads grouped in warps to CUDA cores. Therefore, reducing blocks per kernel with block coarsening, reduces the number of occupied SMs, while thread coarsening reduces the number of threads per block and therefore the number of warps scheduled by each SM, while the number of SMs occupied by the kernel remains the same. Figure 3 depicts a simplified architectural view of mapping between software and hardware resources when a kernel is launched after block and thread coarsening transformation.

Even though both transformations attempt to improve parallel applications' efficiency, their impact seems to highly depend on exogenous factors such as

```
__global__ void square (float *in, float *out){
    int gid=blockIdx.x*blockDim.x+threadIdx.x
  out[gid]=in[gid]*in[gid]; }
```

Listing 1.1. Original squared CUDA kernel

```
__global__ void square_bc (float *in, float *out, int bc){
    int gid=(blockIdx.x*bc)*blockDim.x+(threadIdx.x*bc)
    for (int index=0; index<bc; index++)
      out[gid+index]=in[gid+index]*in[gid+index]; }
```

Listing 1.2. Block coarsened squared kernel

```
__global__ void square_tc (float *in, float *out, int tc){
    int gid=blockIdx.x*(blockDim.x*tc)+(threadIdx.x*tc)
    for (int index=0; index<tc; index++)
      out[gid+index]=in[gid+index]*in[gid+index]; }
```

Listing 1.3. Thread coarsened squared kernels

device architectures, type of kernels, input size and data types. In order to highlight the difference between these transformations and their impacts' variation through different input sizes, we apply both optimizations on syr2k, a linear algebra CUDA kernel hosted in Polybench GPU Suite [10]. Polybench initially launches syr2k kernel with 2 dimensional thread blocks with total 1024 threads each (`blockDim.x` = 32, `blockDim.y` = 32) while we apply the transformations for 1, 2, 4, 8 and 16 factors for block and thread coarsening. The final transformed kernel is evaluated for 2 different input sizes (512×512 and 1024×1024 fl. point input matrices) on a 128-core NVIDIA Maxwell GPU featured in Jetson Nano Development Kit and their experimental results are presented in Fig. 4.

It is clear, that from Fig. 4, we observe trade-offs between performance and power consumption that vary through both transformations and input sizes. More specifically, for 512×512 input matrices, all the block coarsening factors seem to improve performance and degrade power efficiency compared with the initial kernel, while thread coarsening presents a more complicated behaviour with 2, 4 and 8 TCFs to provide the most efficient solution from the performance perspective with big losses in power consumption. On the other hand, for 1024×1024 input matrices, 2, 4 and 8 BCFs seem again to boost performance by burdening the power efficiency, while thread coarsening degrades performance and improve the power for big TCFs. Finally, we clearly discover that for small and big input matrices, both of the optimization techniques deliver an improvement in performance with $\times 1.212$, $\times 1.216$, $\times 1.044$ and $\times 1.033$ speedups on Figs. 4a, 4b, 4c and 4d respectively. For the case of power, only thread coarsening transformation (for TCF = 16) delivers an optimal solution, reducing by 110 mW the initial kernel's power usage.

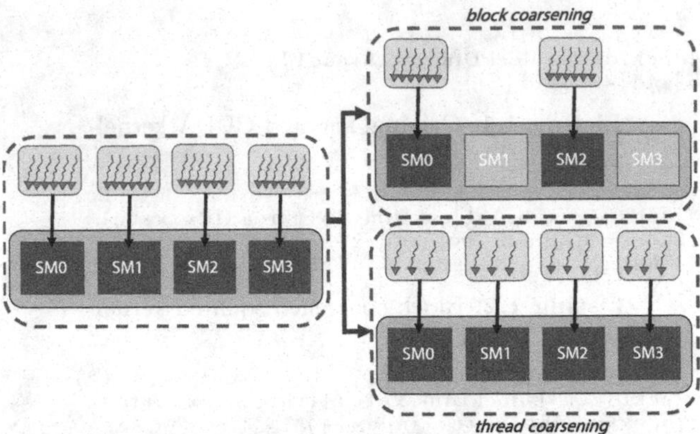

Fig. 3. Block and thread coarsening transformations from hardware perspective

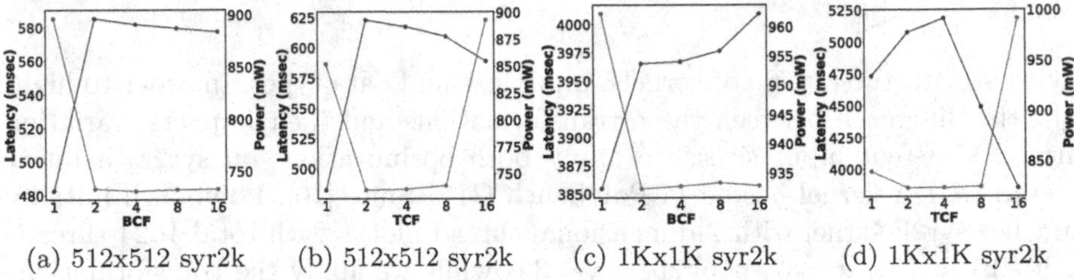

(a) 512x512 syr2k (b) 512x512 syr2k (c) 1Kx1K syr2k (d) 1Kx1K syr2k

Fig. 4. Block (a,c) and thread (b,d) coarsening's latency and power trade-offs for syr2k kernel for various input sizes on 128-core NVIDIA Maxwell GPU

3.4 Automatic Optimization Heuristics

Employing fine-tune implementations on both GPU and FPGA accelerators enables performance and power efficient executions, meeting the SERRANO's objectives set in Subsect. 2.1. However, studying optimization problems and building hand-written heuristics constitutes a time consuming and demanding task, that often leads to suboptimal solutions. Selecting and tuning manually appropriate features is a difficult task even for human experts, mainly because of the large design decisions space and its variation through different hardware devices. Hence, accurate automatic optimization heuristics are necessary for dealing with the complexity and diversity of modern hardware and software, in order to avoid time loss and inaccurate code transformations.

SERRANO aims to simplify this optimization process by building automatic machine learning heuristics able to predict optimal decisions based on representative features of unseen programs. There are several works constructing automatic heuristics for optimization of either serial or parallel programs. Wang et al. [20] use machine learning techniques to optimize applications for multi-cores, while Magni et al. [14] were the first to predict the optimal thread coarsening factor for OpenCL kernels, based on code's static features. Finally, based on their

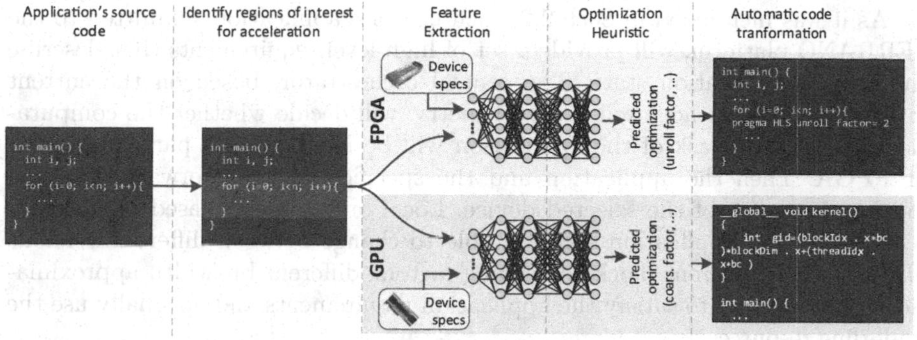

Fig. 5. Generic view of SERRANO's automatic optimization heuristic

works, Cummins et al. [6] were the first to make use of Deep learning models to automatically extract kernel's representative features to be fed to their predictive model for optimal decisions of parallel optimization problems. However, to our knowledge, there is no published work to address automatic optimization transformations as universally as SERRANO aims to do.

In contrast to previous works that build heuristics for specific optimization problems and processors, SERRANO ambitions to construct an end-to-end machine learning based heuristic to automate various applications' optimizations for both GPU and FPGA accelerators. Figure 5 gives a intuitive view of how SERRANO's model will be constructed and its several processing steps.

At first, applications' source codes are planned to be fed into the model as training inputs, where an automatic source-to-source compiler is responsible for converting them to accelerator compiler-compatible representations (CUDA and HLS for our case). Afterwards, through feature engineering, the model will extract the representative code's features in order to feed them to the model for the learning process. Finally, new unseen programs are provided to the trained model in order to automatically make its decisions about accelerators' optimizations problems and provide fine-tuned kernels in terms of both time and power requirements.

3.5 Hardware Accelerated Deployments Within SERRANO

The source-to-source transformation will provide a library of kernels for the computationally intensive tasks of each use case, targeting GPUs and/or FPGAs. Furthermore, different versions of the aforementioned kernels will be produced by applying thread/block coarsening and approximate computing techniques for the GPU and the FPGA case respectively. This library will provide several degrees of freedom to the SERRANO orchestration framework for optimally meeting the application requirements and efficiently using the underline infrastructure. This approach differentiates from former state-of-the-art orchestration schemes [13] that specify the exact resources an application requires.

As it was mentioned in Sect. 2.2, each use case application submitted to the SERRANO platform, will provide a set of high level requirements that describe the desired application state. The central orchestrator, based on the current infrastructure state acquired from telemetry, will decide whether the computationally intensive task of the application will be mapped on a particular GPU or FPGA. Then the application and the specifications are forwarded to the local orchestrator of the selected device. Local orchestrator, based on the current device and application state, is able to change between different versions of this kernel (different block coarsening factors, different bit-width approximations etc.) in order to satisfy the application requirements and optimally use the underline resources.

4 Conclusions and Future Work

In this work, we presented an overview of the SERRANO H2020 project, focusing on the efficient deployment of HW accelerated kernels on the edge-cloud computing continuum. SERRANO aims to create an abstraction layer that will fully exploit the available hardware resources and automate/orchestrate their use. The overall hardware acceleration will be performed in a holistic and automated manner overcoming the existing platform barriers stemming from the heterogeneity of computing units. The efficient utilization of accelerators in both edge and cloud applications will significantly improve the performance and power efficiency of the target workloads while at the same time novel transprecision computing mechanisms will be exploited to examine the accuracy versus resource or speed tradeoffs. Finally, as a future work, SERRANO aims to develop new key concepts and approaches to cloud infrastructures that aim to close existing technology gaps and aspires to have strong innovation potential in a wide number of real-world applications from different markets.

References

1. Gartner Forecasts Worldwide Public Cloud End-User Spending in 2021. https://www.gartner.com/en/newsroom/press-releases/2021-04-21-gartner-forecasts-worldwide-public-cloud-end-user-spending-to-grow-23-percent-in-2021. Accessed 6 Oct 2021
2. The Future of Cloud Computing: Why businesses opt for cloud. https://innovecs.com/blog/future-of-cloud-computing/. Accessed 10 Oct 2021
3. Vitis platform. https://www.xilinx.com/products/design-tools/vitis/vitis-platform.html
4. Xilinx. https://www.xilinx.com/
5. Cong, J., Liu, B., Neuendorffer, S., Noguera, J., Vissers, K., Zhang, Z.: High-level synthesis for FPGAS: From prototyping to deployment. IEEE Trans. Comput.-Aid. Des. Integr. Circ. Syst. **30**(4), 473–491 (2011)
6. Cummins, C., Petoumenos, P., Wang, Z., Leather, H.: End-to-end deep learning of optimization heuristics. In: 2017 26th International Conference on Parallel Architectures and Compilation Techniques (PACT), pp. 219–232. IEEE (2017)

7. Danopoulos, D., Kachris, C., Soudris, D.: A Quantitative Comparison for Image Recognition on Accelerated Heterogeneous Cloud Infrastructures, pp. 171–189 (2019). https://doi.org/10.1201/9780429399602-8
8. Danopoulos, D., Kachris, C., Soudris, D.: FPGA acceleration of approximate KNN indexing on high- dimensional vectors. In: 2019 14th International Symposium on Reconfigurable Communication-centric Systems-on-Chip (ReCoSoC), pp. 59–65 (2019). https://doi.org/10.1109/ReCoSoC48741.2019.9034938
9. Finnerty, A., Ratigner, H.: Reduce power and cost by converting from floating point to fixed point. WP491 (v1. 0) (2017)
10. Grauer-Gray, S., Xu, L., Searles, R., Ayalasomayajula, S., Cavazos, J.: Auto-tuning a high-level language targeted to GPU codes. In: 2012 innovative parallel computing (InPar), pp. 1–10. IEEE (2012)
11. Ko, J.H., Fromm, J., Philipose, M., Tashev, I., Zarar, S.: Precision scaling of neural networks for efficient audio processing. arXiv preprint arXiv:1712.01340 (2017)
12. Koliogeorgi, K., Zervakis, G., Anagnostos, D., Zompakis, N., Siozios, K.: Optimizing SVM classifier through approximate and high level synthesis techniques. In: 2019 8th International Conference on Modern Circuits and Systems Technologies (MOCAST), pp. 1–4. IEEE (2019)
13. Kouris, A., Venieris, S.I., Bouganis, C.S.: Towards efficient on-board deployment of DNNS on intelligent autonomous systems. In: 2019 IEEE Computer Society Annual Symposium on VLSI (ISVLSI), pp. 568–573. IEEE (2019)
14. Magni, A., Dubach, C., O'Boyle, M.: Automatic optimization of thread-coarsening for graphics processors. In: Proceedings of the 23rd International Conference on Parallel Architectures and Compilation, pp. 455–466 (2014)
15. Markidis, S., Der Chien, S.W., Laure, E., Peng, I.B., Vetter, J.S.: Nvidia tensor core programmability, performance & precision. In: 2018 IEEE International Parallel and Distributed Processing Symposium Workshops (IPDPSW), pp. 522–531. IEEE (2018)
16. Sidiroglou-Douskos, S., Misailovic, S., Hoffmann, H., Rinard, M.: Managing performance vs. accuracy trade-offs with loop perforation. In: Proceedings of the 19th ACM SIGSOFT Symposium and the 13th European Conference on Foundations of Software Engineering, pp. 124–134 (2011)
17. Sinha, S., Zhang, W.: Low-power FPGA design using memoization-based approximate computing. IEEE Trans. Very Large Scale Integr. (VLSI) Syst. **24**(8), 2665–2678 (2016)
18. Stanley-Marbell, P., et al.: Exploiting errors for efficiency: a survey from circuits to applications. ACM Comput. Surv. (CSUR) **53**(3), 1–39 (2020)
19. Tziantzioulis, G., Hardavellas, N., Campanoni, S.: Temporal approximate function memoization. IEEE Micro. **38**(4), 60–70 (2018)
20. Wang, Z., O'Boyle, M.F.: Partitioning streaming parallelism for multi-cores: a machine learning based approach. In: Proceedings of the 19th International Conference on Parallel Architectures and Compilation Techniques, pp. 307–318 (2010)

Cross-domain Modelling of Verification and Validation Workflows in the Large Scale European Research Project VALU3S
Invited Paper

Thomas Bauer[1(✉)], Joseba A. Agirre[2], David Fürcho[3], Wolfgang Herzner[4], Bob Hruška[5], Mustafa Karaca[6], David Pereira[7], José Proença[7], Rupert Schlick[4], Robert Sicher[5], Aleš Smrčka[8], Ugur Yayan[6], and Behrooz Sangchoolie[9]

[1] Fraunhofer IESE, Kaiserslautern, Germany
thomas.bauer@iese.fraunhofer.de
[2] Mondragon University, Arrasate-Mondragón, Spain
jaagirre@mondragon.edu
[3] NXP Semiconductors, Hamburg, Germany
davidchristian.furcho@nxp.com
[4] AIT Austrian Institute of Technology, Vienna, Austria
{wolfgang.herzner,rupert.schlick}@ait.ac.at
[5] Lieber Lieber, Vienna, Austria
{bob.hruska,robert.sicher}@lieberlieber.com
[6] Inovasyon Muhendislik Ltd. Sti., Eskisehir, Turkey
{mustafa.karaca,ugur.yayan}@inovasyonmuhendislik.com
[7] ISEP, Porto, Portugal
{drp,pro}@isep.ipp.pt
[8] Brno University of Technology, Brno, Czech Republic
smrcka@fit.vutbr.cz
[9] RISE Research Institutes of Sweden, Gothenburg, Sweden
behrooz.sangchoolie@ri.se

Abstract. The complexity of systems continues to increase rapidly, especially due to the multi-level integration of subsystems from different domains into cyber-physical systems. This results in special challenges for the efficient verification and validation (V&V) of these systems with regard to their requirements and properties. In order to tackle the new challenges and improve the quality assurance processes, the V&V workflows have to be documented and analyzed. In this paper, a novel approach for the workflow modelling of V&V activities is presented. The generic approach is tailorable to different industrial domains and their specific constraints, V&V methods, and toolchains. The outcomes comprise a dedicated modelling notation (VVML) and tool-support using the modelling framework Enterprise Architect for the efficient documentation and implementation of workflows in the use cases. The solution enables the design of re-usable workflow assets such as V&V activities and artifacts that are exchanged between workflows. This work is part

© Springer Nature Switzerland AG 2022
A. Orailoglu et al. (Eds.): SAMOS 2021, LNCS 13227, pp. 368–382, 2022.
https://doi.org/10.1007/978-3-031-04580-6_25

of the large scale European research project VALU3S that deals with the improvement and evaluation of V&V processes in different technical domains, focusing on safety, cybersecurity, and privacy properties.

Keywords: Verification and validation · Safety · Cybersecurity · Privacy · Automated systems · V&V workflows · V&V tool chains

1 Introduction

In complex software-intensive systems, analytical quality assurance activities, especially verification and validation (V&V), on different levels have become crucial for achieving high product quality. The resulting systems have to fulfill a wide range of stakeholder requirements. Depending on the concrete properties to be assessed and the domain of the system being developed, different V&V methods and tools are applied. The underlying V&V process plays a key role for the efficiency of the quality assurance strategy and its implementation as a tool chain in the project. Workflows of the V&V activities have to consider multiple aspects of the development and quality assurance process. V&V workflows are closely linked to the requirements and constraints of the corresponding projects and use cases, as well as the V&V framework, methods and tools that are used.

The remainder of the paper is structured as follows: The VALU3S project with its objectives is introduced in Sect. 2. Section 3 summarizes goals and first results of the different work packages in the project. The workflow modelling approaches with its notation and tool-support is introduced in Sect. 4. Finally, Sect. 5 summarizes the main conclusions.

2 The VALU3S Project

The ECSEL JU (Joint Undertaking) project VALU3S focuses on the V&V of cyber-physical automated systems with respect to safety, cybersecurity and privacy (SCP) requirements. The project aims at the design and implementation of V&V methods, tools and tool chains that reduce the time and effort needed to assure the SCP requirements [1,2]. The main assets of the project and the correlating work package (WP) numbers are illustrated in Fig. 1.

This paper reports on the current status of the activities connected to creation and detailing of V&V workflows. VALU3S also aims to create and evaluate a multi-domain verification and validation framework, which facilitates the evaluation of automated systems from component level to system level. This way, the project provides practitioners with detailed information about all components involved in the V&V process. Such information is then used to facilitate the V&V process through the identification of V&V tools, concepts and processes used in different application domains targeted by the project. These domains are *automotive*, *agriculture*, *railway*, *healthcare*, *aerospace*, and *industrial robotics*.

In order to ensure and show the broad applicability of the results (framework, improved methods and tools, etc.), demonstrators will be built from the 13 use cases selected in the project from the target domains.

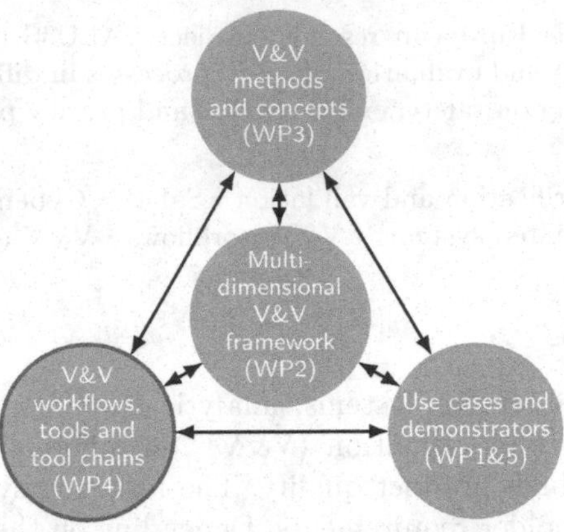

Fig. 1. VALU3S project assets

2.1 Project Objectives

The high-level objective of the project is to design, implement and evaluate state-of-the-art V&V methods and tools that reduce the time and cost needed to verify and validate automated systems with respect to SCP requirements. In order to achieve this objective, the following sub-objectives are defined and are planned to be followed-up on during the execution of the project:

- *Objective 1.* To develop a Multi-layered framework enabling more effective verification and validation
- *Objective 2.* To overcome the SCP gaps and limitations of cyber-physical systems
- *Objective 3.* To present a novel, standards compliant V&V workflow that is generic to reference methods in selected cyber-physical domains
- *Objective 4.* To demonstrate, verify and validate the usefulness and wider acceptance of the proposed framework by realistic pilots
- *Objective 5.* To suggest and validate new as well as state-of-the-art evaluation scenarios for safety, cybersecurity and privacy evaluation
- *Objective 6.* To develop and improve V&V tools and evaluation criteria
- *Objective 7.* To revisit and identify the weaknesses of relevant safety and security standards and develop a concrete strategy to influence the development of new standards
- *Objective 8.* To present guidelines for end users and practitioners as well as to disseminate the project results aiming to increase the awareness on the importance of conducting SCP V&V.

Note that multiple KPIs (key performance indicators) have also been defined to facilitate the monitoring of obtaining the project objectives. Nine of the KPIs defined are used to monitor the project's progress from the technical point of view, while multiple other KPIs are defined to monitor the project's impact through conducting dissemination (8 KPIs), exploitation (7 KPIs), standardisation (1 KPI), and communication (8 KPIs) activities.

3 Project Structure and Work Packages

VALU3S is structured into six technical work packages and one management work package. The following sub-sections describe goals and first results from technical work packages, covering the industrial use cases, the multi-dimensional framework, the V&V method library, the systematic evaluation, and the dissemination and exploitation activities.

3.1 Industrial Use Cases in VALU3S

In WP1, 13 use cases were described in detail, covering all six domains of *automotive*, *agriculture*, *railway*, *healthcare*, *aerospace*, and *industrial robotics*. Some domains include a single use case (e.g., *Aircraft engine controller* in the domain of *aerospace*), while others have multiple (e.g., *Intelligent Traffic Surveillance*, *Car Teleoperation*, *Radar system for ADAS* in the *automotive* domain).

For each use case, several evaluation scenarios, SCP requirements, and test cases were defined and collected in repositories: The evaluation scenarios encompass a high-level classification of the underlying test requirements and a description of what needs to be evaluated and why. The SCP test requirements define a required behavior of a system in a corresponding scenario and will be the basis the systems and demonstrators will later be verified and validated against. The test cases are derived from the evaluation scenarios and test requirements and describe how a test of a certain scenario should be conducted, with regard to safety, cybersecurity and privacy requirements.

The test cases were then mapped on the multi-dimensional framework that was developed in WP2. The test case descriptions were expanded to include references to other framework elements, namely the V&V methods to be used (previously defined in WP3), the components that are tested, and relevant evaluation criteria (as defined in WP5).

In total 57 evaluation scenarios, 239 requirements, and 192 test cases were defined in WP1. To find similarities and possibly synergies between scenarios, requirements, and test cases, a commonality evaluation was conducted, identifying common points across all use cases. This plays an important part in the establishment of a real multi-domain V&V framework and will be taken advantage of during the demonstrator implementation.

3.2 Multi-dimensional V&V Framework

The main objective of WP2 is to create a multi-dimensional layered framework for V&V of automated systems with respect to SCP requirements. The framework will be represented as a web-based repository where all elements of the framework will be stored. Taking as input the VALU3S framework, the Web repository is intended to serve as a searchable catalogue of V&V methods applicable to specific domains and application scenarios. The repository is planned to be updated throughout the course of the project to take into account all the outputs of the project. To this end, the first step is to design a multi-dimensional framework defining a clear structure around the components and elements needed to conduct V&V processes through identification and classification of evaluation methods, tools, environments and concepts that are required to verify and validate automated systems with respect to SCP requirements. The second step is to develop a web repository based in the multi-dimensional framework to store the V&V information created by each of the Use Cases and tasks of VALU3S project. The last step of WP2 is to populate the web repository with the information regarding V&V activities carried out in the project. The Web repository will be populated with the test cases and requirements specification detailed in WP1, V&V methods in WP3, V&V tools identified and developed in WP4 and the evaluation results of the V&V process in WP5. The repository will store also main WP outputs such as V&V methods, processes and tools.

The framework specifies which data related with each V&V activity must be collected and defines the data format. Through a structured classification of the components required for the V&V of automated systems, the framework provides practitioners with detailed information about all components involved in the V&V process. That information facilitates the V&V process through identification of state-of-the-art V&V methods, tools and processes used in different domains, as well as the application of those methods to use cases. The framework is therefore a key instrument to achieve the main objective of the project, which is the design and development of V&V methods and tools that shorten time and lower cost of V&V processes. In order to describe the design and structure of the V&V multi-dimensional framework, a meta-model as a UML class diagram has been created with the V&V methods as its central elements. These methods are categorized using the dimensions, by means of many-to-one and many-to-many relationships between the V&V method entity and the various dimensions. The framework currently has 8 dimensions and is also layered as the evaluation process may include multiple alternatives to choose from in each of the dimensions, see Fig. 2.

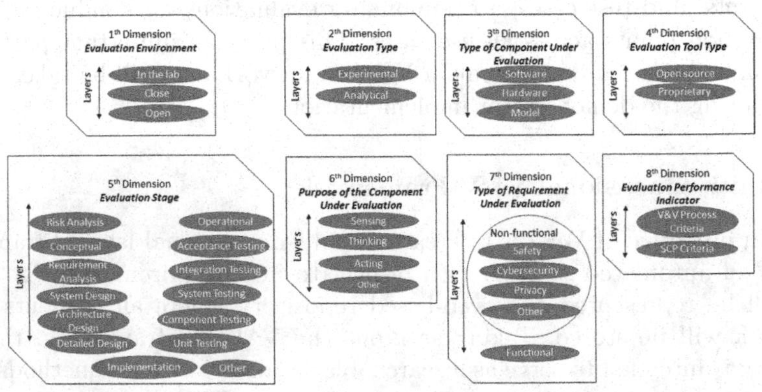

Fig. 2. VALU3S multi-dimensional layered framework

3.3 V&V Method Library

In the project WP3 focuses on developing new methods, method improvements, and innovative combinations of methods for V&V. In a first step, fifty-three V&V methods have been identified, described and characterised [3]. The methods fall into the following (not strictly disjoint) categories:

1. *Injection*: introducing some phenomenon in a system to analyse its response.
2. *Simulation*: studying the behaviour of a model of a system.
3. *Testing*: checking system execution under certain conditions before operation
4. *Runtime verification*: evaluating system execution during operation.
5. *Formal analysis*: for V&V methods with a mathematical basis.
6. *Semi-formal analysis*: for V&V methods that exploit some structured means but without a full mathematical basis.
7. *Informal analysis*: for V&V methods that do not follow any predefined structure or have mathematical basis.

They were analysed for improvement potential from two directions: a) known limitations and weaknesses of the methods and b) needs of the use cases that are currently not sufficiently addressed by the methods. This analysis led to a set of 400 gaps that could be addressed. The gaps fall into one of nine types: Functionality, Accuracy, Scalability, Deployment, Learning Curve, Reference Environment, Costs, Lack of Automation, and Standards. Figure 3 shows the distribution of gaps over these gap types and over the method categories.

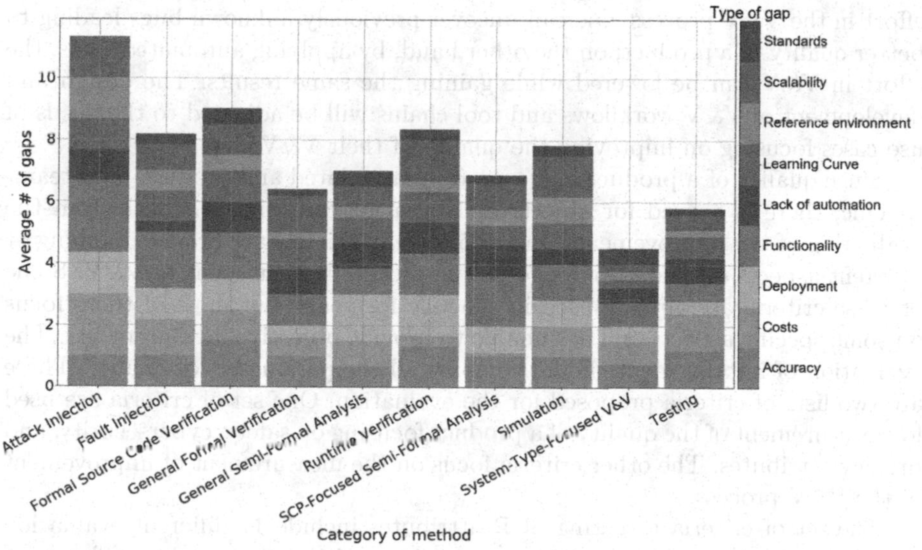

Fig. 3. Identified gap types distributed over method categories

Realistically, only a sub-set of gaps will be successfully solved, but a first collection of planned method improvements and new method combinations already led to sketches for 37 method improvements and 4 new method combinations, addressing 145 of the gaps. The methods and their implementations into tools form the building blocks for the V&V work-flows blocks. But there are also method-internal flows that need to be documented and communicated.

3.4 Demonstration and Evaluation

The VALU3S project is use case driven which means that improvement in engineering processes, especially their V&V parts, is motivated by real problems from industry and will be demonstrated on real development and verification and validation. Some of the designed V&V workflows or their parts will be shared by several use cases targeting some commonalities among them. The commonalities are either in the same domain, namely but not limited to detecting objects using radar in traffic surveillance and in an ADAS system, or across domains like remote control of a car (automotive domain) or a robot (agriculture domain). These workflows can share the same V&V approach using the same toolchain. On the other hand, there is also diversity in engineering processes which comes from different product-specific requirements, the size of engineering team, and/or the team's level of expertise of V&V methods. Improvement of V&V can be achieved by different ways following different V&V workflows.

Improvement of V&V can directly target the quality of developed product and/or the quality of used process to create the product. These two approaches are closely related. By utilising a new verification method which will require more effort in the V&V process, one can uncover previously unknown bugs leading to better quality of a product; on the other hand, by applying automated tools, the effort in V&V can be lowered while gaining the same results. The design and development of V&V workflows and tool chains will be adjusted to the needs of use cases focusing on improving the quality of their V&V.

Since quality of a product and a process are related and product- and team-specific, there is a need for objective criteria for collecting feedback from the evaluation of the improvements. In WP5, several criteria are provided aiming at different aspects of quality of a product and overall effort spent in V&V. Some of these criteria are already used in practice for years, but most of them focus on some specific aspects and are unable to provide objective measurements. The evaluation of improvement should combine all the parameters of quality. There are two lists of criteria proposed for the evaluation. One set of criteria are used for measurement of the quality of a product focusing on safety, cybersecurity, and privacy attributes. The other criteria focus on the measurement of improvement of the V&V process.

The set of criteria targeting SCP attributes include 17 different evaluation criteria, each of which uses different metrics or items to measure. The most commonly used criterion is the number or ratio of fulfilled product requirements in VALU3S, the criterion is used or planned to be used by 9 out of 13 use cases.

There are also 7 completely new criteria previously not documented or defined before.

The set of criteria used for measurement of a V&V process includes 13 evaluation criteria. The most commonly used criterion in practice focuses on the workforce needed for the engineering phases (overall 7 use cases in VALU3S). There are 4 new criteria focusing on time, cost, and effort spent on V&V processes directly or indirectly (see Table 1).

Table 1. Overview of new evaluation criteria

Evaluation criteria for SCP	Evaluation criteria for V&V process
Likelihood of faults and attacks Potential impact of incidents and attacks Reliability measures of decisions Number of attack/incident typologies examined Accuracy of simulated sensor output Simulator environment quality Simulator environment functionality	Time of test execution Joint management of SCP requirements Reduced cost and time for work on certification process and functional safety Workforce required to the user for preparation and running the tool

3.5 Dissemination, Exploitation, and Standardization

WP6 of the project is concerned with ensuring that the work and results of VALU3S are properly conveyed to the target stakeholders and audiences, which include industry and academia members who work on the V&V of automated systems, and standardization bodies that can benefit from the project's outcomes. For that, the several tasks of the work package have planned and defined the necessary activities focused on dissemination, training, exploitation, standardization, and communication that will guarantee the aimed impact of VALU3S' results. The implementation of the plans has already made considerable progresses and the first outcomes are described below.

In terms of *dissemination and training*, the main activities were concerned with the implementation of the internal communication channels, the definition of publication rules, processes, KPIs, and the monitoring of dissemination actions. In terms of training, two training sessions consisting of 11 presentations covering various V&V methods identified and classified under the activities of work package 3 have been organized (the videos of the presentations were made publicly available in the project's YouTube channel [16]).

In what concerns *exploitation*, most of the effort has been directed towards the collection of the necessary information that facilitates identification of exploitable results, the means of exploiting these results, the target stakeholders, and establish the plans to implement the exploitation strategy. To measure the effectiveness of the actions performed within the project, KPIs have been defined for that purpose.

In the context of *standardization*, the focus was given to standards and standardization initiatives related to the work in VALU3S. For that purpose, a survey was designed based on a list of initially identified standards with the objective of collecting further relevant standards and start the evaluation of relevant methods, tools and approaches related to the work planned for the project. After a detailed analysis, a set of initial standards have been defined as the primary focus of the project.

Finally, for *communication* purposes, the focus was given to relevant actions like implementing blog articles with high-level technical content, production of communication materials and, importantly, setting up and triggering the actions for the creation of liaisons with other related R&D projects in order to maximize the impact of dissemination and communication activities. Communication in the project's social media channels has also been a key activity that includes regular posts of partners profiles, announcement of new project publications, and also videos related to activities in the project.

4 Modelling of Verification and Validation Workflows

The efficient conduction of software development and quality assurance activities in complex projects require their systematic description and modelling including their sub-activities, execution steps, and work products that they process and produce and the provision of appropriate tool support for executing the activities. In WP4, a generic V&V workflow design approach and modelling language has been developed to allow tool-supported and highly automated instantiation to specific industrial use cases and implementation as concrete tool chains. The solution have paved the way towards the efficient evaluation and optimization of V&V workflows and tool chains for specific quality properties. The activity has been performed in close cooperation with the V&V method library to support the systematic description, extension, and gap analysis of V&V methods. The following sub-sections give a general introduction into workflows, the project requirements for V&V workflows, and the VALU3S solution assets with the VVML modelling notations and the tool-support for workflow modelling.

4.1 Introduction into Workflow Modelling

A process workflow is an orchestrated and repeatable pattern of activities, enabled by the systematic organization of resources into processes that provide services or process information. It consists of sequences of operations and supports a user task [13]. Process workflows refer to a series of activities or tasks that need to be completed sequentially or in parallel to achieve a business outcome. Process management is about how to create, edit and analyse predictable processes that improve the core of a business.

Basically, a workflow is a sequence of tasks that processes a set of data. Any time data is exchanged between systems and humans, a workflow can be defined. In general, the process is non-variant and proceeds in a sequence determined by actions or pre-defined business rules. In a standard workflow, with the automation of procedures where documents, information or tasks are passed between participants according to a defined set of rules, an overall business goal is aimed to be achieved. In the VALU3S project, a V&V workflow is understood as a reusable V&V activity pattern.

4.2 Workflow Modelling Notations

The application of process workflows for software and systems engineering activities with dedicated models and notations started in the late 1990s s with the introduction BPMN [5] and adaptations of behavior models in standardized modelling languages like UML activity diagrams [6].

BPMN is a graphical illustration of business processes which aims to provide easy and understandable notations for different user groups including business analysts, technical developers, and business managers. It has become part of the OMG standards [5]. BPMN defines workflows with specific patterns and so-called Business Process Diagrams.

UML is a general purpose-modelling language, which is popularly used in software engineering for specifying, visualizing, constructing, and documenting artifacts in software applications [6]. UML provide various notations for representing behavior including Activity Diagrams, which enables the description of sequential and parallel flows of activities.

In given notation formats, BPMN and UML are commonly used in process modelling. There are some differences between BPMN and UML in diagramming the sequence pattern. Both notations use rounded rectangles in activities and utilize directed lines to show the direction of flow [14]. However, UML is a general-purpose visual modelling language that is more than a visual notation tool. BPMN is a modelling notation which aims to be easily understood by all business users [15].

In given modelling languages, it is possible to represent the same workflow in many ways. While flexibility of the modelling notations offer variety of solutions, not each individual is expert in these modelling languages or notations. For the workflow modelling notation, specific requirements and constraints from V&V process stakeholders have been collected in the project:

- simple and clear notation, i.e., providing few element types and few diagrams
- based on behavior modelling approaches in software engineering
- implementable in state of the practice modelling frameworks
- exchange of artifacts between V&V methods
- decomposition of V&V methods as implementation of sequences of lower level activities, which enable the stepwise production of output artifacts
- composition of methods to higher level methods
- preparation for automated and tool-supported analysis of V&V workflows

The generic workflow modelling notations from the previous subsection do not completely fulfill the requirements listed above. Therefore, a novel modelling notation based on a domain-specific language that represents the V&V perspective has been developed.

4.3 Tool-Support for Workflow Modelling with Enterprise Architect

In order to facilitate the application of the modelling approach, tool-support has been provided using the Enterprise Architect (EA), a UML modelling tool by Sparx Systems [4]. In EA, new modelling languages can be created with UML-Profiles, which can be used directly afterwards or can be packaged into an MDG (Model Driven Generation) Technology for more comfortable use. MDG Technologies seamlessly plug into Enterprise Architect to provide additional toolboxes, diagrams, UML profiles, shape scripts, patterns, tagged values and other modelling resources. Such an MDG technology, automatically generates a list of elements and relationships in the Diagram Toolbox, for each of the diagram within the technology, therefore implementing the V&V framework using the MDG Technology rapidly decreases the effort and simplifies the modelling of V&V workflows for VALU3S. EA provides a simple user-friendly interface for modelling of V&V workflows by specially customized diagram types enabling modelling workflow with V&V methods, V&V work products, sequential control flows, quasi parallel control flows, and flow of work products.

4.4 The VVML Modelling Language

In modelling languages such as UML, it is possible to represent the same idea in many ways. While the flexibility that the language has offers its positive aspects, it also brings problems in communicating ideas effectively. By creating a dedicated domain specific language (DSL) that clearly specifies what diagrams and elements can be used in creating a V&V method definition or its workflow, everyone follows a common standardized notation. Modelling V&V workflows falls into a specialized domain that requires a tailored modelling approach for activity models. To meet such requirements, there is a need to develop a UML profile for V&V Modelling Language - shortly VVML profile - introducing a set of model constructs and deploy the UML profile with other extension mechanisms as a modelling framework enabling rapid modelling of V&V workflows. Two levels of modelling are considered:

1. V&V Method Specification
2. V&V Workflow Definition

V&V Method Definition. The V&V method definition enables the design of the base elements of the workflow. It provides an overview of the main V&V method properties such as name, interfaces, artifacts, and constraints. Three element types *Method*, *Artifact*, and *MethodArtifact* are defined (see Fig. 4).

The modelling element *Method* is a unit that represents a process workflow dedicated to a specific V&V phase. It has a defined method type, which is currently used to represent the automation level, here: automated, semi-automated, or manual. The type *Artifact* is an object that is exchanged between methods or activities within methods. It has a dedicated type. An *Artifact* is either an information object or an active unit, i.e., program code or executable. Every

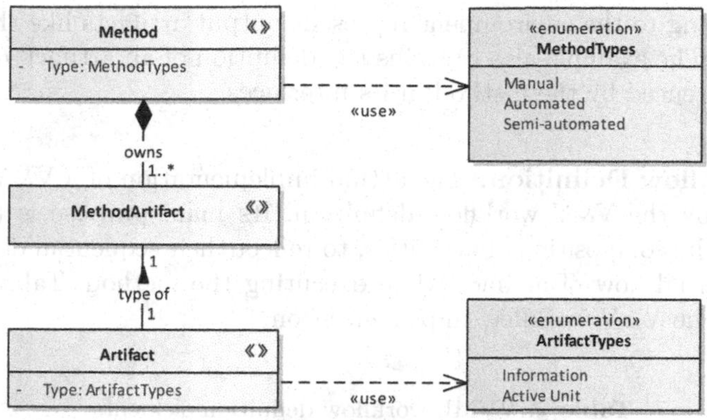

Fig. 4. VVML modelling elements

Method owns a set of *MethodArtifacts*, which represent the method interfaces for the *Artifacts* that they consume or produce. A *Method* shall produce at least one output *Artifact* to show the external use of the *Method*. The meta-model for three main element types of VVML is shown in Fig. 4.

An example for a V&V method definition with its artifacts and interfaces using the EA profile is given in Fig. 5.

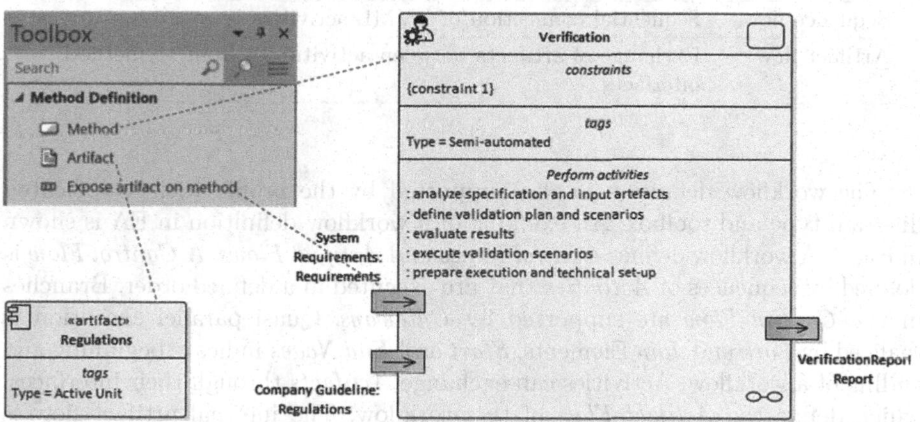

Fig. 5. VVML sample method definition

The EA profile provides a dedicated toolbox for designing new elements, i.e., methods, artifacts, and method interfaces. The method is represented by a yellow box with its name, constraints, tags, and sub-activities. Additionally, the method artifacts as input and output interfaces are annotated as red rectangles with arrows. Interfaces with arrows pointing to the method correspond to inputs such as *Requirements* and *Regulations* in the example. Interfaces with arrows pointing to the environment represent output artifacts like the *Verification Report*. The example also contains the definition of an artifact *Regulations*, which is referenced by the method in its interfaces.

V&V Workflow Definition. The actual implementation of a V&V Workflow is specified by the V&V workflow definition. Its main purpose is to organize and specify the composition of activities, to reflect their sequential dependencies and the internal flow of artifact while executing the method. Table 2 presents elements of the V&V workflow implementation.

Table 2. VVML workflow definition elements

Element	Decription
Start workflow	Node that initiates the beginning of a workflow
Stop workflow	Node that indicates the end of a workflow
Activity	Atomic action that is not further decomposed into steps
Call behavior	Invocation of another method, which is further decomposed in another method workflow diagram
Activity artifact	Activity interface for its input and output artifacts
Gateway	Branching of sequence flow based on condition
Fork/Join	Enables parallel sub-paths of sequence and artifact flows
Sequence flow	Sequential connection of VVML activities
Artifact flow	Exchange of artifacts between activities or from/to method interfaces

The workflow definition is also supported by the profile with a dedicated diagram type and toolbox. An example of a workflow definition in EA is shown in Fig. 6. A workflow defines *Control Flows* and *Artifact Flows*. A *Control Flow* is defined by sequences of *Activities* that are executed in a defined order. Branches in the *Control Flow* are supported by *Gateways*. Quasi parallel execution is realized by *Fork* and *Join* Elements. *Start* and *End Nodes* indicate beginning and ending of a workflow. Activities can exchange *Artifacts* through their interfaces, which define the *Artifact Flow* of the workflow. The internal artifact flow is defined between activities, whereas the external artifact flow is defined from the method interfaces to the activities for method inputs or from the activities to the method interfaces for method outputs. In the example, two method inputs (*Requirements* and *Regulations)* are internally processed and one method output (*VerificationReport*) is provided to the environment.

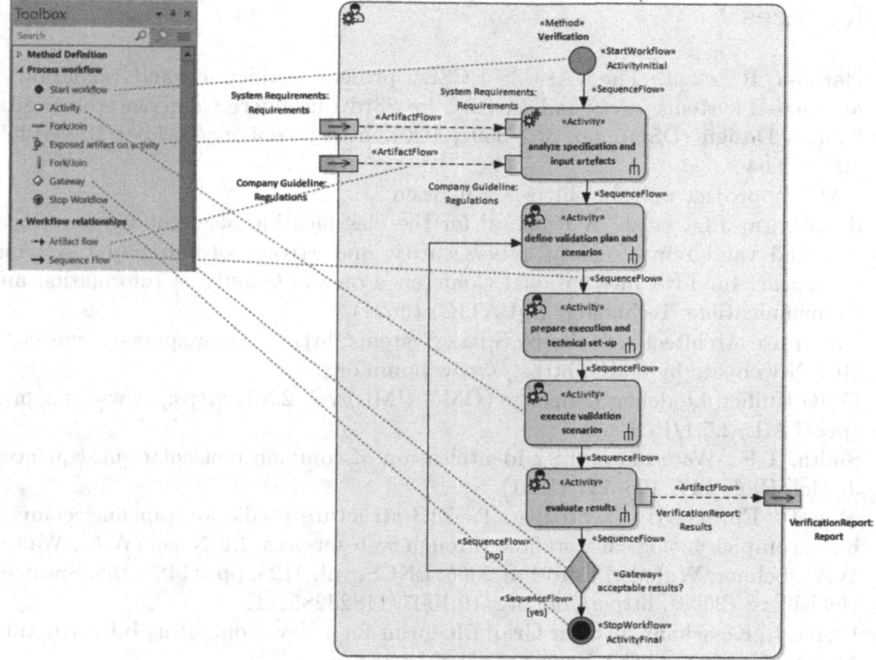

Fig. 6. VVML sample workflow

5 Conclusion

In this paper, the VALU3S ECSEL JU project is presented with its structure and first outcomes of the different work packages, covering the industrial use cases, the multi-domain V&V framework, the V&V methods, workflows and tool chains, the evaluation and demonstration approach, and the dissemination and exploitation activities. The modelling approach of the verification and validation activities is described in detail with its modelling notation VVML and the tool-support using the Enterprise Architect framework. The two levels of VVML are presented. The first one covers the base elements: methods, artifacts, and method interfaces. The second level enables the definition of workflows with sequences of activities and internal artifacts flows.

Acknowledgments. We would like to thank all VALU3S partners for the contributions and feedback. The research leading to this paper has received funding from the ECSEL Joint Undertaking (JU) under grant agreement No 876852. The JU receives support from the European Union's Horizon 2020 research and innovation programme and Austria, Czech Republic, Germany, Ireland, Italy, Portugal, Spain, Sweden, Turkey. The views expressed in this document are the sole responsibility of the authors and do not necessarily reflect the views or position of the European Commission.

References

1. Barbosa, R., et al.: The VALU3S ECSEL project: verification and validation of automated systems safety and security. In: 23rd Euromicro Conference on Digital System Design (DSD), pp. 352–359 (2020). https://doi.org/10.1109/DSD51259.2020.00064
2. VALU3S project web-site. https://valu3s.eu
3. de la Vara, J.L., et al.: A Proposal for the classification of methods for verification and validation of safety, cybersecurity, and privacy of automated systems, to appear. In: 14th International Conference on the Quality of Information and Communications Technology (QUATIC) (2021)
4. Enterprise Architect web-site by Sparx Systems. https://www.sparxsystems.eu/
5. BPMN web-site by OMG. https://www.bpmn.org/
6. OMG Unified Modeling Language (OMG UML) vol. 2.5.1. https://www.omg.org/spec/UML/2.5.1/PDF
7. Smith, T.F., Waterman, M.S.: Identification of common molecular subsequences. J. Mol. Biol. **147**, 195–197 (1981)
8. May, P., Ehrlich, H.-C., Steinke, T.: ZIB structure prediction pipeline: composing a complex biological workflow through web services. In: Nagel, W.E., Walter, W.V., Lehner, W. (eds.) Euro-Par 2006. LNCS, vol. 4128, pp. 1148–1158. Springer, Heidelberg (2006). https://doi.org/10.1007/11823285_121
9. Foster, I., Kesselman, C.: The Grid: Blueprint for a New Computing Infrastructure. Morgan Kaufmann, San Francisco (1999)
10. Czajkowski, K., Fitzgerald, S., Foster, I., Kesselman, C.: Grid information services for distributed resource sharing. In: 10th IEEE International Symposium on High Performance Distributed Computing, pp. 181–184. IEEE Press, New York (2001)
11. Foster, I., Kesselman, C., Nick, J., Tuecke, S.: The Physiology of the Grid: an Open Grid Services Architecture for Distributed Systems Integration. Technical report, Global Grid Forum (2002)
12. National Center for Biotechnology Information. http://www.ncbi.nlm.nih.gov
13. Georgakopoulos, D., Hornick, M., Sheth, A.: An overview of workflow management: from process modeling to workflow automation infrastructure. Distrib. Parallel Databases **3**(2), 119–153 (1995)
14. Khillar, S.: Difference Between UML and BPMN — Difference Between. [online] Differencebetween.net (2021). http://www.differencebetween.net/technology/difference-between-uml-and-bpmn/. Accessed 7 Apr 2021
15. Oliveira, B., Belo, O.: BPMN patterns for ETL conceptual modelling and validation. Found. Intell. Syst. **445–454** (2012). https://doi.org/10.1007/978-3-642-34624-8_50
16. VALU3S Consortium. VALU3S YouTube Channel. https://www.youtube.com/channel/UCBvhaW8hkWgopiJWbFBrIFQ/videos

Special Session on Next Generation Computing

Hardware/Software Co-Design of an Automatically Generated Analog NN

Roland Müller, Maximilian Oppelt, Bijoy Kundu, Bangalore Ramesh Akshay Agashe, Thomas Thönes, Elmar Herzer, Claudia Schuhmann, Soumitro Chakrabarty, Christian Kroos, and Loreto Mateu(✉)

Fraunhofer IIS, Am Wolfsmantel 33, Erlangen 91058, Germany
loreto.mateu@iis.fraunhofer.de
http://www.iis.fraunhofer.de/de/ff/kom/ki/neuromorphic.html

Abstract. This paper presents a partial automated workflow for a hardware and software co-design used to generate analog convolutional neural networks. The developed workflow provides an automated generation of the schematic and layout of analog neural networks itself as well as the verification of the created circuit with an automated simulation setup. The designed application-specific integrated circuit (ASIC) has an energy consumption of 450 nJ (235 nJ for the frontend and 215 nJ for the neural network) and needs 369 µs (362 µs for the front-end and 7 µs for the neural network) per inference.

Keywords: Neuromorphic computing · Analog computing · Hardware and software co-design · Workflow · Integrated circuits · Analog synthesis

1 Introduction

The workflow presented in this paper has been used for an ASIC design in the 22FDX technology of Globalfoundries, which consists of a mixed-signal frontend and an analog neural network [1–3]. It was implemented for the "Pilotinnovationswettbewerb KI-Energieeffizients System" [4] in the KI-Sprung_ADELIA project. The aim of the project was the classification of two minutes electrocardiogram (ECG) data with an energy efficient system based on artificial intelligence.

This paper focuses in describing the hardware/software co-design workflow developed for the automatically generation of the analog convolutional neural network. The special feature of our workflow is the automatic generation of

The authors acknowledge the financial support by the Federal Ministry of Education and Research (BMBF) of Germany in the framework of KI-Sprung_ADELIA (grant number 16ES1144K).

© Springer Nature Switzerland AG 2022
A. Orailoglu et al. (Eds.): SAMOS 2021, LNCS 13227, pp. 385–400, 2022.
https://doi.org/10.1007/978-3-031-04580-6_26

the neural network based on analog neurons that allows the creation of both schematic and layout from the trained network within approx. 30 min.

The topic of neuromorphic computing requires hardware and software co-design due to the complexity of the design task, in order to meet the specifications in terms of accuracy and energy efficiency, for automating tasks and for verification and co-simulation. The resulting analog neural network is a mapping of the neural network algorithm that takes advantage of the workflow and framework developed during the project. Thus, the algorithm and the circuit were developed in parallel decreasing development time. Besides design and software frameworks developed for some fully developed neuromorphic systems like SpiNNaker, IBM's TrueNorth and FACETS/BrainScaleS, there is not much development of hardware/software co-design frameworks for neuromorphic hardware [5].

The paper is structured as follows: Sect. 2 provides an overview of the hardware/software co-design workflow implemented and employed for the automatic generation of the convolutional neural network. In order to obtain a neural network that can be implemented with an analog design, the training should be aware of the constraints at circuit level as explained in Sect. 3. For the automation of the design tasks of the analog neural network, a hierarchical architecture approach has been followed for the layers implemented as described in Sect. 4. Section 5 gives a detailed explanation of the simulation steps followed in our workflow. Finally, Sect. 6 summarizes the conclusions of the paper.

2 Design Workflow for Hardware/Software Co-Design

Figure 1 shows the workflow followed in the design of the analog neural network for the ADELIA ASIC and that can also be employed in other analog implementations of neural networks. The neural network is trained with the limitations and parameters of the hardware design to assure that the accuracy of the integrated circuit network will match the algorithm. After the training has finished, multiple *Data files* are exported. Two of them are the *ONNX* and the *Hyper Parameters* files. *ONNX* is a standard model exchange format to describe the architecture of a neural network whilst the *Hyper Parameters* file gives additional information about the network such as weight and batch normalization quantization values. For the verification at circuit level of the analog neural network, an additional set of files is exported, which contains the values before and after the activation function of the algorithm (*Activation Values*) to be compared with the results of the electrical simulations.

The network generator is an analog synthesis tool built around a Fraunhofer IIS internal automation framework called UnilibPlus, a Python-based Cadence Virtuoso add-on that supplies a framework to automate design tasks similar to the Berkeley Analog Generator [6,7]. The network generator builds the complete analog neural network circuit from the given *ONNX* and *Hyper Parameter* files as well as the *Circuit Building Blocks*. By using the information stored in the given files and the building blocks as the input of the network generator, the flexibility of the circuit generation is assured since changes in the network architecture caused for example by re-training a network or by addressing a different

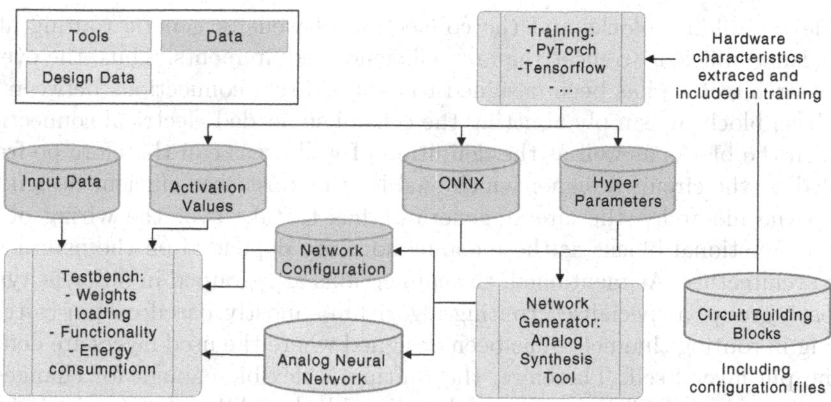

Fig. 1. Workflow from training to simulation of an analog neural network by means of hardware/software co-design.

use case are reflected in these files. The files are automatically created at the end of the training and can afterwards be used to create a new analog neural network circuit using the newly defined architecture. Thus, different network architectures and their corresponding circuits can be created in a time efficient way. The circuit generation flow starts by extracting the needed information such as input and output dimension for fully connected layer or kernel size and stride value for convolutional layer from the *ONNX* and *Hyper Parameter* files. Afterwards, layer by layer will be created in a hierarchical way where the process always starts at the lowest hierarchy level and then combines the results from each level till the layer is complete. The generated layers are then combined to create the top level circuit as described in Sect. 4.

At the lowest hierarchy level, manually designed base level building blocks are used. Dependent on their actual implementation - which the network generator is agnostic to - , different signals must be routed between the blocks and up to the top level. These signals define the physical interface of the blocks and as these interfaces are defined by the blocks them self, each block must be attached with a *configuration file*. The *configuration file* defines the pin naming of analog inputs and outputs, control signals, reference inputs and power supplies where the actual function of the pin itself isn't considered by the network generator. Moreover, the pins are grouped in classes of pins with different types of functionality where the group defines the needed connections and the routing. In addition to that, for layout generation, the access directions of the pins are also used to check the intended signal flow direction. Layout creation also needs the information about the available metal layer and their width and pitch restrictions. Cadence inbuilt PDK functionality together with wire assistant presets are utilized by UnilibPlus to extract the needed definitions. Therefore, no additional external technology configuration is needed. Further on, the layout creation must be flexible and area efficient at the same time. For direct connections between base level building blocks and the connection of wells, a generic routing algorithm isn't sufficient to meet the area efficiency requirements. Thus, the overall circuit architecture has been designed to enable direct connections between the base level blocks by simply abutting the cells. The needed electrical connections between the blocks as well as the definition of well areas can therefore be freely decided by the circuit designer which enables the most area efficient design.

Up the hierarchy, the circuit generator has to take over the wiring of the created functional blocks as these connections are depended on the neural network architecture. As mentioned, the connections are grouped in different types. For each group, a specialised routing algorithm - mostly based on pin-to-trunk routing in routing channels - has been designed where the used layers are defined by the pin layer itself. Therefore, the routing is flexible enough for changes in the architecture of both model and building blocks whilst the circuit designer can still influence the used layers by changing the pin layers. Furthermore, the dynamic selection of layers depending on the pin layers enables the independence from the semiconductor process.

In addition to the circuit generation, *Network Configuration files* are created which are then used to configure the analog neural network. The simulation of the network circuit comprises two steps: 1) weight loading, which also includes the configuration of batch normalization values, both in simulation and down the line to configure the finished ASIC via an external interface and 2) inference. The weight loading step is necessary for configuring the network the first time or for an update of the values if new training data is used to optimize the network performance, by changing some of the weights while keeping the same network structure. Afterwards, the Analog Neural Network circuit can perform the inference with the *Input Data* applied to the input neurons.

3 Hardware-aware Training

We reduce the complexity of the trained model by using quantized network parameters for the forward pass and the backward pass while holding the corresponding floating-point values for gradient updates. This approach ensures that small gradient updates can accumulate in the floating point hold out value over multiple updates/batches. To achieve a high sensitivity and specificity we use hardware-aware training for our deep neural networks by:

- using 7 levels of quantization (three positives, zero and three negatives) for the weights of fully connected and convolutional layers. The 7 levels have been chosen as a trade-off between area, linearity and mismatch.
- using custom levels of quantization for gain and offset on the BatchNorm layers. Offset is quantized to 21 levels centered around zero between -1 and 1. The quantization of gain uses 16 levels.
- using a custom ReLU activation function that is fitted from the transfer function obtained from the designed circuit.

4 Architecture of an Automatically Generated Analog Neural Network

Figure 2 shows the hierarchy of a general neural network with the architecture implemented in the ADELIA ASIC with both fully connected and convolutional layers. Green marked blocks are *base level building blocks* and must be designed manually. Pooling layers like average pool layers are created using the same structure as convolutional layers. By using the *base level building blocks*, the blue marked blocks are created by the automated workflow described in Sect. 2. The different layer types are then built of *functional blocks* and *base level building blocks*. A fully connected layer contains the *functional blocks*: *Column, SRAM Column Control, SRAM Row Control* and *Batch Normalization Config* and the *neuron* building block. A convolutional layer contains the functional blocks: *Filter, Memory, Activation* and *Batch Normalization Config*.

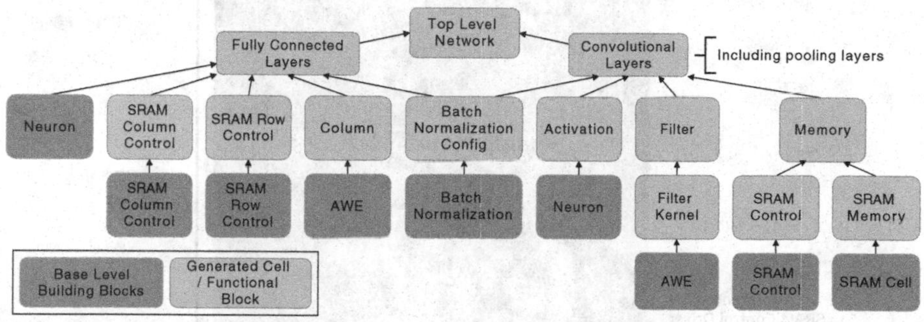

Fig. 2. Network architecture divided in base level building blocks and functional blocks.

The automated workflow enables a manual validation of small examples of the created circuits by the circuit designers to ensure the correct wiring of the block circuits and therefore the correct mapping between the designed network and the implemented hardware. By inspecting, verifying and validating these exemplary circuits, it can be assumed that the addition of neurons to the layers is performed correctly.

Figure 3 shows the connections at the top level of an exemplary analog neural network. The *analog inputs* are located at the left side of the network whilst the *analog outputs* of a layer are connected to the *analog inputs* of the next layer The channels of convolution layers are kept separate when the following layer is also a convolutional layer whereas a wider bus is created if the next layer is a fully connected one. Weight loading requires a *clock* and an *init* signal as well as the *bit lines* used to transfer the current weight value. As shown in Fig. 3, the *bit lines* are connected to all layers in a parallel manner in contrast to the *init* and *clock* signals which are forwarded from one layer to the next. Other connections can be *consecutive connection* that are also forwarded between the

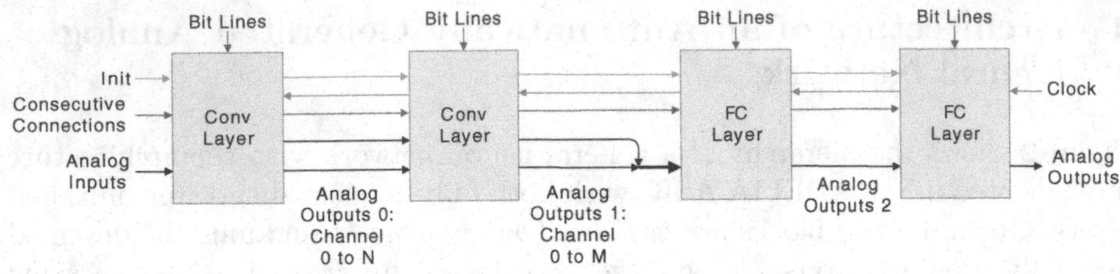

Fig. 3. Top level connections of an exemplary analog neural network.

layers as well as further global connections separate for each layer which are not shown in Fig. 3.

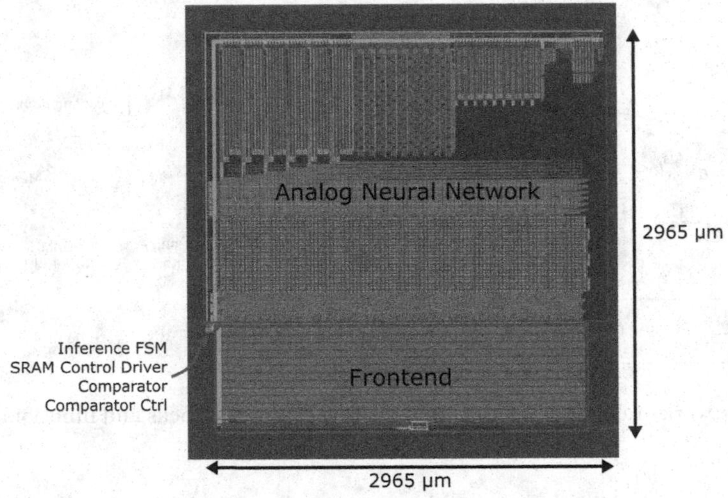

Fig. 4. Top level layout of ADELIA ASIC including the analog neural network.

The ADELIA analog neural network is composed by six layers: three convolutional layers, one average pool and two fully connected layers. The layout generated automatically of the complete analog neural network is shown in Fig. 4. Here, the signal flow starts at the bottom side an ends at the top right corner. All control signals as well as supply pins are located at the lower left corner.

4.1 Fully Connected Layer Architecture

All fully connected layers have the same architecture. Inside a fully connected layer, a multiple of *Column* cells are placed in which the *AWEs* (Analog Weight Emulator) and therefore the weights are contained. Additional to the *Columns*, there will always be *Neuron* cells placed to include the activation function. Since there is SRAM (static random-access memory) inside the *AWEs*, *SRAM Column Control* and *SRAM Row Control* cells for loading the weights are also necessary. The *Batch Normalization Configuration* block is an optative block used to control and optionally store batch normalization offset and gain values.

This section shows the schematic and layout of the last fully connected layer, named as layer 5, with the schematic in Fig. 5 and the layout in Fig. 6. The layer has got 18 analog inputs that are connected to *Column 0* and from there on forwarded to *Column 1*. Thus, each *Column* of layer 5 contains 18 *AWEs* and does the multiplication and accumulation operation for one neuron. Therefore, two *Column* blocks connected to two *Neuron* blocks (*Neuron 0* and *Neuron 1*) are necessary since layer 5 has two neurons. To control the weights loading, the *SRAM Row Control* and the *SRAM Column Control* blocks are placed. Unlike the schematic, the *Neurons* are placed on the right hand side in the layout and not at the bottom. The reason for this is to keep the signal flow from left to right. The vertical size of the *Columns* is adapted to the space needed by the neurons of the previous layer.

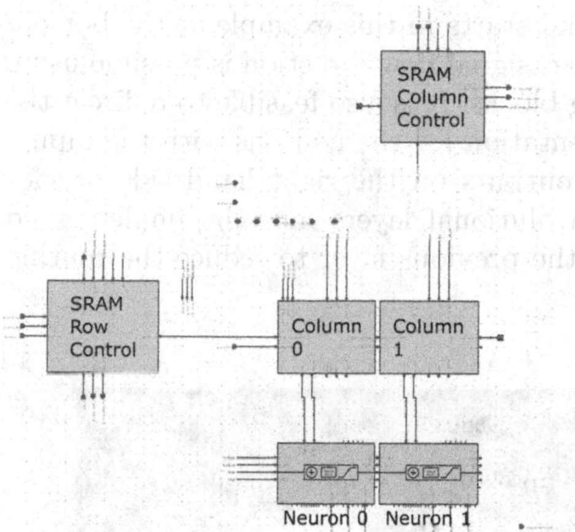

Fig. 5. Schematic of the fully connected layer 5.

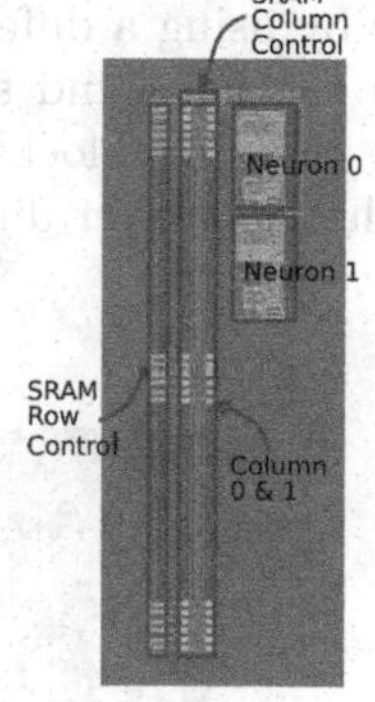

Fig. 6. Layout of the fully connected layer 5.

4.2 Convolutional Layer Architecture

Convolutional layers always consist of multiple *Filter* and *Activation* blocks. The *Filter* contains the *Filter Kernels* which themselves contain the *AWEs*. The *Activation* block contains the *Neurons*. As in the fully connected layers, a *Batch Normalization Config* block will be placed inside the convolutional layers if batch normalization is required.

In this section, the schematic and layout of the first convolutional layer, named layer 0, are presented. All convolutional layers and the average pool layer designed in ADELIA use the same architecture. Layer 0 consists of three *Filters* and therefore three *Activation* blocks. In addition to these blocks, the *Batch Normalization Config* block is required. In the schematic shown in Fig. 7, the signal flow is always from left hand side to right hand side.

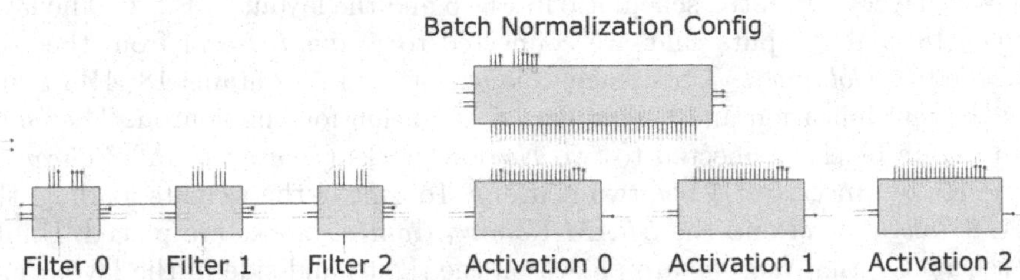

Fig. 7. Schematic of the convolutional layer 0.

Figure 8 displays the layout of layer 0. The signal flow is given by the implementation of the *AWEs* and *Neurons* and starts in this example at the bottom and ends at the top of the figure. Another signal flow direction is possible using a different pin placement in the building blocks. It is also feasible to redirect the signal flow by using a different implementation for the neurons with the inputs located on the left hand side and the outputs on the right hand side or vice versa. The building blocks used in convolutional layers must be implemented in a way the next layer directly fits to the previous layer to reduce the routing complexity.

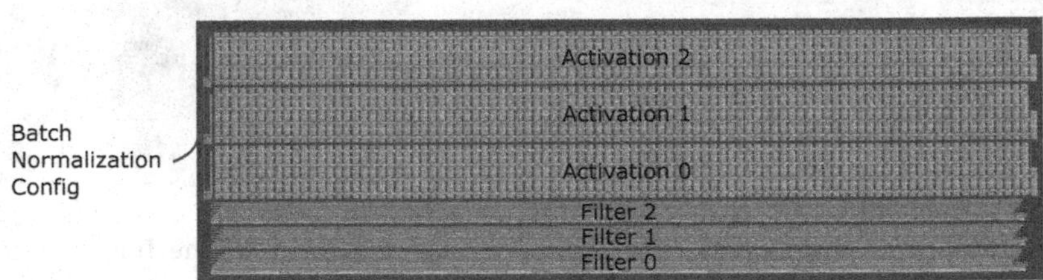

Fig. 8. Layout of the convolutional layer 0.

5 Simulation and Evaluation Workflow for Hardware/Software Co-Design

In Sect. 5.1, we provide an overview of the initial verification concept for the ADELIA ASIC based on electrical simulations. Due to the long simulation time, a simulation and evaluation workflow based on hardware/software co-design had to be implemented. The evaluation of the ASIC is done using Python and PyTorch as described in Sect. 5.2. The correctness of this evaluation is then verified in Sect. 5.3.

The ADELIA ASIC consists of the analog neural network, its control logic including the inference finite state machine, a result comparator and the comparator control circuit as well as a mixed-signal frontend filtering and buffering circuit. All these parts of the circuit have to be simulated and evaluated regarding their correct functionality and their energy consumption.

5.1 Initial Verification Concept of the ADELIA ASIC

As neural networks, during their development and training phase, are a very dynamic structure, where both the internal topology as well as the external interface (number of input and maybe output pins) are prone to frequent changes, a test bench for them needs to be very flexible as well. Moreover, neural networks have thousands of neurons, weights and connections that need to be included by the test bench. An efficient way to create such a test bench for electrical simulations that can handle changes in the DUT (device under test) topology as well as cope with a large number of different input vectors from test signals is to create the test bench dynamically with a scripting language. Network information is gathered from several text files that are created by the Python training tools and the network generator.

The verification process starts with the weight loading step where the weights need to be written to the corresponding configuration blocks built into each synapse circuits, which are labeled as SRAM blocks in Fig. 2. The necessary values are converted into a serial data stream in form of a digital stimulus file for the circuit simulator. After simulation, the binary values now stored in the SRAM cells are saved to a file and automatically filtered and post-processed and the results verified against the data coming from the *ONNX* file corresponding to the trained network. Any bit errors are then reported for further debugging.

During the inference calculation step, the now initialized network is fed with varying input data sets, named as *Input Data* in Fig. 1. The resulting outputs at the end of this second simulation are cross-checked against the known results from the training and verification data sets. In addition, the inter-layer and intra-layer voltages of all layers are saved and processed for debugging purposes of the network circuit when needed. While the test bench tool set created for verification purposes allows the verification of the complete neural network, it became clear during the design process that the simulation times necessary to fully simulate the complete integrated neural network at circuit level are so long, that it is not feasible to do this in a reasonable time with the current state of hardware and simulation tools. We estimated that for the first phase of the simulation, the loading of the weights into SRAM, a simulation time of several years on current generation hardware utilizing 128 CPU cores, which is the current maximum possible with the vendor tools, is necessary. Therefore, analog verification needed to be broken down into more manageable steps. Thus, two complementary simulation workflows, which are presented in the next two sections, were implemented for the verification of the designed ASIC and its comparison with the algorithm.

5.2 ADELIA ASIC Evaluation Based on Python and PyTorch

As stated in Sect. 5.1, an electrical simulation of the complete analog neural network is not feasible for verification due to the long simulation time. Therefore, the functional verification in regards to accuracy metrics and the calculation of the energy consumption has been implemented using Python and PyTorch standard modules.

Inference. The inference step of the evaluation concept calculates the sensitivity and specificity, previously named as accuracy metrics, of the ADELIA ASIC. To ensure correct calculations, the implementation using Python and PyTorch must precisely match the characteristics of the analog hardware. This includes:

- characteristic of the filter used in the frontend,
- quantized weight values and batch normalization factors and
- the transfer function of the activation function.

In general, the inference step executes the same calculations as the hardware aware training described in Sect. 3 but simplifies the user interaction with the script to ensure the usability for non machine learning expects.

The evaluation script starts with loading the trained network from an *ONNX* file and imports them into available PyTorch modules. Afterwards, the input data is loaded from the ECG files given to the script as a command line parameter. The data is then passed through the frontend filter and the network to calculate the result of the network which is then written to the command line. The result for each ECG file must afterwards be compared against the original label of the data to check if the decision taken by the network is correct. Finally, the result of all comparisons between original label and network decision will be taken to calculate sensitivity and specificity. We have reached a sensitivity of 94.37% and a 1-specificity of 4.13% on the test set. These metrics are well above the required minimal sensitivity of 90% and 1-specificity of 20%. Further on, whilst the inference is calculated, the pre- and post-activation values for each neuron are saved internally and written to a file for the calculation of the energy consumption and further debugging.

Energy Consumption. The energy consumption of the ADELIA ASIC can be divided into the contribution of leakage, switching of digital circuitry, static consumption of analog blocks and dynamic consumption of analog blocks. All those different parts the energy consumption consists of have been analyzed for the different circuit blocks. The gathered information is then used by a Python based script that calculates the energy consumption of the complete ADELIA ASIC dependent on the current input data sample. The results for all input data samples are then averaged to calculate the average energy consumption.

Inference Finite State Machine. The inference finite state machine has been created with a standard digital design flow. From there, the power consumption values are given, see Table 1. As these values are power consumption values, they have to be multiplied with the time duration the block is used. Leakage must be considered for the total classification time of 368.6 µs. The switching and internal power consumption is considered only when the analog neural network processes the data, which is for 7.24 µs. Therefore, the energy consumption translates to 26.6 nJ for leakage, 56.64 pJ for switching, and 95.3 pJ of internal energy.

Table 1. Inference finite state machine power consumption.

Type	Power consumption [mW]
Internal power	0.01316327
Switching power	0.00782203
Leakage power	0.07205890
Total	0.0930442

Mixed-signal Frontend. The mixed-signal frontend is divided into three parts: a analog storage, a digital-to-analog converter (DAC, including a downsampler and a buffer) and the frontend finite state machine. The analog storage is divided into 16 identical blocks, all causing switching and leakage energy consumption. As mentioned before, the leakage must be considered for the whole classification time whilst the switching has influence only during the circuit is active. Only one of the 16 blocks gets the data from the DAC and therefore only one of those blocks is active. Thus, taking the switching current of one block and considering its influence for the total storage time of 61.44 µs is enough. The leakage currents are considered for the complete 368.6 µs and are multiplied by 16 to include all blocks. Table 2 shows the voltages, currents and the resulting energy consumption for the analog storage block. The DAC and the finite state machine used in the frontend have both been simulated completely in an analog way. This includes dynamic as well as leakage energy consumption. The DAC consumes 40 µW whilst the finite state machine consumes 6.895 µA * 0.8V = 5.516 µW. The DAC is in use for 61.44 µs and the finite state machine is in use for the whole classification time of 368.6 µs. It translates to 2.46 nJ for the DAC and 2.03 nJ for the state machine.

Table 2. Frontend analog storage energy consumption.

Type	Supply Net	Voltage [V]	Current [μA]	Energy [pJ]
Switching	VDD	0.8	29.31	1441
Switching	VSSM0V2	–0.2	–12.75	157
Leakage	VDD	0.8	0.331×16	1562
Leakage	VDDA0V4	0.4	0.035×16	82.6
Leakage	VDDA	0.8	0.754×16	3557
Leakage	VSSM0V2	–0.2	0.073×16	86.1
Total switching				1598
Total leakage				5287
Total				6886

Analog Neural Network Leakage. The leakage current of the analog neural network must be included in the energy consumption calculation. To simulate the leakage current, the complete network could be placed in a testbench where a DC simulation is performed and the current on the supplies is measured. As the network is large and therefore the circuit simulation takes a long time, a different approach has been chosen. The network consists of blocks which are used multiple times. Therefore, it is enough to simulate each block once and multiply the leakage currents by the number of instances used in the network. Two advantages are gathered from this procedure: the simulation is fast, and the debugging is easy.

Neuron. The neurons are characterized in regards to their operating condition including the input voltage, the load resistance, the load voltage and the batch normalization gain and offset values. This leads to a five dimensional data set containing the energy consumption values for all combinations of parameters. To give an example for a single neuron, Fig. 9 shows a plot of the required energy consumption of one neuron with varying input voltage and load resistance and constant values for the other parameters. The used activation function is a limited ReLU (rectified linear unit) function. It has a constant output value for negative input voltages and a linear rising output voltage for input voltages greater than zero till it hits its maximum output voltage. As expected for such a function, the energy consumption stays constant due to constant output voltage for negative input voltages. For positive input voltages, the energy consumption rises linear with the gradient defined by the load resistance. When the output voltage reaches its maximum value, the energy consumption is again constant because the output voltage stays constant again.

Total Energy Consumption. To calculate the energy consumption of the whole neural network, the operating conditions for each neuron have been extracted during calculating the inference in PyTorch. The information gathered from this step has then be used to get the energy consumption for each neuron from the

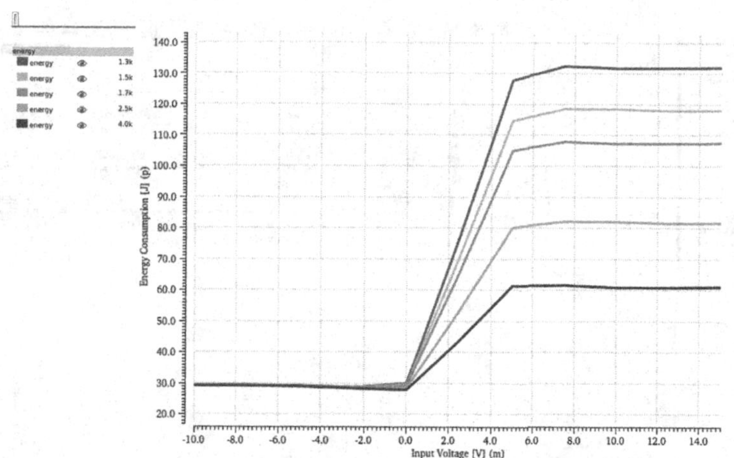

Fig. 9. Neuron energy consumption depended on input voltage and load resistance.

previous mentioned characterization. Adding up all these energy consumption values together with energy consumption of the other blocks leads then to the total energy consumption of the network.

5.3 Electrical Verification of the ADELIA ASIC

In order to prove that the metrics and energy consumption calculated by the evaluation script are correct, at least a subset of the network, specifically the last two fully connected layers that only contain 20 neurons in total, has been simulated in a few hours at circuit level in the time domain.

As shown in Sect. 5.2, the expected post-activation values at the output of each neuron are exported by the evaluation script. To check the correct functionality of the circuits, these values are extracted and converted into analog voltage values, which are then used to drive the last two layers of the network with the correct input signals. The test benches for the analog simulations then again saves all the post-activation output voltages of every neuron in the last two layers at the end of the inference step. For these simulations, the exact same simulation framework as described in Sect. 5.1 has been used.

Figure 10 shows the results of the "inference simulation" for one input vector. The first vertical marker shows the time point when the outputs of all neurons have settled to their final value and are sampled shortly thereafter by the next layer. This time point is extracted in the post-processing part of the simulation and then used to compare the voltage values with the PyTorch results for layer 4. The second vertical marker shows the same decision point for layer 5, which is also the last layer of the network. The differential value between the two outputs corresponds to the decision our network has made with regards to the supplied input vector and is sampled at this point with a differential comparator, in order

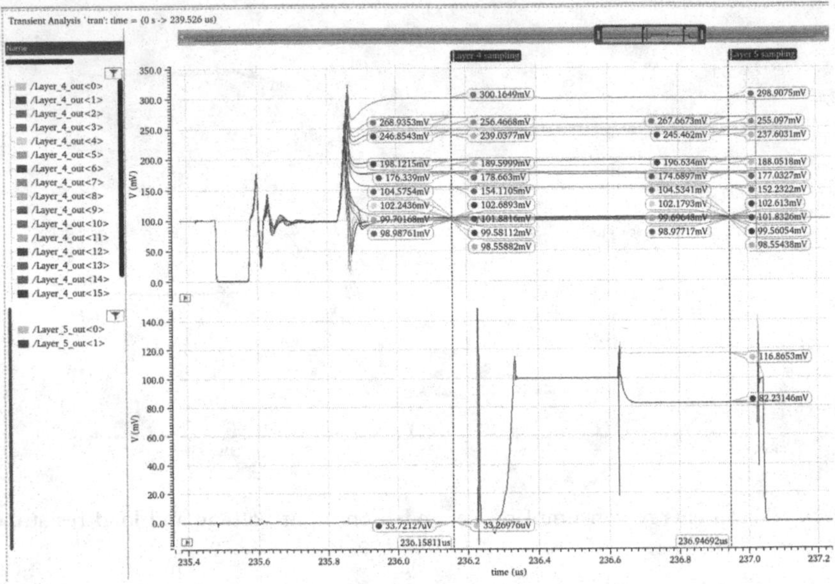

Fig. 10. Inference simulation results for layer 4 and 5.

to give a binary result of "true" or "false". In order to check for validity for a larger set of input vectors, these simulations were scripted and completed for 5 different input vectors. The resulting node voltages are then written to an external file. The results clearly show the network is working as intended.

For all input vectors, small differences between the simulated and the expected value are reported by the simulation. These differences come from the analog nature of the electrical implementation: The voltage limiters that specify the dynamic range of the system are not perfect, but show a few mV of static offset. The gain values of the operational amplifiers are also never perfect in a real implementation and with the circuits being based on switched capacitor topologies, a small error in the output voltages caused by leakage effects and non-perfect gain values are also to be expected. All these error sources do add up, but the outputs of layer 5 are clearly still correct with regards to the binary decision the network would make with regards to the input vector specified. This shows, the network is robust against statistical variations of the node values which further on displays the correct functionality of the network even if small calculation errors occur inside the circuits. We can therefore extrapolate the results to the complete network and predict its correct functionality with high confidence.

In addition to the evaluation of the correct functionality of the circuit, the current consumption of the neural network was simulated in Cadence during the top level-simulation of layers 4 and 5. Table 3 shows the results for the averaged current values over the simulated time frame of 2.192 µs and can be used to compare against the calculated values for layer 4 and 5.

Table 3. Averaged currents for the supply voltage nodes of layers 4 and 5 during layer activity.

Input data Vector	Layer 4 [A] VDDA	Layer 4 [A] VDDA1P8	Layer 4 [A] V_ACT_HI	Layer 5 [A] VDDA	Layer 5 [A] VDDA1P8	sum [A]
0	0.000388917	2.49E–06	7.14E–05	9.11E–06	2.08E–07	0.000472
1	0.0003501	2.27E–06	5.92E–05	8.20E–06	1.88E–07	0.00042
2	0.000385794	2.45E–06	5.54E–05	8.93E–06	2.04E–07	0.000453
3	0.000380152	2.44E–06	6.10E–05	8.92E–06	2.04E–07	0.000453
4	0.000292457	1.96E–06	6.45E–05	6.91E–07	1.51E–07	0.000366
AVG	0.000359484	2.32112E–06	6.2271E–05	7.169E–06	1.909E–07	0.0004328

The results shown in Table 3 translate into a energy consumption of:

$$E_{Layer4} = (359.484\,\mu A \cdot 0.8\,V + 2.32112\,\mu A \cdot 1.8\,V + 62.271\,\mu A \cdot 0.4\,V) \cdot 2.192\,\mu s = 694.1486\,pJ \tag{1}$$

$$E_{Layer5} = (7.169\,\mu A \cdot 0.8\,V + 0.1909\,\mu A \cdot 0.4\,V) \cdot 2.192\,\mu s = 12.7389\,pJ \tag{2}$$

The simulated and the calculated energy consumption values match fairly good, which shows that the calculations are correct.

6 Conclusions and Future Work

The topic of in-memory computing needs to leverage from hardware/software co-design frameworks and workflows. This need is even bigger for an analog in-memory computing implementation since the EDA (electronic design automation) tools are not prepared for automating the design flow. The approach presented in this paper allowed the parallel-in-time design of the neural network algorithm and integrated circuit for an analog convolutional neural network. Moreover, the automatic generation of the schematic and layout for 6 layers, 1,922 neurons and 72,846 synapses takes only approx. 30 min.

The hardware/software co-design workflow presented allows not only an automatic generation of the neural network circuit but also to simulate and evaluate its results. Therefore, instead of simulating months for the evaluation of our ASIC, we just need minutes in order to provide key parameters as inference results, accuracy metrics, energy consumption and latency.

In comparison with other automation frameworks like the Berkeley Analog Generator (BAG) [6,7], layout and schematic creation in our solution is implemented in a similar manner but the full control on generator and backend code enables us to integrate the network generator in the complete design flow. Therefore, area and energy consumption metrics obtained by the network generator can be considered and optimized during training.

Further work is pending for the reduction of the energy consumption per inference from 450 nJ to 225 nJ by shorter power on time of the frontend, switching off all voltage sources except the ones powering the SRAM and re-design of the *Batch Normalization* block. Due to the hardware/software co-design workflow, the re-design of a base level building block is not a time consuming issue since the complete neural network is generated automatically. Therefore, continuous improvement of the base level building blocks can be quickly integrated in the neural network and their improvements evaluated.

References

1. Shafiee, A., et al: ISAAC: a convolutional neural network accelerator with in-situ analog arithmetic in crossbars. ACM SIGARCH Comput. Archit. News **44**(3), 14–26 (2016)
2. Tsai, H., Ambrogio, S., Narayanan, P., Shelby, R.M., Burr, G.W: Recent progress in analog memory-based accelerators for deep learning. J. Phys. Appl. Phys. **51**(28), 283001 (2018). IOP Publishing
3. Lu, J., Young, S., Arel, I., Holleman, J.: A 1 TOPS/W analog deep machine-learning engine with floating-gate storage in 0.13 µm CMOS. IEEE J. Solid-State Circ. **50**(1), 270–281. IEEE (2014)
4. Bekanntmachung des Pilotinnovationswettbewerbs Energieeffizientes KI-System Homepage. https://www.bmbf.de/foerderungen/bekanntmachung-2371.html. Accessed 23 Apr 2021
5. Plank, J.S.: A unified hardware/software co-design framework for neuromorphic computing devices and applications. In: 2017 IEEE International Conference on Rebooting Computing (ICRC), pp. 1–8. IEEE (2017)
6. Crossley, J., et al: BAG: a designer-oriented integrated framework for the development of AMS circuit generators. In: 2013 IEEE/ACM International Conference on Computer-Aided Design (ICCAD), pp. 74–81. IEEE (2013)
7. Chang, E., et al.: BAG2: a process-portable framework for generator-based AMS circuit design. In: 2018 IEEE Custom Integrated Circuits Conference (CICC), pp. 1–8. IEEE (2018)

Mitigating the Effects of RRAM Process Variation on the Accuracy of Artificial Neural Networks

Markus Fritscher[1](✉), Johannes Knödtel[1], Maen Mallah[2], Stefan Pechmann[3], Emilio Perez-Bosch Quesada[4], Tommaso Rizzi[4], Christian Wenger[4,5], and Marc Reichenbach[1]

[1] Chair for Computer Architecture, Friedrich-Alexander-Universität (FAU), Nuremberg, Germany
{markus.fritscher,johannes.knodtel,marc.reichenbach}@fau.de
[2] Fraunhofer IIS, Erlangen, Germany
maen.mallah@iis.fraunhofer.de
[3] Chair of Communications Electronics, University of Bayreuth, Bayreuth, Germany
stefan.pechmann@uni-bayreuth.de
[4] IHP-Leibniz-Institut fur innovative Mikroelektronik Frankfurt (Oder), Frankfurt, Germany
{emilio.quesada,tommaso.rizzi,christian.wenger}@ihp-microelectronics.com
[5] BTU Cottbus-Senftenberg, Cottbus, Germany

Abstract. Weight storage is a key challenge in the efficient implementation of artificial neural networks. Novel memory technologies such as RRAM are able to greatly improve density and introduce non-volatility and multibit capabilities to this component of ANN accelerators. The usage of RRAM in this domain comes with downsides, mainly caused by cycle-to-cycle and device-to-device variability leading to erroneous readouts, greatly affecting digital systems. ANNs have the ability to compensate for this by their inherent redundancy and usually exhibit a gradual deterioration in the accuracy of the task at hand. This means, that slight error rates can be acceptable for weight storage in an ANN accelerator. In this work we link device-to-device variability to the accuracy of an ANN for such an accelerator. From this study, we can estimate how strongly a certain net is affected by a certain device parameter variability. This methodology is then used to present three mitigation strategies and to evaluate how they affect the reaction of the network to variability: a) Dropout Layers b) Fault-Aware Training c) Redundancy. These mitigations are then evaluated by their ability to improve accuracy and to lower hardware overhead by providing data for a real-word example. We improved this network's resilience in such a way that it could tolerate double the variation in one of the device parameters (standard deviation of the oxide thickness can be 0.4 nm instead of 0.2 nm while maintaining sufficient accuracy.)

Keywords: Memristors · RRAM · Device variation · Mixed analog digital integrated circuits · Simulation · Neural networks

© Springer Nature Switzerland AG 2022
A. Orailoglu et al. (Eds.): SAMOS 2021, LNCS 13227, pp. 401–417, 2022.
https://doi.org/10.1007/978-3-031-04580-6_27

1 Introduction

Artificial neural networks (ANN), as part of artificial intelligence, are widely used methods for tasks like the recognition of faces [29], human speech [26] or autonomeous driving [8]. Due to the computational effort involved in the inference of ANNs, many new processing architectures have been developed in recent years. Besides the design of traditional digital accelerators for fast computation of matrix-matrix multiplications, a key research issue is the storage of weights. Modern neural network topologies can exceed several thousands or even billions of weights [17], which renders efficient storage necessary. Moreover, the weight storage should be as close as possible to the computation units, i.e. in best cases implemented as on-chip memory in order to avoid access to external memories e.g. to a DRAM module [28]. This is due to the necessity of accessing memory via a common memory bus that limits throughput and increases power consumption. This poses a problem in classical Von-Neuman architectures.

With the development of the resistive random-access memory (RRAM) technology, a new memory technology is available which is predestined to be used as weight memory: On the one hand, they feature high memory density, especially due to the possibility to store up to 6.5 bits per RRAM device in Multi-Level Cells (MLC) [19], whereby, after appropriate quantization of the network, only one RRAM cell per weight is needed. On the other hand, the technology has the advantage of non-volatility, by which weight matrices on the chip can be retained even with transient power supply.

Despite the outstanding features of the RRAM technology, intrinsic device variabilities, such as cycle-to-cycle (C2C) and device-to-device (D2D) veriations, cause instabilities and downgrade the network's performance. Fortunately ANNs have inherent redundancy, which means that while individual weights may have errors, the overall impact on the functional performance in terms of accuracy might be insignificant.

In 2021, the authors of [7] presented a framework which allows a system evaluation of neural networks running on a digital RRAM-based accelerator architecture regarding the impact of device-to-device (D2D) variations of the RRAM process (see Fig. 1). Aside from the RRAM-based weight storage, the presented architecture is based on conventional digital logic.

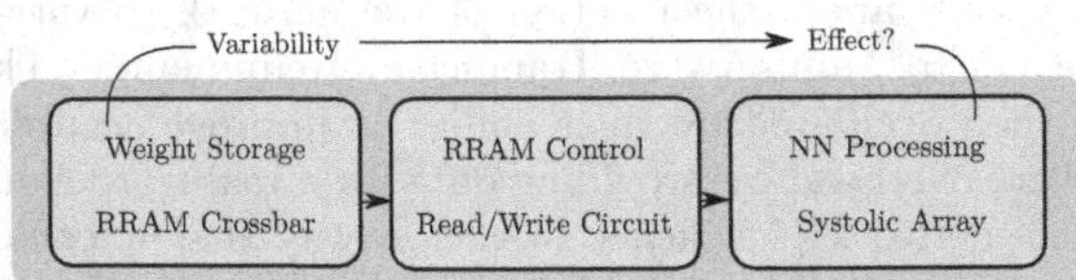

Fig. 1. System's workflow proposed in [7]. The synaptic weights are programmed and stored in a RRAM crossbar and further utilized in a neural network implemented by a systolic array. (Figure taken from [7])

The authors used two different example networks namely handwritten digit recognition on the MNIST dataset and detection of atrial fibrillation in electrocardiogram (ECG) signals, to show how a variation of the oxide thickness in the RRAM manufacturing process affects the recognition accuracy. Despite the analysis presented there, two key questions have not been addressed in the aforementioned paper: (1) Which specific weights in an ANN have a particularly sensitive effect with respect to detection accuracy ("critical weights")? (2) Which mitigations can be applied to protect these critical weights from errors so that the recognition accuracy of the neural network is retained despite the usage of unreliable memory cells?

This paper adresses and answers those questions, building on the work of [7]. Therefore, the contributions of this work are:

- An analysis of how physical variations in the RRAM process affect different weights and how this affects the overall recognition accuracy of ANNs.
- The usage, analysis and evaluation of three approaches (fault-aware training, dropout layer and insertion of redundancy) to make neural networks less susceptible to these variations
- A methodology and its implementation (reference framework) which performs the points mentioned above in an automated way.

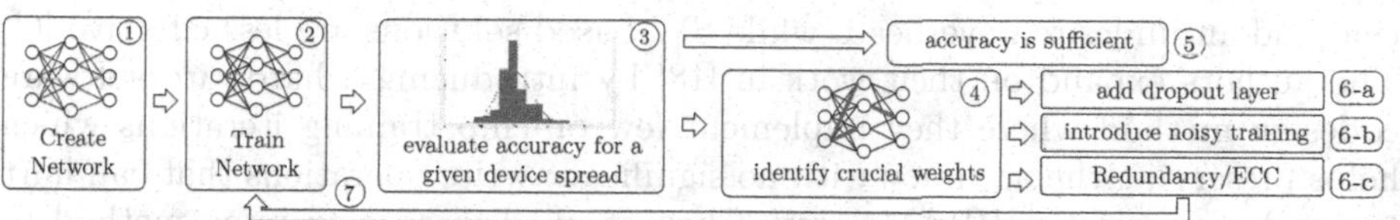

Fig. 2. Methodology and workflow presented in this work.

Figure 2 shows an abstract representation of the methodology and the framework. Steps (1) and (2) correspond to the state-of-the-art procedure for the creation of neural networks. In step (3), the neural network is analyzed with respect to the process variation of the weight memory (analogous to [7]). If the accuracy is sufficient despite process variations (5), the training is finished and an architecture can be created from it. If the accuracy is not sufficient, an analysis of the critical weights (4) follows, which are then additionally secured by 3 mitigations (6a, 6b, 6c). Finally, a retraining (7) is performed and the analysis starts again.

This paper is organized as follows: In Sect. 2, we present other works which also address these problems. Subsequently, in Sect. 3 we show the effect of D2D variations on the accuracy of the ANN, depending on the memory location where errors in the weights storage occur. In Sect. 4, we then present the aforementioned measures to increase accuracy. These are analyzed and evaluated in Sect. 5. Section 6 summarizes the paper and gives an outlook.

2 Related Work

Researchers have found that recent ANNs tend to be too computationally expensive to fit them onto embedded systems [3]. Although several counter-measures (e.g., network compression, pruning, entropy encoding, etc.) have been investigated in literature, the trade-off between computational efficiency and accuracy is still one of the biggest hurdle that designers have to tackle when developing neural network for embedded applications [2,14,24].

Unfortunately, reducing the redundancy of the ANN to make it more computationally efficient can make the network more sensitive to errors [30]. Bianco et al. have concluded, that the efficiency and accuracy of neural networks can be seen as a conflicting (trade-off) problem.

To cope with these challenges, novel technologies have been deployed to implement specialized hardware accelerators. In particular, RRAM devices have gained interest due to their scalability, back-end-of-the-line compatibility, and low energy consumption [20,22,23,25]. Unfortunately, RRAM devices are affected by non-idealities, that hinder their implementation. Possible solutions to these problems are currently pursued by researchers on the material and algorithmic levels [11,13]. While these solutions are tested and the RRAM properties enhanced, the design of a RRAM-based accelerators requires novel techniques able to capture these non-idealities on a broader system level.

Hardware-based solutions to correct the errors cause extra power consumption and an undesired overhead, while SW-based solutions are less effective [6]. The authors expand on their work in [18] by introducing a hardware/software codesign method where they implement few on-chip training iterations which helps preserving the accuracy with no significant write operations that can hurt the endurance of the RRAM array. Chen et al. devised a training method to tackle the variation which prevents large weight values from being mapped to faulty memristors. Charan et al. proposed a joint algorithm-design, where they leverage the knowledge of RRAM variations to train a robust ANN model. Subsequently, they use on-chip memory to adapt the processing to compensate for the performance degradation [5]. Zhang et al. used a low gate voltage on the backpropagation to reduce the effect of the RRAM variations [31].

There has been non-RRAM-specific research of erroneous weights, as described in [16,30]. Zahid et al. characterized the error (faults) as "stuck-at" faults, which assumes that the hardware malfunction will force the activation values to be stuck at a certain value [30]. Salami et al. analyzed different failure modes. Although there has been a lot of research in these different fields, a coherent work which combines these aspects is missing. We combine the research which has been done to transfer device level properties to system level properties using approaches which allow to both analyze and render ANNs with highly quantized weights more resilient. Finally, we map these results to a specific technology (IHP) in order to enable the development and fabrication of ASICs utilizing RRAM for weight storage.

3 Impact of Device Variations

Previous works like [7] have shown that ANNs embedding memristors can be analyzed regarding the effects of device level properties, such as the spread of oxide thickness, on system level properties, such as the accuracy of the network. This is done by extracting the effect of the device level properties on the reliability of the memory cells and simulating a network with defects modeled after these reliability estimations. Such a method bridges the gap between pure device level aspects and system level aspects. While this approach yields valuable data, there are some open questions we address in this work:

1. What effects can be observed in the presence of variations? 2. Depending on the specific weights affected by variations, the net topology and training, the accuracy of the network is affected in different degrees. We want to explore how and to which degree this affects the overall system. 3. How can these effects be mitigated and how do mitigation strategies affect the metrics defined by the previous question?

3.1 Effect of Variations

In order to see the behavior in relation to the variability, we ran several simulations to showcase the overall statistical effects. The simulated interferences are based on RRAM devices with varied device parameters according to the model in [15], which is in turn based on the Stanford-PKU model. We treat the oxide thickness parameter t_{ox} as a normally distributed value around the default thickness and simulate reading the device multiple times in order to introduce a controllable amount of D2D variability to the simulation. This results in a distribution of potentially erroneous values that can be used as weights in the inference. This experiment is run multiple times for a set of standard deviations for the varied t_{ox} parameter using a real-world example for a highly quantized network.

3.2 Networks

Since we will be referring to this network throughout the paper as a recurring example, this subsection will provide a short overview of its task and structure. The network is trained to detect the characteristic pattern of atrial fibrillation (AFib) in ECG signals. This poses a real-world data processing task, as such a network can for example be used in portable medical devices, where it can monitor the health status continuously during the daily routine of the patient.

The structure of the ANN is a simple convolutional feed-forward network as shown in Fig. 3. It consists of a stack of N convolutional layers (Conv) followed by a stack of M fully-connected (FC) layers. These two stacks are separated by a Maxpooling layer which function is to reduce the dimensionality of the activations before the FC layers. All the layers (Conv/FC) comprise three operations: highly quantized Conv/FC, followed by a binary-shift batch normalization (BSBN) and finally a rectified linear unit (ReLU). The BSBN is a batch normalization where the scaling is constrained to powers of 2, yielding only shift operations. All the weights of the Conv and FC layers are quantized to ternary values (−1, 0 and 1) and stored within RRAM cells. This structure is highly optimized for power consumption, it was the winner of the "Pilotinnovationswettbewerb 'Energieeffizientes KI-System"' from the German Federal Ministry of Education and Research (BMBF) for the lowest power consumption in its track [4]. In this work, we use the same structure to analyze not only power consumption but also the error tolerance of the ANN. This involves changing the training routine, increasing the network size to increase redundancy and adding error correction methods.

The starting ANN for the experiments is the original ANN from the competition. It consists of $N = 4$ Conv and $M = 2$ FC stacks. The Conv layers are Conv1D with a filter length of 15 and a stride of 3 to reduce the activations and computational overhead with no need for pooling layers. The Conv layers outputs are 2, 4, 6 and 8 channels. These are followed by a Maxpooling and 2 FC layers with 8 and 2 neurons respectively. This neural network has 1310 ternary weights and 60 BSBN coefficients.

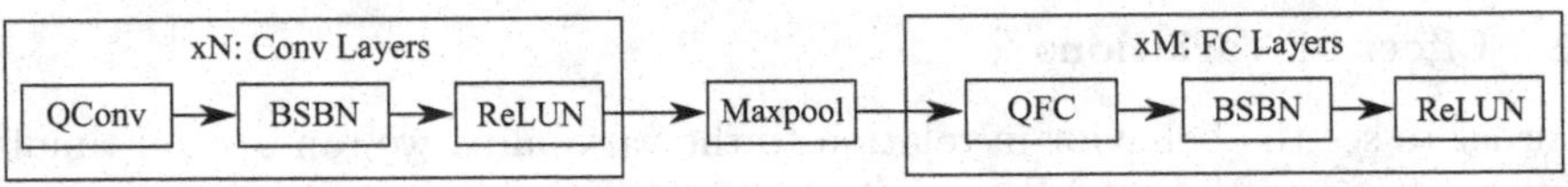

Fig. 3. The ANN we attempt to improve upon to render it more robust against device variations.

3.3 ECG Results

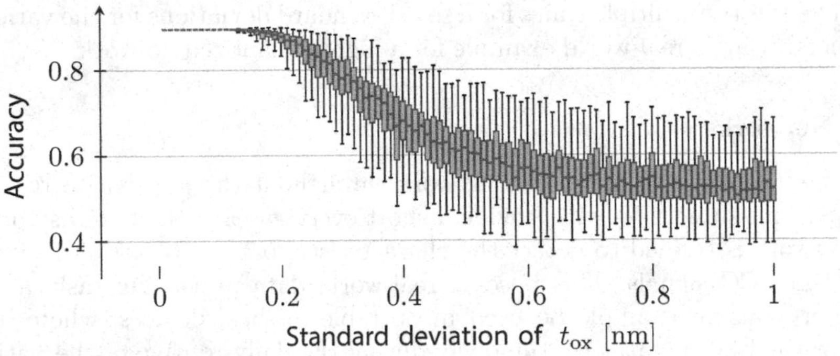

Fig. 4. Boxplot relating the accuracy in the ECG experiment to the standard deviation of the t_{ox} parameter.

This network is now used as the basis for our experiment. It is run with multiple introduced errors according to variations in the RRAM device level parameter t_{ox}, varying the standard deviation from 0 to 1 nm. In Fig. 4, the results are displayed and a few key properties can be deduced:

1. As expected, the mean accuracy is decreasing until it reaches an accuracy which is unacceptable for a binary classification task. 2. The mean values seem to follow the shape of a logistic function. At first the network is mostly unaffected, then starts to be more affected, and finally tapers off. 3. The spread between different experiments with the same amount of variation is increasing.

The analysis of this is considered future work, as it requires large sets of experimental data. The shown dataset already consists of 10.000 data points with a thousand inferences each.

The increasing spread for stronger variations is pointing to individual or small sets of weights being more important than others. In order to find more clues that this is in fact the case, we ran a different simulation. We selected a specific layer from the network, split it into 6 partitions and ran the experiment with variations affecting the whole network as well as only parts of it. The results of this experiment can be found in Fig. 5. Due to the large number of combinations, we only simulate one parameter set per standard deviation value and therefore switched from combining multiple results (as shown in the boxplot in Fig. 4) to evaluating a single sample per $\sigma_{t_{ox}}$.

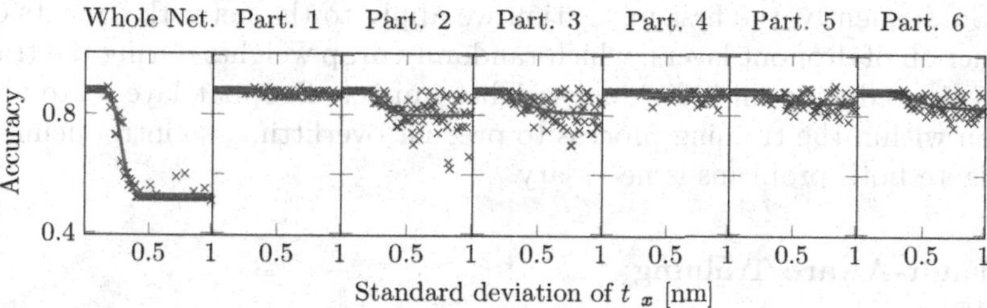

Fig. 5. Results of the partitioned network experiment. The red graphs are fitted logistic functions with offset. (Color figure online)

It can be observed, that the partitions do indeed react differently to variations: While partition 1 and 4 don't show much of an reaction to increased variability, partitions 2 and 3 show a strong reaction. This means that different kinds of mitigations have to be implemented for different parts of the network. We will analyze this further in the following sections.

4 Methodology and Implementation

In Sect. 3 it is shown, that a percentage of weights is stored incorrectly due to non-idealities of the device. In this section, we describe approaches to both analyze the network and render it more robust.

4.1 Analysis

As a first step, we need to consider how the findings presented in the previous section can be addressed, especially the fact that different weights have different importance to the networks performance. Traditional methods, such as determining the gradients of individual neurons of an ANN, are not suitable for this task, as we are dealing with highly quantized networks. As a more appropriate alternative, we used an experimental approach: Faults are injected into specific parts of the network (i.e. individual weights, groups of weights or whole layers) while the rest of the network is unaltered and the accuracy of the network is evaluated. This process is repeated with every layer and yields an estimate for the susceptibility of different layers. In the following we will describe possible mitigations.

4.2 Dropout Layers

A neural network's training process does not optimize for redundancy, the goal lies within maximizing a ANN's accuracy while not overfitting on the training dataset. As a result single weights might be more critical than others, which cannot be mitigated by merely increasing the network size [21]. This is problematic when storing weights within error-prone devices since a single erroneously stored weight might have a large impact on the overall accuracy of the network. Subsequently, the first mitigation we apply to the network consists of the introduction of dropout layers, which randomly drop weights during the training process [1], reducing an individual weights impact. Dropout layers are already common within the training process to prevent overfitting, so introducing them to mitigate both problems is necessary.

4.3 Fault-Aware Training

As the next step, we introduce fault-aware training by applying noise to the training data. Zahid et al. were able to show that "by injecting faults in the convolutional layers during training, highly accurate convolutional neural networks (CNNs) can be trained which exhibits much better error tolerance compared to the original" [30]. Although their focus is on FPGAs utilizing SRAM, the same technique can be applied to RRAM devices. A similar approach was used to introduce faults during the training process of the ANN.

4.4 Redundancy/Error Correction

As a final means of mitigation, we add redundancy to the network. Recent work has investigated redundancy within neural networks as a means to increase overall accuracy [10]. However, when individual weights are stored incorrectly, it might be beneficial to add redundant layers for the sole reason of being more error tolerant. We investigated a) adding redundant layers and b) adding error correction by performing a majority vote on redundantly stored weights. The latter is implemented as follows: Each weight is stored within n storage elements (n being uneven). When a weight is to-be-read, it is read n times and the value which has been stored in most of the elements is returned. If there is a tie between options (e.g. when $[-1, 0, -1]$ is read) the neutral element is returned.

4.5 Technology

We apply our evaluations to an ANN utilizing the RRAM technology provided by the *Leibniz Institut für innovative Mikroelektronik* (IHP). To some extent, RRAM variability is caused by variations in process parameters of the device fabrication. One of these is the oxide thickness, which is used in our experiments to introduce D2D variability to the simulation. A typical standard deviation for the oxide layer in this process is 0.17 nm [9].

4.6 Implementation

A tool is needed in order to apply the theoretical concepts described above to a given ANN. We have built this research upon the framework which has been presented in [7] and which is depicted in Fig. 6a.

The starting point is the creation and training of an ANN with *Traditional NN Training Flow* like Tensorflow. After the training process, the weight matrices containing the weights w_i are extracted. Next, the RRAM cells and the corresponding storage circuitry are characterized using analog simulations run with traditional analog tooling like e.g. Cadence Maestro. The framework utilizes this data to calculate new matrices, which contain the weights w_i' as they would be stored within RRAM arrays of given parameter spreads. Those weight matrices are used to run inferences on the neural network for different σ of a given device parameter. The results of such calculations (evaluated using different $\sigma_{t_{ox}}$) are depicted in Fig. 6b. Two different networks were analyzed, the results for network 1 (handwritten number recognition, based on MNIST dataset) are shown in red, the results for network 2 (AFib detection on ECG network, similar to Sect. 3.2) are shown in blue. As it can be seen, this methodology allows us to deduct the system level property *network accuracy* for a given device parameter *oxide thickness*.

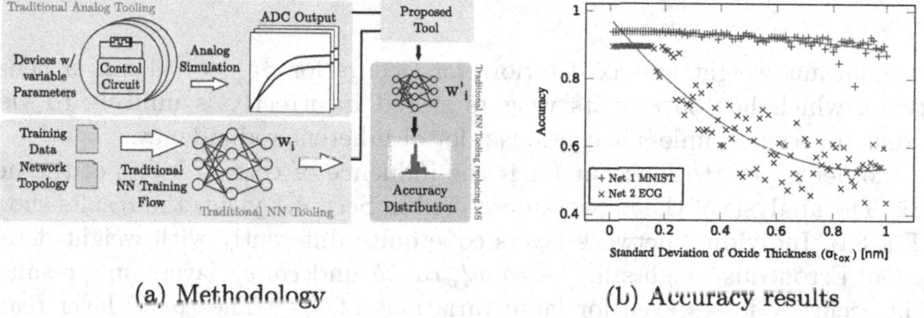

(a) Methodology (b) Accuracy results

Fig. 6. The methodology and instances of analysis results as presented in [7]. Figures adapted from [7].

Figure 2 shows our extensions to this framework. While the initial framework analyzes a given network in regard to robustness against device variations, it is now able to a) determine which weights are crucial for maintaining accuracy and b) apply appropriate countermeasures. This is done repeatedly until the network is robust enough for a given process.

5 Evaluation

After describing our implementation, this section presents the evaluation of the results. In order to ensure a consistent naming scheme we will refer to the four Conv layer stacks of the ECG network described in Sect. 3.2 as *conv4*, *conv5*, *conv6*, *conv7*. We apply different mitigations to the remaining parts of the network, which consists of both a preprocessing step (which was initially included in the network) and a few small fully connected layers.

5.1 Analyzing Degradation Effects

In order to make informed decisions about applying the proposed mitigations, it is necessary to interpret the effects of device variability. In Fig. 7 these effects are plotted by representing the weight storage in a rectangular grid.

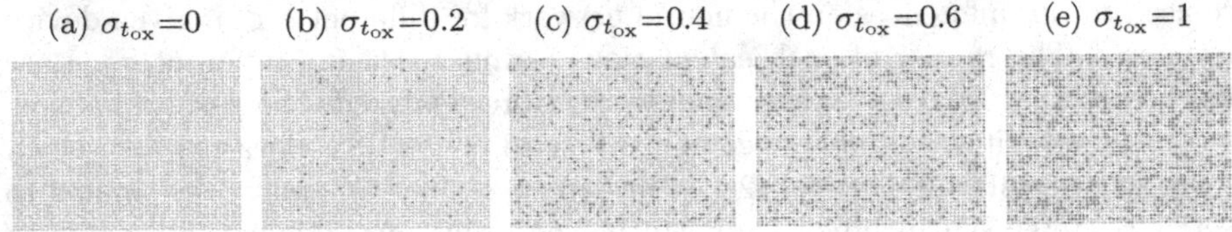

Fig. 7. Erroneously read values in different weight matrices using the *conv6* layer of the ECG network according to different $\sigma_{t_{ox}}$ [nm]. Red fields indicate read errors, while orange fields indicate correctly read values.

Significant weight matrix deterioration occurs for $\sigma_{t_{ox}} > 0.4$ nm; a neural network which has 35% of its weights stored incorrectly is unlikely to yield meaningful results, unless it contains a lot of inherent redundancy.

Another aspect to look out for is the influence of certain layers of the network. The analysis of the network described in Sect. 4.1 yields the results shown in Fig. 8a). Individual network layers cope quite differently with weight deterioration: Erroneous weights in the *conv4*, *conv5* and *conv7* layers only result in slight accuracy losses even for large variations of $\sigma_{t_{ox}}$. The *conv6* layer reacts differently, accuracy strongly decreases even for medium variations of $\sigma_{t_{ox}}$.

In order to view this from another perspective, the results from an "inverse" experiment, where all but a single layer is stored in unreliable RRAM-based storage can be found in Fig. 8b). The results are in line with the ones presented in Fig. 8a): the *conv6* layer shows the largest impact on overall accuracy, validating our previous claims.

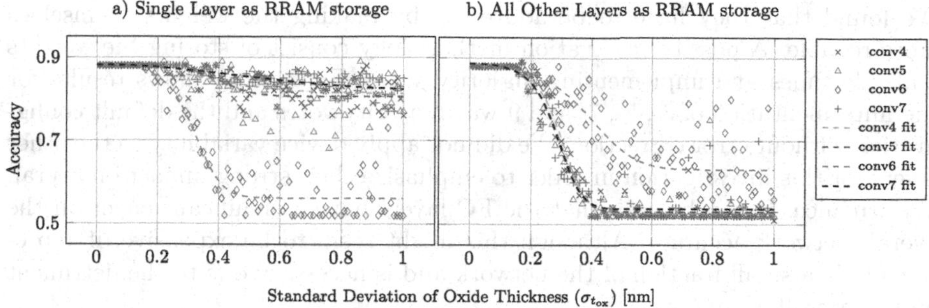

Fig. 8. Effects of variation on accuracy for individual layers

5.2 Applying Mitigations

After presenting an analysis of the effects of unreliable storage on the networks performance, we can use this data in order so study how it affects the proposed mitigation methodologies presented in Sect. 4. In the following we will show these effects by adding mitigations in a sequential manner, meaning that each mitigation is applied to a net that is already treated with all of the previously evaluated mitigations, which aren't sufficient on their own.

Preprocessing: For the task described above, a preprocessing consisting of a non-trainable filter kernel is applied. Since this can be implemented as a convolutional layer, we analyzed whether it makes sense to hardwire this layer, thereby separating it from the actual ANN. This would be unusual for architectures like GPUs, but might be beneficial for our architecture. Implementation based on the existing ANN hardware leads to the results in Fig. 9a), while hardwiring leads to the results depicted in Fig. 9b). This implies that hardwiring this step is necessary for large $\sigma_{t_{ox}}$, but not sufficient on its own.

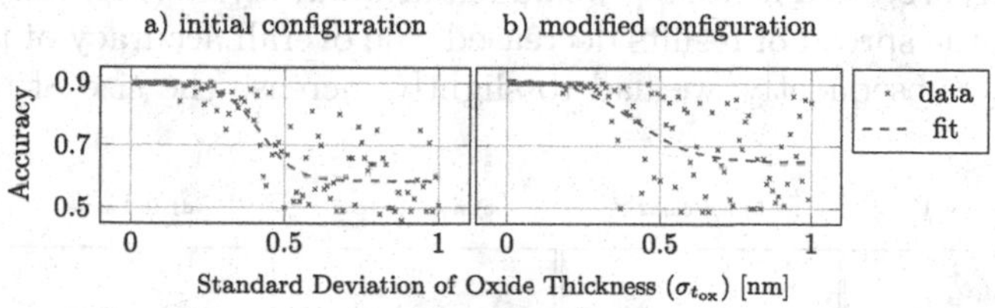

Fig. 9. Accuracy deterioration in different preprocessing configurations: a) (all weights in RRAM storage) and b) (separate hardwired preprocessing layers)

Fully Connected Layers: As described in Sect. 3.2 the overall network architecture consists of a combination of larger convolutional layers and two small fully connected layers. Those FC layers embed a total of 100 weights. This small number of weights renders these layers exceptionally susceptible to variations.

We found that they have to be addressed by making the weights themselves more reliable. A possible mitigation methodology consist of storing the weights multiple times and implementing majority votes. Figure 10a) shows results for the implementation of 3-, 5-, 7- and 9-way majority votes and the default configuration without error correction. We did not apply device variability to the other layers for this investigation in order to emphasize their strong impact on overall performance. It can be seen that the FC layers have a significant effect on the overall network accuracy. Although this might seem to be expensive, it represents only a small fraction of the network and is necessary due to the detriment on the overall accuracy

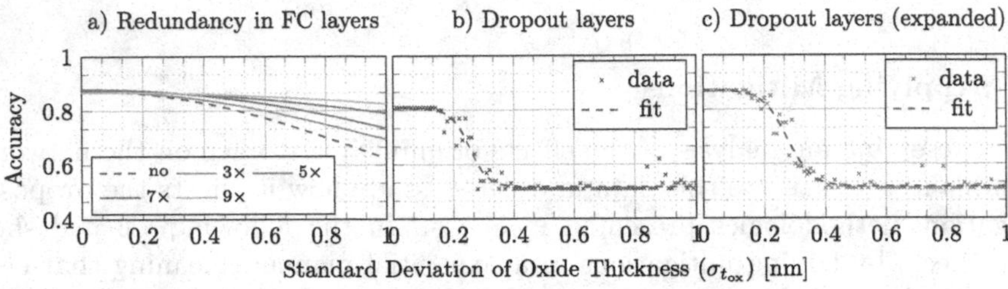

Fig. 10. Accuracy for redundancy in FC layers and insertion of dropout layers

At this point, the user has to select a level of redundancy depending on the process the ANN is supposed to be fabricated in. When using the IHP RRAM technology, 3-way majority vote within the FC layers is likely to achieve reasonable accuracy (not taking the other parts of the network into account), this might not be true for a different process with a deviating $\sigma_{t_{ox}}$. The following sections will assume that reasonable mitigation (using majority votes) has been applied to the FC layers.

Dropout Layers: As a next step we added dropout layers (Fig. 10b)). Unfortunately, while the spread of results decreased, the overall accuracy of the network deteriorated. Subsequently, we had to slightly increase the size of the network

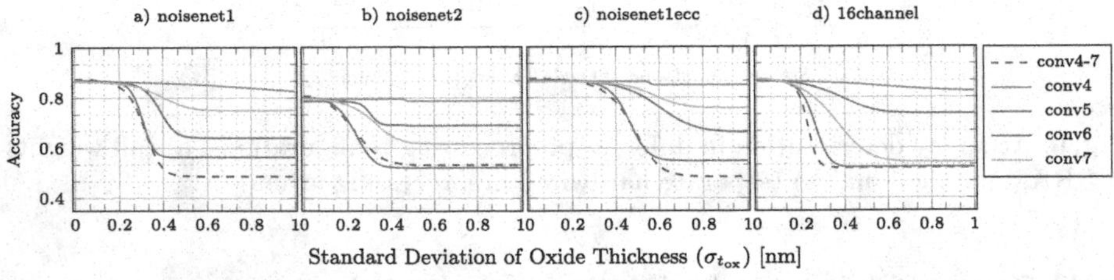

Fig. 11. Performance of different mitigations presented in this paper. The solid lines represent a single layer being investigated, the dashed line represents all of those layers being analyzed at once.

to counter the effects of these layers on the overall accuracy (Fig. 10c)). In the following, we will proceed to use the dropout layers with the expanded network.

Fault-Aware Training: Fault injection during training can be a powerful tool in order to render a network more error tolerant. We trained two networks with differently configured noisy training data. The accuracy results when analyzing both the entire network and individual layers are shown in Fig. 11a) and 11b). The results show that *noisenet2* decreases overall performance while *noisenet1* succeeds in mitigating issues for low to medium device variations.

Redundancy - Expanding Channels: Convolutional ANNs work on different channels, the number of which can be increased utilizing the technique of channel expansion [27] in order to add redundancy. Since the original network is optimized for energy per inference and area, the authors have tried to reduce redundancy as much as possible. While this is not an issue for traditional architectures, it causes problems when utilizing RRAM-based weight storage, since weights might be stored incorrectly. RRAM devices naturally allow for larger storage densities, overall area savings are possible even if more individual storage cells have to be used in order to introduce redundancy. In order to make use of this property, we added 16 additional channels to the *conv6* and *conv7* layers. The results of this experiment can be found in Fig. 11d). It does not seem to improve the network and actually causes *conv7* to be similarly sensitive to device variations as *conv6*.

Redundancy - Error Correction: As we will see within the quantitative analysis, fault tolerant training (applying specific kinds of noise) and expanding network sizes alone were not sufficient. We therefore opted for additional error correction for the network. This comes at a cost, but greatly benefits the accuracy of the resulting system. Since traditional error correction approaches, like error correction codes, require significant chip area [12], it was decided to implement a majority vote based error correction, as described above. Adding ECC to *noisenet1* yields the plot shown in Fig. 11c). This vastly improves robustness and the network is now usable for up to a standard deviation of 0.4 nm of oxide thickness for an accuracy of 87%. The initial network configuration was only able to tolerate a $\sigma_{t_{\mathrm{ox}}}$ of 0.2 nm.

5.3 Quantitative Analysis of Results

When trying to compare these results, a metric must be found that quantifies the improvements gained. This is not trivial, because the accuracy in our model is not a fixed value but dependent on the applied variation strength of the oxide thickness and shows increasing spread with higher variation. Therefore we present different metrics in order capture the various aspects involved, instead of a general score. In this paper we are not focusing on this spread, since it requires very large data sets and therefore causes a significant increase in simulation time. Instead we are generating one accuracy value per variation sample and iterate this process over a range of variations.

Since this data has a rather large amount of noise, which can be seen in the previous plots, we are fitting the data to a logistic function in order to better represent the statistical behavior of the model. In Sect. 3.1 we have shown that this is a good function for this purpose. In the left column of Fig. 12 these fits are displayed.

These fits alone are not yet a quantitative measure for determining the improvement a mitigation such as fault-aware training. Here we are proposing two different metrics (positive values indicate better performing networks):

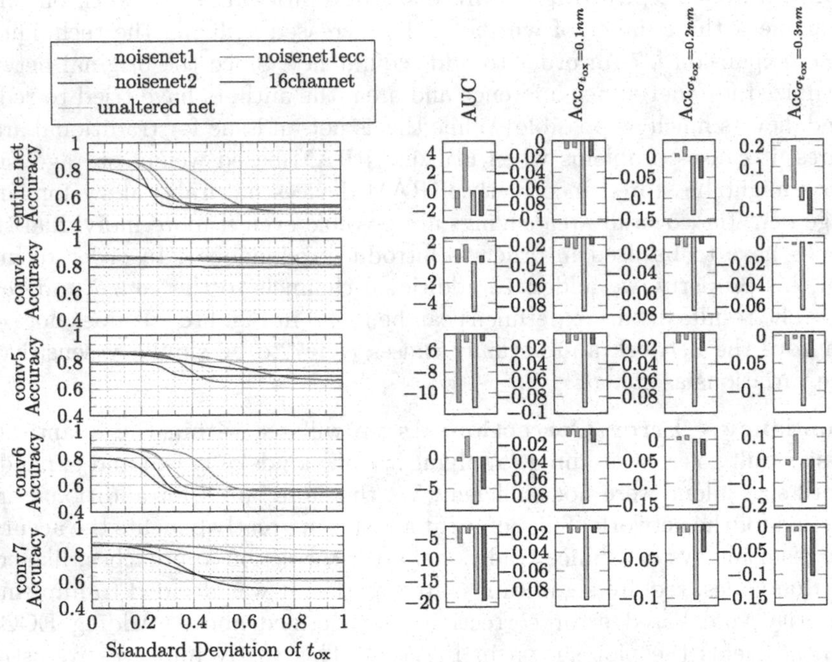

Fig. 12. Evaluation using fits to logistic functions and metrics

1. Area under Curve (AUC): By integrating the difference between the two accuracy curves a rather global metric can be defined that takes the whole spectrum of variations that were measured into account. This is of course dependent on the range of variation strengths that were simulated and needs to be kept in mind when interpreting the results. The results for this metric can be found in column 2 of Fig. 12.

2. Accuracy increase for target variation strength ($Acc_{\sigma_{t_{ox}}=x}$)**:** Here the increase in accuracy is evaluated for a given target variation. This metric only considers a small part of the data and is therefore usually only useful when estimates for the variation strength are available, but under this circumstance it provides a more useful metric. We used 0.1 nm, 0.2 nm and 0.3 nm because these are realistic numbers, as 0.17 nm resembles the variation for the used technology by IHP [9]. The results for this metric can be found in columns 3–5 of Fig. 12.

From the numbers two trends can be seen: Firstly, the stronger the variation, the more effective the mitigations get. Secondly, on a single layer the benefits are marginal at best, but when the mitigations are applied to the whole network, they start to work. For our network we found, that *noisenet1* can yield some benefit in some use cases and *noisenet1ecc* shows similar characteristics but much stronger.

6 Conclusion

In this work we presented a study of different mitigations for issues from read errors introduced by device variations in digital RRAM-based ANN accelerators. These mitigations are then evaluated using an real world example. We have been able to show that a given neural network can be made resilient against a given spread of a selected device parameter for a given fabrication process. However, there still is work to be done regarding the modelling of devices. Although the stochastic variability in RRAM devices still needs further understanding, it is known that this inherent characteristic is not only linked to variations in the thickness of the switching layer. Moreover, the lack of models which are able to accurately mimic the variability of the devices operation is hindering the study of its impact in RRAM-based ANNs. Thus, this work stands as a preliminary assessment of the impact of RRAM variability over quality metrics on system level. As future work, further studies will consider different modeling approaches which capture the device's non-idealities in a more empirical way, e.g. using behavioral models based on experimental measurements.

References

1. Baldi, P., Sadowski, P.: Understanding dropout. Adv. Neural Inf. Process. Syst. **26** (2013)
2. Berthelier, A., et al.: Deep model compression and architecture optimization for embedded systems: a survey. J. Signal Process, Syst., October 2020
3. Bianco, S., et al.: Benchmark analysis of representative deep neural network architectures. IEEE Access 6 (2018)
4. BMBF: Pilotinnovationswettbewerb "Energieeffizientes KI-System" (2021)
5. Charan, G., et al.: Accurate inference with inaccurate RRAM devices: A joint algorithm-design solution. IEEE J. on Exploratory Solid-State Computational Devices and Circuits (2020)
6. Chen, L., et al.: Accelerator-friendly neural-network training: learning variations and defects in RRAM crossbar. In: Design, Autom. Test in Europe Conf. Exhibition (DATE), pp. 19–24 (2017)
7. Fritscher, M., et al.: Simulating large neural networks embedding MLC RRAM as weight storage considering device variations. In: Latin America Symposium on Circuits and Systems (LASCAS), pp. 129–132

8. Grigorescu, S., et al.: A survey of deep learning techniques for autonomous driving. J. Field Robot. **37**(3), 362–386 (2020)
9. Grossi, A., et al.: Impact of intercell and intracell variability on forming and switching parameters in RRAM arrays. IEEE Trans. Electron Dev. **62**(8), 2502–2509 (2015)
10. Medler, D.A., Dawson, M.: Using redundancy to improve the performance of artificial neural networks (1999)
11. Milo, V., et al.: Multilevel HfO2-based RRAM devices for low-power neuromorphic networks. APL Mater. **7**(8), 081120 (2019)
12. Naseer, R., Draper, J.: DEC ECC design to improve memory reliability in sub-100nm technologies. In: 2008 15th IEEE International Conference on Electronics, Circuits and Systems, pp. 586–589 (2008)
13. Pérez, E., et al.: Optimization of multi-level operation in RRAM arrays for in-memory computing. Electronics p. accepted for publication (2021)
14. Radu, V., et al.: Performance aware convolutional neural network channel pruning for embedded GPUs. In: 2019 IEEE International Symposium on Workload Charact. (IISWC), pp. 24–34 (2019)
15. Reuben, J., Biglari, M., Fey, D.: Incorporating variability of resistive RAM in circuit simulations using the Stanford-PKU model. IEEE Trans. Nanotechnol. **19**, 508–518 (2020)
16. Salami, B., Unsal, O.S., Kestelman, A.C.: On the resilience of RTL NN accelerators: fault characterization and mitigation. In: 30th International Symposium on Computer Architecture and High Perform. Computing (SBAC-PAD), pp. 322–329 (2018)
17. Shazeer, N., et al.: Outrageously large neural networks: The sparsely-gated mixture-of-experts layer abs/1701.06538 (2017)
18. Song, Z., et al.: ITT-RNA: Imperfection tolerable training for RRAM-crossbar-based deep neural-network accelerator. IEEE Trans. Comput.-Aided Des. Integr. Circuits Syst. **40**(1), 129–142 (2021)
19. Stathopoulos, S., et al.: Multibit Memory Operation of Metal-Oxide Bi-Layer Memristors. Sci. Rep. **7**(1), 1–7 (2017)
20. Sun, X., et al.: Fully parallel RRAM synaptic array for implementing binary neural network with (+1, −1) weights and (+1, 0) neurons. In: 2018 23rd Asia and South Pacific Design Automation Conference (ASP-DAC), pp. 574–579 (2018)
21. Tan, Y., Nanya, T.: Fault-tolerant back-propagation model and its generalization ability. In: Proceedings of 1993 International Conference on Neural Networks (IJCNN-93-Nagoya, Japan), vol. 3, pp. 2516–2519 (1993)
22. Tang, T., et al.: Binary convolutional neural network on RRAM. In: 22nd Asia and South Pac. Design Automation Conference (ASP-DAC), pp. 782–787 (2017)
23. Tsai, H., et al.: Recent progress in analog memory-based accelerators for deep learning. J. Phys. D Appl. Phys. **51**(28), 283001 (2018)
24. Verhelst, M., Moons, B.: Embedded deep neural network processing: algorithmic and processor techniques bring deep learning to IoT and edge devices. IEEE Solid-State Circuits Mag. **9**(4), 55–65 (2017)
25. Xia, L., et al.: Switched by input: Power efficient structure for RRAM-based convolutional neural network. In: 2016 53nd ACM/EDAC/IEEE Design Automation Conference (DAC), pp. 1–6. IEEE Press (2016)
26. Xiong, W., et al.: Toward human parity in conversational speech recognition. IEEE/ACM Trans. Audio Speech Lang. Process. **25**(12), 2410–2423 (2017)
27. Yang, Y., et al.: Channel expansion convolutional network for image classification. IEEE Access **8** (2020)

28. Yin, S., et al.: XNOR-SRAM: in-memory computing SRAM macro for binary/ternary deep neural networks. IEEE J. Solid-State Circuits **55**(6), 1733–1743 (2020)
29. Yin, X., Liu, X.: Multi-task convolutional neural network for pose-invariant face recognition. IEEE Trans. Image Process. **27**(2), 964–975 (2018)
30. Zahid, U., et al.: FAT: training neural networks for reliable inference under hardware faults. In: 2020 IEEE International Test Conference (ITC), pp. 1–10 (2020)
31. Zhang, Y., et al.: An improved RRAM-based binarized neural network with high variation-tolerated forward/backward propagation module. IEEE Trans. Electron Dev. **67**(2), 469–473 (2020)

SparseMAX: Accelerating Quantum Neural Networks on GPU Clusters Using Sparse-Matrix Kernels

Anand Ravishankar[1,2(✉)], Santhi Natarajan[3], and A. Bharathi Malakreddy[1,2]

[1] BMS Institute of Technology and Management, Yelahanka, Bengaluru 560064, India
[2] Visvesvaraya Technological University, Belagavi, India
anandravishankar12@gmail.com, bharathi_m@bmsit.in
[3] Shiv Nadar University, Chennai 603110, India
santhinatarajan@snuchennai.edu.in

Abstract. The growing popularity of Applied Quantum Mechanics and Artificial Intelligence drives the need for integrating the two fields. Quantum Neural Networks (QNNs) incorporate quantum aspects into classical deep learning networks which are capable of performing universal quantum computations. The dense representation of QNNs presents great challenges in terms of computational cost and noise susceptibility. In this paper, we present SparseMAX, a novel Sparse Quantum Neural Network (SQNN) that is robust to noise and interference for large volumes of network parameters. We also introduce Quantron (ψ), a generalized version of perceptron, which acts on qubits and performs the necessary quantum operations. Based on these insights, we develop 2 GPU kernels. The first kernel estimates the network architecture through a quantum training algorithm. The second kernel accelerates a sparsified version of the network matrices on a GPU cluster. We validate our kernel performance and training algorithm and present the results in terms of inference time, GPU efficiency and scalability. On an average, SparseMAX utilizes 54.83% of our GPU cluster's compute resources, while offering a 41.51$\times$ speedup in terms of serial inference timing measurements for network layer range [120, 1920] and neurons per layer range [1024,4096]

Keywords: Quantum computing · Neural networks · Sparse models · Hardware acceleration

1 Introduction

Researchers have applied Deep Neural Networks (DNN) [1] to a range of scientific and societal applications [2]. Loosely modeled after the complex structure of a biological learning system, DNNs derive an input-output mapping, through an interconnected set of nodes. Researchers have often incorporated concepts from different fields to ascend barriers in reducing the computational cost of training a DNN. The solutions include expediting matrix computations on hardware

© Springer Nature Switzerland AG 2022
A. Orailoglu et al. (Eds.): SAMOS 2021, LNCS 13227, pp. 418–431, 2022.
https://doi.org/10.1007/978-3-031-04580-6_28

accelerators through algorithm-hardware co-design, replacing backpropagation with genetic algorithms for DNN optimization based on natural meta-heuristics, etc. Our paper follows a similar path, by taking inspiration from multiple fields, and presents a architecture capable of improving the exisiting methodology [3].

1.1 Quantum Neural Networks

With the advent of Quantum Computing (QC), integrating the main components of QC with DNNs is an extremely exciting avenue. The eclectic combination of quantum mechanics with neural computation gave rise to Quantum Neural Networks (QNN) [4,5]. QNNs employ quantum entanglement, superposition, and unitary transformations to circumvent the limitations of classic DNNs in handling complex unstructured datasets. QNNs require a generalized perceptron structure and associated activation function to accommodate mathematical formulations of quantum mechanics as against the classical representation [6]. The linear nature of quantum processes serves to be the principle challenge in QNN development, while DNNs have a crucial dependency on non-linearity. Despite these challenges, QNNs present an enticing approach to developing large-scale networks with reduced computational cost [7].

1.2 Injecting Sparsity in a Network

The latency observed, when a QNN is subjected to large volumes of datasets, contributes to substantial overhead [8]. The main technique employed to reduce inference latency is to prune the network. Pruning sparsifies a dense network by trimming off network connections that do not contribute significantly to model performance. However, there exists a trade-off between the amount of sparsity introduced and model validity. Researchers have dwelled on the level of fine tuning to be applied, amongst which element-wise pruning [9] being the most granular and sparsity pattern being the least granular [10] techniques.

1.3 Accelerating Sparse QNN

To accelerate the Sparse QNN (SQNN), the core computations are ported onto accelerator platforms. The matrix computations involved in SQNN development are performed on matrices stored in Compressed Sparse Row (CSR) representation. The feature row and weight column is processed in parallel by assiging them to individual warps and threads. We apply a Block-wise pruning technique with a stride size less than 32 as the GPU architecture limits the thread block size to 32 $\times$ 32. Organizing these blocks along with shared memory offers ultra fine-tuned task and data parallelism, resulting in high throughput and bottleneck elimination.

In this paper, we present SparseMAX, a novel Sparse QNN (SQNN) network architecture with specific shape constraints on the pruning pattern. We also propose two CUDA kernels for accelerated computation of the pruned SQNN. In particular, the primary kernel constructs the QNN architecture by minimizing the error estimate between input and output qubits. The secondary kernel compresses the feature set and weight vector into sparse row representations. The kernel assigns the weight representation to thread blocks and decomposes the Sparse Matrix Multiplication (SMM) across multiple blocks of the GPU to accelerate the multiplication process. We have used the Amazon Graph Challenge Data [3] set consisting of synthetic DNNs created by RadiX-Net with varying numbers of neurons and layers to get inference and scalability results.

2 SparseMAX: A Theoretical Perspective

To develop a QNN, we have modified a basic perceptron into a Quantron (ψ), to incorporate quantum behavior. The modifications are necessary, as quantum functions are linear in nature while neural structures are heavily based on non-linear functions [11]. ψ acts on a set of m input qubits and produces a set of n output qubits for each layer l [12]. Additionally, the qubits are placed in a state of superposition to record and analyze the effect of severing any particular connection. The resulting state space of the neural network composes of the Hilbert state space having N dimensionality, as each ψ has to operate in a probabilistic manner. Let ϕ_{i} be the wave equation representing the ith ψ. At any time t, the action of performing a measurement on the system will describe the dormancy/firing state of any arbitrary ψ. The quantity being measured is the probability amplitude which grows in a deterministic manner. The act of measuring the probability amplitude collapses the curve into a singular value and represented by a Hermitean operator ϕ as shown in Eq. 1.

$$\phi = \sum_{i=1}^{N} \alpha_{\mathrm{i}} |s_{\mathrm{i}}\rangle \tag{1}$$

where α_{i} and $|s_{\mathrm{i}}\rangle$ represents the ith ψ's normalized basis and state. The remainder of the section describes the ψ's construction, the associated quantum functionalities and kernel function.

2.1 ψ (Quantron): Specialized Neuron Architecture

Consider a classical perceptron tasked with obtaining an output y given a set of inputs x_i. Equation 2 describes a perceptron model with weight set i and activation function f.

$$y = f(\sum_{i=1}^{N} w_{\mathrm{i}} x_{\mathrm{i}}) \tag{2}$$

The weight set is updated according to Eq. 3, where $\hat{y}$ is the ground truth and η is the learning rate.

$$w_{\mathrm{i}}(t+1) := w_{\mathrm{i}}(t) + \eta(\hat{y} - y)x_{\mathrm{i}} \tag{3}$$

Constructing a SparseMAX following the learning rule is difficult as there is no analog $\hat{F}$ for the non-linear activation function. The proposed ψ introduces a unitary operation in addition to minor assests to introduce non-linearity into the architecture [13]. The resulting block is similar to a perceptron in terms of functionality with additional quantum layers built on top of it, enabling efficient learning. The ψ takes an input state ρ^{in} and produces an output state ρ^{out} through Eq. 4.

$$\rho^{\mathrm{out}} = U\rho^{\mathrm{in}}U^{\dagger} \tag{4}$$

The ground truth of a ψ exists in a fuzzy state, between connection-existing (1) and connection-severed (0) states, parameterized by the input dataset x and weight set w. The output obtained through the unitary operation is mapped onto the phase of a quantum state $|x_1, \ldots, x_{\mathrm{N}}\rangle$ in an N-dimensional Hilbert state space and an enhanced Kitaev phase-estimation algorithm [14,15] is applied with precision τ. The resulting quantum state $\rho^{\mathrm{out}} = |J_1, \ldots, J_\tau\rangle$ is an initial estimate of ψ. The consistent mapping produced from the input to ρ_{out} replicates classical activation functions with a high degree of similarity.

2.2 Quantum Neural Network

Having defined ψ's functionality, we can now describe the network in detail. The QNN consists of l hidden layers constructing a mapping between ρ^{in} and ρ^{out} as per Eq. 5

$$\rho^{\mathrm{out}} = tr(\mathcal{U}(\rho^{\mathrm{in}} \otimes |J_1, \ldots, J_\tau\rangle_{\mathrm{hidden,out}}\langle J_1, \ldots, J_\tau|)\mathcal{U}^{\dagger}) \tag{5}$$

where $\mathcal{U}$ is the cascaded set of unitary matrices $\mathcal{U} = U^{\mathrm{out}}.U^{\mathrm{out}-1}..U^{l}.U^{l\text{-}1}..U^{\mathrm{in}}$ consisting of ψ acting on input qubits. Given M patterns to learn, the input states ρ_i^{in} are prepared with a projection operator $\rho_i^{\mathrm{in}*}$. The process of preparing the ith input, consists of measuring and renormalizing as per Eq. 6.

$$\rho_{\mathrm{i}}^{\mathrm{in}} = \frac{\rho_i^{\mathrm{in}*}\rho_0\rho_{\mathrm{i}}^{\mathrm{in}*}}{tr(\rho_{\mathrm{i}}^{\mathrm{in}*}\rho_0\rho_{\mathrm{i}}^{\mathrm{in}*})} \tag{6}$$

where ρ_0 is the density matrix. Similarly, output states are defined with the corresponding projection operator $\rho_{\mathrm{i}}^{\mathrm{out}*}$. The measurement ensures a nonlinear behaviour in the QNN.

In order to propogate and optimise the network, two local cost functions are defined: Let E_i denote probability of not finding the input state in the ith state despite it existing in the ith state and let F_i denote probability of finding the input state in the ith state despite it not existing in the ith state. A global cost function $\mathcal{E}$ is defined to improve the network performance by re-adjusting the weight set. Equation 7 formulates the total error for M training samples, with the local errors being depicted in the numerator, parameterized by projection operators $\rho_{\rm i}^{\rm out*}$, $\rho_{\rm i}^{\rm in*}$ and their respective orthogonal complements $Q_{\rm i}^{\rm out}$ and $Q_{\rm i}^{\rm in}$.

$$\mathcal{E} = \sum_{i=1}^{M} \frac{\frac{tr(Q_{\rm i}^{\rm out} U \rho_{\rm i}^{\rm in*} \rho 0 \rho_{\rm i}^{\rm in*} U^{\dagger} Q_{\rm i}^{\rm out})}{tr(\rho_{\rm i}^{in*} \rho_{\rm out} \rho_{\rm i}^{in*})} + \frac{tr(\rho_{\rm i}^{\rm out*} U Q_{\rm i}^{\rm in} \rho 0 Q_{\rm i}^{\rm in} U^{\dagger} \rho_{\rm i}^{\rm out*})}{tr(Q_{\rm i}^{\rm in} \rho_0 Q_{\rm i}^{\rm in})}}{2M} \tag{7}$$

The technique presented above restricts the set of unitary matrices and presents the probability of find one such set within an acceptable probability of error. Gardner [16] suggests the use of the local loss functions E_i and F_i, rather than probing the entire search space of unitary matrices and finding the one corresponding to the minimal cost function.

Code snippet presented in Listing 1.1 displays the CUDA kernel responsible for determining the SparseMAX structure using an accept-reject condition for $\rho^{\rm out}$. The accept-reject condition is based purely on the basis of quantum superposition. The probability $\rho^{\rm out}$ connection surviving is dependent on the output of the super imposed input states fed into ψ.

2.3 Complexity of QNN

To analyze the cost of a SparseMAX, we need to associate a cost with each operation performed. Given k operations being performed on a single qubit, the total complexity is $\mathcal{O}(2^k)$. This forms an upper bound on the cost of training a generic QNN. Quantum Associative networks (QAN) [17] are considered to be a basic version of QNNs. Hence the time complexity of QANs form the lower bound for our architecture. QAN's have a linear time complexity in terms of the number of elements to be folded in the superposition M and the number of dimensions N $\mathcal{O}(MN)$. The remainder of the paper is focused on reducing hypothesized time complexity through the introduction of sparsity into the unitary matrices and finally expediting the training on a GPU cluster.

```
__global__ void calc_features(double* current_fitarray,
  double* memory_fitarray, int data_size, double goal) {

    double theta, c;
    double mx;
    double error, est;
    int xy_data_size = data_size + 1;
    double* x = new double[xy_data_size];
    double* y = new double[xy_data_size];
    bool rho_out;

    memory_fitarray[2 * (data_size)] = log10(num);
    memory_fitarray[2 * (data_size)+1] = log10(pow(
  current_fitarray[0], -2) - 1);
    for (int i = 0; i <= data_size; ++i) {
        x[i] = memory_fitarray[2 * i];
        y[i] = memory_fitarray[2 * i + 1];
```

```
        }
        //Get Unitary Matrix set U and obtain estimate
        U = kitaev_phase_estimate(y[i]);
        est = U*error_interval(x, y, mx, data_size + 1, theta,
        c)*conjugate_transpose(U);
        error = y[data_size] - x[data_size] * theta - c;
        //Check if error is smaller than the estimate
        if (error <= est) {
            rho_out = 1;
        }
        else {
            rho_out = 0;
        }
}
```

Listing 1.1. CUDA Kernel pseudo-code for SparseMAX Error Estimation

3 Sparse Matrix-Matrix Computation on GPU

In the previous section, we define the modified perceptron (ψ) along with the network architecture along with the CUDA kernel for error estimation. In the following section, we introduce sparse models and the relevant nomenclature. Finally, we discuss GPU architecture and the proposed CUDA scheme for decomposing the matrix computations across the processing elements of the GPU.

3.1 Introducing Sparsity and Related Nomenclature

The resources required to train and serve QNN scales with the network architecture and dataset size. However, physical limitations in terms of computational power restrict the availability of these resources. As a result, researchers have looked into neighboring avenues to improve efficiency. The field of finite elements proposes the concept of sparse matrices, which have a high ratio of zero to non-zero elements. Sparsifying the matrix reduces the computation cost associated with the unitary matrices.

An $m \times n$ matrix can be converted into a sparse format if the number of non-zero elements is few enough to bring down the complexity of the model. This reduces the memory requirements drastically by storing only the non-zero elements. There exist multiple data structures for data storage, each optimized for specific operations. In this paper, we adopt the Compressed Sparse Row (CSR) and the Compressed Sparse Column (CSC) representation for our matrices as they support efficient access and matrix operations. Libraries like cuSparse are generally used for executing sparse matrix computations on GPUs. However, porting cuSparse operations on GPUs are unproductive as the hardware design is optimized for dense matrices unless the sparsity ratio is extremely high. We can optimize the performance here by applying constraints on the pruning patterns.

As shown in Fig. 1, there exist three primary pruning techniques for obtaining sparse matrices [18]. The blocks highlighted in blue are placed under scrutiny and

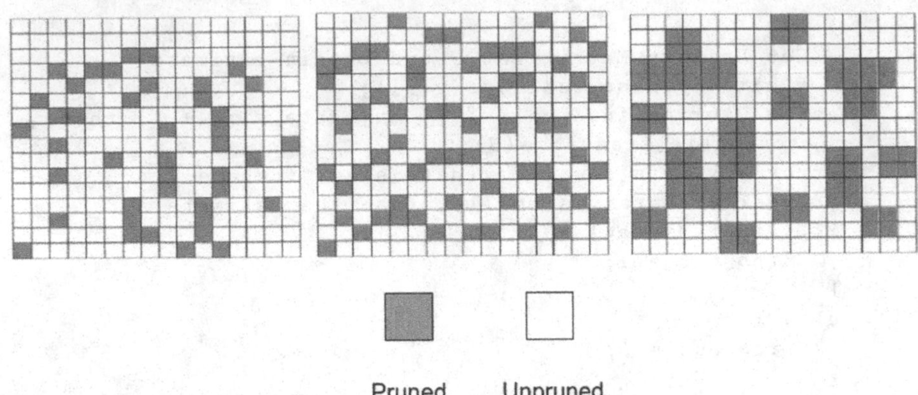

Fig. 1. Three primary pruning techniques for an NXN Matrix (L-R): Element-wise pruning(EW), Vector-wise pruning(VW) (4X1 Vectors), Block-wise pruning(BW) (2X2 Blocks)

the matrix elements corresponding to those blocks can be potentially nullified. In Element-Wise (EW) pruning, we judge each connection based on its importance. Note that this technique does not impose any pattern restriction and hence lacks a structure for acceleration. Moreover, the random distribution of zero elements makes the kernel function's memory access irregular and hence poses a challenge for hardware acceleration. In Vector-Wise (VW) pruning, we divide the matrix into multiple vectors and perform pruning within each vector. A pre-determined set of elements are pruned through a ranking process. This ensures randomness preservation along with a well defined structure. In Block-Wise (BW), we divide the matrix into blocks of pre-determined size and perform pruning within each block. BW provides a generalized version of EW, with the block size increasing on demand. Both VW and BW are well-structured pruning patterns and provide efficient hardware acceleration. However the lack of rigidity in BW forces us to opt for the slower, yet detailed VW.

3.2 Design of Sparse Matrix Computation

A Sparse Matrix Multiplication operation (SpMM) performs the computation $AB = C$, where A is a sparse matrix in CSR format of dimension $m \times k$, B is a dense row major matrix of dimension $k \times n$ and C is a dense matrix of dimension $m \times n$. CSR format stores all non-zero elements of a sparse matrix into a vector. Two additional vectors representing the row and column pointer are used to access values in the sparse matrix. Figure 2 illustrates a sample sparse matrix representation.

The number of access operations performed to fetch data from the GPU's main memory increases as the matrix dimensionality increase, resulting in increased latency. Thread-level parallelism (TLP) aims to keep the GPU optimally functioning such that when a warp needs to perform a memory operation,

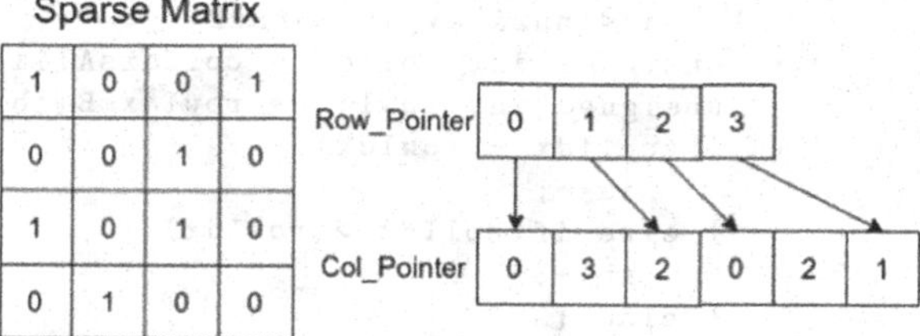

Fig. 2. A 4 × 4 Sparse Matrix decomposed through column and row pointers. The combination of these pointers indicate position of 1 in the matrix.

the scheduler puts the warp to a sleep state and calls one of the warps in the active state. If the occupancy of the SM is high, the warp- switches decrease the latency cost. By assigning each thread an equal workload and by merging memory access operations, we can optimize the overall performance. Any discrepancy in work distribution among threads leads to load-balancing issues [19], as threads assigned less work than others will stay idle for long periods.

In our work, each row of matrix A is assigned to an individual warp and each thread is responsible for loading a column of the matrix B. This leads to the memory access operations being coalesced resulting in optimal scheduling. Each thread has to perform 32 independent operations, which when combined with coalesced memory access for matrix B, significantly reduces the cost of memory operations. Thus, we achieve load balancing by processing instructions in batches of 32. Code snippet provided in Listing 1.2 shows the CUDA kernel responsible for conducting SpMM. SpMM loops over the non-empty feature vectors followed by looping over the non-zero entries in the column vector of the matrix B. Finally, we compute the dot product at the intersection and store the result in matrix C.

```
#define BLOCK_DIM 32
__global__ void spmspm(COOMatrix *result, CSRMatrix *A, CSCMatrix *B, float bias) {
    unsigned int r = blockIdx.y*blockDim.y + threadIdx.y;
    unsigned int c = blockIdx.x*blockDim.x + threadIdx.x;
    unsigned int temp = 0;
    if(r < A->numRows && c < B->numCols) {
        unsigned int rowPtrA = A->rowPtrs[r];
        unsigned int nnzA = A->rowPtrs[r + 1] - rowPtrA;
        if(nnzA > 0){
            unsigned int *colIdxsA = A->colIdxs + rowPtrA;
            float *valueA = A->values + rowPtrA;
            unsigned int colPtrB = B->colPtrs[c];
            unsigned int nnzB = B->colPtrs[c + 1] - colPtrB;
            if(nnzB > 0){
                unsigned int *rowIdxsB = B->rowIdxs + colPtrB;
                float *valueB = B->values + colPtrB;
                float sum = 0;
                unsigned int ia = 0;
                unsigned int ib = 0;
```

```
                while(ia < nnzA && ib < nnzB){
                    unsigned int colIdx = colIdxsA[ia];
                    unsigned int rowIdx = rowIdxsB[ib];
                    if(colIdx < rowIdx) {
                        ia++;
                    } else if(colIdx > rowIdx) {
                        ib++;
                    } else {
                        sum += valueA[ia] * valueB[ib];
                        ia++;
                        ib++;
                    }
                }
                if(sum > THRESHOLD || sum < -THRESHOLD) {
                    sum += bias;

                    if(sum > 0) {
                        if(sum>YMAX) {
                            sum = YMAX;
                        }

                        temp = atomicAdd(&result->nnz, 1);
                        result->colIdxs[temp] = c;
                        result->values[temp] = sum;
                        result->rowIdxs[temp] = r;
                    }
                }
            }
        }
    }
}
```

Listing 1.2. CUDA Kernel pseudo-code for SpMM Computation

4 Results

In this section, we present our empirical results and analysis of the SparseMAX kernels introduced in the previous sections. We have developed the kernels for minimizing the global error. The SparseMAX architecture evolves through these kernels by parametereizing an initial set of 400 prototypes. Each prototype represents a variant of a base network architecture.

4.1 Data Description

The MNIST database of handwritten digits is widely used for training and testing neural networks. It consists of 60,000 28 × 28 pixel images. Each image is resized to 32 × 32 and 64 × 64, with each pixel in range [0,1]. The image pixels are converted into a feature vector and saved as a .tsv file.

The RadiX-Net SDNN generates a wide range of DNNs with varied hyperparameters, produced with the help of mixed radices. In our experimental setup, the base networks evolve to produce different prototypes with a varied number of neurons and layers. The total number of network connections is a function of the number of neurons per layer and the number of layers.

4.2 Accelerator Platform Description

We have conducted the experiments on VEGA, GPU computing cluster. VEGA consists of 2 nodes, each node having 2×18 core Intel Xeon Gold 5220 processors connected to 2×NVIDIA V100 GPUs. We would like to thank the Centre for Artificial Intelligence, TKM College of Engineering, Kerala Technological University, India, for hosting our code on the VEGA HPC Cluster, powered by V100 GPU Cards.

4.3 Dense QNN Configuration

For the network setup, we have used the RadiX generator to randomly generate the dense matrices with different floating-point values. We then train the dense implementations of our prototypes on the MNIST dataset. The base network consists of convolutional layers, followed by hidden layers and a softmax output layer. We have trained the prototypes using the error minimization CUDA snippet provided in Listing 1.1. The network's learning rate is in the range of 0.01 to 0.001, which decreases by a factor of 0.005 after each epoch. The hyperparameters are chosen based on a validation set of 20,000 samples. Figure 3 displays the global cost per prototype in the presence of arbitrary noise. We can observe a dip in the cost at around 800 prototypes after 20 rounds. This shows that the dense format of QNN is resilient to noise, when a large number of prototypes are used.

4.4 Sparsity-Based Results

The following set of results highlights the effect of introducing sparsity into the unitary matrices. Once we read the feature vectors and weights from the .tsv file, we allocate an output vector to create the output matrix C. Subsequently, we convert the vector and weight set into a CSR format. We adopt a double buffering scheme to transfer data to the GPU. At each layer we perform the following actions on the GPU:

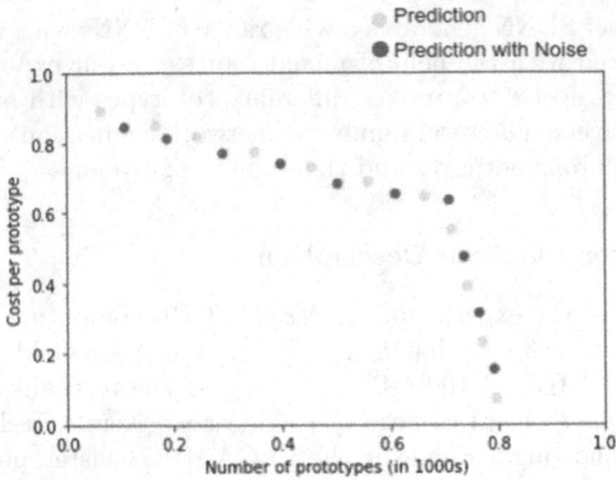

Fig. 3. Error measure of 1000 Dense QNN Prototypes

- Copy data to GPU
- Clear both the co-ordinate lists
- Compute SpMM
- Copy data to co-ordinate list from GPU
- Convert output data to CSR for next layer
- Deallocate memory
- Check Global error

We repeat the entire process for all combinations of neurons per layer and number of layers. Table 1 describes the various timing parameters and Table 2 times the listed parameters for various network configurations. Note that the time taken to perform operations T1 to T8 remain the same for a network with growing depth. However it is worth observing that the processing times T2 and T4 do not follow this trend. These exceptions can be attributed to fact that these measurements relate to operations concerned with weight matrices. The weight matrix set of larger networks will undoubtedly take longer time for performing read and conversion operations. In contrast to, the feature vector remains constant for each network. The relative uniformity indicates the workload distribution and the resultant scalability. Inference time cannot be parametereized in terms of GPU operators and hence increases with an increase in network depth.

Our work emphasizes the scalability of the code as the data size increases along with an increase in the efficiency of GPU usage. While the inference time increases exponentially as the architecture grows, the time spent in performing the SpMM computation remains the same for a fixed number of neurons. The stagnancy of SpMM time directly correlates to optimal workload distribution among warps and threads. When compared to [3], SparseMAX offers 41.51× speedup in terms of serial inference timing measurements for network layer range [120, 1920] and neurons per layer range [1024, 4096].

Table 1. Network operations

Variable	Network operation
T1	Reading Feature vector
T2	Reading Weight vector
T3	Feature Conversion to CSR
T4	Weight Conversion to CSR
T5	Data Transfer to GPU
T6	SpMM Operation
T7	Data Transfer to Co-ordinate Lists
T8	Convert Co-ordinate Lists to CSR
T9	Inference Time

Table 2. Performance metrics for Network Operations for all neuron-layers combinations

Neurons per Layer	Layer Count	Number of Connections	Average Processing time for (in seconds)								
			T1	T2	T3	T4	T5	T6	T7	T8	T9
1024	120	3932160	1.629	1.270	0.380	0.036	0.010	**0.0524**	0.114	0.079	11.385
	480	15728640	1.634	9.131	0.464	0.164	0.007	**0.042**	0.113	0.057	38.497
	1920	62914560	1.637	20.579	0.391	0.687	0.003	**0.0118**	0.040	0.059	149.097
4096	120	15728640	6.458	5.267	3.915	0.153	0.040	**0.659**	0.438	3.138	160.674
	480	62914560	6.435	21.577	3.932	0.651	0.040	**0.654**	0.439	3.146	601.149
	1920	251658240	6.781	84.397	3.962	2.647	0.0398	**0.667**	0.431	3.152	1435.842

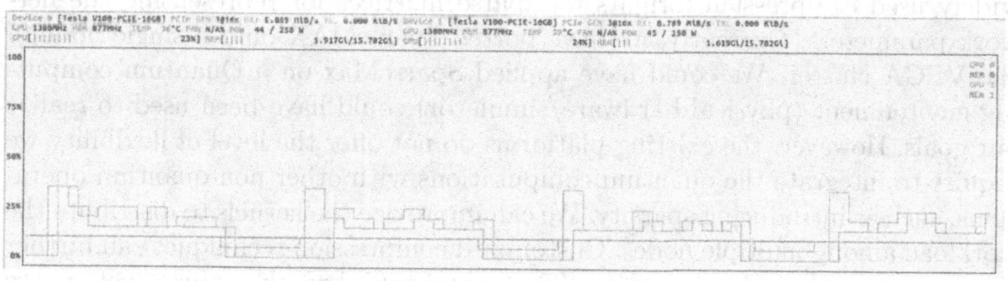

Fig. 4. GPU utilization of a network having 120 layers and 4096 neurons per layer

Figures 4, 5 and 6 represent the GPU utilization for different workloads. We can observe that as the network scales, the GPU performance increases. The memory utilization remains constant for a particular architecture set. The usage of these kernels do not result in any memory spikes and hovers at approximately 40% for any architecture. The CPU readings for both VEGA nodes show increase in CPU utilization with increase in workload. The GPU cluster achieves peak performance at multiple instances for heavy workloads, which further cements the validity of our secondary kernel.

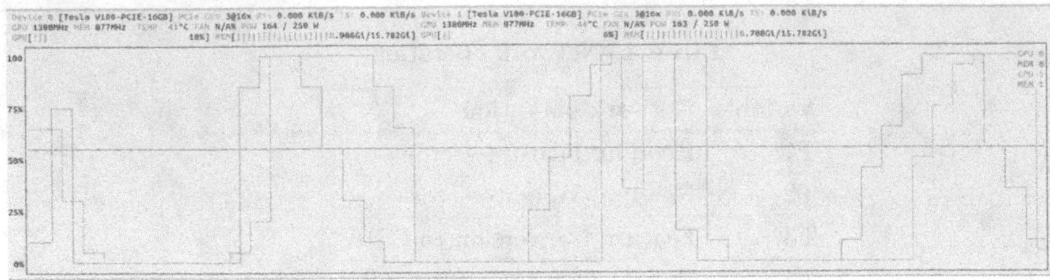

Fig. 5. GPU utilization of a network having 480 layers and 4096 neurons per layer

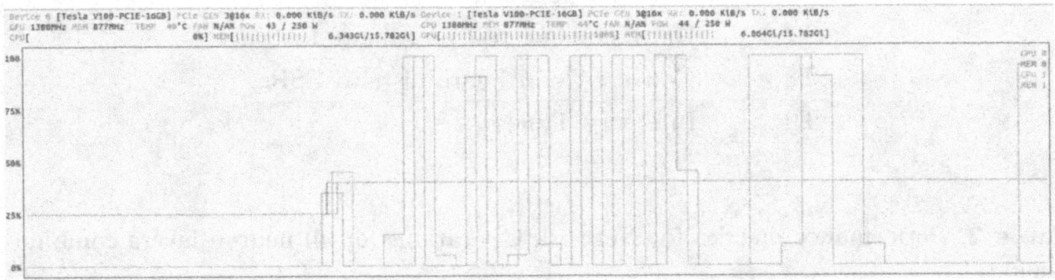

Fig. 6. GPU utilization of a network having 1920 layers and 4096 neurons per layer

5 Conclusion and Future Work

In this work, we introduce SparseMAX, an algorithm-architecture codesign of Sparse Quantum Neural Networks expedited on a GPU cluster. We utilize quantum mechanical aspects to modify and generalize existing DNNs. We employ widely used compression formats for sparse matrices for representing the network parameters. Currently, we have ported SparseMAX onto a single node of the VEGA cluster. We could have applied SparseMax on a Quantum computing environment (physical hardware/simulator) could have been used to realize our goals. However, the existing platforms do not offer the level of flexibility we require to integrate the quantum computations with other non-quantum operations, such as introducing sparsity. We can improvize the kernels to distribute the workload among multiple nodes. Customized compression techniques can further improvise the network parameters. The experimental results conclusively prove the efficacy of SparseMAX over the existing methodology in terms of inference latency [3].

References

1. Hinton, G.E., Osindero, S., Teh, Y.: A fast learning algorithm for deep belief nets. Neural Comput. **18**, 1527–1554 (2006)
2. Hu, H., Liu, Z., An, J.: Mining mobile intelligence for wireless systems: a deep neural network approach. IEEE Comput. Intell. Mag. **15**(1), 24–31 (2020)
3. Jeremy, K., Alford, S., Gadepally, V.: Sparse deep neural network graph challenge (2019)

4. Kak, S.: On quantum neural computing. Adv. Imaging Electron Phys. **94**, 259–313 (1995)
5. Chrisley, R.: Quantum learning. New directions in cognitive science. In: Proceedings of the International Symposium, Saariselka, August 1995, Lapland, Finland. Helsinki: Finnish Association of Artificial Intelligence, pp. 77–89 (1995)
6. Behrman, E.C., Steck, J.E., Kumar, P., Walsh, K.A.: Quantum algorithm design using dynamic learning. Quantum Inf. Comput. **8**(1), 12–29 (2008)
7. Liu, Z., Duan, L.M., Deng, D.L.: Solving quantum master equations with deep quantum neural networks. Phys. Rev. Res. **4**(1), 013097 (2020)
8. Broughton, M., Verdon, G., McCourt, T., et al.: Tensorflow quantum: a software framework for quantum machine learning (2020)
9. Han, S., Pool, J., Tran, J., Dally, W.: Learning both weights and connections for efficient neural network. In: Advances in Neural Information Processing Systems, pp. 1135–1143 (2015)
10. Han, S., et al.: EIE: efficient inference engine on compressed deep neural network. In: Proceedings of the 43rd International Symposium on Computer Architecture, pp. 243–254 (2016)
11. Paula Neto, F.M.D., Ludermir, T.B., Oliveira, W.R.D., Silva, A.J.D.: Quantum perceptron with dynamic internal memory. In: International Joint Conference on Neural Networks (IJCNN), pp. 1–8 (2018)
12. DiAdamo, S., Notzel, J., Zanger, B., Beşe, M.M.: Qunetsim: a software framework for quantum network. IEEE Trans Quantum Eng. **2**, 1–12 (2020)
13. Liu, W., Gao, P., Wang, Y., Yu, W., Zhang, M.: A unitary weights based one-iteration quantum perceptron algorithm for non-ideal training sets. IEEE Access **7**, 36854–36865 (2019)
14. van den Berg, E.: Iterative quantum phase estimation with optimized sample complexity. In: 2020 IEEE International Conference on Quantum Computing and Engineering (QCE), pp. 1–10 (2020)
15. Mohammadbagherpoor, H., Oh, Y., Dreher, P., Singh, A., Yu, X., Rindos, A.J.: An improved implementation approach for quantum phase estimation on quantum computers. In: IEEE International Conference on Rebooting Computing (ICRC), pp. 1–9 (2019)
16. Gardner, E.: Mathematical and general. J. Phys. **21**, 257 (1988)
17. Zhao, J.-Y.: Implementing associative memory with quantum neural networks. In: Proceedings of 2004 International Conference on Machine Learning and Cybernetics, pp. 3197–3200 (2004)
18. Guo, C.: Accelerating sparse DNN models without hardware-support via tile-wise sparsity. In: International Conference for High Performance Computing, Networking, Storage and Analysis, vol. 20, pp. 1–15 (2020)
19. Argueta, A., Chiang, D.: Accelerating sparse matrix operations in neural networks on graphics processing units. In: Accelerating Sparse Matrix Operations in Neural Networks on Graphics Processing Units, vol. 6224, no. 10, pp. 1619-1626 (2019)

SEC-Learn: Sensor Edge Cloud for Federated Learning
Invited Paper

Patrick Aichroth[3], Christoph Antes[4], Pierre Gembatzka[8], Holger Graf[5], David S. Johnson[3], Matthias Jung[4(✉)], Thomas Kämpfe[9], Thomas Kleinberger[4], Thomas Köllmer[3], Thomas Kuhn[4], Christoph Kutter[1], Jens Krüger[10], Dominik M. Loroch[10], Hanna Lukashevich[3], Nellie Laleni[9], Lei Zhang[1], Johannes Leugering[6], Rodrigo Martín Fernández[6], Loreto Mateu[6], Shaown Mojumder[9], Benjamin Prautsch[6], Ferdinand Pscheidl[1], Karsten Roscher[7], Sören Schneickert[4], Frank Vanselow[1], Paul Wallbott[2], Oliver Walter[2], and Nico Weber[10]

[1] Fraunhofer Research Institute for Microsystems and Solid State Technologies EMFT, Munich, Germany
`{christoph.kutter,lei.zhang,ferdinand.pscheidl, frank.vanselow}@emft.fraunhofer.de`

[2] Fraunhofer Institute for Intelligent Analysis and Information Systems IAIS, Sankt Augustin, Germany
`{paul.wallbott,oliver.walter}@iais.fraunhofer.de`

[3] Fraunhofer Institute for Digital Media Technology IDMT, Ilmenau, Germany
`{patrick.aichroth,david.johnson,thomas.kollmer, hanna.lukashevich}@idmt.fraunhofer.de`

[4] Fraunhofer Institute for Experimental Software Engineering IESE, Kaiserslautern, Germany
`{christoph.antes,matthias.jung,thomas.kleinberger,thomas.kuhn, soeren.schneickert}@iese.fraunhofer.de`

[5] Fraunhofer Institute for Computer Graphics Research IGD, Darmstadt, Germany
`holger.graf@igd.fraunhofer.de`

[6] Fraunhofer Institute for Integrated Circuits IIS, Erlangen, Germany
`{johannes.leugering,rodrigo.martin.fernandez,loreto.mateu, benjamin.prautsch}@iis.fraunhofer.de`

[7] Fraunhofer Institute for Cognitive Systems IKS, Munchen, Germany
`karsten.roscher@iks.fraunhofer.de`

[8] Fraunhofer Institute for Microelectronic Circuits and Systems IMS, Duisburg, Germany
`pierre.gembaczka@ims.fraunhofer.de`

[9] Fraunhofer Institute for Photonic Microsystems IPMS, Dresden, Germany
`{thomas.kaempfe,elli.laleni,shaown.mojumder}@ipms.fraunhofer.de`

[10] Fraunhofer Institute for Industrial Mathematics ITWM, Kaiserslautern, Germany
`{jens.krueger,dominik.loroch,nico.weber}@itwm.fraunhofer.de`

Alphabetically sorted author names.

© Springer Nature Switzerland AG 2022
A. Orailoglu et al. (Eds.): SAMOS 2021, LNCS 13227, pp. 432–448, 2022.
https://doi.org/10.1007/978-3-031-04580-6_29

Abstract. Due to the slow-down of Moore's Law and Dennard Scaling, new disruptive computer architectures are mandatory. One such new approach is Neuromorphic Computing, which is inspired by the functionality of the human brain. In this position paper, we present the projected SEC-Learn ecosystem, which combines neuromorphic embedded architectures with Federated Learning in the cloud, and performance with data protection and energy efficiency.

Keywords: SNN · Federated learning · Edge cloud · Neuromorphic hardware · Next generation computing · Virtual prototyping · NVM

1 Introduction

Artificial Intelligence (AI) and *Machine Learning* (ML) have achieved remarkable success in a wide range of products from Industry 4.0, over automotive, consumer, logistics, IoT to smart health applications. In most cases, these AI applications execute on conventional computer architectures like multi-core CPUs or GPUs. However, the computationally and memory-intensive algorithms for the realization of neural networks are pushing these conventional computer architectures to their limits in terms of performance and energy efficiency, due to the gradual decline of Moore's Law and Dennard scaling. Further significant performance leaps will therefore require new, disruptive approaches that at least partially depart from today's prevailing *von Neumann* architectures. In addition to these technical challenges, the limited availability of training data, which is often subject to data protection rules, is an obstacle for many data-intensive applications.

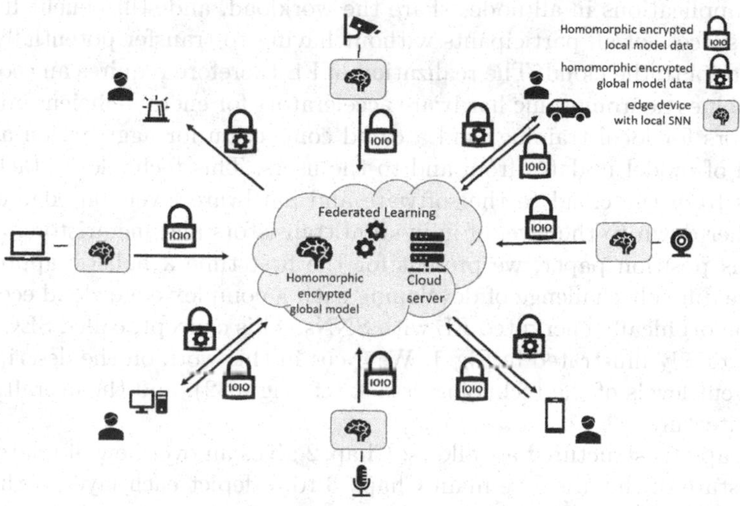

Fig. 1. Sensor edge cloud computing approach

A solution for this problem is to move AI applications to mobile and edge devices, which ensures that the data stays under the control of the users. This requires careful consideration of the load profiles of specific AI applications. For example, during normal inference operation, a neural network typically requires only comparatively little power. Training, however, requires a high amount of computational resources. If the inference has to occur locally whereas the training is to be done for instance on GPUs within a data center, the communication overhead and the energy consumption will increase significantly. Consequently, an alternative is to perform the training in the edge devices, too. This transfer of computation from the cloud to the edge is a growing trend: It is expected that in 2025, the edge AI chipset market will overtake the cloud AI chipset market for the first time[1]. In order to leverage AI and ML on edge devices, local training and inference needs to be supported by new energy efficient neuromorphic processor and memory architectures. Keeping the raw data at the edge, where it originates, without transferring it to the cloud for processing not only optimizes network use, but is also the only way to meet ever-increasing data security and privacy requirements, prevent misuse, and ensure acceptance of distributed applications. The development of specialized neuromorphic hardware promises significant savings in energy consumption, space requirements, latencies and, in sufficiently large quantities, much more cost-effective solutions. In particular, the use of new *Non-Volatile Memory* (NVM) technologies [5] and *Spiking Neural Networks* (SNN) [29] offer the potential for significant improvements.

Despite the clear advantages of local data processing in the edge, the training of a complex AI system typically requires too much data to keep the training completely local. *Federated Learning* (FL) [31], however, offers the ability to train the AI models locally and only feed back improved parameters, i.e. the result of local training, to all connected endpoints via a cloud service. Therefore, AI applications in all nodes share the workload, and still benefit from the learning success of all participants without having to transfer potentially sensitive raw data to the cloud. The realization of FL therefore requires an ecosystem that combines neuromorphic hardware accelerators for energy-efficient inference, accelerators for local training, and a cloud connection for aggregation and distribution of model updates from and to the users. This technology stack spans all layers from the cloud to the software and hardware levels on edge devices, and further down to the level of individual transistors and memristors.

In this position paper, we present for the first time a holistic approach to tackle the difficult challenge of developing such a complex edge cloud ecosystem for homomorphically encrypted FL with SNNs. This concept, called SEC-Learn, is schematically illustrated in Fig. 1. We focus in this work on the description of the different levels of the technology stack (cf. Figure 2), and the overall ecosystem architecture.

The paper is structured as follows: Chap. 2 gives an overview of related work and the state of the art. The main Chaps. 3 to 5 depict each layer of the SEC-Learn ecosystem from the cloud to the memristor, putting emphasis on topics

[1] https://www.eenewseurope.com/news/edge-ai-chip-market-overtake-cloud-2025.

like FL, model aggregation, and edge computing - and outlines challenges and solutions of scaling and efficiency. Chapter 6 presents a virtual prototype and a neural network search tool for the virtual engineering of the SEC-Learn ecosystem. The paper closes with conclusions and considerations on future work.

2 Related Work

In this paper, we focus on *Neuromorphic Computing* (NC) [5] as a key enabler for small embedded edge cloud systems and FL. NC, after several decades of research, has recently seen a resurgence due to the success of deep learning. Besides digital accelerators for conventional *Deep Neural Networks* (DNNs), such as Intel's Movidius/Myriad chip [33], Google's Tensor Processing Units [19] or MIT's Eyeriss processor [7], a growing number of neuromorphic chips target SNNs instead and make use of analog or mixed-signal design. Many of these designs make use of in-memory computing with non-volatile storage cells such as memristors, which is seen as a key technology for overcoming the von Neumann memory bottleneck [16]. One major European initiative, the Human Brain Project [30], aims to provide new tools to better understand the brain and its fundamental mechanisms, and to apply this knowledge to advance the medical and computer sciences. The Human Brain Project therefore develops two hardware-based NC platforms, BrainScaleS[2], and SpiNNaker [12]. The BrainScaleS system uses a mixed-signal approach, employing analog electronics to model up to 1 million neurons and 1 billion synapses, as well as digital communication protocols to model their connections and inter-cellular communication. The SpiNNaker system, by contrast, is a massively parallel, fully digital computing platform targeted at neuroscience, robotics, and computer science applications. Both systems comprise the development of hardware accelerators for SNN models, with a long

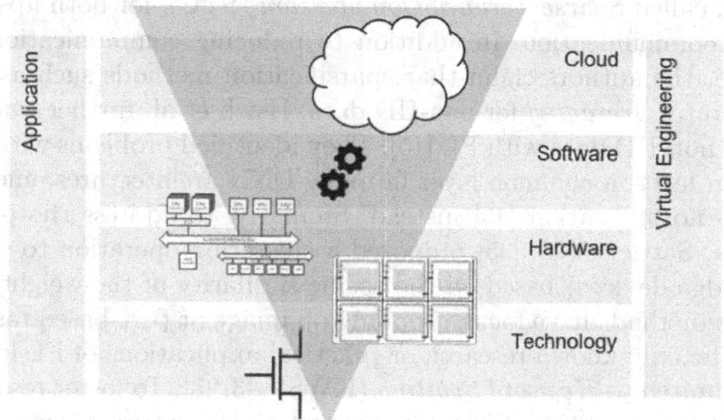

Fig. 2. Technology stack for the SEC-Learn ecosystem

[2] https://brainscales.kip.uni-heidelberg.de/.

history in neuroscience, but have only recently seen applications in ML. Other prominent approaches in this field include IBM's True North architecture [32], Intel's Loihi [10] and Brainchip's AKIDA[3].

The use of SNNs is particularly appealing for hardware development, because it allows to combine the benefits of analog in-memory computing, namely area, latency and power-savings, with those of digital communication, namely improved reliability and better scaling (see also 5.1). However, the event-based operation of SNNs defies conventional training methods and poses a challenge for numerical simulation, and hence, comparatively few mature software tools are available (notable exceptions include NEST [13], Brian [14] and Nengo [1]). While some gradient-based optimization methods, such as surrogate gradient training [34], do exist for SNNs, the prevalent approach for "training" SNNs is therefore the direct conversion of conventional DNNs to SNNs, after being trained. This approach was shown to work remarkably well even for large neural networks [37], and it integrates well into our FL-framework.

FL was proposed as a method to mitigate the security and logistical concerns of storing large amounts of sensitive data in a centralized data center. Instead of storing data centrally, McMahan et al. [31] proposed the FL approach which allows data to remain on distributed devices by training a shared model through the aggregation of weight gradients from models trained locally on the edge devices. To aggregate the weight gradients the authors proposed *federated averaging*, which performs element wise averaging of the weight gradients from participating devices. Kairouz et al. [21] presented a comprehensive overview of FL and its associated challenges. Two of the main challenges for FL include the communication over unreliable networks, and local datasets that are statistically dissimilar, or *Not Independent and Identically Distributed* (non-IID), between edge devices due to the heterogeneous nature distributed data collection.

To address these challenges, Sattler et al. [36] proposed to replace the standard *federated averaging* with an approach that combines sparsification and quantization, called *Sparse Ternary Compression* (STC), for both upstream and downstream communication. In addition to reducing communication bits and training time, the authors claim that sparsification methods such as STC outperform *federated averaging* for non-IID data. Hsieh et al. further evaluated the challenges of non-IID data with FL [15]. They identified problems with the batch normalization layer, a common layer in many DNN architectures, and proposed to use group normalization [43] instead. Similarly, to address the problems of non-IID data, Sattler et al. [35] proposed a clustering operation to group similar clients (edge devices) based on the cosine similarity of the weight gradients. The previous methods have focused mainly on image or text-based tasks. To our knowledge, the only known research or practical applications of FL in the audio domain are limited to *Keyword Spotting* (KWS)[4] [3,25]. To foster research in FL and *Sound Event Detection* (SED), Johnson et al. [18] proposed new FL specific datasets for SED in urban and domestic environments.

[3] https://brainchipinc.com/akida-neuromorphic-system-on-chip/.
[4] https://developer.apple.com/videos/play/wwdc2019/708.

3 The SEC-Learn Ecosystem - From Cloud to Memristor

The SEC-Learn ecosystem combines major concepts of NC with FL. For this disruptive approach, we consider the complete technology stack from cloud, via edge devices, down to the memristor level. Figure 3 illustrates the functional architecture and data flows of the proposed SEC-Learn ecosystem. It is essentially divided into two subsystems: (1) the *Cloud*, which combines and integrates learned knowledge from the field, enabling FL, and (2) the *Edge Devices*, which operate locally in the field and can learn autonomously, resulting in reduced communication with the cloud and bypassing the transfer of individually identifiable sensor data to the cloud.

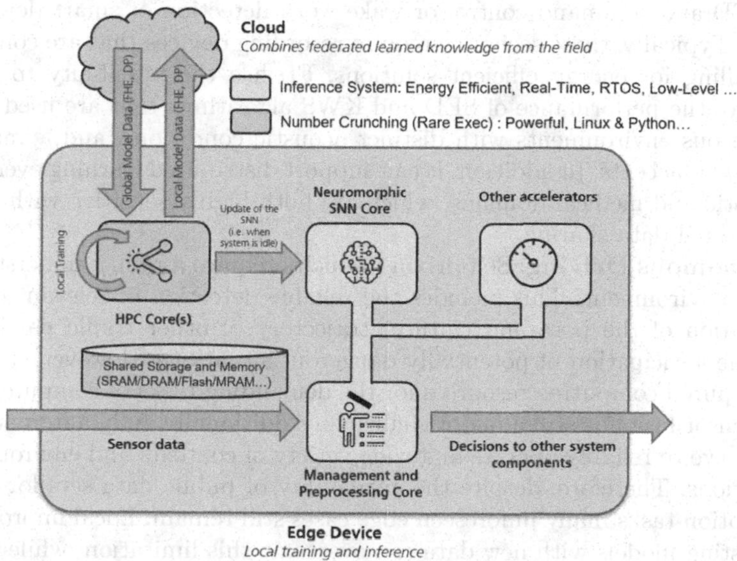

Fig. 3. SEC-Learn ecosystem

In normal operation, the neuromorphic SNN core in the edge device continuously performs inference operations on incoming data, enabling applications that rely on continuous data processing. The key metric for this inference system is energy efficiency, which is the reason why low-power SNN structures are used. The training core, designed as *High Performance Computing* (HPC) core, realizes the local training based on collected data to continuously evolve the AI application in the neuromorphic core. This local training in edge devices reduces communication and computational overhead in the cloud, resulting in massive energy savings. To enable FL and boost the training success, the training core transmits locally learned parameters of the associated NN models to a cloud application that combines, and integrates the federated learned knowledge. New parameter sets are sent back to ecosystem participants, and therefore everyone benefits from each other's experience. As the training process is very computation intensive, the HPC core will have a high power consumption. Therefore, the training process, the communication with the cloud, as well as the updating of the weights in the SNN are performed infrequently compared to inference in order to ensure the energy efficiency of the edge device and thus of the entire ecosystem.

As pilots, we implement the following use cases with the SEC-Learn ecosystem:

- ***Sound Event Detection* (SED) and *Keyword Spotting* (KWS)** are the detection of a predefined set of keywords or sound events from a continuous audio stream. Both are growing research fields with application scenarios in domestic and urban monitoring [18], as well as industrial sound analysis [17] for SED and command control or wake word detection of smart devices for KWS. Typically, these scenarios require recording devices that are constantly on, calling for energy efficient solutions. FL has the possibility to greatly improve the performance of SED and KWS algorithms that are used in heterogeneous environments with distinct acoustic conditions, and a variety of voices and accents. In addition, it can support distributed learning even in the domestic and medical domains, which are both highly sensitive with respect to personal data sharing.
- **Autonomous Driving:** Self-driving vehicles require a robust understanding of the environment. This includes the reliable detection of relevant objects, estimation of the pose and (future) trajectory of other traffic participants and the anticipation of potentially dangerous situations. However, providing the required computing resources for the demanding tasks of computer vision and sensor fusion is still a major challenge. Additionally, fully automated systems have to reliably operate in a wide variety of contexts and environmental conditions. Therefore, despite the availability of public data sets for various perception tasks many unforeseen edge cases still remain. Local improvement of existing models with new data can overcome this limitation, while sharing the learned parameters ensures that all vehicles benefit from scarce events only experienced by very few of them.

To enable the development of system functions while the overall system is not available yet, we develop a virtual prototype (c.f. Sect. 6). This enables the provision of a virtual integration environment that continuously evaluates the performance of *Next Generation Computing* (NGC) components in virtual application contexts and sets parameters for subsequent hardware realization. In the following chapters we will describe the aspects of the SEC-Learn ecosystem in more detail following the path of the technology stack shown in Fig. 2.

4 Cloud and Federated Learning

Some of the most promising AI applications require the collection of vast amounts of data by a large number of independent edge devices. Typical deep learning methods require large centralized datasets for model training, posing significant security and logistical challenges. However, in many cases this data has to remain private. Transmitting it to a central cloud service that realizes training is therefore not feasible. Furthermore, the continuous stream of large amounts of raw data would put a significant load on communication networks. To still enable the training of AI applications with this data, training has to be performed on edge devices, as it must be ensured that the raw data never leaves the device.

FL [31] offers an attractive approach to mitigate these concerns: Instead of sending private data to a centralized data store, FL performs model training directly on many edge devices using locally stored data. The edge devices then share only their updated parameters with a coordination server, which aggregates the shared parameters to update a global model, without the necessity of sharing the actual data. The new global model is then transferred back to the edge devices. This process continues until convergence, or indefinitely if new data is continuously acquired [21].

SEC-Learn will furthermore apply FL to ensure that all ecosystem participants benefit from the shared training efforts. It is based on a cloud-based model aggregation service that combines training data, and provides in regular intervals updated parameter sets for the SNN on edge devices, therefore gradually increasing the quality of the AI applications on the edge.

In [18], we introduced two novel data sets to foster research in FL for SED. To better understand the effects of previously identified challenges associated with non-IID data in FL, we included both IID and non-IID training sets for each use case. Additionally, we contributed the evaluation of three baseline neural network architectures. The results showed that while FL is a promising approach for SED it is prone to challenges with non-IID data similar to previous FL research [15,36].

In real world environments we can have thousands or even more edge devices, of which only a subset may be available during the training procedure. Therefore, we need a fault-tolerant, dynamic runtime environment for handling these circumstances. For this reason, we developed a FL runtime called Fed-DART, which is based on an industry-proven distributed platform for high-performance systems. It enables high scalability on a wide range of participating devices and provides the needed fault-tolerant and dynamic runtime environment. The user can easily implement FL methods without having to deal with the complexity of distributed computing. This is achieved by separating the algorithms from the technical infrastructure. Fed-DART is device-independent and therefore supports a wide range of application options. Furthermore, the integration of Fed-DART is independent of the ML framework used. The user must only write executable Python code for the edge device training procedure and the global aggregation method for the cloud. Fed-DART easily and conveniently integrates into this code by including the respective pip package. The FL runtime is then responsible for the communication exchange and scheduling to the edge devices. In the cloud we define the needed devices for the FL round of a given (valid) task, and the function specified for the task is executed on available edge devices. The current status of the learning progress and the result can be queried at any time. Fed-DART runs in background, is non-blocking and supports multiple types of device populations, which allows to start a local training on specific or randomly selected devices. Fed-DART will run on the SEC-Learn edge device HPC cores.

Once deployed, the SEC-Learn Cloud will have to collect, integrate and redistribute model updates proposed by each edge device based on its individual experience. Even if only the local parameters, and not the training data, are shared with the cloud, it might be still possible to derive potentially sensitive information about the edge devices, by performing so called *Inference Attacks*. A second relevant attack category are *Model Poisoning Attacks*, where a potentially malicious or malfunctioning edge device manipulates the aggregated model by sending invalid model data to the cloud.

For the first (passive) attack, nearly all participants could be potential attackers: the cloud aggregator, one or several colluding edge devices or even the end user of the resulting system. For the (active) model poisoning attack, the focus is set on the edge devices and the cloud. For every application scenario, the sensitivity of the processed data will be assessed to choose the right defense mechanisms, overall there are two promising approaches to mitigate such attacks:

- *Fully Homomorphic Encryption* (FHE): Encryption schemes that allow computations on the ciphertext without decrypting it first. This allows the edge devices to send the model data encrypted to the cloud, while the aggregator is still able to compute a global model *without* access to the plaintext model data.
- *Differential Privacy* (DP): By adding noise to the data sent to the cloud, it is not possible to link back the data to an individual edge device. This helps to prevent that sensitive data is sent to the cloud in the first place, but also potentially makes it harder for an individual attacker to "poison" the model.

Both approaches have downsides in making things computationally more expensive and also potentially degrade the overall system performance. With the help of the virtual prototype (cf. Sect. 6) we will explore the design space of FHE and DP in the respective application scenarios, in order to ensure that security and performance goals are met.

5 Edge Device

As mentioned before, given the vast amount of data captured by each edge device in our use cases, the majority of this deluge of data has to be processed where and when it is produced, i.e., on the edge device itself. This includes the real-time processing of incoming data through a dedicated AI inference accelerator as well as the selection and storage of relevant new data for retraining of the local model through a dedicated training accelerator.

Processing this huge amount of data consumes a significant amount of power in our selected use cases: For example, according to [20] the current control units for autonomous driving like Audi's zFAS, Nvidia's Xavier or Tesla's FSD, have a power consumption between 75 W and 500 W. For both, combustion-engine and electric cars, this power consumption will reduce the driving range significantly. Therefore, it is important to design an edge device which is sufficiently flexible to handle a wide range of functions, and is energy efficient for the sensor processing and inference of neural networks, but also very high performing in the training for the FL. In [4] the Intel's neuromorphic research processor Loihi (Wolf Mountain board) was benchmarked againts CPU (Xeon E5- 2630), GPU (Quadro K4000), Jetson TX1, and Movidius NCS for the keyword spotting application, leading to a lowest mean power consumption of 0.27 mJ per inference for Loihi.

To support these fundamentally different workloads, we rely on an energy efficient design for our heterogeneous platform (cf. Figure 3): The inference system is always active and continuously processes input data. A dedicated RISC-V management core orchestrates the SNN core and other accelerators and stores potential new training data in an energy efficient NVM. The SNN core realizes the neural network processing in hardware and is therefore more efficient than software solutions. An HPC core is used for the training and also implements the cloud communication for FL. It is inactive most of the time to reduce power consumption. Once a certain mass of new training data is collected, and when the system is not in operation mode, training is started on this core. With respect to our use cases, an example for such an idle situation would be the charging of an electric vehicle. In Sect. 5.1 we detail the SNN core of the inference subsystem, and in Sect. 5.2 we describe the HPC core of the training subsystem, respectively.

5.1 The SNN Accelerator Core

In order to minimize power-consumption during the always-on inference operation, we develop a dedicated, mixed-signal inference accelerator for SNNs. This approach combines the respective benefits of both analog and digital design: On the one hand, it allows us to compute the demanding Multiply-Accumulate Operations (MACs), which account for most of the computational cost of DNNs, in very power- and area-efficient analog circuits [42]. On the other hand, the inherently binary, event-driven communication of SNN obviates the need for sensitive analog signal paths and allows for a highly scalable digital package-routing design.

Moreover, by incorporating either *Static Random Access Memories* (SRAM) or NVM elements (or "memristors") such as *Ferroelectric Field-Effect Transistors* (FeFETs) directly into the analog circuit, we can co-localize memory storage and computation and thus minimize data transfers. In the last few years, various architectures [6] have used embedded in-memory computing to overcome limited storage density, to reduce static leakage and to provide a wake-up possibility for extreme low power consumption. The main disadvantage of NVMs to date are their often lower maturity and endurance in comparison to SRAMs.

Since both SNNs and homomorphic encryption are ultimately memory bound operations, they stand to gain considerably from in-memory computing [16], in particular when a weight stationary implementation is chosen, where the coefficients are persistently stored in the NVM cells. However, meeting the low required device-to-device variation in ultra-scaled memory cells is challenging.

In SEC-Learn, we investigate energy efficient, high performance FeFETs as NVM cells. FeFETs have been shown to operate at very high energy efficiency for binary and multi-precision convolutional neural networks [2,39], and we expect this to apply to SNNs, as well. The influence of device-to-device variation on the synaptic behavior of SNNs was investigated, and SNNs were shown to be resilient with respect to such variations, e.g. due to temporal sparsity of the input activation. With optimized peripheral circuits specialized to improve power and area efficiency, the FeFET inaccuracies can be improved both on the single block level and on the overall system level [40]. This makes spike encoded operations possible in the range of < 1fJ per spike. The synaptic efficiency can be extended further by implementation of *Multi-Level Cell* (MLC) storage, which was experimentally shown for 3-bit MLC FeFETs [22,26]. Furthermore, analog switching is possible, which can extent to a larger bitdepth [24].

To combine the benefits of analog in-memory computing and digital communication, we use a hierarchical approach that connects highly integrated, configurable *Neuromorphic Processing Units* (NPUs) through a tiered, heterogeneous *Network-On-Chip* (NoC) infrastructure. Each NPU in this network consists of a small sub-network of custom dual-output integrate-and-fire neurons (akin to the concatenated ReLU activation function in conventional DNNs [38]). The neurons are connected through a crossbar arrangement of synaptic connections that is optimized for some specific type of operation, e.g. 1D convolution or matrix multiplication. These internally analog NPUs are interconnected through a scalable, digital communication network that uses a modified version of the *Address Event Representation* (AER) protocol [9].

The on-chip communication network is critical for performance, and must be designed with the specific requirements of SNNs in mind: Some current neuromorphic designs, such as the MIT EYERISS chip [6], utilize a lightweight mesh network, where the neighbouring processing elements can be directly connected to each other. Most SNN accelerators like SpiNNaker [12], however, use a meshed package-routing system in order to achieve a higher degree of flexibility. We instead opt for a tiled, hierarchical network, which we believe results in an optimal trade-off between latency, area, and design complexity. Figure 4 shows a preliminary chip-level design. A reconfigurable mesh network connects the individual NPUs within each tile, and the tiles are in turn connected through a high-bandwidth ring bus. Such a hierarchical network offers a good compromise for two different types of computations:

- *Intra-layer computation:* Computations within a given SNN layer have to be highly synchronized. A sufficiently large tile of densely interconnected NPUs allows computing an entire NN layer in parallel, which is highly beneficial for performance [27].
- *Inter-layer computation:* Since the data-flow in a deep neural network is mostly unidirectional, individual layers can be processed sequentially. A ring bus is therefore sufficient.

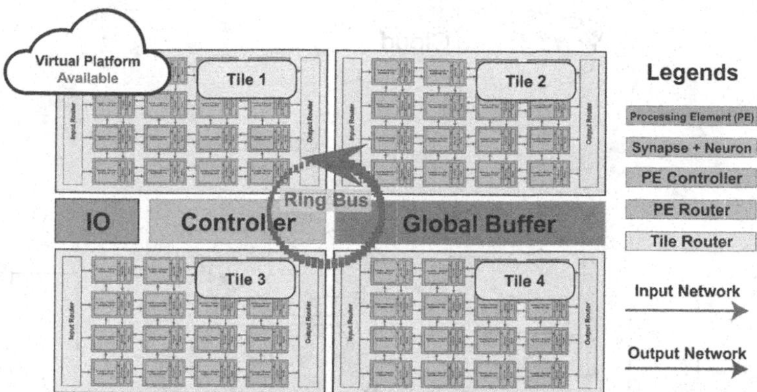

Fig. 4. System-level SNN accelerator design

A critical design challenge arises from the asynchronous, real-time dynamics of SNNs as well as from the use of NVM elements, both of which endow the NPUs with a persistent internal state and thus complicate time-multiplexing. An efficient implementation of an SNN on our hardware therefore requires an optimized, automated mapping of the model onto the available NPUs and tiles to maximally parallelize operations while minimizing data transfer. This process, much alike high-level synthesis on field-programmable gate arrays (FPGAs), requires new algorithms and software tools, which we co-develop alongside the hardware in the SEC-Learn project (c.f. Sect. 6).

5.2 The HPC Training Core

In contrast to the "online" inference, retraining of the model is a more complex and computing intensive operation that should occur "offline", i.e. when the system is idle or connected to a power source. Nevertheless, also during training energy efficiency is key. Due to these fundamentally different requirements, we delegate retraining of the local model to a dedicated training accelerator which will be integrated into the HPC core. The accelerator is based on the *Stencil- and Tensor-Accelerator* (STX) which is developed within the *European Processor Initiative* (EPI)[5]. The STX leverages parts of the PULP architecture [8] for scalable and energy efficient acceleration devices by using software managed scratchpad memories, efficient RISC-V cores and specific acceleration units for tensor and stencil operations. The acceleration units are designed around the concept of local dependencies and staticly structured access patterns such as those encountered in dense calculations like in convolutions or spare calculations such as star-shaped stencil operations. They implement hardware loops and efficient offset address calculations and are fully programmable via openMP. The optimized *Low Level Virtual Machine* (LLVM) compiler backend takes care of the optimization passes and optimal instruction schedules.

[5] https://www.european-processor-initiative.eu/.

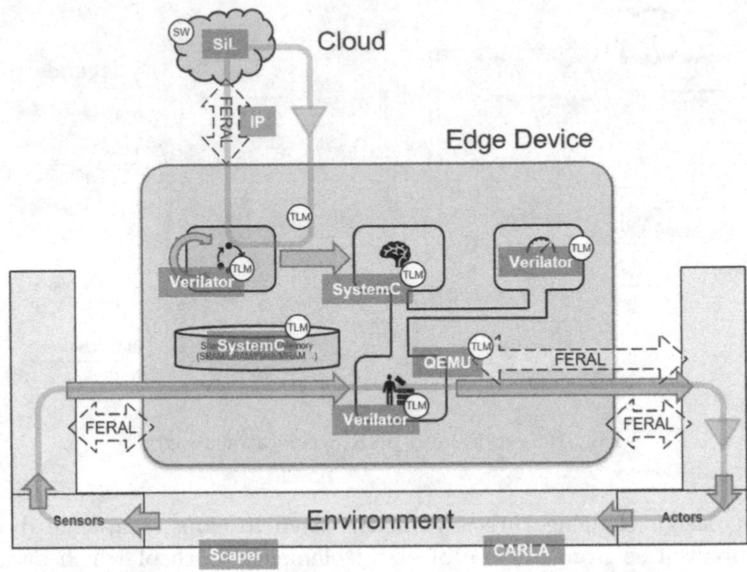

Fig. 5. Virtual prototype of the SEC-Learn ecosystem

6 Virtual Engineering and Neural Network Design

The development of such a complex system as the SEC-Learn ecosystem presented above is a challenging endeavour that requires the seamless integration of many heterogeneous components, each of which is developed by different teams using diverse technologies from the presented technology stack (cf. Figure 2). To ensure a close integration, detect errors early on, and to evaluate all components already during development, we implement a virtual prototype, which consists of software simulation models at various levels of abstraction. Since the ecosystem itself is very heterogeneous, also the virtual platform will consist of heterogeneous simulation models. The main challenge in the design of this virtual prototype is to find the correct level of abstraction in order to find a good trade-off between simulation speed and accuracy. For this reason we use the simulation coupling framework FERAL [23], which offers a seamless integration and time synchronization of the different models of computation. Figure 5 shows the virtual platform of the SEC-Learn ecosystem. It consists of two main simulation loops, first the inference loop and second the training loop.

For the inference loop, for instance, Carla [11] is used for the automotive use case in order to simulate the environment. It is an open-source simulator based on the *Unreal* gaming engine that specifically addresses the needs of autonomous driving research. The environmental data, generated by virtual sensors, is used as stimuli for the simulated edge device.

In order to integrate the SNN accelerator into the entire SEC-Learn virtual platform, a bottom-up modelling approach is followed. Since the goal is to enable an as-fast-as-possible simulation, the analog SNN level has to be abstracted into a more computation-friendly representation. The model, however, must include the major effects of the SNN accelerator. Therefore, we follow a split approach using (1) a non-spiking DNN representation based on TensorFlow [28] and (2) the fast system-level modelling language SystemC/TLM as an interface to the other edge device components. By avoiding transient spiking signals of an analog model, the computation time reduces significantly. At the same time, the non-ideal effects of the transistor-level SNNs are approximated based on characterization of, e.g., neuron accuracy, time-delays, and power consumption. The related accuracy loss is to be traded-off with the simulation speed required. As first step, the TensorFlow model is adapted accordingly to represent the accuracy. Second, it is wrapped by SystemC in order to interface seamlessly with the abstraction levels that support this modelling language, and to include timing effects.

For the simulation of memories we rely on the DRAMSys [41] framework. For the other models, e.g. the training and management core of the edge we are using custom SystemC implementations or *Register-Transfer-Level* (RTL) implementations, which have been converted to SystemC by using the Verilator tool. For the simulation of the training loop we use the *Software In the Loop* (SiL) principle by executing the actual cloud software and coupling it to one edge device by using the FERAL framework.

As mentioned in Sect. 5.1, the target platform has properties that constrain the design space of the DNNs which shall be executed on the device and at the same time yield the desired performance of the application. Using off-the-shelf DNN topologies for this purpose, is not only sub-optimal, but can also negate the efficiency gains from special hardware, if the topology is chosen too unfavorably for the platform. Therefore DNNs must be designed with the hardware in mind. While the design space is too large to be efficiently explored manually, its exploration can be automatized by methods of *Neural Architecture Search* (NAS).

We introduce our optimization framework called *NAS Engine* (NASE), which is specifically designed to incorporate hardware awareness into the exploration process. First, the search space of the NAS is tailored to the underlying hardware platform based on our virtual prototype. So the found topologies are guaranteed to be executable on the SEC-Learn architecture, including aspects like memory size for intermediate values and the quantization of weights and feature maps. Second, the optimization targets and constraints for the hardware are formulated as objectives, which possibly can be non-differentiable functions or look-up tables. NASE is configured for the SNN accelerator by taking into account aspects like the package routing network, on-chip memory constraints, limited range of the weights, robustness to device variations, etc., so that the mapping of the SNN to the NPU tiles can be performed at maximal efficiency, while also ensuring application performance.

Since the number of hardware constraints and objectives is large, it is imperative that the optimization algorithm can efficiently cope with high-dimensional optimization spaces. The selection of DNN candidates in NASE is based on a multi-stage bayesian approach, which allows to identify intelligently promising design space regions and reduces the computational workload. The DNN candidates are trained in parallel by using our own dynamic runtime scheduler for HPC clusters (DART), which is able to not only distribute the training tasks, but also to perform other time-consuming optimizations like quantization fine-tuning, so that NASE scales with complex applications and search spaces.

7 Conclusion and Future Work

In this position paper, we present the SEC-Learn ecosystem, which combines neuromorphic embedded architectures with the idea of federated learning in the cloud. We emphasize that for the holistic development of such an energy efficient and data protecting edge-cloud system all technology levels from the application down to the transistor level must be considered. A virtual prototype is implemented to ensure close integration, and early evaluations. After the successful demonstration with our prototype we plan to manufacture a demonstration chip, and provide performance and power estimations for concrete use cases.

References

1. Bekolay, T., et al.: Nengo: a Python tool for building large-scale functional brain models. Front. Neuroinform. **7**, 48 (2014)
2. Beyer, S., et al.: FeFET: a versatile CMOS compatible device with game-changing potential. In: 2020 IEEE International Memory Workshop (IMW) (2020)
3. Bhowmick, A., et al.: Protection against reconstruction and its applications in private federated learning. arXiv:1812.00984 (2018)
4. Blouw, P., et al.: Benchmarking keyword spotting efficiency on neuromorphic hardware (2018). arXiv: 1812.01739
5. Burr, G.W., et al.: Neuromorphic computing using non-volatile memory. Adv. Phys. X **2**(1), 89–124 (2017)
6. Chen, Y.-H., et al.: 14.5 Eyeriss: an energy-efficient reconfigurable accelerator for deep convolutional neural networks. In: IEEE International Solid-State Circuits Conference (ISSCC), pp. 262–263 (2016)
7. Chen, Y.-H., et al.: Eyeriss v2: a flexible accelerator for emerging deep neural networks on mobile devices. IEEE J. Emerg. Sel. Topics Circ. Syst. **9**(2), 292–308 (2019)
8. Conti, F., et al.: PULP: a ultra-low power parallel accelerator for energy- efficient and flexible embedded vision. J. Signal Process. Syst. **84**(3), 339–354 (2016)
9. Culurciello, E., Etienne-Cummings, R., Boahen, K.: Arbitrated address event representation digital image sensor. In: 2001 IEEE International Solid-State Circuits Conference. Digest of Technical Papers. ISSCC, pp. 92–93 (2001)
10. Davies, M., et al.: Loihi: a neuromorphic manycore processor with on-chip learning. IEEE Micro **38**(1), 82–99 (2018)
11. Dosovitskiy, A., et al.: CARLA: an open urban driving simulator. In: Annual Conference on Robot Learning. Proceedings of Machine Learning Research (PMLR), Vol. 78, pp. 1–16 (2017)

12. Furber, S., Bogdan, P. (eds.) SpiNNaker: A Spiking Neural Network Architecture. Boston-Delft: now publishers Inc. (2020)
13. Gewaltig, M.-O., Diesmann, M.: Nest(Neural simulation tool). Scholarpedia **2**(4), 1430 (2007)
14. Goodman, D.F.M., Brette, R.: The Brian simulator. Front. Neurosci. **3**, 26 (2009)
15. Hsieh, K., et al.: The non-IID data quagmire of decentralized machine learning. In: International Conference on Machine Learning. PMLR, pp. 4387–4398 (2020)
16. Ielmini, D., Wong, H.-S.P.: In-memory computing with resistive switching devices. Nature Electron. **1**(6), 333–343 (2018)
17. Johnson, D.S., Grollmisch, S.: Techniques improving the robustness of deep learning models for industrial sound analysis. In: European Signal Processing Conference (EUSIPCO), pp. 81–85 (2020)
18. Johnson, D.S., et al.: DESED-FL and URBAN-FL: federated learning datasets for sound event detection. eprint: 2102.08833 (2020)
19. Jouppi, N.P., et al.: In-datacenter performance analysis of a tensor processing unit. In: Annual International Symposium on Computer Architecture (ISCA), pp. 1–12 (2017)
20. Jung, M., et al.: Driving into the memory wall: the role of memory for advanced driver assistance systems and autonomous driving. In: International Symposium on Memory Systems (MEMSYS) (2018)
21. Kairouz, P., et al.: Advances and Open Problems in Federated Learning. eprint: 1912.04977 (2019)
22. Kazemi, A., et al.: In-memory nearest neighbor search with FeFET multi- bit content-addressable memories. In: Design Automation & Test in Europe (DATE) (2021)
23. Kuhn, T., et al.: FERAL – framework for simulator coupling on requirements and architecture level. In: ACM/IEEE International Conference on Formal Methods and Models for Codesign (MEMOCODE), pp. 11–22 (2013)
24. Lederer, M., et al.: Ferroelectric field effect transistors as a synapse for neuromorphic application. IEEE Trans. Electron Dev. **68**(5), 652–665 (2021)
25. Leroy, D., et al.: Federated learning for keyword spotting. In: International Conference on Acoustics, Speech, and Signal Processing (ICASSP) (019)
26. Li, C., et al.: A scalable design of multi-bit ferroelectric content addressable memory for data-centric computing. In: IEEE International Electron Device Meeting (IEDM) (2020)
27. Lu, A., et al.: Benchmark of the compute-in-memory-based DNN accelerator with area constraint. IEEE Trans. Very Large Scale Integration (VLSI) Syst. **28**(9), 1945–1952 (2020)
28. Abadi, M., et al.: TensorFlow: large-scale machine learning on heterogeneous systems. Software available from tensorflow.org. (2015)
29. Maass, W., Bishop, C.M. (eds.): Pulsed Neural Networks. A Bradford Book. Cambridge, Mass. MIT Press (2001)
30. Markram, H., et al.: Introducing the human brain project. Procedia Comput. Sci. **7**, 39–42 (2011)
31. McMahan, B., et al.: Communication-efficient learning of deep networks from decentralized data. In: International Conference on Artificial Intelligence and Statistics (AISTATS) (2017)
32. Merolla, P.A., et al.: A million spiking-neuron integrated circuit with a scalable communication network and interface. Science **345**(6197), 668–673 (2014)
33. Moloney, D., et al.: Myriad 2: eye of the computational vision storm. In: 2014 IEEE Hot Chips 26 Symposium (HCS), pp. 1–18 (2014)

34. Neftci, E.O., Mostafa, H., Zenke, F.: Surrogate gradient learning in spiking neural networks: bringing the power of gradient-based optimization to spiking neural networks. IEEE Signal Process. Mag. **36**(6), 51–63 (2019)
35. Sattler, F., Müller, K.-R., Samek, W.: Clustered Federated Learning: Model-Agnostic Distributed Multi-Task Optimization under Privacy Constraints (2019). arXiv:1910.01991
36. Sattler, F., et al.: Robust and communication-efficient federated learning from non-i.i.d. data. IEEE Trans. Neural Netw. Learn. Syst. (2019)
37. Sengupta, A., et al.: Going deeper in spiking neural networks: VGG and residual architectures. Front. Neurosci. **13** (2019)
38. Shang, W., et al.: Understanding and improving convolutional neural networks via concatenated rectified linear units. In: International Conference on Machine Learning, pp. 2217–2225 (2016)
39. Soliman, T., et al.: A ferroelectric FET based in-memory architecture for multi-precision neural networks. In: IEEE International System-on-Chip Conference (SOCC) (2020)
40. Soliman, T., et al.: Ultra low power flexible precision FeFET based analog inmemory computing. In: IEEE International Electron Device Meeting (IEDM) (2020)
41. Steiner, L., et al.: DRAMSys4.0: a fast and cycle-accurate systemc/TLMBased DRAM simulator. In: Embedded Computer Systems: Architectures, Modeling, and Simulation (2020)
42. Sze, V., et al.: Efficient processing of deep neural networks: a tutorial and survey. Proc. IEEE **105**(12), 2295–2329 (2017)
43. Wu, Y., He, K.: Group normalization. In: European Conference on Computervision (ECCV), pp. 3–19 (2018)

Special Session on Insights from Negative Results

(When) Do Multiple Passes Save Energy?

Louis Narmour[1(✉)], Tomofumi Yuki[2], and Sanjay Rajopadhye[1]

[1] Colorado State University, Fort Collins, USA
{louis.narmour,sanjay.rajopadhye}@colostate.edu
[2] Univ Rennes, Inria, Rennes, France
tomofumi.yuki@inria.fr

Abstract. Energy cost continues to be a significant barrier on all modern computing platforms. The common wisdom has been to focus on speed alone through heuristics like "race-to-sleep," a strategy based on the observation that the time-dependent components of total energy tend to dominate. Among different speed-optimal implementations or transformations of a program, however, there is a range of choices to (further) reduce energy. One of them is to execute a program with "multiple passes," which reduces data accesses while retaining speed optimality, and was shown to be effective for stencil computations on CPUs. We try to extend this strategy for a suite of computational kernels on both CPU and GPU platforms based on prior success. We find that the approach does not appear to generalize well due to practical limitations in the hardware present on the systems we studied. Despite this negative result, we illustrate what it would take to be profitable and use it to understand why it appears to be out of reach on current systems today.

Keywords: Energy efficiency · Program transformations · Multiple passes

1 Introduction

Optimizing for energy has become increasingly important in the area of high performance computing. In 2019, the Summit super computer in Oak Ridge National Lab in the United States had a reported power draw of 10,096 kilowatts (kW)[1]. The average cost of electricity in the United States in 2019 was \$0.11 per kilo-watt-hour (kWh)[2]. At these rates, operating Summit continuously at peak performance costs \$1,100 per hour, or \$26,400 per day in electricity alone. Optimization strategies that result in energy savings of even as little as 10% translate into thousands of dollars saved. This is an approximation, of course, but it illustrates the practical need for energy optimality in today's high performance computing systems and the programs that they run.

---

[1] https://www.top500.org/lists/top500/2019/11/.
[2] https://www.eia.gov/electricity/.

© Springer Nature Switzerland AG 2022
A. Orailoglu et al. (Eds.): SAMOS 2021, LNCS 13227, pp. 451–466, 2022.
https://doi.org/10.1007/978-3-031-04580-6_30

Total energy consumption can be thought of as having contributions from time-dependent and time-independent components. Since the time-dependent component is becoming more and more dominant in recent computing platforms, it has been observed that finishing all tasks as quickly as possible and powering everything down is the most energy efficient in many cases [6, 11, 33]. Recent work has shown that there is room for additional energy savings by minimizing portions of the time-independent contributions as well [21, 30, 35]. This suggests that the implementation that minimizes energy is among the set of implementations that also minimizes speed.

In this work, we focus on an approach called multi-pass parallelization [35], which was shown to provide energy savings up to 14% for stencil computations on CPUs by further reducing last level cache (LLC) misses without losing speed. We try to extend this to other computations on other architectures at other levels of the memory hierarchy. Specifically, we look at matrix multiplication on CPUs and stencil computations on graphics processing units (GPUs). From the speed-optimal implementation, provided by high-performance libraries, we ask the question: to what extent are further energy savings possible using multiple passes? We attempt to improve locality beyond reaching the point where there is enough locality for speed. With the speed-optimal implementation as the baseline, we expect to obtain energy savings if we can further reduce data transfers and retain speed optimality.

Counter to our initial expectations, this approach does not appear to generalize well for a variety of different architecture-specific reasons in reality. Even though we can successfully reduce the number of data movements across targeted levels of the memory hierarchy, in some cases, we can not do so without sacrificing speed due to insufficient disk throughput and LLC capacity. Alternatively, in the cases where we do not lose speed, the relative fraction of total energy saved from the reduced memory traffic is too small to matter.

We begin by providing the necessary background about the program transformations used to carry out multiple passes to illustrate how it reduces memory traffic and why this ought to lead to energy savings. Then (in Sect. 4) we discuss how we could extend multiple passes to the following different scenarios: (i) matrix multiplication on CPUs at the LLC to DRAM boundary, (ii) at the DRAM to disk boundary, and (iii) stencil computations on GPUs at the LLC to DRAM boundary. Then (in Sect. 5), we introduce our energy model, and use it to develop profitability constraints (in Sect. 6) to show why each of these cases are ultimately not profitable (in Sect. 8).

2 Background

This section summarizes multi-pass parallelization [35] and illustrates why it is expected to lead to energy savings.

2.1 Optimizing Polyhedral Programs for Speed

Example: The 1D Jacobi (J1D) is a first-order 3-point stencil computation updating an $(N+1)$-element data array over T time steps. The computation of each point depends on three neighboring points from the previous time step.

$$B_{t,i} = \begin{cases} A_i & \text{if } t = 0 \\ B_{t-1,i} & \text{if } 0 < t \leq T \text{ and } (i = 0 \text{ or } i = N) \\ f(B_{t-1,i-1}, B_{t-1,i}, B_{t-1,i+1}) & \text{otherwise} \end{cases} \tag{1}$$

Updating data point i at time step t requires three values from the previous time step: $(i-1)$, i and $(i+1)$. Due to the dependencies, rectangular tiling cannot be applied across the time dimension directly, and a well known technique, *time skewing* [24, 31, 32], is used to enable tiling across the time dimension. As illustrated in Fig. 1 it skews the time dimension with respect to the data space, to make all the dependencies lexicographically positive, and this makes loop blocking legal.

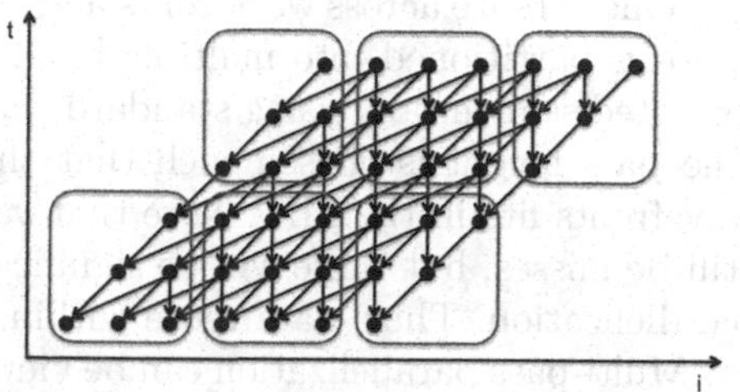

Fig. 1. Rectangular tiling for J1D after time skewing ($T = 5$, $N = 6$).

This produces the tile-graph shown in Fig. 2a where each small square is a tile and arrows show tile dependencies (from consumer to producer). This can be parallelized in a standard way. All the tiles executed at the same time step constitute one *wavefront*, and wavefronts are executed sequentially with a barrier synchronization. The area of the tile corresponds to the computation volume and the perimeter corresponds to the data access. By making tile sizes large enough, the program is fully compute bound and thanks to well developed latency hiding techniques it achieves optimal execution time.

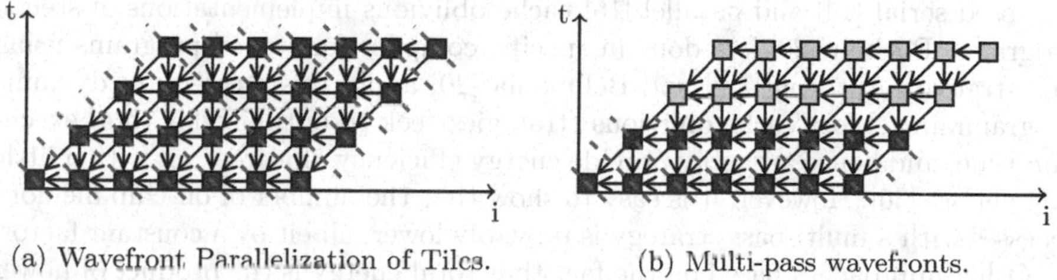

(a) Wavefront Parallelization of Tiles. (b) Multi-pass wavefronts.

Fig. 2. Execution order of tiles for wavefront parallelization and multi-pass. The dashed lines indicate the set of tiles that are executed in parallel.

However, for problem sizes where the program's data footprint exceeds LLC capacity (i.e., most reasonable programs), the perimeter of *every tile* corresponds to an LLC miss, in the steady state. This is because the wavefront schedule executes *all tiles* in a given wavefront before *any tile* in the next one, leading to poor data reuse across wavefronts: by the time a tile's output is required by the next tile (which is in the next wavefront) that data has been evicted from LLC by all the other tiles in the current wavefront. As a result, although such codes are the *fastest*, they are not the *energy optimal* ones [35].

2.2 Multiple Passes Reduce LLC Misses

To achieve reuse across wavefronts and thereby improve energy efficiency, the tile space is partitioned into multiple bands, called passes (see Fig. 2b). Passes are executed sequentially using standard wavefront parallelization within each pass. The pass height is chosen such that the "persistent data" between successive wavefronts fits in the LLC. Note that values needed from the *previous pass* will still be misses, but there will be significantly fewer of these than with wavefront parallelization. Thus, data reuse within one pass is optimized.

Multi-pass parallelization can be viewed as a hierarchical application of tiling, the outer one being passes, and the inner ones the conventional tiling. From here, it follows that if multiple passes can be carried out without losing speed, then the energy that would have been spent on excessive LLC misses resulting from executing all tiles within a wavefront before moving on to the next wavefront can be recouped. However, the ability to do this generally without losing speed is fraught with challenges.

3 Related Work

While this work focuses on the use of multiple passes, there are many other techniques that could be explored with the goal of energy efficiency.

Prokop [13,26] introduced cache-oblivious algorithms, an algorithmic strategy that seeks to minimize data transfers across *all* levels of the memory hierarchy by exploiting a divide-and-conquer execution schedule. Frigo and Strumpen proposed serial [14] and parallel [15] cache oblivious implementations of stencil programs. Pochoir [29] is a domain specific compiler for stencil programs using this strategy. Autogen [7,8] and Bellmania [20] apply this strategy to dynamic programming. Most cache oblivious strategies seek to optimize for total execution time, and hence arguably provide energy efficiency "for free," or with a little extra effort [30]. However, it is easy to show that the number of off-chip memory accesses with a multi-pass strategy is provably lower, albeit by a constant factor.

Other approaches based on the fact that total energy is the product of power and time allow for longer execution times while operating at a lower power to give an overall reduction in energy. Techniques like dynamic frequency and voltage scaling (DVFS) can be used to do this. Yuki and Rajopadhye [33] show that from the perspective of the system as a whole, the use of DVFS in compilers to trade off energy for speed results in negligible savings. So it does not make sense to consider this in the context of multiple passes and further reaffirms the importance of speed-optimality.

However, it is also possible to improve energy efficiency through DVFS without sacrificing speed. The main intuition is that the processor may slow down during memory intensive phases of a program so that the compute power matches the rate at which data is fed to the processors. Earlier work proposed the use of profiling techniques to identify the compute-intensity of program regions to throttle the processor voltage and frequency for energy efficiency [9,19]. Jimborean et al. [21] proposed compiler transformations to decouple kernels into compute-intensive and memory-intensive regions to increase such opportunities for energy savings. Their work is another example of where the compiler is able to improve energy efficiency beyond simply compiling for speed.

4 Extending Multiple Passes

Based on prior success of multiple passes at the LLC to DRAM boundary on CPUs [35], it is reasonable to expect it to be extensible. Multiple passes can be applied to any of the following memory levels: (0) L_x to LLC, (1) LLC to DRAM, (2) DRAM to disk, and (3) disk to network. In this work, levels 0 and 3 are not considered since problems at these scales are either too small to matter or better suited by distributed algorithms, some of which already minimize network communication between nodes [17]. We consider general matrix multiplication (GEMM) on CPUs at levels 1 and 2, and revisit stencils but on GPUs at level 1. GEMM is highly amenable to tiling and tiles can be executed in parallel without the startup overhead of wavefront execution. Stencils can be handled similarly, however there is a wind-up period before substantial parallelism among tiles is exposed, as shown in Fig. 2a. This is not a concern on CPU platforms where there are relatively few processors but becomes a critical limitation on GPUs, where concurrent start is necessary for speed-optimal performance [16,23]. Tiling schemes for stencils that enable concurrent start include: hybrid/hexagonal tiling [16], diamond tiling [28], and overlapped tiling [18,22]. In addition, many high performance stencil generation frameworks exist, for both CPUs and GPUs, that effectively apply these tiling schemes such as StencilGen [27] and AN5D [23]. However, these frameworks focus on speed optimality and do not support multiple passes as is, so we will discuss what it would take to extend them to do so. As mentioned previously, it does not make sense to talk about energy optimality without starting from the speed-optimal implementation as a baseline. To this end, BLAS libraries are used for GEMM [1,34] and AN5D [23] for stencils.

4.1 Matrix Multiply (GEMM)

Recall the standard matrix-matrix product $C = AB$ operation, where $C_{ij} = \sum_k A_{ik}B_{kj}$. Note that the only dependencies here exist along the accumulation dimension k. After tiling, in the 3D tile iteration space, there are entire 2D i-j planes of tiles that can be executed concurrently. This is a special case of wavefront execution, in the sense that each plane of tiles corresponds to a single wavefront and every wavefront contains the same number of tiles.

The same observation from Sect. 2 applies here; for reasonable problem sizes, executing *all tiles* in a given i-j plane before moving on to tiles in the next plane results in poor data reuse across planes. Instead of executing all tiles in a given i-j plane, only process a subset of tiles and then process all of the tiles down the dependence chain along k.

To do this, the full matrix product is decomposed into multiple series of smaller sub-matrix products (along k), where each series updates a single patch of C. The BLAS library is used to carry out the individual sub-matrix products and can think of one sequential series of calls to BLAS as a pass. The pass *size* is chosen such that the volume of data reused across successive sub-matrix products fits within the targeted level of the memory hierarchy. The pass *shape* (i.e., relative tile sizes along each dimension) is chosen such that data reused across successive products is maximized. This shape corresponds to tall thin matrices of A, short stout matrices of B, and as large a patch of C as possible. From this, a single pass consists of the series of tall-thin short-stout (TTSS) sub-matrix products.

BLAS is used as a proxy for the speed-optimal solution and the performance of a single BLAS call on the full problem size as our baseline. By composing smaller BLAS calls on sub-matrix products over multiple passes, we expect to reduce data movements over the baseline without losing speed, thereby improving energy efficiency.

4.2 Stencils

Consider the 2D analog of the first order stencil from Sect. 2 characterized by the following dependencies,

$$S[t+1,i,j] \rightarrow f(S[t,i-1,j], S[t,i+1,j], S[t,i,j], S[t,i,j-1], S[t,i,j+1])$$

where $0 \leq t \leq T$, $1 \leq i < N-1$, and $1 \leq j < N-1$.

N and T together represent the problem size. Each point in the input data grid of size $N \times N$ is repeatedly updated over T time steps from a weighted sum of its adjacent neighboring elements in the previous time step. The prototypical implementation of this corresponds to a series of nested loops where the outer most loop iterates over time, on t.

AN5D generates tiled CUDA code along all dimensions, including time, and supports concurrent start, specifically through the use of overlapped tiling on the inner spatial dimensions [23]. Adopting their notation, let b_T denote the time tile size. The generated code operates as a series of T/b_T CUDA kernel calls, where each kernel call updates the entire $N \times N$ data space over b_T time steps. One of the reasons AN5D obtains good performance is because it accesses global memory (DRAM) only at the bottom and top time steps of each kernel call. The total number of global memory accesses, M_{AN5D}, can be roughly expressed as,

$$M_{\text{AN5D}} = \left(\frac{T}{b_T}\right)(N^2 + (N - 2b_T)^2) = O(N^2T) \tag{2}$$

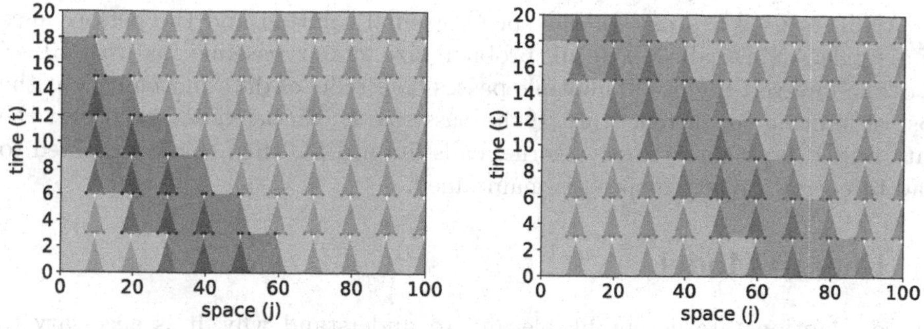

Fig. 3. The projection of the t-i plane from the stencil's t-i-j iteration space. Overlapped tiling of the inner j dimension corresponds to trapezoidal shaped tiles. The left image shows one pass and the right shows the subsequent pass.

Due to the fact that each kernel call touches the entire $N \times N$ data space, many LLC misses are expected across successive calls. From this, the observation that motivates the use of multiple passes is as follows. Instead of processing all of the tiles along the spatial dimensions with each tile step along the time dimension (i.e., with each CUDA kernel call), only process a subset of spatial tiles and then process as many additional tiles along the time dimension as possible subject to the dependencies. This subset of tiles forms a single pass and two different passes are illustrated in Fig. 3. The execution of a pass consists of a series of smaller kernel calls, where each call updates the tiles within the pass boundaries for a specific time tile step. If the pass size is chosen so that the data reused across kernel calls within a pass fits in the LLC, then global memory access will only occur on the pass boundaries.

The iteration space of the p-th pass, described by the pass coordinates p_i and p_j, with a constant pass size P along each spatial dimension is represented by the integer set A_p,

$$A^p := [p_i, p_j, N, T] \rightarrow \{[t, i, j] : 0 \leq i < N,\ \ 0 \leq j < N,\ \ 0 \leq t \leq T, \qquad (3)$$
$$p_i P \leq i + t < (p_i + 1)P,\ \ p_j P \leq j + t < (p_j + 1)P\}$$

Projecting A_p onto the data space, by the function $f : [t, i, j] \rightarrow [i, j]$, and summing over all passes gives the total number of global memory reads $M_{mp} = \sum_p f(A^p)$. Some of the passes along the boundaries will be partial (like the blue pass in Fig. 3) but the total number of global memory reads can be expressed with the following over-approximation,

$$M_{mp} < \left(\frac{N}{P}\right)^2 \Big(P^2 + T(2P - 1)\Big) = O\Big(\frac{N^2 T}{P}\Big) \qquad (4)$$

This only represents the number of global memory reads, but the number of writes is approximately the same and does not change the order. From Eqs. 2 and 4, it follows that the use of multiple passes should reduce the number of global memory accesses by a factor of the pass size P.

AN5D is used a proxy for the speed-optimal solution and the performance of a single AN5D call on the full problem size as our baseline (as with BLAS above). However, the use of multiple passes here reduces data movements at the cost of limiting concurrent start. If the pass size P can be chosen such that the data reused between successive kernel calls fits in LLC then this is expected to lead to energy savings if speed is maintained.

5 Energy Model

These adaptions are not profitable and to understand why, it is necessary to define an energy model and formalize what success would look like within this model. Based on the idea that multiple passes results in fewer data movements, one would like to express energy consumption as a function of the quantity of data movements in relation to execution time.

For a given program and target architecture, the goal is to minimize the total energy consumption, E, which is decomposed into time-dependent and time-independent components. Let $G(T)$ represent the time-dependent portion of energy consumed from simply being powered on for the duration T of program execution. This includes the processing elements, components of the memory subsystem from the on-chip caches all the way down to any non-volatile storage such as spinning disk or solid state drives, the motherboard itself, and any additional peripherals like system fans. Let $H(W)$ represent the time-independent portion of energy consumed due to the actual operational work W necessary to carry out the computation. This includes things like fused-multiply add processing, instruction fetching and decoding, accessing register files, and both on- and off-chip data transfers. The total energy E is expressed as the sum of G and H,

$$E(T, W) = H(W) + G(T) \tag{5}$$

For a particular implementation, let P_i be the average power dissipated by the i-th system component, M_q be the number of data movements across the q-th level of the memory hierarchy (from Sect. 4) and V be the volume of the iteration space of the computation. Then, the total energy is expressed as,

$$E = (\alpha V + \sum_q \beta_q M_q) + (\sum_i \gamma_i P_i T) \tag{6}$$

Now, consider two different implementations that execute instances of the same problem on the same problem size. V in the first term of Eq. 6 is proportional to the problem size (i.e., number of floating point operations performed). Techniques like dynamic voltage and frequency scaling (DVFS) can be used to reduce the contributions of this term but are not used here based on Yuki and Rajopadhye's result [33] showing that the time-dependent component still dominates for the class of programs considered. This analysis assumes that DVFS is not being used and that each implementation contributes equally to the first term, αV. Conversely, the memory traffic could be different if one implementation has higher data locality making more efficient use of data while it resides in faster memory. M_q and T are the variables that can change through implementation and characterize the design space. Among the set of fastest implementations with similar magnitudes of G, the ones that further minimize data transfers M_q across one or more levels of the memory hierarchy are expected to consume less total energy.

6 Conditions for Profitability

For an input program and target architecture, let I_o represent the baseline speed-optimal implementation which requires M_o^q data movements across the q-th level of the memory hierarchy with an execution time T_o. Let I_{mp}, M_{mp}^q, and T_{mp} be the corresponding values of the implementation using multiple passes. Let $\Delta M_q = M_{\text{mp}}^q - M_o^q$ and $\Delta T = T_{\text{mp}} - T_o$ denote the differences over the baseline. Negative values of ΔM_q or ΔT indicate that the multi-pass implementation results in fewer data movements or a smaller execution time respectively.

Conditions: From this, the following conditions must hold for I_{mp} to have a lower energy consumption than I_o,

$$\Delta M_q < 0 \tag{7}$$

$$\Delta T < \epsilon_0 \tag{8}$$

$$\frac{\beta_q}{\sum_i \gamma_i} > \epsilon_1 \tag{9}$$

for some architecture-dependent values of ϵ_0 and ϵ_1. The first condition simply indicates that I_{mp} needs to reduce the number of data movements. The second indicates that I_{mp} did not sacrifice too much speed; ϵ_0 should be close to zero. As for the last condition, recall that β_q represents the energy consumed per unit data transferred across the q-th memory level and γ_i represents the time-dependent portion of energy consumed by the i-th system component. Equation 9 simply states that fraction of energy spent on data movements needs to be large enough for the energy saved from ΔM_q to matter. As shown in the following sections, these conditions do not hold.

7 Experimental Setup

Table 1 displays empirical measurements on energy spent per unit data moved in joules per gigabyte for the LLC to DRAM boundary for the systems evaluated here. These values represent an estimate for β_1 in Eqs. 6 and 9.

Most hardware today exposes performance statistics through performance monitoring units. Most CPUs support the Running Average Power Limit (RAPL) interface [10]. The utilities perf [12] for Intel chips and μProf [4] for AMD chips are used to measure power consumption and LLC misses. For the GPUs, the NVIDIA profiling tools (nvprof) [3] and the NVIDIA management library (NVML) [2] are used to collect measurements on the quantity of data

Table 1. Empirical measurements β_1 for energy spent per unit data transferred across level 1 (LLC and DRAM). We do not calibrate the AMD system because we first confirmed that multiple passes degrade speed.

System	Processor	Model	DRAM (GB)	LLC (MB)	β_1 (J/GB)
1	CPU	Intel Xeon E5-1650V4	16	15.00	0.30
2	CPU	AMD Epyc 7452	500	128.00	–
3	GPU	NVIDIA GTX 1080 Ti	11	2.75	0.19
4	GPU	NVIDIA Titan V	12	4.5	0.21

transferred and energy usage. NVML can be used to programmatically query the GPU device, specifically for the instantaneous power draw.

To obtain a value for energy per unit data transferred, we compare the difference in these counter values between measurements from program implementations that do the same amount of work in the same amount of time. This way we can attribute the change in energy to the change in the quantity of bytes transferred. This is what is reported in Table 1.

8 Evaluation

This section evaluates the multi-pass extensions introduced Sects. 4.1 and 4.2. Intel's Math Kernel Library (MKL) [1] is used for GEMM on the Intel system and BLIS [34] is used for AMD.

8.1 GEMM - CPU at LLC to DRAM

In this scenario, the problem size fits in DRAM. The goal is to minimize data movements between the LLC and DRAM, so tile sizes T_I, T_J, and T_K are chosen such that the data reused across tall thin short stout (TTSS) matrix-matrix products fits within LLC capacity. Then for each patch of C, a series of TTSS calls to MKL or BLIS are issued as shown in Algorithm 1.

Algorithm 1: Multi-pass GEMM

```
Input: A, B, C, T_I, T_J, T_K, N
for each pass do
    ti, tj ← pass;
    c ← getSubMatrix(C, ti, tj);
    for each tk in pass do
        a ← getSubMatrix(A, ti, tk);
        b ← getSubMatrix(B, tk, tj);
        gemm(a, b, c, T_I, T_J, T_K);
```

8.2 Intel - Xeon E5-1650V4

Algorithm 1 describes the multi-pass implementation of square-square matrix multiplication for input matrices A, B, and C with tile sizes T_I, T_J, and T_K.

Let the baseline implementation I_o be the case when $T_I = T_J = T_K = N$ (i.e., making a single library call on the full problem size). Tile size exploration was performed with $T_I = T_J = P$ for values of P in the range $[100, 2500]$ and T_K values in the range $[100, 1000]$. The best performing tile sizes were $T_I = T_J = 1200$ and $T_K = 725$. For each combination of tile sizes, the following values were measured: execution time t, off-chip data transfers M_1, perf power/energy-pkg, and perf power/energy-ram. These are reported in Table 2. The multi-pass implementation successfully reduced the number of data movements by 72%, satisfying Eq. 7. However, there were no tile size configurations that did not violate Eq. 8; all configurations sacrificed speed. This is tightly coupled with the observation that Eq. 9 does not hold either. The extra energy spent due to ΔT, reflected in the increased power/energy-pkg value, is larger than the energy saved from ΔM_1. The 72% reduction in M_1 only resulted in 1.41 J saved, while the additional energy consumed due to a slightly longer execution time was significantly larger, 7.12 J. Even if speed could be maintained, this would only mean energy savings of 2%. From this, one can conclude that the fraction of energy spent on data movements between LLC and DRAM is too small to matter.

Table 2. Best performing multi-pass implementation relative the baseline.

	t (sec)	GFLOPS/sec	%Peak	M_1 (GB)	Energy-pkg (J)	Energy-ram (J)	Total (J)
I_o	0.439	569	82.5	3.47	70.42	3.33	73.75
I_{mp}	0.543	460	66.7	0.97	77.54	1.92	79.46

8.3 AMD - Epyc 7452

Part of the reason for the slowdown in the previous section was due to the fact that the problem size must be large enough for MKL to perform close to machine peak. The same thing holds true for BLIS on the AMD system. This means that multiple calls of smaller sub-problems can not be done without losing speed relative to the baseline, which involves just a single call on the full problem. This is problematic because the sub-problems within a pass must be small enough that they fit in LLC. Figure 4 shows how the performance of BLIS double precision TTSS (N×K by K×N) matrix products varies with problem size for several aspect ratios N/K. The Epyc 7452 has two sockets, and the performance reported here is based on a single socket with 32 physical cores without hyperthreading (i.e., BLIS_NUM_THREADS=32).

BLIS does not attain peak performance for problem sizes below 6K, but the problem sizes exceed LLC capacity. This is enough to conclude that multiple passes can not be applied to save energy.

8.4 GEMM - CPU at DRAM to Disk

In this scenario, the input matrices A, B, and C do not all fit in DRAM together. Unlike the previous case, sub-matrix products within a pass are large enough to

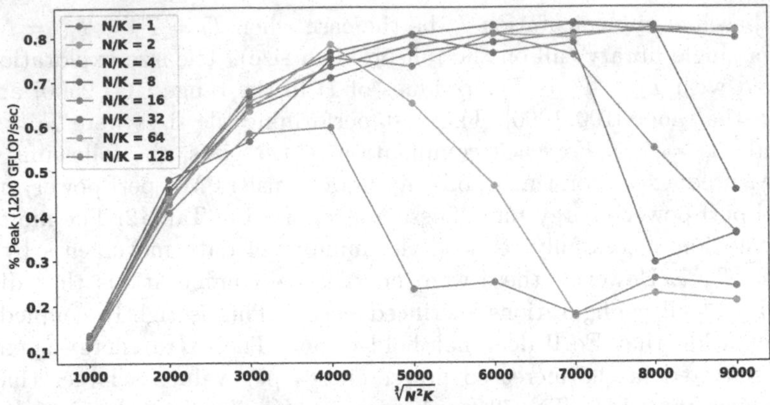

Fig. 4. BLIS performance of tall thin short stout matrix multiplication for increasing problem size and aspect ratio (N/K).

avoid a loss in speed but the time it takes to swap data into DRAM from disk is much greater than the time required to bring data into the LLC from DRAM. So the computation of one sub-matrix product and the communication needed to swap in the next product's tiles from disk must be overlapped. The size of one square tile of C and two tiles of A and B must fit in DRAM,

$$(T_I T_J + 2(T_K T_I + T_K T_J))S < DRAM_{\text{capacity}} \tag{10}$$

where S is the data type size.

On the Intel system, MKL delivers around 500 GFLOPS/sec (75% theoretical machine peak) for single precision square-square inputs and the spinning disk hard drive has an advertised throughput $\mu = 150$ MB/sec. Table-3 shows the minimum throughput needed in order to overlap the communication and computation to keep it compute bound for a range of sub problem sizes. The values in the "Read" column are the size of the next two patches of A and B ($2T_o^2$). The "MKL" column is an estimate of MKL's execution time based off of the problem size and expected performance delivered by MKL ($2T_o^3/(500 \times 10^9)$).

Table 3. Minimum disk throughput μ_{min} needed in order to overlap communication and computation for tiles within a pass. The second column represents the left hand side of Eq. 10 for $T_I = T_J = T_K = T_o$, which must fit in memory.

T_o	DRAM (GB)	Read (MB)	MKL (sec)	μ_{min} (MB/sec)
10000	2.0	800	4.0	200.00
15000	4.5	1800	13.5	133.33
20000	8.0	3200	32.0	100.00
25000	12.5	5000	62.5	80.00
30000	18.0	7200	108.0	66.67

From Table 3, observe that there is sweet-spot range of tile sizes that fits in DRAM (16 GB) without requiring unobtainable disk throughputs (greater than 150 MB/sec).

However, the maximum throughput obtained on the Intel system in Sect. 7, was less than 10 MB/sec which was significantly lower than what was needed. We were unable to figure out why the throughput was so low. In order to keep the problem compute bound with a disk throughput this low, the tiles need to be so large they would no longer fit in memory. Since the minimum throughput necessary to avoid a loss in speed could not be obtained, it was not necessary to further confirm or deny conditions in Eqs. 7 and 9. It is possible that spinning disk drives are simply too slow in this context. Other studies on the energy efficiency of SSDs [5,25] report that SSDs spend 10–20 J/GB on data movements, which is two orders of magnitude higher than what was observed on DRAM shown in Table 1.

8.5 Stencils - GPU at LLC to DRAM

Based on the empirical measurements of β_1 in Table 1, 11–17% of the total energy consumed by AN5D-based stencils can be attributed to data movements which suggests that (Eq. 9) holds and indicates that this scenario can tolerate larger values of ϵ_0 in Eq. 8 with respect to execution time. Despite this, multiple passes can not be carried out without sacrificing speed beyond acceptable levels. The reasoning behind this is as follows. As described in Sect. 4.2 for stencils on GPUs, using multiple passes with a pass size P along each spatial dimension reduces M_1 by a factor P at the cost of limiting concurrent start. Recall that our multi-pass stencil implementation for GPUs is based on a series of calls to a modified AN5D kernel, where each kernel call has a data footprint $\eta = P^2S$ for 2D stencils, where S is the data type size. This must fit in LLC,

$$\eta < LLC_{\text{capacity}} \tag{11}$$

Each CUDA thread block carries out the execution of a single tile. In order for AN5D to obtain speed-optimal performance, it requires the data footprint of individual tiles (each trapezoid in Fig. 3) to be sufficiently large. Among the set of optimal tile sizes reported for the set of generic stencils evaluated by AN5D [23], the smallest tile size configurations have a data footprint of $B = 64$ KB. However, most were larger, as high as 256 KB. This means that our modified AN5D kernel only uses $N_{\text{tiles}} = \eta/B$ tiles. However, concurrent start is necessary in order to obtain good performance on GPUs, because ample parallelism is required in order to keep all of the processing elements busy. On a GPU with N_{SM} streaming multiprocessors (SMs), we need at least N_{SM} tiles that can be executed in parallel. In reality, this number is probably higher in order to effectively hide the latency of the arithmetic units. Minimally,

$$N_{\text{SM}} < N_{\text{tiles}} \tag{12}$$

Together, Eqs. 11 and 12 can be conveyed as,

$$N_{\text{SM}}B < P^2S < LLC_{\text{capacity}} \tag{13}$$

The term $N_{SM}B$ represents a hard lower bound on the data footprint of iterations within a pass. Passes with data footprints below this are not expected to be speed-optimal. For the GeForce GTX 1080 Ti, with $N_{\mathrm{SM}} = 28$, this corresponds to 1.79 MB which is already close to the LLC capacity of 2.75 MB. This is based on the smallest optimal tile sizes reported by AN5D, larger ones ($B = 128$ KB or 256 KB) exceed the 2.75 MB limit. However, for the Titan V with $N_{\mathrm{SM}} = 80$, the value of $N_{\mathrm{SM}}B$ is 5.12 MB which already exceeds the LLC capacity of 4.75 MB using the smallest optimal tile sizes.

Based on this analytical result, the size of the LLC is the limiting factor for GPUs. While multiple passes can be used to reduce data transfers, there does not exist a value of P that is small enough to do so without restricting parallelism beyond acceptable levels.

9 Conclusion

Through experimental and analytical evaluation, we find that the use of multiple passes to obtain energy savings beyond the speed optimal solution is largely not profitable, contrary to prior success with stencils on CPUs. For the LLC to DRAM case on CPUs, the relative fraction of energy spent on data movements was too small to overcome the extra energy spent due to a longer execution time. Even if we could avoid losing speed in this case, the relative magnitude was still too small to matter, less than 2%. In the GPU case however, the fraction of energy spent on data movements was significantly larger but we could not avoid a loss in speed for an entirely different reason, due to a small LLC. Since low disk throughput was the bottleneck and primary reason for the loss in speed in the CPU DRAM to disk case, perhaps solid-state drives may be more appropriate given that they have a much higher throughput. For the case of stencils on GPUs, if the LLC capacity was larger, then we may have been able to avoid a loss in speed. Despite this negative result, now we are in a better position to be able to reason about what such a profitable system looks like.

References

1. Library, I.M.K.: Reference Manual. Intel Corporation, Santa Clara, USA (2019)
2. Nvidia Management Library (NVML), April 2020. https://developer.nvidia.com/nvidia-management-library-nvml
3. Profiler user's guide (2020). https://docs.nvidia.com/cuda/profiler-users-guide/index.html
4. Amd uprof , April 2021. https://developer.amd.com/amd-uprof/
5. Beckmann, A., Meyer, U., Sanders, P., Singler, J.: Energy-efficient sorting using solid state disks. In: International Conference on Green Computing, pp. 191–202 (2010). https://doi.org/10.1109/GREENCOMP.2010.5598309
6. Cho, S., Melhem, R.G.: On the interplay of parallelization, program performance, and energy consumption. IEEE Trans. Parallel Distrib. Syst. **21**(3), 342–353 (2010). https://doi.org/10.1109/TPDS.2009.41

7. Chowdhury, R., et al.: Autogen: automatic discovery of cache-oblivious parallel recursive algorithms for solving dynamic programs. In: Proceedings of the 21st ACM SIGPLAN Symposium on Principles and Practice of Parallel Programming. PPoPP 2016. Association for Computing Machinery, New York (2016). https://doi.org/10.1145/2851141.2851167
8. Chowdhury, R., et al.: Autogen: automatic discovery of efficient recursive divide-8-conquer algorithms for solving dynamic programming problems. ACM Trans. Parallel Comput. **4**(1), 1–30 (2017). https://doi.org/10.1145/3125632
9. Hsu, C.-H., Feng, W.-C.: A power-aware run-time system for high-performance computing. In: Proceedings of the 2005 ACM/IEEE Conference on Supercomputing, pp. 1. SC 2005 (2005). https://doi.org/10.1109/SC.2005.3
10. David, H., Gorbatov, E., Hanebutte, U.R., Khanna, R., Le, C.: RAPL: memory power estimation and capping. In: Proceedings of the 16th ACM/IEEE International Symposium on Low Power Electronics and Design, pp. 189–194. ISLPED 2010 (2010). https://doi.org/10.1145/1840845.1840883
11. Dawson-Haggerty, S., Krioukov, A., Culler, D.: Power optimization-a reality check (2009)
12. Eranian, S.: Perfmon2: a flexible performance monitoring interface for Linux (2010)
13. Frigo, M., Leiserson, C.E., Prokop, H., Ramachandran, S.: Cache-oblivious algorithms. In: FOCS: IEEE Symposium on Foundations of Computer Science, pp. 285–297, October 1999
14. Frigo, M., Strumpen, V.: Cache oblivious stencil computations. In: International Conference on Supercomputing, pp. 361–366. ICS 2005, June 2005
15. Frigo, M., Strumpen, V.: The cache complexity of multithreaded cache oblivious algorithms. In: Proceedings of Eighteenth Annual ACM Symposium on Parallelism in Algorithms and Architectures, pp. 271–280 (2006)
16. Grosser, T., Cohen, A., Holewinski, J., Sadayappan, P., Verdoolaege, S.: Hybrid hexagonal/classical tiling for GPUs. In: Proceedings of Annual IEEE/ACM International Symposium on Code Generation and Optimization, pp. 66–75. CGO 2014 (2014). https://doi.org/10.1145/2544137.2544160
17. Han, D., Nam, Y.M., Lee, J., Park, K., Kim, H., Kim, M.S.: DistME: a fast and elastic distributed matrix computation engine using gpus. In: Proceedings of the 2019 International Conference on Management of Data, pp. 759–774. SIGMOD 2019 (2019). https://doi.org/10.1145/3299869.3319865
18. Holewinski, J., Pouchet, L.N., Sadayappan, P.: High-performance code generation for stencil computations on GPU architectures. In: Proceedings of the 26th ACM International Conference on Supercomputing. pp. 311–320. ICS 2012 (2012). https://doi.org/10.1145/2304576.2304619
19. Hsu, C.H., Kremer, U.: The design, implementation, and evaluation of a compiler algorithm for CPU energy reduction. In: Proceedings of the ACM SIGPLAN 2003 conference on Programming language design and implementation. PLDI 2003, vol. 38, pp. 38–48, May 2003. https://doi.org/10.1145/780822.781137
20. Itzhaky, S., et al.: Deriving divide-and-conquer dynamic programming algorithms using solver-aided transformations. In: Proceedings of ACM SIGPLAN International Conference on Object-Oriented Programming, Systems, Languages, and Applications, pp. 145–164. OOPSLA 2016 (2016)
21. Jimborean, A., Koukos, K., Spiliopoulos, V., Black-Schaffer, D., Kaxiras, S.: Fix the code. don't tweak the hardware: a new compiler approach to voltage-frequency scaling. In: Proceedings of Annual IEEE/ACM International Symposium on Code Generation and Optimization, pp. 262–272. CGO 2014 (2014). https://doi.org/10.1145/2581122.2544161

22. Krishnamoorthy, S., Baskaran, M., Bondhugula, U., Ramanujam, J., Rountev, A., Sadayappan, P.: Effective automatic parallelization of stencil computations. In: Proceedings of the 28th ACM SIGPLAN Conference on Programming Language Design and Implementation, pp. 235–244. PLDI 2007 (2007). https://doi.org/10.1145/1250734.1250761
23. Matsumura, K., Zohouri, H.R., Wahib, M., Endo, T., Matsuoka, S.: AN5D: automated stencil framework for high-degree temporal blocking on GPUs. ACM (2020). https://doi.org/10.1145/3368826.3377904
24. McCalpin, J., Wonnacott, D.: Time skewing: a value-based approach to optimizing for memory locality (1999)
25. Park, S., Kim, Y., Urgaonkar, B., Lee, J., Seo, E.: A comprehensive study of energy efficiency and performance of flash-based SSD. J. Syst. Archit. **57**(4), 354–365 (2011). https://doi.org/10.1016/j.sysarc.2011.01.005
26. Leiserson, C.E.: Cache-Oblivious algorithms. In: Petreschi, R., Persiano, G., Silvestri, R. (eds.) CIAC 2003. LNCS, vol. 2653, p. 5. Springer, Heidelberg (2003). https://doi.org/10.1007/3-540-44849-7_5
27. Rawat, P.S., et al.: Domain-specific optimization and generation of high-performance GPU code for stencil computations. Proc. IEEE **106**(11), 1902–1920 (2018). https://doi.org/10.1109/JPROC.2018.2862896
28. Strzodka, R., Shaheen, M., Pajak, D., Seidel, H.: Cache accurate time skewing in iterative stencil computations. In: Proceedings of the 2011 International Conference on Parallel Processing, pp. 571–581 (2011). https://doi.org/10.1109/ICPP.2011.47
29. Tang, Y., Chowdhury, R.A., Kuszmaul, B.C., Luk, C.K., Leiserson, C.E.: The pochoir stencil compiler. In: Proceedings of ACM Symposium on Parallelism in Algorithms and Architectures. SPAA 2011 (2011)
30. Tithi, J.J., Ganapathi, P., Talati, A., Aggarwal, S., Chowdhury, R.: High-performance energy-efficient recursive dynamic programming with matrix-multiplication-like flexible kernels. In: IEEE International Parallel and Distributed Processing Symposium, pp. 303–312, May 2015
31. Wolf, M.E., Lam, M.S.: A loop transformation theory and an algorithm to maximize parallelism. IEEE Trans. Parallel Distrib. Syst. **2**(4), 452–471 (1991). https://doi.org/10.1109/71.97902
32. Wonnacott, D.: Achieving scalable locality with time skewing. Int. J. Parallel Prog. **30**, 181–221 (1999)
33. Yuki, T., Rajopadhye, S.: Folklore confirmed: compiling for Speed = compiling for energy. In: Caşcaval, C., Montesinos, P. (eds.) LCPC 2013. LNCS, vol. 8664, pp. 169–184. Springer, Cham (2014). https://doi.org/10.1007/978-3-319-09967-5_10
34. Van Zee, F.G., van de Geijn, R.A.: BLIS: A framework for rapidly instantiating BLAS functionality. ACM Trans. Math. Softw. 41(3), 14:1–14:33 (2015). https://doi.org/10.1145/2764454
35. Zou, Y., Rajopadhye, S.: A code generator for energy-efficient wavefront parallelization of uniform dependence computations. IEEE Trans. Parallel Distrib. Syst. **29**, 1923–1936 (2018). https://doi.org/10.1109/TPDS.2017.2709748

Dynamic Network Selection for the Object Detection Task: Why It Matters and What We (Didn't) Achieve.

Emanuele Vitali[1(✉)], Anton Lokhmotov[2], and Gianluca Palermo[1]

[1] Politecnico di Milano, Milano, Italy
emanuele.vitali@polimi.it
[2] Dividiti Ltd., Cambridge, UK

Abstract. In this paper, we want to show the potential benefit of a dynamic auto-tuning approach for the inference process in the Deep Neural Network (DNN) context, tackling the object detection challenge. We benchmarked different neural networks to find the optimal detector for the well-known COCO 17 database [14], and we demonstrate that even if we only consider the quality of the prediction there is not a single optimal network. This is even more evident if we also consider the time to solution as a metric to evaluate, and then select, the most suitable network. This opens to the possibility for an adaptive methodology to switch among different object detection networks according to run-time requirements (e.g. maximum quality subject to a time-to-solution constraint).

Moreover, we demonstrated by developing an ad hoc oracle, that an additional proactive methodology could provide even greater benefits, allowing us to select the best network among the available ones given some characteristics of the processed image. To exploit this method, we need to identify some image features that can be used to steer the decision on the most promising network. Despite the optimization opportunity that has been identified, we were not able to identify a predictor function that validates this attempt neither adopting classical image features nor by using a DNN classifier.

Keywords: Object detection · Application dynamic autotuning

1 Introduction

A lot of progress has been done in the last 10 years in the context of Neural Networks. They have recently been used to solve complex problems such as image classification [12], voice to text [2] or object detection [9]. Since their introduction, they have eclipsed the old methods that were used to perform these tasks. In particular, they have become the de-facto standard in the field of computer vision for image classification and detection [20].

However, since there are a lot of different networks in literature, it is difficult to select the most suitable architecture (in terms of network deployed and hardware architecture used). DNNs are characterized by an accuracy metric. In the

© Springer Nature Switzerland AG 2022
A. Orailoglu et al. (Eds.): SAMOS 2021, LNCS 13227, pp. 467–480, 2022.
https://doi.org/10.1007/978-3-031-04580-6_31

object detection field, this metric is called mAP (mean average precision). This metric tells the user how accurate is the network in finding an object and classifying it. This is not enough, since we may be interested in other characteristics of the network. Sometimes we have to run the network in resource-constrained devices, or we have to perform real-time classification, where the response time is important. As an example in autonomous driving, an approximate detection in a short time is better than an accurate one that comes too late.

An interesting job in classifying several networks by their accuracy and time to solution has been done in [11]. In this work, the authors classify some of the most important object detection networks and provide and compare their performances on a single GPU architecture.

Starting from that work, we benchmarked different networks on different CPU-GPU environments. From that experiment, we found out that there is no single one-fits-all network, even in terms of accuracy on a single image. For this reason, we decided to analyze the problem of autotuning in this field, searching for some characteristics of the application or of the network itself that may enable a runtime network selection, whenever is beneficial. However, we were unable to find a suitable prediction function that can be used to drive the runtime selection, and thus to benefit from this optimization possibility.

The contributions of this paper can be summarized as follow:

- We performed a benchmarking campaign on different object detection networks aimed at exploring accuracy-performance tradeoffs;
- We demonstrate through a simple automotive use case how the dynamic autotuning approach can satisfy changing constraints that a single network was unable to satisfy;
- We built an oracle function based on the benchmarking campaign, that can select the best network among the used ones for every image of the COCO17 dataset, thus evaluating the possible advantage in having a proactive (per image) autotuning approach;
- We highlighted the failed attempts done to employ the proactive method either by finding some image features and training a selector using common machine learning techniques, or adopting an image classification network.

2 Related Works

Thanks to recent advances in the deep learning field, a lot of different models have been proposed to tackle the object detection challenge. These networks have different accuracy and execution times, and selecting the most suitable one is a complex task. Interesting approaches have been proposed considering the dynamic selection of networks for the context of image classification [16,18,22,23]. In [23], the authors propose to select dynamically the image classification network performing the inference, proving that is possible to improve both the accuracy and the inference time thanks to an autotuning approach. There the authors use a K-Nearest-Neighbor predictor to select, among 4 different models, which one is the best to use for every different image. The usage of

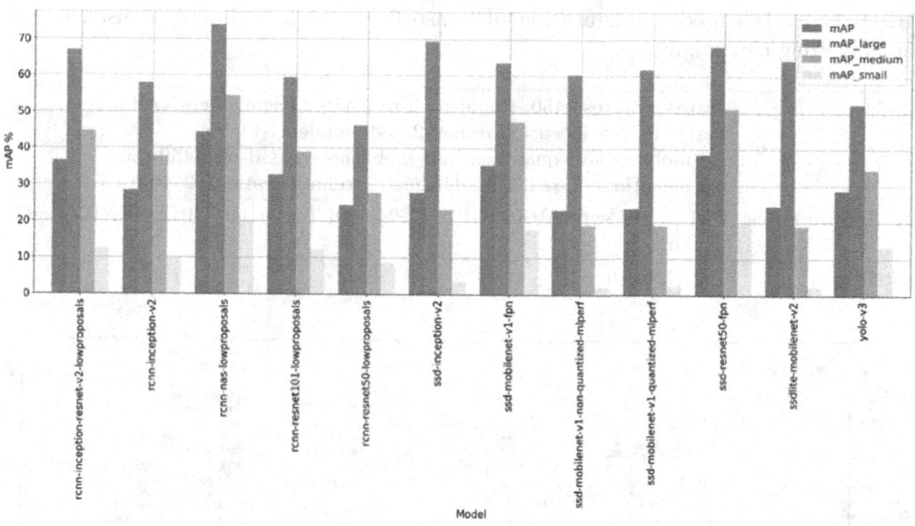

Fig. 1. Results of the benchmarking accuracy campaign.

two networks with a big/LITTLE approach is proposed in [18]. In this work, two different network architectures are created on a chip. One small and fast (the LITTLE architecture) and one that is more accurate and more time-consuming (the big architecture). They perform the inference with the little network and they use the big as a fallback solution only if the little network prediction is deemed not accurate. However, even in this work, the solution is proposed for the image classification challenge. Another dynamic methodology for the image classification has been proposed in [22]. Here the same network is trained several times, with different datasets, and an ensemble of networks is used to perform the inference. The networks are used sequentially and if a certain threshold metric is reached the result is returned without executing the remaining networks. Several other design-time optimizations are proposed in literature to build the networks [21], to compress them [15] or to switch from image processing to more expensive and accurate input (e.g. LIDAR) [16]. All of these work targeting the network selection are done in the context of image classification. Indeed, to the best of our knowledge, there is no work targeting the dynamic selection of the network in the object detection challenge.

3 Motivations

To show the potential benefit of having a self-tuning network selector, we run an extensive benchmarking campaign on different object detection models and platforms. The objective of this campaign is to explore the behavior of different DNN on different platforms and with different configurations. In particular, we tested on CPU (with and without the AVX2 instructions) and GPU (with and without the TensorRT library support). We selected 12 different models.

Table 1. Models used, configuration of Tensorflow and batching sizes used in the benchmarking campaign

Models	Faster-rcnn-resnet50, Faster-rcnn-resnet101, Faster-rcnn-NAS, Faster-RCNN-inception-resnetv2, ssd-mobilenet-v1-fpn, ssd-mobilenet-v1-quantized, ssd-mobilenet-v1, ssd-resnet50-fpn, ssd-inception-v2, ssdlite-mobilenet-v2, rcnn-inception-v2, yolo-v3
TF Configurations	CPU, CPU with AVX2, GPU, GPU with TensorRT, GPU with TensorRT dynamic
Batch sizes	1, 2, 4, 8, 16, 32

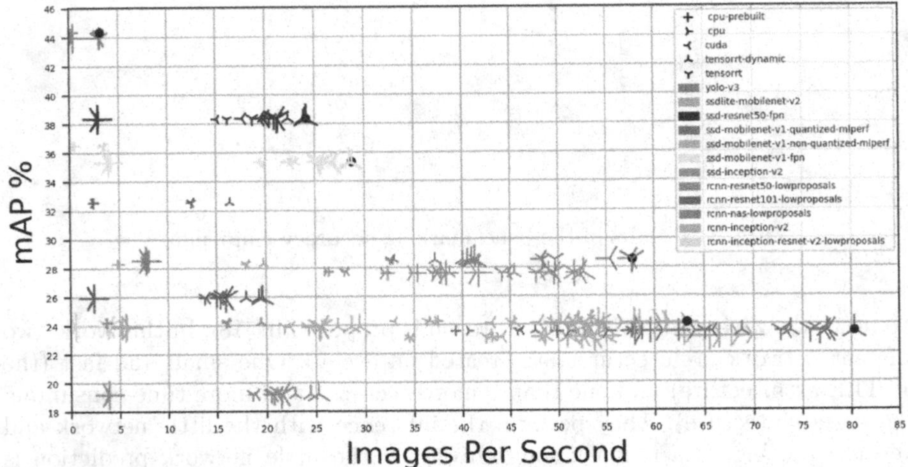

Fig. 2. Result of the benchmarking campaign with the measured accuracy. The batch accuracy loss can be seen in the Faster-RCNN models.

Most of them were coming from the Tensorflow Zoo [1], trying to balance the SSD-based and the Faster-RCNN based models. To those models, we added a reimplementation of the YOLO-v3 network.

From the accuracy point of view, the campaign consists of 24 different experiments (12 models and with or without batch resizing). From the performance point of view, the number of experiments is increased to 360 and the whole Design of Experiment is reported in Table 1. The experiments have been done on the whole validation set of the COCO 2017 dataset.

As a motivation for the proposed idea, we will analyze the results of this benchmarking campaign, firstly from the accuracy point of view, then from the performance perspective and finally, we will analyze the Pareto frontier.

Figure 1 shows the results of the accuracy benchmarking done while differentiating the accuracy also considering the *size* of the object to be identified. In the COCO dataset the objects are divided into three categories, small (up to 32*32 pixels), medium (from 32*32 to 96*96), and large (everything above). The most accurate model is Faster-RCNN-NAS, which reaches the overall mAP of 44%. Usually, a model with a good overall mAP performs consistently well across all three object categories. There are, however, some exceptions: SSD-Inception-v2 has the 2nd best score on large objects, but performs rather poorly on medium and small objects; on the contrary, YOLO-v3 has the 2nd worst score on large objects, but is on the 4th place on small objects and performs OK on medium objects. The bad accuracy obtained on small objects is a well-known problem of SSD-based models. This is why the Feature Pyramid Network (FPN) feature have been introduced. Thanks to this feature, the SSD-ResNet50 and SSD-MobileNet-v1 models are able to reach 2nd and 3rd place on small objects (and on the 2nd and 4th place overall).

The complete result from the exploration can be seen in Fig. 2. Here the color symbolizes the network used for the inference, while the shape is the backend and the size of the marker symbolizes the batch size. We can notice that the GPU backends are faster than the CPU ones and that the bigger points usually have the best performances.

The images in the COCO dataset have different shapes and sizes. For the inference to be performed, they need to be resized to match the model input size. This is usually done inside the network, as a first layer. However, this is not possible when processing a batch of images. In this case, all the images of a batch need to be resized before the inference is performed. This procedure may damage the accuracy: some Faster-RCNN networks have the smallest point (no batch) at a higher accuracy level compared to the largest points of the same network. Besides the Faster-RCNN-NAS, the other Faster-RCNN networks have a *keep-aspect-ratio* layer, which becomes problematic when resizing the images to a unique size. However, batching images can be significant for the performances, so we need to consider this possibility and not just discard it a-priori. Indeed, as we can see from Fig. 2, usually the bigger points have a better performance than the smallest one when we use the same backend. This growth can also be very significant, leading to almost double performances for some networks (YOLO v3 goes from 32 to almost 60 FPS). However, the general behavior is not always true. Some networks show some unexpected results demonstrating how a dynamic selection of the most suitable configuration could be very important in this field. The first is that batching can be detrimental to the performances: this happens when working with the Faster-RCNN-NAS on the CPU. Another interesting result is that some networks perform better on the CPU than the GPU: an example is the ssdlite-mobilenet-v2 network

To conclude the motivational discussion, Fig. 3 shows the best configuration (considering ideal accuracy for the Faster-RCNN networks that have problems with batching). We can notice that there is not a one-fit-all optimal solution, since both the optimal backend and the optimal batch size changes across the different models. Moreover, the networks on the Pareto set are also different if we consider different target accuracy. All these variations strongly suggest that should a network selector function be found like in the methodology proposed in [23] for the image classification challenge, the object detection challenge could largely benefit from an adaptive autotuning approach.

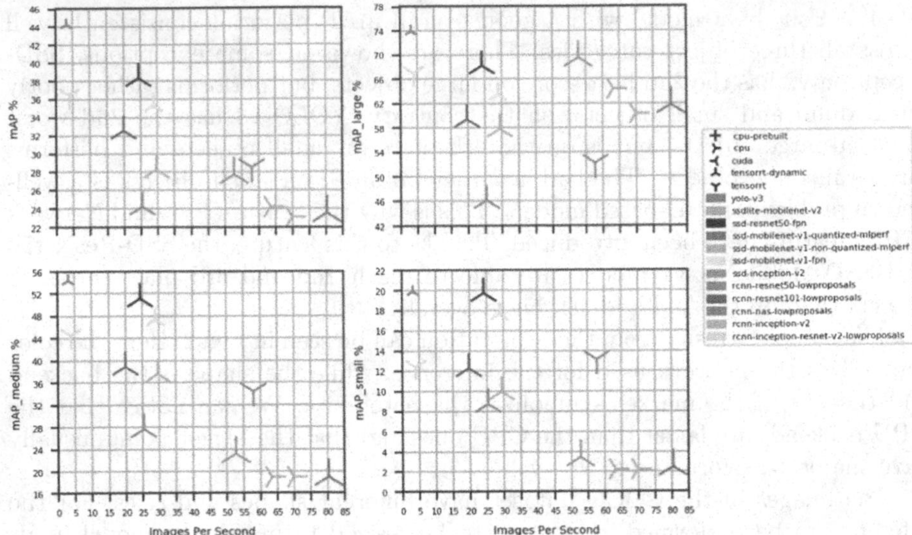

Fig. 3. Best performance for every network at the different accuracy metrics (small, medium and large).

4 The Proposed Approach

In this section, we will see the methodology followed while trying to dynamically select the optimal inference network. At the first time, we will see how exploiting two networks in analyzing a stream of frames can allow adapting to different constraints (maximize the accuracy of the prediction or maximize the frame rate) in a reactive way. With reactive, we mean that the autotuner reacts to the change of the constraints and responds to this change by selecting a different inference network, that can respect the new constraints. This approach follows the traditional reactive autotuning approach, used for example in [3,5–7].

We then try to create a predictor function that can work as an oracle for unknown images. This is a proactive approach that relies on the concept of input feature that is present in some works in literature [13,24]. To create the predictor, we will search for some data features and we use them to create a function that can predict which is the best network to use to perform the inference.

4.1 Reactive Approach

In the reactive approach, the idea is of having the self-tuning module able to react to changes in the system or external conditions. Changes in external conditions are reflected in changes in the constraints. Figure 5 shows the approach from a high-level point of view: we must process a stream of images while respecting some constraints that may change during the runtime. We have a set of networks with different (and known) characteristics in terms of accuracy and time

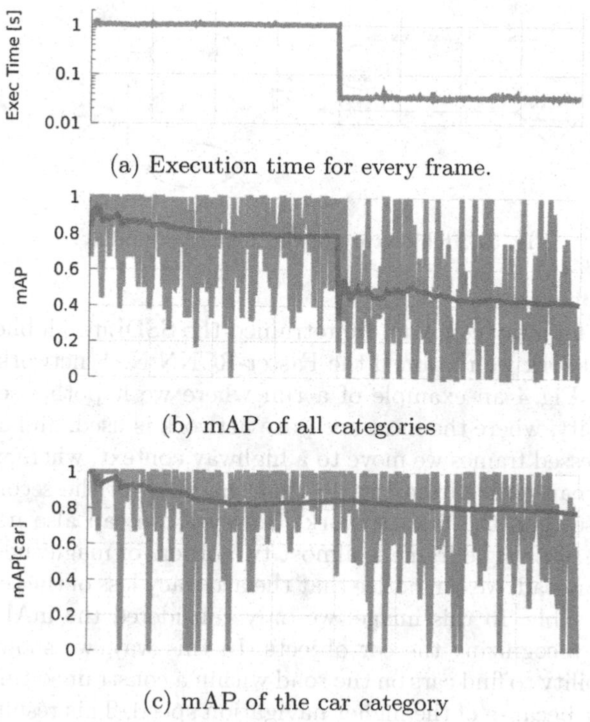

(a) Execution time for every frame.

(b) mAP of all categories

(c) mAP of the car category

Fig. 4. Execution log of the same stream with two different networks, with a change of network in the middle.

to solution. The autotuning module is in charge of selecting the most suitable among them according to the current constraints, interacting with factors that are external from the object detection problem.

To show the validity of this approach, let us suppose a very simplified scenario in the context of autonomous driving, which is one of the most important contexts in the object detection challenge. We need to find the possible obstacles on or near the road, and we need to satisfy a strong constraint on the response time since if the detection arrives too late it is useless. To simplify the approach, let us suppose that we have 2 possible scenarios: highway and city driving. In the first case, we need to have a quick response and we need to identify "big" objects such as cars, while in the second case we have a slower speed, which means that we can use a slower network but we require a greater accuracy since we need to identify the "small" pedestrians.

In this simplified example, the autotuner is in charge of switching from context 1 (city driving) to context 2 (highway) and back whenever a threshold speed is passed. For this experiment, we have used the KITTI dataset [8], which is a dataset created for the autonomous driving context. As the first network (the

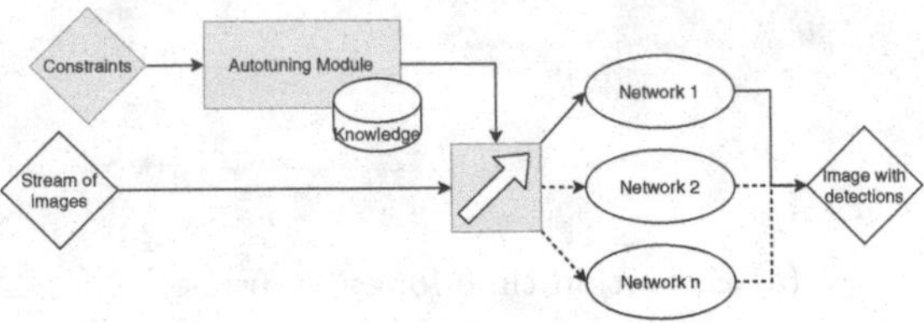

Fig. 5. Architecture of the Reactive module.

fast one for the highway context), we retrained the SSDLite-Mobilenet, while as the accurate network we retrained the Faster-RCNN NAS network.

We show in Fig. 4 an example of a run where we hypothesize to start the trip inside the city, where the most accurate network is used, and after a certain number of processed frames we move to a highway context, where we need faster processing. We can notice from Fig. 4b that the mAP of the second network is noticeably worse than the first network. However, we can also notice that the processing time of a single frame is almost two orders of magnitude faster. If we look at Fig. 4c instead, we can notice that the accuracy loss of the second network is slightly noticeable. In this image, we only considered the mAP obtained by the network in recognizing the car objects. In this way, we show that we can maintain the ability to find cars on the road within a constrained time to solution, which is smaller because of the higher navigation speed. This result confirms the benefit of dynamic network selection in the context of the simplified scenario hypothesized before. Indeed, we can meet the accuracy/response time request in both the contexts, while both the considered networks are not able to do it if taken individually.

The impact of the reactive approach has been demonstrated on a simple use case considering only two networks. However, it can be easily generalized to a more complex one where, as an example, the constraints could be a function of the speed or multiple scenarios (and not only city and highway) can bring to different optimization problems.

4.2 Proactive Approach

An orthogonal approach to the previous approach is the proactive one. The proactive approach to dynamically select the network aims at using characteristics of both the network and the image that is going to be processed to match the image with its best possible network. We believe that if there is not a one-fit-all best network while considering only the accuracy of the prediction, and there may be some features of the images that determine if a network behaves better than other networks in finding objects in that precise image. Thus, we are interested in finding those characteristics of the images, and building a predictor that may be able to select the optimal object detection network.

The first step is to verify that the best network to perform the inference would change across the dataset. We create an oracle function, that selects the best

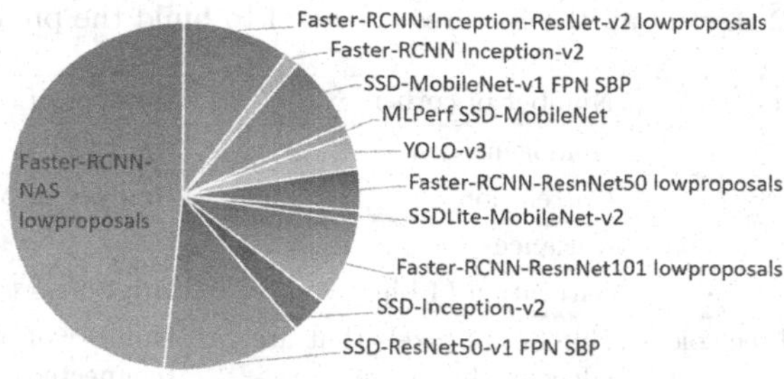

Fig. 6. Composition of the Oracle on the full COCO validation set. All the considered networks are present, which means that they are optimal in predicting some images.

network for all the images of the COCO validation set. In particular, the program selects the highest mAP after evaluating an image with all the networks, and as a tiebreaker, it uses the execution time (the fastest one among the network with the same accuracy wins). Figure 6 reports the pie chart of the oracle. We can notice that almost half of the chart is occupied by the Faster-RCNN NAS, the most accurate network. We expected this network to be dominating. However, this network does not have always the best accuracy. Moreover, the oracle shows that all the different networks are represented which means that they are optimal for at least some images. The second step is to search the data features and a prediction function to drive the network selection proactively given the target image. Figure 7 shows two different attempts that we performed in building the predictor. The first one, which we define "traditional Machine Learning (ML) approach", can be seen in Fig. 7a. The second attempt, where we used neural network techniques, can be seen in Fig. 7b. Figure 7a shows the pipeline that we designed to perform object detection with network selection done with the traditional ML approach. The first step is Feature Extraction, which is a module that is in charge of quickly analyzing the image and extract some features. Then the predictor module is a function in charge of driving the network selection. This function needs to be able to quickly select the network given the data features extracted from the previous step. Finally, the image is forwarded to the object detection network, which performs the detection task and returns the objects detected in the given image. To create the feature extraction module, we need to identify a small set of features that can be quickly extracted from the image.

We started the search of the data features from the ones used in [23] since the authors were already working in the DNN context. Other candidate features are taken from [13]. In this work, four easily obtained characteristics (*mean, variance, local homogeneity, and covariance*) are used to decide how to approximate an image. Moreover, we considered standard image processing features from literature [10]. We extracted all of these features and others using well-known Python packages, such as OpenCV [17] and Skimage [25], collecting in total over 50 image features. The complete list of the considered features is reported in Table 2. We did extract all of these features, however, we are aware that we need to reduce the number of features to use, since getting all of these would be too

Table 2. List of all the features collected to build the predictor.

Number of keypoints	Number of corners	Number of contours
Dissimilarity	Homogeneity	ASM
Energy	Correlation	Number of peaks
Contrast	Variance	Mean
Hues(4 bins)	Saturation (4 bins)	Brightness (4 bins)
Histogram of the three colors (3*8 bins)	Number of pixels that are edges in the image	Number of objects (connected components)
Aspect ratio	Histogram of gradients (8 bins)	

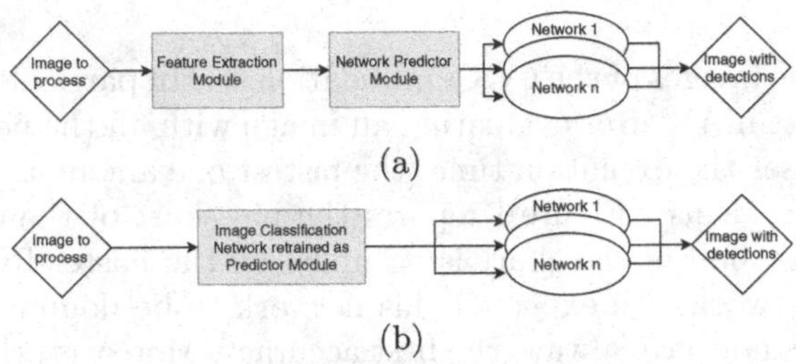

Fig. 7. Structure of the two attempts done in implementing the proactive approach to object detection, using a traditional Machine Learning approach (a) or using an Image Classification Neural Network (b).

time-consuming. Moreover, some of them (for example the connected components) are too expensive in terms of extraction time and have been discarded a priori.

The following step is to build the classifier. To do this, we use both the output of the oracle and the extracted features of the images, since we need to learn the correlation between these features and the best network. We decided to use the scikit library [19] since it is a well-known and verified module for the most common ML algorithms. We used a Principal Component Analysis (PCA) to restrict the space of features, assigning to this methodology the duty of finding out which ones are the most important features that we have to consider. We then passed the output of the PCA to the following step, which is the model training. Before training the model, we have to create the training and the test set. From the available 5000 images (for which we have the array of features with the associated best network), we create a training set of 4500 images, while the other 500 are left as validation set. Since the goal is to implement a classification layer, we have tested most of the classifier engines available in the *scikit-learn* module. Among them, we tested *Decision Tree, Random Forest, Bagging, AdaBoost, Extra Trees, Gradient Boosting, SGD, MLP, KNeighbors*. However, no one of those algorithms was able to provide a robust classifier that could be used as the predictor, as we can notice from Fig. 8. In particular, Fig. 8a shows the result on the complete set of networks. In most cases, the accuracy of the validation set

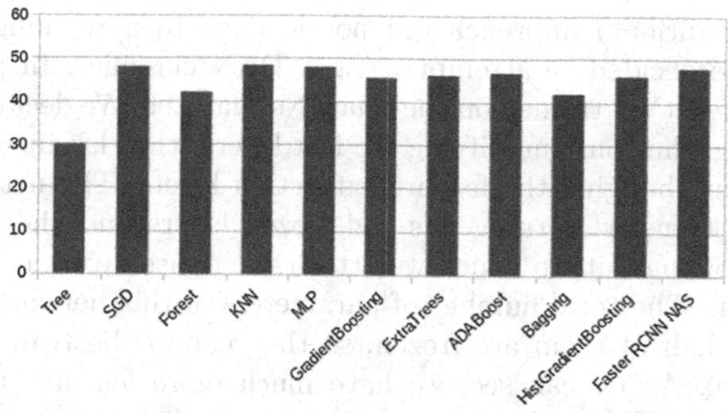

(a) Accuracy of the predictors with all the networks

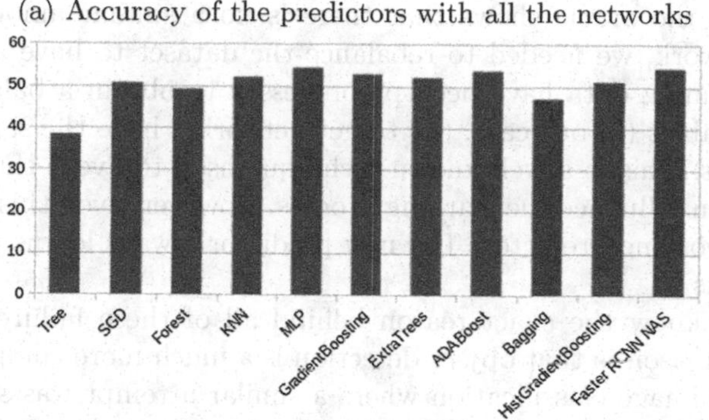

(b) Accuracy of the predictors with a restricted set of networks.

Fig. 8. Results of the training of the different models.

was around 40% which is also the number of occurrences of the most accurate model always (the last column in the figure). The tree predictor is the one that shows the worst result, around 30%. To reduce the noise in the data available for the learning phase, we restricted the number of models. We decided to use only the ones that were Pareto optimal in the benchmarking study. This reduced the number of available models to 6. Nonetheless, even with the reduced number of target networks, the traditional ML classifiers were unable to learn how to predict the best network to use to perform object detection given the image. The result of this final experiment is reported in Fig. 8b. We can notice that even with this reduction in the possible networks there is no valid predictor: the last column (Faster-RCNN-NAS) is the predictor that always selects the Faster-RCNN-NAS network to perform the detection since it is the most accurate one. This predictor has an accuracy of 55%, which means that in more than half of the test images the RCNN-NAS has the optimal accuracy in the reduced validation set. All the predictors have a worse result, meaning that they can guess the optimal network with less accuracy than always selecting the same, and most used, network.

Since the traditional approach did not lead us to a working solution for our problem, we decided to attempt using a DNN classifier. In particular, we selected a MobilenetV2, trained on the ImageNet dataset. We decided to perform transfer learning, thus only modifying the last layers (the classifier layers) of the network, without changing the feature extraction layers. The network we used to perform the transfer learning has 154 frozen layers and the last layer has 1280 features coming out, to which we attach the dense layers used to perform the classification. The total number of parameters of this network is 5,149,771, and more than half of them are frozen, so they cannot be trained during the transfer learning. As we can see, we have much more features than with the previous approach. We used the keras [4] framework to perform the transfer learning. Since the oracle shows that there is no a similar amount of images for all the network, we needed to rebalance the dataset to have a fair training phase. The training data have been preprocessed to obtain a balanced dataset where all the labels (in our case, the target networks) have the same amount of training images. This is a well-known technique used to avoid that the dataset unbalancing can influence the learning process. However, even this approach did not lead to a working predictor. The new predictor always learns to predict one or two networks.

We do not know the exact reason behind all of these failures. We believe that the main reason is that object detection is a much more complex operation if compared to image classification where a similar attempt was successful [23]. Indeed, the DNN used to tackle this challenge are more complex than the classification networks: [11] shows how most object detection networks are composed of two sections, a region proposal network that aims at creating the bounding boxes of the objects, and a feature extractor, which is an image classification network that provides the label to the object extracted with the first stage. We think that this failure may be due to the fact that the image features extracted with traditional image processing or with feature extraction layers trained for the classification problem are not enough. Indeed, these features may not be sufficient to model the region proposal problem. Thus, a different set of features may be needed.

5 Conclusion

In this paper, we studied the possibility of dynamically select the network used to perform inference in the object detection context, where to the best of our knowledge has not been already attempted before. We have shown why a dynamic autotuning methodology could be very profitable for this context, with a large benchmarking campaign that demonstrates that there is no a one-fit-all optimal solution. We have seen that the use of a reactive approach can satisfy changing requirements by exploiting networks that were unable to satisfy the given constraints if taken singularly. We tried also to adopt a proactive approach, that could have been even more profitable if we were able to select in advance the most suitable network for a specific image. While the oracle confirmed our feeling, we were not able to find any feature extraction technique that was able to drive the selection process. Finally, we believe that this work is a good motivational study and our attempts could be useful by other researchers interested in the field.

Acknowledgements. Part of this work was done when Emanuele was an intern in dividiti Ltd, Cambridge. The internship was sponsored by the HIPEAC project, in the European Union's Horizon 2020 research and innovation programme under grant agreement number 871174. Moreover, part of this work has been developed within EVEREST project and funded by the EU Horizon 2020 Programme under grant agreement No 957269.

References

1. Tensorflow zoo. https://github.com/tensorflow/models/blob/master/research/object_detection/g3doc/tf1_detection_zoo.md. Accessed 03 Jan 2021
2. Amodei, D., et al.: Deep speech 2: end-to-end speech recognition in English and mandarin. In: International Conference on Machine Learning, pp. 173–182 (2016)
3. Baek, W., Chilimbi, T.M.: Green: a framework for supporting energy-conscious programming using controlled approximation. In: ACM Sigplan Notices, vol. 45, pp. 198–209. ACM (2010)
4. Chollet, F.: Keras (2015). https://github.com/fchollet/keras
5. Filieri, A., Hoffmann, H., Maggio, M.: Automated multi-objective control for self-adaptive software design. In: Proceedings of the 2015 10th Joint Meeting on Foundations of Software Engineering, pp. 13–24. ACM (2015)
6. Gadioli, D., et al.: Socrates - a seamless online compiler and system runtime autotuning framework for energy-aware applications. In: 2018 Design, Automation Test in Europe Conference Exhibition (DATE), pp. 1143–1146 (2018)
7. Gadioli, D., Vitali, E., Palermo, G., Silvano, C.: margot: a dynamic autotuning framework for self-aware approximate computing. IEEE Trans. Comput. **68**(5), 713–728 (2019)
8. Geiger, A., Lenz, P., Urtasun, R.: Are we ready for autonomous driving? the kitti vision benchmark suite. In: Conference on Computer Vision and Pattern Recognition (CVPR) (2012)
9. Girshick, R., Donahue, J., Darrell, T., Malik, J.: Rich feature hierarchies for accurate object detection and semantic segmentation. In: Proceedings of the IEEE Conference on Computer Vision and Pattern Recognition (CVPR), June 2014
10. Hassaballah, M., Abdelmgeid, A.A., Alshazly, H.A.: Image features detection, description and matching. In: Awad, A.I., Hassaballah, M. (eds.) Image Feature Detectors and Descriptors. SCI, vol. 630, pp. 11–45. Springer, Cham (2016). https://doi.org/10.1007/978-3-319-28854-3_2
11. Huang, J., et al.: Speed/accuracy trade-offs for modern convolutional object detectors. In: Proceedings of the IEEE Conference on Computer Vision and Pattern Recognition, pp. 7310–7311 (2017)
12. Krizhevsky, A., Sutskever, I., Hinton, G.E.: Imagenet classification with deep convolutional neural networks. Commun. ACM **60**(6), 84–90 (2017)
13. Laurenzano, M.A., Hill, P., Samadi, M., Mahlke, S., Mars, J., Tang, L.: Input responsiveness: using canary inputs to dynamically steer approximation. ACM SIGPLAN Notices **51**(6), 161–176 (2016)
14. Lin, T.Y., et al.: Microsoft coco: common objects in context (2014)

15. Liu, S., Lin, Y., Zhou, Z., Nan, K., Liu, H., Du, J.: On-demand deep model compression for mobile devices: a usage-driven model selection framework. In: Proceedings of the 16th Annual International Conference on Mobile Systems, Applications, and Services, MobiSys 2018, pp. 389–400. Association for Computing Machinery, New York (2018)
16. Mazouz, A., Bridges, C.P.: Multi-sensory CNN models for close proximity satellite operations. In: 2019 IEEE Aerospace Conference, pp. 1–7 (2019)
17. OpenCV: Open source computer vision library (2015)
18. Park, E., et al.: Big/little deep neural network for ultra low power inference. In: International Conference on Hardware/Software Codesign and System Synthesis (CODES+ISSS), pp. 124–132 (2015)
19. Pedregosa, F., et al.: Scikit-learn: machine learning in Python. J. Mach. Learn. Res. **12**, 2825–2830 (2011)
20. Russakovsky, O., et al.: Imagenet large scale visual recognition challenge. Int. J. Comput. Vision **115**(3), 211–252 (2015)
21. Tan, M., et al: Mnasnet: platform-aware neural architecture search for mobile. In: Proceedings of IEEE Conference on Computer Vision and Pattern Recognition, pp. 2820–2828 (2019)
22. Tann, H., Hashemi, S., Reda, S.: Flexible deep neural network processing. arXiv preprint arXiv:1801.07353 (2018)
23. Taylor, B., Marco, V.S., Wolff, W., Elkhatib, Y., Wang, Z.: Adaptive deep learning model selection on embedded systems. ACM SIGPLAN Notices **53**(6), 31–43 (2018)
24. Vitali, E., et al.: An efficient Monte Carlo-based probabilistic time-dependent routing calculation targeting a server-side car navigation system. IEEE Trans. Emerg. Top. Comput. (2019)
25. van der Walt, S., et al.: The scikit-image contributors: scikit-image: image processing in Python. PeerJ **2**, e453 (2014)

Sharing-Aware Data Mapping in Software Transactional Memory

Douglas Pereira Pasqualin[1(✉)], Matthias Diener[2], André Rauber Du Bois[1], and Maurício Lima Pilla[1]

[1] Computer Science Graduate Program (PPGC), Universidade Federal de Pelotas, Pelotas, RS, Brazil
{dp.pasqualin,dubois,pilla}@inf.ufpel.edu.br

[2] University of Illinois at Urbana-Champaign, Urbana, IL 61801, USA
mdiener@illinois.edu

Abstract. Software transactional memory (STM) is an abstraction used for thread synchronization that borrows the concept of transactions from databases. It is often easier to use than locks, proving a high-level abstraction for software developers. In current multicore architectures, data locality is an important aspect of STM performance. Sharing-aware mapping is a technique that aims to improve the performance of applications by mapping threads and data (in the form of memory pages) according to their memory access behavior. In prior work, we successfully used information gained from tracking STM variables and STM operations to perform an effective sharing-aware thread mapping. In this paper, we attempt to extend such a mechanism to perform data mapping. Although initial results using a synthetic application were encouraging, data mapping did not improve performance when using realistic workloads. Contrary to thread mapping, where only keeping track of STM operations is sufficient to perform an effective thread mapping, data mapping requires a global vision of memory page accesses of the application to be able to improve the performance, which STM runtimes can not provide.

Keywords: Software transactional memory · Data mapping · Sharing-aware · NUMA

1 Introduction

Multicore processors have been used for many years, due to the higher power consumption and heat dissipation involved on improve the performance of a single CPU core. The number of cores in a single chip is growing every year for server, desktop, and mobile CPUs. Beyond that, NUMA (Non-Uniform Memory Access) architectures are becoming dominant in servers [21]. In these machines, each multiprocessor is connected directly to a local memory module [9]. Data

This study was financed in part by the Coordenação de Aperfeiçoamento de Pessoal de Nível Superior - Brasil (CAPES) - Finance Code 001 and PROCAD/LEAPaD.

© Springer Nature Switzerland AG 2022
A. Orailoglu et al. (Eds.): SAMOS 2021, LNCS 13227, pp. 481–492, 2022.
https://doi.org/10.1007/978-3-031-04580-6_32

can be stored on the local node or on a node that belongs to another processor (remote node). Although programs have transparent access to the entire memory, accessing a remote node implies a higher latency, making the access time non-uniform, i.e., it depends on the location of the data.

To exploit the parallelism available in these multicore machines, the software must be parallel and scalable [11]. In parallel programming, locks still are the most used abstraction for thread synchronization. However, locks are error-prone, making the source code hard to read and debug [1] and they can lead to deadlocks. An alternative abstraction to locks is *Transactional Memory (TM)* [11,12]. The main idea of TM is to enclose critical sections in atomic blocks that will be accessed using transactions, similar to the ones used in databases. Using TM, the programmer only needs to think about which block of code needs to be synchronized and not how to synchronize them. Hence, the TM runtime is responsible to ensure a consistent execution without race conditions or deadlocks. In this paper, we focused on TM implemented in software (STM). Nevertheless, the ideas presented on this paper can be used in any kind of TM.

Although there are several approaches to improving the performance of STM, many of them focus on reducing the number of aborts by using transactional schedulers [20]. An abort is necessary when two transactions access the same shared variable and at least one of them is a writer. However, in current multicore architectures with complex memory hierarchies and different latencies on memory accesses, it is important to consider the locality of the accesses. Using a technique called *sharing-aware thread mapping* [6] which aims to map threads to cores of an application considering their memory access behavior, we were able to improve the performance of STM applications [15–17]. Data mapping, where memory pages are mapped to NUMA nodes considering their memory access behavior, is also important to improve application performance [5].

In prior work, we successfully used information gained from tracking STM operations to dynamically perform an effective sharing-aware thread mapping [15]. However, while attempting to extend such a mechanism to also perform data mapping, we encountered issues due to the lack of global information about the memory access behavior, and discovered that only taking into consideration STM operations is not sufficient to perform an effective sharing-aware data mapping. This paper presents our efforts to implement data mapping using information gained from STM operations, and discusses why this is insufficient for many STM applications.

2 Background: STM and Sharing-Aware-Mapping

2.1 Software Transactional Memory

Software transactional memory (STM) is an abstraction used for thread synchronization that borrows the concept of transactions from databases. Application's critical sections are enclosed in atomic blocks to be executed as a transaction. If a transaction executes without conflicts a *commit* happens, i.e., all shared variable modifications are made visible to other threads. A conflict happens if two distinct transactions access the same shared variable and at least one transaction performs a write operation in the variable. If conflicts are detected, an *abort* is necessary, discarding all operations made in the transaction and restarting it.

2.2 Sharing-Aware Mapping

Data locality is an important factor in modern multicore and NUMA machines. One way to better explore locality is to map threads and data according to their *memory access behavior* [6]. The goal of data mapping is to optimize the usage of memory controllers, by mapping memory pages to the same NUMA node where the core that most accesses it belongs to. On the other hand, thread mapping aims to improve cache usage and interconnections. Thread mapping aims to avoid access to the main memory, prioritizing caches. Oppositely, if an access to the main memory is necessary, data mapping tries to map the memory that needs to be accessed to a local NUMA node, avoiding remote accesses.

Thread and data mapping based on the memory access behavior of applications is called **sharing-aware mapping** [6]. Although the Linux kernel handles thread and data mapping, it does not consider memory access patterns. For instance, the *Completely Fair Scheduler* (CFS) used by default in the Linux kernel mainly focuses on load balancing. For data mapping, the default policy is called *first-touch* [9] where the memory is allocated in the NUMA node where the first access to the memory page is performed.

2.3 Sharing-Aware Mapping in STM

In a previous work [15] we presented a mechanism that, during application execution, keeps track of transactional shared variables to detect the sharing pattern of the STM application and performs sharing-aware **thread mapping** dynamically. The intuition is that the STM runtime has precise information about shared variables and which threads are accessing them. The main objective of thread mapping is to optimize cache usage by mapping threads that access shared variables often closer in the underlying architecture. Hence, contrary to prior works on sharing-aware thread mapping, it is not necessary to keep track of all memory access of the applications, only the STM accesses. Therefore, the proposed mechanism has a low overhead and dynamically performs sharing-aware thread mapping accurately for STM applications. We use the same intuitions to complement such mechanism to include sharing-aware **data mapping**.

3 Related Work

This section presents works that use data mapping to improve the data locality of applications running on shared memory architectures.

`ForestGOMP` [3] is an extension of OpenMP that uses hints provided by application programmers, compiler techniques and hardware counters to perform thread and data placement dynamically. Threads that share data or synchronize often are organized in bubbles. The main objective is to improve the cache usage and try to make each "bubble" accessing the local memory, migrating pages if necessary. The *kernel Memory Affinity Framework* (kMAF) [5] is implemented directly in the Linux kernel, detecting communication patterns of parallel applications and migrate threads and data according to their memory affinity. The *Carrefour* mechanism [4] is also implemented directly in the Linux kernel. However, it uses Instruction-Based Sampling (IBS) available only on AMD processors. Barrera et al. [19] obtain information about characteristics of parallel applications by using instrumentation and hardware performance counters. After that, using machine learning, the collected data is processed resulting in information, for instance, if the application is sensitive to locality and the best thread and data placement.

Analysis tools were proposed to collect information about memory access of applications. These tools help to understand how applications share data. Using Pin instrumentation tool, `Numalize` [7] generates a memory trace of applications and generated information that helps to choose the best placement of threads and data. `TABARNAC` [2] provides a graphical visualization of memory access behavior, such as the distribution of the accesses by threads and data structures. A more recent tool, `NumaMMa` (NUMA MeMory Analyzer) [22] uses hardware counters of a processor to generate memory traces. When the application finishes, `NumaMMa` processes the trace and analyzes the cost of memory accesses of each object and how threads access them. Also, graphical visualization of the processed information is available.

Regarding data mapping for STM applications, as far as we know, only Goés et al. [10] have proposed a mechanism to deal with data mapping. However, their work focuses on a specific sharing pattern of STM application (*worklist*), and their mechanism to exploit memory affinity was implemented inside a new framework. Hence, applications need to be rewritten with this framework to be able to use the memory affinity improvements. Also, their data mapping is based on static page allocation (bind or cyclic).

4 A Mechanism for Sharing-Aware Data Mapping in STM

This section presents our proposed mechanism to dynamically detect memory page accesses and perform data mapping for STM applications.

4.1 Detecting Memory Page Accesses in STM Applications

To perform a sharing-aware data mapping in STM, it is necessary to know which NUMA nodes are accessing each memory page address. In word-based STM implementations, each transactional data access operation, for instance, a transactional read or write, explicitly includes the addresses used in the operation. Hence, it is possible to extract the information of the memory page being accessed by bit-shifting the full memory address.

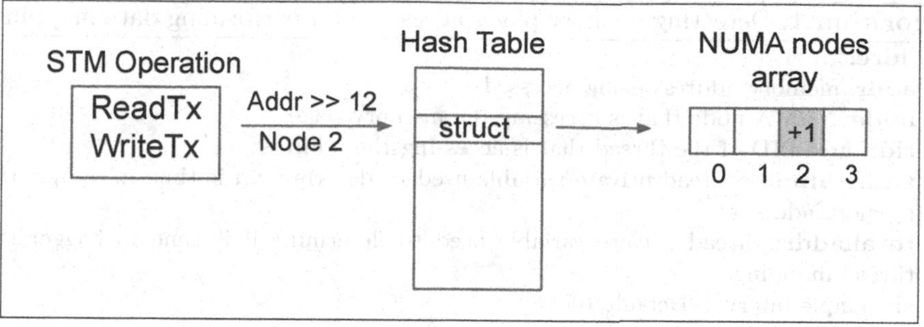

Fig. 1. Mechanism for detecting page accesses. Data structures are shown for a NUMA machine with 4 nodes (0–3).

Since the idea of the proposed mechanism is to detect page access and performing data mapping during runtime, we use the concept of sampling. In order to reduce overhead, we do not track all STM reads and writes, but only a subset of them. Also, to avoid thread synchronization, each thread has its own sampling interval (si) counter. As our previous work showed [15], a sampling interval of **100** presents the best trade-off between overhead and accuracy. In that case, for each thread we sample the memory access once for every 100 accesses. The proposed mechanism is shown in Fig. 1 and detailed in Algorithm 1.

Explaining the Algorithm 1, first, the thread private variable `addr_sample` (line 1) is incremented to verify if is time to sample the memory access. Then, on line 2 we verify if the counter of the current thread is greater than the sampling interval. If true, we zero the variable to be able to detect the next trigger time (line 3), and it is time to sample the page being accessed. Since the STM runtime has access to the full memory address, we first need to bit shift the address to get the information of the memory page (line 4). To keep track of accessed memory pages, a hash table is used, whose keys are memory pages. Each position of the hash table contains a structure with the memory address and an array of size equal to the number of NUMA nodes of the machine (Fig. 1). Each position of this array contains the number of accesses to the memory page performed by each NUMA node. Hence, on line 5, the function `getPageInfo` gets from the hash table the structure containing information about the memory page being accessed. To avoid unnecessary page moves, we only update the number of accesses to this page (line 7) if the page has not been moved already (line 6).

The next part of the algorithm determines when to perform the new data mapping. We have a special variable called *data mapping interval* (dmi) used to determine if it is time to trigger the new data mapping. The idea is to reduce the number of times that the data mapping is triggered because migrate pages in runtime implies overheads. Hence, the data mapping interval is based on the total number of memory addresses. Similar to the sampling interval, to avoid thread synchronization, we decided to track the total number of accessed addresses of only one thread. Therefore, we calculate the new data mapping when the application accessed "data mapping interval" addresses. The lines 8 to 10 are

Algorithm 1. Detecting memory pages accesses and performing data mapping.

Require:

addr: memory address being accessed
node: NUMA node that is accessing the memory page
tid: thread ID of the thread that is accessing the address
addr_sample: thread private variable used to determine if is time to sample the memory address
total_addr: thread private variable used to determine if is time to trigger the thread mapping
si: sample interval. Default 100
dmi: data mapping interval.
PAGE_SIZE_BITS: 12 for page size of 4096 bytes

```
1: addr_sample ← addr_sample + 1
2: if (addr_sample > si) then
3:     addr_sample ← 0
4:     pageaddr ← addr >> PAGE_SIZE_BITS                    ▷ Right shift
5:     elem ← getPageInfo(pageaddr)
6:     if (!elem.moved) then ▷ Verify if the memory page already have been moved
7:         elem.nodes[node] ← elem.nodes[node] + 1 ▷ Increase the amount of access
8: if (tid = 1) then
9:     total_addr ← total_addr + 1
10: if (tid = 1) and (total_addr ≥ dmi) then
11:     Compute new data mapping
12:     dmi ← dmi * 2
```

responsible for keeping track of the amount of memory address accessed, to trigger the data mapping. On line 11, the data mapping is triggered. This step will be explained in Sect. 4.2. Once again, to avoid the overhead of page migrations, after triggering the first data mapping, on the line 12, we double the next *data mapping interval* (dmi).

4.2 Computing the New Data Mapping

This section explains how to the new data mapping is calculated on line 11 of Algorithm 1. Usually, to compute the thread mapping is necessary to rely on complex algorithms or libraries to calculate the best thread placement based on the underline hardware architecture. For data mapping this step is simpler: we verify on the hash table each memory page that not have been moved and which NUMA node has most accessed it. Then, while the application is running, we send this information to the function `move_pages` of the `libnuma` library [13] to perform the page move.

4.3 Implementation

We implemented our proposed mechanism as an extension of our previous work on thread mapping [15] inside the state-of-art STM library `TinySTM` [8], version

1.0.5. The majority of the modifications were made in the file `stm_internal.h`. Algorithm 1 is called inside the functions `stm_write` and `stm_load` of `TinySTM`.

5 Improving STM Applications with Data Mapping

To determine if the proposed mechanism can improve the performance of STM applications, we create an experiment with a synthetic array sum application. This application uses an array of 2^{30} integer elements. In that case, the array uses approximately 4 Gigabytes of memory. We force the array to be initialized with zeros in the main thread. Hence, using the default *first touch* police, all memory will be allocated on the NUMA node of the main thread. To force to use more than one NUMA node, the application was executed using 64 threads (more details of the machine used for run the application will be described in Sect. 5.1). The objective of this application is very simple. On each iteration, it updates the respective array position, incrementing the current value by one. We use the modified `TinySTM` library (Sect. 4.3) with data mapping support for synchronization of shared variables used in the array. Hence, the STM runtime will be aware of all the memory addresses that belong to the array. We iterate through the array thirty times to guarantee that if a memory page is migrated then it will be accessed again in the appropriate NUMA node.

5.1 Methodology

To run the experiments, we used the following NUMA machine (node distances were gathered with `numactl` [13]):

- **Xeon**: 8 Intel Xeon E5-4650 processors and 488 GiB of RAM running Linux kernel 4.19.0-9. Each CPU has 12 2-HT cores, totaling 96 cores. Each CPU corresponds to a NUMA node (for a total of 8 NUMA nodes), and 12× 32 KB L1d, 12× 32 KB L1i, 12× 256 KB L2 and 30 MB L3 cache. Node distances: 50–65. Applications were compiled using gcc 8.3.0.

The default Linux kernel already has routines to improve the memory page balancing of NUMA nodes. It keeps track of the page faults, moving the page automatically to the node that most accessed it. This mechanism is called *NUMA balancing* [18]. For comparison of our proposed mechanism we used the following configurations:

- **Linux-NBOff** is the default Linux CFS scheduler, however with the NUMA balancing mechanism disabled.
- **Linux-NBOn** is the default Linux CFS scheduler with the NUMA balancing mechanism enabled. This approach will be useful to verify if the application is suitable for data mapping, or if the default *first-touch* approach is more effective.
- **STMap** is the mechanism proposed in our previous work [16]. This mechanism detects the communication pattern of threads and performs thread mapping while the application runs.

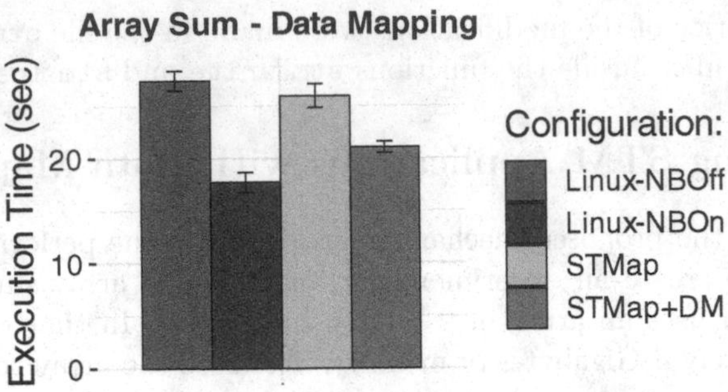

Fig. 2. Execution time of the Array Sum application.

- **STMap+DM** in this approach, we first trigger the thread mapping one time. After that, we begin to keeping track of the memory pages being accessed, triggering the first data mapping on *data mapping interval* of 100,000 addresses. This interval is used by `STMap` [16] to trigger the thread mapping.

It is worth noting that the *NUMA balancing* [18] was enabled only in **Linux-NBOn** approach. In all other approaches, this mechanism was disabled.

5.2 Results

Figure 2 shows the results. It is possible to observe that NUMA balancing (**Linux-NBOn**) reduced the execution time by 35.5% when compared to the same mechanism without the balancing (**Linux-NBOff**). This proves that this synthetic application has an unbalanced memory page allocation. Although it was not possible to beat NUMA balancing, our proposed **STMap+DM** mechanism achieved performance gains of 23.3% when compared to **Linux-NBOff** and, 19% when compared to **STMap**. These results motivate the evaluation of the proposed mechanism using realistic workloads.

6 Evaluation Using Realistic Workloads

6.1 Methodology

The applications used in these experiments were all eight benchmarks (bayes, genome, intruder, kmeans, labyrinth, ssca2, vacation and yada) from the Stanford Transactional Applications for Multi-Processing (`STAMP`) [14], version 0.9.10. The `STAMP` applications represent realistic workloads and is more appropriate to determine the effectiveness of the proposed mechanism. In addition to the configurations previously used to evaluate our proposal, described in Sect. 5.1, we also added two more mechanisms to the comparison:

- **DM-100K** in this approach the thread mapping (STMap) is not used, only data mapping, triggering the first mapping on 100,000 addresses.

– **DM-50K** this approach is used to verify if a more aggressive data mapping is better, triggering the first mapping on 50,000 addresses, i.e., half of the previous configuration.

We run the experiments on the Xeon machine described in Sect. 5.1 using 64 threads. The parameters used to run STAMP are the same as described in [17].

6.2 Results

In general, the results of sharing-aware data mapping were similar for the majority of the applications. Hence, we will not discuss each application individually. Figure 3 show the results. It shows the performance gains of each mechanism using **Linux-NBOff** as a baseline. We also included the average gains (last column, **Average**) over all applications.

Overall, the proposed mechanism does not improve the performance of STM applications. The best gain was achieved by STMap, i.e., only triggering thread mapping. When the data mapping was enabled together with thread mapping (**STMap+DM**) it decreased the performance. In that case, the overhead of the data mapping mechanism was not compensated by a better exploration of the locality of memory pages. Analyzing the performance gains, with exception of Labyrinth, the NUMA balancing mechanism (**Linux-NBOn**) also decreased the performance, with all mechanisms performing better than NUMA Balancing. In that case, for these realistic workloads, the default *first-touch* policy was more effective. Despite our encouraging results in our initial experiment with the synthetic benchmark, these results did not translate into gains for more realistic applications.

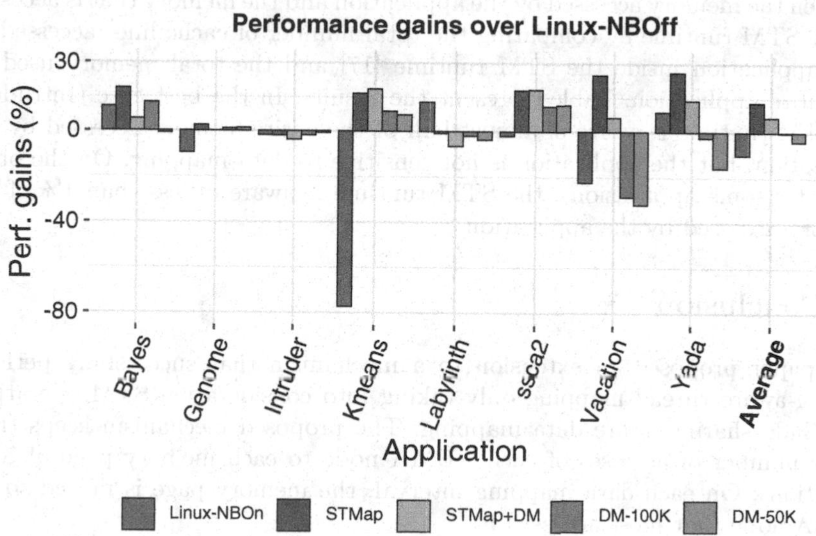

Fig. 3. Performance gains of the mappings when compared to Linux-NBOff.

Table 1. Percentage of memory that the STM runtime is aware of, compared to the total memory accessed by the application.

	Bayes	Genome	Intruder	Kmeans	Labyrinth	Ssca2	Vacation	Yada
Memory seen by STM runtime (%)	0.01	8.8	57.7	0.02	3.9	7.7	26.8	34.9

Although the proposed mechanism in this paper did not improve the performance of realistic STM applications, a synthetic application showed that in specific scenarios it can improve the performance. More specifically, it benefits STM application with atomic blocks that protect a large number of shared variables with distinct memory addresses. On the other hand, applications with few shared variables protected by STM, or those that contain considerable amounts of data *private* to a thread benefit less, since the STM runtime does not have sufficient knowledge about private data that could benefit from data mapping.

Since an STM runtime has precise information about shared variables, this information can be used to choose which threads should be mapped closer to each other to share caches, i.e., it is not necessary a global vision of the application sharing behavior [15,16]. However, for an effective data mapping, a more global view of the memory pages of the application is necessary, not only the ones accessed by the STM runtime. In the synthetic array sum application presented in Sect. 5, the STM runtime was aware of all the 4 Gigabytes of the array, which comprised the vast majority of memory accessed by the application.

Using the realistic workloads, we do not see performance improvements. In the majority of STM applications, the STM runtime is aware of only a small part of the entire memory used of the application. We analyzed the difference between the memory accessed by the application and the memory that is accessed by the STM runtime by comparing the total number of cache lines accessed by each application inside the STM runtime [17] and the total memory used by the entire application. Table 1 present the results. In the best case (Intruder), the STM runtime is aware of almost half of the entire memory accessed by the application, but the application is not sensitive to data mapping. On the other hand, for some applications, the STM runtime is aware of less than 1% of the memory accessed by the application.

7 Conclusion

This paper proposed an extension to a mechanism that successfully perform sharing-aware thread mapping only taking into consideration STM operations to include sharing-aware data mapping. The proposed mechanism keeps track of the number of accesses of each NUMA node to each memory page of STM operations. On each data mapping interval, the memory page is moved to the NUMA node that most accessed it.

Using a synthetic array sum application, we showed that our proposed mechanism is able to increase the performance of STM applications on NUMA machines. However, using more realistic workloads, it was not possible to improve the performance. Based on the experiments, we believe that it is infeasible to perform a sharing-aware data mapping in STM applications by only tracking STM operations because they represent only a fraction of the memory used by the entire application. Furthermore, since even the NUMA Balancing mechanism was not able to improve the performance of these realistic workloads, many STM applications might be generally unaffected by sharing-aware data mapping.

References

1. Anthes, G.: Researchers simplify parallel programming. Commun. ACM **57**(11), 13–15 (2014). https://doi.org/10.1145/2667109
2. Beniamine, D., Diener, M., Huard, G., Navaux, P.O.A.: TABARNAC: visualizing and resolving memory access issues on NUMA architectures. In: Proceedings of the 2nd Workshop on Visual Performance Analysis, VPA 2015, pp. 1:1–1:9. ACM, New York (2015). https://doi.org/10.1145/2835238.2835239
3. Broquedis, F., Furmento, N., Goglin, B., Wacrenier, P.A., Namyst, R.: ForestGOMP: an efficient OpenMP environment for NUMA architectures. Int. J. Parallel Prog. **38**(5), 418–439 (2010). https://doi.org/10.1007/s10766-010-0136-3
4. Dashti, M., et al.: Traffic management: a holistic approach to memory placement on NUMA systems. In: Proceedings of the Eighteenth International Conference on Architectural Support for Programming Languages and Operating Systems, ASPLOS 2013, pp. 381–394. ACM, New York (2013). https://doi.org/10.1145/2451116.2451157
5. Diener, M., Cruz, E.H.M., Alves, M.A.Z., Navaux, P.O.A., Busse, A., Heiß, H.U.: Kernel-based thread and data mapping for improved memory affinity. IEEE Trans. Parallel Distrib. Syst. **27**(9), 2653–2666 (2016). https://doi.org/10.1109/TPDS.2015.2504985
6. Diener, M., Cruz, E.H.M., Alves, M.A.Z., Navaux, P.O.A., Koren, I.: Affinity-based thread and data mapping in shared memory systems. ACM Comput. Surv. **49**(4), 64:1–64:38 (2016). https://doi.org/10.1145/3006385
7. Diener, M., Cruz, E.H., Pilla, L.L., Dupros, F., Navaux, P.O.: Characterizing communication and page usage of parallel applications for thread and data mapping. Performance Evaluation 88–89, 18–36, June 2015. https://doi.org/10.1016/j.peva.2015.03.001
8. Felber, P., Fetzer, C., Riegel, T., Marlier, P.: Time-based software transactional memory. IEEE Trans. Parallel Distrib. Syst. **21**, 1793–1807 (2010). https://doi.org/10.1109/TPDS.2010.49
9. Gaud, F., et al.: Challenges of memory management on modern NUMA systems. Commun. ACM **58**(12), 59–66 (2015). https://doi.org/10.1145/2814328
10. Góes, L.F.W., Ribeiro, C.P., Castro, M., Méhaut, J.-F., Cole, M., Cintra, M.: Automatic skeleton-driven memory affinity for transactional worklist applications. Int. J. Parallel Prog. **42**(2), 365–382 (2013). https://doi.org/10.1007/s10766-013-0253-x
11. Grahn, H.: Transactional memory. J. Parallel Distrib. Comput. **70**(10), 993–1008 (2010). https://doi.org/10.1016/j.jpdc.2010.06.006
12. Harris, T., Larus, J., Rajwar, R.: Transactional Memory, 2nd edn. Morgan and Claypool Publishers, San Rafael (2010). https://doi.org/10.2200/S00272ED1V01Y201006CAC011

13. Kleen, A.: An NUMA API for Linux. Technical report, SUSE Labs, Fürth, Germany, August 2004. http://www.halobates.de/numaapi3.pdf
14. Minh, C.C., Chung, J., Kozyrakis, C., Olukotun, K.: STAMP: stanford transactional applications for multi-processing. In: IEEE International Symposium on Workload Characterization, pp. 35–46. IEEE CS, Washington, DC, USA, September 2008. https://doi.org/10.1109/IISWC.2008.4636089
15. Pasqualin, D.P., Diener, M., Du Bois, A.R., Pilla, M.L.: Online sharing-aware thread mapping in software transactional memory. In: 2020 32nd International Symposium on Computer Architecture and High Performance Computing (SBAC-PAD), pp. 35–42. IEEE CS, Washington, DC, September 2020. https://doi.org/10.1109/SBAC-PAD49847.2020.00016
16. Pasqualin, D.P., Diener, M., Du Bois, A.R., Pilla, M.L.: Thread affinity in software transactional memory. In: 19th International Symposium on Parallel and Distrib. Computing, pp. 180–187. IEEE CS, Washington, DC, USA, July 2020. https://doi.org/10.1109/ISPDC51135.2020.00033
17. Pasqualin, D.P., Diener, M., Du Bois, A.R., Pilla, M.L.: Characterizing the sharing behavior of applications using software transactional memory. In: Wolf, F., Gao, W. (eds.) Bench 2020. LNCS, vol. 12614, pp. 3–21. Springer, Cham (2021). https://doi.org/10.1007/978-3-030-71058-3_1
18. van Riel, R., Feng, S.: Documentation for /proc/sys/kernel/ (2020). https://www.kernel.org/doc/html/latest/admin-guide/sysctl/kernel.html#numa-balancing. Accessed 18 Nov 2020
19. Sánchez Barrera, I., Black-Schaffer, D., Casas, M., Moretó, M., Stupnikova, A., Popov, M.: Modeling and optimizing NUMA effects and prefetching with machine learning. In: Proceedings of the 34th ACM International Conference on Supercomputing, ICS 2020, pp. 1–13. Association for Computing Machinery, New York (2020). https://doi.org/10.1145/3392717.3392765
20. Di Sanzo, P.: Analysis, classification and comparison of scheduling techniques for software transactional memories. IEEE Trans. Parallel Distrib. Syst. **28**(12), 3356–3373 (2017). https://doi.org/10.1109/tpds.2017.2740285
21. Tang, L., Mars, J., Zhang, X., Hagmann, R., Hundt, R., Tune, E.: Optimizing Google's warehouse scale computers: the NUMA experience. In: 2013 IEEE 19th International Symposium on High Performance Computer Architecture (HPCA), pp. 188–197. IEEE Computer Society, Washington, DC, February 2013. https://doi.org/10.1109/HPCA.2013.6522318
22. Trahay, F., Selva, M., Morel, L., Marquet, K.: NumaMMA - NUMA MeMory analyzer. In: Proceedings of the 47th International Conference on Parallel Processing - ICPP 2018, pp. 1–10. Association for Computing Machinery, New York (2018). https://doi.org/10.1145/3225058.3225094

Dead-Ends in FPGAs for Database Acceleration

Anna Drewes(✉), Martin Koppehel, and Thilo Pionteck

Otto-von-Guericke University Magdeburg, Magdeburg, Germany
{anna.drewes,koppehel,pionteck}@ovgu.de

Abstract. In this work we present two case studies of FPGAs in database applications that did not yield the expected results. First, we analyze the issues when synthesizing algorithms that perform small calculations on lots of randomly accessed data, specifically exact lookups in a radix tree. We find that even with manual guidance, the results from high-level synthesis are much slower than the corresponding realization of the algorithm on x86 CPUs. In the second case study, we present a lightweight overlay architecture for streaming query processing which turned out to be too fine-grained to be efficiently placed because the used partitions are quite small. Here, a prototypic implementation revealed resource efficiency limitations related to the interface design of particularly small dynamic reconfiguration partitions. We present approaches to overcome limitations for both case studies.

Keywords: FPGA · HLS · Database · Index structures · Query processing · Dynamic partial reconfiguration

1 Introduction

With the ever increasing scale of databases and the breakdown of Dennard scaling, both industry and academia are researching means to accelerate analytical database processing beyond the limits of classical multi-core CPUs. In the last few years a new demand for increased power efficiency has also become a major driver in data center innovation. While modern CPUs still provide vast processing power, the way forward to higher efficiency leads towards custom compute architectures, not just for database management systems. The compute platforms that evolved from traditional GPUs offer a high degree of data parallelism and can outmatch CPUs in many database tasks. Yet, they are only slightly more customized to their tasks than general purpose CPUs. As the manufacturing of ASICs is out of reach for many for reasons of cost, lead time, and ever changing compute demands, FPGAs are considered the next closest alternative that allows quicker deployment while maintaining the advantage of implementing truly custom hardware accelerators.

Since FPGA design work requires more developer effort than software programming and requires skills usually not found in traditional software development, there have been two broad directions for accelerating database workloads

© Springer Nature Switzerland AG 2022
A. Orailoglu et al. (Eds.): SAMOS 2021, LNCS 13227, pp. 493–504, 2022.
https://doi.org/10.1007/978-3-031-04580-6_33

using FPGAs: Single-function accelerators that can ideally be easily integrated into existing software platforms and overlay architectures that abstract away the low-level lookup table and flipflop design surface of the FPGA into (still customized to the application domain) higher-level compute architectures.

We will present difficulties we encountered in each of the two domains: One case study presents an accelerator design for acceleration of index structures and the other details an reconfigurable overlay architecture for analytical query processing. The rest of this paper is structured as follows: For each of the two FPGA designs for database processing we will give our motivation and then list related work. After describing their architecture, we will present the lessons we learned from our work and we will also highlight new research directions based on the roadblocks we ran into.

2 Case Studies

2.1 High-Level Synthesis for Index Structure Acceleration

Motivation. One of the ideas during our research which initially looked promising was to utilize FPGAs for accelerating the index structure lookup of a database, because they are one of the key performance indicators especially for In-Memory Databases (IMDB). Initially, we took a look at the performance of several index structures on the CPU. We noticed that smart caching is beneficial for most index structures. Here, we identified a performance bottleneck in case the index structure grows, severely impacting the lookup performance (for the CPU case it drops from 200 M Lookups/s to 50 M Lookups/s for larger structures) and therefore the performance of the whole database. In this work we apply high-level synthesis (HLS) to the ART (Adaptive Radix Tree) lookup algorithm and discuss several feasible optimizations to improve the performance.

Related Work. As a consequence, a literature search has been conducted and yielded quite some results. For example, [3] implemented a GPU-accelerated search for the ART index structure, yielding a much better performance than the original CPU-based implementation in [2]. For the classical B+-Tree, there have been several works that accelerate it on GPUs ([1,4,5]). [6] implemented a hash-table using GPUs, which could also be used to index a database. Complementary to the GPU-focused research, common index structures such as the B+-Tree ([7]) and the R-Tree ([8]) have been implemented and evaluated on FPGA platforms, achieving a significant speedup up to 18x compared to the CPU implementation.

Initial Results. ART is a variant of a radix tree that adapts the inner nodes to the number of used children. It knows four node types with 4, 16, 48 and 256 children, named N4 to N256 respectively. Figure 1 outlines the different node sizes in use. In our previous research concerning the ART index structure, we found that an increased memory clock seems to be one of the key factors that contribute to

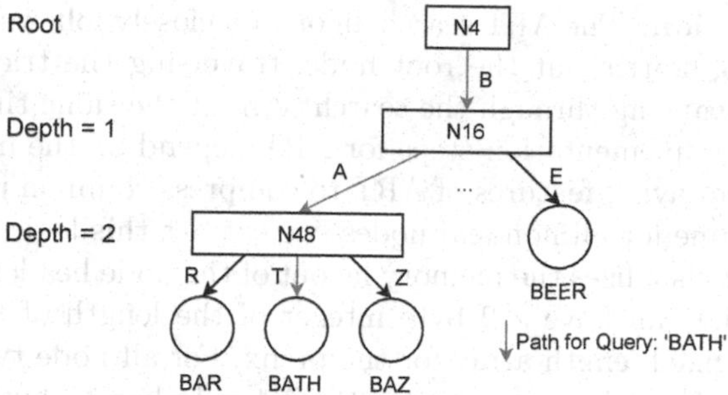

Fig. 1. Visualization of a small ART, including the path for a point query with the key 'BATH'

the overall lookup performance. Several benchmarks on different platforms such as a CUDA-based implementation on GPUs with HBM2, GDDR6X and GDDR5 interfaces confirm that the ART is suitable for a massively parallel lookup and benefits from having a fast memory interface, making both the on-chip SRAM of an FPGA as well as external DDR4 and HBM suitable. The wide availability of HBM-enabled FPGAs for data center applications such as the Xilinx Alveo Cards inspired us to evaluate the performance of ART on this platform. A theoretical analysis of the ART lookup algorithm (see following section) visualized in Fig. 1 indicates that a pipelined FPGA lookup design with an estimated latency of three to five clock cycles per tree layer is feasible. A pipelined design with this throughput and latency should be able to perform around 100 million point queries per second, thus outperforming modern CPUs. In order to ease up the integration and testing of the code, we chose to do our hardware implementation using the Xilinx Vitis High Level Synthesis environment. This environment allows us to dynamically schedule work onto the FPGA using OpenCL on the host side.

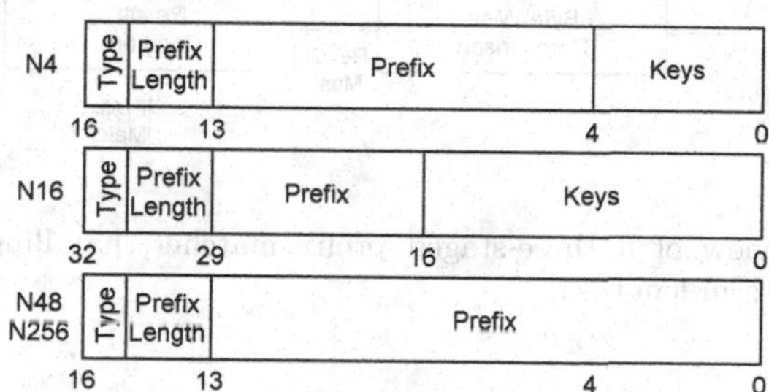

Fig. 2. Memory layout of the ART nodes, showing different layouts depending on the node type

Prefix Compression. The ART search algorithm closely follows the traditional radix tree lookup, starting at the root node, traversing the trie until a leaf is reached, while advancing through the search term at the same time as shown in Fig. 1. The exact implementation steps for ART depend on the node type being used. As the space saving features of ART to compress common prefixes need to be handled the same for all non-leaf nodes, we extract this logic into a separate function. Figure 2 visualizes the memory layout of the node headers, representing the metadata. They all have a 2 byte integer of the length of the compressed path as well as a fixed-length array for the prefix. For all node types except N4, this arrays are 14 bytes in size, whereas the N4 only has 10 bytes. To evaluate a prefix match, it is necessary to perform a byte-wise comparison of the prefix bytes to the current position in the string up to either the maximum prefix length (10 or 14) or the prefix length given in the first two bytes. In theory, a selection of a 14 byte segment from the current position within the search term padded with zeroes is sufficient to decide whether the prefix is a miss, match or a partial match. The latter indicates that only a part of the prefix could be compared because of missing storage within the node. In parallel to this extraction step, a bit mask corresponding to the maximum allowed prefix length is built from the current node type and prefix length. After the 14 byte segment has been extracted, the whole prefix array can be compared byte-wise and transformed into a 14 bit logic vector where a one in each position indicates a match for the specific byte. As a last step, the previously generated bit mask can be applied to the previously generated result vector, whereas a zero result indicates a match. The idea is visualized in Fig. 3.

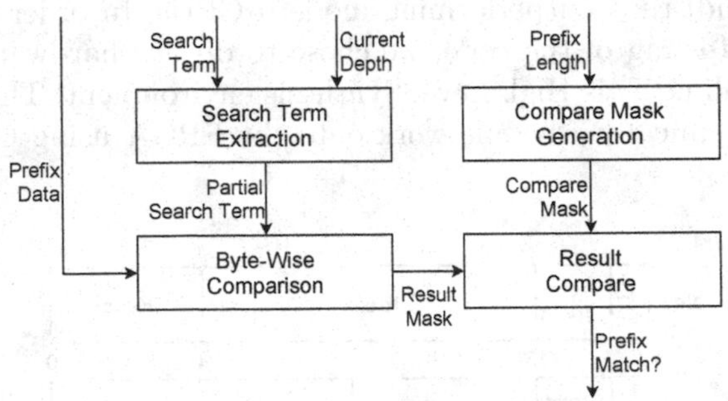

Fig. 3. Schematic view of a three-staged prefix matcher, handling different prefix lengths and search term lengths

We implemented several different approaches and optimizations proposed both by the Xilinx implementation guidelines as well as the tool chain output. In general, Vitis infers extremely complex state machines by not unrolling the prefix compression match loop when generating the logic even if told to do so, yielding an extremely inefficient implementation which requires > 100 cycles to handle the prefix compression. One implemented optimization was the usage of the Xilinx ap_uint type instead of using a byte array to guide the synthesis tool into implementing the logic with multiplexers, which still yielded an overly complex state machine.

Node Handling. After the prefix compression/path expansion has been done, a lookup depending on the node type currently being processed is made. This lookup uses the byte at the current depth of the search term and then compares it against the stored keys. While for both the N4 and N16 objects this is simply a parallel compare, in the case of N48 the original ART implementation used a 256 Byte key array where the index within a values array is encoded. To account for the parallel programming abilities, we changed the memory layout of an N48 to match the layout of N4 and N16 and unroll the comparison loop. For an N256, there is no comparison loop but the processing element needs to index the values array with the current search term byte. For leaves, again it boils down to a simple comparison of the complete key, which can be up to 32 bytes.

During synthesis it quickly became clear that the HLS tool chain would not unroll the comparison loops because in the original algorithm we used as a basis for our work the loops would break upon encountering the first valid element. While this behavior increases the performance on the CPU, it is malicious for high level synthesis because the HLS compiler generates a functionally equivalent version. Therefore the tool chain is not allowed to assume that there will never be two matches for a single node. The resulting implementation of HLS was a variable length pipeline which lead us into the problems hiding the pipeline latency due to a significant amount of random memory accesses, again taking up to 300 clock cycles in the case of an N48, generating a state machine with almost 1700 states.

Compared to the CPU ART implementation for reasonably large trees (1 M to 16 M entries), the CPU outperforms the FPGA implementation by factor 6 when run on a single host thread (250 k Lookups/s on the FPGA vs 1.5 M Lookups/s on the CPU). The implemented design for the tree lookup required around 60 k FFs and 55 k LUTs, which means that in theory we can scale the design up to 6 instances for the Alveo U280 card.

Random Memory Accesses. While modern DRAM implementations claim random access capabilities, there is in fact a penalty when performing truly random accesses. This is due to the clocked command interface and page-oriented setup of DRAM. When hitting a page that hasn't been opened before, the access latency typically is around 50 memory clock cycles. While in FPGAs this behavior is commonly exploited by utilizing on-chip SRAMs instead of external DRAMs, this approach is not feasible for maintaining index structures for very large in-memory databases because those can not fit into the on-chip RAMs. Therefore it is necessary to not only hide the pipelining latency introduced from the steps above, but also the access latency of the off-chip DRAMs. We tried utilizing both the HBMs and the DDR4 RAMs present in the Alveo U280. We found that for naive implementations, DDR4 is beneficial because of its much higher clock rate, leading to less latency in the logic clock domain. On CPUs and GPUs this is typically solved by coalescing small memory transactions into larger chunks, trading wasted bandwidth for improved latency for subsequent transactions. Xilinx also offers such IP core to link into existing designs delivering quite impressive throughput results for random accesses. We found that implementing this IP core brings only marginal improvements in our design because the design itself consists of several pipelines of variable length and therefore is not designed for memory coalescing.

2.2 A Lightweight Reconfigurable Overlay Architecture for Column-Based Analytical Database Processing

Motivation. Analytical database query processing generally describes the task of extracting new information from an existing database by joining tables and filtering/aggregating data. It is a data-intensive and moderately compute-intensive field. Query execution plans for analytical queries can be represented as data flow graphs, which can vary a lot from query to query.

Since the potential for fine-grain spatial parallelism is a big advantage of FPGAs over CPUs and GPUs, our idea was to design a system that would inherently take advantage of this feature. Even with the lower clock rate of FPGAs, creating deep and flexible pipelines of database operators would allow us to attack the performance of CPU- and GPU-based operator-at-a-time systems which do not use runtime compilation. Due to the varied nature of analytical queries, dynamic partial reconfiguration on FPGAs makes it possible to construct custom pipelines at runtime for each query that wouldn't fit in a static design.

Thus, our goal was to implement an overlay of interconnected reconfigurable processing units ideally suited for processing the data flow graphs necessary to compute analytical database queries.

We chose to work with a column-based database. This allows us to only fetch the necessary data columns from memory. Also, the columns can be accessed independently. Finally, using column-based tables reduces the need for highly complex transformation units to rearrange the fields of a row. In order to reduce random memory accesses the FPGA system should also rely more on column scans instead of scatter/gather operators. In contrast to fixed-function accelerators, reconfigurable operators can be smaller and simpler, since it is easy and fast to exchange one operator for another. Also, in contrast to designs that incorporate multiple interconnected fixed accelerators, data flow routing and switching is simplified for reconfigurable overlay architectures, since the function units are adapted to the query. This also applies for the underlying structure and topology of the interconnect.

Related Work. FPGAs have been extensively used as single function accelerators for individual database operators such as sort [9,10], join [9,11], or regular expression matching [12]. While these accelerators are often capable of IO-rate processing, they still require large amounts of data to be transferred between CPU and FPGA since only one part of a query can be accelerated. There are approaches that try to drastically reduce transfer costs through tighter coupling between accelerator and host system [12–14], but these rely on specialized hardware for both the CPU and FPGA. Streaming data between host and accelerator is another approach to deal with limited interface throughput [15]: Since selection relies on table scans, additional DMA copy processes are avoided. In this case, data compression is also utilized to further reduce the bandwidth requirements the row-based format incurs.

There have also been systems proposed which allow for more than one operation to be processed on the FPGA. AxleDB is a programmable query processing platform that implements a full chain of accelerators on a single FPGA [16]. The system contains accelerators for the common database operations which are arranged in a fixed streaming-based ring bus in the order in which they are typically needed. Queries that do not conform to that arrangement require multiple passes. Another disadvantage of this type of system is that all accelerators have to fit on the FPGA at the same time, limiting the amount of resources available to each operator.

A next logical step is to break up the fixed connections between function units, such as proposed in [17]. This system is not specifically targeted at analytical database processing. It consists of a grid of fixed function units which are locally interconnected with a sophisticated communications network. Still, there is the disadvantage that significant over-provisioning of each type of function unit is necessary as not every data flow graph consists of a similar composition of operations.

Dynamic partial reconfiguration can remediate this otherwise static requirement to plan out exactly which function units need to be placed where in the overlay. In [18] this capability of modern FPGAs is used in a smart storage FPGA preprocessor to swap between different large accelerators depending on what kind of preprocessing is needed.

A row-based system which heavily features dynamic partial reconfiguration is proposed in [19]. The system consists of four lanes of 16 reconfigurable function units through each of which data is streamed linearly and one large reconfigurable partition that hosts accelerators for sorting, merging, and hash joins. While this system achieves significant throughput through the accelerator chain, the limited flexibility of the single 128-bit connection between function units causes inefficiencies in placement and utilization, some of which is also due to the system using row-based tables.

Design of the Prototype. Based on our ideas we started to design a prototype on the ZC706 FPGA development board, which contains a Xilinx 7 Series SoC with two ARM cores beside the FPGA fabric. To simplify the mapping of data flow graphs to the overlay architecture, we decided on a homogeneous layout, meaning that it should be possible to place every streaming operator in every tile. With these restrictions we managed to fit a 4 by 7 grid of tiles on the 7Z045

FPGA, as seen in Fig. 4. The tiles are aligned to the FPGA's DSP columns, which are required for several database operators. Figure 5 shows that each tile contains a reconfigurable partition for the function unit plus buffers and small crossbars for data flow routing and access to a light-weight on-chip communications network to exchange configuration packets. All data connections are 32 bits wide.

Figure 4 also shows features that physically limit the size of the overlay: On the top left, there are the two ARM cores. The hard-logic area in which they are contained also consists of a DDR3 memory controller and caches and is marked in gray. The IO-pins for the second DDR3 channel are located in the top right corner. This memory has to be connected to a soft-logic memory controller, which needs to be physically close to these IO-pins and is highlighted in yellow. Finally, on the right hand side, there is the PCIe core, which connects the FPGA to the host system. The PCIe controller is highlighted in pink. All three are wired together into one global memory bus which serves the DMA engines used to feed the overlay architecture. These are depicted in green. To meet timing, the central memory interconnect (shown in blue), the soft DDR3 controller and the various DMA engines all bunch up in the upper part of the FPGA. It was not possible to include another row of tiles and still meet timing since the memory interconnect got restricted. Finally, we also included the capability to stream a column directly between the host system and the overlay. This is especially useful to return intermediate results when CPU and FPGA work in tandem on a single query.

Based on external requirements, there are two different clock domains in the system: The PCIe core and auxiliary logic run at 250 MHz while the rest is clocked at 200 MHz.

For the design of the function units, we used high level synthesis to construct hardware operators from C++ source code. This choice was made to increase productivity and reduce the amount of debugging since that way all operators will automatically comply with the interface protocol.

As the data flow graphs that are typical for analytical query processing usually don't map perfectly to the 2D-grid of our overlay, it is possible to bypass tiles by using them just to buffer and forward up to two independent data streams.

Reconfiguration of Small Function Units. On Xilinx 7 Series devices, reconfigurable partitions generally should span the entire height of a clock region within the chip and can span from a single column to the whole width of the clock region. While it is possible to define partitions smaller than the height of a clock region, in practice the designer limited to exchanging complete columns, since two partitions cannot share the same column. When the size of a reconfigurable region is larger, the resulting rectangular or square partition is usually well-shaped and can be considered a smaller FPGA and will not significantly challenge the router during implementation more than any other design.

But small reconfigurable modules which only span a single column are very long and thin, which makes routing more difficult, and can additionally only

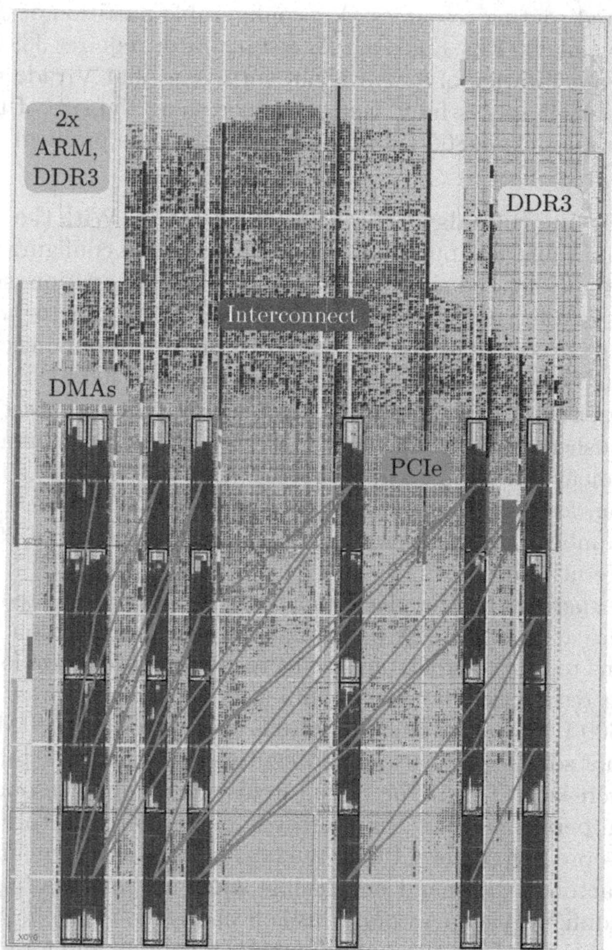

Fig. 4. Physical layout of the FPGA with fixed-function blocks and the reconfigurable partitions of the overlay architecture prototype highlighted

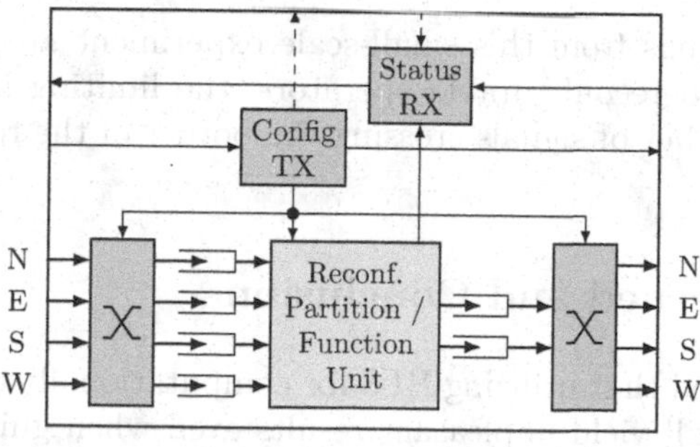

Fig. 5. Schematic of a single tile of the overlay architecture

cover very limited routing resources. A reconfigurable partition of this size contains 400 LUTs and 800 FFs. Since our largest operator requires 368 LUTs which corresponds to a utilization of 92% it is not surprising that Vivado was not able to place and route it successfully. But after increasing the size of the reconfigurable partition to include 800 LUTs (and 1600 FFs) the problem persisted.

Partition-Crossing Signals as the Limiting Factor. With the total of up to four input streams and two output streams, plus the two configuration network interfaces and the elongated shape of the reconfigurable partition, signals across the boundaries of the partitions had become the limiting factor. Summed up, there were 291 partition IO-pins for Vivado to place in the miniscule reconfigurable partition. Only after adding another column with 400 LUTs and 800 FFs to each reconfigurable partition, routing consistently provided successful results. This in turn pushed resource efficiency far lower: While the operator with the largest requirement for LUTs occupies 30% of the available LUTs in a reconfigurable partition, averaged over all operators only 15% of the LUTs are in use. For FFs the numbers are even lower: A maximum utilization of 25% contrasts with an average utilization of 15%.

From our experiments, the place and route process completed successfully when there were at least 3 LUTs per signal crossing the partition border available. This seems to be the minimum size factor required for Vivado to deal with limited routing resources. The relationship also held true in larger experiments (501 I/O vs 1600 LUTs). One thing to note is that introducing SIMD-style data parallelism is not something that can address this issue, since the total number of IO-pins will increase at nearly the same rate as the required resources. Besides, to increase the performance of our prototype overlay architecture to the same level as the 32-core Zen server CPU in the host system would require 4×-SIMD, while only a factor of 3× would be possible while keeping the high number of small-scale reconfigurable operators. This is because the multiplication operator requires 3 out of the 10 DSP slices of a single DSP column and for a single reconfigurable partition to cover two columns of DSP slices would mean a substantial increase in size. But, based on our estimations, even the non-SIMD FPGA overlay architecture is competitive with the CPU implementation in terms of energy consumption.

Our overall findings from this small-scale experiment are that for complex but small HLS-based reconfigurable operators, the limiting factor on resource efficiency is the number of signals crossing the border of the reconfigurable partition.

3 Lessons Learned and Conclusion

In general, we learned that utilizing HLS for computationally cheap but control-flow intense tasks will yield unpleasant results even when guiding the compiler by hand and making functional trade-offs. We showed that both the prefix match and the node lookup itself are realizable in a few clock cycles. Yet, HLS yields a result far from optimal, an underutilization of the compute resources while blocking too many LUTs/FFs. With regards to the lessons learned from both of the experiments, we are now proceeding to implement an optimized version in pure VHDL and to integrate this work into our existing benchmark framework.

In our experiments, we achieved only a fraction of the throughput that a CPU would achieve, at a much higher cost. In general, implementing such lookup engine is feasible by employing a carefully optimized HDL design and scaling the lookup units to Scaling such designs would include instancing of several compute units and a smart management unit to schedule work and memory accesses. We believe utilizing the present HBM memories along with the Xilinx HBM RAMA IP core can deliver the best performance, because each HBM bank has separate memory controllers and interfaces, allowing for more parallel random memory accesses. A further improvement would be a hybrid memory layout, e.g. compacting the upper two first layers into a single node residing in the on-chip PLRAM, effectively removing two off-chip memory transactions per lookup, then utilizing the HBM for traversing the tree and finally placing the leaves into the DDR4 RAMs, with a streaming interface between those stages. Finally, by removing the pipeline dependencies by not processing search terms one by one but processing level-wise, a significant increase in throughput could be achieved.

In the second case study we learned that scaling issues can also come from unexpected limitations, such as routing capabilities and tooling not being able to deal with tight resource limits. One remedy that we will explore in future work is employing code fusion to increase the amount of work done within each function unit while keeping the number of signals into and out of each reconfigurable partition constant. Our overall findings from the second case study are that for complex but small HLS-based reconfigurable operators, the limiting factor on resource efficiency is the number of signals required that cross the border of a reconfigurable partition.

While HLS has proven itself a valuable tool for calculation-heavy use-cases, both case studies revealed problems while tailoring HLS-based code to the specific problems. For both cases we presented the wide range of issues we experienced, ranging from inefficient implementations over memory problems to insufficient resources when dealing with partitioning the FPGA for dynamic reconfiguration. We present several approaches to overcome the highlighted limitations, ranging from a carefully optimized HDL-based implementation to design-time improvements that seek to remedy the limitations encountered.

References

1. Awad, M.A., Saman, A., Johnson, R., Farach-Colton, M., Owens, J.D.: Engineering a high-performance GPU B-Tree (2019). https://doi.org/10.1145/3293883.3295706
2. Leis, V., Kemper, A., Neumann, T.: The adaptive radix tree: ARTful indexing for main-memory databases. In: 2013 IEEE 29th International Conference on Data Engineering (ICDE) (2013). https://doi.org/10.1109/ICDE.2013.6544812

3. Alam, M., Yoginath, S.B., Perumalla, K.S.: Performance of point and range queries for in-memory databases using radix trees on GPUs. In: 2016 IEEE 18th International Conference on High Performance Computing and Communications (2016). https://doi.org/10.1109/HPCC-SmartCity-DSS.2016.0212
4. Kaczmarski, K.: B$^+$-Tree optimized for GPGPU. In: On the Move to Meaningful Internet Systems: OTM 2012 (2012). https://doi.org/10.1007/978-3-642-33615-7_27
5. Fix, J., Wilkes, A., Skadron, K.: Accelerating braided b+ Tree Searches on a GPU with CUDA (2012)
6. Farrell, D.: A simple GPU hash table (2020). https://nosferalatu.com/SimpleGPUHashTable.html
7. Ren, Y., Liao, Z., et al.: A low-latency multi-version key-value store using b-tree on an FPGA-CPU platform (2019). https://doi.org/10.1109/FPL.2019.00058
8. Xiao, X., Shi, T., Vaidya, P., Lee, J.,: R-tree: a hardware implementation. In: Proceedings of the 2008 International Conference on Computer Design, CDES 2008 (2008)
9. Casper, J., Olukotun, K.: Hardware acceleration of database operations. In: Proceedings of the 2014 ACM/SIGDA International Symposium on Field-Programmable Gate Arrays, FPGA 2014 (2014)
10. Sukhwani, B., et al.: Large payload streaming database sort and projection on FPGAs. In: Proceedings of the 25th International Symposium on Computer Architecture and High Performance Computing (2013)
11. R. J. Halstead et al.: Accelerating Join Operation for Relational Databases with FPGAs. In: Proceedings of the IEEE 21st Annual International Symposium on Field-Programmable Custom Computing Machines, FCCM 2013 (2013)
12. István, Z., Sidler, D., Alonso, G.: Runtime parameterizable regular expression operators for databases. In: Proceedings of the IEEE 24th Annual International Symposium on Field-Programmable Custom Computing Machines, FCCM 2016 (2016)
13. Muhsen Owaida et al.: Centaur: a framework for hybrid CPU-FPGA databases. In: Proceedings of the 2017 International Symposium on Field-Programmable Custom Computing Machines, FCCM 2017 (2017)
14. Sidler, D., et al.: doppioDB, a hardware accelerated database. In: Proceedings of the 2017 ACM International Conference on Management of Data, SIGMOD 2017 (2017)
15. Sukhwani, B., et al.: Database analytics acceleration using FPGAs. In: Proceedings of the 21st International Conference on Parallel Architectures and Compilation Techniques, PACT 2012 (2012)
16. Salami, B., et al.: AxleDB: a novel programmable query processing engine on FPGA. In: Microprocessors and Microsystems (MICPRO), vol. 51, pp. 142–164 (2017)
17. Capalija, D., Abdelrahman, T.S.: A high-performance overlay architecture for pipelined execution of data flow graphs. In: Proceedings of the 23rd International Conference on Field programmable Logic and Applications, FPL 2013 (2013)
18. Becher, A., Herrmann, A., Wildermann, S., Teich, J.: ReProVide: towards utilizing heterogeneous partially reconfigurable architectures or near-memory data processing. In: Proceedings of the 1st Workshop on Novel Data Management Ideas on Heterogeneous (Co-)Processors, NoDMC 2019 (2019)
19. Ziener, D., et al.: FPGA-based dynamically reconfigurable SQL query processing. ACM Trans. Reconfigurable Technol. Syst. (TRETS) **9**(4), 1–24 (2016)

The Challenge of Classification Confidence Estimation in Dynamically-Adaptive Neural Networks

Francesco Dall'Occo[2(✉)], Andrés Bueno-Crespo[1], José L. Abellán[1], Davide Bertozzi[2], and Michele Favalli[2]

[1] Universidad Católica San Antonio de Murcia, Murcia, Spain
{abueno,jlabellan}@ucam.edu
[2] University of Ferrara, Ferrara, Italy
{francesco.dallocco,davide.bertozzi,michele.favalli}@unife.it

Abstract. An emerging trend to improve the power efficiency of neural network computations consists of dynamically adapting the network architecture or parameters to different inputs. In particular, many such dynamic network models are able to output 'easy' samples at early exits if a certain confidence-based criterion is satisfied. Traditional methods to estimate inference confidence of a monitored neural network, or of intermediate predictions thereof, include the maximum element of the SoftMax output (score), or the difference between the largest and the second largest score values (score margin). Such methods only rely on a small and position-agnostic subset of the available information at the output of the monitored neural network classifier. For the first time, this paper reports on the lessons learned while trying to extrapolate confidence information from the whole distribution of the classifier outputs rather than from the top scores only. Our experimental campaign indicates that capturing specific patterns associated with misclassifications is nontrivial due to counterintuitive empirical evidence. Rather than disqualifying the approach, this paper calls for further fine-tuning to unfold its potential, and is a first step toward a systematic assessment of confidence-based criteria for dynamically-adaptive neural network computations.

Keywords: Neural network · Runtime adaptivity · Inference confidence · Monitoring neural network

1 Introduction

Neural network classifiers are expected to be widely used in edge computing applications typically featuring strict cost, power and energy constraints [12]. The constrained execution environment has sparked a surge of interest in specialized hardware accelerators, which are reducing energy significantly with respect to traditional parallel processors or GP-GPUs [13].

© Springer Nature Switzerland AG 2022
A. Orailoglu et al. (Eds.): SAMOS 2021, LNCS 13227, pp. 505–522, 2022.
https://doi.org/10.1007/978-3-031-04580-6_34

Although this trend is far from stabilizing, complementary approaches are gaining momentum to augment the power-efficient algorithmic computation of such accelerators with dynamic reconfiguration capability. The key rationale behind this approach consists of adaptively tuning the amount of computation to the execution environment at runtime, thus optimizing power consumption. In particular, the architecture of the neural network model could be dynamically tailored to the input sample at hand [5], thereby avoiding redundant computations for *easy* samples [7,17,18]. Such dynamic neural networks hold promise of remarkable advantages in efficiency over acceleration techniques that deploy static models, which handle *easy* and *hard* input samples with identical computational graphs [8,9,14].

From an implementation standpoint, redundant computation is typically avoided when a certain confidence-based criterion is met on early or intermediate predictions. In classification tasks, the confidence is usually represented by the maximum element of the *SoftMax* output [7,21]. An alternative metric includes the first-order score margin [15], that is, the difference between the largest and the second largest score values of the classifier layer.

These metrics are widely used in deep learning inference frameworks that strive to meet the tight power budgets of embedded systems [10,19]. For instance, in [15] the authors use the simple score margin as a confidence metric to evaluate the predictions of a small, low power/energy neural network and to possibly invoke the use of a bigger one that, however, drains more power and energy. Similarly, in [2] a small network model is dynamically switched to a more complex one when the average confidence score on the latest frames is below a certain threshold, while the large model is switched back to the small one when the score is larger than another threshold value. In order to optimize the weight I/O and storage requirements, the authors in [16] propose a dynamically reconfigurable approach that, in case the score margin does not provide enough confidence in classification, adds resources to a basic neural network in order to perform a more accurate classification while sharing weights across network layers. The work in [10] builds on the general principle of coarse-to-fine computation and cascades network architecture levels consisting of feature transformers, classifiers and confidence threshold comparators to make a decision about early exit.

In general, confidence-based criteria are relatively simple to implement, and generally require no specific training techniques. A trade-off between accuracy and efficiency could be controlled by manipulating the thresholds, which are compared with computed confidence levels and usually tuned on a validation dataset. However, no exploration framework currently exists to determine the comparative capability of the different confidence metrics to discriminate between correct and misclassified samples [5]. In particular, there is a large gap in the open literature between the practical relevance of these metrics and their understanding in terms of: (i) the trade-off they span between confidence quality and complexity of the associated monitoring circuit, (ii) their sensitivity to the distribution of the outputs in the monitored classifier, and (iii) their capability to cope with incorrectly-classified samples with high confidence (overconfidence [3,6]).

This paper is a first step toward bridging this gap, and aims at exploring a hierarchy of confidence-based criteria with growing accuracy and computational complexity for intermediate classifier monitoring in dynamically-adaptive neural network systems. The work consists of two interrelated contributions toward the final goal.

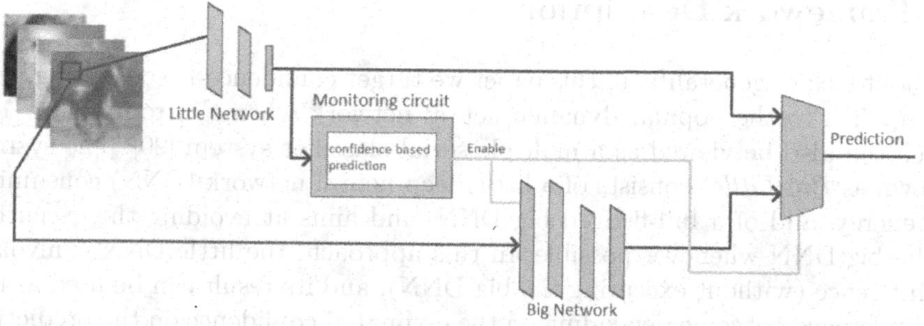

Fig. 1. Big-Little neural network system

On the one hand, we consider the score as the simplest existing metric, and assess the additional capability of the score margin (if any) to distinguish cases featuring the same score. With respect to (partially) related work [10], our analysis investigates the role of post-processing network calibration methods for the effectiveness of these confidence-based metrics. In fact, it has been demonstrated that modern neural networks are often not well calibrated, that is, probability estimates may not be representative of true correctness likelihood [3]. This makes confidence-based decision making challenging due to high sensitivity for threshold setting far away from training data.

On the other hand, for the first time we explore a new monitoring methodology of intermediate classifier outputs that aims at extrapolating confidence information not only from the top(-two) scores like existing metrics, but rather from the whole distribution of the outputs. For this purpose, we instantiate a small neural network-based binary classifier (*MonNet*) fed by the outputs of a monitored neural network. MonNet is trained on the output samples of the monitored classifier when the test set is applied and knowledge of correct/wrong classifications is used for labelling.

Our expectation for this approach is to be able to account both for the position of the scores and for marginal values to better capture specific patterns associated with misclassifications, thus potentially outperforming traditional score and score margin approaches. Counterintuitively, experimental results do not strongly support this expectation, since MonNet does not bring significant advantages over position-agnostic top score-based metrics. In contrast, the empirical evidences reported by the paper seem to indicate that only a few output parameters are correlated to the level of confidence of the monitored classifier.

However, the presented experimental campaign is only a first step, and not a final answer, on the effectiveness of neural network-based monitoring. In fact, the potential of this approach could be better harnessed by extending the set of monitored neural network variables beyond classifier outputs. This is left for future work.

2 Framework Description

Without lack of generality, in this paper we target confidence-based exiting policies applied to the popular dynamic neural network scheme introduced in [15], which can also be viewed as a multiple serial classifier system [20]. The system (known as *Big-Little*) consists of a little deep neural network (DNN) consuming low energy, and of a full-fledged big DNN, and aims at avoiding the execution of the big DNN whenever possible. In this approach, the little DNN is invoked for inference (without executing the big DNN), and its result can be used as the final inference outcome depending on the estimated confidence on the prediction (see Fig. 1). If this is not the case, the big DNN is then executed to deliver the final inference result. This approach aims at low energy by relying on the little DNN for easy samples, while sustaining accuracy by selectively invoking the big DNN on hard samples. In this work, we consider the big network as an oracle, that is, an hypothetical classifier which is always correct. The reason behind that choice is that our focus is on the monitoring circuit of the little network, and on the trade-off between the number of big DNN runs and the maximum achievable accuracy that different confidence-based criteria can strike.

At the same time, we consider a couple of different little neural networks with growing complexity and accuracy, in order to assess their impact over the confidence estimation quality of the monitoring circuit. In particular, two convolutional neural networks with different topologies were considered (see Table 1). One (Little A) is a network based on LeNet [11], but modified in order to obtain a better classification accuracy. This net, like the original LeNet, is composed of three convolutional layers, separated by pooling layers. After the convolutional layers, there is a fully connected section, which includes the output layer and a Softmax activation function.

However, differently from a traditional LeNet, batch normalization and ReLu activation functions were used to reach an accuracy, which is nearly 70%. The other Little network model (Little B) takes advantage of more convolutional layers than Little A, in order to achieve a better accuracy (89%). However, while the size of the network is increased (roughly 7x the number of FLOPs), it is still much smaller compared to most of the state of the art networks [1,4] for the considered dataset, making Little B suitable to play the role of the little network. It is worth noting at this point that the size of the network is believed to be the main factor that may lead to require calibration procedures [3]. This topic will be further analyzed in Sect. 3.

All little networks used in this work are trained on the CIFAR10 dataset. The dataset was partitioned into three sections: 1) the training set X_{train}; 2) the test set X_{test}; 3) the experiment set X_{exp}, which is used for an independent verification of the quality of the monitoring circuit.

Table 1. Topologies of the little neural networks used in this study

Network topology	
Little A	Little B
Conv2D (16), (5 × 5)	Conv2D (32), (3 × 3)
MaxPooling	Conv2D (32), (3 × 3)
Conv2D (32), (5 × 5)	MaxPooling2D
MaxPooling	Conv2D (64), (3 × 3)
Conv2D (500), (1 × 1)	Conv2D (64), (3 × 3)
Dense (10)	MaxPooling2D
	Conv2D (128), (3 × 3)
	Conv2D (128), (3 × 3)
	MaxPooling2D
	Dense (10)

3 Score and Score Margin Binary Classifiers

3.1 Preliminary Definitions

Let us consider a neural network based multiclass classifier with n_x inputs and n_y outputs that is trained in a supervised way. Let us also define a generic input set as $\mathcal{X}$ characterized by the matrix $X \in \mathbb{R}^{n_x+|\mathcal{X}|}$ and the corresponding output set $\mathcal{Y}$ characterized by the (one-hot encoded) labels matrix $Y \in \mathbb{R}^{n_y+|\mathcal{Y}|}$. The neural networks predictions, instead, are described by the set $\hat{\mathcal{Y}}$ to which corresponds the matrix $\hat{Y} \in \mathbb{R}^{n_y+|\mathcal{Y}|}$. Note that X may be one of the followings: 1) the training set; 2) the test set; 3) the validation set that is here added to have a test set for the monitoring circuit, whose parameters are adjusted on the test set of the neural network classifier. Let $\texttt{argpos}(k, \hat{y}^i) : \{1..n_y\} \times \mathbb{R}^{n_y} \rightarrow \{1..n_x\}$ be a function that returns the index of the output of the neural network corresponding to the k-th position in $\hat{y}^i$ sorted in decreasing order. Therefore, $\hat{\alpha}^i = \texttt{argpos}(1, \hat{y}^i) = \texttt{argmax}(\hat{y}^i)$ is the predicted class, while $\hat{\beta}^i = \texttt{argpos}(2, \hat{y}^i)$ is the class with the second position.

If α^i is the class denoted by the labeling of x^i, we can define a variable $\delta^i \in \{0, 1\}$ that holds 1 if the input is correctly classified ($\alpha^i = \hat{\alpha}^i$) and 0 otherwise. Therefore, the accuracy achieved on X is:

$$acc = \frac{1}{|X|} \sum_{i=1}^{|X|} \delta^i$$

The **score** of a prediction $\hat{y}^i$ is $s^i = \hat{y}^i_\alpha$, while its **score margin** is $sm^i = \hat{y}^i_\alpha - \hat{y}^i_\beta$. In case a Softmax layer is used to produce the outputs, the score should mimic the probability that the predicted class is the correct one, while the score margin approximates an uncertainty on such prediction.

Let us now consider a circuit that monitors the neural network. It is a binary classifier that receives the output of the neural network and produces a label $\varphi \in \{0, 1\}$ that denotes the binary trust on the output of the neural network. If $\varphi^i = 0$ the network prediction is untrusted, while if $\varphi = 1$, the network prediction is trusted. Such a circuit may be either a logic circuit that computes scores and compares them to a threshold or a monitoring neural network classifier. The latter is the method proposed in our work.

The simplest methods compare the score or the score margin to a threshold θ which is subject to optimization. In Sect. 3.3, we will discuss the problems related to the choice between these two parameters. For instance, in [15], if $sm^i < \theta$, the monitoring circuit activates a big network providing a more accurate classification than the current one. For an input x^i, the whole system may produce one of the following mutually exclusive events accordingly to the distribution of the mixed random variable (δ, s) or (δ, sm):

- *true negative:* the neural network correctly classifies the input and the monitoring circuit trusts the prediction ($\delta^i = 1 \wedge \varphi^i = 1$);
- *true positive:* the neural network misclassifies the input and the monitoring circuit does not trust the prediction ($\delta^i = 0 \wedge \varphi^i = 0$);
- *false negative:* the neural network misclassifies the input and the monitoring circuit trusts the prediction ($\delta^i = 0 \wedge \varphi^i = 1$);
- *false positive:* the neural network correctly classifies the input and the monitoring circuit does not trust the prediction ($\delta^i = 1 \wedge \varphi^i = 0$);

The numbers of such events are denoted as:

- $TN(X) = \sum_{i=1}^{|X|} \delta^i \varphi^i$ for *true negatives*;
- $TP(X) = \sum_{i=1}^{|X|} (1 - \delta^i)(1 - \varphi^i)$ for *true positives*;
- $FN(X) = \sum_{i=1}^{|X|} (1 - \delta^i)\varphi^i$ for *false negatives*;
- $FP(X) = \sum_{i=1}^{|X|} \delta^i (1 - \varphi^i)$ for *false positives*;

Based on such quantities, the effectiveness of the monitoring circuit can be characterized by defining a true positive rate as: $TPR = TP/(TP + FN)$ which is the probability that a misclassified input is not trusted by the monitoring circuit. While, the false negative rate is defined as $FPR = FP/(TN + FP)$ that is the probability that a correctly classified input is not trusted by the monitoring circuit. In the ideal case, $TPR = 1$ and $FPR = 0$. The behavior of the monitoring circuit as a function of the threshold is summarized by the ROC curve which plots TPR as a function of FPR.

3.2 Overfitting Discussion

As noted in the introduction, modern techniques, such as the use of deep networks to achieve high accuracy, may lead to a mismatch between the score and the score margin values and the actual confidence in the prediction [3]. This problem can be analyzed by estimating the components of the score (score margin) probability density function corresponding to correct cases $(\delta = 1, s)$ $(\delta = 1, sm)$ and misclassifications $(\delta = 0, s)$ $(\delta = 0, sm)$.

Figures 2a and 3a show the distribution for Little A on the CIFAR10 test set, for the score and score margin, respectively. Figures 2c and 3c show the same results applied to Little B.

These results show that overfitting is present both in the very small network little A and in the larger network little B. Therefore, it is not only a problem related to network depth, as pointed by [3], but also to other issues related for instance to activation functions (ReLu instead of sigmoid as in older networks) and training (batch normalization, regularization).

In order to solve this problem, network calibration is necessary. For the purpose of this study, the networks were calibrated using Vector Scaling, which is one of the methods proposed in [3]. Thus, for each network we derived a calibrated counterpart. The impact of calibration on the score margin is shown in Figs. 2b and 3b for Little A on the CIFAR10 test set, while Figs. 2d and 3d show the calibrated results applied to Little B.

The overall comparison of these curves show that calibration reduces the values of s and sm for a small fraction of miscassified samples, thus helping any threshold-based monitoring circuit. However, even if calibration provides better results in separating the distribution of the correctly classified cases from that of misclassifications, such an improvement is not resolutive, because it can be observed that in part it degrades correctly classified scores as well. In addition, the shift in the distribution of misclassified samples is smaller than those shown in [15], thus indicating that different networks are expected to exhibit rather different behaviors from this point of view. These results also show that, in the considered set of networks, the score margin is preferable to the score because of its capability to account for the strength of the second output (β).

With these premises, the empirical method to make use of the score or score margin is to compare them with a chosen threshold that may also undergo optimization, in order to choose the best balance between TPR and FPR for the chosen application.

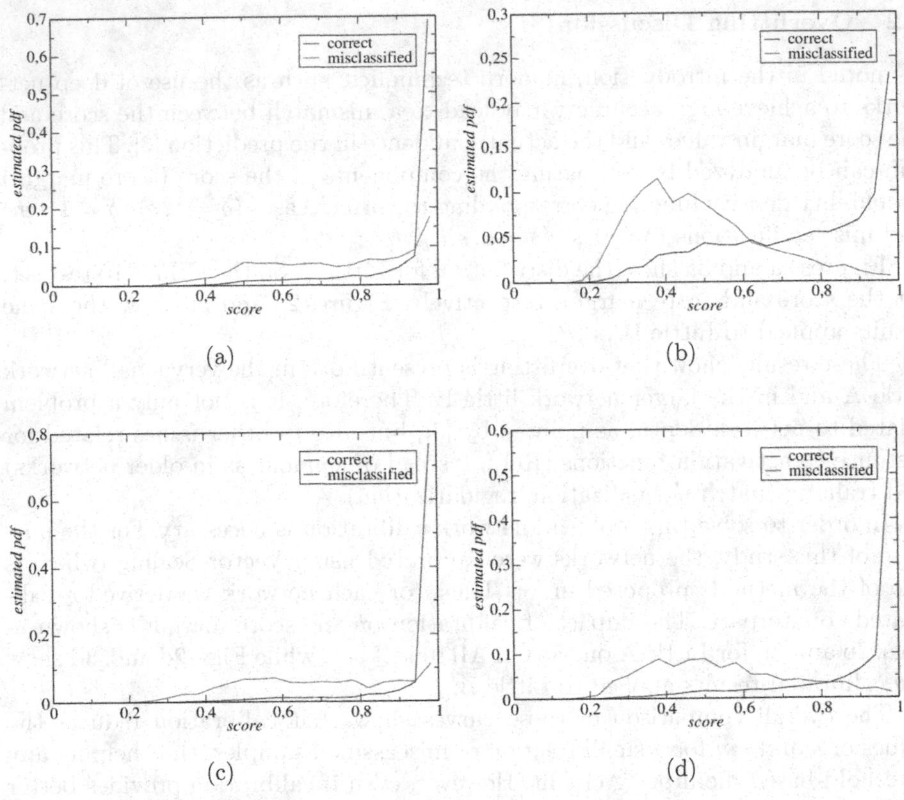

Fig. 2. Components of the score probability density function estimates on the CIFAR10 test set for little A, in the non-calibrated (a) and calibrated (b) cases, and for Little B in the non-calibrated (c) and calibrated (d) cases.

3.3 ROC Curves

By varying the threshold, it is also possible to plot the ROC curves that characterize the capabilities of this method to discriminate between correct and wrong classifications of a given neural network. These curves are also expected to reflect the improvements introduced by the calibration.

The entity of such improvements, in terms of the discrimination capabilities of a score-based monitoring circuit, is shown in Fig. 4a for Little A, while the same data are shown in Fig. 4b in case the score margin is used. Such figures both consider the non-calibrated and the calibrated cases. Figure 5a and b show the ROC curves in the calibrated and non-calibrated cases when considering Little B instead, monitored by using the score and the score margin, respectively.

While the used calibration procedure does not have a large impact on the network's accuracy, which is basically the same, the performances of both the score and the score margin are improved. The ROC curves also show that the score margin works slightly better than the score.

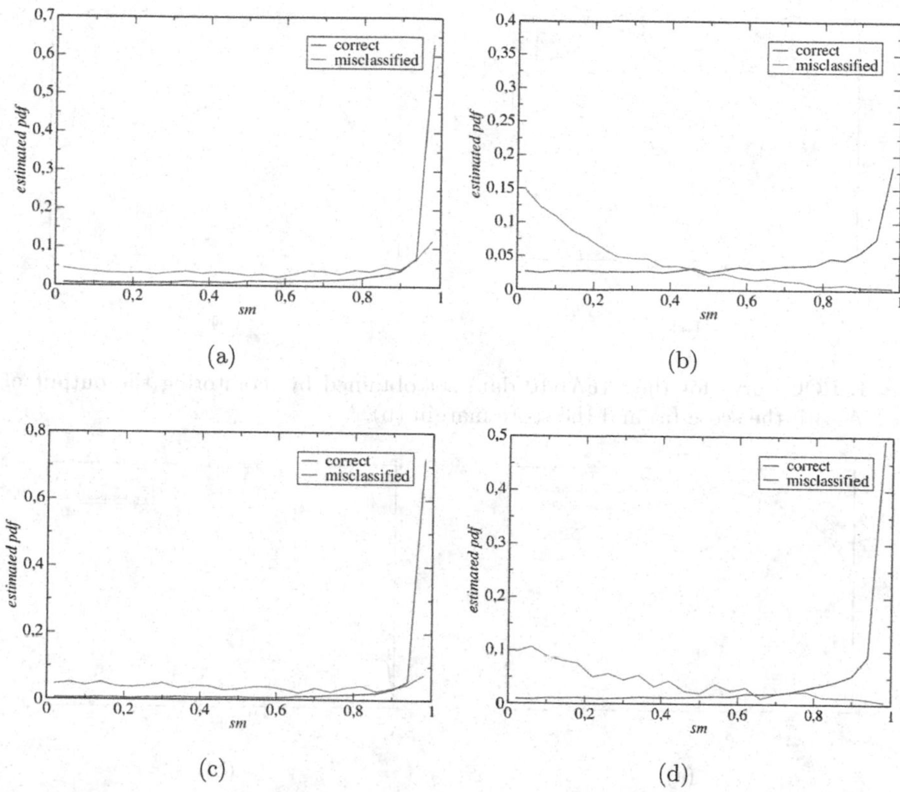

Fig. 3. Score margin probability density function estimates on the CIFAR10 test set for little A, in the non-calibrated (a) and calibrated (b) cases, and for Little B in the non-calibrated (c) and calibrated (d) cases.

3.4 Wider Monitoring Scope

While the use of the score margin allows to implement Big-Little model architectures featuring a reasonable trade-off between computational workload and accuracy, the ROC curves reveal that there is still room for consistent improvements. In fact, a score margin classifier only monitors two outputs of the monitored neural network, and does not account for their positions in the output pattern. Therefore, an intuitive approach for better decision making would consist of extrapolating confidence information from the whole distribution of the monitored classifier outputs rather than from the top two scores only. This could be done with small processing overhead by instantiating a small neural network-based binary classifier capturing specific patterns associated with misclassifications. The wider monitoring capability of this approach holds promise of better

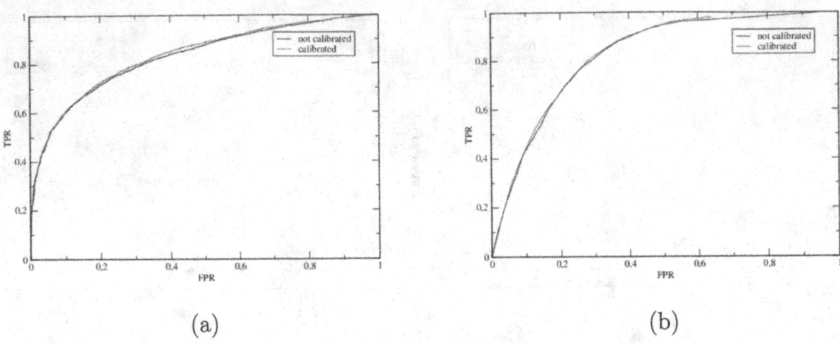

Fig. 4. ROC curve for the CIFAR10 data set obtained by monitoring the output of little A with the score (a) and the score margin (b).

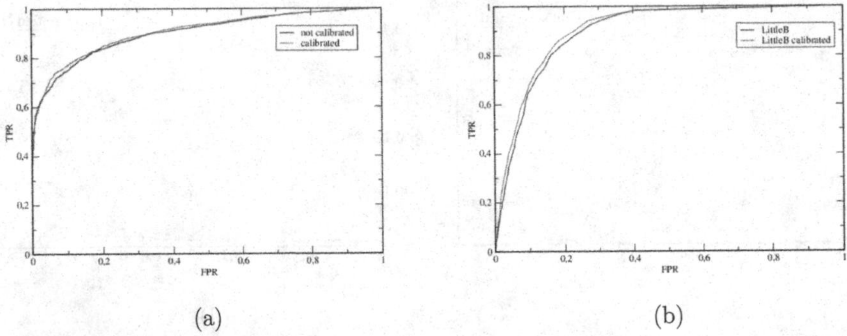

Fig. 5. ROC curve for the CIFAR10 data set obtained by monitoring little B with the score (a) and the score margin (b).

coping with overconfidence, since correctly and incorrectly classified samples with similar high confidence according to the score margin criteria could be better discriminated should they generate different output patterns.

Next, the implementation of the novel decision method is detailed and assessed in depth.

4 MonNet Binary Classifier

MonNet is a small neural network aimed at outperforming state-of-the-art score margin-based confidence estimators. It is deployed as the monitoring circuit in Fig. 1, therefore it uses the output of the little network as input.

Table 2. MonNet configurations depending on the amount of monitored data. The hidden layers are represented with the number of neurons per layer separated by '-'. We assume CIFAR-10 dataset.

Monitored data	MonNet network topology		
	Input layer	Hidden layers	Output layer
All-10 scores (**MN10**)	10	32–10	1
Top-2 scores (**MN2**)	2	12–8	1

For the sake of homogeneous comparison with other metrics, the CIFAR-10 dataset, composed of 50,000 images, was split into three sets as in Sect. 2: (1) X_{train}, with 30,000 samples; (2) X_{test}, composed of 10,000 samples; and (3) X_{exp}, also composed of 10,000 samples. Because of the need to train the MonNet with the output of the little network, out of the 10,000 samples (3), 7,000 were used to train MonNet (of which 1,400 were used to validate while training) and 3,000 were used to test the MonNet. These 10,000 samples have been labelled as hit or miss for the little network, taking into account the success/failure of the prediction. This allows the MonNet to decide whether to trust the little one, or to activate the big one instead. To train and conduct the prediction experiments, we have used TensorFlow 2.4.1. The accuracy results obtained in the Big-Little model have been performed on the 3,000 samples reserved for MonNet testing.

The complexity of the MonNet network topology (i.e., number of hidden layers, type of layers, and number of neurons per layer) heavily depends upon the amount of data to be learnt from the monitored network. Table 2 lists the two scenarios of data to be monitored that we consider in this work. The first row corresponds to our main target, that is, feeding MonNet with all scores from the monitored network's output so that MonNet can learn any specific pattern associate with all scores and their positions in the classifier layer – we assume the CIFAR-10 dataset, thus the input layer of MonNet must be sized with 10 neurons. In addition, for the sake of comparison, we consider the case of using the top-2 scores from the monitored network's output as input to MonNet. This can be understood as a more incremental extension of the Score Margin binary classifier in that, unlike the latter, the values of the largest and the second largest scores are considered for decision making. Regardless the input layer size, MonNet is configured with an output layer composed of 1 neuron to produce the output of the binary classifier ($\varphi \in \{0, 1\}$).

Nonetheless, defining the precise amount and type of hidden layer(s) for each case that achieves the highest binary classification accuracy with the least network resources (e.g., number of inter-layer connections or neuron weights) requires an in-depth design-space exploration and is left for future work. Instead, we conservatively assume a MonNet architecture that is capable of guaranteeing the highest binary-classification accuracy. For that, we have configured MonNet as a simple multi-layer perceptron with the number and size of hidden layers exposed in Table 2. Note that, even without architectural fine-tuning, the Mon-

Net variants targeted by this paper are tiny neural network models that could be efficiently deployed in any heavily-constrained edge computing platform. In fact, their computational complexity in terms of FLOPs is from four to five orders of magnitude lower that the considered little networks.

Table 3. Configurations for the experiments with the Score Margin and MonNet binary classifiers. **AUC** is the area under the curve for the ROC curves (details in Fig. 6). In the table, we also show the confusion matrix embedded in a single cell for each of the cases highlighted in bold font in Tables 4 and 5: matrices' rows represent the target prediction and columns the estimated prediction. "No Trust" is the first row/column and "Trust" is the second row/column).

Network	Calibrated	Binary classifier	Input	AUC	Confusion matrix
Little A	No	Score Margin	Top-2 scores	0.816	520 256 464 1760
		MonNet	All-10 scores	0.819	466 310 357 1867
			Top-2 scores	0.820	525 251 473 1751
	Yes	Score Margin	Top-2 scores	0.826	504 251 443 1802
		MonNet	All-10 scores	0.814	321 435 234 2010
			Top-2 scores	0.830	450 306 347 1897
Little B	No	Score Margin	Top-2 scores	0.891	136 231 91 2542
		MonNet	All-10 scores	0.898	142 225 75 2558
			Top-2 scores	0.890	145 222 95 2538
	Yes	Score Margin	Top-2 scores	0.893	137 206 124 2533
		MonNet	All-10 scores	0.892	91 247 89 2573
			Top-2 scores	0.895	115 223 114 2548

5 Evaluation

5.1 Comparing Monitoring Binary Classifiers

For the experimental analysis, we assume the configurations listed in Table 3. We consider two types of Little neural networks (A and B), whether these networks are calibrated or not, and the input data used by each binary classifier – i.e., the top-2 scores for the calculation of the Score Margin, and the two different types of monitored data exposed in Sect. 4.

To compare the quality of MonNet vs. Score Margin as a binary classifier, Table 3 represents the area under the curve (AUC) for the ROC curves that are illustrated in Fig. 6. Note that the ROC curves for the Score Margin are those discussed in Sect. 2. To plot the ROC curves for the MonNet we followed the same approach as for the Score Margin by varying the threshold of the output classifier layer from 0.0 to 1.0.

At a first glance, we can observe that the ROC curves shown in Fig. 6 are quite similar (almost overlapped) in all cases. A more in-depth analysis considering the AUC column of Table 3 confirms this behavior as the AUC values obtained for MonNet are in the same order of magnitude, considering the first two decimal places of the numbers, with respect to those reported by the Score Margin in both Little networks w/ and w/o calibration cases. The high AUC values are consistent with the large amount of correct predictions made by the binary classifiers (see the left-to-right diagonal values of the confusion matrices). Interestingly, giving as input to MonNet all 10 scores does not yield any

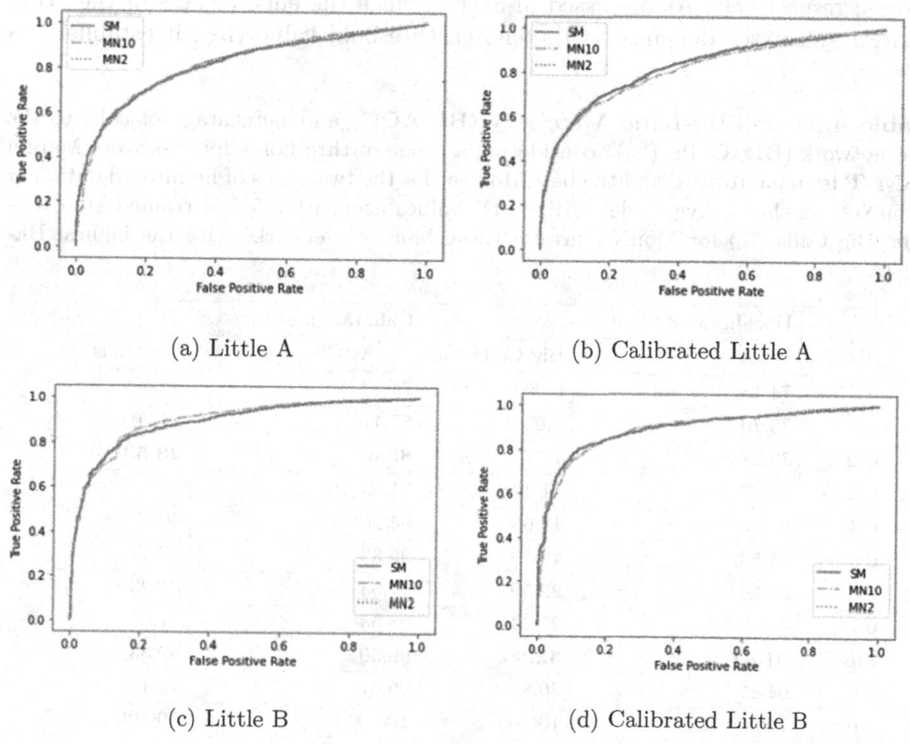

(a) Little A (b) Calibrated Little A

(c) Little B (d) Calibrated Little B

Fig. 6. ROC curves for Score Margin (SM) and the two MonNet configurations (MN10 and MN2) for Little A and Little B with and without calibration.

noticeable benefit on the AUC value when compared with the top-2 scores. This clearly contradicts the original intuition behind the use of MonNet. This counter-intuitive result also occurs in both calibrated Little A and Little B networks.

By considering the confusion matrices it is worth mentioning that MN10 with calibration always presents the minimum number of true positives and the minimum number of positives ($TP + FP$). Therefore, it provides the minimum accuracy increase (when calling the big network) and the minimum number of calls to the big network. In practice, it seems to be overconfident on classifier results, an issue that has no easy explanation (see Sect. 6) and that will be further investigated in future work.

5.2 Assessing the Accuracy-Workload Trade-Off

Next, we conduct a set of experiments to estimate the overall accuracy of the Big-Little model approach using the binary classifiers under test, and the associated computational cost in terms of number of activations of the big network. To evaluate this approach, as explained in Sect. 2, we assume an oracle Big neural network that achieves 100% accuracy for all test images in CIFAR-10.

Tables 4 and 5 show our experimental results for Little A and Little B networks, respectively. As discussed in Sect. 3, since the effectiveness of the Score Margin estimator depends on the chosen threshold value (i.e., it establishes a

Table 4. Overall Big-Little A accuracy (**BL-ACC**) and percentage of calls to the big network (**Big Calls (%)**) considering a range of thresholds for the Score Margin (**SM-T** from 0.0 to 1.0), and the best MonNet for the two types of monitored data. For MonNet, we show "Avg.±Sdev. (Highest)" values using 10 different trained MonNets. The Big Calls (%) for MonNet are for those MonNet networks with the highest BL-ACC.

	Uncalibrated		Calibrated	
SM-T	BL-ACC	Big Calls (%)	BL-ACC	Big Calls (%)
0.0	74.13	0.00	74.83	0.00
0.1	76.70	4.03	83.47	13.70
0.2	78.67	7.57	**88.37**	**23.53**
0.3	80.87	11.43	91.63	31.57
0.4	83.43	15.63	94.20	40.07
0.5	85.53	19.10	96.33	47.37
0.6	87.20	22.50	97.53	54.23
0.7	89.30	27.73	98.53	61.07
0.8	**91.47**	**32.80**	99.30	69.33
0.9	94.17	40.83	99.67	79.13
1.0	100.00	100.00	100.00	100.00
MN10	**88.07±1.27 (89.66)**	**27.43**	**84.62±0.61 (85.50)**	**18.50**
MN2	**88.56±2.86 (91.63)**	**33.26**	**87.08±2.22 (89.80)**	**26.56**

Table 5. Same description as in Table 4 but for Little B.

	Uncalibrated		Calibrated	
SM-T	BL-ACC	Big Calls (%)	BL-ACC	Big Calls (%)
0.0	87.77	0.00	88.57	0.00
0.1	89.57	2.77	91.30	4.70
0.2	91.23	5.20	**93.13**	**8.70**
0.3	**92.30**	**7.57**	94.83	12.27
0.4	93.20	9.70	96.17	16.13
0.5	93.80	11.57	97.13	20.03
0.6	94.77	14.33	98.10	24.37
0.7	95.73	17.70	98.83	29.37
0.8	97.00	21.80	99.20	35.40
0.9	98.17	27.60	99.57	45.17
1.0	100.00	100.00	100.00	100.00
MN10	**92.06±0.26 (92.50)**	**7.23**	**91.59±0.10 (91.76)**	**6.00**
MN2	**92.31±0.21 (92.60)**	**8.00**	**92.08±0.26 (92.56)**	**7.63**

trade-off between number of executions of the big neural network and the loss of inference accuracy), we assume a range of thresholds between 0.0 (i.e., the estimator always trusts the little network, so the big network is never called and the inference accuracy is the same as the little network), and 1.0 (i.e., the estimator never trusts the little network, so the big network is always called and the inference accuracy is the same as the big network). We include these two extreme values in the tables to represent the lower and upper bounds of our little and big networks' prediction accuracy, respectively (note that the prediction accuracy of the little networks are consistent with those described in Sect. 3). For comparison, we also show in the last two rows of the tables the performance of the MonNet network depending on the two types of monitored data (Table 2). In the last case, since training a neural network with different initial weights might change the final prediction accuracy, we have repeated the experiments for MonNet 10 times and we reported the average and standard deviation values. Among all 10 experiments, we select the best result a MonNet can achieve as to the highest overall Big-Little accuracy (it is added in brackets in the tables).

As we can see in Table 4, in the case of the Little A network, the score margin can considerably increase the overall Big-Little prediction accuracy (up to 94.17% with a threshold of 0.9) but at the cost of a large number of calls to the big network (up to 40.83% for the same threshold). The experiments of MonNet reveal that it cannot outperform such high accuracy, but the best trained MonNet networks are very close (up to 91.63%) while at the same time lowering the number of calls to the big network to 33.26%. Considering a similar number of calls to the big network, with a threshold of 0.8 (see the bold font in the table) the Score Margin can achieve similar prediction performance (91.47%).

These results bring out two interesting results. First, MonNet can obtain similar performance to Score Margin for a similar number of calls to the Big network. Second, across the two different configurations for MonNet, we counterintuitively observe that feeding MonNet with all 10 scores does not help increase prediction accuracy. The same trend applies also in the calibrated Little A network, but in this case the Score Margin threshold is 0.2. Even though we have also conducted the same experiments with a more complex little network (Little B), as shown in Table 5, the outcomes are similar and lead to the same conclusions.

Finally, it is worth noticing that calibration makes MonNet with all 10 scores even less effective. This is particularly true in the Little A case (see Table 4). This may depend on calibration heuristics that attenuate the Softmax function. They always decrease the top score, while other scores may be either increased or decreased with respect to the non-calibrated case. Very low scores, instead, are consistently raised by calibration. The impact of this approach on confidence metrics is typically positive for the score margin. If $sm_i > sm_j$ (i and j being two predictions) in the non-calibrated case, calibration increases sm_i/sm_j in the largest majority of cases. Conversely, it is easy to verify that calibration may impair different metrics. For instance, in some cases the score margin takes advantage of calibration, while the Euclidean distance between two classifier outputs is consistently lowered. This may not help also the metric induced by MonNet.

6 Discussion and Conclusions

A crucial operation in most dynamic neural networks for low-power embedded systems consists of deciding whether a neural network module should be evaluated or skipped. Confidence-based criteria are typically used for that, which monitor a small set of output parameters of intermediate classifiers under test. This paper reported on a different monitoring approach, relying on a neural-network based binary classifier (MonNet) to monitor the whole distribution of intermediate classifier outputs.

Overall, our exploration indicates that all confidence estimation strategies under test lead to roughly the same operating points for dynamic neural networks. Therefore, MonNet is not bringing significant advantages over position-agnostic top score-based metrics. In contrast, the following empirical observations emerge. First, the level of confidence of the monitored classifier tends to be revealed only by few, most significant scores. Second, such confidence seems to be better reflected by the absolute value of the top scores rather than their position in the classifier output pattern.

There are a few candidate explanations for the poor performance of MonNet:

- training set unbalanced towards mainly correct classifier predictions;
- MonNet size;
- problems intrinsic to the classifier output distribution.

The unbalanced training set hypothesis is less likely since, in our experiments, MonNet works better with Little B, which is more accurate and has a more unbalanced data set than Little A. At the same time, we experimentally verified that more complex versions of MonNet featuring up to 4 additional hidden layers do not provide remarkable accuracy improvements. As a result, the most likely explanation could reside in the classifier output distribution, which is produced by the normalization operations of the SoftMax layer. These operations might destroy several information about its input distribution (logits). In the case of score and score margin, this problem is partially mitigated by the calibration of the SoftMax layer, which is not effective for MonNet, as shown by our results.

Overall, this paper does not disqualify neural network-based binary classifiers for confidence estimation, but rather calls for fine-tuning of the approach along two directions. First, calibration techniques specifically targeting the use of a monitoring network instead of score-based metrics could be developed. Second, the set of monitored neural network variables could be extended beyond the outputs of the monitored classifier.

References

1. Dosovitskiy, A., et al.: An image is worth 16x16 words: transformers for image recognition at scale. CoRR abs/2010.11929 (2020). https://arxiv.org/abs/2010.11929
2. Du, B.Z., Guo, Q., Zhao, Y., Zhi, T., Chen, Y., Xu, Z.: Self-aware neural network systems: a survey and new perspective. Proc. IEEE **108**(7), 1047–1067 (2020). https://doi.org/10.1109/JPROC.2020.2977722
3. Guo, C., Pleiss, G., Sun, Y., Weinberger, K.Q.: On calibration of modern neural networks. In: Precup, D., Teh, Y.W. (eds.) Proceedings of the 34th International Conference on Machine Learning, ICML 2017, Sydney, NSW, Australia, 6–11 August 2017. Proc. Mach. Learn. Res. **70**, 1321–1330. PMLR (2017). http://proceedings.mlr.press/v70/guo17a.html
4. Han, K., Xiao, A., Wu, E., Guo, J., Xu, C., Wang, Y.: Transformer in transformer. CoRR abs/2103.00112 (2021). https://arxiv.org/abs/2103.00112
5. Han, Y., Huang, G., Song, S., Yang, L., Wang, H., Wang, Y.: Dynamic neural networks: a survey. CoRR abs/2102.04906 (2021). https://arxiv.org/abs/2102.04906
6. Hein, M., Andriushchenko, M., Bitterwolf, J.: Why Relu networks yield high-confidence predictions far away from the training data and how to mitigate the problem. In: 2019 IEEE/CVF Conference on Computer Vision and Pattern Recognition (CVPR), pp. 41–50 (2019)
7. Huang, G., Chen, D., Li, T., Wu, F., van der Maaten, L., Weinberger, K.Q.: Multi-scale dense networks for resource efficient image classification (2018)
8. Huang, G., Liu, S., Maaten, L.v.d., Weinberger, K.Q.: CondenseNet: an efficient denseNet using learned group convolutions. In: 2018 IEEE/CVF Conference on Computer Vision and Pattern Recognition, pp. 2752–2761 (2018). https://doi.org/10.1109/CVPR.2018.00291
9. Hubara, I., Courbariaux, M., Soudry, D., El-Yaniv, R., Bengio, Y.: Binarized neural networks. In: Proceedings of the 30th International Conference on Neural Information Processing Systems. NIPS 2016, pp. 4114–4122. Curran Associates Inc., Red Hook (2016)

10. Jayakodi, N.K., Chatterjee, A., Choi, W., Doppa, J.R., Pande, P.P.: Trading-off accuracy and energy of deep inference on embedded systems: a co-design approach. IEEE Trans. Comput. Aided Des. Integr. Circuits Syst. **37**(11), 2881–2893 (2018). https://doi.org/10.1109/TCAD.2018.2857338
11. Lecun, Y., Bottou, L., Bengio, Y., Haffner, P.: Gradient-based learning applied to document recognition. Proc. IEEE **86**(11), 2278–2324 (1998). https://doi.org/10.1109/5.726791
12. Li, W., Liewig, M.: A survey of AI accelerators for edge environment. In: Rocha, Á., Adeli, H., Reis, L., Costanzo, S., Orovic, I., Moreira, F. (eds.) WorldCIST 2020. AISC, vol. 1160, pp. 35–44. Springer, Heidelberg (2020). https://doi.org/10.1007/978-3-030-45691-7_4
13. Lim, S., Liu, Y.P., Benini, L., Karnik, T., Chang, H.C.: F1: Striking the balance between energy efficiency flexibility: general-purpose vs special-purpose ML processors. In: 2021 IEEE International Solid- State Circuits Conference (ISSCC), vol. 64, pp. 513–516 (2021). https://doi.org/10.1109/ISSCC42613.2021.9365804
14. Liu, Z., Li, J., Shen, Z., Huang, G., Yan, S., Zhang, C.: Learning efficient convolutional networks through network slimming. In: 2017 IEEE International Conference on Computer Vision (ICCV), pp. 2755–2763 (2017)
15. Park, E., Kim, D., Kim, S., Kim, Y.D., Kim, G., Yoon, S., Yoo, S.: Big/little deep neural network for ultra low power inference. In: 2015 International Conference on Hardware/Software Codesign and System Synthesis, CODES+ISSS 2015, pp. 124–132 (2015)
16. Tann, H., Hashemi, S., Bahar, R.I., Reda, S.: Runtime configurable deep neural networks for energy-accuracy trade-off. In: Proceedings of the IEEE/ACM/IFIP International Conference on Hardware/Software Codesign and System Synthesis. CODES 2016. ACM, New York (2016)
17. Teerapittayanon, S., McDanel, B., Kung, H.T.: BranchyNet: fast inference via early exiting from deep neural networks. In: 2016 23rd International Conference on Pattern Recognition (ICPR), pp. 2464–2469 (2016)
18. Veit, A., Belongie, S.: Convolutional networks with adaptive inference graphs. In: Proceedings of the European Conference on Computer Vision (ECCV), September 2018
19. Wang, K., Zhang, D., Li, Y., Zhang, R., Lin, L.: Cost-effective active learning for deep image classification. CoRR abs/1701.03551 (2017). http://arxiv.org/abs/1701.03551
20. Woźniak, M., Graña, M., Corchado, E.: A survey of multiple classifier systems as hybrid systems. Inf. Fusion **16**, 3–17 (2014). https://doi.org/10.1016/j.inffus.2013.04.006, https://www.sciencedirect.com/science/article/pii/S156625351300047X, (Special issue on Inf. Fusion Hybrid Intell. Fusion Syst.)
21. Yang, L., Han, Y., Chen, X., Song, S., Dai, J., Huang, G.: Resolution adaptive networks for efficient inference. In: 2020 IEEE/CVF Conference on Computer Vision and Pattern Recognition (CVPR), pp. 2366–2375 (2020). https://doi.org/10.1109/CVPR42600.2020.00244

Author Index

Printed in the United States
by Baker & Taylor Publisher Services